RESEARCH LIBRARY
OF
COLONIAL AMERICANA

RESEARCH LIBRARY

OF

COLONIAL AMERICANA

WILLIAM BYRD OF VIRGINIA

The London Diary
(1717 - 1721)
and Other Writings

Edited by Louis B. Wright *and*
Marion Tinling

ARNO PRESS
A New York Times Company
New York – 1972

Reprint Edition 1972 by Arno Press Inc.

Copyright © 1958 by Oxford University Press
Reprinted by permission of Louis B. Wright and
Marion Tinling

Reprinted from a copy in
The State Historical Society of Wisconsin Library

LC# 77-141208
ISBN 0-405-03305-2

Research Library of Colonial Americana
ISBN for complete set: 0-405-03270-6
See last pages of this volume for titles.

Manufactured in the United States of America

WILLIAM BYRD OF VIRGINIA

The London Diary
(1717-1721)
and Other Writings

NULLA PALLESCERE CULPA

William Byrd of Westover
in Virginia Esq.

WILLIAM BYRD II

WILLIAM BYRD OF VIRGINIA

The London Diary
(1717 - 1721)
and Other Writings

Edited by Louis B. Wright *and*
Marion Tinling

New York

OXFORD UNIVERSITY PRESS

1958

Printed in the United States of America

PREFACE

THE DIARY printed here is transcribed from a shorthand notebook (Mss 5:1B 9964:1) in the library of the Virginia Historical Society. This shorthand notebook is similar to Byrd's notebooks in the Huntington Library and in the Library of the University of North Carolina. Most of the new portion of the diary concerns Byrd's life in London, though the entries from February 4 until May 19, 1721, record events after his return to Virginia.

The transcription is as accurate as the shorthand will permit. Some symbols are ambiguous and the identification of proper names, which Byrd always wrote in shorthand, has proved particularly baffling. When a word is in doubt it is placed in square brackets. Words that could not be read are indicated by dots within brackets, or by the consonant form indicated by the shorthand. Passages where the manuscript has been trimmed or torn so that the shorthand cannot be deciphered are indicated by a row of dots. The diary is unexpurgated and all the passages that can be deciphered are given as Byrd wrote them.

The limitations of space in this volume have made necessary the abridgment of the *History of the Dividing Line*, *A Journey to the Land of Eden*, and *A Progress to the Mines*. In choosing the selections the editors have tried to include those passages that have the greatest literary and human interest. The text used is that based on the Westover Manuscripts, first published in 1841. Spelling, capitalization, and punctuation have been modernized to increase the ease of reading.

Many letters written by Byrd have been printed in scattered publications or remain in manuscript. A considerable body of his writings is buried in official reports in various public records. It is the hope of the present editors to bring together his letters and eventually to publish them along with a critical edition of his important writings.

The editors wish to thank Mrs. Virginia Freund, executive secretary of the Folger Library, for help with the manuscript and editorial problems.

L. B. W.

M. T.

Note: Byrd's bookplate, from a volume originally in his library, is reproduced through the courtesy of the Library of Congress. The portrait by Kneller is used with the permission of the owner.

Table of Contents

The Life of William Byrd of Virginia
1674-1744

1. MAN OF TWO WORLDS

LIFE on a Virginia plantation in the late seventeenth and the eighteenth centuries frequently reflected the planter's effort to reproduce
the kind of society that the English gentry had evolved in the course
of the centuries. The planter may have been the son of a grocer or a
soapmaker from London or Bristol or he may have derived from even
simpler origins, but, having acquired land, from time immemorial
the symbol of place and position, he set out consciously to imitate the
country gentry as he knew or imagined them. So earnestly did the
wealthier planters apply themselves to this task that they succeeded
in establishing in Virginia, and in some of the other colonies, an
agrarian aristocracy of great social significance in the development
of the new country.

Conditions in Virginia of course were vastly different from the
settled, well-ordered life characteristic of England. Though land in
the new country was easy to come by, human labor was excessively
scarce and costly, homesteads were widely scattered along the creeks
and rivers, and the distance to the nearest market town was measured
by the span of the ocean. The isolation of the Virginia plantations,
especially in the earlier periods, meant loneliness for the settlers and
a complete lack of the varied human relationships that village and

town life in England had provided. Furthermore, slavery added an ingredient unknown in English society in modern times. Yet despite the difference in environment, Englishmen in Virginia established a social group that was recognizably akin to the country gentry of England.

One of the most remarkable examples of the Virginia aristocracy was William Byrd, second of his name in the colony, master of Westover and other plantations, and an urbane aristocrat who conducted himself with equal assurance in the drawing rooms of English noblemen, in the coffeehouses of London, at meetings of the Virginia Council of State, or in a surveyors' camp on the fringes of the Great Dismal Swamp. Though a loyal Virginian devoted to the welfare of the commonwealth, Byrd spent in England more than thirty of his canonical threescore and ten years. Of the first thirty-one years of his life, he spent all but about eight overseas at school, in the business house of the London merchant firm of Perry and Lane, and at the Middle Temple. For a brief period in 1690 he went to Holland to learn something of the business methods of the Dutch. But he never forgot that he was a Virginian who one day would go back to his native country. Later he returned to England for two periods of approximately five years each and lived the life of a gentleman of fashion in London, but if he regretted his final translation to Virginia in 1726 to live out his days at Westover, he gives no indication of it in his diaries. Byrd found it easy to shift from one world to the other without pining for the one he had left.

During most of his adult life he kept a shorthand diary in which he recorded his daily routine: the food he ate, the ills he suffered, the medicine he took, the books he read, the duties he performed, the people he met, and the pleasures as well as the frustrations that were a part of his experience. The first portion of this diary, covering the years from February 6, 1709, to September 29, 1712, came to light in the Huntington Library in 1939 and was published two years later. In the meantime, another portion from August 10, 1739, to August 31, 1741, turned up in the University of North Carolina Library and was published in 1942.[1] A third portion, from December 13, 1717, to

1. *The Secret Diary of William Byrd of Westover, 1709–1712*. Edited by Louis B. Wright and Marion Tinling (Richmond, Va., 1941). And *Another Secret Diary of*

May 19, 1721, was discovered in the library of the Virginia Historical Society. This section is printed in the present volume. The diaries are all in shorthand and were never meant for any eyes except the writer's.

Byrd used small octavo notebooks for his shorthand entries. The volume in the Huntington Library contains approximately one hundred and fifty leaves. On one leaf was written a religious creed and on several preliminary leaves Byrd had transcribed some legal notes from Sir Edward Coke's *Reports*. Interspersed among the latter notes were phrases in shorthand. By overlaying these shorthand symbols with the English words for which they stood, it was possible to build up a shorthand alphabet and decipher the rest of the diary.

The transcription of the three portions of the diary was the work of Mrs. Marion Tinling, at the time of the discovery a member of the Huntington Library staff. She had made the study of archaic shorthand a hobby, but unhappily, she was not able to identify Byrd's type of shorthand immediately. Eventually, however, she discovered in the Huntington Library a copy of the shorthand textbook from which Byrd had learned the skill, William Mason's *A Pen Pluck't from an Eagle's Wing* (1672). This work was reprinted several times and a revised version appeared in 1707 under the title of *La Plume Volante*. It was the system laid down in this revised edition that Byrd used. Like most writers of shorthand, Byrd modified the system to suit his own convenience, and it is impossible to translate certain symbols with precision, for a dot can have any of eight or ten meanings (*of, I, a, the, -ed, -ing,* any vowel, or any of several prefixes). Nevertheless, most of the shorthand is clear and provides a candid picture of the activities of a country gentleman of Virginia.

The value of diaries like Byrd's lies in the uninhibited revelation of facts as they actually were, for Byrd clearly expected his diary to remain secret. The diary not only reveals the most intimate details of Byrd's own character, but it presents a vast amount of minutiae which supply to the social historian concrete facts that make possible a more vivid reconstruction of life in the period. Why Byrd—or anyone, for

William Byrd of Westover, 1739–1741, with Letters and Literary Exercises 1696–1726, edited by Maude H. Woodfin and Marion Tinling (Richmond, Va., 1942).

The discovery of the first portion of Byrd's diary was made while the present writer was searching for materials in the Huntington Library that would throw light

that matter—should write down all the things that the diary-keeper records is a mystery hard to comprehend. Hardly a morsel that he ate fails to get recorded, and there is an interminable notation of the prayers that he said—or, as like as not, forgot. He also meticulously records the intimacies of his sex life, so meticulously indeed that the diary has a considerable value as a case history for students of the psychology of sex.

One of the most significant revelations of the diary is the systematic effort that Byrd made to retain his knowledge of the learned languages—Greek, Latin, and Hebrew—as well as his interest in modern languages, especially Italian and French. He also notes the constant reading and writing of English, though too frequently we are left wondering what books he was reading, what he thought of them, and what literary efforts were engaging his attention. We know from his letters and from a few extant examples like the charming *History of the Dividing Line* that Byrd had a literary flair but was so much a perfectionist that he hesitated to let anything get into print.

William Byrd was a talented and versatile man, one of the most cultivated and ornamental characters of the colonial period. He was also a practical man, a planter ambitious to increase his wealth, a busy politician, an amateur of science and medicine, and an active participant in the social doings of his time. In short, Byrd was a complex character whose rise to prominence provides an instructive revelation of the evolution of the Virginia aristocracy.

2. BYRD'S PARENTAGE AND BACKGROUND

William Byrd II came of substantial middle-class stock. His father, William Byrd I, was the son of John Byrd, a goldsmith of London. John Byrd had married Grace Stegge, daughter of Thomas Stegge, a sea captain and Virginia trader who already had lands in the colony. William Byrd I grew up a promising youth of London and became a favorite of his uncle, Thomas Stegge, Jr., who had also done well for himself in Virginia. This uncle persuaded young Byrd to come

on the intellectual and social history of Virginia in the colonial period. For details concerning the discovery and transcription of the diary, see 'A Shorthand Diary of William Byrd of Westover,' *The Huntington Library Quarterly*, II (1939), 489–96.

to Virginia and when he died in March 1670 he bequeathed to Byrd, then aged eighteen, all of his holdings in Virginia, a considerable estate. As a prosperous planter and trader, Stegge had friends among the wealthier Virginians, and Byrd stepped into an assured social position. His uncle had shown good judgment in choosing the boy as his heir, for young William Byrd set to work to improve his estate and to expand the trade with the Indians that Stegge had begun. In time he became the leading Indian trader in Virginia, with pack trains going as far afield as the Catawba and Cherokee tribes in what is now South Carolina. He also missed no opportunity to acquire land. From his uncle he had inherited more than eighteen hundred acres at the Falls of the James, near the present site of Richmond, and to this estate Byrd added other purchases in the same locality and further down the James, where he later built his plantation house at Westover.

Sometime in 1673 William Byrd I married Mary Horsmanden, daughter of Warham Horsmanden, a Cavalier gentleman who had come to Virginia during the Puritan Revolution but returned to England soon after the marriage of his daughter to Byrd. When Mary met Byrd she was already the widow of Samuel Filmer. The first child of the marriage was a son, born on March 28, 1674, and named after his father, William. Three daughters followed in due course, Susan, Mary, and Ursula. All of the children were sent to England for their education. Susan grew up to marry John Brayne of London and lived out her life in England. Mary came back to marry James Duke. Ursula also returned to Virginia to marry Robert Beverley, the historian, by whom she had one son before she died when she was just short of seventeen.

The industry and shrewdness of William Byrd I made him a rich man by Virginia standards. In his trade with the Indians he found it profitable to barter pots and pans, rum and guns, blankets and cloth for deerskins and beaver and otter pelts. From his less opulent neighbors he took tobacco in exchange for a variety of imported articles, clothing, ammunition, tools, and medicines. Particularly profitable were the servants that he imported for sale: white bond servants to be sold for a term of years, and black slaves. After 1697 when the government restricted the monopoly of the Royal African Company and permitted private owners to employ their ships in the slave trade,

Byrd expanded his slaving activities and in 1699 was the principal owner of a slave ship, the 'William and Jane,' which was captured by a French privateer off the coast of West Africa.[2] Few Virginians at the end of the seventeenth century were more enterprising and successful than William Byrd I.

He also occupied a place of influence among the ruling class of the colony. Even as a young man he served in the House of Burgesses, was a commander of the militia in Charles City County, and held offices in Henrico County. By 1680 he had taken his place on the Council of State, which also served as the highest court in the colony, and in the last year of his life he served as president of the Council. He also served on the building committee of the College of William and Mary. In 1687 Byrd went to England to pursue a request for appointment as auditor and receiver-general of the colony, which he obtained after much maneuvering. Of the public offices that he held, this was the only one that was financially profitable. Most of the wealth that Byrd accumulated came from hard work as a planter and a trader. He succeeded in establishing his name and family as one of the most prosperous and aristocratic in Virginia.

3. WILLIAM BYRD II's EARLY YEARS IN ENGLAND

As a child of seven, young William Byrd was sent to England to be educated. His grandfather, Warham Horsmanden, a country gentle-man of Purleigh in Essex, saw to it that the boy was enrolled in Felsted Grammar School in Essex, which had for headmaster a famous teacher, Christopher Glasscock. Felsted Grammar School had a repu-tation for emphasizing both piety and learning, and though Oliver Cromwell had sent his sons there, that fact did not deter Byrd's Royalist grandfather from recognizing Felsted's worth. William Byrd I himself wrote to the headmaster on March 31, 1685, to express his satisfaction at young William's progress in good learning.[3] A grammar school education in this period meant a thorough grounding in the

2. See Louis B. Wright, 'William Byrd I and the Slave Trade,' *The Huntington Library Quarterly*, VIII (1945), 379–487.

3. Louis B. Wright, *The First Gentlemen of Virginia* (San Marino, Calif., 1940), 320. Previous biographers of Byrd have misspelled Glasscock's name as 'Glassock.'

classics, Latin and Greek, and perhaps Hebrew. At any rate, Byrd received a background in these three languages which he maintained throughout his life.

William Byrd I did not intend for his son to grow up into a mere scholar and apparently had no intention of sending him to either university. When the lad was sixteen he instructed him to proceed to Holland—probably under the care of some of his mercantile correspondents—to serve a brief apprenticeship in Dutch business methods, a training that the elder Byrd from his own experience believed would be useful to him in later life. But William found Holland not to his liking and begged to be allowed to return to England. His father relented and instructed him to report to the firm of Perry & Lane of London to continue his training in business. The counting house of Perry & Lane was not to be the end of Byrd's education, for in April 1692 he entered the Middle Temple and in 1695 was duly admitted to the bar.

As a personable and well-to-do member of one of the Inns of Court, Byrd mingled with the best of London society. Many wits and writers were members of the Inns of Court, and among Byrd's contemporaries at the Middle Temple were the rising dramatist William Congreve and the dramatist and future editor of Shakespeare, Nicholas Rowe. William Wycherley, whose bawdy plays had delighted the wits of the Restoration, was also a friend of Byrd's. With literary friends such as these it is not surprising that Byrd should have developed a taste for the theater and now and then should have turned his own hand to a bit of writing. Another friend at the Middle Temple was Benjamin Lynde of Salem, Massachusetts, who became a noted judge in his native colony. A letter from Byrd to Lynde, written when they were both old men, suggests the gaiety of their lives at Middle Temple. 'If I could persuade our captain of the guard ship to take a cruise to Boston at a proper season,' Byrd writes, 'I would come and beat up your quarters at Salem. I want to see what alteration forty years have wrought in you since we used to intrigue together in the Temple. But matrimony has atoned sufficiently for such backslidings, and now I suppose you have so little fellow feeling left for the naughty jades that you can order them a good whipping without any relenting. But though I should be mistaken, yet at least

I hope your conscience, with the aid of threescore and ten, has gained a complete victory over your constitution, which is almost the case of Sir, your, etc.'[4]

The most influential of Byrd's friends in this period was the distinguished diplomat and virtuoso, Sir Robert Southwell, principal secretary of state for Ireland, and president of the Royal Society from 1690 until 1696. Southwell became his mentor and guide. Through him he met Southwell's learned friend Sir William Petty, the eminent physician Sir Hans Sloane, and many other men of prominence and learning. Through Southwell's influence Byrd was elected on April 29, 1696, to membership in the Royal Society, a great honor for a youth of twenty-two. In the year after his election, he contributed a paper on an albino Negro whom he described as 'dappled.' To the end of his life he treasured his membership in this learned body and three years before his death he wrote sadly to Sir Hans Sloane complaining that he had been left out of the published list of members: 'I take it a little unkindly, Sir, that my name is left out of the yearly list of the Royal Society, of which I have the honor to be one of its ancientest members. I suppose my long absence has made your secretaries rank me in the number of the dead, but pray let them know I am alive and by the help of ginseng hope to survive some years longer.'[5]

Through Southwell Byrd made friends with many scholars and noblemen. Among his life-long friends were Charles Boyle, who became the third Earl of Orrery in 1703; Charles Wager, who was knighted in 1709 and became First Lord of the Admiralty in 1733; John Campbell, who became the second Duke of Argyll in 1703 and was commander for King George I against the rebel Scots in 1715; and John Percival, who was created first Earl of Egmont in 1733 and participated in General Oglethorpe's scheme to establish a colony in Georgia. All of these potentially influential friends and many others besides, both men and women, Byrd met through Sir Robert Southwell's good offices, and it is small wonder that on Byrd's epitaph it was recorded that 'he was early sent to England for his education,

4. Huntington Library MS, Brock 188, II, No. 13.

5. 'Letters of William Byrd II and Sir Hans Sloane Relative to Plants and Minerals in Virginia,' *William and Mary College Quarterly*, 2nd Ser., I (1921), 186–200.

where under the care and direction of Sir Robert Southwell, and ever favored with his particular instructions, he made a happy proficiency in polite and varied learning.'[6] No ambitious colonial could have had a better mentor than Southwell, and Byrd made the most of his opportunities.

Byrd's period of education in England extended from the last years of Charles II's reign until the middle of the reign of William III. Though merely a youth in his teens, he could not have missed the excitement of the Revolution of 1688 and the accession of William and Mary. If the court of those monarchs was less gay and ribald than the courts of their predecessors, London remained much as it had been, and the young beaux of the Inns of Court found much to stimulate their interest. The coming and going of politicians, some of whom Byrd could have met at the Middle Temple, the plays and farces of the theaters, the masquerades and balls which he attended, the gossip of the coffeehouses, and clandestine meetings with women of the town who took his fancy—all of these things, in addition to formal training, were a part of the experience of the young Virginian.

6. The inscription reads:
      Being born to one of the amplest fortunes in this country,
      He was early sent to England for his education,
      Where under the care and direction of Sir Robert Southwell,
      And ever favored with his particular instructions,
      He made a happy proficiency in polite and varied learning.
      By the means of this same noble friend,
      He was introduced to the acquaintance of many of the first persons
        of his age
      For knowledge, wit, virtue, birth, of high station,
      And particularly contracted a most intimate and bosom friendship
      With the learned and illustrious Charles Boyle, Earl of Orrery.
      He was called to the bar in the Middle Temple,
      Studied for some time in the Low Countries,
      Visited the Court of France,
      And was chosen Fellow of the Royal Society.
      Thus eminently fitted for the service and ornament of his country,
      He was made Receiver-General of His Majesty's revenues here,
      Was thrice appointed public agent to the Court and Ministry of
        England,
      And being thirty-seven years a member,
      At last became President of the Council of that Colony.
      To all this were added a great elegance of taste and life,
      The well-bred gentleman and polite companion,
      The splendid economist and prudent father of a family,
      With the constant enemy of all exorbitant power,
      And hearty friend to the liberties of his country.

4. The Beginning of Political Experience

Sometime in 1696 young William Byrd went home to Virginia. He was now a full-fledged lawyer, possessed of the best training a youth could obtain, and at twenty-two was ready to take his place among the ruling class to which he had been born. Through the influence of his father, he was immediately elected a member of the House of Burgesses from Henrico County and sat in the September session of the assembly. His experience at home was short-lived, however, and early in 1697 he returned to London.[7] Precisely what caused him to go back to England after so short a stay at home, we do not know. Perhaps his father had business matters that he preferred to entrust to his son. At any rate, he was in London in April and presented an address from the Virginia assembly to the Board of Trade. Later in the year, on December 27, he represented Sir Edmund Andros, governor of Virginia, at a meeting at Lambeth Palace called by the Archbishop of Canterbury and the Bishop of London to hear charges preferred by the Reverend James Blair that the Governor was thwarting efforts to improve the clergy in Virginia and to develop the College of William and Mary. Blair, the 'commissary' or representative of the Bishop of London who had oversight of the colonial church, was a strong-minded and obstinate Scot unloved by most of his contemporaries. Since Blair would prove an unmitigated annoyance to Byrd for the rest of his life, it is worthy of note that the young lawyer thus early in his career found himself in opposition to the cantankerous Scot.[8] Byrd made an able statement, but the heads of the Church plainly indicated that they were more impressed by the charges of their own representative than by the answers of the twenty-three-year-old lawyer from Virginia. Later Byrd submitted a written statement in amplification of some of the points made in the

7. John Spencer Bassett (ed.), *The Writings of Colonel William Byrd* (New York, 1901), xlv.

8. A detailed account of this episode in Byrd's career is provided by Louis B. Wright, 'William Byrd's Defense of Sir Edmund Andros,' *The William and Mary Quarterly*, 3rd Ser., II (1945), 47–62, which corrects earlier and erroneous statements about the Andros-Blair controversy.

oral argument at Lambeth. He maintained that Andros was a positive friend of the College, that contrary to Blair's testimony, he had never refused a gift of bricks for a college building, and that he had not influenced Virginians to refuse their payments. Indeed, Byrd placed the responsibility for the College's difficulties squarely upon Blair, whom he accused of exaggeration and misrepresentation in efforts to blame others. Blair, he declared, had practiced the maxim, 'throw a great deal of dirt and some of it will stick.' His war upon Governor Andros had been prompted by a desire to 'worm him out of his government' so that he could 'get his righteous patron Mr. Nicholson to succeed him.' As it turned out, Blair managed to have Andros recalled and replaced by Francis Nicholson, then acting Governor of Maryland. But Nicholson fared no better than Andros in keeping the good will of Commissary Blair, who eventually demanded and obtained his dismissal, an event that Byrd had predicted.

The defense of Governor Andros was Byrd's first important legal and political assignment, and it was a prelude to a long career of political activity. In 1698 the Virginia Council appointed him agent for the colony in London and from time to time he was in communication with the Board of Trade on colonial matters. Byrd took a leading part in a controversy between the Crown, represented in Governor Nicholson, and the colony, over Virginia's contribution to the defense of the rest of the colonies. In 1701, with war over the Spanish succession clearly inevitable, the authorities in England instructed the colonies to make preparations for defense. Governor Nicholson transmitted to the House of Burgesses an order from the Crown to furnish monetary assistance to New York and to send men if that colony should be attacked. Nicholson fixed £900 as the proper amount of pecuniary aid and demanded that the House draft legislation to put the colony on a war footing. Instead, the House, with the Council concurring, voted to send an address to the King explaining the impossibility of appropriating that amount and the hazard of raising troops for use outside of the colony. Since William Byrd was in London, he was instructed as agent for the colony to lay the matter before the Board of Trade and to carry the address to the King. The Burgesses and the Council set to work drafting a proper address, and William Byrd I, a member of the Council, was asked to communicate

the wishes of Virginia to his son.[9] All of this so incensed Governor
Nicholson that he refused to authorize the payment of any fee to
Byrd and, to confute Byrd's activities, he sent over a special messenger of his own, one Dionysius Wright, whom he described as an
'old Englander' familiar with the humors of Virginia.

The controversy had some of the elements of later conflicts over
the royal prerogative. Although the Virginians were not eager to
fight outside the colony and were equally indisposed to appropriating
money to be spent by New York, their prime objection to the whole
business was the danger of increasing the prerogatives of the royal
governor. Nicholson high-handedly, in the King's name, had ordered
the colony to do his bidding. The colony refused. And this refusal was
the prelude to controversies in all the colonies that eventually ended
in the War of Independence.

The elaborate address prepared by the House of Burgesses was not
presented to King William as intended because the King died in
March 1702. Byrd then drew up a petition to Queen Anne praying
that he might present the address to her. But he was not granted an
audience. Instead his petition and the address of the House of Burgesses were read by the Privy Council and referred to the Board of
Trade. In the meantime the Privy Council advised the Queen that
communications from the colonies should be addressed to Her Majesty through the royal governors and not through other agents; and
the Privy Council further suggested that she send 'royal letters to the
Governor of Virginia taking notice of the irregularity of this pro-
ceeding and again recommending what has been already proposed
for an assistance' to New York. Despite this rebuke, Byrd sum-
marized the colony's arguments for the Board of Trade, but the latter
also took a cold view of the efforts of the Virginians to circumvent
the royal governor. In the end the Virginians contrived to outwit
Nicholson, who was engaged in a running fight with the great
planters until 1705, when he was at last recalled. As Byrd had predicted earlier, Nicholson soon displeased Commissary Blair, who
joined the planters in ousting him.

In protests to the Board of Trade Byrd also attacked Nicholson for

9. For further details see Louis B. Wright, 'William Byrd's Opposition to Governor Francis Nicholson,' *The Journal of Southern History*, XI (1945), 68–79.

attempting to discourage the production of flax and cotton in Virginia and Maryland at a time when the shortage of shipping brought about by war conditions made imports of clothing extremely scarce. These colonies had tried to stimulate the growing of materials for clothing but Nicholson realized that this innovation might reduce the demand for English textiles and advised the Board of Trade to suppress the planting of flax and cotton. Byrd declared in a memorandum to the Board of Trade that enforcement of a law against the production of clothing would cause the colonials to become Adamites and go naked, and Byrd's brother-in-law, Robert Beverley, remarked sarcastically in his *History and Present State of Virginia* (1705) that Nicholson was 'desiring a charitable law that the planters shall go naked.'[10] Presently shipping eased, the price of tobacco went up, and Virginians forgot about flax and cotton in their devotion to tobacco, the one-crop system that came easiest to them. But they did not forget Nicholson's insistence on more stringent laws to restrain the colonies from producing commodities that might compete with England. Byrd and Beverley kept up a bitter warfare against the Governor, who, Beverley charged, had expressed a desire to hang independent and patriotic Virginians 'with Magna Charta about their necks.'[11]

The two Byrds, father and son, had a personal feud with Nicholson which kept them constantly at war with the Governor. Earlier William Byrd I had obtained the offices of auditor and receiver-general of revenue for Virginia. When receipts were slow during the war that ended with the Treaty of Ryswick in 1697, the senior Byrd had advanced money out of his own pocket to the colonial government with the expectation of being reimbursed out of the quitrents due to the Crown. Nicholson showed no concern over the loan and let Byrd know that he could get his money when and as the duty on tobacco was collected. Furthermore, the Governor set to work to divide the offices of auditor and receiver-general. Though the Byrds staved off the division for the time being, Nicholson did not abandon his plan, and in 1705, a year after the death of the senior Byrd, the two offices were split.

10. Robert Beverley, *The History and Present State of Virginia* (1705). Edited by Louis B. Wright (Chapel Hill, N.C., 1947), 104.

11. Ibid. 107.

Byrd's first period of service for the colony as agent in London gave him an experience that would prove valuable later in his career. He learned the tedious routine of appearing before the Board of Trade, that body vested with the responsibility of advising the Crown on colonial matters. He also learned how to appeal to the Crown and was not abashed when called before the Privy Council, the body that helped to make up the sovereign's mind. Circulating on the fringes of the government and the Court, continuing friendships made earlier, and cultivating other contacts, he led a busy life, profitable to himself and useful to the colony.

5. RETURN TO WESTOVER (1704–1715)

On December 4, 1704, while Byrd was still in London, his father died leaving him heir to all of his landed property in Virginia, a fortune worthy of a young aristocrat. The various plantations and unimproved property totaled 26,231 acres. The best portions of the estate were the lands on the Richmond site and the fourteen-hundred-acre Westover plantation on which the elder Byrd in 1690 had built a comfortable house, furnished with new equipment from Rotterdam.[12] This was a wooden house, later rebuilt by the son in brick. As soon as Byrd could arrange his affairs in London, he sailed for Virginia to take over his inheritance. He arrived in the early spring and at once set about assuming the honors and responsibilities that had been his father's. Already he had been tentatively assured of the offices of auditor and receiver-general, but before he could take them over the posts were divided and in October 1705 Byrd was left with only that of receiver-general. He also applied for his father's place on the Council but others had stronger claims and he had to wait until September 12, 1709, before a vacancy occurred and he could take his place in that body.

As one of the wealthiest and most dazzling young men in the colony, Byrd must have been the target of every matchmaker in Virginia. At any rate, he did not long remain a free man, for on May 4, 1706, he married Lucy Parke, beautiful daughter of Daniel Parke, a

12. Bassett, *Writings*, xxxi, xxxv.

gallant but rakish Virginian who had served with Marlborough on the Continent and had brought the news of the victory at Blenheim to Queen Anne. As a reward for being both a bringer of good news and a graceful courtier, he received the governorship of the Leeward Islands. Parke had married a daughter of Philip Ludwell and had fathered two daughters, Lucy and Frances, both of whom inherited some of their father's violent temper. The father on one occasion demonstrated his own rage by attempting to drag Mrs. James Blair from her pew in Bruton Church because her husband had preached a sermon on adultery pointed particularly at Parke's misconduct.[13]

Though Byrd apparently was passionately fond of his bride Lucy, his life was far from calm, and his household was often in an uproar as a result of his wife's bad disposition. Even so he was luckier than his brother-in-law John Custis, who married Frances. She led Custis such a miserable existence that he provided that his epitaph should state that his bachelor days were the only peaceful ones he had ever known.[14]

Byrd now settled down at Westover to lead the life of a country gentleman, albeit a very hard-working one, for his scattered holdings and his varied activities as planter, lawyer, and auditor required his personal attention and much hard riding to and fro. Like all of his generation, he was land hungry. When Daniel Parke was killed in an uprising in the Leeward Islands in 1710, he left his Virginia estates to his eldest daughter Frances and bequeathed to Lucy only a thousand pounds. Byrd yearned for the lands. Since the will provided that Parke's debts should be paid from the sale of part of his estates, Byrd offered to take over the land that would have to be sold and to assume the obligations for Parke's debts. He never made a worse bargain, for he learned too late that Parke owed his London agent, Micajah Perry, a larger sum than Byrd supposed and in addition had numerous other debts. For the rest of his life, Byrd was saddled with a debt in London as a result of this bargain. Many of his later schemes to colonize land on the frontier were prompted by his need to raise money to

13. Wright, *The First Gentlemen of Virginia*, 80–81.

14. *Memoirs of Washington by his Adopted Son, George Washington Parke Custis with a Memoir of the Author by His Daughter.* Edited by Benson J. Lossing (New York, 1859), 17.

pay off Perry, whom Byrd characterized on more than one occasion
as a grasping usurer.

The details of Byrd's career during this period are clearer than in
the earlier years because entries in his secret diary begin in 1709. This
portion of the diary is the fullest and most complete of any that has yet
come to light. Byrd's daily narrative provides an infinite amount of
detailed information—much of it trivial and repetitious in itself—
which presents in the aggregate a valuable and human picture of plantation life, for Byrd is careful to mention all manner of trifling things,
much as Pepys did.[15] Indeed, though Pepys was more gossipy, the
comparison with his diary is not inappropriate and there are some
striking parallels. Like Pepys, Byrd had his troubles at home, and he
recounts the quarrels with his wife, and an indiscretion now and then.
No trifle is too insignificant to find a place in the journal, even to the
shortening of his coat or the stumbling of his horse, but in such trifles
are unconscious revelations of character and personality not found in
more formal documents.

In this diary Byrd comes to life, and we follow with a living interest the flow of events at Westover. Visitors come and go; slaves
get sick and die—not without a deal of care and medication from the
master; Byrd himself has a cold that lays him low; his daughter is
ailing and his wife is cross; but presently it is spring and the garden
blooms and husband and wife walk together in the twilight with all
quarrels forgotten; ships for England load at the Westover dock
while Byrd hurries his letters and worries about the high rate of
freight and the low price of tobacco; the parson comes to visit and
Mrs. Byrd thinks him unmannerly because he talks Latin with her
husband; a neighbor sends a haunch of venison; meetings of the
Council require Byrd's presence in Williamsburg; he attends court
and is surprised to find a young man on trial for ravishing a homely
woman; he writes an anonymous lampoon on members of the House
of Burgesses, but George Mason gets drunk and reveals the author;
an overseer proves incompetent and has to be discharged; a wind-
storm ravages the crops; the parson preaches a good sermon to a full

15. This section describing the diary for 1709–12 is adapted from a previous essay,
'William Byrd of Westover, An American Pepys,' *The South Atlantic Quarterly*,
XXXIX (1940), 259–74.

church; Byrd spends a wet day planting trees, gets his feet soaked and has to stop to change his stockings; newspapers come from England saying there is no likelihood of peace in Europe; and so the diary runs, an intensely human narrative enumerating thousands of forgotten incidents that throw light on the times and illuminate the character of Virginia's most important man of letters in the Colonial period.

Busy as the master of Westover usually found himself, he followed a routine of reading and study and disliked encroachments upon the time devoted to Hebrew, Greek, Latin, or one of the modern languages, usually French or Italian. Though Byrd was far from an ascetic, he believed a gentleman should cultivate his mind, even at the cost of some exertion; hence he followed a custom of rising early and reading Hebrew and Greek before breakfast; during the rest of the day other less edifying matters might engage him. For instance, on November 2, 1709, he writes:

I rose at 6 o'clock and read a chapter in Hebrew and some Greek in Lucian. I said my prayers and ate milk for breakfast, and settled some accounts, and then went to court where we made an end of the business. We went to dinner about 4 o'clock and I ate boiled beef again. In the evening I went to Dr. B-r-t's, where my wife came this afternoon. Here I found Mrs. Chisweil, my sister Custis, and other ladies. We sat and talked till about 11 o'clock, and then retired to our chambers. I played at [r-m] with Mrs. Chiswell and kissed her on the bed till she was angry and my wife also was uneasy about it, and cried as soon as the company was gone. I neglected to say my prayers, which I should not have done, because I ought to beg pardon for the lust I had for another man's wife. However, I had good health, good thoughts, and good humor, thanks be to God Almighty.

Precisely a month later, on December 2, after noting his daily stint of Greek and Hebrew, he comments: 'In the evening I read more Italian and washed my feet.' The diary frequently mentions the writer's displeasure because he had been interrupted in his reading. Guests in the house, a sudden journey, or something else occasionally interfered with his routine. On November 13, 1709, while visiting Colonel Custis, Byrd was somewhat put out by having to forego his reading in order to hurry off to church:

I rose about 7 o'clock but could read nothing because we were in haste to go to church. I ate milk for breakfast, notwithstanding it was here not very good. About 10 o'clock we rode to church, which is 6 miles off. There was the biggest congregation I ever saw in the country. The people look half dead since the sickness which they had last year. Mr. Dunn preached a good sermon. After church we returned to Colonel Custis' again. About three o'clock we dined and I ate boiled beef. In the evening we drank a bottle of wine pretty freely and were full of mirth and good humor and particularly Colonel Waters. However we were merry and wise and went to bed in good time by my means. I neglected to say my prayers but had good health, good thoughts, and good humor, thanks be to God Almighty.

Though the diary mentions frequent quarrels between Byrd and his wife, he undoubtedly had great affection for her. The daughter of Daniel Parke could hardly have been anything but spoiled and temperamental, and the Byrd household could not have escaped a clash of wills. A crisis occurred on February 5, 1711, when Mrs. Byrd insisted upon plucking her eyebrows in preparation for the Governor's ball in Williamsburg on the Queen's birthday:

I rose about eight o'clock and found my cold still worse. I said my prayers and ate milk and potatoes for breakfast. My wife and I quarreled about her pulling her brows. She threatened she would not go to Williamsburg if she might not pull them; I refused, however, and got the better of her and maintained my authority. . . .

The following day—the day of the ball—Byrd had such a cold that his wife cheerfully offered to stay at home with him, but 'rather than keep her from going, I resolved to go if possible.' After being 'shaved with a very dull razor' and getting off to a bad start by neglecting to say his prayers, Byrd pulled himself together sufficiently to attend the function. He was pleased to find Colonel Carter's wife and daughter there and rather proud that 'the Governor opened the ball with a French dance with my wife,' after which 'we danced country dances for an hour and the company was carried into another room where was a very fine collation of sweetmeats.' 'The Governor,' Byrd reports, 'was very gallant to the ladies and very courteous to

the gentlemen.' This was Lieutenant Governor Alexander Spotswood. The night of the ball was villainously wet and the guests had
trouble getting to their lodgings in Williamsburg:

Colonel Carter's family and Mr. Blair were stopped by the unruliness of
the horses and Daniel Wilkinson was so gallant as to lead the horse himself through all the dirt and rain to Mr. Blair's house. My cold continued
bad. I neglected to say my prayers and had good thoughts, good humor,
but indifferent health, thank God Almighty. It rained all day and all
night. The President [of the Council] had the worst clothes of anybody
there.

That masters were not unmindful of the rights and privileges of
servants and slaves, the diary makes amply clear. For example, on the
day after the ball, the Governor thoughtfully permitted his house-
servants to get drunk in reward for staying sober the day before, as
an entry for February 7, 1711, explains:

I rose at 8 o'clock and found my cold continued. I said my prayers and
ate boiled milk for breakfast. I went to see Mr. Clayton who lay sick of the
gout. About 11 o'clock my wife and I went to wait on the Governor in
the President's coach. We went there to take our leave but were forced
to stay all day. The Governor had made a bargain with his servants that
if they would forbear to drink upon the Queen's birthday, they might be
drunk this day. They observed their contract and did their business very
well and got very drunk today, in such a manner that Mrs. Russell's maid
was forced to lay the [cloth], but the cook in that condition made a shift
to send in a pretty little dinner. I ate some mutton cutlets. In the afternoon
I persuaded my wife to stay all night in town and so it was resolved to
spend the evening in cards. My cold was very bad and I lost my money.
About 10 o'clock the Governor's coach carried us home to our lodgings
where my wife was out of humor and I out of order. I said a short prayer
and had good thoughts and good humor, thank God Almighty.

Byrd himself, though a strict disciplinarian, was a reasonable master.
Sometimes he whipped a slave for disobedience or negligence, but
usually the culprit got off with a threat. During an epidemic among
his slaves in January 1711, he worked hard to save them. Early and
late he was at the quarters giving 'his people' medicine; when they

had slightly improved he provided a bowl of his own best punch to raise their spirits. The plague he regarded as a judgment sent by God for his own sins.

Despite frailties of the flesh confessed in the journal, Byrd was sincerely religious. Indeed, the diary furnishes a needed corrective to the notion that the so-called Cavaliers of Virginia were an utterly worldly race without regard for godliness. As a matter of fact, the gentlemen who made up the ruling class considered religion an essential to a proper life and believed that a civilized society without religion was a contradiction in terms. Like most of his class, Byrd was an Anglican. He attended church, performed his devotions, and read religious books with relish. Because of the great sickness throughout the community at Christmas in 1710, the religious observance was the only notice taken of the holiday. Byrd and his family attended church and he received the communion devoutly, as he is at pains to mention in the diary. Afterward he read a sermon, though he had words with his wife and found it hard to concentrate on a work of piety:

I rose at 5 o'clock and read a chapter in Hebrew and some Greek in Lucian. About 7 o'clock the negro woman died that was mad yesterday. I said my prayers and ate boiled milk for breakfast. The wind blew very strong and it rained exceedingly.... About 11 o'clock we went to church where we had prayers and the Holy Sacrament which I took devoutly. We brought nobody home to dinner. I ate boiled venison. The child was a little better. In the afternoon I took a long walk and I saw several parts of the fence blown down with the wind which blew very hard last night. In the evening I read a sermon in Mr. Norris but a quarrel which I had with my wife hindered my taking much notice of it. However, we were reconciled before we went to bed, but I made the first advance. I neglected to say my prayers but not to eat some milk. I had good health, good thoughts, and indifferent good humor, thank God almighty.

This planter, who also loved the things of this world, frequently found spiritual refreshment in a stout sermon. One of his favorite authors was Archbishop John Tillotson, whose eloquent preaching the young Virginia student may have heard in London.

The eighteenth century was given to excessive eating of meat, but in his diet Byrd exceeded even the usual consumption of flesh. Sometime earlier he had developed a food fad which led him to restrict his choice to one or two dishes at a meal. Almost invariably the staple consisted of a heavy meat, frequently pork or boiled beef. Venison, turkey (both domestic and wild), chicken, duck, goose, partridge, squirrel, and fish were other meats that pleased his palate. Asparagus and green peas were among the few vegetables he deigned to eat. Wine was the staple beverage at Westover, and the cellars were plentifully supplied with good vintages and brandy, from which the master sometimes brewed a powerful punch.

The library at Westover, which numbered more than thirty-six hundred items at Byrd's death, was already one of his proudest possessions. During August 1709, he was busy putting it in order. On August 15 he moved two cases of books into the library and proceeded to arrange them, 'notwithstanding Mr. [Isham] Randolph was here.' In his library the busy planter spent many hours snatched at intervals between multifarious responsibilities.

Byrd was ambitious all his life for the honors and dignities of office. At one time and another he tried to procure through his political friends in England the governorships of both Virginia and Maryland. In 1710 the titular governor of Virginia was George Hamilton, Earl of Orkney, but it was customary to appoint a lieutenant who actually lived in the colony and served as royal administrator. Byrd was angling for this post in 1710 but notes in his diary for March 31 that he had failed:

I met Mr. Bland who brought me several letters from England and among the rest two from Colonel Blakiston who had endeavored to procure the government of Virginia for me at the price of 1000 pounds of my Lady Orkney and that my Lord agreed but the Duke of Marlborough declared that no one but soldiers should have the government of a plantation; so I was disappointed. God's will be done. I ate fish for dinner.

The man who did receive the appointment was a soldier who had been wounded at Blenheim, Alexander Spotswood, a tough-minded Scot who thwarted Byrd on more than one occasion. In the end, however, like Adams and Jefferson in their old age, they became friends.

Byrd had to be satisfied with the honors that came to him as a member of the Council and as commander-in-chief of the militia for Henrico and Charles City counties. The latter appointment gave him much satisfaction, particularly when a threat of a French invasion in August 1711 required a general muster and caused much excitement. In the previous year, September 21, 1710, he notes in his diary his pleasure over the Governor's courtesy and satisfaction at a muster of the Charles City militia:

The Governor was pleased with everything and very complaisant. About ten o'clock Captain Stith came and soon after him Colonel Hill, Mr. Anderson and several others of the militia officers. The Governor was extremely courteous to them. About twelve o'clock Mr. Clayton went to Mrs. Harrison's and then orders were given to bring all the men into the pasture to muster. Just as we got on our horses it began to rain hard; however this did not discourage the Governor but away we rode to the men. It rained half an hour and the Governor mustered them all the while and he presented me to the people to be their colonel and commander-in-chief. About three o'clock we returned to the house and as many of the officers as could sit at the table stayed to dine with the Governor, and the rest went to take part of the hogshead [of punch] in the churchyard. We had a good dinner, well served, with which the Governor seemed to be well pleased. I ate venison for dinner.

Although Byrd was to engage in various controversies with Spotswood, he was eager in this period to keep on the best terms possible with him. For this reason he was upset, as he notes in his diary for January 9, 1712, when someone reported to Spotswood that he had said that no governor ought to be trusted with as much as £20,000. On January 24 he notes that when he called on Spotswood, the Governor 'looked very stiff and cold on me.'

Byrd's difficulties with Spotswood arose from both personal and public problems. Spotswood had come to Virginia determined to increase the prerogatives of the Crown's representative. That brought him into conflict with the Council of State, which in reality was a powerful oligarchy composed of the leading planters.[16]

16. A discussion of Byrd's controversies with Spotswood will be found in Bassett, *Writings*, li-lxxv.

As the man with the best legal training on the Council, Byrd naturally took the lead in the debates with Spotswood, who was determined to curb the Council's authority. The highest court in the colony was the General Court, which in actuality consisted of members
of the Council and the Governor. To enhance the Crown's prerogative, Spotswood in 1710 got a law passed to enable the Governor to
call into force special courts of oyer and terminer to try cases where
the interests of members of the Council might be involved, or any
cases at the Governor's will. The Council at once saw that this would
abridge its own prerogatives and place such authority in the hands of
the Governor that he might exercise tyrannical and arbitrary power.
A long and bitter feud ensued, with an indecisive conclusion. Though
Spotswood won technical victories, in the end the Council kept its
authority. Byrd was the leader of the Council in its fight and helped
to increase its prestige. As one historian has commented, 'instead of
throwing the Councillors, who through abilities and position were the
natural leaders of the community, into an inane espousal of the rights
of the Crown it [the controversy] developed in them a strong colony sense. They felt that they were Virginians first of all.'[17] Byrd's
love of England and English institutions did not obscure for him the
dangers implicit in increasing the royal prerogative and he fought
valiantly and successfully against encroachments on what he con-
ceived to be Virginia's liberties.

Another point of conflict with Spotswood concerned the Governor's criticism of Byrd's administration of the office of receiver-
general, specifically of his collection of the quitrents. Although
Spotswood did not accuse Byrd of dishonesty, he did suggest that the
methods in practice were slipshod and careless, designed to favor the
planters as against the Crown, and in need of overhauling. He asked
Byrd and Philip Ludwell, Jr., the auditor, to make proposals for improving the collection of quitrents but in November 1714 he proposed a scheme of his own. Though Byrd objected strenuously to
Spotswood's plan, the Council passed it and after the first year Spotswood boasted that one third of the Crown lands had yielded more
revenue than all of them had yielded in the previous year. Byrd had
other private grievances against the Governor, not least of them be-

17. Ibid. liii.

ing a law that Spotswood managed to get passed in 1714 creating a company to monopolize the Indian trade.

By 1713 Byrd had an accumulation of private business matters that required him to go to England. For one thing, he wanted to straighten out the involved affairs of his late father-in-law, Daniel Parke, whose debts he had assumed. For another, he wanted to lay before the Board of Trade complaints against the Governor and enlist the help of his friends in getting some of the Governor's laws repealed. But it was not until the late winter of 1714 or early spring of 1715 that Byrd finally sailed for England. He probably did not realize that he would not see Virginia again for another five years.

6. LIFE IN ENGLAND (1715–1720)

Byrd left behind in Virginia his wife and eight-year-old daughter Evelyn. In the autumn after his departure, another daughter, Wilhelmina, was born. Two sons born earlier had died in infancy. When Byrd realized that he probably would have to remain in England for a longer time than he had planned, he sent for Lucy, who arrived apparently in the late summer of 1716, leaving the infant Wilhelmina in Virginia. Byrd was proud of Lucy and was pleased with the reception she received from his friends. But his joy was shortlived. On November 21, 1716, Lucy died of smallpox, the dread malady that carried off so many colonials who made the journey to England. To his brother-in-law, John Custis, Byrd wrote on December 13 to report the sad news. 'Gracious God, what pains did she take to make a voyage hither to seek a grave,' he remarks. 'No stranger ever met with more respect in a strange country than she had done here from many persons of distinction, who all pronounced her an honor to Virginia.'[18]

In the following year Byrd sent for Evelyn. On October 19, 1717, he wrote Custis that Evelyn had arrived some weeks before 'very safe' in the care of Captain Wray and was 'very busy in learning everything that is proper for her.'[19] In April 1719 Wilhelmina, then

18. Ibid. lxxvii.
19. Woodfin, *Another Secret Diary*, xxii, 323.

not yet four years old, came over in the care of Byrd's friend, Captain Isham Randolph. At this time Byrd had his own quarters on a street just off the Strand, but they were probably unsuitable for his children. At any rate, he placed his two daughters with friends or relatives and contented himself with frequent visits, as his diary indicates.

Evelyn grew up into a charming girl, and as the heiress of a Virginia gentleman was a likely catch for any fortune hunter. Such a man, a baronet whose identity has escaped historians, evidently won the heart of the sixteen-year-old girl, for Byrd preserved a copy of an indignant letter that he wrote to the suitor, whose name is disguised in the copy simply as 'Erranti.'

I am informed upon very good evidence [Byrd writes], that you have for some time taken the trouble to follow Amasia [disguised name for Evelyn] with your addresses; that now at last you have played the wise part of a knight errant and pursued her into the country with a pompous equipage that does her and your self much honor. What success these worthy steps have met in the girl, I know not; but they shall never meet with any in the father. I fear your circumstances are not flourishing enough to maintain a wife in such splendor that has nothing, and just such a fortune as that my daughter will prove if she venture to marry without my consent. You are deluded if you believe any part of my estate is settled upon her, or that she has anything independent of my pleasure. I confess you have not deserved it from me but I will however stand your friend so far as to assure you before hand that her portion will be extremely small if she bestows herself upon so clandestine a lover. I have made my will since I heard of your good intention towards me, and have bequeathed my daughter a splendid shilling if she marries any man that tempts her to disobedience . . . [20]

Along with this letter there is a copy of a letter from Byrd to Evelyn forbidding her to marry 'the baronet.'[21] A tradition in the Byrd family has maintained that the nobleman was the Earl of Peterborough, but this seems unlikely as he was an old man at this time. In any case, Evelyn never married and returned to Virginia to die a spinster at thirty. Wilhelmina also returned to Virginia, married Thomas Cham-

20. Ibid. 383–5.
21. Ibid. 381–3.

berlayne of New Kent County, and left numerous descendants.

As a widower of means as well as charm, Byrd himself could expect to find an heiress whose fortune might augment his Virginia estates. The search for such an heiress became his fixed purpose. The diary printed here and the letters in the University of North Carolina letterbook provide a day-by-day account of his amazing pursuit of Mary Smith, daughter of John Smith, Esq., of Beaufort Buildings, a Commissioner of Excise.[22] Beaufort Buildings were in Beaufort Street, west of the Savoy, and were fashionable flats. Byrd lived across the street and could see his beloved from a window in his own flat. John Smith came of a good Lincolnshire family and was both proud and wealthy. In the long series of letters in the North Carolina letterbook, Mary is called Sabina and her father Vigilante.

The letters to Sabina are in the high-flown style learned from French romances and, like the love letters of everybody, except one's own, are a bore. 'The last masquerade wanted no creature but the charming Sabina to make it the most agreeable entertainment in the world,' Byrd writes on March 23, 1717. 'All the goddesses were there but the Queen of Love, who would have appeared to disadvantage in any figure but yours. I fear the old dragon [her father] that guards the golden fruit would not consent to your tasting so much pleasure abroad lest you should come to detest your confinement at home.' He offers her a ticket to the next masquerade ball, a popular form of entertainment in London at the time, and he hopes that she will accept it and be able to attend: 'How shall I know whether my dearest Sabina will please to accept my ticket? If she does, I beg that this may be the gracious signal: let her about ten o'clock lift up the sash and look with consenting smile towards my apartment. Adieu, thou most enchanting of the sex, and may angels without envy guard you from everything that is unfortunate.'[23]

The forty-three-year-old widower pursued his courtship with energy, if not always with success. He tries to arrange for meetings which do not come off. He writes to Mary in invisible ink but the 'elixir' with which she tries to bring out the writing fails to work. The lover fills his letters with sighs over his disappointments and expres-

22. Ibid. 298, 321.
23. Ibid. 298-9.

sions of passionate ecstasy when Mary writes a favorable note. He employs go-betweens to plead for him and enlists the aid of Mary's sister, Lady Dunkellen, and Lord Dunkellen. He sees Mary at a ball or in the presence of friends and believes that she will marry him if her father will consent. Byrd struggles to convince John Smith that he will make a suitable match for his daughter. In the hope of persuading him, he submits a statement of his financial worth, a document, incidentally, of some value to economic historians. His estate, he remarks, 'though it lie so far off as Virginia, is very considerable. I have there about 43,000 acres of land and 220 Negroes at work upon it with a prodigious quantity of stock of every kind . . . What can I tell you for certain is to show how much clear money my returns have yielded the three years since I have been over. In the year 1715 they produced clear of all charge £1716:5-. In the year 1716 they cleared no more than £1535:14:11. But this year they will yield more than £1800.'[24] He promised to settle the whole estate upon Mary Smith except for a dowry of £4,000 which he expected to set aside for his two daughters. On April 7, 1718, he notes in his diary that he had tried to borrow from Micajah Perry £10,000 to settle upon Miss Smith, but that business man was too canny to advance Byrd so large a sum in addition to the money already owed on Daniel Parke's debts. In the end, Smith declared that Byrd's means were insufficient and gave his blessing to the suit of Sir Edward Des Bouverie, son of a wealthy Levant merchant. Mary married Sir Edward on July 8, 1718. Two days afterward, her father died.[25] Presumably Byrd realized that she would soon inherit a fortune, which may explain the eagerness of his suit. Three years after her marriage Mary was dead.

Byrd was not a graceful loser. He had fought for Mary's hand and fortune with the zeal of a trial lawyer and he did not yield until the last stratagem had failed. He had begged, cajoled, and threatened her. 'I have the proper arguments in my strong box to persuade any man of justice and commonsense not to marry a gentlewoman that has proceeded so far with another gentleman,' he wrote her on April 28.[26] And when he realized that all was lost he wrote an ungallant let-

24. Ibid. 322.
25. Ibid. 321.
26. Ibid. 349.

ter to his successful rival. 'Since you did me the honor of a visit the other day,' he commented, 'I have been beating my brains to find out who should write those fine letters which you was pleased to show me. By a certain very gross expression that I remember in one of 'em, I could almost suspect it might come from Mr. Smith himself because it was the very appellation he thought fit to use to his daughter after I had explained to him the encouragement she had given me. For my back was no sooner turned but he went into the next room (convinced as he was of the unfair treatment I had received) and with much tenderness and good breeding called her bitch and jilt.'[27] There had been talk of a duel with Des Bouverie but it blew over. Thus ended an adventure in fortune-hunting, which the reader can follow in the diary and in the letters concerning it which Byrd carefully preserved in the North Carolina notebook.

During the time that he was professing his undying love and loyalty to Mary Smith, Byrd was consoling himself with numerous light-of-loves whom he found in London's bagnios, picked up on the streets, or selected from the choices roaming in St. James's Park. He was also visiting his surgeon for the treatment of a troublesome case of gonorrhea. All of these matters he sets down with care in his diary. For a time he was content to keep as his mistress a certain Mrs. A-l-c, whom he paid two guineas a visit, but at length he dismissed her for infidelity. Throughout his residence in London he was notoriously promiscuous and was not above lying in the grass of St. James's Park with some *fille de joie* whom he had picked up on the street. On one occasion, the diary for October 4, 1718, records, when he found absent Mrs. A-l-n, whose favors he sought, he whiled away the time until she returned by making love to her maid. To complete the evening, after an intimate rendezvous with Mrs. A-l-n, he 'went home and ate a plum cake for supper.' His amours, however, caused him some pangs of conscience, and he periodically resolved to give up wenching. At intervals he went in the morning to St. Clement Danes to ask God to forgive him, but his repentance frequently did not last out the day.

As a man of fashion, Byrd took part in the varied social life on the fringes of the Court of George I. Among his friends were substantial

27. Ibid. 357.

officials of the government and members of the Court circle. He was a frequent visitor at the Spanish Ambassador's where many gay blades gathered, though now and then Byrd notes that he had spent a dull evening there. He enjoyed the masquerade balls with their opportunities for intrigues. He went to the theaters, more for the company than for the plays. On February 1, 1718, he records that he 'went to Will's Coffeehouse and from thence to the play, where I slept.'

A visit to Bridewell Prison, where vagrants and prostitutes were confined, provided more exciting entertainment than the theater. On March 2, 1718, he went with Mr. LeGrande to view the prison and 'to see the people make pins, which was very pretty. Then we saw the ladies beat hemp. Then we went to see the men at fetters, and from thence we went to see a [she lion?].' Cardplaying and other forms of gaming provided frequent amusement for him, but more often than not he lost money, sometimes considerable sums. The coffeehouses took a fair amount of his time, for he was constantly at the Virginia Coffeehouse, Will's Coffeehouse, or the St. James Coffeehouse to read the news and pick up gossip. Sometimes he visited his bookseller to select new titles for his library. For a time he took drawing lessons. When he was in deep distress about his unhappy suit for the hand of Mary Smith he visited a conjuror and fortune-teller for light on his situation. At intervals he went to see his daughters and sometimes took them with him when he called on Micajah Perry and other members of the Perry family who handled his business. He attended church with commendable regularity and gave evidence of a devout regard for his prayers. When Lord Percival came around collecting for the benefit of converts from Popery, Byrd contributed a guinea. If much of his activity seems trivial, it must be remembered that he was making 'contacts' and cultivating people who, he believed, would be useful to him.

For in addition to his private business, Byrd was both unofficially and officially working in the interest of the colony of Virginia. The controversies with Spotswood had grown more heated at home, and in April 1718 the House of Burgesses voted to give Byrd once again the title and a salary as agent for the colony. Spotswood vetoed the action, but the Burgesses went ahead with their plan and agreed to pay Byrd to represent them anyway.[28] In the meantime, Byrd had sold his office of receiver-general to James Roscow for £500. He had found the post difficult to manage by deputy and a continuance in the office gave Spotswood an opening to charge him with negligence if not with misappropriation of the Crown's funds.[29]

On November 17, 1718, Byrd was 'presented to the King as agent of Virginia and I kissed the King's hand, at which Lord Orkney was very angry.' As Spotswood's superior, Orkney of course was opposed to Byrd's mission. In representations before the Board of Trade and in an appeal to the Crown, Byrd pointed out that though Spotswood might have the legal right to establish courts of oyer and terminer and appoint the judges, the exercise of this right might threaten the liberties of the King's subjects in Virginia and would be exceedingly unpopular. The King asked for a report from the Board of Trade but in the end upheld his representative in Virginia. In the meantime, Spotswood had forced the Council to admit his right to appoint the judges, but he quieted their fears somewhat by promising to appoint only members of the Council. Having won this victory, he sought to have Byrd, along with Philip Ludwell and James Blair, removed from the Council. Byrd, he wrote Lord Orkney, had been too long absent from Virginia to hold his place on the Council. The affair dragged on until the spring of 1719 when Byrd capitulated and promised the Board of Trade to make peace with Spotswood provided that they would write conciliatory letters to the Council. For himself he begged that he might have permission to remain in England another year without losing his place on the Council, a request which the King at length granted.[30] Without the King's assurance, Byrd had expressed fear of returning to Virginia in the face of Spotswood's hostility.

One piece of unfinished business that continued to detain Byrd was the search for an heiress. Undiscouraged by the loss of Mary Smith and her fortune, he turned his attention next to a certain Widow Pierson, a resident of Dover Street, whom he had met at the Spanish Ambassador's. His diary from June 1718 until July 1719 records his

28. Bassett, *Writings*, lxxi.
29. Ibid. lxiii.
30. Ibid. lxxiv-lxxv.

diligence in the pursuit of Mrs. Pierson, but she finally turned him down because his daughters were a handicap. Missives in the North Carolina letterbook to Zenobia may have been addressed to Mrs. Pierson.[31] Having lost Mrs. Pierson, in August 1719 he took off for Tunbridge Wells to console himself with the amusements of that fashionable watering place. Though he met many pretty women, including one Sally Cornish, who fascinated him, he made no conquests and was probably glad to get back to London on September 7.

The time was approaching when Byrd would have to return to Virginia. All through November 1719 he was busy winding up his affairs in London and on November 24 he set out for Dover to await the ship that was to take him to Virginia. He embarked on December 9. With him he took at least two white servants, the maids Annie and Hannah. His two daughters he left in England.

The voyage lasted eight weeks and two days. Byrd occupied his time with reading and writing and conversing with the captain. Frequently he notes that he read aloud to the captain, or drank punch or brandy with him. On Sunday, December 27, he records that he 'read a sermon to the captain and my maids till nine o'clock and then I retired and said my prayers but slept indifferently.' Much of the time the weather was rough and the ship rolled incessantly. On January 26, when they were off Cape Hatteras, Byrd was so concerned about the danger that he confesses that he 'slept but indifferently because I had Cape Hatteras in my head. However I said my prayers.' Finally, on February 2, they rounded the Virginia capes and 'sailed in about seven leagues and then came to anchor.' Whether they were headed up the James or the York River, Byrd does not make clear, but two days later after unfavorable winds had prevented further headway, he had the captain send him ashore in the ship's boat. After staying with a certain Captain Smith until February 8, he made his way to Williamsburg, and on February 13 he reached Westover. What he found was not to his liking, for his nephew John Brayne, whom he had sent over from London to look after his affairs, had, among other things, 'spoiled my guns and drunk up abundance of my wine.' But Byrd made the best of it and settled comfortably into plantation life. He notes on February 14 that, 'I began to kiss my girl Annie'—one

31. Woodfin, *Another Secret Diary*, xxv-xxvi, 259-66.

of the maids whom he had brought from England. But Annie was not too eager to be his mistress and sometimes shamed him, and he had the grace to praise her for her own occasional efforts at resistance. On December 26, 1720, he commented that he 'was resolved to avoid playing the fool with Annie' and the next day he wrote that he said his prayers 'and resolved to forbear Annie by God's grace.' On New Year's Eve he strengthened his resolution by reading 'in the *Whole Duty of Man* which edified me very much.' But despite these efforts, he was unable to give up Annie completely. Though not a celibate, at least for a while he would lead a bachelor's life.

During this period Byrd made extensive improvements at Westover, though the rebuilding of the house must have occurred later. At any rate he mentions the receipt of a sloop-load of shingles, and on April 11, 1720, he notes that he gave 'the bricklayer a bottle of rum for laying the bricks.' On the same day he 'put several things in order in the library.' The garden at Westover and his library were his particular pride and he took pleasure in showing them to guests.

Byrd's life was brightened in April 1720 by a sudden and unexpected reconciliation with Spotswood. Ever since his return his relations with the Governor had been strained. Spotswood had also shown great coldness to Philip Ludwell and Commissary James Blair. At a meeting of the Council on April 29 Byrd reports:

. . . there passed abundance of hard words between the Governor and Council about Colonel Ludwell and Mr. Commissary for about two hours till of a sudden the clouds cleared away and we began to be perfectly good friends and we agreed upon terms of lasting reconciliation to the great surprise of ourselves and everybody else. The Governor invited us to dinner and there was illumination all the town over and everybody expressed great joy. The Governor kissed us all round and gave me a kiss more than other people.

Spotswood's reconciliation with the Council did not prevent further political strain between the Governor and individual members, including Byrd, who had long hoped to succeed him, a hope that was dashed in 1722 when Spotswood was removed and Hugh Drysdale was appointed in his place.[32] However, after Spotswood's retirement

32. Leonidas Dodson, *Alexander Spotswood, Governor of Colonial Virginia 1710-1722* (Philadelphia, 1932), 270-71.

to the life of a Virginia planter, he and Byrd exchanged pleasant visits.

At intervals in his diary, Byrd mentions writing something. A part of his leisure at Westover during the winter of 1721 he devoted to writing a treatise on the plague. On February 20 he is writing 'some English concerning the plague,' and on March 16 he remarks that he 'wrote my book fair about the plague and made a good beginning.' On March 22 he 'read over my book about the plague and corrected it till dinner,' and on Sunday, March 26, Colonel Nathaniel Harrison, of Wakefield, came for breakfast and 'I read some of my plague book to him.' Among a number of tracts on the plague published in England in 1721 there was one entitled *A Discourse Concerning the Plague with Some Preservatives Against It. By a Lover of Mankind*.[33] This pamphlet Miss Maude Woodfin identifies as by William Byrd. Although positive proof is lacking, it seems likely from the style and contents that this was Byrd's plague book. If he indeed is the author, this is the only complete work from his pen published in his lifetime. Its propaganda for the use of tobacco as a specific against the plague would at least argue that some interested colonial planter had composed it. Byrd always fancied himself something of a doctor and the subject was congenial to him.

7. IN ENGLAND AGAIN (1721–26)

In the summer of 1721, Byrd sailed again for England. Unhappily, the diary ceases after May 19 and we cannot follow in detail his actions in London. We do not know precisely what prompted this journey so soon after his return to Westover, but it is certain that both personal and colonial matters required his presence in London. At any rate, he was once more appointed agent for the colony. Commissary Blair, now his ally, also went along. And within a year Spotswood was relieved of his post. What influence Byrd had with the Board of Trade and with the politicians in London is a matter of conjecture, but we can be sure he was busy and not in Spotswood's interest.

33. Woodfin, *Another Secret Diary*, 411ff.

Byrd also had not given up his search for an heiress. And he paid court this time to Lady Elizabeth Lee, a widow and a granddaughter of Charles II and his mistress, Barbara Villiers. She too turned him down and later married Edward Young, author of *Night Thoughts*. As he had reproached Mary Smith, so Byrd denounced Elizabeth Lee for encouraging and then rejecting him. She was the 'Charmante' of a series of love letters that he left tied up with a note saying that 'These passionate billets were sent to a lady who had more charm than honor, more wit than discretion.'[34] To various other ladies he paid court without avail until finally he persuaded Maria Taylor, daughter of Thomas Taylor of Kensington, deceased, to marry him on May 7, 1724. Since her mother was still living and seemed to promise trouble, he married Maria and then notified his mother-in-law of the *fait accompli*.[35]

Maria made Byrd a good wife and outlived him by twenty-seven years. He had to be content with her good qualities, however, for she brought with her no material fortune. She bore Byrd four children, Anne, Maria, William, and Jane, all born between 1725 and 1729. William, the only surviving son and heir, was born on September 6, 1728. Byrd several times comments in his letters on the prolific nature of his wife. She clearly was a homeloving soul and much more placid than Lucy Parke. With his marriage to Maria, Byrd entered upon an era of domestic calm that he had not previously known. That he was strictly faithful is to be doubted, for even in his old age his diary for 1739–41 records that he 'played the fool' with Sally and Sarah on several occasions.

The daily record of Byrd's activities in London during this period is lacking but we can surmise that he and Maria occupied themselves with the usual social activities of balls, the theater, and visits with their friends. For much of the time, Maria was pregnant. Byrd was several times before the Board of Trade on business for the colony, and he was in constant touch with some member of the Perry firm about his debts or the sale of his tobacco. Finally in 1726 he and his wife bade farewell to England and came to Virginia. For the rest of his life Byrd would remain on the American side of the Atlantic.

34. Ibid. xxxii–xxxiii.
35. Ibid. xxv.

8. VIRGINIA SQUIRE AND PUBLIC SERVANT (1726–44)

Byrd's plantation and his business affairs required his attention. His life in London had been expensive; his overseers in Virginia had been something less than efficient; and his debts were pressing. He at once set about improving his estates and searching for new ways of adding to his income. He experimented with hemp and grapevines in the hope of finding a money crop in addition to tobacco. He sought for ginseng, an herb which he firmly believed would prove a panacea for most of man's ills and a profitable commodity in the Virginia trade. Like many of his Virginia contemporaries he sought for mineral wealth on his lands and hoped to find mines that could be easily worked. For the rest of his life he was concerned with the exploitation of his landed property in various ways: by farming, by mining, and by the sale or lease of land to immigrants from overseas. These matters kept him extremely busy for the first two or three years after his return.

His letters to his friends in England try to give the impression that he is leading an idyllic life as Horace or Virgil might have described country pleasures and pursuits. In a letter to Charles Boyle, the Earl of Orrery, dated July 5, 1726, Byrd described his patriarchal state:

... Besides the advantage of a pure air, we abound in all kinds of provisions without expense (I mean we who have plantations). I have a large family of my own, and my doors are open to everybody, yet I have no bills to pay, and half-a-crown will rest undisturbed in my pocket for many moons together. Like one of the patriarchs, I have my flocks and my herds, my bondmen and bondwomen, and every sort of trade amongst my own servants so that I live in a kind of independence of everyone but Providence. However this sort of life is without expense, yet it is attended with a great deal of trouble. I must take care to keep all my people to their duty, to set all the springs in motion and to make every one draw his equal share to carry the machine forward. But then 'tis an amusement in this silent country and a continual exercise of our patience and economy. Another thing My Lord, that recommends this country very much: we sit securely under our vines and our fig trees without any danger to our property. We have neither public robbers nor private, which your Lordship will think very strange when we have often needy governors and pilfering convicts sent amongst us. . . . Thus, my Lord, we are very happy in our Canaans if we could but forget the onions and fleshpots of Egypt. . . . [36]

To John, Lord Boyle, he wrote on February 2, 1727, describing the pleasure that his daughters Evelyn and Wilhelmina took in their new life in Virginia: 'My young gentlewomen like everything in the country except the retirement; they can't get the plays, the operas, and the masquerades out of their heads; much less can they forget their friends. However, the lightness of our atmosphere helps them to bear all their losses with more spirit, and that they may amuse themselves the better, they are every day up to their elbows in housewifery, which will qualify them effectually for useful wives and if they live long enough, for notable women.' [37] In an undated letter in the Huntington Library addressed to a Mrs. Armiger, a friend in London, Byrd remarked that 'We that are banish't from these polite pleasures [of London] are forced to take up with rural entertainments. A library, a garden, a grove, and a purling stream are the innocent scenes that divert our leisure.' [38]

A less idyllic and more realistic picture of another side of life in Virginia may be seen in a letter dated June 27, 1729, to an unnamed business correspondent in England concerning a shipment of tobacco and an order of goods for his family:

. . . You will herewith receive the invoice for my family and [I] beg you will please to employ your interest with the tradesmen not to send all the refuse of their shops to Virginia. Desire them to keep them for the customers that never pay them. 'Tis hard we must take all the worst of their people and the worst of their goods too. But now shopkeepers have left off their bands and their frugality and their spouses must be maintained in splendor, 'tis very fit the sweat of our brows should help to support them in it. Luxury is bad enough amongst people of quality but when it gets among that order of men that stand behind counters they must turn cheats and pick-pockets to get it, and the Lord have mercy on

36. *The Virginia Magazine of History and Biography*, XXXII (1924), 26-8.
37. Ibid. 28-30.
38. Huntington Library MS, Brock 188, V, No. 14.

those who are obliged to trust to their honesty. . . . We have yet no tidings
of the 'Williamsburg' so that we are ignorant whether it be war or peace.
I wish [hope?] you know there. Affairs have been so long between hawk
and buzzard that I have not known which to call it for these two years
past. . . . [39]

Despite his arduous duties in the management of his plantations,
Byrd was able in 1728 to accept the leadership of the Virginia commission appointed to collaborate with a similar commission from
North Carolina in settling the long-vexed problem of the boundary
between the two colonies. The line was run in the spring and fall of
1728, and the episode is described in detail in two separate accounts
from Byrd's pen, besides official reports in the public records. The
best known account is *The History of the Dividing Line Betwixt
Virginia and North Carolina Run in the Year of Our Lord 1728*, first
published in 1841 and several times since.[40] The other account is *The
Secret History of the Line*, radically different from the other, which
was not published until 1929.[41] The first version is an entertaining
literary narration of the events, told in an amusing fashion, with many
satirical references to the North Carolinians encountered by the
surveyors. *The Secret History* is less consciously literary and is more
concerned with the squabbles and difficulties between members of
the party. In the *Secret History*, which is hardly more than half as
long as the other version, the names of all the participants are disguised under such pseudonyms as Steady (Byrd himself), Merryman,

39. Huntington Library MS, Brock 188, V, No. 15.

40. This version was printed in 1841 at Petersburg, Va., by Edmund Ruffin with
the title of *The Westover Manuscripts: Containing the History of the Dividing Line
Betwixt Virginia and North Carolina; A Journey to the Land of Eden*, A.D. *1733; and
A Progress to the Mines. Written from 1728 to 1736, and Now First Published*. The
manuscript from which the printed version was made remained in the possession of
members of the Byrd family for many years.
    The principal later versions are: *History of the Dividing Line and Other Notes,
from the Papers of Wm. Byrd, of Westover in Virginia, Esquire*. Edited by Thomas
H. Wynne (2 vols., Richmond, Va., 1866). And *The Writings of Colonel William
Byrd in Virginia, Esq*. Edited by John Spencer Bassett (New York, 1901).

41. *William Byrd's Histories of the Dividing Line Betwixt Virginia and North
Carolina*. Edited by William K. Boyd (Raleigh, N.C., 1929). The manuscript of the
Secret History is preserved in the library of the American Philosophical Society in
Philadelphia. Boyd prints both versions on parallel pages.

Firebrand, Puzzle Cause, Shoebrush, Plausible, etc. The first version goes into much more detail about the appearance of the country, the flora and fauna, and the quality of the people in the border areas. It was evidently written to inform and entertain readers in England. Byrd's *History of the Dividing Line* is one of the most urbane and readable literary productions of the colonial period. It is written with grace and ease and is seasoned with humor—one of the rarest qualities in colonial writing. Byrd was too much a perfectionist to allow it to be printed but he did permit his friends in England to see manuscript copies. In a letter to Peter Collinson, dated July 18, 1736, there is an oblique reference to some of his writing, apparently to a long descriptive letter, perhaps a preview of the *Journey to the Land of Eden*, which Collinson had shown to various of Byrd's friends.

I blush to think it fell into the hand of so many polite judges [Byrd writes]. But I hope as they were great, they were merciful, and looked not upon an Indian scribble with too critical an eye. I am glad they were merry, though the novelty of the subject was all that could make it entertaining.

I was prevented last fall from paying another visit to the Land of Eden, as I intended. But to make myself amends, I shall in September, if I live so long, take a progress to the mountains at the head of the Rappahannock River. Without any regard to the venerable grand climacteric, they have appointed me one of the commissioners to settle the bounds between the King and the Lord Fairfax, whose propriety is confined between [the] Rappahannock and Potomac. . . . But now I come to the most difficult part of your letter to answer, that I mean wherein you desire a sight of my history of the line. I must own it goes against me to deny you such a trifle, but I have one infirmity, never to venture anything unfinished out of my hands. The bashful bears hide their cubs 'till they have licked them into shape, nor am I too proud to follow the example of those modest animals. If Solomon sends lazy people to the ants to learn industry, all authors should not be ashamed to go to the bears to be instructed never to produce any offspring of theirs 'till they have brought it into shape fit to be seen. However I will compound the business with you and compliment you with the perusal of my journal, giving an account of what we did every day during the expedition. This is only the skeleton and ground-work of what I intend, which may sometime or other come to be filled up with vessels and flesh and have a decent skin drawn over all to keep things tight in their places and prevent their looking frightful. I have the materials ready and want only leisure to put them together. I must only desire you not to suffer this journal to go out of your hands, nor a copy of it, unless Sir Charles Wager should have a fancy to see it.[42]

As Byrd indicates here, he was one of the commissioners appointed to survey Lord Fairfax's proprietary domain in the Northern Neck, a task performed in the autumn of 1736.

The explorations of the zone between Virginia and North Carolina opened Byrd's eyes to the opportunity for speculation in frontier lands, and he soon began to acquire territory which he hoped to people with Swiss immigrants. In his zest for speculation in western lands, he was anticipating the fever of speculation which swept the population in succeeding generations. Soon after his return from the survey of the line in 1728, he bought 20,000 acres at the confluence of the Dan and Irvine Rivers.[43] He later added 6,000 acres to this territory, all of which he designated as the Land of Eden. To make a convenient stopping place between Westover and the Land of Eden, he acquired 5,211 acres where the Dan and Staunton rivers join to make the Roanoke, and in 1742 he added 105,000 acres between the Dan River and the North Carolina line, just below where the Hico runs into the Dan. And as one more way station from Westover, he bought 2,429 acres on the Meherrin River. When he died his land-holdings totalled 179,440 acres, surely a princely estate even by colonial standards. Small wonder that he was eager to encourage immigration.

The best colonists for his land, Byrd believed, would be Swiss, and for years he sought to induce German Swiss to come to Virginia. Several times he was disappointed. A certain Mr. Ochs encouraged him to believe that he would bring a colony of his countrymen, but they never materialized. Finally in 1736 Byrd made a contract with Samuel Jenner of Bern, Switzerland, agent for the Helvetian Society, to sell 33,400 acres of land on the Roanoke River, and the following year Jenner published from notes supplied by Byrd *Neu-*

42. Huntington Library MS, Brock 188, III, No. 9.

43. A succinct account of his land acquisitions is given by Boyd, *William Byrd's Histories,* xxv-xxvi.

gefundenes Eden[44] [New-Found Eden], a description of the healthfulness and fruitfulness of the land that ought to have induced any Swiss in search of fertile farms to emigrate. A shipload embarked for Virginia and after a four-months' voyage finally sighted land but wrecked before they could get ashore. Only a handful of survivors managed to reach Byrd's land. Thus ended his hopeful scheme. For the rest of his days he was struggling to find a sale for his property. He was forced at last to solicit Scots, who, he once complained, swarmed over the country like Goths and Vandals.

Except for his inability to raise enough money to pay off his debts to the Perrys in London, Byrd's later years were reasonably serene. His letters and his diary for 1739–41 indicate that he had many reasons to find his life at Westover satisfactory. He was honored by his fellow colonists; he lacked for nothing that he needed; and even if he could not raise sufficient money in sterling to liquidate his debts, he nevertheless held a vast barony, which was the outward symbol of prestige. Sometime after his return from his last trip to England he rebuilt Westover in brick. The date for this reconstruction has been given as 1737 but conclusive evidence is lacking and it was probably rebuilt before that time.[45] Twice since then fire has partially destroyed the building but the present structure gives an indication of Byrd's architectural taste. There Byrd lived like the country gentleman he was, surrounded by a growing family and visited by an endless stream of guests. He took especial pride in his library and the gallery of paintings of his titled friends in England.

Byrd was a characteristic virtuoso of the eighteenth century and a worthy member of the Royal Society, full of projects and schemes for the relief of man's estate. Sometimes these projects coincided with his own self-interest, to be sure, as when late in life he proposed a scheme for draining the Dismal Swamp and planting it in hemp.[46] Botany, natural history, medicine, and other scientific interests oc-

44. *William Byrd's Natural History of Virginia or The Newly Discovered Eden.* Edited and translated from a German version by Richmond C. Beatty and William J. Mulloy (Richmond. Va., 1940).

45. Bassett, *Writings*, lxxxi.

46. Earl G. Swem (ed.), *Description of the Dismal Swamp and a Proposal to Drain the Swamp.* By William Byrd of Westover. Heartman's Historical Series, No. 38 (1922).

cupied much of his time. From his early years he had fancied himself something of a physician and was always ready to prescribe for ailing friends, relatives, and servants. If *A Discourse Concerning the Plague* is from his pen, he should be numbered among those who early recommended inoculation for smallpox; he also had some glimmerings of what today we call psychosomatic medicine. He was constantly in search of remedies for diseases among the plants of the New World. In a letter to Sir Hans Sloane, April 10, 1741, he stresses the virtues of ginseng and snakeroot. Though King Charles II expected ginseng to serve him as an aphrodisiac, it could not work a miracle, Byrd hints, and he adds: 'What I recommend it for is to cheer the animal spirits and feed the flame of life, which I am convinced it will do if regularly taken. And then for the rattlesnake root, I can upon my own experience recommend it for the pleurisy, the rheumatism, and easing of pain in any part that proceeds from inflammation. Others have told me of the strange effects it has in a dropsy and for killing worms.'[47] He hoped Sir Hans would send a qualified naturalist to study the 'excellent simples' of Virginia. Byrd's own zeal to make trial of folk remedies and to recommend them to others persisted throughout his life.

As a man of letters, Byrd's reputation has rested on the *History of the Dividing Line*, the *Journey to the Land of Eden*, and *A Progress to the Mines*. To these should be added his personal letters, many of which show evidences of careful literary craftsmanship. A portion of these letters Byrd took the trouble to preserve in copies bearing fictitious names.[48] Letter-writing in the eighteenth century was an art, as the surviving correspondence of many individuals will attest. Byrd clearly enjoyed writing letters, which gave an outlet for a literary impulse that he felt a need to express. To a relative of his second wife, a certain Mrs. Taylor of London, he wrote on October 10,

47. *William and Mary College Quarterly*, 2nd Ser., I (1921), 199–200.

48. The letterbook in the University of North Carolina Library contains a number of these letters, which are printed by Miss Woodfin, *Another Secret Diary*, 192–387. A few letters addressed to 'Facetia' (Lady Betty Cromwell, who married Edward Southwell in 1703) were privately printed in 1913 in an edition of fifteen copies by Thomas F. Ryan. This little volume bore the ponderous title of *William Byrd, Esqr. Accounts as Solicitor General of the Colonies and Receiver of the Tobacco Tax, 1688–1704. Letters Writ to Facetia by Veramour. Printed from the MS Copy* (1913).

1735, an amusing though somewhat ribald letter describing the discomfiture of an 'Italian Bona Roba' in Virginia who sought to enhance her feminine charms by inflating her breasts with air. He is pleased to have this entertaining tidbit to report, Byrd suggests, because the sources for literary inspiration are often lacking in the country. 'Therefore,' he adds, 'without a little invention it would not be possible for one of us anchorites to carry on a tolerable correspondence, but like French historians, where we don't meet with pretty incidents, we must e'en make them, and lard a little truth with a great deal of fiction.'[49]

Frequently in the three portions of his diary Byrd mentions that he 'wrote English,' evidently some literary exercise that he was composing. His reading of Petronius, mentioned in his diary in March and May, 1712, resulted in his translation of the portion concerned with the Matron of Ephesus. This has survived, along with a few other fragments of writing. Miss Woodfin identified some light verses attributed to 'Mr. Burrard' and published in *Tunbrigalia: Or, Tunbridge Miscellanies for the Year 1719* (London, 1719) as by William Byrd, and she printed a long facetious essay by Byrd entitled 'The Female Creed,' written between 1724 and 1725. None of these pieces adds much to Byrd's literary stature. They merely show that he was following the literary fashion of the day and could turn a skillful phrase.

The entries in the latest portion of Byrd's diary extant, that for 1739–41, show that his zeal for learning continued until his old age. He continued to read the classic languages and to keep up his Hebrew. As he grew older his library, one of the finest in America,[50] occupied more and more of his time. Though he was so worried in his later years by his debts that he seriously thought of selling Westover, the problems of material existence never overwhelmed him because in his library he had an escape from the narrow confines of a backwoods province. Until his death he felt that he was a part of the great world beyond the borders of Virginia and beyond the barriers of time.

One final honor came to Byrd in the last year of his life. He had

49. Bassett, *Writings*, 394-6.

50. A list of the titles in the Byrd library, catalogued in 1777 by J. Stretch just before the library was sold in Philadelphia, is printed in Bassett, *Writings*, pp. 413-43.

long dreamed of political preferment and had yearned in vain for the governorship of Virginia or Maryland. For most of his adult life he had been a member of the Virginia Council of State, and for many years had been the senior member save one. By tradition the senior member was President of the Council, an officer who served as the administrative head of the colony in the absence of a governor. For year after year, Byrd was frustrated in his hope of becoming President of the Council by old Commissary Blair who outranked him and refused to die. Not until 1743 when Blair was eighty-nine did the tough old Scot, who was accustomed to nod in his chair at Council meetings, finally breathe his last and leave room for Byrd.

Byrd died on August 26, 1744, and was buried in the garden at Westover which he loved so well. At some later time a descendant had carved on his tombstone an extended epitaph[51] that mentions his honors but, curiously for an epitaph, says nothing of his piety. Yet Byrd, for all his lapses from moral probity, was genuinely pious. The enumeration of his prayers runs to tedious iteration in his diary. He was frequently repentant for his misconduct; he supported the Anglican establishment and attended church with regularity; and he read sermons with pleasure and presumably with profit. In the notebook containing his diary for 1709–12, he wrote out a religious creed, for the most part orthodox and conventional, but after mentioning his belief in Christ and Resurrection, he concludes with no mention of an orthodox hell or heaven. Instead he declares that 'those who have led good and holy lives here will be rewarded with unspeakable happiness hereafter. But those who have obstinately and impenitently rebelled against God and their own consciences shall go into a state of sorrow and misery.'[52] This was the faith of a gentleman of the eighteenth century whose taste led him to mingle rationalism with his piety.

William Byrd II was an exemplification of an aristocracy that had been developing in Virginia since the early days of its settlement. He was one of the most cultivated members of his class, a group who in general accepted the dictum that privilege carried with it responsibility to society. Though self-interest was never far from his

51. See *supra*, note 6.
52. See Wright, *The First Gentlemen of Virginia*, 346.

thoughts, he nevertheless devoted much of his energy to service to the commonwealth from which he could expect no material reward and little in the way of public acclaim. He represents a society that produced Washington, Jefferson, Madison, Marshall, and a great galaxy of leaders who a little later helped to shape a new nation. Byrd's career is a revealing example of the rise of that influential agrarian aristocracy.

Louis B. Wright

THE SECRET DIARY OF
WILLIAM BYRD OF WESTOVER

from December 13, 1717
to May 19, 1721

December 1717

13. I rose about 8 o'clock and read a chapter in Hebrew and some Greek in Homer. I said my prayers, and had boiled milk for breakfast. The weather was cold and cloudy, the wind northwest, and it rained a little. I wrote a letter to Virginia. About 11 o'clock came Albin[1] to teach me to draw and stayed till almost one. Then I read some English till two and then ate a veal cutlet. After dinner I put several things in order till four and then went to visit Mrs. W-n-m and drank tea with her and stayed till six. Then I went to Sir William Thompson's[2] and sat with him about half an hour and then went to my Lord Percival's[3] and sat with him till 9 o'clock and then went to the Spanish Ambassador's,[4] where I stayed till eleven and then went home in the chair and said my prayers, &c.

1. Eleazar Albin was a teacher of watercolor drawing and a naturalist. In 1720 his *A Natural History of English Insects* was published in London.

2. Sir William Thompson was solicitor general.

3. John, Baron Percival, son of Sir John Percival and Catherine Dering. In 1722 he was created Viscount Percival and in 1733 Earl of Egmont.

4. The Marquis de Monte Leon, ambassador from Spain to the Court of St. James, and a fellow of the Royal Society, was ordered home in October 1718, before the outbreak of war with Spain.

14. I rose about 8 o'clock and read a chapter in Hebrew and some Greek in Homer. I said my prayers, and had boiled milk for breakfast. The weather was cool and clear and there was a very high tide as ever was known. About ten the tailor brought home my new clothes and then I went to the Attorney General,[5] who promised to do my business next week, to forward which I gave the clerk half a guinea. Then I went to the Virginia Coffeehouse[6] and from thence to Mr. Perry's[7] and there found a letter from Virginia. I dined with the old man and ate some roast mutton. After dinner I went to visit Mrs. Perry and stayed there till 4 o'clock and went to Mrs. A-l-c and lay with her. Then I went to Mrs. D-n-s where was D-l-y O-r-d. Here I drank abundance of tea and we stayed till eleven and then I went home in the coach where I said a short prayer. I gave Mrs. A-l-c two guineas.

15. I rose about 8 o'clock and read a chapter in Hebrew and some Greek in Homer. I said my prayers, and had boiled milk for breakfast. The weather was cold and cloudy, the wind west. I went not to church this morning because I had a cold. I read some French till 1 o'clock and then I went to St. James's Coffeehouse[8] to look for Colo-

5. Sir Edward Northey was attorney general (until March 1718).

6. A coffeehouse in the city frequented by Virginia traders, sea captains, and Virginians visiting London. Spotswood complained of the politicking that went on between Virginia business men and London merchants: 'I think it is doing little honor to the government to have its Council appointed in the Virginia Coffeehouse . . . by a merchant in London who has no other rule to judge a man's merit by than by the number of his tobacco hogsheads.' *The Official Letters of Alexander Spotswood*, ed. R. A. Brock (Richmond, 1885), II, 79.

7. Micajah Perry was the London business agent for Byrd, as he had been for his father before him and for many other Virginians. Micajah Perry, the elder, died in 1721, having made a will on December 22, 1720, in which he mentions his granddaughters Mary and Elizabeth, grandsons Micajah and Philip, and daughter Sarah. Sarah was the wife of Micajah's son Richard, who died before his father, on April 16, 1720. 'Old Mrs. Perry' referred to by Byrd was perhaps the widow of Micajah Perry's brother and partner, Richard. Young Micajah was head of the firm after his grandfather's death. See Elizabeth Donnan, 'Eighteenth Century English Merchants: Micajah Perry,' *Journal of Economic and Business History*, IV (1931–2), 70–99; *William and Mary College Quarterly*, 1st Ser., XVII (1908–9), 264.

8. Most famous of Whig coffeehouses, on St. James's Street, facing down Pall Mall.

nel Blakiston[9] but he was not there. Then I went to his house but they told me he dined not at home, so I went to St. James's again. Sir Harry Ashurst[10] asked me to dine with him so I went and ate some roast beef. After dinner we drank a bottle. Here I saw poor Sir Richard Allin.[11] About 7 o'clock I went to Lady Guise's[12] where I sat about two hours and then went home and neglected my prayers, for which God forgive me.

16. I rose about 8 o'clock and read a chapter in Hebrew and some Greek in Homer. I said my prayers, and had boiled milk for breakfast. About 10 o'clock came Colonel Blakiston and reprimanded me for not dining with his wife yesterday. About eleven came Sir Harry Ashurst and stayed about quarter of an hour. Then I wrote letters to Virginia till one and then drew a little till two when I ate a veal cutlet for dinner. In the afternoon I put several things in order and then read Terence till 4 o'clock, when I went to visit Mrs. U-m-s, where I stayed till 7 o'clock and then went to Will's Coffeehouse[13] and about 8 o'clock went with Major Smith[14] to Petcum's[15] assembly where was abundance of company, part of which danced, but I stood so long that I found a great pain in my left thigh which continued very bad; however, I stayed till 12 o'clock and then went home in a chair but neglected to say my prayers.

9. Colonel Nathaniel Blakiston was governor of Maryland from 1698 to 1701, and after that agent for Maryland and Virginia.

10. Sir Harry Ashurst, Bart., was a member of Parliament from New Windsor Borough, Berkshire, 1715-22.

11. Richard Anguish, son and heir of Edmund Anguish, in 1699 assumed the name of Allin and was created a baronet. He married Sir Harry Ashurst's daughter.

12. Anne Russell, second wife of Sir John Guise, 3rd Bart., of Elmore, M.P. for Gloucestershire 1705-10 and for Marlow 1722-7. Pope wrote a satirical poem about a quarrel between Guise and Nicholas Lechmere, published in 1720. Alexander Pope, *Minor Poems*, ed. Norman Ault (London, 1954), 217-18. A sister of Sir John was married to Pope's friend Ned Blount.

13. Will's Coffeehouse, in Bow Street, near Covent Garden, was Byrd's favorite resort. It was a haunt of poets and critics.

14. Major William Smith, of Colonel La Bouchetiere's Regiment of Dragoons, in the Irish Establishment.

15. M. Petcum, or Petkum, was 'resident' of the Duke of Holstein.

17. I rose about 8 o'clock and read a chapter in Hebrew and some Greek in Homer. I neglected my prayers, but had boiled milk for breakfast. The weather was warm. . . . I wrote a letter to Virginia till 11 o'clock and then came old Mr. Perry, with whom I went to visit Horace Walpole[16] and drank tea . . . . I recommended my Cousin Grymes[17] to be his deputy in Virginia. About twelve we took leave and went to Colonel Blakiston's, but he was from home. . . . Mr. Perry and I went to Mrs. . . . and sat with her about an hour and then went home and ate some veal cutlets. After dinner I put [things in] order till . . . o'clock and then I went to visit Mrs. [Misses?] O-r-d, who were from home. Then I went to Will's Coffeehouse, and from thence to the Attorney [General's] and went to Mrs. M-r-l-y, but she was from home. Then I went to Mrs. L-c-b-r and about nine went to the Spanish Ambassador's . . . my lameness worse and about twelve went home in a chair but neglected my prayers, for which God forgive me.

[18.] . . . [I read] Hebrew and some Greek in Homer. I said my prayers, and had boiled milk for breakfast. The weather was warm and . . . continued bad. [I wrote] three letters to Virginia and then sent my man with them [to Mr.] Perry's. I drew a little till dinner and then [put] several things in order, and then read some French till 4 o'clock, when I went to visit Mr. [Leblanc] but he was from home. . . . Went to Lady Burgoyne's[18] and sat with her and Mr. Wren till 7 o'clock. Then I went to Mrs. B-l-d, but she was . . . . I stayed till 9 o'clock and then went to Will's and stayed till eleven and then walked home and said my prayers.

16. Horace Walpole, surveyor and auditor general of plantations; at this time out of favor at court and out of all other offices, along with his brother, Sir Robert Walpole, Earl of Orford.

17. John Grymes, of Brandon, Middlesex County, Virginia, deputy auditor of Virginia. Byrd referred to Virginians who were related to him through the Ludwell family as 'cousins,' though the relationship was through his wife.

18. Lady Burgoyne, widow of Sir Roger Burgoyne, 4th Bart. (who died in 1716), later married Christopher Wren, son of the great architect.

[19.] ... [I read] a chapter in Hebrew and some Greek in Homer. I said my prayers, and had boiled milk for breakfast. The weather was warm and cloudy, ... was better, thank God. About 11 o'clock I went to the Attorney General's and from thence to the Solicitor General's, and returned home about one, painted a little, and read some French till 2 o'clock, and then ate some veal cutlet. After dinner I put several things in order till 4 o'clock and then went to Mrs. A-l-c and from thence to visit my daughter,[19] where I stayed till 6 o'clock and then went into the City to Mr. Lindsay where I played at cards and stayed to supper and ate some roast lamb. Here I stayed till 12 o'clock, and then went home and neglected my prayers.

20. I rose about 8 o'clock and read a chapter in Hebrew and some Greek in Homer. I said my prayers, and had milk for breakfast. The weather was very clear and warm. My maid Marge came and about eleven came Albin to teach me to draw, and stayed till twelve. Then I went to wait on my [Lord] Orrery[20] where I met the Duke of Argyll[21] and drank some chocolate. Then I went to Mr. Blathwayt's,[22] but they were from home. Then I went to walk in the park and met Brownlow Sherard,[23] who invited me to dine with him at St. James's and eat some roast goose. After dinner we sat and talked till ... o'clock, and then I went to Mrs. U-m-s where I played at

19. Evelyn, Byrd's first child, now ten years old, had been brought to England in 1716. She remained in England until after Byrd's second marriage in 1724 and according to tradition was a popular young lady.

20. Charles Boyle, 4th Earl of Orrery, a long-time friend and correspondent of Byrd. Until 1716 he had been lord of the bedchamber to George I. In 1721 he was thrown into the Tower for six months for implication in a Jacobite plot. He was a widower, his wife, Elizabeth Cecil (daughter of the Earl of Exeter), having died in 1708.

21. John Campbell, 2nd Duke of Argyll, was one of the most powerful men in George I's court. From 1718 to 1725 he was lord steward of the household. His wife was Jane Warburton, formerly a maid of honor at Court.

22. William Blathwayt, eldest son of William Blathwayt, of Dyrham Park, who before his death in 1717 was auditor general of the plantations and secretary at war.

23. Brownlow Sherard, son of Richard Sherard of Lobthorpe and brother of Sir John Sherard, 1st Bart., became, in 1730, 3rd Bart. The 'Aunt Sherard' who appears later in the diary was probably of this family, the relationship being through Lucy Parke Byrd.

ombre and stayed till 11 o'clock and then walked home but neglected my prayers.

21. I rose about 8 o'clock and read a chapter in Hebrew and some Greek in Homer. I said my prayers, and had boiled milk for breakfast. The weather was . . . and warm. I wrote some English and drew a little till 1 o'clock, and then went and took a walk in the park till two, and then went to Colonel Blakiston's to [dinner] and ate some fish. Young Mr. M-t-n came there before dinner was done. After dinner I went to Mrs. O-r-d but they were from home. Then to Mrs. Mary O-r-d, was from home; then to Mrs. FitzHerbert's,[24] where I had some toast and ale. Here I stayed till 9 o'clock and then went to Mr. Petcum's where I drank some chocolate and talked abundantly with Mrs. B-r-n-n, a very pretty woman. About 12 o'clock I went home in a chair and neglected my prayers, for which God forgive me.

22. I rose about 8 o'clock and read two chapters in Hebrew and some Greek in Homer. I said my prayers, and had boiled milk for breakfast. The weather was foggy again and cold. My lameness was well again, thank God. I drew a little till 1 o'clock and then went to St. James's Chapel[25] and then into the [lodge] where I [sortied] till 3 o'clock and then went to dine with Mr. Blathwayt, where I ate some roast venison. After dinner we drank a bottle till 6 o'clock and then I went to Mrs. C-r-l, but they were from home; then I went to Mrs. B-r-n[26] and sat with her till eight and there we talked about Miss Smith[27], and she promised to favor me in my love for her. Then

24. Mrs. FitzHerbert may have been a relative of the Southwell family, with whom Byrd was very close; Mary, wife of William FitzHerbert, was an aunt of Edward Southwell's wife. She may have been a relative of the dramatist William Congreve; Anne FitzHerbert was Congreve's paternal grandmother.

25. St. James's Chapel was the most fashionable London church. It was built by Christopher Wren in 1680. From 1709 to 1729 the minister was Samuel Clarke.

26. Possibly Mrs. Richard Brayne, of St. Margaret's, Westminster, mother of Anne Butler Brayne, who in 1724 married Alexander Spotswood, governor of Virginia. When Byrd met Mrs. Spotswood in Virginia he called her 'my old friend'; as she was then a newcomer to Virginia he must have begun the friendship in England.

27. Mary Smith, daughter of John Smith, Esquire, one of the commissioners of excise. Byrd's letters to Miss Smith, whom he addressed as 'Sabina,' have been

I went to Will's Coffeehouse, and from thence walked to Mrs. A-l-c,
where I stayed till 11 o'clock and then went home and said my
[prayers].

23. I rose about 8 o'clock and read two chapters in Hebrew and
some Greek in Homer. I said my prayers, and had boiled milk for
breakfast. The weather was cold and cloudy, the wind northeast. My
cousin Horsmanden[28] called and stayed about half an hour. I drew a
little and then settled some accounts till 2 o'clock and then ate some
battered eggs. After dinner I put several things in order till 4 o'clock.
The maid of the house went away. Then I went to Mrs. B-r-t, but
she was from home. Then I went to the Attorney General's and sat
with him about half an hour, and then went to Mrs. M-r-l-y, but she
was from home. Then I went to Lady Guise's and sat with her till
9 o'clock and then went to St. James's Coffeehouse and drank a dish
of chocolate. Then I went to Court,[29] and from thence to Petcum's,
where I stayed till 12 o'clock, and then went home and said my
prayers, &c.

24. I rose about 8 o'clock and read a chapter in Hebrew and some
Greek in Homer. I said my prayers, and had boiled milk for breakfast. The weather was cold and cloudy, the wind east. About ten
came Mike Perry[30] and brought a letter from Virginia. He stayed
about half an hour. About 12 o'clock I went into the City and dined
with old Mr. Perry. After dinner I went and sat with Dick Perry,
who had the gout. I stayed with him till 4 o'clock and then went to

printed in *Another Secret Diary of William Byrd* (Richmond, Va., 1942), 298ff.
Her sister, Lady Dunkellen, encouraged the match between Mary Smith and Byrd,
but she married Sir Edward Des Bouverie, 2nd Bart., of Wiltshire, in July, 1718,
and died January 3, 1721.

28. Daniel Horsmanden, son of the rector of Purleigh, whose sister Mary was
Byrd's mother. Daniel, born in 1694, was admitted to the Middle Temple in 1721;
in 1731 he was in New York; later he became chief justice of that colony.

29. King George I held a 'drawing room' several times a week.

30. 'Mike' Perry, son of 'Dick' and grandson of old Micajah Perry, carried on
the family business after his grandfather's death in 1721. He became an alderman
and in 1738-9 Lord Mayor of London. See William Purdie Treloar, *A Lord Mayor's
Diary, 1906-7, to Which Is Added the Official Diary of Micajah Perry, Lord Mayor,
1738-9* (London, 1920).

Will's Coffeehouse, and from thence to Mrs. O-r-d, where I stayed the whole evening till 10 o'clock, and then went home in a chair and said my prayers.

25. I rose about 8 o'clock and read a chapter in Hebrew and some Greek in Homer. I said my prayers, and had milk for breakfast. The weather was cold and cloudy. I wrote some English and then drew a little till 2 o'clock and then ate some veal cutlet for dinner. In the afternoon I put several things in order, and then read some French till 4 o'clock, and then went to visit Mrs. U-m-s, where I drank tea and stayed till 8 o'clock. Then I went to Will's Coffeehouse, where I stayed till nine, and then went to visit Mrs. A-l-c, whom I would have laid with but I was not in condition. I stayed with her till 11 o'clock and then went home, where I talked merrily to the maid. I said a short prayer, &c.

26. I rose about 8 o'clock and read a chapter in Hebrew and some Greek in Homer. I said my prayers, and had boiled milk for breakfast. The weather was cold and it rained and blew violently. I wrote some English till 11 o'clock and then came my Lord Percival and stayed about half an hour; then I went to visit Mr. Southwell,[31] whom I found with the gout. Here I stayed till 1 o'clock and then went home and drew a little and then went to Mr. Blathwayt's to dinner and ate some venison pasty. After dinner we drank a bottle of claret and stayed till 5 o'clock, and then Will Blathwayt and I went to the play in Lincoln's Field,[32] where I had the pleasure to sit next to my dear Miss Smith and talked pretty much to her and she was not shy. After the play I went home in a chair and said my prayers but slept indifferently.

31. Edward Southwell, son of Sir Robert Southwell, Byrd's old friend and sponsor, was clerk of the Privy Council. Southwell's first wife, Lady Betty Cromwell, died in 1709, and in August, 1716, he married Anne, daughter of Secretary William Blathwayt. She died a year later in giving birth to their son. The 'Mrs. Southwell' Byrd refers to must be one of Edward's unmarried sisters.

32. The Duke's Theater in Lincoln's Inn Field, the third theater to stand on this site, was built in 1714. Here was presented, in 1717-18, the first opera in English.

27. I rose about 8 o'clock and read a chapter in Hebrew and some Greek in Homer. I said my prayers, and had boiled milk for breakfast. I found myself indisposed a little. The weather was warm and clear. My weakness was worse again. I wrote some English, notwithstanding I was much out of order, till 2 o'clock, and then I ate some battered eggs. After dinner I put several things in order till 4 o'clock, and then I went to visit Mrs. C-r-l, where I drank tea and stayed till seven. Then I went to Mrs. B-r-n, but she was from home. Then I went to Mrs. [or Misses Andrews'] and sat with them till nine, and then went to Court, where was abundance of company, and from thence to the Spanish Ambassador's, where I stayed till twelve, and then went home in the chair and said my prayers.

28. I rose about 8 o'clock and read a chapter in Hebrew and some Greek. I said my prayers, and had boiled milk for breakfast. The weather was cold and cloudy. I was better this morning, thank God. I wrote some English, and drew a little till 2 o'clock, when I ate some veal cutlet. After dinner I put several things in order till 4 o'clock, and then I received a letter from an unknown hand about Mrs. W-n-m. About 4 o'clock I went to visit my daughter and sat with her about half an hour; then I went to visit Mrs. W-n-m, but she could not be seen because her aunt was very bad. Then I went to Mr. D-n-s, but I found him sick. Then I went to Mrs. Lethieullier's[33] and sat there about an hour, and then went to Will's Coffeehouse, where I read the news and sat there till 9 o'clock, and then went to Mrs. A-l-c but could do nothing. About 11 o'clock I went home, where I neglected to say my prayers. It blew very hard all night.

29. I rose about 8 o'clock and read two chapters in Hebrew and three in Greek. I said my prayers, and had boiled milk for breakfast. The weather was rainy and cold, so that I could not resolve to go to

33. In a book of verse, *Tunbrigalia*, published in 1719, a 'Mr. Burrard' had several stanzas on ladies who visited Tunbridge Wells, including 'Mrs. Lethulier.' It is a fair guess that Byrd was the author of these poems. See *Another Secret Diary of William Byrd*, 407–8. There were several members of the prominent Lethieullier family living in London at this time.

church but was devout at home. I read some English and drew a little till 2 o'clock and then ate a teal for dinner. After dinner I put several things in order and then took a nap till 4 o'clock, when I went to visit Mr. Southwell and gave him my petition for the King in Council.[34] Here I stayed till 7 o'clock and then went to Mrs. Mary O-r-d, but she was from home. Then I went to Colonel Blakiston's, but there was nobody at home. Then I went to Mrs. FitzHerbert's, and ate some apple pie with her and stayed till 9 o'clock, and then went home and read some French. I said a short prayer.

[30.] . . . read a chapter in Hebrew and three chapters in Greek. I said my prayers, and had boiled milk for breakfast. The weather was cold and clear. . . . weakness grew worse again. I wrote a letter and then drew a little till 11 o'clock, and then went to Lord Percival's, but he was from home. Then to . . . he was from home. Then to Mrs. O-r-d, but she was from home. Then to Colonel B-l-d A-l-y, and he was from home; then to B-r-g . . . from home; then to Colonel Bladen's[55] and he was from home; then to Lord Foley's[36] and he was indisposed, then to Sir Harry Ashurst's and he was . . . , Mr. F-x-n and he was from home; then I went home and ate some battered eggs for dinner. After dinner I put several things in order till 5 o'clock . . . coffeehouse and stayed till six; then I went to Mrs. B-r-n and stayed there till eight; then I went to Mrs. FitzHerbert's and ate some toast and ale, and . . . o'clock, and then went to Petcum's, where I talked with several ladies but most to Mrs. B-r-n. Here I stayed till 12 o'clock and when I had . . . into the coach, I went home in the chair, where I said my prayers and slept very well.

34. Byrd's petition begged the King to confirm members of the Council, who served as judges of the Virginia General Court, as justices of the biennial courts of over and terminer instead of allowing the lieutenant governor to appoint justices. This was one of the main causes of dispute between Spotswood and the Council members. The petition is in the Public Record Office among the papers of the Commissioners for Trade and Plantations.

35. Colonel Martin Bladen, a Lord Commissioner for Trade and Plantations, 1717 to 1746; M.P. for Stockbridge in Hampshire.

36. Thomas Foley, created Baron Foley of Kidderminster in 1712, was a fellow of the Royal Society.

[31.] . . . o'clock and read a chapter in Hebrew and three in Greek. I said my prayers, and had boiled milk for breakfast. The weather was cold and cloudy . . . a little and danced my dance. Mr. [Leblanc] came with a message from my Lady Mohun[37] about her debt. Then I drew some more [till 1] o'clock, and then took a walk in the park till two and then went to Colonel Blakiston's to dinner, and ate some roast turkey. After dinner we sat and talked and I went to look on the next house.[38] Here I stayed till 5 o'clock and then went to visit Mrs. O-r-d and stayed there till 9 o'clock, and then went to the Spanish Ambassador's, where was abundance of company. I stayed till 12 o'clock, and then went home but neglected to say my prayers, for which God forgive me. This night I began to take an opiate pack for my weakness. It froze very hard.

37. Elizabeth Lawrence, widow of Charles, Lord Mohun, later married Colonel Mordaunt. The debt was one Byrd collected for Daniel Parke's estate.

38. Mary Smith lived in Beaufort Buildings in Beaufort Street, next door to the house where Byrd lodged, which was off the Strand, near Worcester Court.

January 1718

1. I rose about 8 o'clock and read a chapter in Hebrew and three in Greek. I said my prayers, and had boiled milk for breakfast. The weather was clear and frosty, the wind northeast. About 10 o'clock came my surgeon, and soon after him came Colonel [Shutz] and stayed with me about an hour. About 1 o'clock I went to walk in Somerset Gardens and called on Mrs. U-m-s and about two walked to Mrs. D-t-n to dine with the company that use to dine there, but there was nobody, so I was forced to eat some fish by myself. After dinner I took a walk in the Temple[1] and went to see some chambers to be sold. About 4 o'clock I went to see my daughter and found her with a cold. About 6 o'clock I went to Lady Guise's and stayed till eight and then went to Will's Coffeehouse and drank two dishes of

1. Byrd was a member of the Middle Temple.

chocolate, and went from thence with my Lord Bellenden[2] to Court where was dancing. I stayed till twelve and then walked home and said my prayers.

2. I rose about 8 o'clock and read a chapter in Hebrew and four chapters in Greek. I said my prayers, and had boiled milk for breakfast. The weather continued cold and clear. I wrote two letters to two ladies. Then I drew a little till 1 o'clock and then I went to call my daughter to go to Mr. Southwell's to dinner, where I found Hans Hamilton,[3] and I ate some roast hare. After dinner we sat and were merry till five, and then I took leave and carried back my daughter, and then I went to the play and sat near Mrs. O-r-d. After the play I went to Mrs. A-l-c and gave her a flourish and sat with her till 11 o'clock, and then walked home and said my prayers. It continued very cold and froze hard.

3. I rose about 8 o'clock and read a chapter in Hebrew and three chapters in Greek. I said my prayers, and had boiled milk for breakfast. The weather continued frosty and cloudy. My surgeon came again. About 11 o'clock I went to visit Mr. U-t-n, but he was from home. Then I went to the Virginia Coffeehouse, where I stayed about half an hour and then went to Dick Perry's to dinner and ate some venison. After dinner we drank tea and about four I took leave and went home where I drew a little and then read some French till 8 o'clock, and then went to Will's Coffeehouse and stayed there till nine and drank two dishes of chocolate, and then went to Court and because there was but little company I went to the Spanish Ambassador's, where I stayed till twelve, and then went home and said my prayers, &c.

4. I rose about 8 o'clock and read a chapter in Hebrew and three in Greek. I said my prayers, and had boiled milk for breakfast. The

2. John, 3rd Baron Bellenden of Broughton, heritable usher of the Exchequer.

3. Hans Hamilton, quartermaster general under Lord Peterborough in the Spanish campaign, sold his commission as colonel in 1715.

weather was clear and frosty, the wind northeast. About 11 o'clock
I went to visit Mrs. O-r-d and drank tea with her and sat with her
about three hours, and at one returned home and soon after Mr. Ned
Jeffreys[4] came to see me and sat with me about half an hour. About
2 o'clock I ate some battered eggs for dinner. In the afternoon I put
several things in order and then read some English and drew a little
till 5 o'clock, and then went to Mrs. A-l-c and stayed with her about
half an hour. Then I went to Will's Coffeehouse and from thence
to the play where was my dear Kitty Sambrooke,[5] but I did not see
her till after the play, and then I waited on her out and went to Will's
Coffeehouse again, where I drank two dishes of chocolate, and about
eleven walked home and said my prayers, &c. It was very cold and
froze hard.

5. I rose about 8 o'clock and read two chapters in Hebrew and
three in Greek. I neglected to say my prayers, but had boiled milk
for breakfast. The weather was exceedingly cold and clear. However, about eleven I went to Somerset Chapel where I heard a good
sermon. After church I returned home on foot and had some mutton
cutlets for dinner. After dinner I put several things in order and read
some French. Then I drew a little till 4 o'clock, and then walked to
visit Mrs. B-r-t and drank with her, and stayed till 7 o'clock; and
then went to visit Mrs. U-m-s and sat with her about an hour; and
then went to Will's where I drank two dishes of chocolate; and then
went to the Spanish Ambassador's to meet Mrs. O-r-d and stayed till
twelve and then came home in the chair and said my prayers.

4. In 1742 Byrd's sister-in-law wrote him that 'your old acquaintance Ned
Jeffrys departed this life some months ago, he bequeathed the small remainder of
his large fortune entire to Nick's son . . . Young Nick otherways called Jeff is just
married to the only surviving child that Mrs. Morris has left.' *Virginia Magazine of
History and Biography*, xxxvII (1929), 117. John Macky mentions seeing a villa near
Richmond belonging to 'Mr. Geoffreys, rich merchant in London.' *Journey through
England* (London, 1724), I, 66.

5. Probably of the family of Sir Jeremy Sambrooke, Bart. In a gossiping letter from
England in 1742 Mrs. Taylor mentions the death of 'Sir Jeminy Sambrooke' the year
before. Byrd also mentions the Sambrooke family in a letter to Major Otway.
Virginia Magazine of History and Biography, xxxvII (1929), 117 and 101.

6. I rose about 8 o'clock and read two chapters in Hebrew and three in Greek. I said my prayers and had boiled milk for breakfast. It continued to freeze, with cold, clear weather. About 10 o'clock came Albin to teach me to draw and stayed about an hour; then I wrote some English till 2 o'clock, and then ate some mutton cutlets. After dinner I put several things in order till four and then read some French. About 5 o'clock I went to Mr. Nick Jeffreys' where was my Lady and all her daughters, and I played at cards and won five shillings. About 9 o'clock we went to supper and I ate some roast turkey. After supper we drank a bottle till 12 o'clock, and then I went home in the chair and said my prayers, &c.

7. I rose about 8 o'clock and read a chapter in Hebrew and two chapters in Greek. I said my prayers, and had boiled milk for breakfast. The weather was exceedingly cold and clear. About 10 o'clock I went to Mrs. O-r-d to take leave of her, who was to go tomorrow into the country. I drank tea with her and stayed till one o'clock but was interrupted by my Lord Warrington[6] and Mr. Duncombe.[7] Then I went home and ate some battered eggs for dinner. After dinner I put several things in order till 4 o'clock, and then I wrote some English and drew a little till seven, and then went to Will's Coffee-house, from thence to the play, and from thence to Colonel D-m, where I lost ten guineas at basset. I drank some chocolate, and about eleven I went to the Spanish Ambassador's and stayed till twelve, and then came home in a chair and neglected my prayers.

8. I rose about 8 o'clock and read a chapter in Hebrew and three chapters in Greek. I said my prayers, and had boiled milk for breakfast. The weather was warm and cloudy, and it began to thaw and rain a little. About 10 o'clock came Mr. Perry and soon after him two gentlemen from my Lady Mohun to pay five hundred which we received. They stayed till almost 1 o'clock, when I went to my

6. George Booth, 2nd Earl of Warrington.

7. Perhaps a relative of the Duke of Argyll's first wife, Mary, daughter of Thomas Brown (who afterwards assumed the name of Duncombe).

daughter to take her to dine with Mr. U-t-n, who was very courteous to us. I ate some roast duck. After dinner we drank tea till 6 o'clock and then went to the play, and I sent my daughter home. I sat by Mrs. U-m-s. After the play I went to Court, where I stayed, notwithstanding there was no company, till 11 o'clock, and then I went home in the chair but neglected to say my prayers, for which God forgive me.

9. I rose about 8 o'clock and read a chapter in Hebrew and two in Greek. I said my prayers, and had boiled milk for breakfast. The weather was warm and clear and thawing, the wind west. I wrote a letter to Mrs. O-r-d and about 1 o'clock went into the city to Pontack's,[8] where I dined with the members of the Royal Society[9] and ate some fish for dinner. After dinner I went to Garraway's[10] and read the news till 4 o'clock, and then went to Mrs. Lindsay's where I drank tea and stayed till 7 o'clock, and then took leave and went to visit my Lady Henry Powlett,[11] but she was from home; then I went to Mrs. L-c-b-r but she was from home; then to Mrs. U-m-s and they were from home; then I went to Will's Coffeehouse and sat there till 11 o'clock, and then walked home and said my prayers, &c.

10. I rose about 8 o'clock and read a chapter in Hebrew and four chapters in Greek. I said my prayers, and had boiled milk for breakfast. The weather was cold and cloudy, the wind west. About 10 o'clock came Colonel D-m and sat with me about an hour; then I drew a little and read some English till 2 o'clock when I ate some

8. The Royal Society held its dinners at Pontack's, a fashionable French tavern on Abchurch Lane.

9. Byrd became a fellow of the Royal Society April 29, 1696, and was a faithful attendant at its meetings while in London. See Maude L. Woodfin, 'William Byrd and the Royal Society,' *Virginia Magazine of History and Biography*, XL (1932), 23–34, 111–123.

10. Garraway's Coffeehouse in Change Alley, Cornhill, was famous for its wines and played an important part in the city's business life.

11. Catherine, daughter of Charles Parry of Oakfield, Berkshire, wife of Henry Powlett, second son of Charles, 2nd Duke of Bolton. Powlett was M.P. for St. Ives, 1715–22, and in 1754 he succeeded his brother Charles as the 4th Duke of Bolton.

battered eggs. After dinner I put several things in order till 4 o'clock and then went to Lady Guise's and sat disputing with her about an hour and then went to Mrs. B-r-n where I talked of dear Miss Smith. Here I stayed till 9 o'clock and then went to the Spanish Ambassador's, where I talked with several men and ladies till 12 o'clock and then went home in a chair and said my prayers, &c.

11. I rose about 8 o'clock and read a chapter in Hebrew and three chapters in Greek. I said my prayers, and had boiled milk for breakfast. The weather was warm and clear, the wind west. I wrote a letter. About 11 o'clock I got ready to go into the City, and dined with old Mr. Perry, and ate some boiled veal for dinner. After dinner I went to visit Mrs. Perry and stayed with her till 4 o'clock and drank tea. From thence I went to Mrs. Lindsay's and sat with her and drank tea again. We talked of many things and she made some complaints to me of some hardships she endures from her husband. About 7 o'clock he came in and we played at cards till 10 o'clock and then went to supper and I ate some hashed mutton. Mrs. Lindsay was out of humor because her husband would not let her go to the masquerade, but he was, however, not moved.

12. I rose about 8 o'clock and read a chapter in Hebrew and four chapters in Greek. I said my prayers, and had boiled milk for breakfast. The weather was warm and cloudy. About 11 o'clock I went to Somerset Chapel where we had a good sermon. After church I saw my dear Kitty and spoke to her. Then I returned home and had some veal cutlets for dinner. After dinner I put several things in order and read some English till 5 o'clock and then went to Colonel Blakiston's and found the ladies at home and sat with them two hours, and then went to visit Mrs. Mary O-r-d, but she was indisposed; then I went to Mrs. FitzHerbert's where I found Mr. Congreve.[12] Here I stayed about an hour and then went to Mrs. A-l-c and sat with her about an hour, and then walked home and washed my feet and said my prayers, &c.

12. William Congreve, the dramatist, at this time secretary for Jamaica; a member of the Kit-Kat Club.

13. I rose about 8 o'clock and read a chapter in Hebrew and two chapters in Greek. I said my prayers, and had boiled milk for breakfast. The weather was warm and cloudy, or rather, foggy. I wrote several things, and a letter to my Aunt Sherard to condole the death of her son.[13] I drew a little till 2 o'clock, and then had a beefsteak for dinner. In the afternoon I put several things in order till 4 o'clock and then went to Will's Coffeehouse and saw the Duke of Argyll. From thence I went to Sir Robert Raymond[14] about my controversy with Lady Mohun. From thence I went to Somerset House[15] to visit Lady Powlett but she was from home. Then I went to Mrs. U-m-s but they were from home; then to Mrs. L-c-b-r and sat with her till 8 o'clock, and then returned again to Will's Coffeehouse and took up my Lord Orrery and went to Petcum's, and met dear Kitty there and talked pretty much with her. I stayed till twelve and went home in the chair, and neglected to say my prayers, for which God forgive me. It rained abundantly.

14. I rose about 8 o'clock and read a chapter in Hebrew and two in Greek. I said my prayers, and had boiled milk for breakfast. The weather was cloudy and cold. I danced my dance. About 10 o'clock came Mr. Albin to teach me to draw. Then I read some English till two and then ate some battered eggs. After dinner I put several things in order till 5 o'clock and then I went to visit Mrs. W-n-m but she was gone to bury her aunt in the country. Then I went to Mrs. L-f-l-r but she was from home. Then I went to see my daughter and sat with her about an hour and then went to my Lady Guise's where I found Sir Roger Braidshaigh[16] and took him with me to Will's Coffeehouse, where I read the news and drank two dishes of choco-

13. George Sherard, captain in the First Foot Guards, 'found dead upon Datchet Common' on January 5. *Historical Register*, Chronological Diary (London, 1714-38), v, 3. Daniel Parke in 1710 mentioned a 'cousin Sherard (now in the Guards)' who had been in the Leeward Islands. *Calendar of State Papers, America and the West Indies,* September 9, 1710.

14. Sir Robert Raymond was M.P. for Ludlow; in 1724 he became chief justice.

15. Somerset House on the Strand belonged to the royal family; at this time it was used as a residence for numerous 'poor relations' of the nobility.

16. Sir Roger Braidshaigh, 3rd Bart.

late, and then went to Sir Harry Ashurst's where we danced. About twelve we went to supper, and I ate some fowl and bacon and then danced till two and then I went home and neglected my prayers.

15. I rose about 8 o'clock and read a chapter in Hebrew and three in Greek. I said my prayers, and had boiled milk for breakfast. The weather was clear and cold, the wind east. Marge came this morning to desire me to give her a character. I wrote a letter to Virginia and put several things in order till about 1 o'clock and then my coach brought my daughter to go dine with Colonel Blakiston, where I ate some fish for dinner. The Colonel offered to give me two hundred to quit my pretension to the two thousand of the quitrents. I played at piquet and won a guinea of Colonel [Shutz]. About five I went with my daughter to Mrs. B-r-n but she saw no company; then I went to Mrs. C-r-l and drank tea and danced, because Mr. A-b-y was there and so was Colonel Holmes.[17] From hence I went about 9 o'clock to Court, where I saw nobody I liked; however, I stayed till 11 o'clock and then went home in the chair and neglected my prayers.

16. I rose about 8 o'clock and read a chapter in Hebrew and two in Greek. I said my prayers, and had boiled milk for breakfast. The weather was cold and clear, the wind northeast. My tailor came about my habit for the masquerade and a [gentle]woman came about my maid Marge. About 12 o'clock I went into the City and dined with young Mr. Perry and ate some boiled beef, and young Mr. W-r-k dined with us. After dinner we drank some coffee and I sat and talked till 4 o'clock, and then went to Will's Coffeehouse and read the news, and then to the play, where was nobody that I cared for. After the play I went to Will's again and drank a dish of chocolate and sat till 11 o'clock, and then went home in a chair because it snowed. I said my prayers, &c.

17. I rose about 8 o'clock and read a chapter in Hebrew and three chapters in Greek. I said my prayers, and had boiled milk for break-

17. Colonel Richard Holmes, regimental lieutenant colonel, retired in 1717.

Entries in the Diary for March 13-17, 1718

fast. The weather was cold and it snowed all the morning, the wind northeast. Mr. Albin came to teach me to draw, and then I wrote a letter to Virginia. Then I danced my dance, and about 2 o'clock I ate some battered eggs. After dinner I put several things in order till 4 o'clock, and then I went to Will's Coffeehouse, where I stayed about an hour, and then went to Sir Robert Raymond's chambers but he had not done my business; so I went to Mr. Southwell's but there was nobody home; then to my Lord Percival's, but nobody at home; then to Mrs. Mary O-r-d, but there was nobody at home; then to Mrs. FitzHerbert's and sat with her and had some toast and ale. About 9 o'clock I went to the Spanish Ambassador's, but it was a dull night; however, I stayed till 12 o'clock, and then went home in the chair and said my prayers.

18. I rose about 8 o'clock and read a chapter in Hebrew and some Greek. I said my prayers, and had boiled milk for breakfast. The weather was cold and cloudy and it snowed all the morning, the wind northeast. I danced my dance. Then I wrote a letter to Virginia, and then read some English till 2 o'clock, and then ate some mutton cutlets. After dinner I put several things in order, and then wrote a letter to Mrs. O-r-d. About five I went to Will's Coffeehouse and from thence with my Lord Bellenden to the play in Lincoln's Inn Field which was bespoke by Kitty Sambrooke who sat not far from me. I went away before it was done to Colonel D-m where I lost four pounds. Here I stayed till 12 o'clock, and then went home in the chair and said a short prayer. I gave Mrs. A-l-c two guineas.

19. I rose about 8 o'clock and read a chapter in Hebrew and three chapters in Greek. I said my prayers, and had boiled milk for breakfast. The weather was cold and cloudy, the wind northeast. and it snowed a little all the morning, which, however, did not hinder me from calling for my daughter about 12 o'clock and carrying her to Mr. Lindsay's to dinner, who was very kind to her. I ate some boiled chicken for dinner, and Mr. A-d-l-n dined there likewise. After dinner we sat and talked till 4 o'clock and then drank tea. About six Mr.

Lindsay went to Sir Robert D-s-r and left me and his wife together, and I gave her a ticket for the masquerade and she told me her dress. Here I stayed till supper (only I sent away my daughter about seven) and I ate some roast lamb, and went home about eleven and said my prayers. I kissed the maid till my seed ran from me.

20. I rose about 8 o'clock and read a chapter in Hebrew and three in Greek. I said my prayers, and had boiled milk for breakfast. The weather was cold and cloudy, the wind northeast. My surgeon came to me and thought my weakness better. I wrote a letter to Mrs. U-m-s to excuse my not giving her a ticket to the masquerade. I read some English till 1 o'clock and then came Mr. Lindsay, and I went with him to hire a habit for the masquerade, and returned home again about two, and then I ate some battered eggs for dinner. In the afternoon I put several things in order till 4 o'clock, and then I went to visit Mrs. W-n-m and sat with her about two hours, and discovered that she knew of the writing the letter I received without a name. Then I went to Will's Coffeehouse and drank a dish of chocolate, and then went to Mrs. A-l-c and sat with her about an hour, and then went to Court and from thence to Petcum's, where I stayed till 12 o'clock, and then walked home, where I said my prayers. I had a looseness.

21. I rose about 8 o'clock and read a chapter in Hebrew and three chapters in Greek. I said my prayers, and had boiled milk for breakfast. The weather was cold and clear, the wind northeast. About ten came Albin to teach me to draw. Then came my tailor with my habit, and then came Mike Perry and sat a quarter of an hour with me. Then I read some English till 2 o'clock, and then ate some mutton cutlets. After dinner I put several things in order till 3 o'clock and wrote some English; then read some French till 7 o'clock, when Sir Roger Braidshaigh came and after him Mr. Lindsay and dressed at my lodgings. Then we went to show ourselves at Lady Guise's and about nine to the masquerade, where was abundance of good company but nothing remarkable. I stayed till 4 o'clock, and then went home and neglected my prayers.

22. I rose about 12 o'clock and read a chapter in Hebrew and three chapters in Greek. I said my prayers, and had boiled milk for breakfast. The weather continued cold and cloudy, the wind northwest. Mr. F-s came to see me and stayed about half an hour. Then I read some French till 2 o'clock, and then ate some battered eggs for dinner. In the afternoon I put several things in order till 4 o'clock, and then went to Mrs. B-r-n, but she was indisposed; then I went to Mrs. [or Misses Andrews'] and drank tea with them, and stayed till seven; and then went to Will's Coffeehouse and stayed till 9 o'clock, and then called in at the play, and then walked home, where I read some French and said my prayers, &c. I dreamed that Miss Smith called me dear and was in bed with me.

23. I rose about 8 o'clock and read a chapter in Hebrew and two chapters in Greek. I said my prayers and had boiled milk for breakfast. The weather was very cold and cloudy, the wind northeast. My surgeon came to see me, and I had a [s-p-n-y] brought me from Mrs. Sherard. I wrote a letter to dear Miss Smith. About one o'clock I went to the City to Garraway's Coffeehouse, and from thence to Pontack's to dinner and ate some fish. After dinner I went again to Garraway's and read the news, and then went to Will's and from thence to Mrs. FitzHerbert's, where I stayed about two hours, and heard Mrs. Robinson[18] sing. About eight I went away and returned to Will's, where I stayed all the evening till 11 o'clock, and then went home in the chair and said my prayers. It thawed very much and rained.

24. I rose about 8 o'clock and read a chapter in Hebrew and two in Greek. I said my prayers, and had boiled milk for breakfast. The weather was warm and cloudy, the wind west. I took a purge and had three stools. I received a letter from dear Miss Smith which forbade me to write but not to hope. My bookseller came with his bill and I paid him. I ate some mutton cutlets for dinner. After dinner I

18. Anastasia Robinson, a noted soprano. In 1722 or later she was secretly married to the Earl of Peterborough, and was long afterward acknowledged as his wife.

read some English and put several things in order till 5 o'clock, and then went to Sir Robert Raymond's chambers but found him not; then I called at the play, and went from thence to my Lady Dunkellen's,[19] but she was from home; then to Mrs. Lethieullier's, but she was from home; then to Mrs. M-r-l-y and sat with her till nine, and then went to the Spanish Ambassador's, where I stayed till twelve, and then went home in the chair and said my prayers, &c. I slept very ill.

25. I rose about 8 o'clock and read a chapter in Hebrew and a chapter in Greek. I said my prayers, and had boiled milk for breakfast. The weather was clear and cold. About 11 o'clock I went to the Duke of Argyll's, who received me kindly and invited me to dinner. Then I went to Mrs. Southwell's and sat with her about an hour; then I went to Mr. Blathwayt's and stayed half an hour; and then to the Court of Requests, where I won four pounds at play. Here I drank two dishes of chocolate, and about 3 o'clock went to the Duke of Argyll's, where I stayed two hours before the Duke came home. Miss Lepell[20] dined here, and I ate some roast chicken. The Duke was merry and gave us some tokay. About seven I waited on the Duke to the coffeehouse, and asked him for his picture,[21] which he promised me. I took Major [Stewart][22] to the play in Lincoln's Inn where I stayed, and went from thence home, where I neglected to say my prayers.

26. I rose about 8 o'clock and read a chapter in Hebrew and three chapters in Greek. I said my prayers, and had milk for breakfast. The weather was clear and cold, the wind northwest. I went not to

19. Anne Smith, sister of 'Sabina,' married (as the widow of Hugh Parker) Michael, Lord Dunkellen, eldest son of the Earl of Clanricade.

20. Mary Lepell, daughter of Brigadier General Nicholas Lepell, groom of the bedchamber to George, Prince of Denmark, was a maid of honor. She later married John Hervey, styled Lord Hervey.

21. A portrait of the Duke of Argyll by Kneller was among Byrd's treasures at Westover.

22. Possibly Major Mathew Stewart.

church till 12 o'clock, and then I went to St. James's Chapel, and after that to Court, where I stayed till 3 o'clock and then walked through the park and dined with Mr. Blathwayt and ate some roast beef. After dinner we drank a bottle till 5 o'clock, and then I went to Colonel Blakiston's, where I stayed till eight; and then went to Will's Coffeehouse, and from thence to Mrs. A-l-c and scolded at her for not making my shirts. About eleven I went home and found a great pain in my toe. I kissed the maid and my seed came from me, and neglected my prayers, for all which God forgive me.

27. I rose about 8 o'clock and read a chapter in Hebrew and three chapters in Greek. I said my prayers, and had boiled milk for breakfast. The weather was cold and clear, the wind northwest. About 11 o'clock I went to my Lord Percival's but he was come at the same time to me. Then I went to Colonel Paget's,[23] but he was from home; then I went to Horace Walpole's, but he was from home. Then to Major Dives',[24] but he was from home; then to my Lord Orrery's and I found him and drank a dish of chocolate with him, and then went home, where I read some English till 2 o'clock and then ate some battered eggs for dinner. In the afternoon I wrote some English till 5 o'clock, and then went to Will's Coffeehouse, and from thence to the play, where I saw a very pretty woman, Mrs. F-l-t. Then I went to Court, and from thence to Petcum's, where was abundance of company, and I stayed till twelve and then went home in the chair and said my prayers.

28. I rose about 8 o'clock and read a chapter in Hebrew and three chapters in Greek. I said my prayers, and had boiled milk for breakfast. The weather was clear and cold, the wind northeast and blowing hard. I wrote a letter to Mrs. O-r-d. About ten came Mr. Albin to teach me to draw. I read English till 2 o'clock, and then ate some

23. Thomas Paget, lieutenant colonel of the first troop of Horse Grenadier Guards, was grandson of the 5th Baron Paget. Later, as a brigadier general, he was governor of Minorca.

24. Lewis Dives, major of the Second Life Guards.

mutton cutlets. After dinner I put several things in order and wrote some English till 4 o'clock, and then went to visit my cousin Horsmanden, but he was from home. Then I went to see my daughter, and sat with her about an hour. Then I went to Lady Guise's and stayed about two hours, and then went to Will's Coffeehouse and drank two dishes of chocolate, and about 10 o'clock went to the Spanish Ambassador's, where I stayed till 12 o'clock, and then came home in a chair and said my prayers.

29. I rose about 8 o'clock and read a chapter in Hebrew and two in Greek. I said my prayers, and had boiled milk for breakfast. The weather was very cold and clear, the wind northeast. I wrote some English till 12 o'clock, and then went into the City and dined with old Mr. Perry and ate some roast beef. After dinner I went to Dick Perry's and sat there till 4 o'clock and then walked to Garraway's and sent to Mr. Lindsay, but they were from home; then I went to visit Mrs. U-m-s, but they were from home; then to my Lady Powlett's and sat there about an hour, and then went to Will's Coffeehouse, where I saw the Duke of Argyll. Then I went to the play, and from thence to Court, where I stayed till 11 o'clock and then walked home and said my prayers.

30. I rose about 9 o'clock, and read a chapter in Hebrew and two chapters in Greek. I said my prayers, and had boiled milk for breakfast. The weather was cold and cloudy, the wind northeast. I wrote a letter to Mrs. O-r-d and then drew a little till 2 o'clock and then ate some battered eggs. After dinner I put several things in order, and then read some English till five, and then went to Will's Coffeehouse, where I drank two dishes of chocolate, and stayed till 8 o'clock; and then went to Lady Guise's, where I stayed all the evening and ate some roasted goose for supper. About 12 o'clock I took leave and went home in the chair and said my prayers, and kissed the maid till I polluted myself, for which God forgive me. The weather was warmer, and it thawed.

31. I rose about 8 o'clock and read a chapter in Hebrew and four in Greek. I said my prayers, and had boiled milk for breakfast. The weather was cold and cloudy. About ten my drawing master came to me and stayed about an hour. I sent for twelve bottles of wine from Mr. U-t-n. I wrote a letter to Virginia till 2 o'clock and then ate some mutton cutlets. After dinner I put several things in order and read some English till 5 o'clock, and then went to visit Mrs. W-n-m but she was from home. Then I went to my Lady Dunkellen's, and sat with her about half an hour, and then went to both playhouses, and from thence to Will's Coffeehouse, where I drank two dishes of chocolate and stayed till 9 o'clock, and then went to the Spanish Ambassador's, where I won three pounds at basset and came home about twelve in a chair and said my prayers. I slept very well, thank God.

February 1718

1. I rose about 8 o'clock and read two chapters in Hebrew and two in Greek. I said my prayers, and had boiled milk for breakfast. The weather was cold and cloudy, the wind northwest. About eleven I went to Mr. U-t-n and sat with him about quarter of an hour. Then I went to Lord Harry Powlett's but he was from home; then I went to Spring Garden[1] and stayed with Mrs. Southwell about half an hour, and then went to my Lord Percival's, but he was from home; then I went home, where I drew a little and wrote a letter to Virginia. About 2 o'clock I went again to Mr. Southwell's to dinner and ate some broiled pork. Tom W-n dined there too. From hence I went to Will's Coffeehouse and from thence to the play, where I slept. After the play I returned to Will's and drank two dishes of chocolate, and went home about eleven and said my prayers.

1. Spring Garden was originally part of the pleasure gardens of Whitehall Palace; the Southwell family leased a house here, and at the time of Edward Southwell's death in 1730 he owned most of the gardens.

2. I rose about 8 o'clock and read two chapters in Hebrew and two chapters in Greek. I said my prayers, and had boiled milk for breakfast. The weather was cloudy and cold, the wind east. About 11 o'clock I went to Somerset Chapel, where we had a pretty good sermon. After church I went home with the U-m-s and warmed myself and stayed about half an hour and then went home, where I ate some beefsteak for dinner. In the afternoon I put several things in order, and danced my dance till 4 o'clock and then went to Mrs. B-r-n in hopes of meeting dear Miss Smith. There I drank coffee, and sat with Mrs. B-r-n three hours and talked most of the time about Miss Smith. Then I went to Lady Guise's and sat with her about an hour, and then went to the Spanish Ambassador's where was scarce any women; however, I stayed till 12 o'clock and then went home in the chair and said my prayers. I slept pretty well, thank God.

3. I rose about 8 o'clock and read two chapters in Hebrew and two chapters in Greek. I said my prayers, and had boiled milk for breakfast. The weather was clear and warm, the wind northwest. About 11 o'clock I went to Colonel Blakiston's and drank a dish of chocolate and stayed about an hour; then I went to Lord Percival's, but he was from home. Then I went to the Cockpit[2] to speak with Mr. Beake,[3] and then to the Court of Requests, where I won three guineas and drank a dish of chocolate, and about 2 o'clock returned home and ate some battered eggs for dinner. In the afternoon I put several things in order and then read some English till 4 o'clock, and then danced my dance. About five I went into the City to Mr. Lindsay's where I saw dear Kitty Sambrooke and we drank tea together but then she went away and Mrs. Lindsay and I talked and played at cards till Mr. Lindsay came, and then we all played till ten, and then I ate some hashed mutton for supper. About twelve I went home and said my prayers.

2. Once a place for cockfighting in Whitehall, the Cockpit was at this time used for Privy Council offices.

3. Thomas Beake was a clerk of the Privy Council.

4. I rose about 8 o'clock and read two chapters in Hebrew and two chapters in Greek. I said my prayers, and had boiled milk for breakfast. The weather was cold and cloudy. About ten Mr. Albin came and taught me to draw. About twelve I went to the Cockpit to get my representation to the Council of Trade from the Council office.[4] Then I went to the coffeehouse and read the news and drank a dish of chocolate, and then returned home and at two ate some mutton cutlets for dinner. In the afternoon I put several things in order, and about 5 o'clock went to the play where Miss Smith and Kitty Sambrooke both were. I had bespoke the play[5] so that it was lucky enough. However I waited on Kitty Sambrooke out, and then went to the coffeehouse and drank two dishes of chocolate, and then went to the Spanish Ambassador's where I stayed till twelve and then went home.

5. I rose about 8 o'clock and read a chapter in Hebrew and two chapters in Greek. I said my prayers, and had boiled milk for breakfast. The weather was cold and cloudy, the wind west. About 11 o'clock came my Lord Dunkellen and stayed with me about half an hour, and then I went to the Council of Trade and carried my representation from the King in Council, and then went to the coffeehouse and drank a dish of chocolate. Then I went to Court, where I stayed till 2 o'clock, and then went to dine with Mr. U-t-n, and ate some roast pork. His brother and sister dined with us. About 4 o'clock I went to my Lady Powlett's and drank tea, and about 6 o'clock went to the play in Lincoln's Inn Field where were several ladies of my acquaintance. After the play I went to Will's Coffeehouse and drank two dishes of chocolate and then walked home and said my prayers. About 4 o'clock in the morning somebody opened the door of my chamber but when I spoke retired again, but I know not who.

4. Byrd's petition to the King on the courts of oyer and terminer in Virginia was referred by the Privy Council to the Commissioners for Trade and Plantations on February 2; it was read in the latter body on February 5, as is shown by the endorsements on the petition found in the Public Record Office.

5. Byrd's statement that he 'bespoke' the play would seem to imply that he had asked the company to produce that play; however, he may simply mean that he had chosen the playhouse for the party.

6. I rose about 8 o'clock and read a chapter in Hebrew and three in Greek. I said my prayers, and had boiled milk for breakfast. The weather was cold and cloudy, the wind northwest. About 10 o'clock I sent to borrow of Mr. Jeffreys his Marquis dress for the masquerade. About twelve I went to Mrs. U-m-s and sat there about an hour and gave a guinea to Mr. U-m-s to give to some poor people. Then I went home and ate some mutton cutlets for dinner. In the afternoon I put several things in order till five and then came Sir Harry Ashurst and stayed till seven; then I dressed myself in the habit of the Marquis and went to Mrs. B-r-t, and from thence to Lady Guise's, and from thence to my Lady Foley's,[6] and about ten went to the masquerade, where I was well diverted. About twelve I ate some neat's tongue with Mrs. Hoar[7] and after that met several of my acquaintances and particularly a little Dutchwoman that I liked and [. . .]. I stayed till 6 o'clock, having kept up my spirits with chocolate. I neglected my prayers, for which God forgive me.

7. I rose about 12 o'clock and read a chapter in Hebrew and some Greek. Then I said my prayers, and had boiled milk for breakfast. The weather was clear and warm, the wind southwest, but violent. About 3 o'clock I went to dinner and ate some battered eggs. In the afternoon I put several things in order till 4 o'clock and then came Daniel Horsmanden and stayed about quarter of an hour. About five I went to his lodgings and carried him to visit my daughter, where we stayed about an hour, and then I went to visit Mrs. W-n-m but found her not; then I went to Mrs. Lethieullier's but she was from home; then I went to Will's and my Lord Orrery desired me to go with him to the play in Lincoln's Inn Field, where I saw dear Miss Smith and led her out in spite of the old fellow that offered his hand. From hence I went with Colonel Blathwayt[8] to the chocolate house and had two glasses of jelly and won five shillings at [f-r-n].

6. Mary, only daughter of Thomas Strode, sergeant at law, wife of Thomas, Baron Foley of Kidderminster.

7. Perhaps Mary, wife of Charles Hoar, a sister of Sir Charles Buck. See *Another Secret Diary of William Byrd*, 407 n.

8. John Blathwayt, lieutenant colonel of the First Life Guards, was brother of William Blathwayt and son of the late auditor general William Blathwayt.

Then we went to the Spanish Ambassador's, where I stayed till twelve and then came home and said my prayers.

8. I rose about 8 o'clock and read a chapter in Hebrew and a chapter in Greek. I said my prayers, and had boiled milk for breakfast. The weather was cold and cloudy, and the wind continued violent at southwest. About 10 o'clock I had the honor of a visit from my Lord Percival who stayed with me about an hour, and after him came Tom Beake, to whom I discovered a project of getting the government of Virginia and he undertook it. He stayed till 12 o'clock; then I drew a little and read some English till two when I had some mutton cutlets for dinner. In the afternoon I put several things in order till 5 o'clock and then I went to visit Mrs. B-r-t and drank tea with her till 6 o'clock and then went to the play in Covent Garden[9] and led out Mrs. W-n-m; and then I went to the coffeehouse where I stayed till 11 o'clock and then walked home and said my prayers.

9. I rose about 8 o'clock and read a chapter in Hebrew and three chapters in Greek. I said my prayers and had boiled milk for breakfast. The weather was cold and it rained all the morning, the wind southwest. This hindered me from going to church. I drew a little and read some English. Mr. Blathwayt sent to invite me to dinner but I chose rather to stay at home and eat some beefsteak. After dinner I put several things in order till 5 o'clock and then I went to Mrs. B-r-n where I had the pleasure to talk of my dear Miss Smith. Here I stayed till 7 o'clock and then went to Mrs. FitzHerbert's where I drank some strong beer and ate some toast and then went to the Ambassador's where I lost four pounds. Here I was very bright and stayed till 12 o'clock and then went home in a chair and kissed the maid till I polluted myself. I said my prayers.

10. I rose about 8 o'clock and read a chapter in Hebrew and two chapters in Greek. I said my prayers and had boiled milk for break-

9. At the Covent Garden Theater *Othello* was being played.

fast. The weather was warm and cloudy, the wind southwest. About 11 o'clock I went to my Lord Dunkellen's but he was from home. Then to Mr. Sambrooke's, but he was from home. Then to Mr. N-l-r where I met Mr. B-r-n-t-n, a man of good sense. Then I went to take my daughter and Miss Page[10] to Mr. Perry's where we dined and I ate some roast mutton. After dinner we drank tea and stayed till 5 o'clock and then I carried home the girls and went to the playhouse, and from thence to a conjuror called Old Abram but he was from home. Then to Will's and from thence after I had drunk two dishes of chocolate I went to Petcum's where I played and lost ten pounds. Here I stayed till 1 o'clock and then went home and said my prayers. I dreamed that I was in great danger of my life but on my earnest prayer was delivered.

11. I rose about 8 o'clock and read a chapter in Hebrew and two in Greek. I said my prayers, and had boiled milk for breakfast. The weather was warm and cloudy, the wind southwest. About ten came Mrs. A-l-c and stayed about half an hour. Then came Albin to teach me to draw. I danced my dance. About twelve came Mr. Horsmanden and stayed about quarter of an hour. About 2 o'clock I ate some mutton cutlets for dinner. In the afternoon I put several things in order till 4 o'clock and then went to visit Mrs. M-n-l-y, who came home yesterday, and drank tea with her. Then I went to Mrs. W-n-m but she was from home; then to Mr. D-n-s who was very sick; then to Mr. Jeffreys' where I drank tea again; then to Will's Coffeehouse where I drank two dishes of chocolate and about nine went with Mr. Jeffreys to the Spanish Ambassador's where I stayed till 12 o'clock and then went home in the chair and said my prayers. I felt myself that my weakness is better, thank God.

12. I rose about 8 o'clock and read a chapter in Hebrew but no Greek because I was to go out soon. I said my prayers and had boiled milk for breakfast. The weather was clear and warm, the wind . . . place and told me everything would be fortunate this year. Then I

10. Probably the daughter of Byrd's fellow Councillor in Virginia, Colonel Mann Page.

went home to my own coach, and went into the City to my book-seller and from thence to the Virginia Coffeehouse; and from thence to Mr. Perry's and dined with the old man and ate some roast mutton. After dinner I wrote a letter to Virginia and then went to visit Mrs. B-r-n to tell her about the conjurer, and about 9 o'clock went to Will's Coffeehouse and stayed there till 11 o'clock and then walked home and said my prayers.

13. I rose about 8 o'clock and read a chapter in Hebrew and four chapters in Greek. I said my prayers, and had boiled milk for break-fast. The weather was clear and warm, the wind south. About 11 o'clock I went to the Cockpit and spoke to Sir Charles Cook[11] about my business but he gave me a short answer, and returned again. Then I went to the coffeehouse and drank two dishes of chocolate and then spoke with Mr. Beake about the business I had with him. Then I went to Mrs. Southwell's and drank another dish of chocolate and then went home and drew a little till 2 o'clock and then ate battered eggs. After dinner I put several things in order and wrote a letter to Virginia and danced my dance and about 5 o'clock went to Mrs. O-r-d who was out; then to Mrs. Paget's, who was out; then to Mrs. FitzHerbert's where I stayed to supper and ate some apple pie and about nine went to Will's Coffeehouse and stayed till eleven and then walked home and was so sleepy I could not say my prayers, for which God forgive me. I slept very ill and had bad dreams.

14. I rose about 8 o'clock and read a chapter in Hebrew and four chapters in Greek. I said my prayers, and had boiled milk for break-fast. The weather was warm and cloudy, the wind southwest. About 10 o'clock came Mr. Albin to show me to draw. About 12 o'clock came Mr. Southwell and sat with me about half an hour. I wrote a long account for Virginia. About 2 o'clock I ate some mutton cutlets. After dinner I put several things in order and then wrote a letter till 5 o'clock and then went to visit Mrs. A-l-c at Westminster and drank tea with her till 7 o'clock and then called at Mrs. D-n-s but she was from home; then at my Lady Burgoyne's, but she was from home;

11. Sir Charles Cook was a Lord Commissioner for Trade and Plantations.

then I went to Mrs. C-r-y where I saw Mrs. S-t-r-t and stayed till 9 o'clock and then went to Will's Coffeehouse and drank two dishes of chocolate. I went to the Spanish Ambassador's where I saw Mrs. W-n-m that looked a little out of countenance upon me. About twelve I went home and said my prayers.

15. I rose about 8 o'clock and read a chapter in Hebrew and four chapters in Greek. I said my prayers, and had boiled milk for breakfast. The weather was warm and cloudy, the wind west. I wrote a long letter to Mrs. O-r-d which took me up till dinner, when I ate some roast mutton. After dinner I put several things in order till 4 o'clock and then drew a little till five, and then went to Will's Coffeehouse and read the news till six and then went to the play, where I saw Mrs. W-n-m but she gave herself very grave airs. After the play I went to the coffeehouse and drank two dishes of chocolate. About eleven I went home and said my prayers.

16. I rose about 8 o'clock and read a chapter in Hebrew and no Greek. I said my prayers, and had boiled milk for breakfast. The weather was warm and cloudy, the wind east. About 11 o'clock I went to Somerset Chapel where we had but an indifferent sermon. After church I called on my Lord Harry Powlett to inquire how my Lady did. Then I went with Mr. U-t-n to St. James's where I talked with my friend Sir Charles Wager [12] and went to my Lord Percival's to dinner and ate some roast duck. After dinner we sat and talked till five and then I went to Colonel Blakiston's and stayed till seven and then went to Mrs. Mary O-r-d and stayed till nine, and was very sleepy so that I went home and washed my feet and said my prayers, &c.

17. I rose about 8 o'clock and read a chapter in Hebrew and two chapters in Greek. I said my prayers, and had boiled milk for break-

12. Sir Charles Wager, a Lord Commissioner of the Admiralty, 1718–33, was a long-time friend and correspondent of Byrd.

fast. The weather was clear and warm, the wind southwest. About 9 o'clock came John Randolph [13] to take his leave and took two of my letters; then came my Lord Dunkellen and brought me a message from my dear Miss Smith that there was a match proposed to her but she would not accept it till she had heard what I had to propose, for that she could be happier with me than any man. I let my Lord know that I would wait on him next day with what I had to say on that subject, and so he took his leave. Then I dressed me and went into the City with an intent to dine with Jack [Willis] but his wife was just brought to bed. However, he and I and Tom Randolph [13] dined together at the tavern and I ate some salmon. About three I went to Will's Coffeehouse, and from thence to Mrs. C-r-l where I drank tea and then to Mrs. B-r-n to let her know my success and about 9 o'clock went home and wrote a state of my circumstances [14] by way of proposal. I said my prayers, &c.

18. I rose about 6 o'clock to write my business fair, but read nothing because I was to go out. However, I said my prayers, and had boiled milk for breakfast. The weather was warm and clear. About 10 o'clock I went to my Lord Dunkellen with an account of my estate by way of letter, which my Lord approved and said he would show to my Lady Dunkellen and Miss Smith and consult with them how to proceed. Here I drank two dishes of chocolate. Then I went to the Duke of Argyll's and found him better than he had been. I stayed with him about half an hour and then went with him to the Court of Requests where I drank another dish of chocolate and about 1 o'clock went home and ate some battered eggs for dinner. In the afternoon I put several things in order and then danced my dance. Then I read some English and drew a little. About 5 o'clock I went to

13. John was the fourth son of Colonel William Randolph I of Virginia. He was a lawyer, and in 1732 was knighted. Tom was the second son of Colonel Randolph.

14. This remarkable document, a copy of which is preserved in Byrd's North Carolina letterbook as an undated letter 'To Vigilante,' is printed in *Another Secret Diary of William Byrd*, 321–24. In it Byrd tells Smith about his property in Virginia, his descent 'from the family of my name at Broxon in Cheshire,' and refers him to the Perrys and to his friends Lord Percival and Mr. Southwell for a character.

visit Mrs. B-r-t and stayed till seven, and then went to Lady Guise's and stayed till nine and then went to Will's Coffeehouse, where I stayed till eleven and drank two dishes of chocolate and then went home in a chair because it rained. I said my prayers and slept indifferently.

19. I rose about 8 o'clock and read a chapter in Hebrew but no Greek because I wrote a letter to Mr. Smith to propose myself for his daughter. However, I said my prayers and had boiled milk for breakfast. The weather was cold and cloudy. I received a letter from my Lord Dunkellen to meet him at Leveridge's Coffeehouse, which I did accordingly and there he brought me directions from Miss Smith how to make my proposal to her father shorter than I had done to my Lord, which I agreed to do and went home and did it accordingly. About 3 o'clock I ate some mutton cutlets. After dinner I put several things in order till four and then danced my dance. About five I went to see my daughter and sat with her about an hour and then went to visit Mrs. U-m-s but they were from home. Then I went to Lady Powlett's and drank tea with her; then I went to the coffeehouse and drank two dishes of chocolate and then went to Court where I talked with Mrs. R-d-r. About twelve I went home and said my prayers.

20. I rose about 8 o'clock and read a chapter in Hebrew and two chapters in Greek. I said my prayers, and had boiled milk for breakfast. The weather was warm and cloudy, the wind west. I danced my dance and wrote several letters till 11 o'clock and then I went into the City to the Virginia Coffeehouse and from thence to Mr. Dick Perry's where I dined and ate some roast veal for dinner. Then I discovered to him my affair with Miss Smith and desired their favor, which they promised me. About 4 o'clock I returned home, where I put several things in order and then dressed me in the habit of a running footman to go to the masquerade, but first I showed myself to my landlady and then went to Mrs. B-r-n and from thence to Mrs. C-r-l and from thence to Mrs. FitzHerbert's where I found my Lady

Frances B-l-n. Then to Colonel Blakiston's and went with the ladies to Mr. C-r-n-b-r and then to the masquerade where I kept with Miss T-r-n-s-f-l all the night. Here I stayed till six in the morning, and then went home in the chair. I neglected to say my prayers.

21. I rose about 12 o'clock and read a chapter in Hebrew and a chapter in Greek. I said my prayers, and had boiled milk for breakfast. The weather was clear and warm, the wind west. I danced my dance, and sent the things home which I had borrowed for the masquerade. About 2 o'clock I ate some battered eggs for dinner. In the afternoon I put several things in order till 4 o'clock and then went to my Lord Dunkellen's but neither he nor my Lady were at home. Then went into the City to Mrs. Lindsay's and drank tea with her, then came a man, Mr. [Tryon] (a young man) and we played at cards till supper, when I ate some chicken. Here I stayed till 11 o'clock and then took leave and went home, where I kissed the maid till I polluted myself, for which God forgive me. I said my prayers and was disturbed in my sleep.

22. I rose about 8 o'clock and read a chapter in Hebrew and a chapter in Greek. I said my prayers and had boiled milk for breakfast. I received a letter from my Lord Dunkellen and met him about 10 o'clock at Leveridge's Coffeehouse, where he told me that Mr. Smith could not be brought to look on my circumstances but that Miss Smith was resolved to endeavor to bring him to it, for that she remained firm in my favor and told me I must have patience, which I promised I would. Then I returned home again and wrote a letter to Colonel Nicholson[15] and Colonel Blakiston to desire them to speak a good word for me in case they should be asked about me. Then I wrote a letter to Virginia, and about 5 o'clock made Colonel Nicholson a visit and he promised to do me all the favor he could. Then I went to Mrs. A-l-c and gave her two guineas and drank tea. Then I called on

15. Colonel Francis Nicholson, lieutenant governor of Virginia, 1690–94 and 1698–1705; governor of Maryland 1695–7; governor of Acadia, 1713–19; and governor of South Carolina, 1719–28. In 1720 he was knighted.

Mrs. D-n-s but she was from home. Then I went to visit Mrs. S-t-r-t but she was from home. Then to Mrs. C-r-y but she was from home; then to Mrs. U-m-s but they were from home; then to Mrs. L-c-b-r where I stayed two hours and then went to Will's and from thence home and said my prayers.

23. I rose about 8 o'clock and read a chapter in Hebrew and three chapters in Greek. I said my prayers and had boiled milk for breakfast. The weather was cold and cloudy, the wind west. I did not go to church but wrote a letter to my dear Miss Smith till 1 o'clock and then went to Colonel Blakiston's to dinner by invitation but found Mrs. Blakiston indisposed. I ate some boiled beef for dinner. After dinner we went to sit with Mrs. Blakiston and found her better. I told them the story of my love, without naming my mistress. About 5 o'clock I went to Mrs. B-r-n and sat with her about an hour, and then went to Lady Guise's and sat with her two hours, but was very sleepy. About nine I went to the Spanish Ambassador's, where I met my Lord Dunkellen who told me I might write if I could do it without giving suspicion to Mr. Smith. Here I stayed till 11 o'clock and then went home, where I said my prayers, &c. I slept better, thank God.

24. I rose about 8 o'clock and read a chapter in Hebrew and three chapters in Greek. I said my prayers, and had boiled milk for breakfast. The weather was warm and clear, the wind west. About 10 o'clock I went to the Cockpit and gave in a letter to the Council of Trade to desire them to consider my petition referred to them by the King. Then I went to Mr. Blathwayt's but both the brothers were out. Then I went to Mrs. Southwell's and sat with her about an hour and drank tea, and then went home and danced my dance. About two I ate some veal cutlets for dinner. In the afternoon I took a nap and put several things in order till 5 o'clock and then went to Will's Coffeehouse and from thence to the play. After the play I went to Court, and from thence to Petcum's where was abundance of company.

Here I stayed till 12 o'clock and then went home in a chair and kissed the maid till I committed uncleanness, for which God forgive me. I slept pretty well.

25. I rose about 7 o'clock and read a chapter in Hebrew and three chapters in Greek. I said my prayers, and had boiled milk for breakfast. The weather was cloudy and warm, the wind west. About 9 o'clock came Mr. Perry and Mr. M-s, the lawyer, about our business with Mrs. Sherard and stayed about half an hour, and then I danced my dance. The maid of the house came to complain of my man Rob for calling her names and I found them both in the wrong. About 12 o'clock I wrote some English till two and then had a beefsteak for dinner. After dinner I put several things in order till 5 o'clock and then went to see my daughter and sat with her till 6 o'clock and then went to visit Mrs. W-n-m but she was from home; then I called at the playhouse but did not stay; then I went to Will's and drank a dish of chocolate and about nine went to the Spanish Ambassador's where I played at commerce and lost nothing but played at hazard and lost six pounds. About twelve I went home and said my prayers.

26. I rose about 7 o'clock and read a chapter in Hebrew and three chapters in Greek. I said my prayers, and had boiled milk for breakfast. The weather was clear and cold, the wind west. I danced my dance. I drew a little till 11 o'clock and then went to Somerset Chapel where we had only prayers. Then I came home and Mr. N-c-l-r called to see me and stayed about half an hour. Then I wrote some English till 2 o'clock and then ate some battered eggs. After dinner I put several things in order and then read some English. About 5 o'clock I received a letter from my dear Miss Smith that was not unkind. Then I went to visit Mrs. U-m-s and drank tea and stayed all the evening and about 10 o'clock supped with them, and ate some eggs. About twelve I walked home and neglected to say my prayers, for which God forgive me.

27. I rose about 7 o'clock and read a chapter in Hebrew and a chapter in Greek. I said my prayers, and had boiled milk for breakfast. The weather was cold and cloudy, the wind west. I wrote a long letter to my dear Miss Smith in answer to hers, which took me up all the morning till 2 o'clock, and then I ate some mutton steak for dinner. In the afternoon I put several things in order and wrote more English till 5 o'clock and then went to the coffeehouse and from thence to the play, where I sat by Betty Southwell.[16] After the play I went to Major Dives' where I played at hazard and basset and lost twenty-one pounds and went home about 12 o'clock and said no prayers, &c.

28. I rose about 7 o'clock and read a chapter in Hebrew and some three in Greek. I said my prayers, and had boiled milk for breakfast. The weather was warm and cloudy, the wind west. I wrote some English and then got ready to go into the City, and dined with Mr. Perry and ate some roast beef. After dinner I went and sat with Mrs. Perry till 4 o'clock and then went to visit Mrs. Lindsay but because she was going out I stayed but half an hour, and then went home and danced my dance. About six I went to Mrs. A-l-c and drank tea with her and stayed till eight and then went to Will's Coffeehouse where I read the news and stayed till 10 o'clock and drank a dish of chocolate. Then I walked home and washed my feet and said my prayers, &c. I slept pretty well, thank God. This evening came a cousin of my dear Miss Smith to Will's Coffeehouse with design to observe me; what he observed I know not, but he reported favorably, as my Lady Dunkellen told me afterwards.

16. Betty Southwell was Edward Southwell's sister.

March 1718

1. I rose about 7 o'clock and read a chapter in Hebrew and three chapters in Greek. I said my prayers, and had boiled milk for breakfast. The weather was clear and cold, the wind northwest. I wrote some English till 10 o'clock and then prepared to go out, and about eleven I went to Colonel Bladen's but found him not; then to the Duke of Argyll's, who received me very kindly and invited me to dinner; then to Mr. Southwell's, where I drank tea and about 1 o'clock went home and wrote some English till 3 o'clock, and then returned to the Duke of Argyll's to dinner where I ate some boiled chicken. My Lord Bute[1] and his lady dined here and so did Jenny Smith, one of the maids of honor. Here I stayed till 6 o'clock and then went with my Lord Islay[2] to Will's Coffeehouse and from thence to Mr. Lindsay's. I found him out of humor. We played at cards and I stayed till supper and then ate some broiled fowl and about 12 o'clock went home and said my prayers, &c.

2. I rose about 8 o'clock and read a chapter in Hebrew and three chapters in Greek. I said my prayers, and had boiled milk for breakfast. The weather was clear and warm, the wind northwest. I wrote some English and about 12 o'clock went to St. James's Chapel and from thence to Court, where I spoke with the Solicitor General and Colonel Bladen; about 2 o'clock I went with Captain O-m-r-k to Mr. Southwell's to dinner and ate some boiled pork. After dinner we drank tea and I sat with Mrs. Southwell till six and then went to Colonel Blakiston's, where I stayed till nine, and then I went to the Spanish Ambassador's where was few women; however, I stayed till 12 o'clock and then went home in the chair and kissed the maid till I committed uncleanness, for which God forgive me.

1. James Stewart, 2nd Earl Bute, and his wife, Anne, sister of the Earl of Argyll.

2. Archibald Campbell, Viscount and Duke of Islay, brother of the Duke of Argyll. He married Anne Whitfield, daughter of Major Walter Whitfield.

3. I rose about 7 o'clock and read a chapter in Hebrew and three chapters in Greek. I said my prayers, and had boiled milk for breakfast. The weather was cold and cloudy, the wind west. I wrote some English till 11 o'clock and then came Mr. LeGrande[3] and I went with him to Bridewell[4] to see the people make pins, which was very pretty. Then we saw the ladies beat hemp. Then we went to see the men at fetters, and from thence we went to see a [she lion] and then I went home and danced my dance till 2 o'clock, and then ate some battered eggs. After dinner I put several things in order and then wrote more English till 6 o'clock and then went to Will's Coffeehouse, where I read the news. Then I went to visit Mrs. B-r-n, but she was indisposed. Then I went to Mrs. C-r-l but they were out; then I went to Mrs. [Andrews'] and drank tea with them till 9 o'clock, and then I went to Court and from thence to Petcum's, where I met my Lady Dunkellen who told me several things about dear Miss Smith. I won two guineas and about 12 o'clock went home and said my prayers, &c.

4. I rose about 7 o'clock and read a chapter in Hebrew and three chapters in Greek. I said my prayers, and had boiled milk for breakfast. The weather was cold and clear, the wind west. I wrote some English till 11 o'clock and then came Albin to teach me to draw and stayed till twelve, and then I discontinued to learn. I danced my dance, and read some English till 2 o'clock, and then ate some mutton cutlets. After dinner I put several things in order till 5 o'clock and then went to Will's Coffeehouse and from thence to the play, where I sat by Mrs. Lindsay. After the play I went to the Spanish Ambassador's where I stayed till about twelve and then walked home, it being late and the streets clean. I said my prayers, &c.

5. I rose about 7 o'clock and read nothing because I wrote a letter to my dear Miss Smith. I neglected to say my prayers, but had boiled milk for breakfast. The weather was clear and warm. About 10 o'clock I went to visit Mrs. Southwell to consult about our tickets,

3. Lewis LeGrande married Helena Southwell, sister of Edward Southwell.

4. Bridewell was a prison and workhouse for vagrants and prostitutes. It was open to visitors.

but she had company with her. However, I drank tea and then Sir Roger Braidshaigh and I went to see the [White Widow] and I laid out six pounds with her. Then I went home and wrote some English till 2 o'clock, and then returned to Mr. Southwell's to dinner and ate some fish. After dinner we drank tea and about 5 o'clock I went home and wrote some English and about six went to Will's Coffeehouse and from thence to visit Lady Powlett where I drank caudle and about nine returned to Will's again, where I sat till eleven and then walked home where I said my prayers and slept but indifferently.

6. I rose about 7 o'clock and wrote a letter to my dear Miss Smith. I read a chapter in Hebrew and three in Greek. I said my prayers, and had boiled milk for breakfast. The weather was warm and clear. I danced my dance, and about 11 o'clock I went to the Cockpit and drank a dish of chocolate and read the news. I went up and spoke with Mr. Beake and then returned home. Colonel Blakiston came to me and stayed about half an hour. About 2 o'clock I ate some battered eggs. After dinner I put several things in order and then . . . Then I went to see my daughter where I stayed about an hour; then I went to my Lady Dunkellen's but she was from home; then to Mrs. W-n-m but she was from home; then to Lady Guise's where I stayed till 10 o'clock, and then went to Will's where I stayed half an hour, and then walked home and was so sleepy I could not say my prayers.

7. I rose about 8 o'clock and read a chapter in Hebrew and three in Greek. I said my prayers, and had boiled milk for breakfast. The weather was cold and cloudy, the wind west. Mike Perry called to desire me to go to the Court of Requests. Mr. Albin then came to bring some prints. I danced my dance. About 12 o'clock I went to the Court of Requests to solicit against the bill for Dover pier [5] and spoke to several lords. I drank a dish of chocolate. Here I stayed till 2 o'clock and then went in the chair to dine with Sir Roger Braidshaigh

5. A bill for the repair of Dover Harbor was passed on March 17. Byrd's opposition was based on his feeling that the additional duties on trade and navigation applied to the upkeep of the harbor were an unwarranted burden on the Virginia trade.

at Mr. Southwell's and ate some salt fish. After dinner we sat and talked till 5 o'clock, and then I went to Mrs. A-l-c and drank tea. Then I went to Lady Burgoyne's and sat with her till 8 o'clock. Then I went to Mrs. O-r-d, but she was from home. Then I went to St. James's Coffeehouse and ate a jelly, and then to the Spanish Ambassador's where I stayed till twelve and then went home in the chair and said my prayers.

8. I rose about 8 o'clock and read a chapter in Hebrew and three chapters in Hebrew [sic]. I said my prayers, and had boiled milk for breakfast. The weather was warm and cloudy, the wind west. I danced my dance. I read some English till 11 o'clock, then came Daniel Horsmanden and stayed quarter of an hour. Then I went to the Cockpit to the Council office to speak with Mr. Beake; then I took a turn in the park till 2 o'clock and then went home and ate some battered eggs for dinner. After dinner I put several things in order till 4 o'clock and then read some English till five and then went to the play in Lincoln's Inn, where I talked to my Lady Dunkellen. After the play I went to the other house and led out Mrs. R-d-r. Then I went to Will's and drank two dishes of chocolate and about eleven went home, where I said my prayers, &c.

9. I rose about 7 o'clock and read a chapter in Hebrew and four chapters in Greek. I said my prayers, and had boiled milk for breakfast. The weather was cold and clear, the wind east. I danced my dance, and about 11 o'clock got ready to go into the City to dine with Mr. Lindsay, where I ate some roast beef. After dinner I went with them to church where we had an indifferent sermon. After church Mr. Lindsay and Tom [Tryon] [6] went with me to the park where we found it very dusty, so we went away soon to the Cocoa Tree,[7] where I drank some tea. Then I went to Mrs. B-r-n and talked of dear Miss Smith. About 9 o'clock I went to Will's Coffeehouse where I

6. Perhaps Thomas Tryon, a West India merchant, director of the Royal Exchange Assurance.

7. A chocolate house in St. James's Street.

drank two dishes of chocolate and stayed till 11 o'clock, and then walked home and said my prayers.

10. I rose about 7 o'clock and read two chapters in Hebrew and three in Greek. I said my prayers, and had boiled milk for breakfast. The weather was warm and clear, the wind east. I danced my dance. I wrote some English till 2 o'clock and then ate some battered eggs. After dinner I put several things in order till 4 o'clock and then my cousin Horsmanden came and stayed about half an hour. I received a letter from Mrs. O-r-d. About 6 o'clock I went to Will's and read the news. About seven I went to Mrs. [Andrews'] and drank tea and ate cake and stayed till nine; and then went to Court where was abundance of people. Then I went to Petcum's where I played and won three guineas. I talked to several ladies and stayed till 12 o'clock and about 12 o'clock went home, where I said my prayers. I slept indifferently.

11. I rose about 8 o'clock and read a chapter in Hebrew and a chapter in Greek. I said my prayers, and had boiled milk for breakfast. The weather was warm and clear, the wind east. About nine came my surgeon and found my running pretty well. About eleven came my Lord Percival and I gave him a guinea for the new converts from popery. He stayed about half an hour. I wrote a letter to my dear Miss Smith till 2 o'clock and then I ate some mutton cutlets. After dinner I finished my letter and about 5 o'clock went to visit my Lady Dunkellen where we talked abundance about Miss Smith and both my Lady and my Lord pretended much to be my friends. Here I stayed till 7 o'clock and then went to Mr. Jeffreys' and drank caudle. Then I went to the Spanish Ambassador's where I won four pounds, and about twelve walked home and neglected my prayers.

12. I rose about 8 o'clock and read a chapter in Hebrew and two chapters in Greek. I said my prayers, and had boiled milk for breakfast. The weather was warm and clear, the wind west. I danced my dance, and read some English till 11 o'clock and then went to Mrs.

Southwell's and sat with her about an hour, and then Sir Roger Braid-shaigh and I went and walked an hour in the park and then went and dined with Lady Guise, where I ate some salt fish. While I was there my man brought me a letter from my dear Miss Smith that gave me abundance of concern because therein I was forbid to write any more. About 5 o'clock I went home and from thence to Will's Coffeehouse, where I stayed about an hour and then went to visit Mrs. S-t-r-t but she was out. Then I went to Mrs. C-r-y but she was out. Then I went to Mrs. U-m-s and they were out; then to Mrs. L-c-b-r where I stayed till 9 o'clock and then went to Court where was abundance of company. From hence I walked home about eleven and found a letter from my Lord Dunkellen to inform me that Miss Smith would be in the park tomorrow. I said my prayers and slept pretty well, thank God.

13. I rose about 8 o'clock and read a chapter in Hebrew and three in Greek. I said my prayers, and had boiled milk for breakfast. The weather was clear and warm, the wind west. My Lord Percival called upon me to bring the roll for subscriptions. Then came my Lord Bellenden and stayed about half an hour. About 11 o'clock I went to the Duke of Argyll's but he was from home. Then I went to my Lord Orrery's where I drank a dish of chocolate and then went to walk in the Mall and there saw my dear Miss Smith but did not speak to her because she looked a little askew. About three I returned home and ate some mutton cutlets and after dinner took a little nap, and about six went to Mrs. FitzHerbert's and sat the whole evening and ate some toast and cheese; and about eleven walked home but neglected my prayers. I dreamed this night that I kissed Miss Smith very much and that her father would die this morning; God's will be done. The wind came about and it was very cold.

14. I rose about 8 o'clock and read a chapter in Hebrew and three in Greek. I said my prayers, and had boiled milk for breakfast. The weather was cold and cloudy, the wind northeast. About 10 o'clock came Daniel Horsmanden and I paid his bill for my suit in chancery. I danced my dance. Then I wrote some English till 2 o'clock, and then

ate some battered eggs. After dinner I put some things in order and then wrote more English till 5 o'clock and then went to visit Mrs. A-l-c whom I found resolved to be [salivated for a surfeit?] Then I went to Mrs. B-r-n and sat with her till nine and then went to Will's Coffeehouse and drank two dishes of chocolate, and then went with my Lord Dunkellen to the Spanish Ambassador's, where I met my Lady, who told me that Miss Smith told her father she could not so soon forget me, when he proposed another match to her. My Lady told abundance of good things on the same subject. I lost five guineas and went home about one and neglected my prayers.

15. I rose about 8 o'clock and read nothing in Hebrew nor in Greek. However, I said my prayers, and had boiled milk for breakfast. The weather was cold and cloudy, the wind east. I wrote a letter to Miss Smith with intent to give it her in the evening at the music, but her brother sent me word she would not be there. About 2 o'clock I ate mutton cutlets. After dinner I put several things in order and took a nap till five, and then went to Will's and from thence about six I went with my Lord Bellenden to the music, where I saw my Lady Dunkellen, who told me several things about Miss Smith that displeased me. Then I went home with my Lord Dunkellen where my Lady told me that Miss Smith thought me [more shy] and that it was impossible our affair could succeed. I stayed to supper and ate some lamb stones and about 1 o'clock went home very melancholy and neglected to say my prayers.

16. I rose about 8 o'clock and read a chapter in Hebrew and four chapters in Greek. I said my prayers, and had boiled milk for breakfast. The weather was clear and warm, the wind west. I danced my dance. About twelve I went to St. James's Chapel and after church went home with Mr. Blathwayt and ate some calf's head for dinner. Our company were Sir Thomas Samwell,[8] Colonel Nevill,[9] Mr.

8. Sir Thomas Samwell, 2nd Bart., M.P. for Coventry, 1715–22.

9. Clement Nevill, lieutenant colonel of Munden's Dragoons, 1715–43.

West,[10] Mr. N-t-n. We drank nothing but Burgundy. About five I
ran away and went to Mrs. U-m-s but stayed there very little but
went to Lady Powlett's and sat there two hours and then went to
Will's Coffeehouse and ate a jelly. Here I stayed till 10 o'clock and
then walked home and washed my feet. I said my prayers and slept
pretty well, thank God.

17. I rose about 7 o'clock and read a chapter in Hebrew and three
chapters in Greek. I said my prayers, and had boiled milk for breakfast. The weather was clear and cold, the wind west. My mind was
much disturbed about my mistress. About 11 o'clock I went to the
Duke of Argyll and begged five guineas of him for charity. He was
so good as to invite me to dinner. Then I went to my Lord Orrery
who gave me some chocolate but would give me no charity About
one I went home and wrote some English till three and then returned
to the Duke of Argyll's to dinner, where dined an agreeable woman
called Mrs. L-n-t-n. I ate some boiled chicken. After dinner we drank
a bottle of Burgundy. Then I carried the Duke to Will's Coffeehouse,
where I found my Lord Dunkellen, who invited me to his house to
play at hazard, where I went, and lost twenty pounds. About twelve
we went to supper and I ate some green goose. We played till 3
o'clock and then was forced to walk home. I neglected my prayers,
&c.

18. I rose about 8 o'clock and read a chapter in Hebrew and some
Greek. I said my prayers, and had boiled milk for breakfast. The
weather was cloudy and cold, the wind northwest . . . and went home
about one and read some English till two and then ate some boiled
eggs. After dinner I put some things in order and took a nap till five
and then went to Will's Coffeehouse. About six I went to the new
playhouse where there was but indifferent company and I slept.
After the play I returned to Will's and drank two dishes of chocolate
and read the news. About eleven I walked home and said my prayers,
&c. I slept pretty well, thank God, though my neighbor disturbed me.

10. Probably Richard West, counsel for the Board of Trade.

19. I rose about 7 o'clock and read a chapter in Hebrew and three chapters in Greek. I said my prayers, and had boiled milk for breakfast. The weather was cold and cloudy, the wind west. I danced my dance and wrote a letter to Mr. Southwell. About 11 o'clock I went to see my daughter, where I stayed till twelve, and then went into the City to Mr. Perry's where I dined with his lady, but Jane was from home. After dinner we drank and about four I went home and met my dear Miss Smith in her coach and she gave me a gracious bow. Then I went to Will's Coffeehouse and read the news and then went to visit Mrs. C-r-l, but they were from home. Then I went to Mrs. B-r-n and talked two hours about my mistress. Then I went to Court, where I saw Mrs. W-n-m and took no notice of her because she gave herself airs. About twelve I came home in the chair and said my prayers. I dreamed that I saw Miss Smith almost naked and drew her to me.

20. I rose about 8 o'clock and read a chapter in Hebrew and four chapters in Greek. I said my prayers, and had boiled milk for breakfast. The weather was cloudy and cold, the wind west. I danced my dance. I wrote some English and was very uneasy about my mistress. About 1 o'clock I went down and dined with my landlord, Mr. M-n-l-y, and ate some roast veal for dinner. My Lord Dunkellen sent me a letter to let me know that my mistress could not be at the play this evening. However, I resolved to go, but went first to the coffeehouse. At the play I saw the lady come that Miss Smith should have come with. After the play I went to Will's again and from thence a company of us went to the W-l-s Ambassador's where were abundance of sad company. I drank a dish of chocolate and then walked home and said my prayers, &c.

21. I rose about 7 o'clock and read a chapter in Hebrew and four chapters in Greek. I said my prayers, and had boiled milk for breakfast. The weather was clear and warm, the wind west. I danced my dance and wrote some English. A man came to pay me some money from Mr. L-d. About 11 o'clock came Colonel Blathwayt and stayed about half an hour. About twelve I went to my Lord Percival's but

he was from home. Then I went to the Cockpit and spoke with Tom Beake; then to Ozinda's Chocolate House where I drank some chocolate, and about 2 o'clock went to Mr. Southwell's to dinner and ate some salt fish. Mrs. Bellenden [11] and my Lord Finch [12] dined there. After dinner we drank tea and about 7 o'clock I went again to my Lord Percival's and sat with him about an hour. Then I went to Court and from thence to the Spanish Ambassador's where I talked abundance to my Lady Dunkellen about Miss Smith but I could not well understand her. I stayed till 1 o'clock and then went home in the chair and said my prayers.

22. I rose about 7 o'clock and read a chapter in Hebrew and a chapter in Greek. I said my prayers, and had boiled milk for breakfast. The weather was clear and cold, the wind west. I wrote some English till 11 o'clock and then went to visit Mr. G-n-y but he was from home. Then I went to Brigadier Russell's [13] and he showed me his ship and several rarities. Then I returned home and wrote more English till two and then ate some battered eggs. After dinner I put some things in order and wrote more English till 5 o'clock and then went to Will's Coffeehouse, where I read the news and then went with my Lord Orrery to the opera, where I had the pleasure to ogle my dear Miss Smith but was forbid to speak to her or lead her out, which I submitted to with great difficulty. I went and ate a jelly at the chocolate house and then went home and said my prayers.

23. I rose about 7 o'clock and read a chapter in Hebrew and some two chapters in Greek. I said my prayers, and had boiled milk for breakfast. The weather was cloudy and cold, the wind west. I danced my dance, and about 11 o'clock went to Somerset Chapel where I heard a good sermon. After church I just called on Mrs. U-m-s and

11. Perhaps Mary Bellenden, sister of Lord Bellenden, a maid of honor.

12. Daniel Finch, later 8th Earl of Winchelsea, Earl of Nottingham, styled Lord Finch until 1730. M.P. for Rutland, 1710–29; a fellow of the Royal Society.

13. Richard Russell, brigadier general of the First Foot Guards, 1710–22; perhaps related to Anne Russell, Lady Guise.

then went to dine with Mr. U-t-n and ate some roast beef. After dinner we sat and talked till 5 o'clock and then I went to Mrs. A-l-c and
drank tea with her and about seven went to Mrs. D-n-s but she was
from home; then I went to Mrs. FitzHerbert's, and ate some apple
pie, and about nine went to the Spanish Ambassador's where I met my
Lady Dunkellen who told me abundance about my mistress but nothing good. About twelve I went home and said my prayers.

24. I rose about 6 o'clock and read nothing, because I wrote a long
letter to Miss Smith. However, I said my prayers, and had boiled milk
for breakfast. The weather was cloudy and cold. About eleven I received a letter from my Lord Dunkellen to tell me my Lady would
speak with me, so I sent for a coach and went to wait on her and she
told me abundance about my mistress and encouraged me to write
and seemed very friendly. About 2 o'clock I returned home and had a
beefsteak for dinner. After dinner I put several things in order and
then finished my letter to Miss Smith. About 6 o'clock I went to Will's
Coffeehouse and read the news and then went to visit Mrs. Ch-f-n
and Mrs. S-t-r-t where I drank tea and played at cards and about 9
o'clock went to supper and I ate some eggs. About ten we went to
Mr. Petcum's where was abundance of company. I stayed till 12
o'clock and then came home in the chair and said my prayers, &c.

25. I rose about 8 o'clock and read a chapter in Hebrew and four
chapters in Greek. I said my prayers, and had boiled milk for breakfast. The weather was cold and clear, the wind west. I danced my
dance and then drew a little; then I wrote some Hebrew words till 2
o'clock, and then ate some battered eggs for dinner. After dinner I
put several things in order and then wrote more Hebrew. About
four Miss Smith went out, very melancholy, and did not look up at
all. About five I went to Will's and read the news and about six went
with my Lord Orrery to the opera[14] because he gave me a ticket. We
saw two handsome women in the gallery and went to them upon their

14. This was the first performance of *The Lady's Triumph* at Lincoln's Inn
Fields.

invitation, but went away without coming to any business. About nine I went to Mr. C-r-y, where was abundance of company because of Jenny Jeffreys' birthday. Here I supped and ate some chicken and asparagus and about twelve went home.

26. I rose about 7 o'clock and read a chapter in Hebrew and three in Greek. I said my prayers and had milk for breakfast. The weather was cold and clear, the wind west. I danced my dance and then wrote several things. About eleven came Mr. [Leblanc] and gave me satisfaction about my Lady Mohun's debt. Then I went to my Lord Percival's, but he was from home; then to Colonel Paget's, but he was from home. Then to Colonel Blathwayt's, but he was from home; then to Mr. D-m, but he was from home; then to my Lord Orrery's, but he was likewise from home; then to Ozinda's Chocolate House where I won four pounds. About two I went to dine with Colonel Blakiston and ate some boiled beef. After dinner we sat and talked till five and then I went to Will's and sent away the coach because it rained. Here I stayed till seven and then went with Jack into the City and I called at Mrs. Lindsay's but she was out; then I went to Garraway's and from thence back to Will's where I drank two dishes of chocolate and then went with my Lord L-s-f-l to the tavern where we had rack punch and ate some eggs. About twelve I walked home and said my prayers, &c.

27. I rose about 8 o'clock and read a chapter in Hebrew and a chapter in Greek. I said my prayers, and ate boiled milk for breakfast. The weather was clear and cold, the wind northwest. About 10 o'clock came my cousin Horsmanden and stayed half an hour. About eleven I went to visit my daughter and stayed about half an hour, and then went to Mr. Dick Perry's to dinner and ate some boiled mutton. After dinner we sat and talked till four and then drank tea and then returned home, and about six went to Will's Coffeehouse and read the news, and then went to the play where I slept. After the play I went to Will's again and lost five pounds at piquet. I drank two dishes of chocolate and about 12 o'clock walked home and said my prayers.

28. I rose about 7 o'clock, and read a chapter in Hebrew and three chapters in Greek. I said my prayers, and had boiled milk for breakfast. The weather was cold and cloudy, the wind northwest. I danced my dance. I wrote a letter to my dear Miss Smith. About 2 o'clock I ate some battered eggs for dinner. After dinner I put several things in order and took a nap. About 4 o'clock came my cousin Horsmanden and stayed till five, and then we went to the park, and after that I went to Mrs. FitzHerbert's and ate some toast and ale. About nine I went to Court and from thence to the Spanish Ambassador's, where I found my Lady Dunkellen who told me Miss Smith was out of humor with me and said I had written a bullying letter to her, with abundance of other things that put me out of humor. However, I stayed till twelve and then went home in a chair.

29. I rose about 8 o'clock and read a chapter in Hebrew and two chapters in Greek. I said my prayers, and had boiled milk for breakfast. The weather was cloudy and cold, the wind southeast. I wrote some English till 11 o'clock and then I went to the Cockpit and put my letters into the post. Then I went to Mrs. Southwell's, where I drank a dish of chocolate, and about twelve went home and learned that one Mr. Orlebar,[15] a master in chancery, had been to speak with me from Miss Smith. My Lord Orrery came and stayed above an hour and invited me to dine with him tomorrow. About 2 o'clock I went to Mr. Southwell's to dinner and ate some roast veal. After dinner Mr. Southwell and I talked about business till five and then I went to Mrs. A-l-c and gave her ten guineas to [flux]. About seven I went to Mrs. D-n-s, where I drank tea and stayed till 10 o'clock and then went to Will's Coffeehouse, where I saw my Lord Dunkellen and lost a guinea on his head. About eleven I walked home and said my prayers.

30. I rose about . . . southeast. Miss Smith went out and would not look at me as she used to do. I danced my dance and did not go to

15. John Orlebar, a master in chancery, was related to the Smyth family of Ashton and perhaps to Mary Smith. See Frederica St. John Orlebar, *The Orlebar Chronicles . . . 1553–1733* (London, 1930).

church till 1 o'clock and then I went to St. James's Chapel, and about 2 o'clock went to my Lord Orrery's to dinner and ate some ragout of veal. There I met Mr. W-t-r-s, who is a very pleasant man. After dinner we drank a bottle and about 7 o'clock went to Will's Coffee-house and from thence my Lord Orrery and I went to visit two gentlewomen we had met at the play and my Lord rogered one of them but I did nothing. About nine my Lord set me down at the Ambassador's where I stayed till 12 o'clock and then went home in the chair, and said my prayers. I slept pretty well, thank God.

31. I rose about 7 o'clock and read a chapter in Hebrew and some Greek. I said my prayers, and had boiled milk for breakfast. The weather was warm and cloudy, the wind southwest. About 10 o'clock came Colonel Blakiston and stayed about half an hour. Then came Mr. Orlebar with a message from Miss Smith that I should not trouble her any more with my letters or addresses, and returned my letter that I wrote last to her. I was very much concerned but said little to him, but when he was gone I cried exceedingly. However, about 11 o'clock I went to my Lord Dunkellen's, who was out, but my Lady invited me in and I told her the message I had received, but she advised to continue writing. I stayed with her two hours and then returned home and ate some battered eggs. After dinner I put several things in order and wrote some English till 6 o'clock and then went to Will's and stayed till seven and then went to Mrs. [Andrews'] and drank tea. From thence I went to Court, and from thence to Petcum's where I stayed till twelve, and then went home and said my prayers.

April 1718

1. I rose about 7 o'clock and read a chapter in Hebrew and three chapters in Greek. I said my prayers and had boiled milk for breakfast. The weather was cold and cloudy, the wind west. I wrote a

letter to Mr. Orlebar containing the whole story of my love of Miss Smith and sent it by my servant. I danced my dance and read some English till 2 o'clock, when I ate some mutton cutlets. After dinner I put several things in order till 4 o'clock and then took a nap; then read some English till five, and then went to Will's Coffeehouse and stayed there till seven and then went to Mrs. B-r-n and told her how my affair stood with Miss Smith, whom she blamed extremely. Then I went to my Lady Guise's and sat with her till almost 10 o'clock and then went to the Spanish Ambassador's where I lost four guineas and about twelve went home and said my prayers.

2. I rose about 7 o'clock and read a chapter in Hebrew and three chapters in Greek. I said my prayers, and had boiled milk for breakfast. The weather was warm and cloudy, the wind southwest. I danced my dance. About 11 o'clock I went to visit my Lord Percival but found him not. Then I went to Mr. G-n-y but found him not. Then I went to my Lord Orrery and sat with him about an hour and drank a dish of chocolate. Then I went to my Lord Foley but found him not. Then I returned home and wrote some English till two and then ate some battered eggs. After dinner I put several things in order and took a nap. About six I went to Will's Coffeehouse and in the way met Miss Smith but she would not look at me. Here I stayed the whole evening, and lost a guinea on Colonel Cecil's[1] head at piquet. I drank two dishes of chocolate and about eleven went home and said my prayers.

3. I rose about 7 o'clock and read a chapter in Hebrew and three chapters in Greek. I said my prayers, and had boiled milk for breakfast. The weather was clear and warm, the wind west. I wrote a letter to Mrs. O-r-d. About 11 o'clock I went to visit my daughter and stayed with her about an hour, and then went to Garraway's Coffeehouse where I talked with several of my acquaintances till two, and then went to Pontack's to dinner where I ate some fish. After dinner

1. Colonel William Cecil, equerry to George I. He was sent to the Tower in 1744 as a Jacobite conspirator.

I returned again to Garraway's and talked with the milliner till four, and then went to Mr. Lindsay's where I drank tea and stayed till six. Then I returned home and adjusted myself and then went to Mrs. FitzHerbert's and told her all my grief and ate some apple pie with her and saw a woman just like Miss Smith. About nine I returned to Will's Coffeehouse and went with some gentlemen to the W-l-s Ambassador's and stayed till eleven and then went home and dreamed that Miss Smith was favorable again, thank God.

4. I rose about 7 o'clock and read a chapter in Hebrew and three chapters in Greek. I said my prayers, and had boiled milk for breakfast. The weather was clear and warm, the wind west. I danced my dance and wrote some English. About ten I went again to Old Abram and he gave me hope that my mistress would be kind again, notwithstanding all her displeasure. Then I returned home and wrote more English till 2 o'clock and then ate some battered eggs. After dinner I put several things in order and then drew a little and read some English till five and then went to Will's and from thence to the park and carried Mr. P-l. Then I returned to Will's and went with my Lord Orrery to visit two gentlewomen at Wotton but I did nothing. Then I went to Court and from thence to the Spanish Ambassador's where was my dear Miss Smith but I could do no more than look at her because she was with Lady Dunkellen. When she went I went home about 12 o'clock and said my prayers.

5. I rose about 7 o'clock and read a chapter in Hebrew and three chapters in Greek. I said my prayers, and had boiled milk for breakfast. The weather was clear and warm, the wind west. I wrote a letter to Mrs. H-n-t-n to excuse my not going to her tomorrow because I resolve to keep myself for my dear Miss Smith. Abut 11 o'clock I went to my Lord Dunkellen's but he was from home. However, I saw my Lady and we talked about my dear Miss Smith. She gave me some comfort and some despair. However, she persuaded me to write to her and go to church and so did my Lord, who came home after-

wards. About one I went to Devereux Court[2] with intent to find the company with Sir John Sherard[3] but he did not dine there. However, I dined by myself and ate two roast pigeons. Then I went to the coffeehouse and read the news. About five I went home and adjusted myself and then went to the music for the benefit of Mr. Robinson,[4] where I sat by Mrs. R-d-r. When this was done, I went to Will's Coffeehouse where my Lord Dunkellen came to tell me that Miss Smith had refused Mr. P-t a gentleman of 3000 pounds a year and excused herself to her father on account of her inclination to me. I ate some cake and milk and about twelve went home in a chair and said my prayers.

6. I rose about seven and read a chapter in Hebrew and three chapters in Greek. I said my prayers, and had boiled milk for breakfast. The weather was clear and cold, the wind west. About 10 o'clock, because Miss Smith did not go to church, I went to take leave of my Lord Orrery before he went out of town and he gave me a bottle of [c-l-b], where I drank a dish of chocolate and about eleven went to Somerset Chapel where I saw Mr. U-t-n. After church I returned home and ate two roast pigeons for dinner. After dinner . . . About five I went to Will's Coffeehouse and carried my Lord Bellenden to the park. Then I went to my Lord Percival's but he was from home. Then I went to Mrs. FitzHerbert's and had some bread and cheese and then went to the Spanish Ambassador's where I was very dull and went home before 12 o'clock and said my prayers, &c.

7. I rose about 7 o'clock and read a chapter in Hebrew and three chapters in Greek. I said my prayers, and had boiled milk for breakfast. The weather was cold and clear, the wind southeast. I wrote a letter to excuse myself from going to Mrs. H-n-t-n. Then came Mr. G-n-y and stayed about quarter of an hour. Then I wrote a letter to

2. The Grecian Coffeehouse and Tom's Coffeehouse were in Devereux Court.

3. Sir John Sherard, Bart., son of Richard Sherard of Lobthorpe.

4. Thomas Robinson, blind father of the singer Anastasia Robinson. The concert was held at the Haymarket Theatre.

Mr. Perry to borrow ten thousand pounds to settle upon my mistress. Then I wrote a letter to Miss Smith till 2 o'clock, when I ate some battered eggs for dinner. In the afternoon I put several things in order and then finished my letter to Miss Smith and about 5 o'clock went to Will's Coffeehouse and from thence went to Lady Powlett's where I drank tea and stayed about an hour and then took leave. Then I went to Mrs. U-m-s, who were from home. Then I went to Mrs. Ch-g-n but she was from home. Then to Mrs. C-r-y where I stayed about an hour, and then went to Court and from thence to Petcum's where I stayed till past eleven and then went home in a chair and said my prayers.

8. I rose about 7 o'clock and read a chapter in Hebrew and three chapters in Greek. I said my prayers, and had boiled milk for breakfast. The weather was warm and cloudy, the wind west. I drew a little till 11 o'clock and then went into the City to the Virginia Coffeehouse where I learned that my vessel came out with the *Harrison* that was arrived from hence. I went to Mr. Perry's and received my answer that they could not let me have the money, which I could not take unkindly. I dined with Dick Perry, where I found my daughter, and ate some salt fish. After dinner I sat and talked till four and then went to Sir Charles Wager's but he was out of town. Then I went to Mr. [Tryon's] and drank tea and about six went to Mr. Lindsay's where we played at cards till ten and then went to supper and I ate some roast lamb. Here I stayed till 12 o'clock and then I went home in a coach and said my prayers.

9. I rose about 7 o'clock and read a chapter in Hebrew and three chapters in Greek. I said my prayers, and had boiled milk for breakfast. The weather was cold and cloudy, the wind northwest, and I had a little cold. I danced my dance and about 11 o'clock went to visit Mrs. Southwell and stayed with her about an hour, and then returned home and read some Greek in Homer till 2 o'clock, and then I ate some battered eggs for dinner. In the afternoon I put several things in order and then took a nap till five, when I had the pleasure

to see my mistress at the window for half an hour, where I made distant love. Then I went to Mrs. B-r-t and drank tea and stayed till 8 o'clock and then went to Will's Coffeehouse and stayed all the evening because when I sent to Mrs. U-m-s they were not at home. About ten I went home and said my prayers.

10. I rose about 8 o'clock and read a chapter in Hebrew and some Greek in Homer. I said my prayers, and had boiled milk for breakfast. The weather was cold and cloudy and it rained, the wind west. My surgeon came to me and agreed to my going into the cold baths. My cold continued but not violent. I danced my dance. About 1 o'clock I went into the City and dined at Pontack's and ate some teal. After dinner we went to Garraway's Coffeehouse and about 4 o'clock went and talked with the seamstress. Then I went home and found several letters from Virginia. About five I went to Will's Coffeehouse and from thence took my Lord Bellenden to the park. In the evening I went to Mrs. B-r-n, but she was from home. Then I went to Lady Guise's and stayed till ten and then went to Will's Coffeehouse, and from thence home and took some milk and rosemary for my cold. I said my prayers. I woke in the night and could scarcely fetch my breath, which lasted about an hour.

11. I rose about 8 o'clock and read a chapter in Hebrew and some Greek in Homer. I said my prayers, and had boiled milk for breakfast. The weather was clear and warm, the wind west. I danced my dance and wrote some English and then drew a little. Miss Smith went out and would not look at me. About 2 o'clock I ate some battered eggs. After dinner I put several things in order till 3 o'clock and then read some French till five, when I went to Will's Coffeehouse and from thence with Mr. P-ch-y to the park and then returned to Will's again, and then went to Mrs. Ch-g-n but she was from home. Then to Mrs. U-m-s and found them and stayed till 10 o'clock and then walked home and said my prayers. I was troubled again with a difficulty of breathing that was very troublesome.

12. I rose about 8 o'clock and found my breathing difficult. However, I read a chapter in Hebrew and some Greek. I said my prayers, and had boiled milk for breakfast. The weather was clear and cold. Mr. Albin came and brought me some prints. My cold continued, which made me resolve to go to Kensington about 12 o'clock to dine with Mr. [Boyle] where I walked in his garden till one and then ate some boiled pork for dinner. In the afternoon we walked again and about five took leave and I went to St. James's Coffeehouse where I took up Mr. P-l-t and went to the park and having set him down I called at the Smyrna⁵ and walked from thence to the Cocoa Tree, and went with Mr. . . . . from thence to Will's Coffeehouse, where I stayed the whole evening and ate some cake and milk, and about ten walked home and found letters from Virginia which displeased me. I neglected my prayers, for which God forgive me, but I slept better than I had done two nights before.

13. I rose about 7 o'clock and read a chapter in Hebrew and some Greek in Homer. I said my prayers, and had boiled milk for breakfast. The weather was warm and cloudy, the wind west. About 10 o'clock I went to church at St. Clement's where I saw Miss Smith and put her in all the confusion in the world, her face glowing and her eyes looking conscious both of love and shame; however, she would not look at me or salute me the whole time, but hid herself behind those that sat with her in the pew. After church I went and walked in Somerset Garden and met Mrs. U-m-s, who invited me to dinner and I ate some roast beef. After dinner we drank tea and about five I went home and read some French till six, when my cousin Horsmanden came and I carried him to Kensington Garden where we walked till eight and then I set him down and went to Mrs. Ch-g-n where I ate some crayfish for supper. About eleven I took leave and went home in a chair and said my prayers.

14. I rose about 7 o'clock and read a chapter in Hebrew but no Greek, because I was to go out soon. However, I ate my milk for

5. The Smyrna Coffeehouse was in Pall Mall.

breakfast, and said a short prayer. The weather was clear and warm. About 10 o'clock Mr. G-n-y came and told me his friend had undertaken my business about the government of Virginia and did not doubt but it would succeed. About eleven I went to the City with design to dine with Mr. Perry but learned they were from home; but afterwards I met with Mr. Lindsay who took me home with him, where I dined and ate some roast mutton and fish for dinner. After dinner we played at piquet till five and then I went home and then found Mr. [Tryon] at the play and we went to my Lord Mayor's, where I danced with Miss Perry till 11 o'clock and then Mr. [Tryon] carried me and another gentleman to the coffeehouse, where we ate some toast and butter and drank two bottles of rack punch and were merry till about 2 o'clock, and then I went home and said my prayers.

15. I rose about 8 o'clock and read a chapter in Hebrew and some Greek in Homer. I said my prayers, and wanted milk for breakfast. The weather was clear and warm, the wind west. About eleven I went to visit my cousins Horsmanden [6]—just come to town—and sat with them till one and then went into the City to dine with Mr. [Tryon] and ate some chicken and asparagus. After dinner Mr. Lindsay came and then about four Mr. [Tryon] and I walked to Mr. Perry's to drink tea and about seven we took Mike and went to the sheriff's entertainment, but I did not dance only one minuet, and about ten I returned by myself to Mr. [Tryon's] and ate some asparagus and eggs [or goose] and found Mr. Lindsay and his spouse there. I stayed till 1 o'clock and then went home and said my prayers.

16. I rose about 8 o'clock and read nothing because I wrote a letter to Miss Smith. However, I ate some boiled milk for breakfast, but neglected my prayers. The weather was cloudy and so was my understanding, for I could not write a letter in five hours. About 2 o'clock I went again to Mr. [Tryon's,] where we drank chocolate and about 3 o'clock went to Drapers' Hall [7] to dine with Sir Har-

6. Daniel Horsmanden's sisters, Susanna and Ursula ('Suky' and 'Nutty'), daughters of the rector of Purleigh.

7. Drapers' Hall, in Throgmorton Street, where members of the Draper's Company held meetings and parties.

court Masters [8] and ate some bacon for dinner. After dinner we drank tea and about 8 o'clock we danced and my partner was Kitty Sambrooke and I talked abundance to her and we danced till 11 o'clock, and then my partner and Mrs. Lindsay went home. I stayed till twelve and then took leave of Sir Harcourt Masters and went home and said my prayers.

17. I rose about 8 o'clock and read a chapter in Hebrew and some Greek in Homer. I said my prayers, and had boiled milk for breakfast. The weather was cloudy and warm, the wind west. I finished my letter to my dear Miss Smith and about 12 o'clock came my cousin Daniel Horsmanden and stayed with me about half an hour. At two I ate some mutton cutlets for dinner. In the afternoon I put several things in order and took a nap till five and then prepared my things for the masquerade and dressed me in the [sight] of my mistress. About eight I first showed my habit to my landlady, then I went to Mrs. B-r-t, then to Lady Guise's and about 10 o'clock I went to Haymarket, where was abundance of company and I was exceedingly well entertained and particularly I put one woman's hand upon my business and spent. I met with pretty Mrs. H-n-t-n who was a great romp. Here I stayed till 5 o'clock in the morning and then went home in the chair and neglected to say my prayers.

18. I rose about 10 o'clock and read a chapter in Hebrew and some Greek in Homer. I said my prayers, and had boiled milk for breakfast. The weather was warm and cloudy, the wind west. About 10 o'clock I received my letter back again that I wrote to Miss Smith, but I am sure she had read it. I wrote some English till 2 o'clock and then ate some battered eggs. After dinner I put several things in order and then took a nap. Then I read some French till five, when I went to visit Mrs. U-m-s where I drank tea, and then called at the play and afterwards went to Will's Coffeehouse, where I found my Lord Dunkellen, who told me Miss Smith had shown my letter to her father. He told me many other things. Then I ate a jelly and went to

8. Sir Harcourt Masters was a director of the South Sea Company.

visit Mrs. H-n-t-n and would have laid with her but she thought
herself too dirty. About ten I went to the Spanish Ambassador's
where I saw my cousins Horsmanden and several other ladies of my
acquaintance. About twelve I went home and said my prayers.

19. I rose about 8 o'clock and read a chapter in Hebrew and some
Greek in Homer. I said my prayers, and had boiled milk for breakfast. The weather was clear and cold, the wind west. About 11 o'clock
I went to visit Mr. G-n-y but found him not. However, I left a letter
for him. Then I went to my Lord Stanhope's [9] who was very courteous to me. This morning I sent a letter to Mrs. H-n-t-n to excuse
my not coming to her this evening, for fear I should lay with her.
About 1 o'clock came Colonel Blathwayt and sat with me about
half an hour and then I wrote some English till two and then ate
some roast pigeon. After dinner I put several things in order till four
and then took a nap. About five came Mr. Lindsay and stayed half
an hour with me. About six I went to Will's Coffeehouse and read
the news and then came my Lord Dunkellen, with whom I talked
abundance about Miss Smith. We went to the park that we might
talk enough of her. In the evening I set him down at Ozinda's and
went to Mrs. FitzHerbert's and ate some toast and cheese, and then
went to Will's and stayed there till eleven and then walked home and
washed my feet but neglected my prayers, for which God forgive
me.

20. I rose about 7 o'clock and read a chapter in Hebrew and some
Greek. I said my prayers, and had boiled milk for breakfast. The
weather was clear and cold, the wind west. About 10 o'clock I went
to St. Clement's Church where I saw my mistress but she would not
look at me. After church I went into the City and dined with Mr.
Lindsay and ate some roast beef. In the afternoon we went to church
and heard a charity sermon from Dr. Sherlock [10] and I gave five

9. James Stanhope, created Earl Stanhope on April 14, 1718, was secretary of
state for the northern department.

10. Thomas Sherlock, dean of Chichester in 1718; master of the Temple and
master of St. Catharine's Hall, Cambridge.

shillings. Then we returned to Mr. Lindsay's and drank tea and then I sent for my daughter and carried her with us to the park, where there was a great crowd. Then we went to the lodge and ate cheese cake and then returned again to Mr. Lindsay's, where I ate some rabbit for supper and stayed till 11 o'clock, and then went home and neglected my prayers.

21. I rose about 7 o'clock and read a chapter in Hebrew and some Greek in Homer. I said my prayers, and had boiled milk for breakfast. The weather was cloudy and warm, the wind west. I wrote a submissive letter to dear Miss Smith. A man brought me news of the arrival of my brigantine, thank God. I danced my dance. About 2 o'clock I ate some battered eggs. After dinner I took a nap and read some French till 5 o'clock and then I went to take leave of Mr. Southwell that was going into the country. Then I went to Mrs. B-r-t and drank tea; then I went to Will's Coffeehouse for half an hour, and then went to visit Mrs. B-r-n and stayed with her till 9 o'clock, and then went to Ozinda's Chocolate House where I won two guineas in betting. I stayed till 11 o'clock and went home in the chair and said my prayers.

22. I rose about 8 o'clock and read nothing because I wrote two letters, one to Miss Smith and one to her father. I said my prayers, and had boiled milk for breakfast. The weather was clear and warm. Captain Turner, commander of my brig, came and brought me some letters from Virginia. About eleven I went to visit my cousins Horsmanden but they were from home, and then went to Mr. D-n-s but he was indisposed. Then I went to the Virginia Coffeehouse, and from thence to Garraway's and from thence home, where I ate some veal cutlets for dinner. In the afternoon I put several things in order and then took a nap, and then wrote some English till five. Then I went to Will's Coffeehouse, and from thence to the play in Lincoln's Inn Field. After the play I returned to Will's and from thence to the Spanish Ambassador's, where I stayed till twelve and then walked home and said my prayers.

23. I rose about 8 o'clock and read a chapter in Hebrew and some Greek in Homer. I said my prayers, and had boiled milk for breakfast. The weather was clear and warm, the wind west. About 10 o'clock came my Aunt Sherard and stayed about half an hour. About eleven I went to my Lord Percival's and he was out; then to Mr. G-n-y and stayed with him quarter of an hour; then to Colonel Blakiston's but he was out. Then to my Lord Orrery's where I drank some chocolate and stayed about an hour. Then I went to my Lord Islay's about some of his [gimcracks] and came home about 1 o'clock and wrote a letter till two and then went to my Lord Orrery's to dinner and my Lord Windsor and my Lord Islay dined there and I ate some pigeon pie. After dinner we drank Burgundy till six, and then went to Will's Coffeehouse, and from thence I went to the play, and from thence to Mrs. U-m-s where I ate a jelly and stayed till twelve, and then walked home and neglected my prayers, for which God forgive me.

24. I rose about 8 o'clock and read a chapter in Hebrew and some Greek in Homer. I said my prayers, and had boiled milk for breakfast. The weather was warm and cloudy, the wind east. I wrote a full copy of the letter [or letters] to my mistress. About 11 o'clock came Colonel Blakiston and stayed about half an hour and invited me to dinner, and accordingly I went about 2 o'clock and ate some roast beef. After dinner we sat and talked till 4 o'clock, and then I took a walk to Mrs. B-r-n where I was to meet a woman that pretended to tell fortunes but knew nothing of the matter. However, I gave her a crown because she said I should have my mistress in a short time. Here I stayed till 7 o'clock, and then went to Mrs. FitzHerbert's and sat with her till 9 o'clock, and then walked to Will's Coffeehouse where I played at piquet till 1 o'clock, and lost three guineas, and then walked home and said my prayers.

25. I rose about 8 o'clock and read a chapter in Hebrew and some Greek. I said my prayers, and had boiled milk for breakfast. The weather was clear and warm, the wind southwest. I wrote my letter fair to my mistress and saw her go out with her father. About 11

o'clock I went to visit my cousins Horsmanden, but they were from home. Then went to visit my daughter but she was not come to school. Then I went to the Virginia Coffeehouse and from thence to Dick Perry's where I dined and ate some fish for dinner. After dinner we drank tea and about five I went home and adjusted myself and then went to the play, and from thence to the park, and from thence to the Mall, and from thence to Ozinda's where we heard a [d-k] speak. From thence to the Spanish Ambassador's where I stayed till twelve and then came home in the chair and said my prayers and dreamed good dreams.

26. I rose about 7 o'clock and read a chapter in Hebrew and some Greek in Homer. I said my prayers, and had boiled milk for breakfast. The weather was clear and warm, the wind west. I received my letter back from Miss Smith, with a very cross one from herself that gave me much concern. About 11 o'clock I went to Mr. Horsmanden's chambers where I found his sisters and drank tea with them and afterwards went and walked in [Gray's Inn?] walk till 3 o'clock and then went to dine with my cousin Horsmanden. In the afternoon I went to Mrs. B-r-n and from thence to the park with my cousin Horsmanden and then walked in St. James's Park and walked towards Will's and picked up a girl in the street and committed uncleanness with her. Then I went to Will's where I saw my Lord Dunkellen, who told me there was a proposal of Sir Edward Des Bouverie [11] again. About eleven I walked home and neglected my prayers, for which God forgive me.

27. I rose about 7 o'clock and read a chapter in Hebrew and some Greek. I said my prayers, and had boiled milk for breakfast. The weather was clear and hot, the wind west. About 9 o'clock I got ready to go to St. Clement's Church where I saw Mrs. Smith in all the confusion in the world. After church I walked in Somerset Garden and then went home and ate some veal cutlets. After dinner I put several

11. Sir Edward Des Bouverie, 2nd Bart., of Longford Castle, Wiltshire; M.P. for Shaftesbury, 1718–34. The marriage to Mary Smith took place at Somerset House Chapel, July 7.

things in order and then took a nap. Then I began a letter to Miss Smith and about five went to Will's Coffeehouse and from thence to visit my Aunt Sherard, where I drank tea and stayed till 8 o'clock, and then went to my Lord Percival's but he was from home; then to Mrs. FitzHerbert's, where I ate some bread and cheese; and then went to the Spanish Ambassador's, where I was very gay and went home about twelve but neglected my prayers.

28. I rose about 7 o'clock and read a chapter in Hebrew and some Greek in Lucian. I said my prayers, and had boiled milk for breakfast. The weather was hot and clear, the wind west. I made an end of my letter to Miss Smith and found myself very melancholy. About 2 o'clock I ate some battered eggs. After dinner I put things in order and then wrote some English till 5 o'clock, and then went to Will's Coffeehouse and read the news. About six I went to visit Mrs. Ch-g-n and drank tea with them and at seven returned to Will's and went from thence to my Lady Guise's, where I stayed about an hour, and then went to Petcum's where I talked with the ladies till twelve and then went home in the chair and said my prayers. I slept indifferently.

29. I rose about 8 o'clock and read a chapter in Hebrew and some Greek in Lucian. I said my prayers, and had boiled milk for breakfast. The weather was cold and cloudy, the wind west. I danced my dance and put several things in order and then read some letters from Virginia. About 12 o'clock came my cousin Horsmanden and while he was here I received a message from Mr. Smith that he desired to speak with me and I promised to go about 5 o'clock. About 2 o'clock I went to Mr. U-t-n to dinner and found him in an ague. My Lord Bellenden and Mr. [Clark] dined there and I ate some boiled chicken. After dinner I drank a bottle of champagne to give me some spirit and then went to Mr. Smith, with whom I had abundance of discourse about the encouragement his daughter had given me, and at last he agreed, though he would not give his consent nor would his daughter marry me. About six I went to Will's Coffeehouse and from thence to the park with my Lord Bellenden and Mr. [Clark] and afterwards

went to Will's and from thence with my Lord Dunkellen to Mrs. O-r-t-g-l-y where we saw my Lady and discoursed about this matter till 12 o'clock and then went home in the chair and said my prayers.

30. I rose about 6 o'clock and read nothing because I wrote a long letter to Mr. Smith. I said my prayers, and had boiled milk for breakfast. The weather was cloudy and cold, the wind northwest. About 10 o'clock came Lord Percival and Mr. U-t-n and stayed an hour, and then I went to visit my cousins Horsmanden and drank tea with them. Then I went to Leveridge's Coffeehouse to meet my Lord Dunkellen and I showed him the letter I wrote to Mr. Smith, which he desired to show to his Lady and send me again. Then I went home and read some Greek till two, and then ate some battered eggs. After dinner I took a nap till four, and then read some English till five, and then went to Mr. Lindsay's in the City where I drank tea, and then we played at cards till ten, and then I ate some pigeon and asparagus. After supper we played again and I won in all about ten shillings and went home about 1 o'clock and said my prayers. I dreamed this night that Mr. Smith invited me to dinner and was very kind to me.

May 1718

1. I rose about 8 o'clock and read a chapter in Hebrew and some Greek in Lucian. I said my prayers, and had boiled milk for breakfast. The weather was cold and cloudy. My tailor brought me some rich waistcoats but I liked none of them. About 11 o'clock I went to visit my cousins Horsmanden again and drank tea with them. I sent for my daughter to see them, but about 1 o'clock I took my leave and went to Pontack's, where I dined and ate some boiled beef. After dinner I went to Garraway's Coffeehouse and read the news, and about 4 o'clock went home, and about six went to Will's Coffeehouse, where I saw my Lord Dunkellen, who told me he left my mistress

crying and had not eaten anything all day. I lost two guineas in bet-ting to my Lord Orrery. Then I went to Mrs. B-r-n, who told me she had consulted Old Abram about me and he promised I should suc-ceed. Then I went to Mrs. FitzHerbert's and sat with her till 10 o'clock and then walked home but took a woman into a coach and committed uncleanness. Then I went home and prayed to God to forgive me.

2. I rose about 8 o'clock and read a chapter in Hebrew and some Greek in Lucian. I said my prayers, and had boiled milk for break-fast. The weather was clear and cold, the wind west. About 11 o'clock I went to the Virginia Coffeehouse where I found my cousin Hors-manden, and then I walked to Mr. Perry's, where I dined with Dick and ate some fish. After dinner we played at cards and drank some rack punch, and then I set Mrs. C-r-d-k home and drank tea with her, and then I went to Will's Coffeehouse and ate some jellies. From thence I went to the Spanish Ambassador's where I talked with sev-eral ladies and about 12 o'clock walked home and said my prayers. I dreamed that I spoke to my mistress.

3. I rose about 8 o'clock and read a chapter in Hebrew and some Greek in Lucian. I said my prayers, and had boiled milk for break-fast. The weather was clear and cold, the wind west. About 11 o'clock came Brigadier L-n-s-t-n and I just saw him and then went to visit my Lord Islay but he was from home; then I went to my Lord Or-rery's and drank chocolate with him and about one returned home, where my cousin Horsmanden came to me and carried me to his sis-ters', where I dined and ate some broiled lamb. After dinner I re-ceived a letter from my Lord Dunkellen. About five Daniel and I went to his chambers where I wrote a letter to Mr. Smith. Then we went to Ozinda's Chocolate House where I met my Lord Dunkellen, who told me all the news. Then I went to the Cocoa Tree, where I saw my rival and despised him. Then we went to Will's, where I played at piquet and won two guineas. About one I walked home and slept indifferently but neglected my prayers.

4. I rose about 8 o'clock and read a chapter in Hebrew and some Greek in Lucian. I said my prayers, and had boiled milk for breakfast. The weather was cold and cloudy. Miss Smith went not to church. Therefore I did not go to St. Clement's but to Somerset Chapel, but before it began I walked in the garden and about eleven went to chapel where I slept, God forgive me. I dined with Mr. U-t-n and ate some roast beef. After dinner we sat and talked and about four I walked again a little in the garden, and then walked to Mrs. B-r-t, where I drank tea and stayed till 6 o'clock and then went to Will's Coffeehouse and carried Daniel Horsmanden to the park and afterwards we walked in St. James's Park and then to Ozinda's, where I drank a dish of chocolate and then walked to the Spanish Ambassador's, where I talked with several ladies till twelve and then walked home and said my prayers, &c.

5. I rose about 8 o'clock and read a chapter in Hebrew but no Greek. I said my prayers, and had boiled milk for breakfast. The weather was clear and warm, the wind southwest. About eight I went to Leveridge's to meet my Lord Dunkellen, who told me the whole business was settled about the settlement, and that now was the time for me to move if I intended. I told him I would observe my word, let happen what would. About nine I returned home and my Lord Percival came to me and stayed about half an hour. Then I wrote some English till two and then ate some battered eggs for dinner. After dinner I put several things in order and then took a nap till 5 and then came Daniel Horsmanden and stayed half an hour. Then I saw my rival come to visit Mr. Smith, which gave me little concern. About six I went to Will's and from thence to walk in the park and then to Ozinda's to meet my Lord Dunkellen again and drank two dishes of chocolate, and then walked to Petcum's where I stayed till twelve and then walked home and said my prayers.

6. I rose about 7 o'clock and read nothing because I wrote to my Lord Dunkellen. I said my prayers, and had boiled milk for breakfast. The weather was cold and cloudy, the wind northeast. I sent a letter to my Lord Dunkellen about eleven and it worked just as we

designed. Then I went to my cousins Horsmanden and drank tea with them and sat with them till almost one, and then went home and wrote a letter to Miss Smith. About two I ate a pigeon pie for dinner. In the afternoon I put several things in order, and then took a nap till four, when Daniel Horsmanden came and stayed with me till five and then I went to see Mrs. A-l-c and gave her two guineas. Then I went to Will's Coffeehouse where I saw my Lord Dunkellen, who told me the distraction my letter had made in the family. About ten I went to the Spanish Ambassador's where I lost four guineas. I gave my cousin Horsmanden two tickets and walked home about 12 o'clock but neglected my prayers.

7. I rose about 8 o'clock and read a chapter in Hebrew and some Greek in Lucian. I said my prayers, and had boiled milk for breakfast. The weather was cloudy and warm, the wind west. I received a letter from my Lord Dunkellen to meet him at Ozinda's about 12 o'clock where I went accordingly and found him and he showed me a letter he was to write to my rival. I drank a dish of chocolate and then went to dine with my cousin Horsmanden and ate some broiled veal. After dinner we drank tea and my cousin Ch-d-k came, whom I was glad to see. About five I went to Daniel's chambers and from thence to Mr. D-n-s where we drank tea again and spent the evening till 10 o'clock and then I went to Will's to meet my Lord Dunkellen who was gone. I walked home and washed my feet and said my prayers.

8. I rose about 8 o'clock and read a chapter in Hebrew and some Greek in Lucian. I said my prayers, and had boiled milk for breakfast. The weather was warm and cloudy. About ten came my rival, Sir Edward Des Bouverie, and brought Captain W-n[1] with him. He told me he had received a letter from me, which I denied. But I told him the whole story of my affair with Miss Smith, which he allowed to be wrong in her and yet told me he would proceed, to which I said much good may it do him. About twelve I went to Ozinda's, where I saw

1. Perhaps Maurice Wynne of Carnarvon, Esq., a captain in Vesey's Foot Regiment.

my Lord Dunkellen. Then I went to my cousin Horsmanden's where I dined and ate some roast veal. After dinner I went home, where Mr. Lindsay came to me and about eight I dressed myself for the masquerade and then went to my cousin Horsmanden's, where I drank some chocolate, and about ten we went and I was very well diverted and spent most of the night with one woman. Here I met with a woman that I hugged till I spent. I stayed till 6 o'clock in the morning and then went home in the chair.

9. I rose about 10 o'clock and read nothing, because Captain Turner came and hindered me. However, I said my prayers and had boiled milk for breakfast. The weather was clear and cold. About twelve I went to Ozinda's to meet my Lord Dunkellen and lost two guineas in betting against my Lord Portmore.[2] About 2 o'clock I returned home and ate some battered eggs. After dinner I took a nap and then wrote a letter to my rival till six and then went to Will's Coffeehouse, where I met my cousin Horsmanden, and then went to the park, and from thence returned again to Will's and had a lady call upon me with whom I had made an assignation at the masquerade. We went and sat at the tavern door in a coach and had some Rhenish wine and agreed to meet again tomorrow. Then I returned to Will's and went with my Lord L-s-f-l and several others to the tavern and I ate some lobster and stayed till twelve and then walked home, but neglected my prayers.

10. I rose about 8 o'clock and read nothing because I wrote a letter to my rival. I said my prayers, and had boiled milk for breakfast. The weather was hot and clear, the wind west. About eleven I went to visit my daughter and went from thence into the City and dined with Mrs. Perry and ate some bacon and eggs. After dinner we sat and talked and then drank tea till 4 o'clock and then I walked to the Exchange, where my coach stayed, in which I went home and wrote my letter to my rival fair. About six came Mr. Lindsay and sat with me about half an hour. About seven I went to Will's Coffeehouse and

2. David Colyear, 1st Earl of Portmore.

read the news and ate a jelly and stayed till almost nine, when a lady called upon me and we went and supped at the tavern and ate some chicken and asparagus and drank Burgundy but she would not let me do anything. We stayed till 11 o'clock and then I walked home and neglected my prayers. This day my man Jacob came to me.

11. I rose about 8 o'clock and read a chapter in Hebrew and some Greek in Lucian. I said my prayers, and had boiled milk for breakfast. The weather was hot and clear. About 11 o'clock I went to Somerset Chapel where we had a very dull sermon. After church I went to my Lord Percival's to dinner and ate some fricassee of rabbits. When we had dined we went to Kensington to make our court and stayed about an hour and then returned to my Lord Percival's and drank tea till five and then went to St. James's Chapel to prayers. Then I went to Colonel Blakiston's where I found Mr. [Shutz] and his lady. Then I went to Mrs. A-l-c who was from home. Then to Mrs. Sherard's, but they were from home. Then to Mrs. T-l-s where I stayed quarter of an hour, and then walked in the park, where I found my daughter with Mrs. [*or* Misses] Horsmanden. Then Daniel and I went to Ozinda's where I drank two dishes of chocolate, and then went to the Spanish Ambassador's and about twelve went home in a chair and said my prayers.

12. I rose about 7 o'clock and read a chapter in Hebrew and some Greek in Lucian. I said my prayers, and had boiled milk for breakfast. The weather was clear and warm, the wind west. About nine came Ben Bradley [3] and stayed about half an hour. Then came Mr. G-n-y and told me my affair would succeed but required time because the ministers were busy. Then came Mrs. A-l-c and told me she had taken a lodging at Chelsea and stayed about half an hour. About 11 o'clock I went to . . . cousins Horsmanden and drank tea with them and found my daughter there. Then Daniel and I went to see a Spaniard that made foils, and then walked in Somerset Garden till 2 o'clock and then went to my cousin's to dinner and I ate some veal.

3. Ben Bradley, a Virginia merchant of London.

After dinner we all took a nap and then I set my daughter home and went home, where I wrote English till six, and then went to Will's Coffeehouse and from thence to Mrs. B-r-n whom I found very sick. Then I went to Mrs. C-r-l but found them not. Then to Lady Guise's where I stayed half an hour. Then to Mrs. [or Misses Andrews'] but they were from home; then to Mrs. U-m-s but they were from home; then to Lady Powlett's where I stayed about an hour and then P-n-y U-m-s, D-l-y [Clark], and Peg Bellenden [4] walked in the garden till ten, and then I walked to Will's and drank two dishes of chocolate and then went to Petcum's where there was a quarrel but no harm. About twelve I walked home and said my prayers.

13. I rose about 8 o'clock and read a chapter in Hebrew and some Greek in Lucian. I said my prayers, and had boiled milk for breakfast. The weather was hot and clear, the wind southwest. I expected my masquerade woman to come to drink tea with me but she disappointed me. About 12 o'clock I went to Ozinda's Chocolate House and lost two guineas in betting. About 2 o'clock I returned home and ate some battered eggs for dinner. After dinner I put several things in order and then took a nap and read some French till 6 o'clock, and then went to my cousins Horsmanden and drank tea with them and Mrs. [or Misses Sands] and Sir Wilfred Lawson [5] and his brother came there. Here we spent the evening till 10 o'clock and drank chocolate. Then we went to the Spanish Ambassador's where I stayed till 12 o'clock and then I walked home and said my prayers.

14. I rose about 8 o'clock and read a chapter in Hebrew and some Greek in Lucian. I said my prayers, and had boiled milk for breakfast. The weather was clear and warm, the wind southwest. About 11 o'clock I went to Mr. G-n-y but he was out. Then I went to Sir Wilfred Lawson's and drank a dish of chocolate. Then I went to William L-m and stayed with him about half an hour; then to the coffee-

4. Margaret Bellenden, sister of Lord Bellenden; a maid of honor.

5. Sir Wilfred Lawson, 3rd Bart., M.P. for Cockermouth, 1722-37. His brother is later referred to as 'Jack' Lawson.

house and read the news, and about 2 o'clock went to my cousins Horsmanden to dinner and ate some fish. After dinner we took a nap by consent and about 5 o'clock I went home, and from thence to the coffeehouse, where I quarreled with a woman because she would not change me a guinea. Then I went to the play and stayed it out. After the play I picked up a woman and carried her to the tavern and ate some roast chicken and lay with her, for which God forgive me. About 12 o'clock I walked home and neglected my prayers.

15. I rose about 7 o'clock and read nothing because I prepared to go upon the water with some ladies. I said my prayers, and ate some boiled milk for breakfast. The weather was clear and hot, the wind southwest. About 9 o'clock I went to Mrs. [or Misses Sands'] lodging, where the company was to meet in order to go by water in a barge, but it was eleven before we all were ready and Sir Wilfred Lawson and his brother, I and Daniel Horsmanden, my two cousins Horsmanden and the two Misses [Sands] and Mrs. O-r-t-y made up the company. At eleven we went aboard and went through the bridge in our barge of six horses and we had a bigger boat rowed by [...]. We played at commerce and [little plays] and were merry while the barge rowed down to Dagenham Breach,[6] which was in a fair way of being finished. Then we returned, but by the way we ate some ham and chicken and ate some salmon. Then we walked in Greenwich Park, where we saw Colonel [Cunningham] and the fortune he had married. When it was dark we went aboard and ate some lobster and tongue and drank Burgundy and champagne and by ten got to Tower Stairs where we found our coaches and there parted and I carried the two [Sands] and Mrs. O-r-t-y home and then went home myself, but neglected my prayers. It rained this night.

16. I rose about 8 o'clock and read a chapter in Hebrew and some Greek in Lucian. I said my prayers, and had boiled milk for break-

6. At Dagenham, about eleven miles from London, the Thames in 1707 overflowed about a thousand acres of land, forming a sandbank halfway across the river. It remained in this state for many years and was finally reclaimed by Captain Perry at an expense of forty thousand pounds. Samuel Lewis, *Topographical Dictionary of England*, (London, 1844), II, 1.

fast. The weather was cloudy and warm and rained a little. Captain Turner brought our account of my brigantine which I examined and found so extravagant I resolved to sell the brig. I danced my dance and wrote several things till 2 o'clock, when I ate some battered eggs. After dinner I put several things in order and took a nap till 4 o'clock, and then read some French till five, and then went to visit my daughter and sat with her half an hour. Then I went to visit my cousins Horsmanden and drank tea with them. About eight came Mr. [Sands] and Sir Wilfred Lawson and we were merry and drank chocolate and about 10 o'clock I went to the Spanish Ambassador's where I played at commerce and lost three guineas. Here I was told that Sir Edward Des Bouverie had challenged me and I refused, which I declared to be a lie. About 12 o'clock I went home and neglected my prayers.

17. I rose about 6 o'clock and read nothing because I prepared to go to Isleworth to visit Colonel [Shutz]. However, I said my prayers and had boiled milk for breakfast. The weather was cold and clear, the wind west. About 8 o'clock I got into the coach and was about two hours going to Colonel [Shutz's] and came time enough to drink chocolate with them and then the Colonel and I took a walk for about two hours and when we returned we found Daniel Dering.[7] We played at commerce till 2 o'clock and then I ate some roast veal for dinner. After dinner we played at cards again and I lost twenty-five shillings and about 6 o'clock took leave and returned to London and went to the tavern to meet a woman that failed me, so I took a walk and picked up a woman and put her into a coach and committed uncleanness. Then I walked home and neglected my prayers.

18. I rose about 8 o'clock and read a chapter in Hebrew and some Greek in Homer. I said my prayers, and had boiled milk for breakfast. The weather was cloudy and it rained a little, the wind west. About eleven I went to Somerset House Chapel where we had an indifferent sermon. After church it rained so much that I was carried in a chair to the coach and then went to dine in Devonshire Street with

7. Daniel Dering, a relative of Lord Percival.

my cousin Horsmanden and ate some roast beef. After dinner I took a nap and about 6 o'clock went to visit Mrs. [Sands] and then went to the park, and about 9 o'clock went to Mrs. [Sands] again, where came Mrs. B-n-x and her daughter and we were very merry till 12 o'clock and then I went home in a chair and said my prayers.

19. I rose about 8 o'clock and read a chapter in Hebrew and some Greek in Lucian. I said my prayers and had boiled milk for breakfast. The weather was cloudy and cold, the wind west. About eleven came my cousin Horsmanden and we went to Sir Wilfred Lawson's and paid the charge of our entertainment by water. Here I drank two dishes of chocolate and then went to Ozinda's to meet my Lord Dunkellen, who told me abundance about my rival and his mistress and particularly that he had retained another second in the room of Captain W-n who was gone into the country. Here I lost five pounds betting upon the wrong side. About two we went to dine with my cousin Horsmanden and I ate some roast mutton. After dinner we drank tea and about five I went home, and from thence to Will's Coffeehouse, where I read the news, and then went with my cousin Horsmanden to the park and then I went to Mrs. FitzHerbert's and ate some bread and cheese, and then went to Petcum's where I stayed till twelve and then went home in a chair and neglected my prayers.

20. I rose about 8 o'clock and read a chapter in Hebrew and some Greek in Lucian. I said my prayers, and had boiled milk for breakfast. The weather was cloudy and cool. About 11 o'clock came Mrs. P-l-ing, whom I met at the masquerade, and drank tea with me and stayed till 1 o'clock. Then I went to my cousin Horsmanden's to dinner and ate some lamb. After dinner I took a nap and about 4 o'clock went to Chelsea to see Mrs. A-l-c and drank tea with her and stayed till seven, and then returned and went to visit my Aunt Sherard, where I stayed till nine, and then went to Ozinda's and drank a dish of chocolate, and then went to the Spanish Ambassador's and stayed till twelve, and then went home in a chair and neglected my prayers.

21. I rose about 8 o'clock and read nothing because I wrote a long letter to my Lord Dunkellen. I said my prayers, and ate boiled milk for breakfast. The weather was warm and clear. About eleven I went to my cousin Horsmanden's where I drank tea and settled my journey into the country with Sir Wilfred Lawson. About twelve I went into the City and dined with old Mr. Perry and ate some boiled beef. After dinner I sat and talked and drank tea and about four went to Mr. Lindsay's and sat half an hour with him and then went home and from thence to my Lady Guise's and stayed about an hour; and then went to Will's, and from thence to Mrs. U-m-s but they were from home. Then I walked in the garden and found them there. Then I took a walk to pick up a woman but could not find one to my mind and went home about eleven and neglected my prayers. It rained and thundered much.

22. I rose about 8 o'clock and read a chapter in Hebrew and some Greek in Lucian. I said my prayers, and had milk for breakfast. The weather was hot and clear, the wind west. I agreed about a chariot with the coachmaker. About 11 o'clock I went to Mrs. Parker's about some lace. Then I went to my Lord Orrery's where I drank chocolate and stayed about an hour, and then went home and packed up my things and about 2 o'clock ate some battered eggs for dinner. After dinner I put several things in order till 4 o'clock and then went to Sir Wilfred Lawson's lodgings and from thence we went in the chaise over the river to Deptford where we saw my cousins Horsmanden and drank tea with them. Here we stayed about an hour and then went to Greenwich and after giving the necessary orders walked in the park and met Colonel [Cunningham] and his lady. About nine we went home and ate some salmon for supper and my landlady supped with us. About twelve we went to bed and I neglected my prayers, for which God forgive me.

23. I rose about 7 o'clock and read a chapter in Hebrew and some Greek in Homer. I said my prayers and had milk for breakfast. The weather was clear and hot, the wind southwest. In the morning Daniel Horsmanden came to us and about ten we walked in the park and

from thence to G-r-s T-s-r where we drank chocolate and played at piquet and I lost ten shillings. About two we went home to dinner and I ate some mackerel. After dinner we went to see the new church[8] and the hall of the hospital[9] and then walked through the park to G-r-s T-s-r where we met my cousins Horsmanden who came in a chaise we had sent for them. We played at cards and were merry and then went and walked in the park and entertained them with Burgundy and champagne, and about 9 o'clock took leave and we afterwards took a walk and then went home to supper and ate some roast chicken and my landlady supped with us and we talked till 11 o'clock and then retired. I said my prayers, &c.

24. I rose about 8 o'clock and read a chapter in Hebrew and some Greek in Homer. I said my prayers, and ate some milk for breakfast. The weather was hot and clear, the wind west. About 11 o'clock we walked through the park to G-r-s T-s-r where we read the news and drank some chocolate. Then we played at piquet till 1 o'clock, when my Lord L-s-f-l called there [...]. About two we walked through the park home and ate some roast beef for dinner and my landlady dined with us. After dinner we went to visit my cousins Horsmanden and played at commerce and then walked about the King's yard and in the evening took leave and returned home and walked in the park till 10 o'clock and then ate some eggs for supper. I said my prayers.

25. I rose about 8 o'clock and read a chapter in Hebrew and some Greek. I said my prayers, and had milk for breakfast. The weather was clear and warm, the wind west. About 10 o'clock we went to church and my landlord carried us into Misses Robinsons' pew, who are pretty sort of women and after church we walked with them in the park, where Daniel Horsmanden and his brother came to us and dined with us and I ate some roast rabbit for dinner. In the afternoon

8. St. Alphage's Church, rebuilt in 1718 by Nicholas Hawksmoor and John James.

9. Greenwich Hospital, a hospital for seamen, built on the ruins of a royal mansion after 1705. It was designed by Christopher Wren. The great hall, called the 'Painted Hall,' was adorned with paintings by James Thornhill.

we carried some wine into the park and drank it there and about 5 o'clock went to G-r-s T-s-r where was but little company. Then we walked in the park where was abundance, but very indifferent. My cousin Horsmanden came here. We walked till 9 o'clock and then went home to supper and I ate some eggs but neglected my prayers.

26. I rose about 7 o'clock and read two chapters in Hebrew and some Greek in Homer. I said my prayers, and had cold milk for breakfast. The weather was hot and clear, the wind west. I wrote a letter to Sir Wilfred as from an old man that took notice of him yesterday at church, which he believed to be a true letter. About 11 o'clock we walked through the park to G-r-s T-s-r and drank a dish of chocolate and played at piquet till two and then walked through the park to our lodgings where Mr. Horsmanden dined with us and I ate some mackerel. After dinner we went into the park to meet our ladies but they came not. However, in the evening my cousins Horsmanden came and we walked with them and gave them some champagne. In the evening we returned home and ate some cold roast beef. I neglected my prayers.

27. I rose about 7 o'clock and read a chapter in Hebrew and some Greek in Homer. I said my prayers and ate some milk for breakfast. The weather was very hot and clear. About 10 o'clock Will [Tryon] came to visit us and walked with us to see General Withers' [10] house which was very pretty and the furniture very well fancied. Then we proceeded to G-r-s T-s-r and drank some chocolate and about two returned to our lodgings with Mr. [Tryon] and my cousin Daniel and ate some boiled mutton for dinner. After dinner we paid our reckoning and went to see the Carolina yacht which was very fine and neat, and then proceeded by water to London and by the way called aboard a ship where we got a flask of champagne and when we got ashore saw the lions and drank a bottle of claret till the chaise came and then I went home but found neither of my servants, but they came at last and I scolded at them. In the evening I went to

10. Henry Withers, lieutenant general of the First Foot Guards.

Will's and from thence took a walk and picked up a woman and went home with her and committed uncleanness, for which God forgive me. About twelve I went home and quarreled with my man Jacob because he would not come to me. I neglected my prayers.

28. I rose about 7 o'clock and read a chapter in Hebrew and some Greek in Homer. I said my prayers and had boiled milk for breakfast. The weather was hot and clear, the wind west. I dressed me very fine to go to Kensington, being the King's birthday, and about twelve went to Sir Wilfred Lawson's and we went together and found a great crowd in the gallery where the King saw company. People were not very fine. About 2 o'clock I went to Lady Jeffreys' to dinner and ate some fish. After dinner we drank tea and about five I went to Mr. [Boyle's], but everybody was gone to Court. Then I went to Mr. W-r-k, and sat with him about an hour and then returned to Lady Jeffreys' and waited on the young ladies to Court. The company went into the garden and the dancing was there and the company walked about the garden. About 10 o'clock the fireworks were fired and were very fine. The little Princesses danced till eleven. About twelve I went away but could not find my servants. I neglected my prayers, for which God forgive me.

29. I rose about 8 o'clock and read a chapter in Hebrew and some Greek in Lucian. I said my prayers, and had boiled milk for breakfast. The weather was cold and cloudy, the wind west, blowing very fiercely. About 10 o'clock came Mr. Horsmanden and stayed about half an hour. I read some English and about 1 o'clock went to Garraway's Coffeehouse and there I met Tom R-l and Mr. Cecil,[11] and we went to dine at the [Chapelhouse] and I ate some mutton steak. After dinner we went to T-l-y to buy some things and from thence I went home, where I adjusted myself and then went to Will's, where I read the news and then walked to the woman I picked up the other night and there committed uncleanness. Then I went to visit Mrs. B-r-t and drank tea and then stayed to supper and ate some cold lamb. About twelve I walked home, where I neglected my prayers.

11. Lord Orrery's wife, Elizabeth Cecil, who died in 1708, was a daughter of the 5th Earl of Exeter; Mr. Cecil was probably of this family.

30. I rose about 6 o'clock and read nothing because I prepared to go to Petersham to the Duke of Argyll's[12] with Colonel Cecil. I said my prayers, and had milk for breakfast. The weather was cold and cloudy. About nine I called on Colonel Cecil and we went to Petersham through the King's Gate to the Duke of Argyll's who was just going to the [Fair?] with my Lady Duchess.[13] However, he ordered Mr. W-s-c-m to entertain us with all the house afforded. We walked in the garden before dinner and ate some strawberries and about 3 o'clock went to dinner and I ate some boiled beef. We had Burgundy and champagne and Colonel Burgess[14] dined with us. We stayed till 6 o'clock and then took leave and returned to town, where I picked up a woman in the street and lay with her at the Union Tavern and then went to the Spanish Ambassador's where I stayed till twelve and then went home in a chair and neglected my prayers, for which God forgive me.

31. I rose about 8 o'clock and read a chapter in Hebrew and some Greek in Lucian. I said my prayers and had milk for breakfast. The weather was clear and hot, the wind west. About 11 o'clock came my cousin Daniel and stayed a quarter of an hour, and then I went to visit Mr. G-n-y but he was from home. Then I went to Lord Percival's but he was from home; then to Mr. Blathwayt's but he was from home; then to Sir Charles Wager at the Admiralty and found him. Then to Sir Wilfred Lawson's but he was from home; then to Ozinda's where I bet but neither won nor lost. Then I went home and ate some battered eggs for dinner. In the afternoon I put several things in order and read some English till five and then went to Chelsea to Mrs. A-l-c and drank tea with her and stayed till eight and then returned to town and went to Mrs. U-m-s and stayed to supper and ate some peas, and about twelve walked home and said my prayers.

12. Sudbrook House, built by the Duke of Argyll at Petersham.

13. Jane Warburton, formerly maid of honor, was the second wife of the Duke of Argyll.

14. Elisha Burgess, lieutenant colonel of Palmes' Regiment of Dragoons.

June 1718

1. I rose about 8 o'clock and read a chapter in Hebrew and some Greek in Lucian. I said my prayers, and had milk for breakfast. The weather was clear and warm. About 11 o'clock I went to Somerset Chapel where we had a good sermon. After church I went home and adjusted myself and then went to Sir Wilfred Lawson's to dinner and ate some mackerel and his brother dined with us. After dinner we drank Burgundy till four and then Sir Wilfred and I went in his coach and six to Deptford where we made a visit to my cousins Horsmanden and then proceeded to Greenwich where we first went to the coffeehouse and from thence to the park where we walked till 10 o'clock and then returned to London and I went home and washed my feet and said my prayers.

2. I rose about 8 o'clock and read a chapter in Hebrew and some Greek in Lucian. I said my prayers, and had milk for breakfast. The weather was cloudy and warm. About 11 o'clock I went to visit my daughter and found her well, thank God. Then I went to Mr. Perry's and dined with Dick and ate some mackerel. After dinner Mr. [Tryon] came in and some ladies from Philadelphia and we drank some Burgundy till 7 o'clock and then I set Mr. [Tryon] down and went to Will's Coffeehouse where I read the news and went to walk in the park and walked with Mrs. C-t-l-r and then went to Ozinda's and from thence I walked home and prepared for my journey. I neglected to say my prayers, for which God forgive me.

3. I rose about 3 o'clock and read nothing because I prepared for my journey to [Guildford]. I said my prayers and about five went to Sir Wilfred Lawson's where I drank chocolate for breakfast. We stayed till six for one of our company that did not come, and then we went into the coach and went to Cobham, a little town about fifteen miles from London, and there ate some bread and butter and then proceeded to R-d-ing[1] where we put ourselves in order and about 1 o'clock dined at the Lion and ate some boiled chicken for dinner. Mr. B-r-t-n and I got into the coach and took two girls of the town with us and went to the race, where was abundance of company and the King, and my Lord Stamford's grey won the plate. Our girls were very coy and therefore we did nothing with them, so we set them down in the evening and took a walk till nine and then supped at the Lion and I ate some trout for supper. We lay at the [Hatter] in pretty good lodgings and I said my prayers and slept pretty well, thank God.

4. I rose about 8 o'clock and read some Greek but no Hebrew. I said my prayers, and had milk for breakfast. The weather was cold and cloudy. We gave half a guinea for our lodgings this night. About 11 o'clock we went to the coffeehouse and about twelve we got into the coach and drove to Hampton Court[2] where we saw the royal apartments and walked in the garden. About 2 o'clock we dined at the Mitre and ate some stewed crab for dinner, and Mr. H-l and Mr. C-t dined with us and so did Mr. B-r-t-n that went with us. About 8 o'clock we got to London and went to the play and after the play we went to Mrs. W-d-l-n-t-n, a decent bawd, where we had two ladies to divert us and Sir Wilfred and Mr. B-r-t-n lay with one of them but I did nothing but gave half a guinea to one of them and about 12 o'clock we went home and I neglected to say my prayers, for which God forgive me.

5. I rose about 8 o'clock and read a chapter in Hebrew and some Greek in Lucian. I said my prayers, and had milk for breakfast. The weather was cloudy and cold, the wind northwest. About 12 o'clock I went to Mr. G-n-y but he was from home, then to my Lord Percival's, who was from home; then to Ozinda's, from whence I went with Lord Windsor and walked round the park and then lost two

1. This may be an error on Byrd's part for Orking. Reading was too far away for him to have reached in so short a time.

2. Hampton Court is a royal palace on the Thames.

guineas in betting. Then I returned home and ate some battered eggs for dinner. In the afternoon I put several things in order till 5 o'clock and then went to Mrs. B-r-t and drank tea, and then went to my cousin Daniel's chambers where I found his two sisters and the two Misses [Sands], where we were very merry and I ate some cold beef and bacon for supper. I found a sore throat come upon me. However, I sat up there till 2 o'clock and then Sir Wilfred set me down. I neglected to say my prayers and was much out of order and slept indifferently.

6. I rose about 8 o'clock and found myself much out of order. However I read a chapter in Hebrew and some Greek in Lucian. I said my prayers, and had milk for breakfast. About 11 o'clock I went into the City and dined with old Mr. Perry and ate roast beef but had very little stomach, being much out of order. After dinner I went to Dick Perry's and sat with him about an hour and then went to Mr. [Tryon's] where I drank tea and by a start threw a dish of tea into my own face. Then I went to visit Mr. Lindsay and stayed about quarter of an hour and then went home; and from thence to visit Mrs. [Sands], where my cousins Horsmanden were. Here I stayed till 8 o'clock and then went home and drank some [sack whey?] and went to bed and sweated pretty much. I said my prayers.

7. I rose about 9 o'clock and found myself a little better, thank God. I read a chapter in Hebrew and some Greek in Lucian. I said my prayers, and had boiled milk for breakfast. It rained almost all day. About eleven Mr. [Philips] came and let me blood, which did me abundance of good, and I gave him half a guinea. However, I was but indifferent all day. About 1 o'clock my cousin Daniel came to see me and stayed about half an hour. At two I had a boiled chicken for dinner. After dinner I put several things in order till 5 o'clock, and then I went to Chelsea to visit Mrs. A-l-c and drank tea with her and stayed till 8 o'clock and walked through the park and then went to Will's Coffeehouse, where I saw my Lord Dunkellen who told me my mistress was to have fifteen hundred pounds laid out upon her

wedding clothes. About 10 o'clock I went home and ate some boiled milk and in half an hour went to bed and said a short prayer. I slept pretty well and sweated a little.

8. I rose about 8 o'clock and read a chapter in Hebrew and some Greek in Lucian. I said my prayers, and had milk for breakfast. The weather was clear and warm, the wind west. I found myself pretty well, thank God. Therefore I went to Somerset Chapel about eleven, where we had a pretty good sermon. After church I went home, where I read some English till 1 o'clock and then I ate a veal cutlet for dinner. After dinner I put several things in order and then took a nap and about 5 o'clock went to my Lady Guise, whom I found very sick. I stayed there till six and then returned to Will's to meet my Lord Bellenden to carry me to the park but he disappointed me. However I stayed an hour for him and then went to visit Mrs. Fitz-Herbert, who was not at home. Then I went to Mrs. Blakiston's and sat with her about an hour; then I went to Mrs. B-r-t but she was from home. Then I returned to Will's and ate a jelly and then went home and ate some cold milk and said my prayers.

9. I rose about 8 o'clock and found myself not very well. I read a chapter in Hebrew and some Greek in Lucian. I said my prayers and ate milk for breakfast. Captain Posford [3] came and sat with me about an hour and then my Lord Bellenden came to excuse his having disappointed me yesterday, and stayed half an hour. Then I read some English and then paid my landlady a quarter's rent. About two I ate some battered eggs for dinner. After dinner I put several things in order till four, when Daniel Horsmanden came and went with me to visit Mrs. [Sands] where we stayed till seven and then went to the park and from thence to St. James's Park where I walked about an hour and then went to Will's Coffeehouse and ate a jelly and read the news and about eleven went home and wrote a letter. I said my prayers.

3. Captain Posford, who carried goods between Virginia and England, is frequently mentioned in letters of Byrd and other tobacco planters of Virginia.

10. I rose about 8 o'clock and read a chapter in Hebrew and some Greek in Lucian. I said my prayers, and had milk for breakfast. The weather was clear and cold, the wind southwest. About 11 o'clock came my cousin Daniel Horsmanden and went with me to visit Sir Wilfred Lawson but he was from home. Then I went to my Lord Percival to take my leave of him before he went out of England but he was from home. Then I went to Mrs. [Sands] and found Miss Grace indisposed. Then we went to the [chapelhouse] and dined on mutton steak. After dinner we went to the Tower and took boat to Deptford and drank tea with my cousins Horsmanden and then went to Greenwich to walk in the park where we stayed till 9 o'clock and then set the ladies home and proceeded to London and when I came home I found my man Jacob very drunk. However, I went to the Spanish Ambassador's and stayed there till 12 o'clock and then Daniel set me home where I said my prayers.

11. I rose about 8 o'clock and read a chapter in Hebrew and some Greek in Lucian. I said my prayers, and had milk for breakfast. The weather was cloudy and it rained abundantly. I turned Jacob away because he was drunk and paid him his wages. I wrote a letter till 2 o'clock and then ate a broiled chicken for dinner. In the afternoon I wrote more English till 4 o'clock when my cousin Daniel came and stayed with me till five, when I went to Mrs. B-r-t and found her not at home. Then I went to Mrs. [Andrews] and drank tea with them. Then I went to Will's Coffeehouse and read the news and sat there till 8 o'clock and then carried my Lord Orrery and my Lord Windsor to St. James's Park and walked there about an hour and then went to Ozinda's and drank a dish of chocolate, and then I walked home and endeavoured to pick up a woman, but could not, thank God. I said my prayers, &c.

12. I rose about 8 o'clock and read a chapter in Hebrew and some Greek in Lucian. I said my prayers, and had milk for breakfast. The weather was clear and warm, the wind west. About 11 o'clock I went to my Lord Orrery's but he was from home; then I went to Sir

Wilfred Lawson's, who was likewise from home. Then I went to my coachmaker's to see my chariot and liked it. Then I went home and ate some mutton steak for dinner. In the afternoon I took a nap and wrote some English till 5 o'clock and then went to visit Mrs. [Sands] where I found my cousin Horsmanden. Here I stayed and played at cards till 12 o'clock and then took leave and went home where I neglected to say my prayers, for which God forgive me.

13. I rose about 8 o'clock and read a chapter in Hebrew and some Greek in Lucian. I said my prayers and had milk for breakfast. The weather was clear and warm, the wind west. Mr. G-n-y was with me to let me know he could do nothing in my affair about the government of Virginia. About 11 o'clock I visited Mrs. [Sands] and sat with them half an hour, and then went to my Lord Orrery's where I stayed about half an hour and then went to Ozinda's where I met Sir Wilfred Lawson and Mr. B-r-t-n and went to dine with them at the Thatched House[4] and ate some boiled chicken for dinner. Both these gentlemen told me they were clapped by Mrs. W-l-m. After dinner I went with them to the surgeon and then I took leave of them and went home and received several letters from Virginia. About 6 o'clock I went to Will's Coffeehouse and read the news. Then I walked in the park and then drank a dish of chocolate at Ozinda's and went to the Spanish Ambassador's. About twelve I went home in a chair and said my prayers.

14. I rose about 7 o'clock and read a chapter in Hebrew and some Greek in Lucian. I said my prayers, and had milk for breakfast. The weather was clear and warm, the wind southwest. I wrote some English till 11 o'clock. I went to my Lord Bellenden's but he was from home; then to Mr. O-r-d but he was from home; then to Mr. B-r-t-n and sat with him about an hour and then I went to see the burning engine in the Privy Garden, and was well pleased with it. Then I went home and ate a roast rabbit. After dinner I took a nap till five and then went to Chelsea and at the College a gentlewoman came and

4. A tavern in St. James's Street.

told me she desired to speak with me, so I got out and walked with her in the college walk and she told me Mrs. A-l-c had commerce with another man and showed me several of her letters. I thanked her and took leave and returned to London, and went to the park and afterwards to Mrs. FitzHerbert's. From thence I took a walk and picked up a woman and carried her to the tavern and committed uncleanness and ate some roast fowl. About 1 o'clock I went home and neglected my prayers, for which God forgive me.

15. I rose about 8 o'clock and read a chapter in Hebrew and some Greek in Lucian. I said my prayers, and had milk for breakfast. The weather was clear and warm, the wind west. This day my new chariot came out and about 11 o'clock I went to Somerset Chapel and heard a pretty good sermon. After church I walked in the garden with Penny U-m-s and Mrs. H-r-c-r and then dined with Mrs. U-m-s and ate some roast beef. After dinner we drank tea till 5 o'clock and then I went to visit Mrs. Southwell and drank tea again and would have carried Mr. Southwell to the park but we discovered that my coachman was drunk so I set him down at White's Chocolate House[5] and then went to Mrs. [Sands'] where I stayed till 9 o'clock and then went to Ozinda's Chocolate House and from thence to the Spanish Ambassador's and walked home at twelve and neglected my prayers.

16. I rose about 8 o'clock and read a chapter in Hebrew and some Greek in Lucian. I said my prayers, and had milk for breakfast. The weather was cloudy and warm, the wind southwest. About 10 o'clock Colonel [Shutz] came to see me but did not stay because my chariot was come. About twelve I went to the Virginia Coffeehouse and saw Captain Randolph[6] just come from Virginia. Then I went to Mr. Perry's and dined with Mike and ate some fish. After dinner I wrote a letter and then went and sat with Mrs. Cole, a milliner, and ate some cherries. Then I went to Chelsea and saw Mrs. A-l-c

5. A gambling club and chocolate house in St. James's Street.

6. Probably Edward Randolph, youngest of the seven sons of Colonel William Randolph of Virginia. Like his brother Isham, he was a sea captain.

for the last time because she had played the whore. However I drank tea with her and about 8 o'clock returned to London and went to Will's where I read the news and then went to the Union Tavern to meet a young woman who supped with me and I ate some roast chicken and then we went to the bagnio in Silver Street, where I lay all night with her and rogered her three times and found her very straight and unprecocious and very sweet and agreeable. I slept very little.

17. I rose about 8 o'clock and drank two dishes of chocolate and about 9 o'clock took leave of my mistress and then went home, where I read a chapter in Hebrew and some Greek in Lucian. I received a letter from Virginia from my cousin Brayne.[7] Captain Turner brought me part of the money for the brig. I received the news that my daughter was indisposed and that they feared it would be the smallpox. My cousin Daniel came and stayed half an hour. About 2 o'clock I ate some battered eggs for dinner. After dinner I took a nap for about an hour and at 5 o'clock went to see my daughter and found her much better, thank God. Then I called on my cousin Daniel to take him to the park but he could not go, so I went to Mrs. B-r-n and sat with her about an hour. Then I went to Mrs. C-r-l but they were from home. Then I went to Mrs. Blakiston and found Mrs. [Shutz] there and stayed till ten and then went to the Spanish Ambassador's and from thence went with Sir Wilfred Lawson to the Three Tuns where we supped and I ate some fricasseed chicken. There were two whores, with one of which two of the company lay in condoms, but I did nothing but went home about two.

18. I rose about 8 o'clock and read a chapter in Hebrew and some Greek in Lucian. I said my prayers, and had milk for breakfast. The

7. Byrd sent John Brayne, orphaned son of his sister Susan, to Virginia in 1717 'to make himself acquainted with my affairs' (Byrd to John Custis, October 19, 1717, MS, New York Public Library). Two other children, William and Susan Brayne, had been sent from England to Virginia in 1710 and lived with Byrd at Westover for some years. See *The Secret Diary of William Byrd*.

weather was cold and cloudy, the wind west. Captain Turner was with me and stayed about half an hour. Then came my coachmaker whom I paid for my chariot. I wrote a letter to Mrs. A-l-c to take my leave of her forever. About 2 o'clock I ate a beefsteak for dinner. In the afternoon I took a nap till 4 o'clock and then came my cousin Horsmanden and I went with him to Misses [Sands'] but they were from home. Then we went to Mrs. D-n-s where we drank tea and ate sweet biscuits. I read several things to them out of my book and we stayed till 10 o'clock and then took leave. Then we went to the coffeehouse and read the news and about eleven I went home and said my prayers.

19. I rose about 8 o'clock and read a chapter in Hebrew and some Greek in Lucian. I said my prayers, and had milk for breakfast. The weather was cloudy and cold, the wind west. Captain Turner came and paid me my money for the brigantine, which I sold to him for one hundred and sixty pounds. About 10 o'clock came Captain Randolph and stayed with me about an hour and then I went to visit Sir Wilfred Lawson and stayed with him half an hour. Then I went to Mr. B-r-t-n and found his clap very bad. Then I went to Ozinda's and won a guinea in betting. Then I went home and ate some battered eggs. After dinner I wrote some English till five and then came my cousin Daniel and we went to Misses [Sands'] but they were from home, and then I went to Mrs. FitzHerbert's where I drank two dishes of chocolate and afterwards ate some raspberries and cream. Here I stayed till 11 o'clock where was also Lady Anne and Lady Barbara Shirley.[8] Then I went home and said my prayers.

20. I rose about 9 o'clock and read a chapter in Hebrew and some Greek in Lucian. I said my prayers and had milk for breakfast. The weather was cloudy and cold, and threatened rain. I wrote some English till 11 o'clock and then came Mrs. Wilkinson and I gave her some of my linen to mend. About twelve I went as far as Poplar to dine with Captain Posford and there met Captain Randolph. I ate some

8. Daughters of Robert Shirley, 1st Earl Ferrers.

boiled beef. After dinner we remembered our friends in Virginia till 6 o'clock and then I returned to London and went to Will's Coffee-house where I lost twenty-six shillings at piquet, and about 11 o'clock went to the Spanish Ambassador's where I stayed till twelve and then came home in the chair and said my prayers. My gleet was much better.

21. I rose about 8 o'clock and read a chapter in Hebrew and some Greek in Lucian. I said my prayers, and had milk for breakfast. The weather was cloudy and warm, the wind west. My running was much worse again. I wrote a letter to my cousin Suky Horsmanden till 2 o'clock and then I ate some battered eggs. After dinner I put several things in order and then read some English till 5 o'clock when Mr. Lindsay came and stayed about half an hour. Then I went to Mrs. B-r-t where I drank tea and stayed till 8 o'clock, when I went to walk in the park and met Sir Wilfred Lawson and walked with him. I also walked with Mrs. [Noel] and about ten went to St. James's Coffeehouse, from whence I went with Sir Wilfred, Colonel Lowther[9] and Mr. B-r-t-n and ate some minced veal, and about twelve went home and neglected my prayers.

22. I rose about 8 o'clock and read a chapter in Hebrew and some Greek in Lucian. I said my prayers, and had milk for breakfast. The weather was clear and warm, the wind west. I wrote two letters, and about 11 o'clock went into the City to Mr. Lindsay's to dinner and ate some roast beef. After dinner we went to church where I slept, for which God forgive me. After church Mr. Lindsay set me home and I read some English till 6 o'clock and then went to my Lady Guise's where I stayed about an hour, and then went to Colonel Blakiston's who was from home. Then to Mrs. Mary O-r-d but she was in the country. Then to Mrs. Southwell's, who was from home; then I walked through the park to my Aunt Sherard's where I stayed till 10 o'clock and then went to Ozinda's Chocolate House and drank a dish of chocolate. Then I walked to the Spanish Ambassador's

9. Anthony Lowther, lieutenant colonel of the Coldstream Guards.

where I talked abundance to the widow Pierson.[10] About twelve I
went home in the chair and said my prayers.

23. I rose about 8 o'clock and read a chapter in Hebrew and some
Greek in Lucian. I said my prayers and had milk for breakfast. The
weather was cloudy and hot, the wind west. About 9 o'clock Colonel
Blakiston and his son came to see me but would not stay because Mrs.
Blakiston was in the coach. About ten I went to Sir Wilfred Lawson's
and we went to Major F-r-b-r to see Mr. Lawson [ride]. Then I
went with him to see the horse of Mr. W-l-k. Then we went into the
City to Garraway's Coffeehouse and talked to several girls. About
three we dined at Pontack's and I ate some fish. After dinner we
drank a bottle till 6 o'clock and then I went to Will's Coffeehouse
and won four guineas at piquet. About nine I went to the Union in
Longacre[11] where my mistress met me and I rogered her. I ate some
veal for supper. I agreed to give her twenty pounds a year to take
care of my linen, &c. About eleven I went home and neglected my
prayers.

24. I rose about 7 o'clock and read a chapter in Hebrew and some
Greek in Lucian. I said my prayers, and had milk for breakfast. The
weather was hot and cloudy, the wind west. I read some English till
11 o'clock and then went to visit my daughter and found her pretty
well, thank God. From thence I went into the City and dined with
Dick Perry whose lady and daughter were come to town. I ate some
boiled beef for dinner. After dinner I went to Garraway's Coffeehouse and read the news and then went and sat with Molly Cole till
4 o'clock, when I went home and about six went to Mrs. U-m-s
where I drank tea and saw a person [or parson] who desired to go to
Virginia. About eight I went to my Aunt Sherard's and took leave of
my cousin Smith who is going to Ireland. About ten I went to

10. It is likely that the letters Byrd addressed to 'Zenobia' (*Another Secret Diary
of William Byrd,* 261-6) were to Mrs. Pierson, to whom he paid court for some
months in the spring of 1719.

11. Longacre was a street filled with taverns, bagnios, and other places of
amusement.

Ozinda's and drank a dish of chocolate, and then went to the Spanish Ambassador's where I talked to Mrs. Walker and Miss [Noel]. About twelve I walked home and said my prayers.

25. I rose about 7 o'clock and took some pills. I read a chapter in Hebrew and some Greek in Lucian. I said my prayers, and had boiled milk for breakfast. The weather was clear and warm, the wind west. I wrote some English and danced my dance till 2 o'clock and then ate some boiled chicken. After dinner I put several things in order till four and then came Daniel Horsmanden and I went with him to Mrs. [Sands'] where we sat till 8 o'clock and then we went to walk in the park and joined Mrs. D-n-s and Mrs. A-l-d-n. Then we went to the tavern and ate some lobster and drank a bottle of French wine and about one o'clock walked home and said my prayers. My running was very bad. My physic worked but once.

26. I rose about 8 o'clock and read a chapter in Hebrew and some Greek in Lucian. I said my prayers and had milk for breakfast. The weather was clear and cold, the wind west. I wrote some verse. About eleven came Daniel Horsmanden and stayed half an hour, and about one I went to Ozinda's, where I lost four guineas and about two returned home and ate some battered eggs for dinner. After dinner I put some things in order and then took a nap till 5 o'clock, when Daniel Horsmanden came and we went to the park, where we had appointed to meet some ladies but they failed. Then we went to Spring Gardens where we picked up two women and carried them into the arbor and ate some cold veal and about 10 o'clock we carried them to the bagnio, where we bathed and lay with them all night and I rogered mine twice and slept pretty well, but neglected my prayers.

27. I rose about 8 o'clock and took leave of the ladies and went home and read a chapter in Hebrew and some Greek in Lucian. I said my prayers and had milk for breakfast. The weather was cloudy and warm, the wind west. Annie Wilkinson came to me but I did noth-

ing. I wrote some English till 2 o'clock and then ate some veal cutlets. After dinner I put several things in order and then took a nap till 5 o'clock and then went to Mrs. U-m-s where I drank tea and sat with them till 8 o'clock, and then went to the play and from thence to the Mall where I walked till 10 o'clock, and then went to Ozinda's and drank two dishes of chocolate and read the news, and then walked to the Spanish Ambassador's where I talked much to the widow Pierson, and about 12 o'clock walked home where I said my prayers.

28. I rose about 7 o'clock and read a chapter in Hebrew and some Greek in Homer. I said my prayers, and had milk for breakfast. The weather was warm and clear, the wind west. My running was much better, thank God. I wrote some English till 11 o'clock and then went to visit Mrs. Southwell and sat with her about an hour and then went to Ozinda's where I won three guineas. About 2 o'clock I returned to Mr. Southwell's to dinner and ate some beefsteak. After dinner we went to Bayswater to see [Jones's iron works?]. Then we went to Spring Gardens where we ate a cheesecake and walked about two hours and then returned and I walked home, but by the way we called at Will's Coffeehouse and ate a jelly. About eleven I went home and washed my feet and said my prayers.

29. I rose about 7 o'clock and read a chapter in Hebrew and some Greek in Homer. I said my prayers and had milk for breakfast. The weather was warm and clear, the wind west. About 11 o'clock I went to Somerset Chapel and heard a pretty good sermon. After church I talked about half an hour with Mrs. U-m-s and Mrs. Gunning.[12] My Lord Bellenden invited me to dinner but I excused myself and went home and ate battered eggs. After dinner I put several things in order and then wrote some English till 5 o'clock, when I went to Mrs. [Andrews'] but they were from home. Then I went to Lady Guise's where I stayed two hours. Then I went to Mrs. FitzHerbert's and ate some bread and cheese, and then went to the

12. Mrs. John Gunning was housekeeper in Somerset House. She was the mother of three celebrated beauties, the Duchess of Argyll and Hamilton, the Countess of Coventry, and Mrs. Travers.

Spanish Ambassador's where I stayed till 12 o'clock and then walked home and said my prayers.

30. I rose about 7 o'clock and read a chapter in Hebrew and some Greek. I said my prayers, and had milk for breakfast. The weather was clear and hot, the wind west. I danced my dance and wrote a letter till 11 o'clock and then I went to see my daughter and found her well, thank God. Then I went to Mr. Perry's and dined with the old gentleman and ate some minced veal. After dinner we sat and talked till 3 o'clock and then I walked to Garraway's Coffeehouse and then called upon Molly Cole and then went home where I stayed till six and then went to Mrs. B-r-t and stayed till 9 o'clock and then went to the Union Tavern where I met Mrs. Wilkinson. We had a broiled chicken for supper and then I rogered her and walked home about 12 o'clock and neglected my prayers, for which God forgive me. It was very hot this day and my running was abundantly better.

July 1718

1. I rose about 8 o'clock and read a chapter in Hebrew and some Greek in Lucian. I said my prayers and had milk for breakfast. The weather was cold and cloudy, the wind southeast. I wrote a letter and about 11 o'clock went to visit Mrs. Southwell, where I found Mrs. FitzHerbert who was to dine there, which made me resolve to dine there likewise. However I went first to Ozinda's, where I won fifty shillings and then returned to Mr. Southwell's to dinner, where I found also Captain M-n-g-y. I ate some boiled beef and after dinner we drank a bottle till 6 o'clock and then I went to Misses [Sands'] but they were from home. Then to Mrs. B-r-n who was away from

home; then to Mrs. C-r-l where I found the Duchess of Wharton[1] who is a pretty woman. Then I went to my Aunt Sherard's but she was from home. Then to Mrs. D-l-y where I stayed till 9 o'clock, and then went to Will's Coffeehouse where I played at piquet and lost three guineas, and about 1 o'clock went home and neglected my prayers.

2. I rose about 8 o'clock and read a chapter in Hebrew and some Greek in Lucian. I said my prayers, and had milk for breakfast. The weather was cold and cloudy, the wind southeast. I wrote some English and put several things in order till 2 o'clock and then ate some battered eggs for dinner. After dinner I put several things in order and wrote more English till 5 o'clock and read some French. Then I went to Colonel Blakiston's where I stayed till 7 o'clock and then went to Lady Guise's where I stayed till 8 and then walked with Colonel Guise[2] in the park till ten and then walked home and picked up a woman and set her down in a coach and committed uncleanness, and about 12 o'clock I went home and neglected my prayers.

3. I rose about 8 o'clock and read a chapter in Hebrew and some Greek in Lucian. I said my prayers and had milk for breakfast. The weather was warm and cloudy, the wind west. I danced my dance. About 11 o'clock came Annie Wilkinson with some of my linen, and then came Sir Charles Wager and invited me to dinner. About twelve he went away and I read some French till one and then went into the City and called at my bookseller's and then went to Sir Charles Wager's, where I ate some boiled rabbit. About eight I took my leave and went and took up my daughter and then carried her to Mrs. B-r-t's where we had tea, and fruit for Miss. We stayed till 8 o'clock and then I went to the coffeehouse, and from thence to the bagnio where I bathed and lay with Annie Wilkinson till 12 o'clock and then went home in a coach and neglected my prayers.

1. Martha, daughter of Major General Holmes, married in 1715 the Marquess of Wharton.

2. John Guise, captain and lieutenant colonel of the First Foot Guards, stepson of Lady Guise; a fellow of the Royal Society.

4. I rose about 8 o'clock and read a chapter in Hebrew and some Greek in Lucian. I said my prayers, and had milk for breakfast. The weather was hot and clear, the wind west. About 9 o'clock came Mrs. A-l-c but met with an indifferent reception, notwithstanding she took on sadly. I read some French. I danced my dance, and wrote some English till 2 o'clock and then ate some broiled herring for dinner. After dinner I put several things in order and then took a nap till about five and then I went to my Lord Foley's and stayed till 7 o'clock; then I went to visit Mrs. [Sands'] and drank tea and stayed till nine, and then went to Ozinda's and lost a guinea. About ten I went to the Spanish Ambassador's where I talked to the widow Pierson and about twelve walked home, but neglected to say my prayers.

5. I rose about 8 o'clock and read a chapter in Hebrew and some Greek in Lucian. I said my prayers, and had milk for breakfast. The weather was hot and clear, the wind southeast. I wrote a letter and about 10 o'clock Mr. Horsmanden came and stayed about half an hour. Then came Mr. Lindsay and I read a letter to him which I wrote to his wife. I ate some battered eggs for dinner. In the afternoon I put several things in order and then read some French till 4 o'clock, when my cousin Horsmanden came and we went in my chariot to the Tower and there took boat for Greenwich, where we went to the chocolate house and I drank two dishes of chocolate. Then we walked in the park till 9 o'clock, and then returned to London in our boat and went to the tavern where we had some lamb for supper and drank a bottle of French wine. About one o'clock we walked home, where I neglected our [sic] prayers, for which God forgive me.

6. I rose about 8 o'clock and read a chapter in Hebrew and some Greek in Lucian. I said my prayers, and had milk for breakfast. The weather was warm and clear, the wind northeast. I went not to church because I was to dine with Mr. Lindsay; accordingly I went there about 12 o'clock and ate some roast beef. After dinner I took a

little nap, that I might not sleep at church in the afternoon. About three we went to church and heard a good sermon about the resurrection. After church we went in Mr. Lindsay's chariot to G-r-s T-s-r on Blackheath where was abundance of company. I drank some chocolate. We could not walk in the park because it rained so we returned to London, where I ate some [r-g-s-c] and then went to the Spanish Ambassador's and stayed till twelve and then went home, but neglected my prayers.

7. I rose about 8 o'clock and found myself griped. I read a chapter in Hebrew and some Greek in Lucian. I said my prayers. It rained a little, the wind west. I wrote some Hebrew words till 2 o'clock and then I ate some battered eggs for dinner. In the afternoon I put several things in order and then took a nap till 5 o'clock and then came Daniel Horsmanden and stayed about half an hour. Then I went to Mrs. [Andrews'] but they were from home. Then I went to Mrs. B-r-n and stayed there till 7 o'clock and then went to walk in the park and joined Jenny [Noel] and walked with her and her cousin. Then I walked home and endeavored to pick up a woman but could not meet with one I liked, but went home about 11 o'clock and neglected my prayers, for which God forgive me.

8. I rose about 8 o'clock and read a chapter in Hebrew and some Greek in Lucian. I said my prayers and had milk for breakfast. The weather was clear and warm, the wind west. Mrs. Wilkinson brought me home some linen. About 11 o'clock I went to the Virginia Coffeehouse and from thence to dinner with Dick Perry, where I found Jack [Willis]. I ate some Virginia pork and drank some [r-m-t-k]. After dinner I wrote a letter to Mrs. Perry about the marriage of my mistress, Miss Smith, who was married this day. About four I returned home, after having laid out some five pounds in travel. I read some English and then went to visit Mrs. B-r-t and drank tea. Then I took a walk in the park and then went to Ozinda's where I bet and won two and a half guineas. About one I walked home and said my prayers.

9. I rose about 8 o'clock and read a chapter in Hebrew and some Greek in Lucian. I said my prayers and had milk for breakfast. The weather was cloudy and cold, the wind west. I danced my dance. About 11 o'clock came Daniel Horsmanden and stayed half an hour and then I went to Mrs. Southwell's and sat about an hour with her and then went to Ozinda's and won a guinea. About two I went to Colonel Blakiston's to dinner and ate some fried lamb. Mrs. Blakiston was indisposed. After dinner we sat with her till 5 o'clock and then I went to Mrs. B-r-n where was the woman that tells fortunes, to whom I gave a crown. Then I went to Will's Coffeehouse and drank a dish of chocolate, and about ten went to the bagnio and bathed and then lay all night with Annie Wilkinson and rogered her twice. I neglected my prayers.

10. I rose about 8 o'clock and went home, where I read a chapter in Hebrew and some Greek in Lucian. I said my prayers and had milk for breakfast. The weather was hot and clear, the wind west. I had several letters from Virginia. I danced my dance. I read some French till 1 o'clock and then I went into the City and dined at Pontack's and ate some fish. After dinner we went to Garraway's and drank a dish of tea, and then I paid my milliner for six neckcloths. Then I called upon my daughter and carried her to Colonel Blakiston's and from thence to Mrs. FitzHerbert's, who was not at home, so I sent my daughter home and walked in the park and then went to Ozinda's and won four and a half guineas, and about 12 o'clock walked home and met a woman by the way and committed uncleanness, for which God forgive me.

11. I rose about 8 o'clock and read a chapter in Hebrew and some Greek in Lucian. I said my prayers and had milk for breakfast. The weather was cloudy and warm. My neighbor Smith died last night. I danced my dance and then came Mr. G-l-n to persuade me to subscribe to his great pair of globes. About twelve I went to the Virginia Coffeehouse and Brigadier L-n-s-t-n with me. From thence I went to old Mr. Perry's and ate some roast beef with him. After dinner

we sat and talked about Virginia affairs. Then I walked to Garraway's Coffeehouse and read the news and about 4 o'clock went home and wrote some English and about six went to Will's Coffeehouse and played at piquet with Colonel Cecil and won a guinea. Then I drank a dish of chocolate and went to the Spanish Ambassador's where I stayed till 12 o'clock and then walked home and said my prayers.

12. I rose about 8 o'clock and read a chapter in Hebrew and some Greek in Lucian. I said my prayers and had milk for breakfast. The weather was cloudy and hot, the wind west. I wrote some English. My cousin Daniel came and told me he was going to Purleigh. About 2 o'clock I ate some battered eggs for dinner. In the afternoon I put several things in order till 5 o'clock and then went to Mrs. U-m-s where I drank tea and stayed till 8 o'clock and then went to Mrs. B-r-t where I found my Lord Tyrconnel.[3] Here I lent Mrs. B-r-t six guineas and stayed to supper, and about 12 o'clock walked home, notwithstanding it had rained. When I came home my man was fallen asleep and it was a good while before I got in. I neglected my prayers, for which God forgive me. It rained pretty much.

13. I rose about 5 o'clock to prepare for my journey to my Lord Orrery's. I read some Hebrew but no Greek. I said my prayers and had milk for breakfast. The weather was hot and clear. About 7 o'clock I went to Colonel Cecil's lodgings and then we went to know if Lord Boyle[4] had any command to his father and about nine we went in the coach and four horses to my Lord Orrery's, who lives two miles from Windsor.[5] We got there by 1 o'clock and saved our dinner, and I ate some young turkey. After dinner we drank tea and

3. Sir John Brownlow, 5th Bart., on June 23, 1718, was created Baron Charleville and Viscount Tyrconnel; he married his cousin, Eleanor, daughter of Sir John Brownlow, 3rd Bart., and Alice Sherard.

4. John Boyle, only son of the Earl of Orrery. He became 5th Earl Orrery in 1731, and in 1753 Earl of Cork.

5. Lord Orrery's home was Britwell.

about 5 o'clock rode out through abundance of pretty lanes and saw Burnham Common which is a pretty place. About seven we returned and walked in the garden till eight and then we went to supper and I ate some battered eggs. Then we walked for an hour and then went to bed and I said my prayers.

14. I rose about 7 o'clock and read a chapter in Hebrew and some Greek in Lucian. I said my prayers, and had cold milk for breakfast. The weather was hot and cloudy. About 8 o'clock my Lord Orrery came to me and soon after we went to breakfast, and I ate some milk, as I said before. When I was dressed Colonel Cecil and I played at billiards but he beat me. Then we played at piquet and he beat me, and then my Lord Orrery and P-g-y played at billiards against Colonel Cecil and me till 1 o'clock and then we went to dinner and I ate some stewed crab. After dinner Colonel Cecil and I played at piquet till 6 o'clock and I won a guinea. Then we rode out and saw the great house at Taplow[6] and returned about eight and before nine went to supper, and I ate some milk. Then we took a walk in the garden till ten and then we all retired to our chambers and I said my prayers.

15. I rose about 7 o'clock and read a chapter in Hebrew and some Greek. I said my prayers and about eight my Lord Orrery came to me and we went down to breakfast and I ate some milk. Then Colonel Cecil and I played at piquet and I lost two guineas. About one we went to dinner and I ate some veal and bacon. After dinner we played again at piquet and I lost a little. About 6 o'clock we rode out, notwithstanding it threatened rain and the wind blew violently, which made the dust very troublesome. About eight we returned and I ate some milk for supper and then we took a walk in the garden till 10 o'clock and then we retired to our chambers, where I read some English and said my prayers. I slept very well.

6. Cliveden (or Cliefden), home of the Earl of Orkney, now preserved by the National Trust.

16. I rose about 7 o'clock and read a chapter in Hebrew and some Greek. I said my prayers and had milk for breakfast. The weather continued clear and cold, the wind southwest. About nine Colonel Cecil went to London and then my Lord and I played at billiards. Then we played at bowls till dinner and I ate some roast veal. After dinner we played at piquet and P-g-y played with us. About six we were about to ride out but it began to rain and prevented us so we all three played a pool at piquet again till nine and then my Lord and I ate some pudding for supper. After supper we played again and I won a little. About ten we retired to our chambers, where I said my prayers and slept pretty well, thank God. It rained all night pretty much.

17. I rose about 7 o'clock and read a chapter in Hebrew and some Greek. I said my prayers, and had milk for breakfast. The weather was clear and cloudy, the wind west. I walked into the garden and read some English and danced my dance. About twelve we played at billiards till dinner and then I ate some roast goose. After dinner we played a pool at piquet till 5 o'clock and then drank tea till six and then my Lord and I rode out and found it very pleasant. About eight we returned home and I found I had scratched my cheek with a bramble. Then we played at piquet again and I lost a little. About nine we went to supper and I ate some battered eggs. After supper we played again at piquet till ten and then we parted. I said my prayers and slept pretty well, thank God.

18. I rose about 7 o'clock, and read a chapter in Hebrew and some Greek. I said my prayers, and ate some milk for breakfast. The weather was cloudy and it rained a little. I read the news and about 11 o'clock we played at billiards and about twelve came three parsons that my Lord had invited to dinner. We made them play at billiards with us till dinner and then I ate some mutton. After dinner we sat and talked till 4 o'clock and then drank tea. Then the three parsons went away and my Lord and P-g-y and I played at piquet till 6

o'clock and then we rode out for three or four miles and then returned and played at piquet again till supper, and then I ate some milk. Then we played at piquet till 10 o'clock and then went to bed. I said my prayers.

19. I rose about 6 o'clock and read a chapter in Hebrew and some Greek. I said my prayers and had milk for breakfast. The weather was cloudy and cold, the wind northwest. About 9 o'clock my Lord Orrery and I rode to my Lord Orkney's[7] at Cliveden but he was gone to London. The house and situation seem very fine. Then we returned home and played at billiards till dinner and I ate some roast mutton. After dinner we played at piquet till four and then we drank tea, and about five I took leave of my Lord Orrery and my Lady and returned to London, where I arrived without any accident about 9 o'clock and took a walk to pick up a woman but met with none to my mind. About eleven I went home and put several things in order. I neglected my prayers, for which God forgive me.

20. I rose about 7 o'clock and read a chapter in Hebrew and some Greek in Lucian. I said my prayers and had milk for breakfast. The weather was warm and cloudy, the wind northwest. About ten I went to see my Lord Boyle to give him a letter from his father. I likewise called on Colonel Blathwayt but he was from home. Then I went to church at Somerset Chapel where I slept away a pretty good sermon. After church I went home and ate some battered eggs for dinner. After dinner I put several things in order and read some English till 5 o'clock, and then went to Mrs. M-r-l-y and drank some tea. Then I went to Will's Coffeehouse and ate a jelly and about eight went to visit Mrs. B-r-t, and then went to the Spanish Ambassador's till twelve and then came home and said my prayers.

7. Lord George Hamilton, created Earl of Orkney, governor general of Virginia 1710-37, governor of Edinburgh Castle, and a lord of the bedchamber. Orkney never visited Virginia, but left the administration of the colony to his lieutenant governors.

21. I rose about 7 o'clock and read a chapter in Hebrew and some Greek in Homer. I said my prayers, and had milk for breakfast. The weather was warm and cloudy, the wind west. About 11 o'clock I went to visit Mrs. Southwell but everybody was out. Then I went into the City and read the news at Garraway's Coffeehouse and then went to dine with old Mr. Perry, where I found a letter from Virginia. I ate some roast mutton. After dinner I wrote a letter into the country and then went to visit my daughter whom I found in good health, thank God. Then I went to Lady Guise's where I stayed till 7 o'clock and then went to walk in the park, where I met Mr. C-p-r and then picked up two women and carried them to supper and ate some Scotch collops and then went with one of them to the bagnio and lay with her all night and rogered her three times to her great satisfaction.

22. I rose about 8 o'clock and went home and read a chapter in Hebrew and some Greek in Homer. I said my prayers and had milk for breakfast. About nine came John F-l to see me and then came my cousin Horsmanden and stayed about half an hour. I read some English till 2 o'clock and then ate some battered eggs for dinner. In the afternoon I put several things in order and then took a nap. About five I went to Mrs. C-r-y but she was from home; then to Mrs. [Sands'] and drank tea and stayed till 9 o'clock, and then went to Will's Coffeehouse and had two dishes of chocolate. Then I went to the Spanish Ambassador's where I talked a great deal to Mrs. Pierson, and about twelve went home in a chair and found some letters from Virginia. I neglected my prayers, for which God forgive me.

23. I rose about 8 o'clock and read two chapters in Hebrew and some Greek in Homer. I said my prayers, and had milk for breakfast. About nine came Mr. [Howe] to take measure of me for new clothes. About 11 o'clock I went into the City to the Virginia Coffeehouse and from thence I went to Mr. Perry's and dined with Dick, whose wife and daughter were come to town. I ate some pigeon pie. After dinner Mrs. Perry went out of town and I went to Mr. Lindsay's and

from thence made a visit to Mrs. U-m-s but they were from home. Then I went to Mrs. [Andrews'] but they were from home; then to Mrs. B-r-n where I sat about an hour and then went to walk in the park and joined my Lord Fairfax.[8] Then I went to Will's Coffeehouse and won a guinea and then went home and said my prayers.

24. I rose about 8 o'clock and read a chapter in Hebrew and some Greek in Homer. I said my prayers and had milk for breakfast. About nine came Captain Isham Randolph[9] and stayed about half an hour. I wrote more letters and read some English till 1 o'clock and then [went] to carry my daughter to dine with Mrs. U-m-s, where I ate some Virginia ham. After dinner we took a nap by consent and then we drank tea, when one Captain Hamilton[10] came in. About six I took leave and went with my daughter to the park where Mrs. [Noel] presented her with some fruit. Then I sent my daughter home and walked in St. James's Park where I met Mrs. [Noel] with Mrs. [. . .] and walked with them till 9 o'clock and then walked to Will's, where I ate a jelly and then walked home and neglected my prayers.

25. I rose about 6 o'clock and read a chapter in Hebrew and some Greek. I said my prayers and had milk for breakfast. The weather was cloudy and cold. About 8 o'clock Mr. [Lindsay] called on me and we went into his chariot drawn by four horses and we went to Uxbridge, where we dined and I ate some trout, for which this town is famous. This town lives only by the thoroughfare. In the afternoon we proceeded through Beaconsfield to Wycombe[11] and walked

8. Thomas, 6th Baron Fairfax of Cameron, was proprietor of the Northern Neck of Virginia.

9. Captain Isham Randolph, of Dungeness, in Virginia, third son of Colonel William Randolph I of Turkey Island.

10. Perhaps Robert Hamilton, a captain in Orkney's Regiment of Foot and probably a relative of Lord Orkney.

11. Almost the entire village of West Wycombe has been preserved by the National Trust.

up to the hill where had been a fortification. This place derives a great trade with [meal and malt]. We ate some roast mutton for supper, and then played at piquet and I lost ten shillings. About 10 o'clock we went to bed and I said my prayers. It rained in the night. My running began again.

26. I rose about 7 o'clock and read a little Greek. I neglected to say my prayers but had milk for breakfast. The weather was cloudy and cold. About 8 o'clock we got into the coach and passed by Little Wycombe where is a good house of Sir Francis Dashwood.[12] About 2 o'clock we got to Oxford, where we took a private lodging and ate some beefsteak to stay our stomachs. Then we walked about the town and played at piquet. About seven came Mrs. Lindsay and her mother. After talking about two hours we went to supper and I ate some rabbit and about 10 o'clock I went to my lodgings where I put several things in order and said my prayers. My running was violent.

27. I rose about 7 o'clock and read some Greek. I neglected my prayers, and had milk for breakfast. I was angry with my man for lying so long in bed. However I got ready to go to Mr. Lindsay's about nine and sat with them till ten and then we went to Saint Mary's to church and heard a good sermon. After church we walked home and invited Dr. G-r-n-d-s to dine with us, who was very obliging. After dinner we drank tea and about 4 o'clock we went to Magdalene College Chapel where we had an anthem well performed. Then we walked in the garden and Magdalene Grove and then went to Dr. G-r-n-d-s chambers and had wine and fruit. We went to the Physic Garden and then walked home and had roast duck for supper and Mr. C-t-s-r supped with us. About ten I went home and said my prayers. My running was extremely bad.

12. Sir Francis Dashwood, created a baronet in 1707. His house at West Wycombe now belongs to the National Trust. His son, a notorious profligate, founded the 'Order of the Monks of Medmenham' and helped to found the Dilettante Society.

28. I rose about 7 o'clock and read some Greek. I said a short prayer, and had milk for breakfast. My running was very bad. The weather was warm and cloudy. About 10 o'clock we went to Mr. C-t-s-r chambers where we had tea. Then we went to see several colleges and other rarities till dinner and then I ate some boiled mutton. After dinner we drank tea till 4 o'clock and then we had Mr. Tryon[13] and Mr. F-l-x come in, who went with us to see more colleges and other places. We found the Duke of Portland[14] at the public library and I spoke to him. In the evening we walked in Merton Grove and then went home, where we played at commerce and then went to supper and I ate some cold chicken. We sat till 11 o'clock and then parted and I said my prayers.

29. I rose about 7 o'clock and read some Greek and wrote some English. I said my prayers and had milk for breakfast. It rained almost all the morning. However about 11 o'clock we all went to the library where we saw abundance of rarities, particularly some rare manuscripts and medals. Here we spent two hours and then went to Magdalene College to dine with Dr. G-r-n-d-s and were well entertained. I ate some roast mutton. After dinner we drank tea and then walked round Magdalene College meadow. Then we went to Christ Church to the chambers of Mr. Tryon who afterwards carried us to see the library of that college which was small but pretty. Then we went to see the great bell over the gateway. Then we played at cards till supper and I ate some roast duck. Then we played and were merry till 11 o'clock and then I went home and said my prayers. My running continued bad.

30. I rose about 7 o'clock and read a chapter in Hebrew and some Greek. I said my prayers and ate some milk for breakfast. About 9 o'clock I drank two dishes of chocolate and about ten we went to

13. Charles Tryon, son of Charles Tryon of Bulwich, Northamptonshire, matriculated at Christ Church, September 2, 1717, aged 14.

14. Henry Bentinck, created Duke of Portland in 1715, a lord of the bedchamber.

Blenheim [15] with two coaches and four horses. About twelve we got there and saw the house and garden which were extremely fine. We then saw the bridge which was also fine and remarkable for the middle arch and the engine to raise the water. We went about two hours and then went to the [Bear] Inn to dinner and I ate some boiled mutton. After dinner we stayed till 6 o'clock, and then came back to Oxford, and then walked in Merton Grove and about nine went to supper and I ate some roast rabbit. About ten I took leave and then took a walk.

31. I rose about 6 o'clock and read some Greek. I said my prayers and ate some milk for breakfast. When we came to pay the reckoning Mr. Lindsay would not let me pay anything but for my lodging and for the milk I had had for breakfast. About 9 o'clock we took leave of Mrs. Lindsay and her mother and returned home by Henley, where we dined, and I ate some boiled pigeon. I won two parties at piquet of Mr. Lindsay. About 6 o'clock we proceeded to Windsor, where we had roast duck for supper and about twelve went to bed, but I neglected to say my prayers, for which God of his excessive goodness forgive me. We arrived here so late we could not see Windsor Castle. My running continued bad.

15. Blenheim was the seat of the Duke of Marlborough. A description of the house and the bridge in May 1717 may be found in Thomas Hearne, *Remarks and Collections* (Oxford, 1902), VI, 57.

August 1718

1. I rose about 5 o'clock and made a shift to get away from hence about six. I neglected to say my prayers, for which God forgive me. About nine we breakfasted at Islip and Mr. Sh-y and I drank two

dishes of chocolate. About ten we proceeded to London, where I found several letters from Virginia, by which I learned that all was well, thank God. I had likewise two letters out of the country. I read some English till 3 o'clock and then ate some battered eggs for dinner. In the afternoon I put several things in order till 5 o'clock and then came my cousin Horsmanden and we went together to see my daughter, who was not well, but was indisposed with the [measles]; however, she was pretty well again, thank God. Then we went to Misses [Sands'] and drank tea with them and stayed till 7 o'clock, and then took a walk with him in the park, where was very little company. We endeavored to pick up some girls but were disappointed. Then I went to the coffeehouse and read the news and walked home about 11 o'clock and said my prayers. My running was better, because I used the injection.

2. I rose about 7 o'clock and read a chapter in Hebrew and some Greek in Homer. I said my prayers, and had milk for breakfast. The weather was warm and cloudy, the wind west. About 10 o'clock came Mr. Southwell and I told him I could not possibly go with him to France, for which he seemed to be very much concerned. He stayed with me till twelve and invited me to dinner. I wrote a letter and about 2 o'clock went to Mr. Southwell's and ate some boiled veal. After dinner he gave us a bottle of [spruce] wine. About 5 o'clock I took leave and went to Lady Guise's where I stayed till 7 o'clock and then went to St. James's Park where I picked up a woman that was with a child and went home with her and committed uncleanness with her, and then walked home and neglected my prayers.

3. I rose about 7 o'clock and read a chapter in Hebrew and some Greek in Homer. I said my prayers, and had milk for breakfast. The weather was cloudy and warm. About 11 o'clock I went to Somerset Chapel and heard an indifferent sermon. After church I returned home and wrote some English till 2 o'clock and then ate some battered eggs. After dinner I put several things in order and then wrote more English till 5 o'clock, when I went to visit Mrs. B-r-t and she

told me she was going to France. While I was there my Lady Cust [1] came. Then I went to Mrs. FitzHerbert's and stayed with her all the evening and ate some cold veal for supper. About ten I walked to Will's Coffeehouse and stayed till eleven and then walked home and said my prayers, &c.

4. I rose about 7 o'clock and read a chapter in Hebrew and some Greek in Homer. I said my prayers, and had milk for breakfast. About nine came a parson that intended for Virginia and desired my recommendation. I wrote some English till 11 o'clock and then went to visit my daughter, whom I found pretty well again, thank God. Then I went into the City and dined with Mr. Perry and found abundance of letters from Virginia. I ate some roast mutton. After dinner I read my letters and wrote one to Colonel Blakiston at Tunbridge. About 5 o'clock I went home and put several things in order till six and then went to Mrs. B-r-n where I drank coffee. Then I walked in the park and lay with a woman on the grass. Then I went to Will's Coffeehouse and lost two guineas at piquet. About twelve I went home and neglected my prayers.

5. I rose about 7 o'clock and read a chapter in Hebrew and some Greek in Homer. I said my prayers and had milk for breakfast. The weather was hot and clear, the wind west. Annie Wilkinson came and brought me some linen. About 11 o'clock I went into the City to the Virginia Coffeehouse and went with Jack [Willis] to Captain Randolph's to dinner and he gave us a Virginia ham and chicken. There we saw his lady, a pretty kind of woman. After dinner we drank some rack punch and Jack Carter [2] came to us. About 7 o'clock we returned and I walked home and picked up two women and committed uncleanness with the last of them because the first would not. I gave the last a mutton cutlet and some Rhenish wine. About eleven I went home and repented of what I had done and begged pardon of God Almighty.

1. Anne, daughter of Sir William Brownlow, 4th Bart., wife of Sir Richard Cust, 2nd Bart.

2. Son of Robert ('King') Carter of Corotoman, Virginia, and a student at one of the Inns of Court.

6. I rose about 7 o'clock and read a chapter in Hebrew and some Greek in Homer. I said my prayers, and had milk for breakfast. The weather was cloudy and warm, the wind west. I wrote some English till 11 o'clock and then went to visit my Lord Orrery but found him not at home; however, I saw his housekeeper and told her I would come again. Then I went to Mr. Blathwayt's and carried him a bill of exchange from Virginia. Then I went to Mr. Southwell's; then to my Lord Orrery's again; then to Ozinda's, where I read the news, and then to Mr. Southwell's to dinner, where I ate some goose, and Ned Blount[3] dined with us. After dinner we drank tea and about five I took leave of Mr. Southwell and wished him a good voyage to France. Then I went to Will's Coffeehouse, where I stayed all the evening and played at piquet and won a guinea, and about 11 o'clock walked home and said my prayers.

7. I rose about 7 o'clock and read a chapter in Hebrew and some Greek in Homer. I said my prayers, and had milk for breakfast. The weather was cold and cloudy, the wind west. I wrote some English till 11 o'clock and then came Captain John Turner. About 12 o'clock I went to the Virginia Coffeehouse and from thence to Mr. John [Willis'] to dine where I saw his brother, just come from Virginia. I ate some roast pork for dinner. In the afternoon we drank some rack punch till five and then I took leave and went to Leveridge's Coffeehouse, where I met my Lord Dunkellen and discoursed him about his good sister. Then I went to Will's Coffeehouse and played at piquet and lost a guinea to Colonel Cecil. I ate two jellies. About twelve I walked home and said my prayers.

8. I rose about 7 o'clock and read a chapter in Hebrew and some Greek in Homer. I said my prayers, and had milk for breakfast. The weather was warm and clear. My bookcase came home. About 12 o'clock I went to my Lord Orrery's but he was from home, so I sat with the housekeeper about half an hour but he came not, so I re-

3. Edward Blount, whose wife, Anne, was a sister of Lord Guise.

turned home again, where I put some of my books into my new case. About 2 o'clock I ate some battered eggs for dinner. In the afternoon I put several things in order and was busy again with my books till 5 o'clock, when I went to visit Daniel Horsmanden, and about six went to Will's Coffeehouse and from thence to St. James's Park where I walked with my old friend Mr. O-r-d till it was dark and then I picked up a woman and walked with her upon the grass and a man came and took my sword from my side in great fury, but after much swaggering he gave it me again, when he found he could not fright me. Then I walked home and said my prayers.

9. I rose about 7 o'clock and read a chapter in Hebrew and some Greek. I said my prayers, and had milk for breakfast. The weather was very hot and clear, the wind west. I never was so uneasy with the heat since I came to England. I wrote a letter into the country. About 1 o'clock came my Lord Orrery and sat with me about half an hour. I ate some broiled chicken for dinner. In the afternoon I put several things in order and settled my books in order. About five I went to Mrs. D-n-s where I drank tea and ate some wafers. Then I read to them some things of my own writing which they all commended extremely. We were very merry till 11 o'clock and then I went home and by the way set Mr. F-r-y home, who was with us. I said my prayers.

10. I rose about 7 o'clock and read a chapter in Hebrew and some Greek in Homer. I said my prayers, and had milk for breakfast. It was very hot again and clear, the wind southeast. I wrote a long letter to Virginia. It was exceedingly hot. About 2 o'clock I went to Mr. Blathwayt's to dinner and ate some roast beef. After dinner we drank a bottle of Burgundy and then had some tea. About 6 o'clock I went to visit Misses [Sands] and sat with them till 7 o'clock and then took a walk in the park and walked with Mrs. D-n-s. On my return I met with an old acquaintance and took her into the coach and lay with her, for which God forgive me. I neglected to say my prayers.

11. I rose about 7 o'clock and read a chapter in Hebrew and some Greek. I said my prayers and had milk for breakfast. The weather was cloudy and warm, the wind southeast and blowing pretty hard, which made it cooler. About 11 o'clock I went to visit my daughter and found her pretty well, thank God. Then I went to Mr. Lindsay's in the City but he was from home. Then I went and dined with old Mr. Perry and ate some minced veal. After dinner I read some letters from Virginia. About 3 o'clock I went to Mrs. Cole and sat an hour with her, and then went to visit Daniel Horsmanden who had a sore leg. Then I went to Lady Guise's and stayed there till 8 o'clock and then went to Mrs. B-r-t and stayed till ten and then I walked home and said my prayers.

12. I rose about 7 o'clock and read a chapter in Hebrew and some Greek. I said my prayers, and had milk for breakfast. The weather was clear and cold, the wind southeast. About 9 o'clock came Parson L-c-y and I gave him a [note again?]. I wrote a long letter to Virginia. Then I danced my dance and read some English till 2 o'clock, when I ate some battered eggs. After dinner I put several things in order and then wrote another letter to Virginia. About 5 o'clock I went to Mrs. B-r-n but she had taken physic and was not to be seen. Then I went to Mrs. C-r-l but she was from home. Then I went to my Aunt Sherard and sat with her till 7 o'clock, and then took a walk in the park till 9 o'clock, and then went to Will's Coffeehouse where I had a cake and some milk. Then I played at piquet with Colonel Cecil and won a guinea. About 12 o'clock I went home and said my prayers. I dreamed I rogered my Lady Des Bouverie.

13. I rose about 8 o'clock and read a chapter in Hebrew and some Greek in Homer. I said my prayers, and had milk for breakfast. The weather was cold and cloudy, the wind southeast. I wrote a letter and about 11 o'clock went to visit my cousin Horsmanden and found him better. From him I went into the City and dined with my friend Mr. Lindsay who had lately lost nine hundred pounds and was in a spleen about it. I ate some roast veal. After dinner I went away be-

cause the man came in that was to pay him the money. Then I went to the coffeehouse and drank a dish of tea and about 4 o'clock returned home and wrote a letter and about six went to Will's Coffeehouse and went from thence with my Lord Fairfax to the park and walked till seven and then went to Mrs. FitzHerbert's where I met Mrs. Southwell and little mistress. I ate some roast rabbit and drank some punch till I was drunk. I walked home and endeavored to pick up a whore but could not, so went home.

14. I rose about 7 o'clock and found myself indisposed after my debauch. However, I read a chapter in Hebrew and Greek in Homer. I said my prayers, and had milk for breakfast. The weather was cloudy and warm. I wrote two letters to Virginia and danced my dance. I read some English till 2 o'clock and read some letters likewise and then ate battered eggs for dinner. After dinner I put several things in order till 3 o'clock and then wrote another letter to Virginia. About 5 o'clock I wrote a letter to my milliner. Then I went to Mrs. B-r-t and drank tea till seven and then walked in the park with Mrs. D-n-s and Mrs. [Noel]. Then I picked up a woman and went home with her and ate some mutton steak and committed uncleanness. About one o'clock I went home and neglected my prayers.

15. I rose about 7 o'clock and read a chapter in Hebrew and some Greek in Homer. I said my prayers and had milk for breakfast. The weather was clear and warm, the wind west. I danced my dance and then wrote a letter to Virginia. About 11 o'clock I went with my cousin Horsmanden, that I met by the way, to see my daughter, whom I found very well, thank God. Then I went to dine with Mr. Perry and ate some chicken and bacon. After dinner I wrote a letter to Virginia and then went home and settled several accounts till 6 o'clock and then went to Mrs. B-r-n and drank some coffee with her. Then I walked in the park with some merry ladies and then went to the bagnio with Annie Wilkinson and rogered her but once and about 12 o'clock went home and said a short prayer. It rained in the night.

16. I rose about 8 o'clock and read a chapter in Hebrew and some Greek in Homer. I said my prayers and had milk for breakfast. The weather was cloudy and cold, the wind northwest. About eleven I went to visit Mrs. Southwell and found her not. Then I went to my cousin Horsmanden and found him pretty well so that we resolved to go to Tunbridge tomorrow. I dined with him and ate some roast pig. After dinner we went into the City and sat half an hour with Molly Cole and then went home and prepared for my journey. In the evening I went to visit Mrs. A-l-n, a mistress of mine, and she treated me with a bottle of Rhenish wine and I rogered her well and gave her a guinea. About 11 o'clock I went home and neglected to say my prayers.

17. I rose about 5 o'clock and got everything ready for our journey. I ate a seed cake and about 6 o'clock we set out with six horses for Tunbridge. I said a short prayer. We stopped at Farnborough and I ate some milk. Then we proceeded to Sevenoaks where we had some roast goose for dinner. Here Ned Jeffreys overtook us. About 3 o'clock we set out from hence and about five got to Tunbridge and found that Mrs. Blakiston had taken lodgings for us on Mount Sion. We went upon the Walk where I saw abundance of men of my acquaintance and some ladies. I stayed till 9 o'clock and then walked home and supped with Mrs. Blakiston and ate some roast beef. I put my things in order and said my prayers.

18. I rose about 7 o'clock and read a chapter in Hebrew and some Greek. I neglected my prayers, but had milk for breakfast. The weather was cold and cloudy. I wrote some English till 11 o'clock and then we went upon the Walk and I played and won two guineas and talked to several ladies till 2 o'clock, and then we dined with Mrs. Blakiston and ate some roast fowl for dinner. After dinner we went to see the cold baths and walked about the place till 5 o'clock, and then we returned again to the Walk where I played again and won two guineas more. I talked to several ladies till 9 o'clock, and then we went home and ate some apple pasties. Then I went to my chamber

and wrote some English till eleven and then said my prayers. I slept very indifferently.

19. I rose about 7 o'clock and read a chapter in Hebrew and some Greek. I neglected my prayers, and had milk for breakfast. The weather was cold and cloudy, the wind west. I wrote a letter to Virginia and about 12 o'clock we went upon the Walk and I played and lost a little. I gave five shillings to a poor man whose house had been burnt. I talked a pretty deal to Mrs. W-l-s. About 2 o'clock we went home to dinner and I ate some roast rabbit. After dinner I wrote some English till 5 o'clock and then went upon the Walk and played a little and won what I lost in the morning. About 10 o'clock we went to the play and afterwards to the public ball, where we stayed till 11 o'clock and then came home and ate some apple pie for supper. I said my prayers.

20. I rose about 6 o'clock and read a chapter in Hebrew and some Greek. I said my prayers, and had milk for breakfast. The weather was cold and cloudy, the wind northwest. About 9 o'clock we went to see the iron furnace about five miles off, where I learnt the whole process of melting iron. By the way we were almost stuck fast in a narrow lane. About 12 o'clock we returned to the Walk where I played and lost eleven guineas to Mrs. Bellenden and my Lady Dorset. [4] About two I went home to dinner and I ate some fish. Daniel Horsmanden dined with my Lady Chapman. [5] After dinner I made a visit to Mrs. Jeffreys and drank tea and then went to the Walk where I talked to Mrs. B-n-y and her daughter and to my Lady Herbert [6] and about ten went home and ate some broiled mutton for sup-

4. Elizabeth, daughter of Lieutenant General Colyear, wife of the 7th Earl (later 1st Duke) of Dorset. Maid of honor to Queen Anne and first lady of the bedchamber and mistress of the robes to Caroline as Princess of Wales and Queen. Her home was at Knole, Sevenoaks, Kent.

5. Elizabeth, daughter of Thomas Webb, wife of Sir William Chapman, a director of the South Sea Company.

6. Mary, daughter of John Wallop, wife of Henry, Baron Herbert of Cherbury; first lady of the bedchamber to Anne, Princess of Orange.

per. I had a looseness all day and it worked four times. I said my prayers.

21. I rose about 7 o'clock and read a chapter in Hebrew and some Greek. I neglected my prayers, and had milk for breakfast. The weather was cold and clear. I wrote some English and about 11 o'clock went to church. I lent my coach to Daniel Horsmanden to make a visit. After church I went upon the Walk, where I played and lost a guinea. Then I talked with several women till 2 o'clock and then went home to dinner and I ate some rabbit and onions. After dinner I put several things in order till 4 o'clock and then I wrote some English till five and then fell asleep. About six I went to the wells where I found Miss B-n-y and joined her and then walked with several till about eight and then sat with my Mrs. W-l-s. About nine we came home, ate some beef for supper. I said my prayers.

22. I rose about 7 o'clock and read a chapter in Hebrew and some Greek. I neglected my prayers and had milk for breakfast. The weather was clear and cold. I wrote some English till 12 o'clock and then we went upon the Walk where I was out of humor very much. I played and lost three guineas. About 2 o'clock I went to dine with my Lord Dunkellen and ate some roast partridge for dinner. In the afternoon we sat and talked and my Lady told me abundance about my Lord's playing and drinking and desired to speak with me alone. About five I took leave and returned to the Walk and walked about till 7 o'clock and then played at piquet till nine with Mrs. Pulteney [7] and won two guineas and then played at hazard and won one guinea more, and went home about eleven and ate some broiled mutton for supper. I said my prayers. Colonel Blakiston came down this evening.

23. I rose about 7 o'clock and read a chapter in Hebrew and some Greek. I neglected my prayers, but had milk for breakfast. The weather was clear and very hot, the wind southwest. I wrote some

7. Wife of Daniel Pulteney, a Lord Commissioner of Trade.

English till eleven and then we went to church; then went upon the Walk and played at piquet again with Mrs. Pulteney and lost two guineas. About two I went home and ate some fish for dinner. After dinner I drank tea with Mrs. Jeffreys and then returned again to the Walk and walked about till 7 o'clock and then played again at piquet and lost a guinea to Mrs. Pulteney. About 8 o'clock we went to the ball and saw them dance and talked to several women, and about twelve came home and ate some minced veal for supper. I said my prayers.

24. I rose about 7 o'clock and read a chapter in Hebrew and some Greek. I neglected my prayers, but had milk for breakfast. The weather was clear and warm, the wind southwest. I wrote some English till 10 o'clock and then we went to the Walk in my chariot where we walked about half an hour and then went to church where we had a good sermon and abundance of company. After church we returned to the Walk and stayed till one and then went home and ate some boiled beef for dinner. After dinner I wrote more English till 4 o'clock and then we went again to church and heard another sermon. Then we went to the Walk where I drank two dishes of chocolate and walked with several ladies and particularly with Mrs. C-p-r with whom we drank a cold tankard. I walked with her and Mrs. B-n-y. About nine we went home and ate some cold beef for supper and were very merry. I said my prayers &c.

25. I rose about 7 o'clock and read nothing because I finished a lampoon.[8] I neglected my prayers, but had milk for breakfast. The weather was clear till 11 o'clock and then it rained a good shower. However, we went to church and then upon the Walk where I played at the ace of hearts and lost three guineas. About two o'clock we returned to dinner and ate some roast pigeon. After dinner I was very sleepy and took a nap and about 4 o'clock we went with Mrs. Jeffreys and Miss A-s-t-n to see the rocks, and about six returned to

8. Some of the verses Byrd wrote in Tunbridge were printed in *Tunbrigalia* in 1719. See *Another Secret Diary of William Byrd*, 399-409.

the wells where I stayed about half an hour and then was sent for by my Lady Dunkellen to tell me her misfortunes. I gave her the best advice I could and about eight returned to the wells where I walked much with Mrs. C-p-r and about eleven came home and ate a cold pigeon for supper, and we drank a bottle of champagne. About one o'clock we retired and I neglected my prayers.

26. I rose about 7 o'clock and read a chapter in Hebrew and some Greek. I neglected my prayers but had milk for breakfast. The weather was cloudy and warm. I wrote some English till 10 o'clock and then went upon the Walk and from thence to church, and then returned to the Walk again, where I read the lampoon to several ladies and gentlemen and particularly to Mr. Pulteney and his lady. I played at piquet with one of the Cornishes and won two guineas and about 2 o'clock went home to dinner and ate some fish. After dinner we drank a bottle of champagne and then I wrote some English till five and then went to the Walk and treated Mrs. Pulteney and Mrs. O-r-n-y. In the evening I went to the ball and danced there a French dance and then walked home with Mrs. C-p-r and then walked home and said my prayers.

27. I rose about 6 o'clock and read a chapter in Hebrew and some Greek. I neglected to say my prayers and ate some milk for breakfast. The weather was cloudy and warm. About 8 o'clock we went in my chariot and six horses to see Penshurst, the house of my Lord Leicester[9] where there was very good pictures. About twelve we returned to the wells where I lost a guinea at piquet to Mrs. Cornish. I ate some boiled chicken for dinner. In the afternoon I took a nap till 4 o'clock, when I beat my man Ralph because he was out of the way. About six we walked to the wells, where I talked to abundance of women and particularly to Mrs. [Cambridge], whom I love dearly. I treated several ladies with jellies and about 11 o'clock walked home and ate some apple pie for supper. I neglected my prayers.

9. John, 6th Earl of Leicester, a lord of the bedchamber.

28. I rose about 6 o'clock and read nothing because I was obliged to get ready to wait on Mrs. B-n-y to Penshurst. I neglected to say my prayers but had boiled milk for breakfast. The weather was clear and hot. About 8 o'clock we called on Mrs. B-n-y and her fair daughter and went to Penshurst in my coach and six horses and saw the pictures and drank chocolate, and about 11 o'clock returned and got to the Walk by one and played and lost eighteen guineas. About 2 o'clock we went to dine with Mr. M-l-n-r and he gave us a haunch of venison and treated us very handsomely. About 4 o'clock I went home and put up my things and about five went to the wells where I treated several ladies with tea and Mrs. Pulteney among the rest. Miss B-n-y said something to desire us to stay to dine tomorrow at the [Fishpond]. Therefore we resolved to stay. I ate jelly and several things and about 11 o'clock went home and said my prayers. My throat was very sore.

29. I rose about 7 o'clock and read a chapter in Hebrew and some Greek. I neglected my prayers and had milk for breakfast. The weather was cold and cloudy and about 10 o'clock it rained. About eleven I went to church in the chariot and after church walked upon the Walk but did not play. I talked abundance to Mrs. C-p-r. About 2 o'clock I carried Mrs. Masters to Mrs. B-n-y in my coach and six and then waited on them to the [Fishpond] where we entertained very handsomely and I ate some stewed crab. We entertained them abundantly with a blind harper and a juggler. After dinner we walked in the garden and about seven went to the Walk and stared with the rest upon an eclipse of the moon. I talked with several women and treated Miss M-n-l-f and Miss N-n-m. About ten we took leave of the Walk and went home to receive the good wishes of Colonel Blakiston and his lady, with whom we sat up till eleven. I neglected my prayers, for which God forgive me.

30. I rose about 4 o'clock and prepared for my journey, and about six we took leave and went away in my coach and six. I said my prayers but ate nothing. The weather was cold and clear, and the dust

was laid. We gave the horses some hay and our people some breakfast at Sevenoaks but we ate nothing. About 8 o'clock we proceeded to Farnborough, where we got about ten and there we baited the horses and ate some ham and bread and butter. We stayed here till 1 o'clock and then went to make G-r-s T-s-r a visit where we drank some rack punch. About 2 o'clock we proceeded to London and I got home about 4 o'clock and found everything in order, thank God. I unpacked my things and changed my clothes and then read some English till 7 o'clock and then went to Mrs. A-l-n where I ate some broiled fowl for supper and then went to bed and rogered her once. I got up again about twelve and walked home, where I neglected to say my prayers, for which God forgive me. My throat continued sore.

31. I rose about 8 o'clock and read a chapter in Hebrew and some Greek in Homer. I neglected my prayers, but had boiled milk for breakfast. I quarreled with my man Ralph for telling me a lie and gave him warning. About 11 o'clock I went to Somerset Chapel and heard a good sermon. After church I dined with Mrs. U-m-s and ate some roast beef. I found P-n-y pretty well again, thank God. After dinner we sat and talked till four and then came Mrs. M-r-l-y and her sister and we drank tea till five when I called at Will's Coffeehouse and took Mr. O-r-d and went with him to Kensington Garden where I saw Mrs. [Cambridge] and several others of our Tunbridge acquaintants. Then I set Mr. O-r-d down at Will's and read the news and then went home and took some boiled milk. I neglected to say my prayers.

September 1718

1. I rose about 7 o'clock and read a chapter in Hebrew and some Greek in Homer. I said my prayers, and had boiled milk for breakfast. The weather was cloudy and warm, the wind southwest. I danced my dance. I wrote a letter to Virginia and some other things till about 2 o'clock. I went to dine with Mr. U-t-n and one Mr. D-l-t-n dined there likewise. I ate some boiled fowl and bacon. After dinner we drank a bottle of wine till 5 o'clock and then I went to visit Mrs. U-m-s and drank coffee with them. About 6 o'clock I went to visit Mrs. M-r-l-y but she was from home. Then I went to Lady Guise's and stayed there till about 9 o'clock and then went home because of my sore throat and read some English. I said my prayers, &c.

2. I rose about 7 o'clock and read a chapter in Hebrew and some Greek in Homer. I said my prayers, and had boiled milk for breakfast. The weather was cloudy and it rained pretty much about 9 o'clock. About 7 o'clock [*sic*] I went to Mrs. U-m-s and carried them to Fulham in my Lady Stanley's coach to dine with the Bishop of London [1] and ate some ragout. After dinner we walked in the garden and ate some fruit and about five we drank a dish of chocolate to keep us from fainting. Then we returned to London and I walked in the park and then walked to Will's Coffeehouse and read the news and then walked home; but by the way I picked up a young girl and carried her to the tavern and gave her some mutton cutlets and committed uncleanness with her, and then walked home and neglected my prayers.

3. I rose about 7 o'clock and wrote a letter to Colonel Blakiston. Then I read a chapter in Hebrew and some Greek in Homer. I said my prayers and had boiled milk for breakfast. About 8 o'clock came

1. John Robinson, Bishop of London.

Captain [Willis] and stayed about half an hour and then came Daniel Horsmanden who was going to Tunbridge again to endeavor to get Miss B-n-y and I lent him thirty guineas for his expedition. About 11 o'clock I went to see P-n-y U-m-s and went from thence into the City and dined with Dick Perry, where I saw my daughter, who was perfectly well, thank God. I ate some boiled tongue for dinner. In the afternoon I wrote a letter to Virginia and about 5 o'clock went to Mr. Lindsay's, but he was from home, so I went to Mr. [Philips] where I found Will [Tryon] and Dr. T-s-n and drank some tea, and about six went to my Lord Percival's, who was just come from France, but found them not. Then I went home and wrote two letters, ate some milk, and said my prayers.

4. I rose about 8 o'clock and read a chapter in Hebrew and some Greek in Homer. I said my prayers, and had boiled milk for breakfast. The weather was cloudy and it rained pretty much but held up again before eleven, when I went to visit Mrs. Southwell, but she was from home. Then I went to my Lord Orrery's and found him at home and had a dish of chocolate. Then I went to Mrs. LeGrande's but she was gone out of town; then to Ozinda's, where I read the news, and then returned to Lord Orrery's to dinner and ate some fish. After dinner we sat and talked till five and then went to the coffeehouse, from whence I went to visit Mrs. C-p-r and stayed till 9 o'clock and then went home and wrote more letters to Virginia and then said my prayers.

5. I rose about 7 o'clock and read a chapter in Hebrew and some Greek in Homer. I said my prayers, and had boiled milk for breakfast. The weather was clear and warm, the wind southwest. I danced my dance and then wrote a long letter till 2 o'clock, when I ate some battered eggs for dinner. In the afternoon I put several things in order and then wrote more English till 5 o'clock, when I went to visit Mrs. B-r-n but her husband was sick, so I could not see her. Then I went to Mrs. C-r-l and found Brigadier C-r-l come home. Here I stayed half an hour and then went to Mrs. [Sands] and sat there half an hour and then went and walked in the park. About 8 o'clock I went

to take leave of Mrs. U-m-s and about nine went home and ate some boiled milk. I said my prayers and read some English.

6. I rose about 7 o'clock and read a chapter in Hebrew and some Greek in Homer. I said my prayers and had boiled milk for breakfast. The weather was clear and cold, the wind east. I wrote several letters and about 11 o'clock went to visit Mrs. Southwell but she was gone to Richmond. Then I returned home because I saw my Lord Orrery's coach go toward my lodgings, but I missed him. I wrote more letters till 2 o'clock, and then ate some battered eggs for dinner. After dinner I put several things in order and wrote another letter. About 5 o'clock I went to Will's Coffeehouse and there I agreed with Lord Orrery to go with him tomorrow into the country. Then I played at piquet with Colonel Cecil and won two guineas and about 10 o'clock went home and said my prayers and ate some milk and cake for supper.

7. I rose about 7 o'clock and read a chapter in Hebrew and some Greek in Homer. I said my prayers, and had boiled milk for breakfast. The weather was cold and cloudy. I paid Mr. O-f-l-n his account to this day and put several things in order and prepared to go out of town, and about 1 o'clock I went first to my Lady Guise's and stayed about half an hour and then went to my Lord Orrery's, where I ate some boiled chicken for dinner, and Colonel Cecil dined with us and gave us a bottle of champagne. After dinner we drank tea and about 4 o'clock I went out of town with my Lord in his coach and six and about eight got to his house in the country, where I ate some milk for supper. Then we took a walk in the garden, notwithstanding it was dark, and about 9 o'clock retired and I said my prayers.

8. I rose about 6 o'clock and first shaved myself, then read a chapter in Hebrew, and then went down and ate some milk for breakfast. The weather was clear and warm, the wind east. I walked a turn in the garden; then I read some Greek and wrote a letter to Virginia; then we played at billiards and then at bowls till about 2 o'clock, and

then we went to dinner and I ate some boiled mutton. After dinner we played at billiards again, and then drank tea, and then rode out for about an hour, and when we returned I walked by myself in the garden for an hour. When it was dark we played at piquet till 8 o'clock, and then I ate some pudding for supper, and then we played at piquet again till nine, and then we retired and I said my prayers. My sore throat continued bad.

9. I rose about 6 o'clock and I shaved myself, and then read a chapter in Hebrew and some Greek. Then I went down and ate some milk for breakfast. The weather was clear and warm. I cut my finger, which bled very much. I wrote a letter to Virginia, and then we played at billiards and bowls till dinner and then I ate some roast veal. After dinner we played again at billiards till 4 o'clock and then drank tea. Then we rode out till six and then I walked by myself in the garden till seven and then we played at piquet till eight and then ate some broiled turkey for supper. While we ate Colonel Cecil came. After supper I lost a guinea to Colonel Cecil at piquet. About ten we retired and I said my prayers. My throat continued bad.

10. I rose about 6 o'clock and read a chapter in Hebrew and some Greek. I neglected to say my prayers, but had milk for breakfast. The weather was clear and warm. About 9 o'clock Colonel Cecil and I sat down to piquet again and played five parties and I won a guinea. I danced my dance, and then played at bowls till dinner, and then ate some boiled pork. After dinner we drank tea and about 4 o'clock my Lord and I rode two miles with Colonel Cecil and then came round by the lane home. Then I took a walk and danced my dance again. In the evening we played at piquet and about eight we supped and I ate some apple pie. After supper we played again at piquet till nine and then we retired. I said my prayers. My throat continued sore.

11. I rose about 6 o'clock and read a chapter in Hebrew and some Greek. I said my prayers and had milk for breakfast. The weather was clear and cold, the wind east. My man came late to me, which made me angry with him. I danced my dance and then wrote a letter to Virginia. About twelve we played at billiards and then at bowls

till dinner, when I ate some roast duck. After dinner we played at billiards again till 4 o'clock, and then drank tea, and then rode out. Then I walked about an hour in the garden. In the evening we played at cards and I won about six shillings. About 8 o'clock we ate some sausage paste for supper and after supper played again at piquet till 12 o'clock. I said my prayers. My throat continued sore.

12. I rose about 6 o'clock but read nothing because I prepared to go visit my Lord Harry Powlett. However I ate some milk for breakfast and about 7 o'clock got on horseback and went through Maidenhead and through Henley and as far as Nettlebed and about 10 o'clock got to my Lord Powlett's and drank some chocolate. Then we walked in the garden and talked till one o'clock, when my Lord Harry came home with one Mr. [Able]. I ate some pigeon pie for dinner. In the afternoon we drank a bottle till 5 o'clock and then I took leave and returned back to my Lord Orrery's where I got about 8 o'clock and ate some boiled milk and then retired and said my prayers. I was very much tired with my journey. I sweated much in the night.

13. I rose about 6 o'clock and read a chapter in Hebrew and some Greek. I said my prayers, and had milk for breakfast. The weather was clear and warm, the wind east. I walked in the garden, and then wrote two letters to Virginia. Then we played at billiards till dinner, when I ate some fish. After dinner we played again at billiards till four and then drank some tea and about five rode out. In the evening I took a walk and danced my dance in the garden, and then read the news. Then we played at piquet and supped about 8 o'clock, and then played at cards again and I lost. Then we were sleepy and retired and read a little English and then said my prayers. I slept but indifferently.

14. I rose about 6 o'clock and read a chapter in Hebrew and some Greek. I said my prayers and had milk for breakfast. The weather was clear and cold, the wind northeast. About 10 o'clock we walked to Burnham church and Mr. T-t gave us a pretty good sermon. My

Lord Windsor came back to dinner and I ate some roast beef and drank a bottle after dinner till 4 o'clock, and then we drank tea. Then we rode with my Lord Windsor as far as Maidenhead and then returned and I walked in the garden and danced my dance. Then we sat and talked till eight and then ate some pudding for supper. Then we walked about the rooms till nine and then retired to our apartments, where I said my prayers. I slept pretty well, thank God.

15. I rose about 6 o'clock and read a chapter in Hebrew and some Greek. I said my prayers, and had milk for breakfast. The weather was cloudy and cold, the wind northeast. I wrote a letter to Virginia till 12 o'clock and then we played at billiards and then at bowls till dinner, and then I ate some roast pork. After dinner we played again at billiards till 4 o'clock and then drank tea and then went to take the air in the coach and six; when we returned I took my walk and danced my dance, and then played at cards till supper, when I ate some battered eggs, and then played again at cards till 9 o'clock and then we retired and I said my prayers. My sore throat was better, thank God.

16. I rose about 6 o'clock and read a chapter in Hebrew and some Greek. I neglected my prayers, but had milk for breakfast. The weather was cloudy and cold, the wind northeast. I wrote two letters to Virginia. About 12 o'clock we played at billiards, and about 2 o'clock went to dinner and I ate some fish. After dinner we played again at billiards till four and then drank [tea]. Then we rode out and afterwards I walked in the garden and danced my dance. In the evening we played at cards till supper and read the news. I ate some pudding for supper. After supper we played again at cards and I lost my money. About 9 o'clock we retired and I washed my feet. I said my prayers. I slept indifferently but my throat was better, thank God.

17. I rose about 6 o'clock and read a chapter in Hebrew and some Greek. I neglected my prayers, but ate milk for breakfast. The weather was clear again, the wind northeast, but it was cold. I read some English and then wrote more letters to Virginia. About twelve we went to billiards and then to bowls, and then to dinner, and I ate some tongue and udder. After dinner came Mr. A-r-s and Mr. T-t and

drank tea with us. Then we went out in the coach and six and saw my Lord Wharton's [2] house at Uborn. When we returned I danced my dance and walked in the garden till seven, and then we played at piquet and I lost my money. About nine we retired and I read some English. I said my prayers.

18. I rose about 6 o'clock and read a chapter in Hebrew and some Greek. I neglected my prayers, and had milk for breakfast. The weather was clear and cold, the wind northeast. I wrote more letters to Virginia till 12 o'clock. A small quantity of seed came from me. We played at billiards and then at bowls till dinner when I ate some roast pigeon. After dinner we played again at billiards till 4 o'clock and then drank tea. Then we rode out and afterwards I danced my dance and walked for about half an hour. Then we played at cards till eight, then supped, then played again till nine, and then we retired and I said my prayers.

19. I rose about 6 o'clock and read a chapter in Hebrew and some Greek. I said my prayers, and had milk for breakfast. The weather was cold and cloudy, the wind northeast. My eye was very sore by some accident in the night. I wrote some English till 12 o'clock and then we played at billiards till dinner when I ate some boiled goose. After dinner we played again at billiards till four and then drank tea, and then rode out and in the evening I walked in the garden and danced my dance. Then we played at piquet till eight, and then ate some calves' feet for supper. After supper we walked about the halls till nine and then retired and I said my prayers.

20. I rose about 6 o'clock and read a chapter in Hebrew and some Greek. I said my prayers and had milk for breakfast. The weather was cloudy and cold, the wind southeast. I walked in the garden and then wrote a letter to Virginia. About 12 o'clock we played at billiards, and then at bowls, till dinner, when I ate some roast veal. After

2. Philip, 2nd Marquess of Wharton, created Duke of Wharton in January, 1718. Uborn, his home, 'with its gardens, stables, and other offices, is inferior to very few in the kingdom,' reported John Macky in *Journey through England* (London, 1724), I, 53.

dinner we played again at billiards till four and then drank tea. Then we rode out and then I walked in the garden and danced my dance. In the evening we played at cards and I read the news till supper and then I ate some boiled milk. Then we walked about till nine and then retired and I said my prayers.

21. I rose about 6 o'clock and read two chapters in Hebrew and some Greek. I said my prayers, and had milk for breakfast. The weather was cold and cloudy, the wind east. I wrote a letter to Virginia. About 10 o'clock we walked to church and had a pretty good sermon from a stranger. After church we returned home and I wrote some English till dinner, and then I ate some roast beef. After dinner we walked till 3 o'clock and then we drank tea and afterwards went to take the air in the coach and six. In the evening I took a walk and Madam walked with me. Then we talked till supper and I ate some toasted cheese. Then we walked again till 9 o'clock and then retired and I said my prayers.

22. I rose about 7 o'clock and read a chapter in Hebrew and some Greek. I said my prayers and had milk for breakfast. The weather was cold and cloudy, the wind east. I wrote some English till 11 o'clock and then we went to the fair, where we saw the maids stand in a row to be hired. We returned about one and Madam and I walked in the garden and then we played at bowls till dinner and I ate some fricassee of chicken. After dinner my Lord and I went in the chaise to D-r-s-t horserace where we saw General Evans [3] and Mr. A-l-t's new horses run [. . .] and they ran three heats. There were two coaches and six, one of four, and three of two, and two chaises. We returned about 7 o'clock and played at piquet till supper and then ate some fried pudding. Then we walked about till nine and then retired. I said my prayers.

23. I rose about 7 o'clock and read a chapter in Hebrew and some Greek. I neglected my prayers and had milk for breakfast. The

3. William Evans, major general of a regiment of dragoons, had accompanied Argyll on his march to Aberdeen in 1716.

weather was cold and cloudy, the wind northeast. I wrote some English and then wrote a letter to Virginia. About twelve we played at
billiards and then at bowls till dinner, when I ate some tongue and udder. After dinner we played again at billiards till four and then drank
tea. Then we rode out and after that walked and danced my dance.
In the evening we played at piquet till eight and then ate some milk
for supper, and then played again at piquet till nine and then retired
and I wrote a letter. I said my prayers.

24. I rose about 6 o'clock and read a chapter in Hebrew and some
Greek. I neglected my prayers, and had milk for breakfast. The
weather was clear and cold, the wind northeast. I wrote some English
and read some English till twelve, and then we played at billiards and
then at bowls till dinner, when I ate some roast veal. When we had
almost done Colonel Boyle came in, my Lord's cousin. About 2
o'clock we went again to the races, where we diverted ourselves till
the evening, and then returned home in the chaise and played at
piquet and I lost a crown. We ate milk for supper and about ten retired. I said my prayers.

25. I rose about 6 o'clock and read nothing because I prepared to
go away. However, I said my prayers, and had milk for breakfast.
The weather was cloudy and warm, the wind west. About 9 o'clock I
gave thirty-five shillings among the servants and then took my leave
and went in my Lord Orrery's chaise to Maidenhead where I ate
some roast chicken and about 12 o'clock went in the Abingdon
coach to Nettlebed and from thence walked to my Lord Harry Powlett's but my Lord was from home. However, I found my Lady and
the two Misses U-m-s. We drank tea and there came one Mrs. T-r-
p-n. In the evening we played at cards and I won five shillings. About
9 o'clock we went to supper and I ate some battered eggs and about
eleven retired and I said my prayers. It rained very much this night.

26. I rose about 7 o'clock and read a chapter in Hebrew and some
Greek. I said my prayers, and ate milk for breakfast. The weather
was cold and cloudy and the wind southwest and blowing fiercely.

About eleven we took a walk and returned about twelve, when I took a little nap and wrote some English till 2 o'clock, when I ate some pigeon pie for dinner. After dinner we walked again in the garden and ate fruit. Then we drank tea and read the news and then walked again in the garden. Then I read some English to the ladies till nine, when I ate some rice milk. Then Lady Powlett and I played at piquet and we sat and talked till eleven and then retired. I said my prayers.

27. I rose about 7 o'clock and read a chapter in Hebrew and some Greek. I said my prayers and ate milk for breakfast. The weather was cold and cloudy, the wind southwest. I dreamed last night that I saw a bloody sword in the air that gave me abundance of concern. I walked with P-n-y U-m-s about a mile and then came home and found Mr. Parry, my Lady's brother, the parson, and I walked with him. I ate some tongue and udder for dinner. After dinner P-n-y U-m-s and I walked again till the evening, when Mr. Parry and his wife came and we played at cards till nine and then my Lord Harry came with one Mr. T-r-f-y and I ate some pheasant for supper; and then we drank a bottle till 12 o'clock and then we retired. I said my prayers. I slept indifferently.

28. I rose about 7 o'clock and read a chapter in Hebrew and some Greek. I said my prayers, and had milk for breakfast. The weather was windy and warm and it rained a pretty deal, the wind southwest. I read some English. My Lord Harry had a toothache violently. We talked till dinner and then I ate some fish. After dinner we read the news and about four I took a walk and then drank tea and then P-n-y and I walked again. In the evening we played at little proverbs and played till nine and then we ate hare for supper. Then we played again till 11 o'clock and then retired and I said my prayers. I slept but indifferently. It blew very hard all night.

29. I rose about 7 o'clock and read nothing in Hebrew nor in Greek. I said my prayers, and had milk for breakfast. The wind continued to blow and it rained a little. About 10 o'clock we set out for Mr. LeGrande's and rode through Reading and got to Mr. LeGrande's

about 1 o'clock and dined there, and I ate some roast beef. After dinner we went to the races on the Common by the house where were several coaches and some of the ladies came home with us and we drank some coffee. About 7 o'clock my Lord and Lady Powlett with Mrs. U-m-s went away and I ate some [r-t-s-c] for supper. Then we sat and talked till ten and then retired and I said my prayers.

30. I rose about 7 o'clock and read a chapter in Hebrew and some Greek. I said my prayers, and had boiled milk for breakfast. The weather was cold and cloudy and it rained. However, this did not discourage us from going about 12 o'clock to visit Mr. [Clark] at the Priory. Mr. LeGrande and I went in the chaise and got there about 1 o'clock and I ate some boiled beef for dinner. After dinner we drank a bottle till 4 o'clock and then went about half a mile in the rain to the coffeehouse, where we played at cards and were merry till nine and then returned home to supper and I ate some milk porridge. After supper we played at cards and sat up all night at play and were merry and went home about 6 o'clock and I went to bed and lay till one. I neglected to say my prayers. It rained very much.

October 1718

1. I rose about 1 o'clock and read nothing. I neglected to say my prayers, but about 2 o'clock ate some tongue and udder for dinner. After dinner it rained so that we could not walk, so we played at piquet till five, and then drank coffee. Then I read the news and looked over some prints and then played at piquet again till 9 o'clock and then ate some rice milk. After supper we sat and talked of old stories and I told them the story of my love with Miss Smith. About 10 o'clock we retired and I put several things in order and I said my prayers. It rained abundantly.

2. I rose about 7 o'clock and read a chapter in Hebrew but no Greek. However, I said my prayers and had three dishes of chocolate for breakfast. It continued to rain abundantly all day. I read some English and conversed with Mrs. LeGrande till 2 o'clock and then I ate some fried udder and eggs. After dinner I read English again till 4 o'clock and then we went to the coffeehouse at Sonning where were Lady Rich,[1] Lady Blackett,[2] and several other ladies. We drank coffee and ate cake and played at commerce and I lost my money. Here we stayed till 9 o'clock and then returned home and I ate some rice milk for supper and about 12 o'clock retired. I put up my things and said my prayers.

3. I rose about 6 o'clock and got ready to go away. I said my prayers and then drank three dishes of chocolate. About 7 o'clock I took leave of Mr. LeGrande and his lady and went in their chaise to meet the Reading coach and about 8 o'clock went into it and had six people beside myself. We had not gone two miles before we were overturned, but thank God nobody was hurt. The rest of the journey was performed well and I was well pleased with one of our women, Mrs. C-n-s-t-ble. We dined about two o'clock at Slough and I ate some roast mutton. Then we proceeded to Turnham Green where I ate a good plum cake and about 8 o'clock I got to my lodgings, where I put my things in order and ate some boiled milk for supper. I said my prayers to thank God for our deliverance.

4. I rose about 7 o'clock and read a chapter in Hebrew and some Greek. I said my prayers and had boiled milk for breakfast. The weather was cold and clear, the wind west. About 11 o'clock came Mrs. Wilkinson and brought me some linen. Then I went into the City and dined with old Mr. Perry who gave me several letters from Virginia. I ate some cold roast beef. After dinner I received a hundred pounds and then went to visit Dick Perry who was exceedingly bad of the gout. Here I drank tea and about 4 o'clock went to Molly

1. Elizabeth, wife of Sir Robert Rich, 4th Bart., a groom of the bedchamber to George, Prince of Wales; M.P. for Dunwich.

2. Probably the widow of Sir Edward Blackett, alderman, who died April 23, 1718.

Cole's and sat with her half an hour. Then I went home and wrote a letter into the country and then looked in at the play. Then I went to visit Mrs. A-l-n and committed uncleanness with the maid because the mistress was not at home. However, when the mistress came I rogered her and about 12 o'clock went home and ate a plum cake for supper. I neglected my prayers, for which God forgive me.

5. I rose about 7 o'clock and read a chapter in Hebrew and some Greek in Homer. I said my prayers and had boiled milk for breakfast. The weather was fair and cool, the wind west. About 11 o'clock I walked to Somerset Chapel and heard a good sermon. Then I walked in the garden with my Lord Bellenden till 1 o'clock and then returned home and ate some battered eggs for dinner. In the afternoon I put several things in order and danced my dance. About 5 o'clock I walked to Will's Coffeehouse and then I walked to the park, and after took a turn, and then went to Mrs. FitzHerbert's and ate some toast and cheese with her and about 9 o'clock walked home and said my prayers. It rained and blew violently in the night.

6. I rose about 7 o'clock and read a chapter in Hebrew and some Greek in Lucian. I said my prayers, and had boiled milk for breakfast. The weather was cloudy and warm and the wind continued to blow hard and it rained sometimes. However, about 11 o'clock I went to Spring Gardens to visit Mr. Southwell but he was from home. However, I saw his sister and sat with her half an hour and then went to Colonel Blakiston and paid him the twenty-five guineas I owed him. Then I returned again to Mr. Southwell's where I dined and ate some roast beef, and after dinner we drank tea, and about five I went to Lady Guise's and sat with her till 8 o'clock, and then went to Will's Coffeehouse and ate some milk and cake. About 10 o'clock I went home and said my prayers.

7. I rose about 7 o'clock and read a chapter in Hebrew and some Greek in Lucian. I said my prayers and had boiled milk for breakfast. The weather was cold and clear, the wind northwest. I wrote three letters to Virginia till 2 o'clock, and then went to dine with Mr.

Southwell and ate some boiled beef. Mrs. FitzHerbert dined there likewise. After dinner we drank tea till 5 o'clock and then I went to Will's Coffeehouse. From thence to the play, and from thence to visit my daughter, and sat with her till 8 o'clock, and then walked about till ten but could pick no woman that I liked. About ten I went home and wrote some English but found myself dull and therefore went to bed. I neglected to say my prayers.

8. I rose about 7 o'clock and read a chapter in Hebrew and some Greek in Lucian. I said my prayers and had boiled milk for breakfast. The weather was warm and very windy and it rained sometimes. I wrote an epitaph upon Colonel Nott[3] at the request of Colonel Blakiston. I expected Molly Cole but the wet weather prevented her. I ate some battered eggs for dinner. After dinner I put several things in order and then wrote a letter till 5 o'clock, and then I went to visit Mrs. B-r-n and drank some coffee with her. Then I went to Mrs. A-l-n but her lord was with her. Then I walked the street and picked up a woman and carried her to the tavern and gave her a broiled chicken for supper but she could provoke me to do nothing because my roger would not stand with all she could do. About ten I went home and said my prayers.

9. I rose about 7 o'clock and read a chapter in Hebrew and some Greek in Lucian. I said my prayers and had boiled milk for breakfast. The weather was cold and cloudy, and it rained, the wind west. About 10 o'clock came my cousin Horsmanden and sat with me till twelve and then we went into the city and dined at the Beefsteak House in the Old Jewry and I ate some beefsteak. Then we went to visit Mrs. M-n-l-v but she was from home. Then we went to Mrs. B-n-y and drank tea with them and sat there about two hours, and then went to Will's Coffeehouse, where I read the news and ate some milk and cake for supper. Here I sat and talked till 10 o'clock, and then walked home and said my prayers.

3. Edward Nott, brother-in-law of Colonel Blakiston, was lieutenant governor of Virginia from August, 1705, until his death in 1706. In May, 1718, the Virginia Assembly ordered a marble monument in memory of Nott to be erected in the churchyard at Williamsburg. The epitaph may be found in *Another Secret Diary of William Byrd*, 359-60.

10. I rose about 7 o'clock and read a chapter in Hebrew and some Greek in Lucian. I said my prayers and had boiled milk for breakfast. The weather was clear and warm, the wind west. About 9 o'clock came Colonel Blakiston and stayed about a half an hour. Then came Mr. Albin and showed me several things and about 12 o'clock came Mrs. Cole whom I kissed and made love to for about an hour, and then ate some battered eggs for dinner. After dinner I put several things in order and packed up my things. About 5 o'clock I went to visit Mrs. A-l-n and rogered her and gave her a guinea and then took leave and returned home and wrote a letter. Then I went away with my portmantle to the inn where I ate a roast chicken for supper and about 11 o'clock Mr. Horsmanden came to me. I said my prayers and slept indifferently.

11. I rose about 6 o'clock and said my prayers and then went into the Maldon coach, only Mr. Horsmanden and I went to Hart Street where we ate a mutton pie and drank some milk. Then we proceeded to Brentwood, where we ate some boiled beef for dinner. About 1 o'clock we got into the coach again and I took a nap and got without any misfortune to Danbury, where my uncle's chaise met us and we proceeded to Purleigh, where I found my uncle and the ladies[4] well. We sat and talked till 8 o'clock and then I ate some pigs [p-t-y] for supper. After supper we sat and talked of old stories till ten and then I took my leave and said my prayers. It blew very hard.

12. I rose about 7 o'clock and read a chapter in Hebrew and some Greek. I said my prayers, and had boiled milk for breakfast. The weather was clear and cold, the wind southwest. About 11 o'clock we went to church and had only prayers. About one we went to dinner and I ate some boiled beef. After dinner we talked about an hour and then went again to church and my uncle gave us a good sermon. After church we drank tea and then took a walk in the gar-

4. Daniel Horsmanden, rector of Purleigh, and his wife and daughters, Ursula and Susan. Purleigh Church stands on a hill between Chelmsford and the North Sea, a few miles from Maldon. The benefice remained in the Horsmanden family until about 1770. *The Virginia Magazine of History and Biography*, xv (1907–8), 314–17.

den till the evening, when we sat and talked till 8 o'clock and then I ate some rice milk for supper, though the company had many other things. After supper we went to romp and eat walnuts till 10 o'clock and then retired to our chambers, where I said my prayers.

13. I rose about 7 o'clock and read a chapter in Hebrew and some Greek in [Epistles]. I said my prayers, and had boiled milk for breakfast. The weather was cold and clear, the wind southwest. I danced my dance and then read some English and took a walk till dinner and then ate some fowl and bacon. After dinner we sat and talked till four o'clock and then Daniel and I took a walk till five. In the evening we played at commerce till 9 o'clock and then I ate some hasty pudding. Then we romped till eleven and then retired and I said my prayers. I slept very indifferently and had disagreeable dreams.

14. I rose about 8 o'clock and read a chapter in Hebrew and some Greek. I said my prayers, and had boiled milk for breakfast. The weather was clear and cold, the wind southwest and driving. I wrote some English and read some English till dinner, when I ate boiled rabbit and onions. After dinner we talked a little and then took a walk with the girls and romped with them in the fields. In the evening I read more English till night and then we played at commerce and I lost my money. Then we went to supper and I ate some milk porridge. After supper we played at romping and danced several dances. I said my prayers. I slept indifferently. It rained abundantly.

15. I rose about 7 o'clock and read a chapter in Hebrew and some Greek. I said my prayers, and had boiled milk for breakfast. The weather was clear and cold, the wind southwest. I danced my dance. About 11 o'clock we went to Danbury Place to dinner and I ate some boiled beef. Mr. Humphrey would not speak to me. After dinner we played at commerce and I won a little. About 7 o'clock we took leave and returned home, where we ate some apple pie for supper. After supper we romped very much till 11 o'clock and then we retired and I said my prayers.

16. I rose about 8 o'clock and read a chapter in Hebrew and some Greek. I said my prayers and had boiled milk for breakfast. The weather was cold and cloudy, the wind west. I danced my dance and then wrote some English till one o'clock, when Mr. P-l-x-n and Mr. Humphrey came to dinner and I ate some beef. After dinner we sat and talked till 4 o'clock and then drank tea and then the gentlemen went away and I took a walk in the garden. Then we played at cards till 8 o'clock and then went to supper and I ate some buttered rice. After supper we played at cards again and I won twelve shillings and about twelve we retired and I said my prayers. I slept very indifferently and had troublesome dreams.

17. I rose about 8 o'clock and read a chapter in Hebrew and some Greek. I said my prayers, and had boiled milk for breakfast. The weather was cold and clear, the wind west. I danced my dance. After breakfast I wrote some English and then read several of my letters that I had writ to my uncle formerly. About 2 o'clock we sat down to dinner and I ate some roast pork. After dinner we talked a little and then took a walk in the fields and returned at five. I had a looseness. Then we drank tea, then played at cards and I lost eight shillings. I ate some milk porridge for supper. Then we played at passage and I won twenty-eight shillings. About eleven we retired to our chambers and I said my prayers.

18. I rose about 8 o'clock and read two chapters in Hebrew and some Greek. I said my prayers and had boiled milk for breakfast. The weather was cold and clear, the wind northwest. I read some of my old letters to my uncle and then I wrote a love letter for Daniel. About 2 o'clock I ate some stewed beef. After dinner we took a walk all about the fields and in the evening drank some tea. Then we played at commerce and I lost six shillings. Then I ate some boiled milk for supper. After supper we romped till 11 o'clock and then we retired, and I said my prayers. I slept very ill.

19. I rose about 8 o'clock and read a chapter in Hebrew and some Greek. I said my prayers and had boiled milk for breakfast. The

weather was cold and cloudy, the wind northwest and high. We did not go to church this morning because my uncle got up late, but I read some English till dinner and then ate some boiled beef. After dinner we sat and talked till two and then went to church and my uncle gave us a good sermon. After church we drank some tea and then read the news till 8 o'clock when we ate some milk porridge for supper. Then we sat and talked till ten, and then retired and I said my prayers.

20. I rose about 8 o'clock and read a chapter in Hebrew and some Greek. I said my prayers and had boiled milk for breakfast. The weather was warm and cloudy and it rained a little, the wind west. I read some English to my cousin and then danced my dance and wrote a letter till dinner, when I ate some pork boiled. After dinner we sat and talked and then I read more English till 4 o'clock, when I drank tea. Then we played at cards and I lost ten shillings. About 9 o'clock I ate some rice milk for supper. Then we romped till eleven and then retired and said my prayers. I slept very well, thank God.

21. I rose about 2 o'clock and read a chapter in Hebrew and some Greek. I said my prayers and had boiled milk for breakfast. The weather was cloudy and warm, the wind northeast. I danced my dance and then read some English. This morning my cousin Bunty[5] went to London. I ate some boiled tongue for dinner. In the afternoon we walked in the garden till 4 o'clock and then drank some coffee. In the evening we played at loo and I won four shillings. I ate four eggs for supper, and after supper played again at loo till 11 o'clock and then retired. I said my prayers.

22. I rose about 8 o'clock and read a chapter in Hebrew and some Greek. I said my prayers and had boiled milk for breakfast. The weather was cloudy and warm, the wind northwest, and it rained. I danced my dance and then read some English till dinner, when I ate some fish. After dinner we sat and talked and then walked till four when we drank tea. Then we went to cards and I won five shillings.

5. Barrington Horsmanden.

I ate some barley milk for supper. After supper we played again at cards and I won a shilling. About 12 o'clock we retired and I said my prayers. I slept indifferently well, thank God.

23. I rose about 8 o'clock and read a chapter in Hebrew and some Greek. I said my prayers and had milk for breakfast. The weather was warm and clear, the wind northwest. I danced my dance and then read some English. Then I packed up my things till dinner, when I ate roast turkey. After dinner we romped a little; then I took a walk till tea time and in the evening played at cards and I won a little. I ate some battered eggs for supper. After supper we sat and talked till 11 o'clock and then took leave of all our friends because we intended by God's blessing to go early in the morning. I said my prayers.

24. I rose about 5 o'clock because my cousin Daniel and I were to go to meet the Maldon coach. However, we ate our milk first and I said my prayers, and about 7 o'clock got to Danbury where we went into the stagecoach and about 11 o'clock got to Brentwood where we ate some pork and peas for dinner. After dinner we got into the coach again about one and proceeded on our journey with a young gentlewoman and an old one; the young one pretended to have seen my cousin Suky Horsmanden in the King's coach, not knowing who we were, but we discovered ourselves and the woman was confused and asked pardon. Then I went to Mr. Perry's where I ate some cold beef, and I picked up a woman and carried her to the tavern and committed uncleanness, for which God forgive me. Then I came home and said my prayers.

25. I rose about 8 o'clock and read a chapter in Hebrew and some Greek in Lucian. I said my prayers and had milk for breakfast. The weather was cold and clear, the wind west. About 9 o'clock I went with Mr. Horsmanden to the cold baths. I danced my dance. About 11 o'clock came Mr. Page[6] and sat with me two hours and we talked of Virginia. About two I ate some battered eggs. After dinner I put several things in order and had a chaldron of coals laid in that cost thirty-two shillings. Then I wrote a letter to my uncle Horsmanden

6. Perhaps John Page of Virginia.

and about 6 o'clock I went to the play and had the pleasure to sit next to Mrs. Lindsay. After the play I went to Will's and read the news, and then went home and said my prayers.

26. I rose about 8 o'clock and read a chapter in Hebrew and some Greek in Lucian. I said my prayers and had milk for breakfast. The weather was warm and clear, the wind southwest. About 10 o'clock D-k came to me and thanked me for offering to be his security, but that it was done already. I lent him five guineas. About 11 o'clock I went to Somerset Chapel where we had a good sermon. After church I went to St. James's Chapel where I saw several of my acquaintances, and about two returned home and ate a roast chicken for dinner. In the afternoon I put several things in order till 4 o'clock and then read some English till five and then went to visit my daughter, whom I found well, thank God, and there saw Miss Page just come from Virginia. Then I went to Lady Dunkellen, who told me all her grievances and kept me till 10 o'clock. Then I called at Will's and took a dish of chocolate and then went home and said my prayers.

27. I rose about 8 o'clock and read a chapter in Hebrew and no Greek, because I was hindered by some visitors. However, I said my prayers and had milk for breakfast. The weather was cold and cloudy, the wind west. My cousin Horsmanden came and went with me to the cold baths, but there was not water enough, so I returned home again. Then came Annie Wilkinson and I gave her some work. About 11 o'clock I went to my Lord Orrery's and drank chocolate. Then I returned home and danced my dance and then returned to my Lord Orrery's to dinner and ate some herring. After dinner we talked of several things till 5 o'clock and then we went into the City and called on my milliner and one Mrs. Q-r and then returned to Will's and drank some tea and then my Lord Orrery, my Lord Islay, and I went to the new playhouse, but came away before it was half done and went to Will's again, where I had some milk and cake. About ten I walked home and said my prayers.

28. I rose about 8 o'clock and read a chapter in Hebrew and some Greek. I said my prayers and had milk for breakfast. The weather

was cold and cloudy, the wind west. I danced my dance. About 11 o'clock my coachman disappointed me, so I was forced to go into the City in a hack, and dined with Dick Perry and ate pork and peas. After dinner we drank tea and about 5 o'clock went to meet my cousin Horsmanden at Garraway's Coffeehouse. Then we went to the milliner and from thence to Will's Coffeehouse and read the news. Then we made a visit to Mrs. A-s-t-n, and then I returned to Will's again where I had a cake and some milk. About 10 o'clock I went home and settled some accounts and then said my prayers.

29. I rose about 8 o'clock and read a chapter in Hebrew and some Greek in Lucian. I said my prayers and had milk for breakfast. The weather was cloudy and cold, the wind southeast, and it rained a little. I danced my dance. Mrs. Wilkinson came and brought my ruffles. I wrote a letter to my cousin Horsmanden. About 2 o'clock I ate some battered eggs. After dinner I put several things in order and then read some English till 5 o'clock, when I went to Mrs. Lindsay's where we played at cards and I won twenty-five shillings and Mr. G-l-s-t-n was there. Then Mr. [Tryon] came in and I ate some wild duck for supper and after supper drank a glass and about 12 o'clock went home in a hack and said my prayers.

30. I rose about 8 o'clock and went into the cold bath with my cousin Horsmanden. Then I read a chapter in Hebrew, but no Greek. I said a short prayer and had boiled milk for breakfast. The weather was cloudy and warm, the wind southeast. About 11 o'clock I went to the Duke of Argyll's and stayed with him about an hour, and then set Peter Campbell down at St. James's and then went to Pontack's to dinner and ate some fish. After dinner we called at Garraway's and then proceeded to Crane Court,[7] where I stayed till five and then went to Will's and from thence to the play. After the play we went with two women of my acquaintance to the tavern and ate some wild duck and kissed our ladies till 11 o'clock and then I walked home and said my prayers. I committed uncleanness with one of the women while I was kissing her.

7. Crane Court, off Fleet Street, where the Royal Society held its meetings.

31. I rose about 8 o'clock and read a chapter in Hebrew and some Greek in Lucian. I said my prayers and had boiled milk for breakfast. The weather was cold and cloudy, the wind northeast and blowing violently. I danced my dance. About 10 o'clock came Daniel Horsmanden and stayed about half an hour. Then wrote a letter to Virginia till 2 o'clock and then ate some battered eggs. After dinner I put several things in order and then danced again. About 5 o'clock I went to Will's Coffeehouse and read the news and about six went to Lady Guise's where I stayed till 9 o'clock. Then I went to St. James's Coffeehouse and drank two dishes of chocolate and went with Colonel Blakiston to the drawing room, where were few ladies. About eleven I walked home and said my prayers.

November 1718

1. I rose about 8 o'clock and read a chapter in Hebrew and some Greek in Lucian. I said my prayers, and had milk for breakfast. The weather was cold and cloudy, the wind northeast. I danced my dance. My cousin Horsmanden and I went into the cold baths. About 11 o'clock I went to Mrs. Southwell's and sat with her half an hour, and then went to Mr. Blathwayt's and found the Colonel. Here I stayed about an hour, and then went home and had a beefsteak for dinner. After dinner I put several things in order and had just light enough to read a little English and then went to Will's Coffeehouse and from thence to the play, where I found indifferent women. Then I went to the coffeehouse again and had some cake and milk, and then walked about the streets half an hour and then went home and said my prayers.

2. I rose about 8 o'clock and read a chapter in Hebrew and some Greek in Lucian. I said my prayers devoutly and had milk for break-

fast. The weather was cold and cloudy, the wind northeast. I danced my dance. Then I wrote a letter to Virginia and about 2 o'clock went to Somerset House and dined with Tom U-t-n, where I found Sam M–, Mr. C-l-f [. . .]. I ate some roast beef. After dinner we drank some champagne till 5 o'clock and then I called on my cousin Horsmanden and went to visit my daughter and Miss Page and stayed about half an hour and then went to visit Mrs. N-n-m where we had birthday cake and tea and stayed till 9 o'clock and then I set Mr. Horsmanden home and went to Will's Coffeehouse and stayed there till eleven, and then walked home and said my prayers.

3. I rose about 8 o'clock and read a chapter in Hebrew and some Greek in Lucian. I said my prayers, and had milk for breakfast. I had a running again come upon me without provocation. The weather was warm and cloudy, the wind west. I wrote some English and danced my dance till 1 o'clock and then Mr. Horsmanden came and we went together to Colonel Blakiston's where we dined and I ate some boiled goose. After dinner Colonel [Shutz] and I played at piquet and I lost a guinea. Then we went to the play where we met two women in B-r-t-n box but could not persuade them to go with us, so I went to Will's and had some cake and milk and stayed there till 10 o'clock and then walked home and said my prayers. My running grew worse.

4. I rose about 8 o'clock and read a chapter in Hebrew and some Greek in Lucian. I said my prayers and had milk for breakfast. My running was much better, thank God. I danced my dance. I put some things in order till 11 o'clock and then went to visit Mr. Page and from thence went into the City and dined with old Mr. Perry and had boiled beef. After dinner I went to visit Mrs. Perry and drank tea till 5 o'clock and then went to the play with Mr. Page and was well diverted. Mrs. Lindsay was there and talked all the while with Jack H-r-v-y. After the play I went to Will's Coffeehouse and read the news and drank two dishes of chocolate, and then walked home where I wrote a letter to my daughter and said my prayers. I had a nocturnal pollution. My running was well again.

5. I rose about 7 o'clock and read two chapters in Hebrew and some Greek in Lucian. I said my prayers, and had milk for breakfast. The weather was cold and cloudy, the wind southeast. About ten came my milliner and I rogered her. Then I danced my dance and wrote a letter to Virginia and then read some English till 2 o'clock and then ate some battered eggs. After dinner I put several things in order and then read more English till four and then took a nap till five and then went to visit Mrs. D-n-s where I drank tea. Here I stayed till nine and then went to St. James's Coffeehouse where I drank a dish of chocolate and then went to Court where I saw Miss B-n-y and stayed till 11 o'clock and then walked home and said my prayers.

6. I rose about 8 o'clock and read a chapter in Hebrew and some Greek in Lucian. I said my prayers, and had milk for breakfast. The weather was clear and cold, the wind southwest. I danced my dance. About ten o'clock came Mr. P-l-n-t-n and I paid his bill. About 11 o'clock I went to visit Mrs. Southwell and stayed with her till one and then I went into the City and dined with Pontack and ate some boiled beef. After dinner I went to Garraway's Coffeehouse and read the news and then I went to see Molly Cole and about five went to Will's Coffeehouse and from thence to the tavern with two ladies that called upon me at Will's. I went with them to the tavern and we ate some roast fowl and were merry, notwithstanding Mr. Horsmanden followed us. About twelve I set the ladies home and I returned and said my prayers.

7. I rose about 8 o'clock and read a chapter in Hebrew and some Greek in Lucian. I said no prayers, but had milk for breakfast. The weather was clear and cold, the wind southeast. I danced my dance. About 11 o'clock came Colonel Blakiston and Mr. Horsmanden and I went with the Colonel into the City to the Virginia Coffeehouse and then we dined with Dick Perry and I ate fish for dinner. After dinner we drank tea and then I went to Mr. Horsmanden's lodgings and from thence to the play. After the play we went to Will's where I drank two dishes of chocolate and then we went to Court where we

met Sir Wilfred Lawson and went to the tavern and ate some hogs' feet for supper. About twelve I went home and said my prayers.

8. I rose about 8 o'clock and read a chapter in Hebrew and some Greek in Lucian. I neglected my prayers but had milk for breakfast. The weather was cold and cloudy, the wind northwest. About 11 o'clock came Molly Cole and brought me my [g-n]. We drank tea and she stayed with me till 1 o'clock. I danced my dance and about two I ate some battered eggs. After dinner I put several things in order and about 3 o'clock went to Mr. Horsmanden's chambers and from thence to the Temple where we looked upon some chambers which I liked very well. Then we went to Lincoln's Inn to the coffee-house and from thence to the play, where was abundance of company. After the play I went to Will's and had some cake and milk and then walked home and said my prayers.

9. I rose about 8 o'clock and read a chapter in Hebrew and some Greek in Lucian. I neglected my prayers, but had milk for breakfast. The weather was cold and cloudy, the wind northeast. I danced my dance. About 12 o'clock came Colonel Blathwayt and stayed about half an hour, and then we went together to Court where I met with several of my friends and particularly my Lord Percival and Sir Charles Wager, and I went home to dine with the last and ate some boiled beef. After dinner we went to O-r-m-n Chapel where we had a good sermon from Mr. B-s-c-o. After church we drank tea and then I went to my Lord Dunkellen's and sat all the evening with my Lady Buck and Mrs. Sebright.[1] About 9 o'clock I went to Will's Coffeehouse and drank two dishes of chocolate. I said my prayers. I slept very ill.

10. I rose about 8 o'clock and read a chapter in Hebrew and some Greek in Lucian. I neglected my prayers, but had milk for breakfast. The weather was cold and cloudy, the wind east. About 10 o'clock

1. Wife of Sir Charles Buck, Bart., of Hamby Grange and the Grove, and her sister; they were the daughters of Sir Edward Sebright, 3rd Bart.

came Mrs. D-n and I gave her a letter to write to the Lady [Philips].[2] Then came the woman that sold capes. Then I danced my dance and my Lord Percival came and stayed about half an hour. Then I went to Lord Orrery's and stayed an hour and then returned home and wrote a letter to Virginia, and then ate battered eggs for dinner. After dinner I put several things in order till four, and then came Mr. Horsmanden. Then I went to Mrs. M-r-l-y and sat with her about an hour. Then I went to Lady Guise's and stayed till eight, and then went to St. James's Coffeehouse and drank a dish of chocolate and then went to Court and about eleven walked home and said my prayers. Sir Wilfred Lawson presented me to Mr. Craggs.[3] I slept pretty well, thank God.

11. I rose about 8 o'clock and read a chapter in Hebrew and some Greek in Lucian. I said my prayers and had milk for breakfast. The weather was cold and cloudy, the wind southeast. I danced my dance. Mrs. D-n came and brought the letter to my Lady [Philips], which I sent away. About twelve I went to Lincoln's Inn Coffeehouse and read the news and then saw the chambers of Sir George Cooke [4] and then went home and read several things from Virginia. Then I ate some beefsteak and then wrote some English. About five I went to Mr. Horsmanden's but he was from home. Then I went to visit my daughter and stayed about an hour and then went to Mr. M-l-n-r and drank some rack punch. About nine I went to the coffeehouse and from thence I walked and picked up a wench and couched her and then went home and said my prayers.

12. I rose about 8 o'clock and read a chapter in Hebrew and some Greek in Lucian. I said my prayers, and had milk for breakfast. The weather was cold and cloudy, the wind southwest. I danced my dance. About 11 o'clock came Mr. Horsmanden and I gave him a case to carry to Sir Robert Raymond. Then I went to the Virginia Coffeehouse and then to Mr. Perry's and dined with the old gentle-

2. Probably the wife (or widow) of Sir Ambrose Philips.

3. James Craggs, the younger, one of the principal secretaries of state.

4. Barrister, son of Sir Henry Cooke, Bart., M.P.

man and ate boiled beef. After dinner I made a visit to Mrs. Perry and drank tea. Then I went to Mr. Horsmanden's chambers and from thence to the play where the French people acted. From the play I went to Court where I stayed till 11 o'clock and then walked home and said my prayers. I saw a picture of the King in little, very well performed.

13. I rose about 8 o'clock and found I had a cold. However, I read a chapter in Hebrew and some Greek in Lucian. I said my prayers, and had milk for breakfast. The weather was cold and clear, the wind southwest. I danced my dance and my milliner came but did not stay. About 12 o'clock I went to the Cockpit and spoke with Tom Beake and drank a dish of chocolate. Then I went to Garraway's Coffeehouse and from thence to Pontack's where I dined and ate some fish. After dinner we went to Crane Court, and about six I went to Will's and stayed about half an hour and then went to visit Mrs. Fitz-Herbert's and ate some turkey and cheese. About nine I walked home and by the way endeavoured to pick up a whore but could not, so I went home and said my prayers. I slept pretty well.

14. I rose about 8 o'clock and read a chapter in Hebrew and some Greek in Lucian. I said my prayers and had milk for breakfast. The weather was cold and clear, the wind east. I danced my dance. I wrote a letter to my Lady Mohun. About 2 o'clock my cousin Horsmanden dined with me and we had some boiled rabbit. After dinner I put several things in order and wrote some English. My coachman went away for want of a greatcoat. About 5 o'clock I sent to Mrs. U-m-s but they were from home. Then I went to Mrs. B-r-n and drank some coffee. Then I went to Misses [Sands'] but they were out; then to my Lord Percival's, but they were out. Then to St. James's Coffeehouse where I read the news and drank chocolate. Then to Court where was pretty Mrs. F-t-r-m-t-n. About eleven I came home with Mr. Horsmanden and said my prayers. The wind blew hard.

15. I rose about 8 o'clock and read two chapters in Hebrew and some Greek. I said my prayers, and had milk for breakfast. The

weather was cold and cloudy and it rained pretty much, the wind west. I danced my dance and then came my cousin Horsmanden. I wrote a letter to Mr. B-r-n-t and ate some battered eggs for dinner. After dinner I put several things in order and then went to Mrs. U-m-s and drank tea till 6 o'clock and then went to the play, where I sat by Sir Wilfred Lawson and notwithstanding Mrs. Lindsay, Mrs. [Cambridge], and Mrs. Sambrooke were there, I went away with Sir Wilfred to Mother W-d-l-n-t-n and lay with a [c-s-n] whore. We ate some ducks for supper and came away about 2 o'clock, and I said my prayers.

16. I rose about 8 o'clock and read a chapter in Hebrew and some Greek. I said my prayers, and had milk for breakfast. The weather was cold and cloudy and it rained all morning so that I went not to church. I danced my dance and read some English till 1 o'clock and then ate some beefsteak. After dinner I put several things in order and then took a nap. About 5 o'clock I went to visit Mrs. Blathwayt[5] and drank tea with them both. Here I stayed till seven and then called at the Virginia Coffeehouse, and then went to visit Mrs. [Sands] where I met Sir Wilfred Lawson and we were very merry till 11 o'clock and then I went home and said my prayers. I slept but indifferently.

17. I rose about 8 o'clock and read a chapter in Hebrew and some Greek. I said my prayers, and had milk for breakfast. The weather was clear and warm, the wind southwest. About 10 o'clock came Colonel Blakiston and stayed about an hour. Then came my milliner and put my linen in order. Then came Mr. Page and stayed till 2 o'clock, when I ate some roast fowl for dinner. After dinner I put several things in order and about 5 o'clock went to visit Mrs. A-s-t-n but she was from home. Then I went to Lady Guise's, and about 8 o'clock went to St. James's Coffeehouse and there met Sir Wilfred Lawson and went with him to Court where Mr. Craggs presented me to the King as Agent of Virginia and I kissed the King's hand, at which Lord Orkney was very angry. Then I went to the drawing

5. William Blathwayt had married Thomasina Ambrose at Gray's Inn Chapel on August 17.

room where Lord Orkney scolded at Craggs. Then Sir Wilfred and
I went to the tavern and had some hogs' feet for supper and about 1
o'clock I went home in the chaise. I slept very ill.

18. I rose about 8 o'clock and read nothing because I wrote a long
letter to Sir Wilfred Lawson about my agency. However, I said a
short prayer and had milk for breakfast. About 10 o'clock came my
countryman Mr. Fox[6] just come out of prison. I found he wanted
money so I gave him two guineas. About 11 o'clock I went to my
Lord Stanhope's but he was from home. Then I went into the City
and dined with Dick Perry and ate some roast beef. After dinner we
drank tea till 4 o'clock and then I called upon my milliner by the
Exchange and then went to my cousin Horsmanden but he was from
home. Then I went to visit Mrs. C-p and sat with her the whole evening, and about nine ate some roast chicken for supper. We played
also at piquet. About nine came my old acquaintance Mrs. B-l-g-r-v
who lives next door. Here I stayed till eleven and then went home
and said my prayers. I had a nocturnal pollution.

19. I rose about 8 o'clock and read two chapters in Hebrew and
some Greek. I said my prayers, and had milk for breakfast. The
weather was cloudy and warm and it rained, the wind southwest.
About 11 o'clock I went to visit Sir Wilfred Lawson but found him
at St. James's Coffeehouse where I drank a dish of chocolate. Then I
went to Colonel Blakiston's but he was from home. However I saw
Colonel [Shutz] for quarter of an hour. Then I went to Lord Orrery's but he was from home. However, I saw his housekeeper and
kissed her. Then I went home and had some battered eggs and cold
chicken. After dinner I put some things in order till 5 o'clock and
then went to the play in Lincoln's Inn Field. After the play I went
to Court, where I saw Mrs. W-n-m and about 11 o'clock came home
and said my prayers.

6. John Fox, a Virginian, conducted an ephemeral English literary weekly, *The
Wanderer*. From his files he compiled a book entitled *Motto's of the Wanderers*
(1718) dedicated to Byrd. Byrd's letter to Fox appears in a copy of the book now
in the Harvard College Library. See Kenneth Ballard Murdock, 'William Byrd and
the Virginian Author of *The Wanderer*, *Harvard Studies and Notes in Philology and
Literature*, XVII (1935), 129–36.

20. I rose about 8 o'clock and read a chapter in Hebrew and some Greek in Lucian. I said my prayers, and had milk for breakfast. The weather was warm and cloudy, the wind southwest. About 10 o'clock came Dr. L-m-s and made me a long visit and stayed till 12 o'clock. Then I danced my dance and read some English till one when Sir Wilfred Lawson came and we went to dine at Pontack's and ate some fish. After dinner we went to Crane Court and I proposed Sir Wilfred Lawson to be a member. Then we went to the play and about 7 o'clock we went to my milliner's in the City and carried them to supper at the Three Tuns in Chandos Street where we had pheasant and woodcock and made the ladies merry till 12 o'clock and then I walked home in the coach [sic] without rogering my nymph. My running returned.

21. I rose about 8 o'clock and read two chapters in Hebrew and some Greek in Lucian. I said my prayers, and had milk for breakfast. The weather was warm and clear, the wind southwest. I danced my dance. My running was better. I wrote some English. About 10 o'clock came Colonel Blakiston and stayed about half an hour. Then came Annie Wilkinson and did some work for me. About 2 o'clock I had some battered eggs for dinner. In the afternoon I put several things in order till 4 o'clock and then went to visit my daughter and stayed with her till 6 o'clock and then went to Lady Dunkellen's and she told me all her grief and complaints against my Lord. Then I went to Mrs. N-n-m but she was from home. Then I went to Will's Coffeehouse and drank two dishes of chocolate. Then I went to Court and about eleven returned home in a chair and said my prayers. I slept but indifferently.

22. I rose about 8 o'clock and read a chapter in Hebrew and some Greek in Lucian. I said my prayers, and had milk for breakfast. The weather was cloudy and warm and it rained. I danced my dance and then wrote a letter till 12 o'clock, and then I went to visit Mrs. Southwell and stayed about an hour with her, and then went to Colonel Blakiston's to dinner and ate some roast turkey. After dinner I played with Colonel [Shutz] at piquet and won a crown. Then I went to

the play and there saw Mrs. W-l-c-r and led her out. Then I went to Will's Coffeehouse and ate a jelly and then walked home and said my prayers.

23. I rose about 2 o'clock and read a chapter in Hebrew and some Greek in Lucian. I said my prayers and had milk for breakfast. The weather was clear and warm, the wind west. I went not to church but read some English. I danced my dance and about 1 o'clock ate some biscuits and cheese and then went to Court where I saw several of my friends. About 2 o'clock I went to dine with Mr. Southwell where Mr. LeGrande and Mr. [Chester] also dined and I ate some veal and bacon. After dinner we drank a bottle and about 5 o'clock I set Mr. LeGrande down and then went to Lady Guise's where I stayed till 7 o'clock and then went to Mrs. [Sands'] and sat there two hours and about 10 o'clock went home and read some English and then said my prayers.

24. I rose about 8 o'clock and read a chapter in Hebrew and some Greek in Lucian. I neglected my prayers, but had milk for breakfast. The weather was clear and cold, the wind west. I danced my dance and read some English till 11 o'clock and then went to visit Mr. U-t-n and about 12 o'clock went to the milliners' and persuaded them to go to the play tomorrow. Then I went to the Virginia Coffeehouse and Mr. [Willis] invited me home to dinner with Dr. L-m-s and I ate some roast veal. After dinner we walked to Garraway's Coffeehouse where I read the news and about 5 o'clock went to Mr. Lindsay's where I saw Mrs. Cornish and drank tea. Here I stayed all the evening and played at piquet till supper, when I ate some roast lamb. About 12 o'clock I went home and said my prayers. I slept very badly.

25. I rose about 8 o'clock and read two chapters in Hebrew and some Greek in Lucian. I said my prayers and had milk for breakfast. The weather was cold and cloudy. About 9 o'clock came Mr. Perry and then came my milliner and then came my cousin Horsmanden and stayed till 12 o'clock, and then I read some English till two and then I ate some battered eggs. After dinner I put several things in

order and then danced my dance. About 5 o'clock I went to Will's and read the news and then Sir Wilfred Lawson and I went to the play to B-r-t-n box to meet our milliners and they came to us. After the play we went to the Three Tuns and had a fricassee of chicken. We kissed and were merry till 12 o'clock and then went home, and I said my prayers.

26. I rose about 8 o'clock and read a chapter in Hebrew and some Greek in Lucian. I said my prayers, and had milk for breakfast. The weather was cold and cloudy, the wind west. About 10 o'clock came Colonel Blathwayt and brought me my masquerade ticket. I wrote some English till 2 o'clock and then I ate some beefsteak. After dinner I put several things in order and then wrote more English till 4 o'clock, and then I went to the play in Lincoln's Inn where the French acted before the King and tumbled very well. From the play I came home directly in a chair and ate some bread and cheese. I found myself indisposed with a sore throat and therefore went soon to bed and said my prayers. I slept very ill being light headed all night.

27. I rose about 8 o'clock and read three chapters in Hebrew and some Greek in Lucian. I said my prayers and had milk for breakfast. The weather was cloudy and cold. I found myself much indisposed and my head still out of order, so that I could only write a little and then dozed till 2 o'clock in the great chair and then ate some boiled chicken and broth. After dinner I found myself so bad that I resolved not to go to the masquerade and therefore sent my ticket to Mrs. Lindsay with a very gallant letter. In the evening came Mrs. Wilkinson and stayed till 8 o'clock and then came my two milliners in masquerade and after them Sir Wilfred Lawson and they stayed with me till 10 o'clock. Then I took some Gascoigne powder and slept pretty well, thank God.

28. I rose about 8 o'clock and found myself much better, thank God. I read two chapters in Hebrew and some Greek in Lucian. I said my prayers, and had milk for breakfast. I danced my dance and

then wrote some English till 2 o'clock and then ate some milk porridge for dinner. After dinner I put several things in order and then
wrote a letter to my daughter and about 4 o'clock carried it myself.
I stayed with her about an hour and then went to the coffeehouse
where I found the Duke of Argyll and my Lord Orrery. Here I
stayed till 8 o'clock and then went to Lady Guise's where I found
Sir Roger Braidshaigh. Here I stayed till 9 o'clock and then went
home and had some milk porridge for supper. I said my prayers. I
slept pretty well, thank God.

29. I rose about 8 o'clock and read two chapters in Hebrew and
some Greek in Lucian. I said my prayers and had milk for breakfast.
I found myself much better, thank God. I wrote some English. About
11 o'clock came Dr. L-m-s and Mike Perry and stayed till one; then
I wrote more English till two and ate some battered eggs. After dinner I put several things in order and about 4 o'clock went to visit Mrs.
U-m-s and drank tea and about 8 o'clock went to Will's Coffeehouse
and read the news and stayed there till 10 o'clock and then walked
home and said my prayers. I continued much better, thank God.

30. I rose about 8 o'clock and read a chapter in Hebrew and some
Greek. I said my prayers and had milk for breakfast. I found myself
pretty well and grew strong again. I wrote some English till 1 o'clock
and then went to Court where I saw my friend Sir Wilfred Lawson
and when the King came from chapel took Sir Roger Braidshaigh and
went to dine with Lady Guise and I ate some boiled venison. Here
we stayed till 5 o'clock and then went to Will's where I stayed with
Lord Orrery till eight, and then went to Mrs. [Sands'] where I
stayed till ten, and then went home and said my prayers.

December 1718

1. I rose about 8 o'clock and read nothing because I was obliged to write a long letter to Virginia. However, I said my prayers, and had milk for breakfast. About 11 o'clock my Lord Percival called upon me and I waited on him to the Royal Society to our yearly meeting. When we had chosen our officers we went to Garraway's and from thence to Pontack's where about forty of us dined and I ate some fish. After dinner we returned to Garraway's and then I carried Lord Percival back and set him down at the Temple. Then I went to Mrs. A-s-t-n but she was from home, then to Will's, and from thence I went with Lord Orrery to the play where I saw my mistress, my Lady Bouverie. Then I went to Court, where was a great crowd, and about eleven I walked home and said my prayers.

2. I rose about 8 o'clock and read nothing because I was obliged to write more letters to Virginia. However, I said my prayers, and had milk for breakfast. The weather was clear and warm, the wind west. About ten came Mrs. D-n-s and I gave her a letter to Lady [Philips]. About twelve I went into the City and dined with Mr Perry and ate some boiled beef. After dinner I went to visit Mrs. Perry and there drank some wine and stayed till four. Then I sent to Mr. Lindsay but they were from home. Then I went to Will's Coffeehouse and from thence to Mrs. [Andrews'] and drank tea. About 9 o'clock I returned to Will's again and ate a jelly and drank some milk. About eleven I went home and settled some accounts and said my prayers.

3. I rose about 8 o'clock and read a chapter in Hebrew and ne Greek. I said a short prayer and had milk for breakfast. About 1 o'clock came Annie Wilkinson. About 11 o'clock I went to my Lor Percival's and with him I went to the meeting of the committee abou

the French prisoners. Then I went to Lord Orrery's but he was from home, and then to Sir Wilfred Lawson's and with him to the Court of Requests where I saw several of my acquaintances. Then about 2 o'clock I went to Mr. Southwell's to dinner and ate some fricassee of chicken, and Phil Percival was there. I consulted Mr. Southwell about my business with the Council of Trade, then went to the French play and after the play walked home and endeavored to pick up a whore by the way but could not succeed. So I went home and said my prayers.

4. I rose about 8 o'clock and read a chapter in Hebrew and some Greek in Lucian. I said my prayers, and had milk for breakfast. The weather was cold and cloudy, the wind northwest. I danced my dance and wrote a letter to the Council of Trade.[1] About 1 o'clock I went to Will's and read the news and then went to my Lord Percival's to dinner and ate some boiled beef and drank abundance of Burgundy. About five we played at commerce and I lost ten shillings. About six I went to Mrs. FitzHerbert's and sat with her till 8 o'clock and then came home and wrote a letter to Purleigh. I said my prayers.

5. I rose about 8 o'clock and read a chapter in Hebrew and some Greek in Lucian. I said my prayers, and had milk for breakfast. The weather was warm and clear, the wind west. About 11 o'clock came Mr. U-t-n and gave me five guineas for the new converts. Then I went to the Duke of Argyll's but he was from home. Then I went to my Lord Orrery's but I found only Madam there and kissed her for half an hour and then went home and danced my dance. About 2 o'clock I had some battered eggs for dinner. In the afternoon I put several things in order till four and then wrote some English till six and then went to Will's Coffeehouse and from thence to Mrs. B-r-n and then to St. James's Coffeehouse where I had a dish of chocolate, and then went to Court and came home about eleven and said my prayers.

1. Byrd wrote a petition to the Board of Trade that no members of the Virginia Council be removed on Governor Spotswood's accusations until they had presented their cases.

6. I rose about 8 o'clock and read a chapter in Hebrew and some Greek in Lucian. I said my prayers and had milk for breakfast. The weather was warm and clear, the wind northwest. I danced my dance and wrote two letters till 2 o'clock, and then ate some beef-steak for dinner. After dinner I put several things in order and then danced my dance again. About four I called on Miss A-s-t-n but she was from home. Then I went to the coffeehouse and from thence to the play where I saw Kitty Sambrooke but came away as soon as the play was done. Then I took a walk and picked up a whore but did nothing. I ate a plum cake and about eleven walked home and said my prayers.

7. I rose about 8 o'clock and read two chapters in Hebrew and some Greek in Lucian. I said my prayers, and had milk for breakfast. The weather was cold and cloudy, the wind northeast. About 11 o'clock I went to Mr. Lindsay's in the City where I dined and ate some roast beef. After dinner we went to church where we had an excellent sermon. After church we returned to Mr. Lindsay's and drank tea and then sat and talked all the evening till nine and then we had some teal for supper. Then we drank a bottle and were merry till eleven and then I took leave and went home in my own chariot and said my prayers.

8. I rose about 8 o'clock and read a chapter in Hebrew and some Greek. I said my prayers and had milk for breakfast. The weather was clear and cold, the wind west. I danced my dance. About 9 o'clock came my cousin Horsmanden and stayed about half an hour. Then came Colonel Blathwayt and then my Lord Orrery and stayed till 2 o'clock. Then I ate some battered eggs for dinner. After dinner I put several things in order and about 4 o'clock went to the Temple with my cousin Horsmanden to discourse Sir George Cooke about his chambers in Lincoln's Inn. Then I went to Will's where I saw the Duke of Argyll. About 9 o'clock I went to St. James's Coffeehouse and drank a dish of chocolate and then went to Court, where there was a ball, and I got almost drunk and came home about 1 o'clock and said my prayers.

9. I rose about 8 o'clock and read a chapter in Hebrew and some Greek. I said my prayers, and had milk for breakfast. The weather was cloudy and cold, the wind northwest. I danced my dance. About 10 o'clock I went to Mr. Southwell's where I drank tea and stayed till eleven. Then I went to the Cockpit where I talked with Mr. B-m-f-l. Then I went home and danced again. Then about 2 o'clock I returned again to Mr. Southwell's where I ate some boiled beef. After dinner we sat and drank a bottle till 5 o'clock and then I took a coach and called on my milliner. My daughter had the chariot to go to the ball. About 6 o'clock I went to Mrs. Lindsay's where I drank tea and chocolate and then took a walk and picked up a woman and put her into the coach and committed uncleanness. Then I went to Will's and had some cake and milk and read the news. Then I went home in a chair because it rained and said my prayers.

10. I rose about 8 o'clock and read a chapter in Hebrew and some Greek in Lucian. I said a short prayer, and had milk for breakfast. The weather was cloudy and cold. About 11 o'clock I went into the City and dined with Dick Perry. After dinner we drank tea and then I went to Mrs. Lindsay's and drank tea again. About 6 o'clock came Mr. M-r-s and about seven we went together to Mr. G-r-s-c-t ball and stayed there till 10 o'clock and then I returned to Mr. Lindsay's and ate some hasty pudding for supper. Then we sat and chatted till 12 o'clock and then I returned home and said my prayers. My land-lady was extremely ill.

11. I rose about 8 o'clock and read a chapter in Hebrew and some Greek in Lucian. I said no prayers, but had boiled milk for breakfast. The weather was clear and cold, the wind northwest. I danced my dance and wrote some English. Colonel Blakiston and his son came about 11 o'clock and stayed half an hour. The Colonel told me the Council of Trade took my letter very ill. About 1 o'clock I went into the city to dine at Pontack's and ate some boiled beef. After dinner we called at Garraway's and from thence we went to Crane Court where my friend Sir Wilfred Lawson was chosen. About 6 o'clock I went to visit Mrs. F-p-s to meet my Lady Dunkellen and

she told me her story. I drank two dishes of chocolate. About 11 o'clock I walked home and said my prayers.

12. I rose about 8 o'clock and read two chapters in Hebrew and some Greek in Lucian. I said my prayers, and had milk for breakfast. The weather was very cold and clear. I danced my dance and about 11 o'clock went to the Duke of Argyll's and stayed there about an hour and then returned home and called on Mrs. H-r-s but she was from home. I wrote some English till two and then ate some battered eggs. After dinner I put several things in order and then danced again and wrote more English. Then I read some English till 5 o'clock and went to Will's Coffeehouse, and read the news. Then I called in at the play and went from thence to Lady Guise's and there met Lord Tyrconnel's daughter. Then I went to St. James's Coffeehouse and drank two dishes of chocolate. Then went to Court and thence walked home and said my prayers.

13. I rose about 8 o'clock and read a chapter in Hebrew and some Greek in Lucian. I said my prayers and had milk for breakfast. The weather was clear and cold, the wind north. I danced my dance. About 11 o'clock I went to my Lord Percival's and stayed about half an hour. Then I went to Mr. Southwell's and sat with Betty till one o'clock and then walked in the park with Colonel Gay[2] till two. Then I went to dine with Mr. Southwell and ate some beefsteak, and after dinner we drank a bottle of wine. About five we went to the play where I found myself very dull. After the play I went to the coffeehouse and drank two dishes of chocolate and talked with my cousin Horsmanden and he walked home with me lest I should pick up a whore. I said my prayers and washed my feet.

14. I rose about 8 o'clock and read a chapter in Hebrew and some Greek in Lucian. I said my prayers, and had milk for breakfast. The weather was cold and cloudy, the wind east. I danced my dance and about 11 o'clock went to Somerset Chapel and heard a good sermon.

2. Alexander Gay, formerly (until November 1717) lieutenant colonel in Meredith's Regiment of Foot.

After church I went and dined with P-n-y U-m-s and ate some boiled beef. In the afternoon we drank tea and about 5 o'clock came Mrs. A-l-b-r-th and Mrs. Bellenden and her sister. Here I stayed till 6 o'clock and then went to Will's Coffeehouse. Then I took my cousin Horsmanden and went to Mrs. [Sands'] where we found Sir Wilfred Lawson and his brother. About nine I called on my neighbor H-r-s and sat with her till 11 o'clock and then walked home and said my prayers.

15. I rose about 8 o'clock and read two chapters in Hebrew and some Greek. I said my prayers, and had milk for breakfast. The weather was cold and cloudy, the wind northwest. I danced my dance. About 11 o'clock I went to my Lord Orrery's and there drank two dishes of chocolate, and about 1 o'clock I went home and danced my dance again till 2 o'clock and then ate some battered eggs for dinner. After dinner I put several things in order till 4 o'clock and then danced my dance again, and read some English. About five I went to Will's Coffeehouse and read the news and about six went to visit Mrs. [Andrews] but they were from home. Then I went to Colonel Blakiston's and stayed there about two hours, and then went to St. James's Coffeehouse and drank a dish of chocolate. Then I went to Court and about eleven walked home and said my prayers.

16. I rose about 8 o'clock and read a chapter in Hebrew and some Greek. I said my prayers and had milk for breakfast. The weather was very cold, the wind northeast. About 11 o'clock came old Mr. Perry and talked of his reception by the Council of Trade. I danced my dance and read some English till 2 o'clock and then ate some beefsteak. After dinner I put several things in order till 5 o'clock and then Mrs. Lindsay came to visit me by herself and half an hour after Mr. Lindsay also came and drank tea with me and stayed till seven and then I went in the dress of a running footman to my Lady Guise's and from thence I went to Lord Orrery's and there ate some broiled turkey. Then I went with my Lord to the masquerade where I was but indifferently diverted. However I stayed till 5 o'clock in the

morning and drank three dishes of chocolate. About five I rode home and neglected to say my prayers, for which God forgive me. I was not well diverted this masquerade.

17. I rose about 8 o'clock to go to the house of office and then went to bed again and lay till one. Then I rose and read a chapter in Hebrew and some Greek in Lucian. I danced my dance and had some milk for breakfast and about 3 o'clock ate some battered eggs. After dinner I put several things in order and about 5 o'clock went to Mrs. Lindsay's where we played at hazard and I won a guinea. Then we played at slam and I lost a little. However, we were very merry. About seven we drank tea and about ten we went to supper and I ate some broiled goose. Then we sat and talked till twelve and then I went home and neglected to say my prayers. This day war was proclaimed against Spain.[3]

18. I rose about 8 o'clock and read a chapter in Hebrew and some Greek in Lucian. I said my prayers, and had milk for breakfast. The weather was cold and cloudy, the wind northeast, and it both rained and snowed. About 11 o'clock I went to the committee of the converts and gave them Mr. U-t-n's five guineas. About one I endeavored to go to Pontack's but was stopped so long that it would have been too late, so I went home and danced my dance and then ate some beefsteak for dinner. After dinner I put several things in order and then wrote a letter to my cousin Suky Horsmanden. About 5 o'clock I went to visit my cousin Daniel and stayed about half an hour and then went to my daughter's and carried her to Mrs. [Sands'] where we drank tea and stayed till nine and my daughter set me to Will's and she went home. Here I read the news and had a cake and some milk and about eleven walked home and said my prayers.

19. I rose about 8 o'clock and read a chapter in Hebrew but no Greek because I was hindered. However, I said my prayers and had

3. 'War was declared against Spain in the usual places within the cities of London and Westminster, and with the usual solemnities,' *Historical Register, Chronological Diary.*

milk for breakfast. The weather was cold and cloudy, the wind northwest. I perceived I had a cold in my head. About 12 o'clock I went to the Virginia Coffeehouse and from thence to Mr. Perry's and dined with the old gentleman and ate some roast beef. After dinner I received a hundred pounds and then went to visit Mrs. Perry and drank tea with them and then went to the playhouse in Lincoln's Inn and had a quarrel with several footmen about wearing their hats. I sat by Mr. Southwell. After the play I went to Court, where I talked abundance to the widow Pierson and about 11 o'clock went home in the chair and said my prayers.

20. I rose about 9 o'clock and read a chapter in Hebrew and some Greek in Lucian. I said a short prayer, and had milk for breakfast. The weather continued cold, the wind northeast. My cold grew worse. However, I went about 11 o'clock to my Lord Orrery's where I drank a dish of chocolate and from thence I went to my Lord Islay's but he was from home. Then I went to the Court of Requests and recommended the tobacco law to some Lords. About 2 o'clock I went to Mr. U-t-n and by the way found pretty Mrs. F-r-m-m-t-n in some distress because a cart was run upon her coach. I went to her and offered her my chariot, which, however, she would not accept. I ate some boiled beef for dinner. Sir Harry Ashurst dined with us and my Lord Bellenden. About 6 o'clock I went to the play, where I was diverted very well. After the play I went to the coffeehouse and read the news till eleven and then walked home and found little fire, notwithstanding it was cold, for which I scolded at my man.

21. I rose about 8 o'clock and was angry with my man for not getting up and gave him warning. I read a chapter in Hebrew and some Greek in Lucian. The weather was extremely cold, the wind northeast. My cold continued, so that I went not to church. I danced my dance. About 1 o'clock I ate some battered eggs for dinner. After dinner I put several things in order till 4 o'clock and then I wrote a letter to my daughter. Then I made a visit to my landlady and drank some caudle. About 5 o'clock I went to the coffeehouse and then went to visit my Lord Foley and stayed till eight and then went

to Lady Guise's and stayed till nine and then went home and ate some cake and cheese. I neglected to say my prayers, for which God forgive me. I began to have a fire in my chamber.

22. I rose about 8 o'clock and read a chapter in Hebrew and some Greek in Lucian. I said my prayers, and had milk for breakfast. It continued very cold, the wind northeast. My cold was worse. I danced my dance. I wrote a letter to my cousin Nutty Horsmanden,[4] and about 2 o'clock ate some broiled chicken. After dinner I put several things in order and danced my dance again and about 5 o'clock went to visit Mrs. P-n and Mrs. M-r-s but the first was from home. However, I drank tea with the last and stayed till 7 o'clock and then went to Colonel Blakiston's and stayed till nine, and then went to the coffeehouse and drank two dishes of chocolate, and then went to Court and stayed there till 11 o'clock, and then went home in a chair and said my prayers.

23. I rose about 8 o'clock and read a chapter in Hebrew and some Greek in Lucian. I said a short prayer, and had milk for breakfast. The weather was cold and cloudy, the wind north. My cold was still bad but was turned to a cough. Annie Wilkinson came and I scolded at her for not bringing my things. Then came Colonel Blakiston and proposed to me the government of Maryland and said he would manage it for me. About [. . .] I went to Mrs. Southwell's and then walked in the park. Then I went to the Court of Requests and about 2 o'clock went back to Mr. Southwell's again for dinner and I ate some boiled beef. After dinner we sat and talked till 4 o'clock and then went to visit a whore but she was from home, so I went to Will's and sat there till eight and then went to visit Mrs. U-m-s and stayed till ten and then walked home, ate some cake, and said my prayers.

24. I rose about 8 o'clock and read a chapter in Hebrew and some Greek in Lucian. I said my prayers, and had milk for breakfast. The weather was cold and cloudy and it rained all the morning, the wind north. I danced my dance and then wrote a letter to Purleigh. About

4. Ursula.

one o'clock I went to Will's and read the news and then went to Mr. Southwell's to dinner where the Muscovite Ambassador[5] dined also and I ate some fish. After dinner we sat and talked of several things relating to his country. About 5 o'clock I went away and called upon Mrs. [...], a lady of pleasure, but she was not at home. Then I went to Will's and from thence to Mrs. B-r-n and drank some coffee. Then I went to Lady Guise's and sat with her till 9 o'clock and then went home and ate some milk porridge, and said my prayers. My cold continued bad. I committed uncleanness this night.

25. I rose about 8 o'clock and read a chapter in Hebrew and some Greek in Lucian. I said my prayers, and had milk for breakfast. The weather was cold and cloudy, the wind north. I danced my dance and wrote some English and then read some English till 2 o'clock and then my coachman came and let me know my chariot was out of order, so I took a hack and went to Lady Guise's where I ate some roast beef for dinner. After dinner we sat and talked till 6 o'clock and then I went to visit Mrs. FitzHerbert but notwithstanding it was her day she was from home. Then I went to Mrs. L-c-b-r and sat there till 9 o'clock and then walked to Will's Coffeehouse and ate a jelly and read the news. About ten I went home and read some English and said my prayers.

26. I rose about 8 o'clock and read some Hebrew and some Greek in Lucian. I said my prayers, and had milk for breakfast. The weather was warm and cloudy, the wind west. My cold continued. I danced my dance and then read some English till 2 o'clock and then ate some battered eggs. After dinner I put several things in order till 5 o'clock. Then I went to visit Mr. U-m-s where I drank some tea and stayed till 8 o'clock and Mr. U-t-n came in while I was there. Then I went to Will's Coffeehouse and drank two dishes of chocolate and about nine went to Court and carried Mr. G-r-d-n with me. There was little company, so about eleven I went home and said my prayers.

27. I rose about 8 o'clock and read a chapter in Hebrew and some Greek in Lucian. I said my prayers, and had milk for breakfast. The

5. M. Wesselowski, envoy from the Czar of Muscovy.

weather was warm and cloudy and it rained a little. I danced my dance and then wrote some English till 1 o'clock and then went to Will's Coffeehouse and read the news and then went to dine with Mrs. U-t-n and ate some broiled turkey. After dinner I went to Mrs. U-m-s and drank tea and then went to Mrs. [Andrews'] and stayed till 9 o'clock and then called at the playhouse and then went to Will's Coffeehouse and had a cake and some milk for supper. I stayed till 10 o'clock and then went home in a chair because it rained and said my prayers. My cough was violent.

28. I rose about 8 o'clock and read some Hebrew and some Greek in Lucian. I said a short prayer and had milk for breakfast. The weather was warm and cloudy, the wind west, and it rained a little. I danced my dance and wrote a little English. About 12 o'clock I went into the City to Mr. Lindsay's but he was gone into the country with his family so I went to Sir Charles Wager's and dined there, but because he dines late we ate some oysters and about three we dined and I ate some roast turkey. About five we drank tea and then I took leave and went to Will's Coffeehouse and met my Lord Dunkellen and told him what I heard of him and his lady. About seven I went to Mr. [Sands'] where I met Sir Wilfred Lawson and stayed till ten and then went home and said my prayers. My cough was violent. I took some Anderson's pills.

29. I rose about 8 o'clock and read a chapter in Hebrew and some Greek in Lucian. I said my prayers, and had milk porridge for breakfast. The weather was cold and cloudy, the wind west. About 10 o'clock came Annie Wilkinson and brought one shirt and I scolded at her. Then came Mike Perry and stayed about half an hour. Then came my Lord Percival and stayed half an hour. Then I danced my dance and then wrote some English till 2 o'clock and then ate some boiled chicken. After dinner I put several things in order and wrote more English till 5 o'clock and then went to visit Mrs. P-n and Mrs. M-r-s and drank tea. Here I stayed till 7 o'clock and then went to Colonel Blakiston's and stayed there till nine and then went to Court where was abundance of company. About eleven I returned home in the chair and said my prayers. My pills worked three times with me.

30. I rose about 8 o'clock and read some Hebrew and some Greek. I said my prayers, and had milk porridge for breakfast. The weather was cold and cloudy, the wind northwest, and it rained a little. I wrote three letters and about 12 o'clock went into the City and dined with Mr. Perry and ate some boiled pork. After dinner we drank tea. I chid my daughter for not writing to me but gave her four half guineas, as I did Miss Page. About 5 o'clock I went to Will's Coffeehouse and set Phil Perry [6] down by the way at the Temple. Then I went to the play and after the play came home but did not find my man, for which I was very angry with him. I ate some cold chicken for supper and wrote some English and said my prayers. I took some [dogwood].

31. I rose about 8 o'clock and read a chapter in Hebrew and some Greek in Lucian. I said my prayers and had milk porridge for breakfast. The weather was clear and cold, the wind west. I wrote some English till 11 o'clock and then came Mr. Horsmanden and stayed quarter of an hour. Then I went to the Duke of Argyll's and stayed with him about an hour. Then I went to Ozinda's and drank some [egg cider]. Then I walked in the Mall till 2 o'clock and then went home and had some beefsteak for dinner. In the afternoon I set some things in order and then wrote two letters to Virginia till 7 o'clock and then went to Will's Coffeehouse and from thence to my Lady Guise's where I sat about an hour, and then went to Court where was very few people. About eleven I returned in a chair, ate some milk porridge, and said my prayers. It rained extremely.

6. Son of Richard Perry.

January 1719

1. I rose about 8 o'clock and read some Hebrew and some Greek in Lucian. I said my prayers, and had milk porridge for breakfast. The weather was cloudy and cold, the wind west. I danced my dance. Then I wrote a letter to Virginia and about 2 o'clock dined with my landlord, who invited me to dinner, and I ate some boiled turkey. After dinner we sat and talked till 4 o'clock and then drank tea. About 5 o'clock I went to Will's and read the news and then looked in at the play, and from thence went to visit Mrs. U-m-s and sat with them till eight, and then I went to Court, where there was a ball and abundance of company. I talked to very few because I had a cold. About twelve I returned home in the chair, ate some milk porridge, and said my prayers. My cough troubled me very much.

2. I rose about 8 o'clock and read a chapter in Hebrew and some Greek in Lucian. I said my prayers, and had milk porridge for breakfast. The weather was cold and cloudy, the wind west. I danced my dance and then wrote some letters to Virginia till 2 o'clock and then had some battered eggs. After dinner I put several things in order and then danced my dance again and then wrote more letters. I resolved not to go out because of my cough and because I had so many letters to write. About 8 o'clock I had some milk porridge again and then read some English till 10 o'clock and said my prayers. I slept pretty well, thank God.

3. About 7 o'clock I drank asses' milk and rose about eight and read some Hebrew and some Greek in Lucian. I said my prayers, and had milk porridge for breakfast. The weather was cloudy and cold, the wind west. About 11 o'clock my cousin Horsmanden came and stayed till twelve and then I wrote two letters to Virginia and about

two I ate some boiled chicken. After dinner I put several things in
order and danced my dance. About 5 I went to Will's Coffeehouse
and read the news. Then I went into the City to Mr. Lindsay's notwithstanding Mrs. Lindsay was out of town. Here I played at dice
and won about ten shillings. About eight I drank two dishes of chocolate and about nine returned home and made a visit to my landlady
and ate some cake. I read some English and said my prayers. I slept
pretty well.

4. I rose about 8 o'clock, having drunk my asses' milk in bed. I
read some Hebrew and some Greek in Lucian. I said my prayers and
had milk porridge for breakfast. I wrote a letter to Virginia and then
danced my dance and then wrote more letters till 2 o'clock and then
ate some brains for dinner. In the afternoon I wrote more letters and
danced my dance again, and about 5 o'clock went to Will's Coffeehouse and drank some tea and milk. About seven I went to visit Mrs.
[Sands] where was Harriet Smith, a pretty girl. Here I stayed till
10 o'clock and then returned home, where I read some English and
then ate some milk porridge for supper. I said my prayers and took
[dogwood] which made me sleep pretty well and cough but little.

5. I rose about eight having drunk my asses' milk in bed. I read a
chapter in Hebrew and some Greek in Lucian. I said my prayers,
and had milk porridge for breakfast. The weather was cold and
cloudy and rained abundantly. However about 12 o'clock I went to
the Virginia Coffeehouse where I learned that Mr. F-l-d died there
of an apoplexy. I gave my letters to Major B-k-r-t-n and Captain
Ned Randolph. Then I went and dined with old Mr. Perry and ate
some ham and bacon. After dinner I went to Dick Perry's and drank
tea and saw my daughter, who had a cold. Then I went to the play
and then to Will's and then to Colonel Blakiston's but they were from
home. Then to Mrs. FitzHerbert's but found her not, and then to
St. James's Coffeehouse, where I read the news and then went to
Court but there were so few people the King did not come out so I
went home, ate some milk porridge, and said my prayers and took
[dogwood] and slept indifferently.

6. I drank my asses' milk and rose about 8 o'clock and read a chapter in Hebrew and some Greek in Lucian. I said my prayers, and had milk porridge for breakfast. The weather was clear and warm, the wind northwest. I wrote a letter and some other things in English till 2 o'clock and then ate some brains for dinner. After dinner I put several things in order till 4 o'clock and then I danced my dance. About 5 o'clock I went to Will's Coffeehouse and read the news and then went to my Lord Percival's where I found abundance of company met together to be merry.[1] We played at basset and I won two guineas. Then we drew king and queen. Then came three women in masks and stayed about half an hour. Then we played at [little plays] and were merry. We had some punch which did me good for my cold. About 11 o'clock we took leave and went to Court where was abundance of company, where the King played at dice and several danced. I stayed till 1 o'clock and then walked home and neglected my prayers. However I slept pretty well, thank God.

7. I drank my asses' milk and rose about 8 o'clock and read some Hebrew and some Greek in Lucian. I said my prayers, and had milk porridge for breakfast. The weather was clear and cold, the wind north. I danced my dance and about 11 o'clock went to Colonel Blakiston's but he was from home. However, I overtook him and we walked through the park and then I walked round and then went to visit Mrs. Southwell where I saw D-l-y [Clark]. Then I walked to Ozinda's and about two walked home with Mr. Southwell and dined with him and ate some fish for dinner. After dinner we sat and talked till five and then I took leave and went to Will's and read the news and stayed there till 7 o'clock and then went to visit my Lady Guise where I found Lady G-l-s-n, and stayed till 10 o'clock and then went home and found no fire. I said my prayers and took [dogwood].

8. I rose about 8 o'clock, having drunk my asses' milk. I read a chapter in Hebrew and some Greek in Lucian. I said my prayers,

1. The festivities were in celebration of Twelfth Night.

and had milk porridge for breakfast. The weather was cold and cloudy. About 10 o'clock I received a letter from Mrs. Perry that my daughter had the signs of the smallpox, so I went away, after having Mr. M-n-l-y promise that my daughter should be with me. I found [her] bad of a pain in the head but very [lively]. I dined here and ate some beef boiled. After dinner I stayed and we drank tea, and then I went to Will's Coffeehouse and read the news and then went to the play and there agreed to go to the girls. After the play I picked up a woman, walking home, and carried her to the alehouse in Westminster but she could not stay. However, we agreed to meet again. The landlady was courteous to me and lent me a shilling to go home in a coach. I found by Mr. M-n-l-y that my daughter was better, thank God. I said my prayers.

9. I drank asses' milk and rose about 8 o'clock and read a chapter in Hebrew and some Greek in Lucian. I said my prayers, and had milk porridge for breakfast. The weather was cloudy and warm. About 11 o'clock I went to Mrs. Southwell's and sat with her about half an hour and then went to Lord Percival's but he was from home, and then I went to my Lord Orrery's and drank some chocolate and about 1 o'clock went home and wrote a letter to Virginia and about 2 o'clock ate some brains. After dinner I put several things in order and then danced my dance and about 5 o'clock went to Mr. Perry's to see my daughter and found her much better, thank God. About 6 o'clock I went to Mr. Lindsay's and lost five guineas at hazard and about ten went to supper and I ate some oysters. About twelve I came home and said my prayers.

10. I rose about 8 o'clock, having taken my asses' milk, and read a chapter in Hebrew and some Greek in Lucian. I said my prayers, and had milk porridge for breakfast. The weather was warm and cloudy, the wind west. I danced my dance. Annie Wilkinson came to endeavor to get money of me but I refused her. I wrote a letter to Purleigh till 2 o'clock and then ate some battered eggs for dinner. After dinner I put several things in order and then read some English and danced my dance again. About five I went to Will's Coffeehouse and read the news. Then I went to the play where I had an occasion

to do a civil thing to the Duke of Buckingham.[2] After the play I went to visit a whore but she was from home. Then I went to Will's and had a cake and some milk. Then I walked home and took some [dogwood]. I said my prayers.

11. I rose about 8 o'clock, having taken my asses' milk, and read some Hebrew and some Greek in Lucian. I said my prayers, and had milk porridge for breakfast. The weather was warm and cloudy. About 11 o'clock I went to Somerset Chapel where we had an indifferent sermon. After church I returned home and danced my dance. Then I read some English till 1 o'clock and then ate some roast fowl for dinner. In the afternoon I put several things in order and then read more English till 5 o'clock and then went to meet my mistress at the alehouse in Westminster, where we drank some punch and ate some fowl. I said my prayers.

12. I rose about 8 o'clock, having drunk my asses' milk and read a chapter in Hebrew and some Greek in Lucian. I said my prayers, and had milk porridge for breakfast. The weather was warm and cloudy. I danced my dance and then wrote some English. Annie Wilkinson came and I gave her a guinea. Then I read some English till 2 o'clock and then ate some battered eggs. After dinner I put several things in order and then read more English till 5 o'clock and then I went to Mrs. M-r-s and drank some tea. Here came Mrs. H-s and I sat and talked till 7 o'clock, and then went to Colonel Blakiston's and found them at cards. I stayed till 9 o'clock and then went to Court where was very indifferent company. About eleven I went home in the chair and ate some cake and cheese and said my prayers.

13. I rose about 8 o'clock, having drunk my asses' milk, and read a chapter in Hebrew and some Greek in Lucian. I said my prayers, and had milk porridge for breakfast. The weather was warm and cloudy, the wind west. About 11 o'clock I went to Mrs. U-m-s and gave P-n-y a ticket for the masquerade. Then I went to Mr. Perry's and dined with Dick and ate some pork and peas. About three I went

2. John Sheffield, Duke of Buckingham.

home and was in a fury with my man for not being at home according to my orders. Then I got things ready for to dress me for the masquerade and about eight went to Mrs. M-r-s in a Mogul's habit and from thence to my Lord Percival's where I ate some chicken for supper. About 11 o'clock I went to the masquerade and was pretty well diverted but exceeding tired. I returned home about 5 o'clock and slept till eleven.

14. I rose about 11 o'clock, having had my asses' milk, and read a chapter in Hebrew and some Greek in Lucian. I said my prayers and had milk porridge for breakfast. I danced my dance. Then I read some English and then took a nap till 3 o'clock and then ate some battered eggs for dinner. In the afternoon I put several things in order and then read more English. About five I went to Will's Coffeehouse and read the news. About 6 o'clock a lady came to call me and I went with her to the tavern and ate some boiled chicken. From hence we went to the bagnio where I lay with my woman for about an hour and then got up again and I went home and washed myself. I said my prayers.

15. I rose about 8 o'clock, having taken my asses' milk. I read a chapter in Hebrew and some Greek in Lucian. I said my prayers, and had milk porridge for breakfast. The weather was clear and warm, the wind west. I danced my dance. About 12 o'clock my Lord Foley came and stayed about an hour. Then came Sir Wilfred Lawson and I went with him to Pontack's where I ate some fish for dinner. About 4 o'clock we went to Crane Court where Sir Wilfred was received into the Society. From hence I went to visit Mrs. F-r-y, the lady I met with at the masquerade, and drank tea with her and stayed about an hour, and then went to Lady Guise's and stayed till 9 o'clock and then went to Will's, read the news, and lost a guinea by betting on Colonel Cecil. About eleven I walked home and said my prayers.

16. I rose about 8 o'clock, having taken my asses' milk, and read some Hebrew and some Greek in Lucian. I said my prayers, and had

milk porridge for breakfast. The weather was clear and cold, the wind west. I danced my dance. About 11 o'clock I went to the Duke of Argyll's and stayed about an hour and then went to my Lord Orrery's where I drank some chocolate and after an hour went to Mr. Blathwayt's but they were from home. Then I walked in the Mall till 2 o'clock with Colonel Hales.[3] Then I went with Sir Roger Braidshaigh to my Lady Guise's and ate some fish for dinner. Here I stayed till 6 o'clock, and then went to Will's and from thence to Mrs. [Andrews'] but they were from home. Then to visit D-l-y [Clark] and stayed there till 9 o'clock and then went to Court where was a ball. Here I stayed till 12 o'clock and then went home in the chair and said my prayers and slept pretty well.

17. I rose about 8 o'clock, having drunk asses' milk, and read some Hebrew and some Greek in Lucian. I said my prayers, and had milk porridge for breakfast. The weather was clear and cold, the wind west. I danced my dance and wrote a letter. About 1 o'clock I went to walk in the Mall, where there was abundance of company. Here I walked till 2 o'clock and then Sir Roger Braidshaigh and I went to Mr. Southwell's to dinner and found Lord Percival and Daniel Dering there. I ate some beefsteak. Mr. Southwell was gayer than ordinary. About five we took leave and went to Will's and from thence to the play, which was indifferent enough. After the play I went to Will's again and had some milk and cake and read the news. About ten I walked home and said my prayers.

18. I rose about 8 o'clock, having drunk my asses' milk. I read a chapter in Hebrew and some Greek in Lucian. I said my prayers, and had milk porridge for breakfast. The weather was cold and cloudy, the wind northeast. This morning Sir Samuel Garth[4] died. This morning I danced my dance and wrote a letter to my daughter. About twelve I went to St. James's Chapel and stayed till the King

3. Thomas Hales, colonel of a regiment of foot on the Irish Establishment, disbanded in 1718.

4. Sir Samuel Garth, one of the physicians in ordinary to the King and physician general to the army; a fellow of the Royal Society and a member of the Kit-Kat Club.

came out and then Mr. Blathwayt and I walked through the park and I dined with him and ate some roast beef. About five we drank tea and at six I went to Mrs. [Sands'] but they were from home. Then I went to Colonel Blakiston's and stayed about an hour and then went to Will's where I had some cake and milk. Then I went to Kitty C-d-g-n and played with her and gave a guinea [entrance] but did nothing. Then I walked home and said my prayers.

19. I rose about 8 o'clock, having taken my asses' milk, and read a chapter in Hebrew and some Greek in Lucian. I said my prayers, and had milk porridge for breakfast. The weather was cold and cloudy, the wind northeast. I danced my dance and then wrote a letter to Purleigh. About 2 o'clock I ate some battered eggs for dinner. After dinner I put several things in order and then danced again. About 4 o'clock I went to visit Mrs. U-m-s and drank tea and about 6 o'clock I went to the play in Lincoln's Inn. After the play I went to Will's and drank two dishes of chocolate and then went to Court where were abundance of pretty girls, particularly Miss F-l-m-n. About eleven I went home in the chair and said my prayers.

20. I rose about 8 o'clock, having had my asses' milk, and read a chapter in Hebrew and some Greek in Lucian. I said my prayers, and had milk porridge for breakfast. The weather cold and cloudy, the wind northwest. I danced my dance. About 11 o'clock I went to Mr. Horsmanden's but he was from home. Then I went to Mrs. S-t-r-d-g to visit my daughter and Miss Page and found them very well. Then I went and dined with old Mr. Perry and ate some boiled beef. After dinner I went to visit Mrs. Perry and drank tea with her. There came in Mrs. T-r-n-t of Pennsylvania. About six I went away and called at both playhouses and then went to Will's Coffeehouse and read the news and drank two dishes of chocolate. About 8 o'clock Mrs. S-t-r-d called on me and we went to the bagnio and lay there all night and I rogered her three times with vigor.

21. I rose about 10 o'clock and went home, where I read some Hebrew and some Greek. I said my prayers and had milk porridge

for breakfast. The weather was cold and cloudy. About twelve came my Lord Orrery and stayed about an hour. Then I read some English till two when I ate some brains for dinner. After dinner I put several things in order and then dressed me and about 4 o'clock went to Mrs. Lindsay's, and sat with her two hours and drank tea; about seven came home Mr. Lindsay. We played at cards. About eight we drank chocolate and about that time came home Mr. Lindsay [sic]. About ten we went to supper and I ate some fricassee. Then we played again at cards and Will [Tryon] was with us. About twelve I went home and said my prayers.

22. I rose about 8 o'clock, having drunk my asses' milk, and read some Hebrew and some Greek in Lucian. I said my prayers, and had milk porridge for breakfast. The weather was clear and cold, the wind northwest. About ten Mr. A-w-r-th came and told me the steps he had made relating to the encouragement of hemp. I settled several matters and wrote some English and about one o'clock went to Will's Coffeehouse to meet Mr. A-s-r-t and from thence went to Mr. U-t-n to dinner and ate some fowl and bacon. There dined Margaret Bellenden and P-n-y U-m-s. After dinner we were merry till five and then I went to Will's and from thence to visit Mrs. [Andrews] and sat with them and drank tea till 9 o'clock and then returned to Will's again and ate a cake and milk. About eleven I walked home and said my prayers.

23. I rose about 8 o'clock, having drunk my asses' milk, and read a chapter in Hebrew and some Greek in Lucian. I said my prayers, and had milk porridge for breakfast. The weather was warm and cloudy, the wind west. I danced my dance. About 10 o'clock came Mr. Horsmanden and stayed half an hour. Then came Sir Roger Braidshaigh and stayed half an hour more. Annie Wilkinson came likewise. I wrote some English till 2 o'clock, when I ate a beefsteak for dinner. In the afternoon I settled several matters and danced again. I drank tea with my landlady and then went to Mrs. B-r-n but she was indisposed so I went to Mrs. M-r-s and drank tea there again. Then I went to Colonel Blakiston's who was likewise from home. Then to Mrs. FitzHerbert's who was from home. Then to Lord

Percival's where I lost twelve shillings at cards. About nine I went to Court where was abundance of company. About eleven I came home in the chair and said my prayers.

24. I rose about 8 o'clock, having drunk my asses' milk, and read a chapter in Hebrew and some Greek in Lucian. I said my prayers, and had milk porridge for breakfast. The weather was warm and cloudy, the wind west. I wrote a letter to my daughter and about 11 o'clock went to visit my Lord Orrery where I drank a dish of chocolate. Then I went to visit Mrs. Southwell and stayed there about an hour. Then I went to the Court of Requests where I talked with Sir Charles Wager and Colonel Blakiston. About two I returned to my Lord Orrery's to dinner and ate some roast fowl and sausage and stayed till five. Then we went to the coffeehouse and from thence I went to the play where I saw my old mistress and Mrs. [Coatsworth]. Then I went to the coffeehouse again and from thence went to a whore that was from home. Then I walked home and said my prayers.

25. I rose about 8 o'clock, having drunk my asses' milk, and read a chapter in Hebrew and some Greek in Lucian. I said my prayers, and had milk porridge for breakfast. The weather was warm and cloudy. I danced my dance and about 11 o'clock went to take up my daughter to carry her to dine with Mrs. Lindsay. I found her with a great cold. However, we went there and I ate some fricassee. After dinner we sat and talked while Mr. Lindsay went to church and when he returned we drank tea and Mrs. [Tryon] and her daughter came in to us. About 5 o'clock I took leave and carried home my daughter and then went to see Mrs. F-r-y and sat there till seven and then went to Will's and had some chocolate. Then I went to Mrs. C-d-g-n but she was out, so I walked home, ate a cake, and said my prayers.

26. I rose about 8 o'clock, having taken my asses' milk, and read a chapter in Hebrew and some Greek in Lucian. I said my prayers and had milk porridge for breakfast. About 10 o'clock came Annie Wilkinson and I rogered her. About one o'clock I went to Will's and

read the news and then went to Mr. U-t-n to dinner and ate some boiled beef. After dinner we went and sat with the U-m-s and drank tea and about 5 o'clock I went to Will's where I sat the whole evening till 9 o'clock and then went to Court where were abundance of pretty women, and Mrs. F-r-m-t-n among the rest with whom I talked abundantly, and then said many things to Mrs. B-r-n. Here I stayed till eleven and then went home in a chair and said my prayers.

27. I rose about 8 o'clock, having had my asses' milk, and read a chapter in Hebrew and some Greek in Lucian. I said my prayers and had milk porridge for breakfast. The wind was west and it rained. Captain [Blakiston] came to borrow a habit for the masquerade and I lent him one. About eleven I went to visit my daughter and offered a ticket to Miss Page but she would not accept. Then I went to Mr. Lindsay's where I dined and ate some roast veal. I gave Mrs. Lindsay a ticket. After dinner we sat and talked, Miss [Coatsworth] being there. About four I went to Garraway's Coffeehouse and from thence to Mrs. Cole the milliner. Then I came home and Annie Wilkinson came and stayed till seven. I got ready my dress which was a gray domino and a red head. About eight Mr. Lindsay and Mr. Jackson came to my lodgings and I carried Mr. Jackson to Lady Guise's and from thence we went to the masquerade where I was not much diverted but stayed till 6 o'clock and then came home, much tired, in a chair and neglected my prayers.

28. I rose about 11 o'clock, having had my asses' milk, and read a chapter in Hebrew and some Greek in Homer. I said my prayers, and had milk porridge for breakfast. I danced my dance. About one o'clock my Lord Percival came and stayed about half an hour. I read some English till 3 o'clock and then ate some brains. After dinner I put several things in order till 5 o'clock and then I went to see Mrs. U-m-s where I drank tea and stayed till six and then went to Will's, where I met my Lord Orrery and went with him to Mrs. Smith a [g-t] woman that lives in Queen Street where I met with Mrs. C-r-t-n-y and went to bed with her and rogered her two times. We lay till 10 o'clock and then rose and I went to Will's and ate a jelly and then walked home and said Lord have mercy on me.

29. I rose about 8 o'clock, having had my asses' milk, and read a chapter in Hebrew and some Greek in Lucian. I said my prayers, and had milk porridge for breakfast. The weather was cold and cloudy, the wind east. I danced my dance. About 10 o'clock came Colonel Blakiston and stayed about half an hour. About one o'clock I went to Will's Coffeehouse and read the news and then went to Colonel Blakiston's to dinner and ate some boiled beef. After dinner Colonel [Shutz] and I played at piquet and I won a guinea. Then I went and called in at the play and then went to Will's Coffeehouse and from thence I went to Mrs. C-d-g-n but she was out so I went to Betty S-t-r-d and drank some wine with her and then went to the bagnio and lay all night and rogered her four times.

30. I rose about 8 o'clock and gave my girl a guinea and about nine went home and found no fire, which put me out of humor. However, I read some Hebrew and some Greek in Lucian. I found I had taken cold in my expedition. I wrote a letter to Mrs. C-r-t-n-y to excuse my not meeting her because she was a married woman. About 12 o'clock Mr. Page came and sat about an hour with me. I ate some battered eggs for dinner but the butter was very rank. About 3 o'clock came my cousin Horsmanden and stayed about half an hour. Then I wrote more English till four when Sir Harry Ashurst came and sat with me about an hour. I resolved not to go out because I had a cold, read some English and wrote several things. I ate some milk porridge for supper and said my prayers.

31. I rose about 8 o'clock and found my cold bad; however, I read some Hebrew and some Greek in Lucian. I said my prayers, and had milk porridge for breakfast. The weather was cold and cloudy, the wind northeast, and it rained violently. I danced my dance and then wrote some English till 2 o'clock, when Captain W-t-r-g came and I paid him fifteen pounds that Mrs. Byrd had borrowed of him. I ate some beefsteak for dinner. In the afternoon I put several things in order and danced my dance again. It rained so much and my cold was so bad that I resolved not to go out and therefore wrote more English and read the news. Then I read other English and had milk porridge for supper. I said my prayers.

February 1719

1. I rose about 8 o'clock and read a chapter in Hebrew and some Greek in Lucian. My cold continued bad. I said my prayers, and had milk porridge for breakfast. The weather was cold and cloudy, the wind east. I danced my dance. I went to Sir Charles Wager's to dinner where I found several persons. I ate some hare pie. After dinner we sat and talked of several things till 5 o'clock and then I went to Lady Guise's where I stayed till 7 o'clock and then went to Mrs. Smith's where I found a handsome young woman but I was so out of order I did nothing but caress her and promised her a ticket for the masquerade. We drank tea. I was much indisposed about 10 o'clock and went home and took some [dogwood] which made me not sleep at all. I neglected my prayers.

2. I found myself much indisposed so I rose not till 9 o'clock. I read some Hebrew but no Greek because my head was out of order, which made me send to Mr. [Philips] to let me blood and lost ten ounces. Mrs. Wilkinson came and stayed about an hour. I had some milk porridge for breakfast and some mutton boiled with broth for dinner. In the afternoon I took a nap and found myself better, thank God. However my head was so bad I could not read. About 6 o'clock Mr. Lindsay and his lady and Mr. Jackson came. I gave them some tea and then we played at cards and I lost three shillings. Mr. Lindsay was much out of humor with his wife for no reason. They stayed till 10 o'clock and then retired and I ate some broth and said my prayers.

3. I rose about 8 o'clock, having had a good night, thank God, and read some Hebrew and some Greek in Lucian. I found myself much better. I said my prayers, and had milk porridge for breakfast. The weather was warm and cloudy. However about twelve I ventured out to my Lord Orrery's, where I stayed till two and then returned home where I danced my dance and ate some boiled chicken for dinner. In the afternoon I wrote a letter and about five went to the coffeehouse and read the news and went with General Ross to the play where I thought I saw the gentlewoman I rogered on Wednesday last. From the play I returned home and ate some milk porridge for supper. I read some English and said my prayers. I slept pretty well, thank God.

4. I rose about 8 o'clock and found myself better. I read some Hebrew and no Greek because I wrote a petition for the merchants to sign concerning the Council of Virginia. I said my prayers, and had milk porridge for breakfast. The weather was cold and cloudy, the wind northwest. About 11 o'clock came Colonel Blakiston and stayed with me about half an hour. I went to the Virginia Coffeehouse and from thence to Mrs. Perry's and dined with Dick Perry and ate some veal for dinner. After dinner we sat and talked till four and then drank tea and about five I went to Mr. Lindsay's and there found Mrs. Lindsay with a sore throat and Mrs. [Coatsworth] with her. We played at cards to divert her and about 10 o'clock I ate some rice milk. About eleven I took leave and went home and said my prayers and slept pretty well.

5. I rose about 8 o'clock and found myself pretty well, thank God. I read a chapter in Hebrew and some Greek in Lucian. I said my prayers, and had milk porridge for breakfast. The weather was warm and cloudy. I danced my dance and wrote a letter in English. About one I went into the City and found my Lord Percival at Garraway's and went with him to Pontack's to dinner and ate some fish. After dinner we went to the meeting of the Society where we had nothing but trifles. Then I went to Will's Coffeehouse and from thence I met Molly C-t-n at Mrs. Smith's and went to bed with her and rogered her two times. About ten we rose and I ate some boiled chicken for supper. About twelve I went home in the chair and said my prayers. I coughed pretty much.

6. I rose about 8 o'clock and read a chapter in Hebrew and some Greek in Lucian. I said my prayers and had milk porridge for breakfast. The weather was warm and cloudy. About 10 o'clock came Annie Wilkinson and stayed about an hour and then came my Lord Orrery and sat with me about an hour. Then I danced my dance and read some English till 2 o'clock and then ate some brains for dinner. In the afternoon I put several things in order and about 5 o'clock went to Mrs. U-m-s but they were from home. Then to Mrs. M-r-s where I drank tea and stayed chattering till 9 o'clock. Then I went to Court where I talked most to my Lady Buck. Here I stayed till eleven and then went home in the chair. This night the Duke of Argyll had his white staff.[1] I said my prayers and had milk porridge.

7. I rose about 8 o'clock and read a chapter in Hebrew and some Greek in Lucian. I said my prayers, and had milk porridge for breakfast. The weather was warm and cloudy, the wind west and violent. About eleven I went to the Duke of Argyll's, where I saw a vast number of people that came to give him joy, people that wished . . . having before. About twelve I went to visit Mrs. Southwell and sat there an hour and then went to Ozinda's and about two went with Sir Roger Braidshaigh to dine with Mr. Southwell and there was Mr. George Clarke.[2] I ate some beefsteak. About five we went to the play, where was abundance of company. After the play I went to Will's and ate a jelly and then came home and ate some milk porridge. I said my prayers.

8. I rose about 8 o'clock and read a chapter in Hebrew and some Greek in Lucian. I said my prayers, and had milk porridge for breakfast. The weather was clear and warm, the wind southwest. I danced my dance and about 11 o'clock went to Somerset Chapel where we had but an indifferent sermon. After church I returned home and danced my dance again and ate some battered eggs for dinner. In the afternoon I put several things in order till 4 o'clock and then danced my dance again, read some English, and about five I went to visit my

1. The Duke was made lord steward of the household.

2. George Clarke was M.P. for the University of Oxford.

daughter and stayed there till about six, and then went to meet Mrs.
C-r-t-n-y at Mrs. Smith's. Here we supped and I ate some boiled
chicken, and then we went to bed and I rogered her once and gave
her a guinea and so went home about twelve and said my prayers.

9. I rose about 8 o'clock and read a chapter in Hebrew and some
Greek in Lucian. I neglected my prayers, but had milk porridge for
breakfast. The weather was cloudy and warm, the wind southwest.
About eleven came Annie Wilkinson came to me and brought me an
invitation from her sister to her house in the evening. About eleven
came Colonel Blathwayt and stayed with me about an hour. Then I
had some veal cutlets for dinner. After dinner I put several things in
order and about five I went to Will's Coffeehouse and read the news
and about six Annie Wilkinson called upon me and we [went] to
her sister's, who I found a woman of very good sense.[3] She gave us
tea and wine. Here I stayed till about 10 o'clock and then I went
home and dressed for the masquerade and then called on my mistress
at Mrs. Smith's and carried her to the masquerade, where I was pretty
well diverted and stayed till 6 o'clock in the morning and came home
and neglected my prayers.

10. I rose about 11 o'clock and read a chapter in Hebrew and
some Greek in Lucian. I neglected my prayers, but had milk porridge
for breakfast. The weather was warm and cloudy, the wind southwest. About twelve came my Lord Orrery's housekeeper to desire
me to speak to the Duke of Argyll for a place for her husband, which
I promised to do. I ate some battered eggs for dinner but was seized
with a bad headache which went off again in an hour. I took a nap
till five and then I went to Will's Coffeehouse and from thence to my
Lady Guise's, where I was ready to fall asleep. I stayed till nine and
then went home and said my prayers.

11. I rose about 8 o'clock and found the pain in my head returned.
However, I said my prayers, and had milk porridge for breakfast.

3. Mrs. B-s, Annie Wilkinson's sister, was the 'Cleora' of Byrd's letters. See *Another Secret Diary of William Byrd*, 361.

I read some Hebrew and some Greek. The weather was cold and cloudy. I wrote a letter to the Duke of Argyll about my Lord Orrery's housekeeper. About 11 o'clock I went to my Lord Orrery's and drank a dish of [...]. Here I stayed till 1 o'clock and then went to Ozinda's and about two Mr. P-ch-y and I returned to my Lord Orrery's to dinner and I ate boiled pigeon and bacon. After dinner we drank a bottle till five and then went to Will's where my Lord Islay talked to me abundantly about himself and the Duke of Argyll. About 6 o'clock P-ch-y and I went to Mrs. Pierson's and stayed about half an hour. Then I went to Mrs. [Sands'] but they were from home. Then to Mrs. U-m-s, but they were from home. Then I went to Mrs. A-l-t and sat with them till 10 o'clock and then went home and ate some milk porridge for supper, and said my prayers.

12. I rose about 8 o'clock and read a chapter in Hebrew and some Greek in Lucian. I said my prayers, and had milk porridge for breakfast. The weather was cold and cloudy, the wind northeast. I danced my dance, and about eleven went into the City to Mr. Perry's and dined with the old man and went after dinner to visit Dick, who was very much indisposed with a cold. I ate some roast mutton for dinner. In the afternoon we drank some tea. About five I took leave and went to Mrs. Lindsay's where I played at cards and lost fifty shillings. About eleven we went to supper and I ate some frumenty and then went home and said my prayers. My ague in my head came again but less violently than yesterday.

13. I rose about 8 o'clock and read some Hebrew and some Greek in Lucian. I said my prayers, and had milk for breakfast. The weather was cold and cloudy, the wind east. I danced my dance. About 10 o'clock came Annie Wilkinson and talked of her sister. About twelve I went to visit Mr. Sambrooke but he was from home; then I went to Mr. N-l-r but he was from home; then to Mr. Horsmanden, but he was from home; then to Mr. Page but he was from home; then I went home and ate some beefsteak. After dinner I put several things in order and then took a nap till 5 o'clock. I stayed half an hour for my man and then went to visit Mrs. [Andrews] and drank tea there and

stayed till nine and then went to Ozinda's and from thence to Court where I stayed till eleven and then came home in the chair and said my prayers.

14. I rose about 8 o'clock and read some Hebrew and some Greek in Lucian. I said my prayers and had milk porridge for breakfast. The weather was cold and cloudy, the wind northeast. About 10 o'clock came Julius Caesar Parke[4] and sat with me about an hour. Then came Colonel Blakiston and Colonel G-r-th. and stayed about an hour. Then I danced my dance and wrote some English. About one I ate some battered eggs for dinner. After dinner I put several things in order and then wrote more English till 5 o'clock and then I danced my dance again and then went to the play of Tom Killigrew's which had abundance of wit in it and was well liked by almost everybody.[5] After the play I went to the coffeehouse and ate a jelly and about 10 o'clock walked home, ate some milk porridge, and said my prayers.

15. I rose about 8 o'clock and read some Hebrew and some Greek in Lucian. I said my prayers and had milk porridge for breakfast. The weather was clear and cold, the wind northeast. I danced my dance and wrote some English till 11 o'clock and then went into the City to Mr. Lindsay's where I dined and ate some roast beef. After dinner we went to Will [Tryon's] who had his mistress with him. Here we drank tea and I stayed till 5 o'clock and then went to my good friend Mrs. Smith where the girl I was to meet disappointed me. I sent to Mrs. C-r-t-n-y but she was from home. Then my friend sent for the widow J-n-s who came and we went to bed and I rogered her twice and about ten we had a broiled chicken for supper and about twelve we parted and I went home and neglected my prayers.

4. Julius Caesar Parke, illegitimate son of Byrd's father-in-law, Daniel Parke; he was a lieutenant in Major Primrose's Regiment of Foot. Parke left a legacy to 'my godson Julius Caesar Parke.' See *Virginia Magazine of History and Biography*, xx (1912), 372–81.

5. This was the first performance of Killigrew's *Chit-Chat*, dedicated to the Duke of Argyll, at the Drury Lane Theatre. The play, 'owing to the great zeal of the author's friends, was acted eleven times.' John Genest, *Some Account of the English Stage* (Bath, 1832), II, 641-2.

16. I rose about 8 o'clock and read some Hebrew and some Greek in Lucian. I said my prayers, and the weather was clear and cloudy, the wind northeast. About 10 o'clock Mr. Smith, the bookseller, came and I paid his bill. I danced my dance and wrote a letter and then wrote several other things till 2 o'clock and then I ate some beefsteak. After dinner I put several things in order till 5 o'clock and I danced my dance again and then went to Will's Coffeehouse and read the news and stayed till 7 o'clock and then went to my Lord Percival's where I sat till nine and then went to Court where my Lord Islay was very drunk. About eleven I walked home and ate my milk porridge and then said my prayers and slept pretty well, thank God.

17. I rose about 8 o'clock and read a chapter in Hebrew and some Greek in Lucian. I said my prayers and had milk porridge for breakfast. The weather was cold and clear, the wind east. About ten came Annie Wilkinson and told me her sister would come to see me tomorrow night. Then came Mr. Parke and sat with me half an hour. About eleven I went to my Lord Orrery's where I drank some chocolate and went with my Lord Ch-m-b-r-n to walk in the park where I walked two hours and then dined at the King's Arms in Pall Mall. I won my dinner at piquet and ate some boiled beef. After dinner we played at basset and I neither won nor lost. About six I went to the play, being Tom Killigrew's still where I saw Kitty Sambrooke and took no notice of her. After the play I went to Will's and from thence to see Betty S-t-r-d and went with her to the bagnio where we lay all night and I rogered twice.

18. I rose about 8 o'clock and went home where I read some Hebrew and some Greek in Lucian. I said my prayers, and had milk porridge for breakfast. The weather was cold and cloudy, the wind west. I read some French and then danced my dance. About 2 o'clock I went to dine with Mr. U-t-n and ate some tripe for dinner. In the afternoon we sat and chatted till 5 o'clock and then I went home and prepared for Mrs. B-s who with her sister was to spend the evening with me. About 6 o'clock they came and first I gave them tea and afterwards wine of two sorts. We were pretty dull. However, I kept

them till 9 o'clock and then I set things in order, ate some milk porridge and then said my prayers and slept pretty well, thank God.

19. I rose about 8 o'clock and read some Hebrew and some Greek in Lucian. I said my prayers, and had milk porridge for breakfast. The weather was cold and cloudy, the wind southwest. I wrote a letter and danced my dance. About 12 o'clock I went into the City to Mr. Perry and dined with Dick and ate some boiled beef. After dinner we sat and talked till four and then drank tea. About five I went and called in at the play and went from thence to Will's Coffeehouse and from thence to Mrs. FitzHerbert's where I ate some bread and cheese and stayed till nine. Then I returned home and found no fire, which made me go and complain to the mistress who was much concerned. I read some English and had milk porridge for supper, then said my prayers.

20. I rose about 8 o'clock and read some Hebrew and some Greek in Lucian. I said my prayers, and had milk porridge for breakfast. The weather was clear and cold, the wind west. I danced my dance, and about eleven went to Lord Islay's but he was from home; then to the Duke of Argyll's where I stayed about half an hour; then to Mrs. Southwell's where I stayed half an hour and then walked in the park till 2 o'clock and then went home where I ate some battered eggs. After dinner I put several things in order till four and then danced my dance again. Then I went to Mrs. U-m-s where I drank tea and went about six to Mrs. Smith's where I met Mrs. C-t-n and rogered twice. About ten we rose and I ate some broiled chicken and stayed till twelve and then went home and said my prayers.

21. I rose about 8 o'clock and read some Hebrew and some Greek in Lucian. I neglected my prayers, but had milk porridge for breakfast. The weather was cold and cloudy, the wind west. About 11 o'clock Captain Tom H-s-r came and told me he had brought me a [hogshead?] of wine from Lisbon. He stayed about half an hour. I wrote to my daughter and about twelve went to Colonel Blakiston's where I drank a dish of chocolate. Then I went to Sir Wilfred Law-

son's and stayed half an hour; then to Ozinda's and from thence about two to Mr. Southwell's to dinner and ate some beefsteak. Dan Jones dined with us. We sat and talked after dinner till five and then I went to Mrs. Robinson's music[6] where was abundance of good company and particularly my old mistress Lady Bouverie. I sat by my Lord Peterborough[7] and Mrs. Johnson and was very merry. I led Mrs. [Coatsworth] out and then went home to my milk porridge and said my prayers.

22. I rose about 8 o'clock and read a chapter in Hebrew and some Greek in Lucian. I neglected my prayers, and had milk porridge for breakfast. The weather was warm and clear, the wind west. I danced my dance and about eleven went to Somerset Chapel where we had an indifferent sermon. After church I walked in the garden with Mr. U-t-n and about two dined with Mrs. U-m-s and my daughter was of the party. I ate some good ham and chicken. After dinner we sat and talked till 4 o'clock and then drank tea and then came in Mr. U-t-n and my Lord Bellenden. About five I sent away my daughter and I went to Will's Coffeehouse where Dr. B-f-l entertained the company very much. About 7 o'clock I went to Mrs. [Sands'] where I found Sir Wilfred Lawson and we were merry till ten and then I came home and said my prayers.

23. I rose about 8 o'clock and read a chapter in Hebrew and some Greek in Lucian. I said my prayers, and had milk porridge for breakfast. The weather was warm and cloudy, the wind west. I danced my dance and about 11 o'clock went to Mr. U-m-s and took them up and carried them through the King's Gate to the Bishop of London's where we dined and I ate some roast chicken. After dinner

6. This was a command performance at the Haymarket Theatre, attended by George I.

7. Charles Mordaunt, 3rd Earl of Peterborough. He secretly married, about 1722, the singer, Anastasia Robinson. The tradition that Byrd's daughter Evelyn was courted by the Earl of Peterborough and that she died of a broken heart because her father objected to the match seems quite unsupported by the known facts.

the Bishop gave us some strong water. Then Miss P-n-y and I walked in the garden and about 5 o'clock took leave and returned to London again and I drank tea with my lady and about 8 o'clock walked to Mrs. J-n-s in Young Street and sat with her till 9 o'clock and then went to Court where I talked abundance to Mrs. S-n-l-t-n and about eleven walked home, ate milk porridge, and said my prayers.

24. I rose about 8 o'clock and read a chapter in Hebrew and some Greek in Lucian. I said my prayers, and had milk porridge for breakfast. The weather was warm and cloudy, the wind west. I danced my dance and about 10 o'clock came Annie Wilkinson and I scolded at her for not bringing my shirts. About eleven I went to visit my daughter and found she had a rash. Then I went to Mr. Perry's and dined at the old gentleman's but did not find him at home. I ate some boiled beef. After dinner I went to visit Mrs. Perry and drank tea. About four I took my leave, went to Mrs. B-s but she was from home. Then I went to Mrs. U-m-s where I met Mrs. Lindsay and drank tea again. About eight I went to my Lady Guise's and stayed till nine and then went to Will's where I received a message from Lady Dunkellen to meet her tomorrow night. About ten I walked home and ate milk porridge and said my prayers.

25. I rose about 8 o'clock and read a chapter in Hebrew and some Greek in Lucian. I said my prayers and had milk porridge for breakfast. The weather was clear and cold, the wind west. About 10 o'clock came Mr. Parke and stayed half an hour. Then came Sir Roger Braidshaigh and stayed half an hour. Then I went to the Duke of Argyll's but he was from home; then to my Lord Islay's, who was also from home; then to my Lord Orrery's who was in the country; then to my Lord Percival's, who was likewise in the country; then to Mr. Blathwayt's who was from home; then to Mrs. Southwell's, with whom I sat half an hour and then went to my mistress J-n-s and then went home and ate some battered eggs for dinner. After dinner I put several things in order and danced my dance and then read some English till five and then went to visit Mrs. B-s and drank tea till seven and then went to meet my Lady Dunkellen and sat with her till

eleven o'clock and then walked home, ate my milk porridge, and said my prayers.

26. I rose about 8 o'clock and read two chapters in Hebrew and some Greek in Lucian. I said my prayers and had milk porridge for breakfast. The weather was clear and warm, the wind west. About eleven I went to the Committee of Council about Colonel Hunter's business and stayed about an hour, and then went into the City to Pontack's and ate some fish. After dinner I went to Garraway's and spoke to my Lord G-l-v-r-s about the government of Maryland but he told me it was disposed of. Then I called on my milliner Mrs. Cole and then went to the play where I talked with Annie [Coatsworth] and about seven went to my friend Mrs. Smith and met Mrs. J-n-s there and rogered her twice and then ate some boiled chicken and about twelve returned home and said my prayers.

27. I rose about 8 o'clock and read a chapter in Hebrew and some Greek in Lucian. I said my prayers and had milk porridge for break-fast. The weather was clear and warm, the wind west. I danced my dance and about 11 o'clock came Mr. Page and after him Mr. Lindsay and stayed till 1 o'clock and then I went to the Mall and walked with Brigadier Windsor[8] and there was abundance of company. I walked there two hours and then went to dine with Mrs. Southwell and ate salt fish. After dinner we drank a bottle till six and then drank tea and then I went to Will's where my Lady Dunkellen sent for me and I stayed with her till nine and then went to Court where I saw nobody I liked. About eleven I walked home, ate some milk porridge, and said my prayers.

28. I rose about 8 o'clock and read two chapters in Hebrew and some Greek in Lucian. I said my prayers, and had milk porridge for breakfast. The weather was clear and warm, the wind northwest. I danced my dance. I wrote a letter to my daughter and another to my

8. Andrews Windsor, a brigadier general, commanded the 28th Foot from 1711 to his retirement in 1715. Youngest brother of Thomas, Viscount Windsor.

Lady Mohun and a third to my cousin Suky Horsmanden. About two I ate some battered eggs. After dinner I put several things in order and then wrote some English till 5 o'clock and then I went to the concert for the use of the other Mrs. Robinson[9] where was abundance of good company and I sat by D-l-y [Clark] and in sight of Lady Bouverie. Then I walked to the coffeehouse and read the news and then called on Mrs. C-d-g-n and then came home to my milk porridge and said my prayers.

March 1719

1. I rose about 7 o'clock and read a chapter in Hebrew and some Greek in Lucian. I said my prayers, and had milk porridge for breakfast. The weather was cold and cloudy, the wind northwest. I danced my dance and about 12 o'clock came Colonel Blathwayt and stayed about half an hour, and then I went with him to St. James's Chapel and talked with several people. About 2 o'clock I went to Mr. Blathwayt's in the chair and ate some roast beef for dinner. After dinner we sat and talked till 5 o'clock and then drank tea and about six I went to visit Mrs. B-s, where I saw her aunt and other sister. Here I sat in a grave way till 10 o'clock, and then took my leave and went home, where I ate a cake and some cheese and then said my prayers.

2. I rose about 8 o'clock and read two chapters in Hebrew and some Greek in Lucian. I said my prayers and had milk porridge for breakfast. The weather was cold and clear, the wind northwest. I danced my dance and about 10 o'clock came Annie Wilkinson. About 11 o'clock I went to Colonel Blakiston's and proposed to go

9. A concert at the Haymarket Theatre for the benefit of Anastasia Robinson's sister.

to Virginia to make peace between the Governor and the Council upon the Governor's own plan.[1] Then I went to my Lord Orrery's, where I drank a dish of chocolate and then went to Ozinda's and then walked in the park with Captain Rogers and about two we went to dine with Ned Southwell and I ate some roast mutton. After dinner I went home to adjust myself and then called at the play and then at the coffeehouse and then went to visit Mrs. [Andrews] and drank tea and then went to Court where I talked much to the widow Pierson and led her to her coach and then came home in the chair, ate my milk porridge, and said my prayers.

3. I rose about 8 o'clock and neglected the chapter in Hebrew and the Greek in Lucian because I wrote some terms of peace between the Governor of Virginia and the Council. I neglected my prayers likewise, but ate milk porridge for breakfast. The weather was cloudy and cold. About 10 o'clock came Tom Rogers and stayed quarter of an hour. Then came Mike Perry to tell me his father would be glad to see me. Then came Annie Wilkinson with some linen. About eleven I went to see my daughter and found her indisposed. Then I went to Mr. Perry's and dined with the old man and ate some boiled beef. After dinner I went to visit Dick and drank tea till five and then went to Mr. Lindsay's where we played at cards and I won three pounds for which Mrs. Lindsay was out of humor. I ate some pigeon for supper, and about twelve went home and reprimanded my man for being out of the way. I said my prayers.

1. Byrd wrote to the Board of Trade offering 'either by my going over my self, or by letter, that I will unfeignedly employ all the credit I have with the gentlemen of the Council, to dispose them to a sincere pacification, upon the terms of the Lieut. Governour's own plan.' His letter goes on to specify the terms, which seem rather to be Byrd's own notions of a peaceful settlement than Spotswood's: the Council members alone (except in extraordinary emergency) were to act as a court of oyer and terminer; the minutes of each Council meeting were to be read in the next succeeding meeting; the Act of Assembly giving the Governor power to 'lay out what money he should think fit upon the Governor's house' was to be repealed; the Lieutenant Governor was to be told to let all members of the Council, Court, and Assembly give their opinions frankly 'without reproaching or ridiculing'; and neither side (Governor or Council) was to complain to the Board without having first given a true copy of the complaint to the party complained of. Public Record Office, C.O. 1318, 557, endorsed 'Letter from Mr. Byrd with propositions for a reconciliation between the Lieutenant Governor and the Council of Virginia, received 24 March, read 8th April, 1719.'

4. I rose about 8 o'clock and read a chapter in Hebrew and some Greek in Lucian. I neglected my prayers but had milk porridge for breakfast. The weather was clear and cold, the wind southwest. About 10 o'clock I received a letter from Mrs. B-s inviting me to come and see her. Then I went to Colonel Blakiston's and with him to my Lord Orkney's who received me very coldly and we had a sort of a scold; however, at last he heard my proposal about peace between his deputy and the Council. Then I called at Lord Percival's but he was from home. Then I went to Mr. Page and stayed about half an hour with him and then went home and danced my dance and ate some battered eggs for dinner. In the afternoon I read some English till 5 o'clock and then sent to Mrs. U-m-s but they were from home. Then to the coffeehouse and read the news and about 7 o'clock I went to Mrs. B-s and was merry with her till twelve, then drank two dishes of chocolate, then went home, ate milk porridge, and said my prayers.

5. I rose about 7 o'clock and read two chapters in Hebrew and some Greek in Lucian. I said my prayers, and had milk porridge for breakfast. The weather was warm and cloudy, the wind west. I wrote a letter to Mr. [Annesley] for Lady Dunkellen. About 11 o'clock came a young woman to inquire after Colonel Jenings[2] in Virginia. About one I went to Garraway's and then to Pontack's to dine with the Royal Society and I ate some boiled beef. After dinner we went to Crane Court where we saw several curious things in anatomy by Mr. B-n-r-y. Then I went to the play for the benefit of Mr. Mills[3] where I sat near Lady Bouverie. After the play I went to Will's and sat there till ten when Mrs. S-t-r-d called for me in a hack and we went to the bagnio where I rogered her but once and neglected my prayers.

6. I rose about 8 o'clock and took leave of my mistress and went home, where I read a chapter in Hebrew and no Greek. I said my prayers, and had milk porridge for breakfast. The weather was clear

2. Edmund Jenings was president of the Council of Virginia. He had emigrated to Virginia as a young man, and served as a member of the Council from 1701 to 1727.

3. John Mills, actor at Drury Lane for forty years. The play was *Venice Preserved*, a command performance for the Prince of Wales.

and warm, the wind west. Annie Wilkinson came and brought my things. I wrote a letter to Mrs. B-s and about one I went to St. James's Park and walked till almost three and then went to dine with Mr. Southwell and I ate some broiled beef. After dinner I looked over several books in the library and about five went to Hyde Park by myself and then went to visit Mrs. M-r-s and drank tea there, and about 9 o'clock I went to Court where I talked with several and returned on Saturday. I walked home, ate milk porridge, and said my prayers.

7. I rose about 8 o'clock and read two chapters in Hebrew and some Greek in Lucian. I said my prayers, and had milk porridge for breakfast. The weather was cloudy and warm, and it rained a little. I danced my dance. I wrote some English and a letter to Suky Horsmanden till 12 o'clock and then I ate some battered eggs. After dinner I put several things in order and then took a nap till 5 o'clock and then I went to the coffeehouse and stayed there till seven and then went to visit Mrs. B-s, where I found Mr. Campbell who stayed till 9 o'clock. Then we were merry till ten and then I ate some Scotch collops. After supper we sported very much and talked till three in the morning and then I went home and then returned home [sic].

8. I rose about 9 o'clock and read a chapter in Hebrew and some Greek in Lucian. I neglected my prayers, but had milk porridge for breakfast. The weather was clear and warm. About eleven I went to Somerset Chapel and heard but an indifferent sermon. After church I walked in the garden about half an hour and then went to dine with Mrs. U-m-s and ate some boiled mutton. After dinner we sat and talked till four and then drank tea. Then I went with Lord Bellenden to Hyde Park and about seven returned to Will's Coffeehouse, where I read the news, and then went to my Lord Harry Powlett's and stayed there till nine because D-l-y [Clark] was there. Then I returned again to the coffeehouse and about 10 o'clock picked up a pretty woman and went to the tavern and had a broiled fowl. I found the woman [entrancing] and gave her a crown and committed uncleanness with her and returned home about 12 o'clock and neglected my prayers.

9. I rose about 8 o'clock and read a chapter in Hebrew and little Greek. I said my prayers, and had milk porridge for breakfast. The weather was cold and cloudy, the wind east. I wrote a letter to Mrs. B-s. About 10 o'clock came Annie Wilkinson and put my linen in order. At 11 o'clock I went to the committee for relieving poor prisoners and then went to my Lord Orrery's but he was from home, but I saw his housekeeper. Then I went home and danced my dance and then wrote some English till two, when I ate some battered eggs. After dinner I took a nap till four when my cousin Horsmanden came and went with me to the play and afterwards waited on the widow Pierson out. Then I went to the coffeehouse, ate a jelly, read the news, and then walked home and had milk porridge and said my prayers.

10. I rose about 8 o'clock and read a chapter in Hebrew and some Greek in Lucian. I neglected my prayers, but had milk porridge for breakfast. The weather was clear and warm, the wind northwest. I wrote a letter to Mrs. B-s and received one from her, very obliging. About 11 o'clock I went to the Duke of Argyll's and stayed about quarter of an hour. Then I went to Colonel Blakiston's but he was from home. Then to Lord Percival's but he was from home. Then to Sir Wilfred Lawson's but he was from home; then to Mr. Southwell's where I stayed about an hour and then went to walk in Somerset Garden and dined with Mr. U-t-n and ate pork and peas. After dinner I went to Lady Powlett's and had coffee. Then I talked to Mrs. Lindsay in her coach at Somerset House gate and went to the Marquis DuQuesne[4] and stayed there about an hour and then went to Will's and read the news till ten, and then went to the tavern to meet a maid and ate a beefsteak and then committed uncleanness with her and about 12 o'clock went home and said my prayers. I slept very indifferently.

11. I rose about 8 o'clock and read two chapters in Hebrew and some Greek in Lucian. I said my prayers, and had milk porridge for

4. Gabriel, Marquis DuQuesne, a colonel of the first troop of Horse Grenadier Guards, married Elizabeth, daughter of Sir Roger Braidshaigh.

breakfast. The weather was clear and cold, the wind west. I danced my dance. About 10 o'clock came Annie Wilkinson and set my linen in order. About 11 o'clock I went to my cousin Horsmanden's and went then into the City to Mr. Perry's and dined with the old gentleman and ate some cold beef. After dinner I went to Garraway's Coffeehouse and drank some tea and then went to Molly Cole's and stayed there till 4 o'clock and then went to Will's where I found Sir George Beaumont[5] and carried him to the park and then returned again to Will's till nine and then went to Court. About eleven I walked home, ate my milk porridge, and said my prayers.

12. I rose about 8 o'clock and read a chapter in Hebrew and some Greek in Lucian. I said my prayers, and had milk porridge for breakfast. The weather was clear and warm, the wind southwest. I danced my dance. About 11 o'clock came my Lord Percival and stayed about half an hour. Then came my Lord Orrery and stayed about an hour and then I went with him to the Court of Requests, from whence I went to walk in the park, where was abundance of company. About 3 o'clock I went home and ate some broiled chicken for dinner. After dinner I took a nap and about 5 o'clock went to visit Mrs. Pierson but she was from home; then I went to Colonel Blakiston's where I found them playing at cards. Here I stayed an hour, and then went to Mrs. FitzHerbert's, and ate some toast and cheese. Then I went to Will's where my mistress called on me and carried me to the bagnio where I lay all night and rogered her twice.

13. I rose about 8 o'clock and went home and read a chapter in Hebrew and some Greek in Lucian. I said my prayers, and had milk porridge for breakfast. The weather was clear and warm. About ten came Mrs. Wilkinson and put my linen in order. I danced my dance and bought a hat for myself and brought up another for my coachman. About 2 o'clock I ate some battered eggs. After dinner I put several things in order and then took a nap till 4 o'clock and then read some English till my cousin Horsmanden came, with whom I went to the park, where was much company. Afterwards I called at Mrs. Pierson's but she was from home; then at my Lord Percival's, who

5. Sir George Beaumont, 4th Bart., M.P. for Leicester, a lord of the admiralty.

was from home; then at Mrs. M-r-s where I drank tea and stayed till nine, when I went to Court, where I saw Mrs. Pierson and said abundance of fine things to her. About twelve I came home in the chair, ate my milk porridge, and said my prayers.

14. I rose about 8 o'clock and read a chapter in Hebrew and some Greek in Lucian. I said my prayers, and had milk porridge for breakfast. I found a great pain in my loins occasioned by wind. The weather was cold and cloudy. I danced my dance, and at 11 o'clock went to visit Sir Roger Braidshaigh and carried him some tobacco. Then I went to Betty Southwell's and sat with her about an hour and then went home and danced my dance again, and then ate some beefsteak for dinner. In the afternoon I put several things in order till 5 o'clock and then went to visit the widow Pierson and drank tea with her and stayed about an hour and then went to Mrs. Smith's to meet a new mistress who was pretty and well humored. I went to bed with her and rogered her three times and about eleven rose to supper and ate some young rabbit. About twelve I took leave and walked home and said my prayers.

15. I rose about 8 o'clock and read a chapter in Hebrew and some Greek in Lucian. I said my prayers, and had milk porridge for breakfast. The weather was cold and clear, the wind northeast. My back was very bad; however I danced my dance, and then wrote some English till 1 o'clock, when I ate some battered eggs for dinner and strained my back with carrying of coals. After dinner I put several things in order and took a nap and then read some English till 5 o'clock and then went to Will's to meet my cousin Horsmanden to carry him to the park and we went there and found abundance of coaches. From hence we went to visit Mrs. [Sands] and sat there till 10 o'clock and then went to Will's and from thence I went home, ate my milk porridge and said my prayers. I took four of Anderson's pills.

16. I rose about 8 o'clock and found my back very bad. I read two chapters in Hebrew and some Greek in Lucian. I said my prayers, and had milk porridge for breakfast. The weather was very cold and

clear, the wind northwest. About 10 o'clock came Colonel Blakiston and stayed about half an hour. Then came Annie Wilkinson and put my linen in order. I danced my dance and read some English till 2 o'clock and then I ate some boiled mutton. After dinner I put several things in order and read more English till 5 o'clock and then went to the play for the benefit of Mrs. Porter.[6] I sat by my Lady Buck. After the play I went to Court where was but indifferent company. About twelve I walked home and ate some broth and said my prayers.

17. I rose about 8 o'clock and found my back better, thank God. I read a chapter in Hebrew and some Greek in Lucian. I said my prayers, and had milk porridge for breakfast. The weather was clear and very cold, the wind northeast. I danced my dance. About 12 o'clock came Mrs. Cole and drank tea with me and I did nothing to her but only kiss her. I wrote a letter into the country and about 3 o'clock ate some battered eggs. After dinner I put several things in order and danced my dance again. About 5 o'clock I went to Will's and read the news and about seven went to my Lady Guise's and sat with her about an hour and then went to Mrs. U-m-s and found them not at home. Then I called at the play and then walked home and ate some bread and cheese and said my prayers.

18. I rose about 8 o'clock and found my back better, thank God. I read two chapters in Hebrew and some Greek in Lucian. I said my prayers, and had milk porridge for breakfast. The weather was clear and cold, the wind northeast. I danced my dance. About 11 o'clock came the Marquis DuQuesne and stayed half an hour and then I went to my Lord Orrery's but he was out. Then to Colonel Blakiston's where I drank a dish of chocolate. Then to my Lord Percival's and then took a turn in the park and then returned to my Lord Percival's to dinner and ate some boiled chicken. After dinner I went to view my Lord's new house and then drank tea. Then I went to the widow Pierson's and stayed till 9 o'clock and then went to Court where I stayed till 12 o'clock and then walked home and ate milk porridge and then said my prayers.

6. Mary Porter, actress at Drury Lane Theatre. The play was *The Chances*.

19. I rose about 8 o'clock and found my back still better, thank God. I read two chapters in Hebrew and some Greek in Lucian. I said my prayers, and had milk porridge for breakfast. The weather was clear and cold, the wind northeast. I danced my dance and wrote a letter to Mrs. B-s. About one I went into the City to Garraway's and from thence to Pontack's to dinner and ate some roast mutton. After dinner I went to my bookseller and from thence proceeded to Crane Court where I stayed till 5 o'clock and then went to visit Mrs. U-m-s and drank tea with them. About 8 o'clock came Mrs. Lindsay to dress for my Lord Ch-t-n's masquerade and I agreed to stay there till she came back from thence to keep her husband in good temper. I ate some broiled mutton, played at cards, and stayed till 5 o'clock in the morning, went home in the chair and said my prayers.

20. I rose about 9 o'clock and read a chapter in Hebrew and some Greek in Lucian. I said my prayers, and had milk porridge for breakfast. The weather was clear and cold, the wind violent at northeast. I danced my dance. About ten came Annie Wilkinson to put my linen in order. Then came Colonel Blathwayt and sat with me half an hour. Then came Mr. Horsmanden and brought the opinion of Sir Robert Raymond about Mr. Blair's case, which was against the poor parson.[7]

7. James Blair, Commissary of the Bishop of London in Virginia, was involved in a series of controversies with Governor Spotswood. The present one seems to have arisen out of a difference of opinion as to whether the Governor had the right to appoint ministers (as Spotswood believed) or whether vestries had the right to choose their ministers (as the vestries believed and as was actually the custom). This point flared into controversy in 1718 over the rector of James City Parish, of which Ludwell and Blair were vestrymen. Hugh Jones, of the College of William and Mary, sided with the Governor, but the Commissary had most of the Assembly and the vestries on his side. In the convention which the clergy held in Virginia in April, 1719, the question arose as to whether Blair was ordained in the Anglican Church. As a matter of fact he was an ordained minister of the Church of Scotland. To bring the matter to a show-down, the vestry of Bruton Parish presented Blair to the Governor for induction as their minister, and the Governor refused to induct him. The Governor had the opinions of Richard West and Sir William Thompson that he had the right of appointment. But Sir Robert Raymond had rendered an opinion that the vestry had the right to choose a minister and present him for induction. Only if they let six months elapse without doing this could the Governor send them a minister of his choice. With these diverse opinions, the two sides decided to present the matter to the General Court and then to appeal the decision (whichever way it went) to the King in Council. However, the removal of Spotswood in 1722 put an end to the case. (See references to the Commissary in this diary, 1720-21.) George M. Brydon, *Virginia's Mother Church* 1 (Richmond, 1947), 344-53.

About 2 o'clock I danced my dance and then ate some battered eggs. After dinner I put several things in order and then went to visit my daughter and reproved her for not writing to me, which made her cry. Then I went to Mrs. Lindsay's where I found the Misses U-m-s. We drank tea, played at cards, and about ten went to supper and I ate some fricassee of lamb. I won about twenty shillings and about twelve I came home with the Misses U-m-s and then went to my own lodging and said my prayers.

21. I rose about 8 o'clock and read a chapter in Hebrew and some Greek in Lucian. I said my prayers, and had milk porridge for breakfast. The weather was clear and cold, the wind northeast. I danced my dance and about 11 o'clock went to the Duke of Argyll's but I did not see him notwithstanding he was from home [*sic*]. Then I went to my Lord Islay's and was let in with much to do and stayed till twelve and then went to Spring Gardens and stayed there till dinner and ate some beefsteak. After dinner we drank a bottle till five and then I went and set Phil Percival home, and then went to the opera house to hear the music [8] and found abundance of company and sat by Mrs. Lindsay but Colonel Gay came and carried her out. I walked to Mrs. Smith's and sent to Mrs. C-r-t-n-y and she came and we drank a bottle of wine, and then I walked home and said my prayers.

22. I rose about 8 o'clock and read a chapter in Hebrew and some Greek in Lucian. I said my prayers, and had milk porridge for breakfast. The weather was clear and cold, the wind northeast. I danced my dance and read some English till one o'clock, and then went to Sir Charles Wager's to dinner but Sir Charles did not come home so that I dined with the ladies and ate some roast veal. After dinner we went to O-r-m-n Chapel where I saw Mrs. W-n-m. After church I went back with my Lady Wager and stayed till 5 o'clock and then went to Will's Coffeehouse, then to Lady Powlett's who was from home; then to Mrs. B-r-n with whom I drank some coffee and about 7 o'clock went to Mrs. Pierson's who was from home. Then to

8. A concert by Mrs. Robinson at the Haymarket Theatre.

Colonel Blakiston's where I stayed till 9 o'clock and then went home and said my prayers.

23. I rose about 8 o'clock and read a chapter in Hebrew and some Greek in Lucian. I said my prayers, and had milk porridge for breakfast. The weather was clear and cold, the wind northeast. I danced my dance. About 10 o'clock came Annie Wilkinson and put my linen in order. About 12 o'clock I went into the City and dined with Mike Perry and ate some hashed beef. After dinner we sat and talked till 3 o'clock and then came John P-s with whom I walked to Garraway's and from thence I went in my chariot home and put myself in order and then went to Will's Coffeehouse and read the news and about seven went to visit Mrs. [Andrews] and drank tea with them and about nine went to Court where was but little company. I stayed till eleven, then walked home, ate milk porridge, and said my prayers.

24. I rose about 8 o'clock and read a chapter in Hebrew and some Greek in Lucian. I neglected my prayers, but had milk porridge for breakfast. The weather was cold and cloudy, the wind north. I danced my dance. About 11 o'clock came Mrs. C-r-t-n-y and I entertained her with tea and lent her two guineas. About 1 o'clock came Mr. Sambrooke and stayed about half an hour. About three I ate some battered eggs. After dinner I put several things in order and read some English till five and then went to visit Mrs. U-m-s and drank tea. About seven I went to the music of Mrs. Robinson, where was a pretty deal of company. Then I walked to Will's and ate a jelly and about eleven walked home, said my prayers, and ate milk porridge.

25. I rose about 8 o'clock and read a chapter in Hebrew and some Greek in Lucian. I neglected my prayers, and had milk porridge for breakfast. The weather was cold and cloudy, the wind northwest. It rained pretty hard almost all day. About ten came Annie Wilkinson and set my linen in order. About twelve I went to my Lord Orrery's but he was from home. Then to my Lord Percival's who was not to be spoken with. Then I went to Colonel Blathwayt's and saw the Colonel and sat with him half an hour, and then went to West-

minster where I spoke to several lords in favor of the merchants against the clause in the East India Company bill. About 2 o'clock I went home with Colonel Blakiston to dinner where I found Lady Susan Fane[9] who dined there likewise, and I ate some pigeon pie. After dinner we drank tea and about five I went to Mrs. Pierson's and drank tea also, and stayed three hours and about nine went to Will's in expectation of Mrs. S-t-r-d but she came not so I went home and said my prayers.

26. I rose about 8 o'clock and read a chapter in Hebrew and some Greek in Lucian. I neglected my prayers, and had milk porridge for breakfast. The weather was clear and warm, the wind west. I wrote a letter to Mrs. B-s and danced my dance. About 2 o'clock I ate a beef-steak. After dinner I put several things in order till four and then I went to visit Mrs. S-t-n that is kept by Colonel Lumley[10] and while I was there the Colonel came in, that put us all into some confusion; however, I sat about half an hour after he came and drank some tea and then went to Mrs. FitzHerbert's where I read in Lucian to her and then ate some battered eggs for supper. About nine I went to Will's where my mistress called on me and we went to the bagnio and lay all night. I neglected my prayers and rogered once.

27. I rose about 8 o'clock and got home about nine and read a chapter in Hebrew and some Greek in Lucian. I said my prayers, and had milk porridge for breakfast. The weather was warm and clear, the wind west. I danced my dance and put several things in order till 1 o'clock and then went to visit Mr. Page and carried him to Somer-set Garden where I met Mrs. U-m-s and invited myself to dinner and ate salt fish. After dinner we sat and talked till five and then drank tea. Then I called on Mr. Page and carried him to the park where we saw several pretty women. Then we returned to Will's Coffeehouse where I read the news and stayed till ten and then walked home

9. Lady Susan Fane, daughter of Vere Fane, 4th Earl of Westmoreland, and sister of Thomas, the 6th Earl; her sister, Lady Mary Fane, married Sir Francis Dashwood.

10. Thomas Lumley, lieutenant colonel of Lord Hinchinbrooke's Regiment of Foot. Lumley succeeded his brother Richard as Earl of Scarborough in 1740.

where I ate milk porridge and said my prayers. I slept pretty well, thank God.

28. I rose about 8 o'clock and read a chapter in Hebrew and some Greek in Lucian. I said my prayers, and had milk porridge for breakfast. The weather was clear and cold, the wind southeast. I danced my dance, then wrote a letter to my cousin Suky Horsmanden and paid for my lodgings. About one I went to Mrs. Parker's to settle accounts with her and about two went to Mr. U-t-n to dinner and ate some boiled lamb. After dinner we sat and talked till 4 o'clock and then went to Mrs. U-m-s and drank tea till six; then I went to Will's Coffeehouse and from thence to Lady Guise's where I found Madame Kielmansegge[11] and her daughter. I stayed about an hour and then returned to Will's Coffeehouse again, where Mr. W-c-m and I talked about the bad consequences of luxury. About ten I walked home, ate milk porridge, and said my prayers.

29. I rose about 7 o'clock and read a chapter in Hebrew and some Greek in Lucian. I said my prayers, and had milk porridge for breakfast. The weather was clear and cool, the wind northeast. I danced my dance and put several things in order till 12 o'clock and then I went into the city and dined with Mr. Lindsay and ate some roast beef. After dinner we went to church, where I slept a little. After church I returned to Mr. Lindsay's and drank tea with Mrs. [Tryon] and Mrs. Ch-m-n-s. About 7 o'clock I went to Will's Coffeehouse and after a little stay went to the widow Pierson's and sat with her two hours and about 10 o'clock went home, where I washed my feet and said my prayers.

30. I rose about 7 o'clock and read a chapter in Hebrew and some Greek in Lucian. I said my prayers and had milk porridge for breakfast. The weather was cloudy and cold, the wind northwest. I danced my dance. Annie Wilkinson came and mended my linen and read

11. Madame Kielmansegge, widow of Johann Kielmansegge, master of the horse to George I, was the King's mistress. In 1721 she was created Countess of Leinster, in 1722 Baroness of Brentford and Countess of Darlington. She had several children by George I.

some English till 2 o'clock. My Lord Percival was here about twelve. I ate some battered eggs for dinner. In the afternoon I put several things in order and had a letter from Mrs. B-s. About five I went to the play where I sat next to Mrs. B-l-r. After the play I went home with Mrs. A-s-t-n. Then I went to the coffeehouse and then ate a seed cake and walked home, had my milk porridge, and said my prayers.

31. I rose about 8 o'clock and read a chapter in Hebrew and some Greek in Lucian. I said my prayers, and had milk porridge for breakfast. The weather was cloudy and cold, the wind northeast. I danced my dance. About 11 o'clock I went to Colonel Blakiston's but he was from home. Then to Sir Wilfred Lawson's but he was from home; then to my Lord Percival's and I sat with him about an hour and then went to Mrs. Southwell's and sat about half an hour, and then went to Will's Coffeehouse and read the news and about 8 o'clock went to Sir Charles Wager's to dinner and ate some roast beef. Here I found Mr. R-g-b-y, a man of good sense. About five I took leave and went to Lady Guise's and sat with her half an hour; then to Mrs. Smith's and met a new woman and went to bed and could not roger her; however, I gave her three guineas, came home, and said my prayers. I was angry with my man for not getting ready my milk.

April 1719

1. I rose about 7 o'clock and read a chapter in Hebrew and some Greek in Lucian. I said my prayers, and had milk porridge for breakfast. The weather was cold and cloudy, the wind east. I danced my dance and about 11 o'clock went to visit Mr. Sambrooke but he was from home. Then I went to my daughter and stayed with her about an hour and then went to dine with Dick Perry and ate some roast

pigeon. After dinner we sat and talked till four and then drank tea. About five I went away and called at the playhouse in Lincoln's Inn where I saw two acts and then went with Mr. G-r-d-n to Drapers' Hall where was very bad company. However, I stayed till 11 o'clock and then came home, ate my milk porridge, and said my prayers. I slept very indifferently.

2. I rose about 7 o'clock and read two chapters in Hebrew and some Greek in Lucian. I neglected my prayers and had milk porridge for breakfast. The weather was cloudy and cold, the wind east. I wrote a letter to Mrs. B-s till 1 o'clock and then Colonel Blathwayt called upon me; however, he did not stay, because I was obliged to go into the City and dine at Pontack's where I ate some fish. After dinner we went to Crane Court where we had several letters about the ball of fire that was seen in the sky on the nineteenth of last month. About 6 o'clock I walked home and wrote some English and put several things in order till 8 o'clock and then I dressed myself for the masquerade in a domino and about 8 o'clock went to my Lady Guise's where I found several ladies and several misses come. About 10 o'clock I went to the masquerade where I met Mrs. Pierson and declared my whole mind to her which she received pretty peacefully and seemed not displeased in the least. I spent most of my time with her and went away about 6 o'clock, when she did, and neglected my prayers.

3. I rose about 11 o'clock and read a chapter in Hebrew and some Greek in Lucian. I said my prayers, and had milk porridge for breakfast. The weather was cold and cloudy, the wind east. About 12 o'clock came Annie Wilkinson to take care of my linen. I danced my dance and about 2 o'clock ate some battered eggs for dinner. In the afternoon I put several things in order till 5 o'clock and then I drank tea with my landlady and my daughter came to me in order to go to the park and there we went but there was but little company. Then I went to Mrs. Pierson's but sent home my daughter. I said many things to Mrs. Pierson about my love but was interrupted by company. However, I stayed till 10 o'clock and then went to Court where I

talked to the Duke of Argyll. About eleven I came home in a chair, ate my milk porridge, and said my prayers. I received a letter from Virginia.

4. I rose about 8 o'clock and read a chapter in Hebrew and some Greek in Lucian. I said my prayers, and had milk porridge for breakfast. The weather was cold and cloudy, the wind north. I danced my dance and about 11 o'clock went to the Duke of Argyll's but he was from home. Then to my Lord Islay's and found him, and stayed about half an hour and then went with Brigadier Sutton[1] and set him down and then went to Colonel Blakiston's who was from home; however, I saw Mrs. Blakiston who invited me to dinner, but I went home first and read some English. About 1 o'clock came Mr. N-l-r and stayed half an hour. Then I returned to Colonel Blakiston's and ate some tripe. After dinner Colonel G-r-th came in and there I stayed till six and then went to the play and sat next to my Lady Buck. After the play I went to Will's and read the news and then went home, ate milk porridge and said my prayers.

5. I rose about 7 o'clock and read a chapter in Hebrew and some Greek in Lucian. I said my prayers, and had milk porridge for breakfast. The weather was cold and cloudy, the wind east. I danced my dance, notwithstanding I found I had a great cold. I read some English till 2 o'clock and then went down and dined with my landlord, and ate some ham and chicken. Mrs. M-n-l-y brother dined with us. After dinner we sat and talked till 4 o'clock and then drank tea till five and then went to Will's Coffeehouse and there took Mr. G-r-d-n and went to the park, notwithstanding it was very cold, and found abundance of company. Then I set Mr. G-r-d-n down at St. James's Coffeehouse and went to the widow Pierson's and sat with her all alone till ten and made love to her which she took not unkindly but let me kiss her hand. Then I went home where I found the fire out. I ate milk porridge and said my prayers. My cold was very bad.

6. I rose about 8 o'clock and read a chapter in Hebrew and some Greek in Lucian. I said my prayers, and had milk porridge for break-

1. Richard Sutton, brigadier general.

fast. The weather was cold and cloudy, the wind northwest. I danced my dance and wrote a letter to Suky Horsmanden till 2 o'clock and then ate some battered eggs. After dinner I put several things in order and read some English till 4 o'clock and then went to Mrs. Pierson's but she was from home. Then I went to Kensington to see the house upon the wall of the King's garden but did not like it. Then I returned to town and went to Mrs. B-r-n where I drank three dishes of chocolate. About 8 o'clock I went to Will's Coffeehouse, where I found the Duke of Argyll. Here I stayed till 11 o'clock and talked with Mr. P-ch-y about my widow. Then I went home, ate my milk porridge, and said my prayers.

7. I rose about 7 o'clock and read neither Hebrew nor Greek but wrote a letter to Mrs. B-s. I neglected to say my prayers, but had milk porridge for breakfast. The weather was cold and cloudy, the wind northeast. About eleven came Annie Wilkinson and did my linen. Then I went into the City to Mr. Perry's and dined with Mrs. Perry because neither of the gentlemen were at home, and ate some cold beef for dinner. After dinner we sat and talked till 3 o'clock and then I went to Garraway's and read the news and then went to Mrs. U-m-s and drank tea and about six went to Mrs. Smith's where I met Molly J-n-s and could not lie with her, to my great grief. We rose about nine and ate some boiled chicken for supper and I went home in a chair about twelve and said my prayers.

8. I rose about 8 o'clock and read two chapters in Hebrew and some Greek in Lucian. I neglected my prayers, but had milk porridge for breakfast. The weather was clear and warm, the wind west. About 11 o'clock I went to my Lord Orrery's, where I drank a dish of chocolate. Here I saw the Duke of Buckingham, my Lord Strafford, Sir Thomas Hanmer[2] and others. Then I went to Mr. Southwell's and sat there an hour and then went to Mr. U-t-n to dinner where was my Lord Harry Powlett and my Lord Bellenden. I ate some boiled beef. After dinner we went to Mrs. U-m-s and from thence to the playhouse in Lincoln's Inn, Mrs. Lindsay having made

2. Sir Thomas Hanmer, Bart., was speaker of the House of Commons under Queen Anne.

me take a ticket, and at the play I sat by my Lady Bouverie. After the play I went to Court and from thence with my Lord Tyrconnel to supper where was Mr. Johnson and Mr. Archer.[3] I ate some chicken and asparagus and sat and talked till one o'clock and then I went home and neglected my prayers. I received letters from Virginia.

9. I rose about 8 o'clock and read a chapter in Hebrew and some Greek in Lucian. I neglected my prayers, but had milk porridge for breakfast. The weather was warm and cloudy. I read my letters from Virginia till 12 o'clock and then came Mrs. B-s and I gave her some tea. I kissed her very much and made her promise to call me tomorrow at the coffeehouse and go to supper. About 3 o'clock she went away and I ate nothing but cake for dinner. About 5 o'clock I went to Mrs. Pierson's but she was from home. Then I went to Will's Coffeehouse and read the news and about 6 o'clock went into the City to Mrs. Lindsay's where I lost thirty shillings. I ate some cold chicken for supper with [p-r-t-l-c] onions. About 1 o'clock I got home and neglected my prayers.

10. I rose about 8 o'clock and read a chapter in Hebrew and some Greek in Lucian. I said my prayers, and had milk porridge for breakfast. The weather was warm and clear, the wind west. About 11 o'clock came Annie Wilkinson and I was angry with her for coming so late and so I was with my servant for not getting ready in time. Then I went to the Duke of Argyll's but he was from home; then to my Lord Percival's; then to Mr. Blathwayt's and found the Colonel and sat with him till he dressed and then went to Court where the Duke of Argyll overtook me and I walked with him in the park till he went to the House of Lords and then I walked with several persons and about 3 o'clock Colonel Gay and I dined at the tavern and I ate some boiled beef. After dinner I walked to St. James's Coffeehouse and from thence to Mrs. Pierson's but she was from home; then to Colonel Blakiston's where I stayed about half an hour and then went with Sir Wilfred Lawson to the park and from thence to Will's

3. Perhaps Thomas Archer, groom porter under Queen Anne, George I, and George II. He was the architect of numerous great buildings, including St. John's Church, Westminster.

and from thence to Court where I found my widow and talked much to her and led her out and then went home to my milk porridge, and then said my prayers.

11. I rose about 8 o'clock and read a chapter in Hebrew and some Greek in Lucian. I said my prayers, and had milk porridge for breakfast. The weather was warm and clear, the wind west. I danced my dance. I wrote a letter to excuse myself from meeting Mrs. B-s upon mere conscience. I wrote some English till 2 o'clock and then ate some battered eggs for dinner. After dinner I put several things in order till 5 o'clock and then went to Mrs. Pierson's where was abundance of company. Here I drank tea and then some of the company went away and others played at ombre. Mrs. Pierson seemed very well inclined, so much that the company took notice of it. I sat very much with Mrs. Pierson's cousin and all my affair seemed to go right. About ten I took leave and returned home to my milk porridge and said my prayers.

12. I rose about 8 o'clock and read a chapter in Hebrew and some Greek in Lucian. I said my prayers and had milk porridge for breakfast. The weather was clear and warm, the wind west. About 11 o'clock I walked to Somerset Chapel where we had a very indifferent sermon from Mr. S-ing. After church I walked a little in the garden and then went to dine with Mr. U-t-n and ate some roast beef. After dinner we drank a bottle of Burgundy and then I went to drink tea with Mrs. U-m-s and about five carried Lord Bellenden to Kensington Garden where we found abundance of company. About 8 o'clock at Dover Street and sat about an hour and Mrs. Pierson told me what I desired could not be because of my children. Then I took my leave and went home in the chair, ate my milk porridge and said my prayers.

13. I rose about 8 o'clock and read a chapter in Hebrew and some Greek in Lucian. I said my prayers, and had milk porridge for breakfast. The weather was clear and warm, the wind west. Annie Wilkinson [came] and did my linen. About eleven came Sir Harry Ashurst and stayed half an hour and then I set him down and went to my

Lord Orrery's where I found the Duke of Argyll and drank a dish of chocolate. About 1 o'clock I went to Mrs. Southwell's and stayed half an hour and then set Mr. Southwell to my Lord Percival's and then went home and danced my dance and ate battered eggs for dinner. In the afternoon I set several things in order and then wrote a letter to Mrs. B-s in answer to one she wrote me to borrow one hundred and fifty pounds. About 6 o'clock I went to Mrs. U-m-s but they were from home; then to Lady Powlett's but she was asleep; then to Will's where I read the news; then to Lady Guise's till nine and then to Ozinda's where I drank a dish of chocolate, and then went to Court. When I came home my man was asleep and I beat him. I said my prayers.

14. I rose about 8 o'clock and read a chapter in Hebrew and some Greek in Lucian. I said my prayers and had milk porridge for breakfast. The weather was cold and cloudy. My man gave me warning. I received a letter from Virginia. I wrote a letter to Mrs. B-s to refuse to lend her fifty pounds. I wrote a letter likewise to my daughter. About 12 o'clock I went into the City to the Virginia Coffeehouse and from thence to Mr. Perry's and dined with the old gentleman and ate some roast beef. After dinner I went to visit Mrs. Perry and drank tea. About 5 o'clock I set Mr. Carter home and went to the play but stayed not there but went to Lady Powlett's and drank some caudle. From thence I went to Will's, read the news and had two dishes of chocolate, and about 10 o'clock went with Mrs. S-t-r-d to the bagnio and rogered her once.

15. I rose about 8 o'clock and went home where I read a chapter in Hebrew but no Greek. I hired a man recommended by my peruke-maker. I wrote some English till 10 o'clock when my cousin Horsmanden came and told me everybody was well at Purleigh. I wrote a letter to my Lord Orkney and about 2 o'clock ate some roast chicken for dinner. After dinner I put several things in order and took a nap till 4 o'clock and then went to visit Mrs. Pierson and sat with her a pretty while alone. She persisted in her objection against being a

mother-in-law. We drank tea. My Lord Wallingford[4] was there. Here I stayed till 9 o'clock and then went to St. James's Coffeehouse and drank a dish of chocolate. Then I went to Court where I saw Mrs. Pierson again. About twelve I walked home and found several letters from Virginia. I ate my milk porridge and said my prayers.

16. I rose about 8 o'clock and read a chapter in Hebrew and some Greek in Lucian. I neglected my prayers, and had milk porridge for breakfast. The weather was cold and cloudy, the wind northwest. About 9 o'clock came Mr. Southwell and told me my Lord Orkney and the Council of Trade had recommended Mr. Beverley[5] to be of the Council in my stead and that he spoke to the Duke of Argyll about it, who took the thing with great concern. About 11 o'clock I went to the Duke of Argyll and begged him to speak to Lord Stanhope or Mr. Craggs to get me confirmed in the Council, which he promised to do. Then I went to Lord Orrery's where I drank a dish of chocolate and saw the Duke of Argyll there again. Then I went to Sir Wilfred Lawson's and with him went to Court where I spoke to Lord Stanhope who promised my business should be done. Then I returned to my Lord Orrery's to dinner and ate some boiled beef. After dinner we went to Will's and from thence I went to the play where I sat by Mrs. Lindsay. After the play I went home and wrote to the Duke of Argyll, ate milk, and said my prayers.

17. I rose about 8 o'clock and read a chapter in Hebrew and some Greek in Lucian. I neglected my prayers, and had milk porridge for breakfast. The weather was cold and cloudy, the wind southwest. I wrote a letter to Mrs. Perry concerning my little daughter[6] just come from Virginia. About ten came Colonel Blakiston and my cousin Horsmanden and stayed about an hour. I danced my dance. About 1 o'clock I went to Court but saw not the Duke of Argyll there so I

4. Probably Charles Knollys, son of the 3rd Earl of Banbury, baptized as 'Viscount Wallingford,' engaged in a lifelong fight to establish his legitimacy as the 4th Earl.

5. Peter Beverley, Treasurer of Virginia.

6. Wilhelmina Byrd, second surviving child of Byrd and Lucy Parke, now three and a half years old.

went to dine with Mrs. [Sutton][7] and ate some pigeon and asparagus. After dinner I went to Colonel Blakiston and sat with him half an hour and then went to Mrs. Pierson but she was from home. Then I went to Will's Coffeehouse and read the news. Here I sat till 9 o'clock and then went to Court where I saw Mrs. Pierson and talked with Mrs. Howard[8] for the first time. About twelve I came home and said my prayers.

18. I rose about 8 o'clock and read a chapter in Hebrew and some Greek in Lucian. I neglected my prayers, and had milk porridge for breakfast. The weather was cold and cloudy, the wind southwest. I paid my man his wages and discharged him but my other man came not, so about 11 o'clock I went into the City to Mr. Perry's and dined with Dick Perry and ate some beefsteak. After dinner we sat and talked till 4 o'clock and then drank tea. Then I went home and put some things in order till five and then I went to the play, where I sat by the widow Pierson and she was kind enough. After the play I went to Will's and read the news and about eleven walked home and found my man still there and the other sent word he could not serve me, I believe by my other man's desire. I ate my milk porridge and said my prayers.

19. I rose about 8 o'clock and read a chapter in Hebrew and some Greek in Lucian. I said my prayers, and had milk porridge for breakfast. The weather was cold and cloudy, the wind southwest. I danced my dance and about 12 o'clock went to Court but the King was gone to church before I came. However, I saw several persons of my acquaintance. I went about 1 o'clock with Daniel Dering to my Lord Percival's to dinner and ate some roast mutton. After dinner we went to see the new house and then we saw Mrs. T-l-r's house which was very fine. Then we drank tea and then I went to St. James's Coffeehouse where I met with Jack Lawson and carried him to the park where was abundance of company. About 8 o'clock I went to visit

7. Perhaps the wife of Brigadier General Sutton.

8. Henrietta Howard, afterwards Countess of Suffolk, lady in waiting to the Princess of Wales and mistress of Prince George.

Mrs. P-r-s-l where I sat till ten and then went home and washed my feet. I ate no supper but said my prayers.

20. I rose about 7 o'clock and read a chapter in Hebrew and some Greek in Lucian. I neglected to say my prayers, but ate milk porridge for breakfast. The weather cold and cloudy, the wind southwest. About 10 o'clock came Annie Wilkinson to mend my linen. Then I went to the Duke of Argyll's but he was gone out of town. Then I went to Lord Islay's who received me very kindly and advised me to bribe the German[9] to get the governorship of Virginia and told me he would put me in the way. Then I went to the Cockpit and gave six guineas to B-n-f-l to retain two counsels for the Assembly of Virginia against their Governor. Then I went to Court where I spoke to Mr. Secretary Craggs who promised to get me leave to stay in England and keep my Council place. Then I went with Sir Wilfred Lawson to see his new house which was a good one. About 2 o'clock I went to dine with Mr. Southwell and ate some broiled beef. After dinner we drank tea and about 5 o'clock I went to Will's Coffeehouse and from thence to Mrs. [Andrews] and from thence to Court, where I talked with pretty Miss Howard. About twelve I went home, ate milk porridge, and said my prayers.

21. I rose about 7 o'clock and read a chapter in Hebrew and some Greek in Lucian. I said my prayers, and had milk porridge for breakfast. The weather was clear and cold, the wind west. I danced my dance. I wrote some letters to Virginia till 2 o'clock and then I ate some roast chicken for dinner. After dinner I put several things in order and then took a nap and danced again till 5 o'clock and then I went to visit Mrs. Pierson where I drank tea and sat and talked merrily till 7 o'clock and then I went to Will's Coffeehouse to meet Sir Wilfred Lawson to carry him to Mrs. S-n-l-t-n to a ball where was Mrs. S-t-b-r-k whom I did not think very pretty. I danced with

9. Andreas Gottlieb, Baron von Bernstorff, adviser to King George. On June 9, 1718, the Duchess of Orleans wrote of him, 'The man is a real devil, and a wicked devil too. He has this inducement to make trouble, that so long as the King is on bad terms with the Prince of Wales, the minister can dispose of places without interference.' Lewis Benjamin, *The First George in Hanover and England,* by Lewis Melville [pseud.], (London, 1908), I, 239.

Mrs. Pierson and was merry. We had nothing but some cakes for supper and wine. We danced till 4 o'clock and then I went home and neglected my prayers.

22. About 10 o'clock before I rose Mr. Bradley brought me a packet from Virginia. Then I rose and read nothing because I was obliged to go into the City. However, I ate some milk porridge and about 12 o'clock went in the hack to Mr. Perry's where I found several letters from Virginia. After dinner, which was salmon, I went up and wrote a letter to Virginia and about 5 o'clock went to Will's Coffeehouse and from thence to Mrs. Pierson's where I drank tea and made love. My Lord Maynard[10] came in, discovering good sense in his conversation. About 9 o'clock I carried Mr. O-s-b-r-t-n to Court where was but indifferent company. However, I stayed till 11 o'clock and then walked home, ate my milk, said my prayers, and went to bed.

23. I rose about 7 o'clock and read a chapter in Hebrew and some Greek in Lucian. I said my prayers, and had milk porridge for breakfast. The weather was cold and clear, the wind southeast. About 11 o'clock I went to the Duke of Argyll's who was gone out; then to my Lord Islay's, who was very busy. Then I went to the Cockpit and spoke with Mr. S-t-n-n about my Council place. Then to the coffeehouse to meet Mr. B-n-f-l about our Virginia business, and then to court where I spoke with Lord Islay and Mr. Secretary Craggs about my business. About 2 o'clock I went to Colonel Blakiston's to dinner and ate some fish. Colonel Blakiston had the gout. After dinner came in Colonel G-r-th. About 5 o'clock I went to visit my daughter and stayed an hour and then went to Will's and sat there till 8 o'clock. Then I was carried by a woman I met in the street to a pretty French-woman with whom I supped and gave her some chicken and asparagus but did not roger her. About twelve I went home and neglected my prayers.

24. I rose about 7 o'clock but read nothing because I wrote a petition to the King concerning my Council place. I neglected to say

10. Henry Maynard, 4th Baron Maynard.

my prayers, but had milk porridge for breakfast. The weather was clear and cold, the wind violent at east. I wrote some English. Annie Wilkinson came to take care of my linen. About ten came Daniel Horsmanden and stayed half an hour. About eleven came Mr. Page and stayed half an hour and about twelve my Lord Orrery came and stayed an hour. Then I ate some battered eggs. After dinner I put several things in order and wrote some English and took a little nap till 5 o'clock and then I went to Colonel Blakiston's and carried his paper concerning the quitrents of Virginia. Then I went to Mrs. Pierson who was from home. Then I went to Mrs. FitzHerbert's and drank and found Mr. Congreve and stayed till 9 o'clock and then went to Court where I met Mrs. Pierson and talked pretty much to her and walked home and said my prayers and ate some milk porridge.

25. I rose about 7 o'clock and read a chapter in Hebrew and some Greek in Lucian. I neglected my prayers, but had milk porridge for breakfast. The weather was cloudy and warm, the wind south. About 9 o'clock came Captain Turner lately arrived from Virginia and brought me some letters. About ten came my Lord Percival and stayed about half an hour. About eleven I went to the Duke of Argyll's but he was from home. Then to Lord Islay's who was from home; then to my Lord Orrery's where I drank a dish of chocolate and wished him a good journey into the country. Then to Mrs. Southwell's and sat with her till 1 o'clock and then went to Court where I spoke to the Duke of Argyll who was very kind to me. About 2 o'clock I went home with Sir Charles Wager and ate some of a Spanish [o-l-y] for dinner. Here I stayed till 6 o'clock and then went to the widow Pierson's where I stayed till 10 o'clock and then walked home, ate my milk, and said my prayers.

26. I rose about 7 o'clock and read a chapter in Hebrew and some Greek in Lucian. I neglected my prayers but had milk porridge for breakfast. The weather was cloudy and warm, the wind southwest. About 11 o'clock I walked to Somerset Chapel where we had a very indifferent sermon from a stranger. After church I walked in the gardens with several ladies and about 2 o'clock dined with Mrs. U-m-s

and ate some roast beef. After dinner we sat and talked till 4 o'clock and then drank tea. About five came Mrs. Lindsay and her husband and I carried the last to Kensington Garden where I walked with several. About nine I went to Mrs. U-m-s where I found my Lord Sussex and about ten I walked home, ate my milk, washed my feet, and said my prayers.

27. I rose about 7 o'clock and read a chapter in Hebrew and some Greek in Lucian. I said my prayers, and had milk porridge for breakfast. The weather was warm and cloudy, the wind southwest. I danced my dance and wrote some English till 12 o'clock and then went into the City to Garraway's Coffeehouse and read the news. Then I went to Mrs. Lindsay's to dinner and ate some fish. After dinner I went to make a visit to young Mrs. [Tryon] to wish her joy on her marriage. Here I drank tea and about 6 o'clock went to make a visit to Mrs. S-n-l-t-n where I stayed about an hour and then went to Will's and stayed half an hour. Then I went to Mrs. B-r-n where I drank three dishes of chocolate and then went to court and talked abundantly to Mrs. Howard. In coming home I took a woman into the coach and committed uncleanness and then went home and said my prayers. In the morning I went to Hatton Garden to visit my daughter.

28. I rose about 7 o'clock and read a chapter in Hebrew and some Greek in Lucian. I said my prayers, and had milk porridge for breakfast. The weather was warm and clear, the wind east. I danced my dance and wrote a letter to Mr. B-r-n-t in Scotland. I put several things in order till 1 o'clock and then went to Court where I spoke to the Duke of Argyll and my Lord Islay. About 2 o'clock I went to Mr. Southwell's to dinner where my Lord Ashburnam,[11] Mrs. Bellenden, and Robin Moore dined and I ate some boiled beef. After dinner we sat and talked till 7 o'clock and then four of us walked in the aisles of the park. Then we returned about 8 o'clock and I walked to Mrs. Pierson's where I stayed till ten and then walked home and said my prayers.

11. John, 3rd Baron Ashburnam.

29. I rose about 7 o'clock and read a chapter in Hebrew and some Greek in Lucian. I said my prayers, and had milk for breakfast. The weather was cloudy and cold, the wind east. About 9 o'clock came Captain W-l-s and stayed half an hour. I danced my dance. About 11 o'clock came Captain Randolph and brought my little daughter with him who appeared much better than I had heard. He was so kind as to offer to take care of her till she was cured of the itch. About 12 o'clock I sent six bottles of wine to Mr. U-m-s and twelve to Colonel Blakiston. Then I went to Sir Wilfred Lawson and waited on him to Court and from thence home with him to dinner where I ate some fish. After dinner we went to Kensington Garden and stayed there till eight and then returned to St. James's Coffeehouse where I drank a dish of chocolate and then went to Court where I saw Mrs. [Noel]. About twelve I walked home and said my prayers.

30. I rose about 7 o'clock and read a chapter in Hebrew and some Greek in Lucian. I said my prayers, and had milk for breakfast. The weather was cloudy and cold, the wind east. About nine I paid Mr. H-l-n twenty-five pounds for my coach. Then I danced my dance and wrote a letter to my Lady Mohun. About eleven I went to Lord Islay's who told me the King's going to Hanover was a great hindrance to my affairs. Then I went to the Duke of Argyll's and from thence to my Lord Percival's, who was from home. Then to visit Mrs. Southwell, where I drank a dish of chocolate. Then I went home where Sir Wilfred Lawson came to see me and we went to Pontack's to dinner and I ate some boiled beef. After dinner we went to my milliner's and from thence to Crane Court where we stayed till 5 o'clock and then we went to Mrs. Pierson who was from home. Then we went to Kensington Garden where we walked till 8 o'clock and then returned and I went to see my French whore where I supped and ate some fricassee of chicken. I gave the whore two guineas and committed uncleanness and then went home in the chair and said my prayers.

May 1719

1. I rose about 8 o'clock and read a chapter in Hebrew and some Greek in Lucian. I said my prayers, and had milk for breakfast. The weather was clear and cold, the wind east. About 10 o'clock came Annie Wilkinson and took care of my linen. I danced my dance and about 11 o'clock went to visit my daughter where I stayed about half an hour and then went to the Virginia Coffeehouse, and from thence to Mr. Perry's where I dined and ate some roast mutton. After dinner we drank tea and then I took leave and went home where I adjusted myself and then danced my dance again. Then I went to my Lady Guise's where I stayed an hour, and then went to Mrs. FitzHerbert's, where we supped and I ate some fricassee of chicken. Margaret Bellenden was there and we were very merry. I said my prayers.

2. I rose about 7 o'clock and read a chapter in Hebrew and some Greek in Lucian. I said my prayers and had milk for breakfast. The weather was clear and cold, the wind east. I danced my dance and then wrote some English till one o'clock and then went to Court where I spoke to several of my friends. Then I went to St. James's Coffeehouse and ate a jelly and then went to Sir Wilfred Lawson's and ate some mackerel. After dinner we drank a bottle till six and then we went to Kensington Garden and walked there two hours and we found the King there himself. About 8 o'clock I made a visit to Colonel Blakiston, where I stayed till 10 o'clock and then walked home and I met with an old mistress and saw her home to her lodging and then came home and said my prayers.

3. I rose about 8 o'clock and read a chapter in Hebrew and some Greek in Lucian. I said my prayers, and ate milk for breakfast. The weather was cold and cloudy, the wind east. I danced my dance and

wrote some English till 1 o'clock and then I went to dine with Lady Guise and ate some mackerel. After dinner we both took a nap and about five drank some coffee. Then I went to Will's Coffeehouse and from thence to visit Mrs. [Sands] where I found Mrs. G-n-s who is very elegant of speech. Here I stayed till 10 o'clock and then went home and washed my feet and said my prayers.

4. I rose about 8 o'clock and read a chapter in Hebrew and some Greek in Lucian. I said my prayers, and had milk for breakfast. The weather was cold and cloudy, the wind east. I danced my dance. About 9 o'clock came Daniel Horsmanden and stayed about half an hour. Then came Annie Wilkinson and adjusted my linen. About 11 o'clock I went to my Lord Orrery's but he was from home; then to Mrs. LeGrande's and sat with her about an hour and then went to Mrs. J-n-s in Young Street and then home, where I wrote a letter to Virginia. About 2 o'clock I ate a roast chicken. After dinner I put several things in order and then took a nap. About six I went to the play where I sat by the widow Pierson. After the play I went to Court and talked to Mrs. Howard and about 11 o'clock walked home and said my prayers.

5. I rose about 7 o'clock and read a chapter in Hebrew and some Greek in Lucian. I said my prayers, and had milk for breakfast. The weather was cold and cloudy, the wind east. I wrote two letters and about 11 o'clock went to Mr. Horsmanden's lodgings and from thence to Hatton Garden, then to the Virginia Coffeehouse, and from thence my cousin Horsmanden and I went with Isham Randolph to his house to dinner and my mouth was so sore I could eat nothing but chicken. After dinner we saw my little daughter. There dined with us Mr. Russell and Mrs. D-s-s. Here we were merry and I gave Isham Randolph twelve guineas for bringing my daughter over. About five we went to London and so to the park where we went to the lodge with Mrs. P-n and ate some cheesecake. From thence I went to Somerset House to Mrs. U-m-s where I stayed and ate an egg and then walked home and said my prayers. My mouth continued bad. It rained a little.

6. I rose about 7 o'clock and read a chapter in Hebrew and some Greek in Lucian. I said my prayers, and had milk for breakfast. My mouth was better. The weather was cloudy and warm, the wind west. About 10 o'clock came Mr. F-s and stayed about half an hour. I wrote a letter to Virginia. About 12 o'clock I called on Mrs. S-t-r-d-k and went to Mr. Perry's and dined with the old gentleman and ate some cold beef. After dinner I went to visit Mrs. Perry and drank tea and about five went to Will's Coffeehouse and read the news and talked with the Duke of Argyll and my Lord Islay. About 8 o'clock I went to Mrs. Pierson's but she was from home. Then I walked in the park and walked with Mrs. G-n-s and Sally Cornish and picked up a whore afterwards that committed uncleanness, for which God forgive me. Then I went to Court and talked to Miss Howard and about eleven walked home and said my prayers.

7. I rose about 7 o'clock and read a chapter in Hebrew and some Greek in Lucian. I said my prayers, and had milk for breakfast. My mouth was better, thank God. The weather was cloudy and warm, and it rained. I danced my dance and wrote a letter to Virginia till 1 o'clock, and then I went into the City to Pontack's to dinner, where I ate some boiled beef. After dinner we went to Crane Court to the meeting of the Royal Society where I stayed till five and then went to Mr. Horsmanden's lodging but he was from home. Then I went to Will's where I read the news and then carried Mr. G-r-d-n to Kensington Garden where we walked two hours and some part of the time I was with Mrs. G-n-s. About 9 o'clock I went to visit Mr. Percival where I was very merry till 11 o'clock and then I took leave and went home where I said my prayers, &c.

8. I rose about 7 o'clock and read a chapter in Hebrew and some Greek in Lucian. I said my prayers and had milk for breakfast. The weather was cloudy and warm, the wind west. I wrote a letter to Virginia and some other things till 1 o'clock and then came Daniel Horsmanden and stayed half an hour and then I went to Court where I spoke with the Duke of Argyll and then went to Colonel Blakiston's to dinner and ate some boiled veal and bacon. After dinner we

played at piquet and I lost a guinea. About 7 o'clock Colonel Blakiston and I went to the park where some of the Council of Trade saw us together. Then we walked in St. James's Park till nine and then I went to the coffeehouse and drank some chocolate. Then I went to Court and talked abundance to Mrs. Howard and made Mrs. Pierson jealous. About twelve I walked home and said my prayers.

9. I rose about 7 o'clock and read a chapter in Hebrew and some Greek in Lucian. I said my prayers, and had milk for breakfast. The weather was warm and cloudy, the wind west. I danced my dance. About 11 o'clock came Mr. Lindsay and told me I must go with him to Epsom in the afternoon, which I promised to do, so I went to my Lord Orrery's, but he was from home; then to Mrs. Southwell's where I stayed about half an hour, and then went home and got ready for my journey. About 2 o'clock came my Lord Orrery to me and stayed about half an hour. I ate a roast chicken for dinner. About 3 o'clock came Mr. Lindsay and we went in my chariot and six horses over the ferry to Epsom and got there about 7 o'clock. We put ourselves in order and went to the Long Room where we found Mrs. Lindsay and Mrs. U-m-s. I played at the ace of hearts and lost a guinea. About 11 o'clock we went home to supper and Colonel Murray[1] and Mr. Ingraham[2] supped with us and I ate some chicken and asparagus. We sat up till 3 o'clock and then I went to my lodging and neglected my prayers.

10. I rose about 8 o'clock and read nothing. However, I said my prayers, and had milk for breakfast. It had rained in the night, but this morning the weather was cloudy and cold. About 10 o'clock we went to church where I saw dear Mrs. [Cambridge]. Colonel Murray and Mr. Ingraham dined with us and I ate some chicken fricassee for dinner. After dinner we drank tea till 4 o'clock and then we went all hands to my Lady Dudley Fielding's park, which is very pretty and so is the house. Then we went to my Lord Guilford's[3]

1. Honorable Robert Murray, captain and lieutenant colonel, Third Foot Guards, brother of John, Earl of Dunmore.

2. Perhaps Arthur Ingraham, director of the South Sea Company.

3. Francis, 2nd Baron Guilford, owned Durdans at Epsom.

and walked in his garden and then to Mr. Diston's,[4] whose garden is very pretty, and then to my Lord Baltimore's,[5] which is a place run to ruin; however, the chapel and staircase are fine. In the evening we returned home and ate roast duck for supper. Colonel Murray and Ingraham supped with us. However, we parted about 12 o'clock and I went home and said my prayers.

11. I rose about 7 o'clock and read a chapter in Hebrew and some Greek. I said my prayers, and had milk for breakfast. The weather was warm and cloudy. About 10 o'clock Mr. Lindsay and I went through Leatherhead to my Lord Paisley's,[6] who lives in a bad house well set near the river. Neither my Lord nor Lady were at home, so we went to Mr. Arthur Moore's house at Petersham which is fine set and the garden lovely but ill kept. About 2 o'clock we returned home and I took a nap till three when we dined and I ate some veal and bacon. After dinner we went to see a race between Lord Baltimore and young Colonel Pitt,[7] who rode themselves, and my Lord beat. Then I went home and read English till 8 o'clock when we went to the Long Room where I lost five pounds at everything. Then I talked to Mrs. [Cambridge] and my Lady Guilford,[8] who is still an adorable woman. About eleven we went home to supper and I ate some cold chicken. Mr. Will G-r and Mr. F-r-m-n supped with us and we sat up till 3 o'clock and I neglected my prayers.

4. Alderman Josiah Diston, whose house was Woodcote Grove.

5. Charles Calvert, 5th Baron Baltimore, became governor of Maryland in 1732. His house at Epsom was Woodcote Park.

6. Lord Paisley, son of the 6th Earl of Abercorn. He was a fellow of the Royal Society.

7. Thomas Pitt, second son of the Governor of St. George, created Baron Londonderry on June 3, 1719.

8. Alice, wife of the 2nd Baron Guilford, was a daughter of Sir John Brownlow, Bart., and Alice Sherard. Her sister Elizabeth married the Earl of Exeter, and her sister Eleanor married Lord Tyrconnel. In a letter written by Byrd to 'Facetia' in 1703 he reports 'Lord Guilford is coupled to Mrs. Brownlow, and the gods alone can tell what will be produced by the conjunction of so much fat and good humor.' *William Byrd Esqr. Accounts as Solicitor General of the Colonies & Receiver of the Tobacco Tax 1688-1704. Letters Writ to Facetia by Veramour &c. Printed from the MS Copy* (privately printed by T. F. Ryan, 1913), 16.

12. I rose about 7 o'clock and read a chapter in Hebrew and some Greek. I said my prayers, and had milk for breakfast. The weather was cold and cloudy, the wind west. About 9 o'clock we returned to London in my chariot and six and got there by twelve and I went to the Virginia Coffeehouse, where I found Colonel Blakiston and then I went with him to dine with old Mr. Perry and ate some boiled beef. After dinner I just called on Mrs. Perry and then I went to visit P-n-y U-m-s and drank tea with her. Then I went home, then to Will's, then to the play, and then to visit Mrs. Pierson, who was from home. Then I walked to Mrs. Smith's who could not get me a mistress. Then I walked in St. James's Park and then picked up a woman that was pursued by a footman and carried her to the tavern where we had a veal cutlet with great innocence till twelve and then I walked home and said my prayers.

13. I rose about 8 o'clock and read a chapter in Hebrew and some Greek in Lucian. I said my prayers, and had milk for breakfast. The weather was cold and cloudy, the wind west, and it blew violently. I danced my dance and about 11 o'clock went to the Duke of Argyll's but he was from home. Then to Mrs. Southwell's where I sat about an hour. Then I returned home and wrote two letters to Virginia and put several things in order till 2 o'clock when I was angry with my man about my dinner. I ate some veal cutlets. After dinner I put several things in order till 5 o'clock and then I went to the widow Pierson's, where I stayed till 9 o'clock and then went to Will's where I had two dishes of chocolate. Then I went to my kind Mrs. Smith where I met a fine young woman, with whom I ate some rabbit fricassee and then we went to bed together and I rogered her three times and neglected my prayers.

14. I rose about 9 o'clock and we drank coffee and [cockscombs] for breakfast. About eleven I went home and read a chapter in Hebrew and some Greek in Lucian. I neglected my prayers, but ate some milk. About twelve Mr. Horsmanden came and then Brigadier L-n-s-t-n, and about two I went to dine with Colonel Blakiston, where I ate some boiled mutton. After dinner the Colonel and I played at piquet and he won every game. About 6 o'clock I went to

Ozinda's Chocolate House where I was to meet my cousin Horsmanden to carry him to the park, where we went and I saw dear Mrs. Howard there, and afterwards again at St. James's Park, where I walked with Sir Wilfred Lawson and saw the widow without speaking to her. About nine I walked to Will's and had some milk and a cake and then walked home and said my prayers.

15. I rose about 7 o'clock and read a chapter in Hebrew and some Greek in Lucian. I said my prayers, and had milk for breakfast. The weather was cold and cloudy, the wind west and blowing hard. About ten came Annie Wilkinson to examine my linen. About 11 o'clock I went to Mrs. S-t-r-d-x to inquire after my little daughter who was a little better. Then I went to the Virginia Coffeehouse, and from thence to Dick Perry's to dinner, where my daughter was and I ate some roast mutton. After dinner we sat and talked till four and then drank tea. Then I just called at Mr. Lindsay's for half an hour and then went home and set Mr. Lindsay down by my house. About six I looked into the play and then went to Will's Coffeehouse where I stayed till 8 o'clock and then went to Lady Guise's where I sat till ten and then went home, ate a cake, and said my prayers.

16. I rose about 7 o'clock and read a chapter in Hebrew and some Greek in Lucian. I said my prayers and had milk for breakfast. The weather was cold and cloudy, the wind west. I danced my dance, and about 11 o'clock went to my Lord Islay's and stayed with him half an hour and he showed me two engines, one for driving the [piles], the other for making [rivers deep]. Then I went to Mr. LeGrande's where I stayed about an hour, and then went to visit Mrs. Southwell where I stayed to dinner and ate some roast mutton. Tom Southwell and his brother[9] dined with us. About 5 o'clock I went to visit Mrs. Pierson but she was from home. Then I went to Mrs. Howard's for the first time and stayed about an hour. Then I went to St. James's Park and walked there and would not join Mrs. Pierson. I drank some warm milk and then walked home and said my prayers.

9. Probably sons of Thomas Southwell, in 1717 created Baron Southwell of Castle Mattress; they were related to Edward Southwell's family. In 1720 Baron Southwell was succeeded by his son Thomas.

17. I rose about 8 o'clock and read a chapter·in Hebrew and some Greek in Lucian. I said my prayers, and had milk for breakfast. The weather was cold and cloudy, the wind west. I danced my dance, and wrote two letters to Virginia till 1 o'clock and then I went to St. James's Coffeehouse where I drank a dish of chocolate and about 3 o'clock went to Sir Wilfred Lawson to dinner and Mr. T-l-k dined with us. I ate some roast pigeon and asparagus. After dinner we drank a glass till 6 o'clock and then Sir Wilfred and I went to the park where was abundance of company and my widow and Mrs. Howard among the rest. At night I set my friend down at St. James's Coffeehouse and went to Dover Street to visit the widow and sat with her about two hours and then walked home and said my prayers.

18. I rose about 7 o'clock and read a chapter in Hebrew and some Greek in Lucian. I said my prayers, and had milk for breakfast. The weather was warm and clear, the wind west. I danced my dance, and wrote letters to Virginia till 10 o'clock and then came Annie Wilkinson and mended my linen. About eleven came Mr. LeGrande and we went together to see the wax anatomy, which was exceedingly fine. Here I stayed two hours and then I went home and dined on bread and cheese because my man was out of the way. After dinner I put several things in order and wrote another letter to Virginia. About five I went to Mr. Southwell's and found there Lady Dorothy [Southwell] [10] who sings and plays exceedingly fine. In the afternoon I walked in the street and endeavored to pick up a whore but could not so I ate more cake and went home and said my prayers and slept very well.

19. I rose about 7 o'clock and read a chapter in Hebrew and some Greek in Lucian. I said my prayers, and had milk for breakfast. The weather was clear and warm, the wind southwest. I danced my dance and wrote a letter to Virginia till 11 o'clock and then I went to the Virginia Coffeehouse, where I met Captain Randolph and Mr. Carter and we went to Captain Randolph's to dinner and I ate some boiled beef. After dinner we drank a bottle of rack punch and were merry till 7 o'clock and then went to Mr. Perry's where we stayed to sup-

10. Perhaps a sister of Thomas Southwell.

per and I ate some pigeon. After supper I walked home and looked for a woman, but could not find one so about eleven I went home and said my prayers.

20. I rose about 7 o'clock and read a chapter in Hebrew and some Greek in Lucian. I said my prayers, and had milk for breakfast. The weather was warm and cloudy, the wind southwest. I washed my feet and wrote a letter till 11 o'clock and then I went to visit Mr. V-n-n but he was from home. Then to the Cockpit to the Council office and then to Mrs. Southwell's and sat with her till 1 o'clock and then I went to Mrs. U-m-s and stayed there half an hour, and then walked home and ate a roast chicken for dinner barely done. After dinner I put several things in order and took a nap till five and then I went to Mrs. Pierson's, but she was from home; then to Mrs. Blakiston's and sat with her about half an hour, and then to Mrs. B-r-n where I drank some milk coffee, and then to Will's where I drank a dish of chocolate and then went to Mother Smith's, where I supped with Betty G-r-n-r and then we went to bed and I rogered her two times very powerfully.

21. I rose about 8 o'clock and paid my mistress a guinea and my mother another, and then I went home in a coach. There I read a chapter in Hebrew and some Greek in Lucian. I danced my dance and then wrote a letter and about 1 o'clock went to Pontack's to dinner and ate some boiled beef. Afterwards my dear Duke of Argyll came there and was very kind in inviting me to his house in the country to stay as long as I would. After dinner I went and sat with the Duke and my Lord Islay till five and then we went to the Temple where I took [...]. I walked to Misses U-m-s who were going to the play with Mrs. Lindsay and I went likewise and was jawed to death so that I did not stay it out but went to walk in the park where was abundance of company. About ten I walked to the coffeehouse and from thence home and said my prayers.

22. I rose about 7 o'clock and read a chapter in Hebrew and some Greek in Lucian. I neglected my prayers, but had milk for breakfast. The weather was clear and warm, the wind southeast. About 10

o'clock came Annie Wilkinson to mend my linen. However I wrote several things and read several papers relating to my country. About 2 o'clock I went to Sir Charles Wager's to dinner where I ate some mackerel for dinner. After dinner we sat and talked till five and then I set Mr. B-r-n-t who dined with us in Panton Square and went to Mrs. Pierson's where I put the question and was flatly refused so I resolved to say no more about it. However, I stayed till 8 o'clock and then went to walk in the park and joined Mrs. C-r-d. About ten I walked home and said my prayers.

23. I rose about 7 o'clock and read a chapter in Hebrew and some Greek in Lucian. I neglected my prayers, but had milk for breakfast. The weather was clear and warm, the wind southeast. I wrote a letter to Purleigh till 10 o'clock and then came my tailor with some altered clothes. About 11 o'clock I went to Mrs. LeGrande's and stayed there about half an hour; then I went to Mrs. Southwell's and stayed two hours and found Colonel Blathwayt and Mr. Moore. Then I returned home and wrote more letters till 3 o'clock and then I read some English and had battered eggs for dinner. After dinner I put several things in order and then read English till 5 o'clock and then went to Will's where I talked with Sir George Markham[11] about an hour and then went to Mrs. M-r-s and stayed about quarter of an hour and then to the Mall where I walked till 9 o'clock and then drank some milk and then walked to my Lady Dunkellen's levee, and then walked home and by the way bought a cheesecake. I said my prayers.

24. I rose about 7 o'clock and read a chapter in Hebrew and some Greek in Lucian. I said my prayers, and had milk for breakfast. The weather was clear and hot, the wind southeast, but very little of it. I danced my dance and about 11 o'clock walked to Somerset Chapel, where I slept, God forgive me. After church Mr. U-t-n invited me to dinner where I ate some salmon. His sister dined with us and two other gentlewomen. About 5 o'clock I went to visit the widow Pierson but she was from home. Then to Colonel Blakiston's but nobody was at home; then to Mrs. FitzHerbert's where I met Congreve and Mrs. LeGrande and stayed about two hours. Then I went to Lady

11. Sir George Markham, Bart., was a fellow of the Royal Society.

Guise's and stayed about an hour and then walked home and by the way picked up a woman and committed uncleanness with her and went home about eleven and said my prayers.

25. I rose about 7 o'clock and read a chapter in Hebrew and some Greek in Lucian. I said no prayers but had milk for breakfast. The weather continued very warm and clear, the wind southeast. I wrote abundance of Hebrew till 2 o'clock and then read some English till three when I ate some roast chicken. After dinner I put several things in order and took a nap till four. Then I read English till five and then went into the City to Mr. Dick Perry's where was Mrs. C-r-d-k and we played at cards and I lost ten shillings. About nine we went to supper and I ate some ham and cold chicken and drank some rack punch. About eleven we took leave and I walked home where I said my prayers.

26. I rose about 7 o'clock and read a chapter in Hebrew and some Greek in Lucian. I said no prayers, but had milk for breakfast. The weather was clear and very hot, the wind still southeast. I wrote some Hebrew till 11 o'clock and then went to Mr. J-n-n but he was from home. Then to my Lord Islay's but he was from home. Then to my Lord Orrery's, but he was from home; then to Mrs. Southwell's and sat with her about an hour and then went to the Cockpit and saw Mr. Beake and then went home and ate some battered eggs. After dinner I put several things in order and read some French till 5 o'clock and then went to visit Mrs. Pierson; then I went to Will's Coffeehouse and saw my Lord Orrery and then took a walk to Mrs. S-t-r-d but she was from home. Then I picked up a woman and carried her to the tavern and ate some roast lamb. I was very wanton till 12 o'clock and then walked home and said my prayers. This was the hottest day I ever felt at the time of year.

27. I rose about 7 o'clock and read a chapter in Hebrew and some Greek in Lucian. I said my prayers, and had milk for breakfast. The weather was much cooler. However, it was warm and clear, the wind northeast. I danced my dance. About 11 o'clock I went to my Lord Orrery's where I drank a dish of chocolate and about twelve went

with my Lord Orrery and Lord B-n-l-y to see the [burning glass]. Then I went to the Council office and found my business was not yet done. Then I went to St. James's Coffeehouse and there had a jelly. About two I went to my Lord Orrery's where I dined with my Lord B-n-l-y and ate some fish. After dinner we drank a bottle of champagne and about 5 o'clock went to see the anatomy of wax and stayed there two hours and then went to Will's and from thence to St. James's Park with Mr. Ashley where I walked till ten and joined Mrs. [Andrews]. Then I walked home and said my prayers.

28. I rose about 7 o'clock and read a chapter in Hebrew and some Greek. I neglected my prayers, but had milk for breakfast. The weather was still warm and clear and very dry, the wind north. About eleven came Annie Wilkinson but I would not speak with her. I was disappointed in the coming of Mrs. B-s who wrote me word she would come and breakfast with me, so I read some English and ate some bread and butter because I was to dine late and about 3 o'clock went to dine with Sir Wilfred Lawson and ate some mutton. After dinner we talked a little and about 6 o'clock went to Kensington in Sir Wilfred's coach where there was a ball in the gardens and several ladies and among the rest Miss Perry whom I stuck most to and she complained I squeezed her hand. Here I stayed till 1 o'clock and then came home and neglected my prayers.

29. I rose about 8 o'clock and read a chapter in Hebrew and some Greek in Lucian. I said my prayers, and had milk for breakfast. The weather continued hot but was a little cloudy. I read some English till 11 o'clock and then came Colonel Blakiston and stayed about half an hour and then I went to Mrs. S-t-r-d-x to inquire after my little daughter and found she was better. Then I went into the City to Garraway's Coffeehouse where I read the news and then went to Mr. Lindsay's to dinner and ate some fish. After dinner we played at faro and I won forty shillings. About 6 o'clock I went to Will's Coffeehouse, and from thence to Lady Guise's and then returned to Will's where Margaret G-t-n called on me and I went with her to the bagnio where I rogered her three times with vigor, twice at night and once in the morning. I neglected my prayers.

30. I rose about 8 o'clock. I gave my mistress a crown and then went home, where I read a chapter in Hebrew but no Greek. I neglected my prayers, but had milk for breakfast. The weather continued clear and cold, the wind east. I wrote a letter to my daughter and about 11 o'clock went to St. James's Coffeehouse where I found Mr. U-t-n and went in his chariot to Fulham to the Bishop of London with intent to dine with him but he was just going to London. I was set over the river to Putney to visit my Aunt Sherard but she was from home. Then I took a boat and went to Vauxhall and dined upon a roast chicken at Spring Garden. After dinner I took a nap in the arbor till 6 o'clock and then took a walk and joined three women and gave them Rhenish wine and cheesecake, but about nine went to London alone and went to Will's Coffeehouse and drank some milk and about eleven walked home and neglected my prayers.

31. I rose about 8 o'clock and read a chapter in Hebrew and some Greek in Lucian. I neglected my prayers, and had milk for breakfast. The weather continued warm and dry, the wind northeast. Before 11 o'clock I walked to Somerset Chapel where I slept, for which God forgive me, and after church went to dine with Mrs. U-m-s and ate some bacon and cauliflower. After dinner we drank tea till five and then I went to Mrs. S-n-l-t-n where I found Mrs. Pierson and stayed there till eight and then went to Will's Coffeehouse and drank some milk and about ten walked home where I washed my feet and said my prayers but found my man late, which made me very angry with him. However, I kept my temper pretty well, thank God.

June 1719

1. I rose about 6 o'clock and read a chapter in Hebrew and some Greek in Lucian. I said my prayers, and had milk for breakfast. The weather was cold and cloudy, the wind northeast. I found a little

running and used my injection. I danced my dance. About ten came
Annie Wilkinson and mended my linen. About 11 o'clock I went to
Mr. V-n-n but he was from home. Then to my Lord Islay's who was
from home, then to Mrs. U-m-s and paid my money for the lottery.
Then to Garraway's where I read the news, then to Mr. Perry's
where I dined with the old gentleman and ate minced veal. After
dinner I went to visit Mrs. Perry where I drank tea and about 5
o'clock went to Will's and from thence to Mrs. C-r-d and they were
from home. Then to Mrs. Pierson's and I found her alone and sat with
her two hours and then went and walked in the park till ten and then
walked to Will's, ate some milk, and walked home and said my
prayers.

2. I rose about 6 o'clock and read a chapter in Hebrew and some
Greek in Lucian. I said my prayers, and had milk for breakfast. The
weather was clear and warm, the wind northeast. I danced my dance
and read some English till 11 o'clock and then went to Lord Islay's
and sat with him about an hour and then went to the Cockpit to speak
with Tom Beake. Then to Mrs. Southwell's where I sat till 2 o'clock
and then went home and had a roast chicken for dinner. After dinner
I put several things in order and took a nap till five and then read some
English till six and then went to Tom's Coffeehouse and stayed till
eight and then I carried Mr. Buckhurst to the St. James's Park to walk
where I stayed till nine, and then drank some milk and walked home,
where I said my prayers, &c.

3. I rose about 7 o'clock and read a chapter in Hebrew and some
Greek in Lucian. I said my prayers and had milk for breakfast. The
weather continued warm and dry, the wind northeast. About 10
o'clock came Captain Tom Ward who was going to Virginia. I
danced my dance and read the papers sent me from Virginia till 2
o'clock and then I went to dine with Sir Wilfred Lawson and ate
some mackerel. After dinner we went to Kensington to the young
Princesses' Court [1] where we stayed about an hour and then returned
and walked in St. James's Park till 9 o'clock and then I went to Will's

1. The three young princesses (daughters of the Prince of Wales) lived with the
King at the Royal Palace.

Coffeehouse and drank two dishes of chocolate. About ten came Betty S-t-r-d and I went with her to the bagnio and lay with her all night and rogered her twice. It threatened rain.

4. I rose about 8 o'clock and went home, where I read a chapter in Hebrew and some Greek in Lucian. I said my prayers, and had milk for breakfast. It continued very hot and dry, the wind southwest. About ten came Captain Ward again and after him my cousin Horsmanden who stayed half an hour. I read some English and took a short nap till 1 o'clock and then I went into the City and dined at Pontack's and ate some roast goose. After dinner we went to Crane Court and from thence I went to visit Mrs. Pierson but she was from home. Then I went to Mrs. FitzHerbert's and drank tea. Then I went to walk in the park and walked with Mrs. Pierson and about ten walked home and ate a seed cake. I said my prayers.

5. I rose about 7 o'clock and read a chapter in Hebrew and some Greek in Lucian. I said my prayers, and had milk for breakfast. The weather continued warm and dry, the wind northeast. I wrote two letters to Virginia and about 11 o'clock went to Mrs. U-m-s about the business of the lottery. Then I went to the Virginia Coffeehouse to meet Captain Ward who was going to Virginia and from thence we went to dine with old Mr. Perry and I ate some boiled fowl and bacon. After dinner we parted and I went to visit Mrs. Perry and drank tea with her. Then I went to Tom's Coffeehouse and from thence to visit Mrs. [Andrews] where I stayed about an hour and then walked in the park and then bought a cake and walked home and said my prayers. I slept pretty well, thank God.

6. I rose about 6 o'clock and read a chapter in Hebrew and some Greek in Lucian. I said my prayers and had milk for breakfast. The weather continued warm and dry, the wind northeast. I danced my dance and then wrote a letter to my cousin Nutty Horsmanden till 2 o'clock and then I walked to Mr. U-t-n to dinner and ate some boiled mutton. Mrs. U-t-n dined with us. After dinner I went to Mrs. U-m-s and drank tea till 5 o'clock and then came Mrs. Lindsay and invited me to dinner tomorrow. About 7 o'clock I went to Mrs. Pierson's and

sat with her till ten. She seemed pretty gracious but would not consent. Then I walked to Will's Coffeehouse and by the way ate two plum cakes and there I drank some milk and then walked home and said my prayers.

7. I rose about 7 o'clock and read a chapter in Hebrew and some Greek in Lucian. I said my prayers, and had milk for breakfast. The weather was cold and clear, the wind east and . . . I danced my dance. Tom Ward called upon me about ten. My coachman came in a blue coat because he had dirtied mine, but I sent him back again and went in a hack to Mr. Lindsay's to dinner and ate some roast beef. After dinner we went to church, where I slept, for which God forgive me. After church we drank tea with Mr. H-s and Mr. G-r-d-n. About 8 o'clock I walked all the way to Will's Coffeehouse, where I drank some milk for supper. Here I sat about an hour and then walked home and said my prayers.

8. I rose about 6 o'clock and read a chapter in Hebrew and some Greek in Lucian. I said my prayers, and had milk for breakfast. The weather was cold and cloudy and it rained a little, the wind west. I danced my dance and scolded at Mr. H-l-n about the coachman who brought his clothes in a dirty condition. I wrote some English till 12 o'clock and then I went to meet Captain Ward at Dick Perry's where we dined and I ate some fish. After dinner we sat and talked till three and then we parted but I stayed with the ladies and drank tea. About five I went to Mr. Horsmanden's but he was from home; then to Will's Coffeehouse, and from thence to Lady Guise's where I found old Mr. V-n-n. About nine I went to see Mrs. Smith and walked home and took a girl into the coach and diverted myself and then went to Will's and had some milk and toast. Then I walked home and said my prayers.

9. I rose about 6 o'clock and read two chapters in Hebrew and some Greek in Lucian. I said my prayers, and had milk for breakfast. The weather was cloudy and cold, the wind northwest. I danced my dance and about 11 o'clock went to my Lord Islay's and saw his library. I stayed with him till twelve and then went to the Cockpit to

look for the Duke of Argyll where I spoke to him and about one returned home and read some English till two and then ate a roast chicken. After dinner I took a nap and then read more English till five and then went to visit Mrs. Pierson where I found Sir Will Leman. Here I ate some cherries and stayed till 9 o'clock and then went to Will's from whence I walked to Mrs. Smith's and supped with Mrs. G-r-d-n-r and then lay with her all night and rogered her twice.

10. I rose about 8 o'clock and gave a half guinea to the poor and then went home where I read a chapter in Hebrew and some Greek in Lucian. I said my prayers, and had milk for breakfast. The weather was clear and warm. About 9 o'clock came Tom Ward and stayed quarter of an hour. I danced my dance and about twelve went to visit Mrs. Southwell and stayed about an hour and then went to meet Tom Ward and dined with him at the tavern and ate some fish. After dinner I walked home and wrote a letter to Mr. Perry and then read some English till seven and then walked to Will's and from thence to St. James's Park where I walked with Horace Walpole and then with Mrs. D-n-s who had got [on the white r-s] and had been affronted before I came. About ten I walked home and said my prayers.

11. I rose about 7 o'clock and read two chapters in Hebrew and some Greek in Lucian. I said my prayers, and had milk for breakfast. The weather was cold and cloudy, the wind west. I wrote a letter to Virginia and paid my coachmaker's bill. About 12 o'clock I went to Mr. Horsmanden's chamber and from thence to see my daughter where I stayed till 1 o'clock and then went to Will's and from thence to Mr. U-t-n to dinner where I ate some beans and bacon. After dinner we drank a bottle of Burgundy and then drank some tea. About 6 o'clock I went to Mrs. C-r-d and by the way I met the guards that were sent against the weavers.[2] I stayed with Mrs. C-r-d till 10 o'clock and then went to Mrs. U-m-s where I ate a boiled egg and stayed till 12 o'clock and then walked home and said my prayers.

2. The silk weavers, out of work because of the increased use of calico, rioted, and it was necessary to call out the guards on June 11, 12, and 13.

12. I rose about 7 o'clock and read a chapter in Hebrew and some Greek in Lucian. I said my prayers, and had milk for breakfast. The weather was cold and cloudy, the wind southwest. About 11 o'clock I went to Sir Wilfred Lawson's and sat with him about an hour and then went to Colonel Blakiston's and drank a dish of chocolate and then went to Somerset House and dined with Mrs. U-m-s and ate some mutton steak. After dinner I took a nap and about 6 o'clock came Mr. Lindsay and his wife, Colonel Murray, and Mr. Will [Tryon] and we went in a barge upon the river and had very good music. We had ham and cold chicken and very good wine of several sorts and went to Mortlake where we went ashore and dined till 2 o'clock and then returned to London where we got about four and I went home but neglected my prayers.

13. I rose about 9 o'clock and read a chapter in Hebrew and some Greek in Lucian. I said my prayers, and had milk for breakfast. The weather was cold and cloudy, having rained abundance yesterday. I received a letter from Captain Ward which made me resolve not to go out of town to the Duke of Argyll's as I intended. About 12 o'clock came Mr. N-l-r and stayed about half an hour. I read some English till 1 o'clock and then I went to Colonel Blakiston's to dinner where was Colonel Lowther and Colonel [Folliot]. I ate some ham and chicken. After dinner came in young M-t-n-y and we drank a glass till 5 o'clock and then I went to the widow Pierson's but she was from home. Then to Lady Dunkellen's but she was from home. Then to Mrs. M-r-s but she was from home; then to Mrs. [Sands'] where I stayed two hours and then went to walk in the park where was abundance of company. About ten I walked home and endeavored to pick up a whore but could not. I said my prayers.

14. I rose about 8 o'clock and read two chapters in Hebrew and some Greek in Lucian. I said my prayers, and had milk for breakfast. The weather was cold and cloudy, and it rained abundance for three hours together. I wrote a letter to Virginia and read some English till 1 o'clock and then went to St. James's Coffeehouse and read the news. Here I drank a dish of chocolate. About 2 o'clock I went to dine with Sir Wilfred Lawson and ate some boiled mutton. After dinner we

drank a bottle till 6 o'clock and then went to the park where was abundance of company. Then we walked in St. James's Park and I joined Mrs. [Noel] and Mrs. D-n-s and then walked home, and ate a cake by the way. I said my prayers.

15. I rose about 7 o'clock and read a chapter in Hebrew and some Greek in Lucian. I said my prayers and had milk for breakfast. The weather was cold and clear, the wind west. About 9 o'clock came Mr. Perry to take me with him to Mr. [Burchett] [3] and I went but he refused us what we desired. Then I went to the Cockpit and spoke to several people and then went to Mrs. Southwell's and stayed about an hour and then went to Mrs. U-m-s and desired them to speak to Mrs. Lindsay about all her conduct with Colonel Murray, which she promised to do. Then I went home to dinner and ate a roast chicken. After dinner I put several things in order and took a nap and about 6 o'clock went to visit Mrs. Pierson but she was from home. Then I went to Hyde Park by myself and then to St. James's Park where I walked with Mrs. Pierson and then went and supped with Mrs. U-m-s and ate some eggs and stayed till twelve and then walked home and said my prayers.

16. I rose about 7 o'clock and read a chapter in Hebrew and some Greek in Lucian. I neglected my prayers, but had milk for breakfast. The weather was clear and warm, the wind southwest. About 9 o'clock I went to the Duke of Argyll's and found him at my Lord Is-lay's and told him I would go see him tomorrow. Here I stayed till ten and then went home and read some English till eleven and then went to Mr. Horsmanden's who was from home, then to my daughter who was well, then to Mr. Perry's and dined with Dick and ate some Virginia pork. About four I went home and put all my matters in order for my journey and about eight went and walked in St. James's Park, notwithstanding it had rained abundance. Here I picked up a whore that made me commit uncleanness and I gave her half a crown. About eleven I came home and did not find my man, for which I was a little angry.

3. Perhaps Josiah Burchett, secretary to the Admiralty.

17. I rose about 6 o'clock and read nothing at all because I prepared to go to Petersham to the Duke of Argyll's. However, I said a short prayer, and had milk for breakfast. The weather was clear and warm. About 9 o'clock I went to Colonel Blakiston's and stayed about half an hour and then proceeded on my journey and got to the Duke's house about 12 o'clock. He received me very kindly and we walked about and talked till 2 o'clock and then we dined and I ate some beans and bacon. Colonel S-t-r-d and Mr. G-r-d-n dined with us and after dinner James Campbell and his wife came in and we drank tea and then walked about the garden till 9 o'clock and then we went to supper and Mr. C-b-r-n supped with us and I ate some eggs. After supper we sat and talked till eleven and then I was conducted to the house in the garden where I lay and said my prayers.

18. I rose about 6 o'clock and read a chapter in Hebrew and some Greek in Isocrates. I said a short prayer, and had milk for breakfast. The weather was clear and warm. About 9 o'clock I walked about the garden and then read some English. Then I danced a little and then Mr. C-b-r-n came to see me at my apartment. About 2 o'clock Tom Harrison, Sir Robert Gordon and Mr. Abercromby came to dine with the Duke and James Campbell. I ate some stewed beef. After dinner we talked a little and then played at ninepins and then at bowls and in the evening the Duke, the Duchess, and I took a walk about the garden till 9 o'clock when we went to supper and I ate some lobster. Then we sat and talked till eleven and then I retired and said my prayers. It rained all night, thank God.

19. I rose about 6 o'clock and read two chapters in Hebrew and some Greek. I neglected my prayers, and had milk for breakfast. The weather continued cloudy and was cold, the wind southwest. I danced my dance and about 11 o'clock Mr. C-b-r-n and I went to Lord Percival's where we drank some chocolate. We stayed about an hour and then returned to the Duke's again where we found my Lord Shannon[4] and Colonel Middleton[5] and old Mr. L-t-n that

4. Richard Boyle, Viscount Shannon, son of the Honorable Richard Boyle.

5. John Middleton, brevet colonel, had served in the Duke of Argyll's regiment; he was governor of Tynemouth Castle.

dined with us, and I ate some boiled beef. After dinner we drank a bottle till 6 o'clock and then the company went away and my Lord Duke and I walked to Ham Walk [6] and were overtaken by the rain. When we came home we found Molly B-r-n-n and drank tea with her. She was grown better. I ate some salad for supper and about twelve went home and said my prayers.

20. I rose about 6 o'clock and read a chapter in Hebrew and some Greek. I neglected my prayers, and had milk for breakfast. The weather was warm and clear, the wind southwest. I read some English till 11 o'clock and then I went in my chariot to Kew to visit Sir Charles Norris and drank a dish of chocolate, and about two returned to the Duke's where I found my Lord B-n-l-y, my Lord Islay, my Lord L-s-f-r, Mr. J-k and Mr. P-ch-y and I ate some fish for dinner. We drank a bottle till 6 o'clock and then went to bowls and I lost two shillings. About eight the company went away and my Lord, Lady Duchess, Harry B-l-n-n and I walked about the grounds till nine and then we ate some eggs for supper, and then drank a bottle of wine till twelve and then I went to my lodging.

21. I rose about 6 o'clock and read a chapter in Hebrew and some Greek. I said my prayers, and had milk for breakfast. The weather was cloudy and warm, the wind southwest. It rained two hours; however, about 10 o'clock I went to church and heard an indifferent sermon. After church I returned home and walked in the garden till dinner when Miss Howe [7] and Miss Lepell dined with us and I ate some roast beef. After dinner we drank tea and then took a walk and about 6 o'clock my Lord B-l-s-n and John Montgomery came and walked with us and then the ladies went away. James Campbell and Major B-d came also but did not stay but the other gentlemen did and supped with my Lord Duke and I ate an egg. About twelve we parted and I said my prayers.

6. Ham House, near the Duke of Argyll's estate, was the Jacobean seat of the Earl of Dysart.

7. Sophia Howe, maid of honor to the Princess of Wales.

22. I rose about 6 o'clock and read no hing because I prepared to go to my Lord Shannon's with the Duke of Argyll, and accordingly after I had eat some milk I waited on his Grace to Mr. L-t-n who has a very pretty house and garden. Here my Lord Shannon met us together with Colonel W-t-m, and Colonel Middleton was with him and Mr. Abercromby. We went to see some land which his Grace had a mind to purchase and about 2 o'clock arrived at my Lord Shannon's where I ate some tongue for dinner. After dinner we drank pretty much and I went away with the Duke about 7 o'clock and rode gently and got home about ten and I ate some rice milk for supper. About twelve we parted and I said my prayers.

23. I rose about 6 o'clock and read some Greek and then packed up my things in order to come to London, and took leave of the Duke and Duchess that came about 8 o'clock, but I stayed till eleven; in the meantime I had my milk for breakfast. About eleven I came away and gave money to the maid, the butler, the cook, and one of the grooms. I went to dine with Lord Percival but he was gone to London, which made me resolve to dine with Sir Charles Norris, but before dinner we went to the coffeehouse at Richmond, where I read the news and talked to Mrs. C-l-m-n who lives next door. About two we returned to Sir Charles' where I ate some chicken and bacon and drank some Smyrna wine. About five I set out for London where I got about seven and went to Mrs. Pierson's but she was from home; then I walked in the park and afterwards picked up a girl called Molly York and carried her to the bagnio and lay all night with her and rogered her twice.

24. I rose about 8 o'clock and went home and read a chapter in Hebrew and some Greek in Lucian. I said my prayers, and had milk for breakfast. The weather was cold and cloudy. About eleven I went to the Duke of Argyll's and stayed with him about an hour, and then went to Mr. Southwell's who invited me to dinner. This made me go home and write some English and about 2 o'clock went to dine with Mr. Southwell, where I found the Marquis of M-r-m-n and Count B-r-n-b-r. I ate some mutton cutlets. After dinner the company drank a merry bottle but I drank tea with Mrs. Southwell and

then went to Will's and from thence to Dover Street but Mrs. Pierson was from home. Then to Mrs. C-r-d and I sat with them half an hour and then went to walk in the park where I walked with Mrs. D-n-s. Then I went again to the coffeehouse and had milk, then went home and said my prayers.

25. I rose about 7 o'clock and read a chapter in Hebrew and some Greek in Lucian. I said my prayers, and had milk for breakfast. The weather was cloudy and cold, the wind southwest. I danced my dance. About 11 o'clock I went to the Cockpit and wrote a letter to the Duke of Argyll to put him in mind of my affair in Council and stayed till he came out and spoke to him. My business came on in Council and the Duke spoke extremely in my favor. However, the matter was referred to a committee.[8] Then I went home and ate some mutton cutlets for dinner. After dinner I put several things in order and took a nap and about 6 o'clock went to the committee to try the business of Mr. G-r-d-n and stayed there till 9 o'clock and then went to Will's, drank two dishes of chocolate, and about ten Betty S-t-r-d came to me and we went to the bagnio where we lay all night and I rogered twice.

26. I rose about 8 o'clock and went home, where I read a chapter in Hebrew and some Greek in Lucian. I neglected my prayers, but had milk for breakfast. The weather was cold and cloudy. About 11 o'clock I went to Mr. Horsmanden's and from thence to the Virginia Coffeehouse and from thence to old Mr. Perry's to dinner and ate some roast beef. After dinner I examined some of Mr. Perry's books to look for my leave to come here. Then I went to visit Mrs. Perry and about four went away to Mr. Southwell's who advised me to get my business put off till the King came. Then I went to Mrs. Pierson's and sat with her about two hours and found her gracious. Then I went to Will's and from thence to Mrs. U-m-s where I ate an egg but was very sleepy and went home before 12 o'clock and neglected my prayers.

8. Byrd's petition for leave of absence from Virginia while retaining his seat in the Council was referred to the Lords of the Committee of the Privy Council. *Calendar of State Papers, Virginia and West Indies*, June 25, 1719.

27. I rose about 8 o'clock and read a chapter in Hebrew and some Greek in Lucian. I said my prayers, and had milk for breakfast. The weather was cold and cloudy and it rained pretty much. However, about 11 o'clock I went to my Lord Islay's but he was from home; then to Mrs. S-t-r-d-x to see my daughter and found her pretty well. About [. . .] o'clock I went home and read some English till two and then ate a roast chicken for dinner. After dinner I put several things in order and then took a nap till five and then read more English. Then I went to Mr. Horsmanden's lodging and from thence we went to see the chambers at Lincoln's Inn and made Mr. M-d a visit. Then I went to walk in the park and drank some milk and in returning home picked up a girl and carried her to the tavern and ate some broiled lamb but did nothing but talk till twelve and then went home and neglected my prayers.

28. I rose about 8 o'clock and read a chapter in Hebrew and some Greek in Lucian. I said my prayers, and had milk for breakfast. The weather was warm and clear. About 11 o'clock came Mr. Page and went with me to church at Somerset Chapel. After church I walked home and read some English till 2 o'clock and then ate a broiled chicken for dinner. After dinner I read some English and took a nap and read till six and then came Mr. Horsmanden and I carried him to the park where we ate some cherries. About eight we walked in St. James's Park till nine and then I went to my Lady Dunkellen's who told me she was going to Ireland. I sat with her till eleven and then walked home and said my prayers. I slept very ill.

29. I rose about 6 o'clock and read a chapter in Hebrew and some Greek in Lucian. I said my prayers, and had milk for breakfast. The weather was cloudy and warm. About 10 o'clock I went to visit Mrs. Pierson and drank tea with her, and about eleven proceeded to Petersham to the Duke of Argyll's and by the way read some English. I arrived at the Duke's about 2 o'clock where I found Parson G-r-d-n, my Lord Islay and several other gentlemen and I ate some goose giblets. After dinner we drank a bottle till 5 o'clock and then played at bowls and I won five shillings. In the evening we took a walk with the Duchess till nine and then I ate some rice milk for supper and

after supper drank a bottle and about twelve I was laid in the best apartment and neglected my prayers.

30. I rose about 6 o'clock and read some English only. I said my prayers but had not time to eat my breakfast because I came to town with the Duke and we went into the coach at 8 o'clock and got to town about ten and I went and drank tea with Mrs. Southwell and then went home and put my house in order and wrote some English till two and then returned to Mr. Southwell's to dinner and my Lord Percival and Daniel Dering dined there too. I ate some boiled beef. After dinner I went to Lady Guise's that I found indisposed. However I stayed till eight and then went to walk in the park and walked with Mrs. D-n-s and some other ladies. Then I picked up a woman and felt her and then went home and neglected my prayers.

July 1719

1. I rose about 8 o'clock and read two chapters in Hebrew and some Greek in Lucian. I said my prayers, and had milk for breakfast. The weather was exceedingly hot and clear, the wind southwest. However, I danced my dance, and then read some English and settled several accounts. Mr. Albin came and brought me a set of [. . .]. About 2 o'clock I ate some boiled chicken. After dinner I put several things in order and took a nap and then wrote a letter and read some English till 6 o'clock and then called on Mrs. C-r-d but she was from home. Then I went to Mrs. Pierson's but she was from home. Then to Mrs. [Sands'] where I drank tea and stayed till 8 o'clock, and then walked in the park, and then went to the coffeehouse and ate some milk, and then walked home and gave a girl half a crown that was going into a flux tomorrow. I said my prayers.

2. I rose about 7 o'clock and read two chapters in Hebrew and Greek in Lucian. I said my prayers, and had milk for breakfast. The weather was clear and very hot. I danced my dance and about 11 o'clock I went to see my daughters and learned that the youngest had been very bad but was better, thank God. Then I went to Mr. Page and went with him to the coffeehouse and read the news and about two went to dine with Mr. U-t-n where I found my Lord Bellenden, my Lord Harry Powlett and Mr. [Clark]. I ate some roast mutton and we drank abundance till five and then I went to Mr. Horsmanden's lodging and carried him to Spring Garden by water, where we picked up two girls and I lay with one of them all night at the bagnio and rogered her twice. Her name is Margaret M-c-n-y.

3. I rose about eight and went home, where I read a chapter in Hebrew and some Greek in Lucian. I neglected my prayers, but had milk for breakfast. The weather continued very hot and clear. About eleven I went and took up Mr. Page and carried him to the Virginia Coffeehouse and from thence to old Mr. Perry's to dinner where I ate some roast beef. I took a hundred pounds; then I walked to Mr. Lindsay's and sat with him about an hour and then went home and read some English. Then I went to Mr. Horsmanden's lodgings and he told me he had agreed about the chambers in Lincoln's Inn for nine hundred guineas. Then we went to walk in the park till we were tired, and then I went to Will's and from thence home about 11 o'clock and said my prayers.

4. I rose about 7 o'clock and read a chapter in Hebrew and some Greek in Lucian. I said my prayers, and had milk for breakfast. The weather was clear and hot, the wind southwest. I danced my dance. I wrote a letter to Suky Horsmanden and then read some English till 2 o'clock and then ate some roast chicken. After dinner I put several things in order and then read more English till 6 o'clock and then went to Mrs. Pierson's where I stayed till 9 o'clock and then went to meet Mary York at the Union Tavern where we had a broiled chicken for supper. I gave her half a guinea and did nothing for it. About 12 o'clock I walked home and said my prayers. It rained a little and thundered in the night but I slept so sound I did not hear it.

5. I rose about 7 o'clock and read two chapters in Hebrew and some Greek in Lucian. I said my prayers, and had milk for breakfast. The weather continued extremely hot. However, I danced my dance and went not to church because the weather was intolerable. I read some English till 2 o'clock and then ate some battered eggs. After dinner I put several things in order, and then took a nap till four, and then read more English till five, and then went to visit Mrs. [Andrews] where I drank tea and complained at the weather. About eight I went to walk in the park where I walked with Mrs. [Andrews] and was forced to walk home with them because I could get no coach. About eleven I walked home and said my prayers. It rained a little in the night.

6. I rose about 7 o'clock and read two chapters in Hebrew and some Greek in Lucian. I said my prayers, and had milk for breakfast. The weather was clear, the wind northwest. About 11 o'clock I went to visit my Lord Orrery and drank a dish of chocolate with him. Then I went to Mr. Southwell's and took leave of him because he was going out of England to Ireland. Then I went and dined with Lord Orrery and ate some fish. About 5 o'clock we went to Will's where I read the news, and about seven my Lord and I went to Spring Garden and walked there and from thence to St. James's Park and about 10 o'clock I walked home and said my prayers.

7. I rose about 7 o'clock and read two chapters in Hebrew and some Greek in Lucian. I said my prayers and had milk for break-fast. The weather was pretty cool, the wind northwest. I danced my dance and about 11 o'clock went to the Cockpit to visit the Duke of Argyll but the regent sat so long that I could not stay, because I was invited to dinner by my landlady, where I ate some fowl and bacon. After dinner we drank tea till 5 o'clock and then I went up and read some English till six and then went to visit Mrs. Pierson and sat with her till 9 o'clock and she refused me again. Then I went to meet Mary York and went with her to the bagnio but my man had the curiosity to [dog me] before the coach. Here I lay all night and rogered her twice.

8. I rose about 8 o'clock and went home where I scolded at my man for [dogging me] last night. I read a chapter in Hebrew and some Greek in Lucian. I said my prayers and danced my dance. About eleven came Mr. Albin and brought me some glass. Then came Colonel Blakiston and sat with me about half an hour. I read some English till 2 o'clock and then went to Sir Charles Wager's but he was gone to Chelsea so I returned home to my lodging and had broiled chicken for dinner. In the afternoon I took a nap and then read some English till 6 o'clock and then went to Mr. Horsmanden's and from thence to Will's Coffeehouse where I found Lord Orrery and Lord Windsor and walked with them in Somerset Garden and then to finish my walk went to the park and walked with Mrs. [Andrews] and then returned to Will's and ate some milk and about 11 o'clock went home and said my prayers.

9. I rose about 7 o'clock and read a chapter in Hebrew and some Greek in Lucian. I said my prayers, and had milk for breakfast. The weather was cold, the wind southeast. I danced my dance, and read some English till 11 o'clock and then went to the Virginia Coffeehouse where I learned that twenty of the Virginia ships were arrived. Then I went to dine with old Mr. Perry and got his note for five hundred pounds to purchase chambers in Lincoln's Inn. I ate some young [fawn] for dinner. After dinner I read several letters from Virginia and then went to Garraway's Coffeehouse and from thence to my milliner's and then went to Mr. Horsmanden's and then to Lincoln's Inn. Then I went home and read some letters and about 7 o'clock went to Will's and from thence to St. James's Park with my cousin Horsmanden and Mr. Page with whom I went afterwards to Leveridge's where we had a cold chicken and some rack punch. About twelve I went home and said my prayers.

10. I rose about 6 o'clock and went at eight to Daniel Horsmanden's and from thence to Sir George Cooke's chambers to execute the covenant and take possession of my chambers at Lincoln's Inn, which I did accordingly and about 10 o'clock walked home and read several letters from Virginia till 1 o'clock and then came my Lord Orrery and stayed about an hour and then I ate some mutton steaks for

dinner. After dinner I put several things in order and then took a nap and read some English till five. Then I went to my chambers and saw several things and then went to Lady Guise's where I met Mr. V-n-n. Here I sat till eight and then walked in the park with Mrs. [Noel]. In going home I picked up a gentlewoman, carried her to the tavern where we ate lobster, and then went to the bagnio. The woman's name was R-s-m-l.

11. I rose about 8 o'clock and read a chapter in Hebrew and some Greek in Lucian. I said my prayers, and had milk for breakfast. The weather was warm and clear. I wrote two letters and danced my dance. I read some English till 2 o'clock and then ate some battered eggs for dinner. After dinner I wrote a letter to Virginia and then took a nap and then read more English. I gave my man Ralph warning to go next week. About five I went to Lincoln's Inn to my chambers and Mr. M-d came to see me and congratulate my being so near him. Then I went with Mr. Horsmanden to walk in the park and then we walked to Will's where I had some milk. About eleven I went home and said my prayers.

12. I rose about 7 o'clock and read a chapter in Hebrew and some Greek in Lucian. I said my prayers and had milk for breakfast. The weather was cold and cloudy, the wind northwest. I danced my dance. About 11 o'clock came Mr. Page and I carried him to Lincoln's Inn and from thence to the City but I went and dined with Mr. Lindsay and had roast beef for dinner. In the afternoon we went to church, where I slept, for which God forgive me. After church we drank tea and I went to Will [Tryon's] where I drank some champagne and about 7 o'clock went to Daniel Horsmanden's where I found John Page. With these gentlemen I went to St. James's Park where we walked till 9 o'clock and then I met with two French women and went home with them but nothing came of it so I walked home and said my prayers.

13. I rose about 5 o'clock and read a chapter in Hebrew but no Greek because I got ready to go to Mr. [Tryon's] with design to go to Northolt. Accordingly about 7 o'clock I went to Mr. [Tryon's]

but nobody was ready so we sent to Mrs. [*sic*] to get up and come to us, which she did and I ate some chocolate for breakfast. About 9 o'clock we set out in the coach and four and went through Highgate, where I was sworn. Then we proceeded to Northolt which is about twelve miles from London. We got there about one and I ate some beans and bacon. We sat and talked till 5 o'clock and then went to the wells where a new long room is built and there was abundance of company and I danced three dances with Mrs. [Coatsworth]. Kitty Sambrooke was here and I talked abundance to her, and so was Mrs. [Cambridge] who was very obliging to me. About 11 o'clock we went home and got to town about two, very tired. However, I walked home from the coach and said my prayers.

14. I rose about 7 o'clock and read a chapter in Hebrew and some Greek in Lucian. I neglected my prayers, but had milk for breakfast. The weather continued hot and dry. About 11 o'clock I went to my Lord Orrery's where I drank a dish of chocolate and there was Lord Windsor and Lord Bathurst.[1] Then I went to the Cockpit to do some business and then returned to my Lord Orrery's to dinner and ate some mutton cutlets. After dinner we had a bottle of champagne and then went to the coffeehouse and read the news. Then I went to see my daughters and learned that my youngest had the smallpox, but very favorably. Then I went to walk in St. James's Park and found Will [Tryon] and Daniel Horsmanden and then took a turn with Mrs. D-n-s and returned to Will's, had some milk, and walked home, and said my prayers.

15. I rose about 7 o'clock and read a chapter in Hebrew and some Greek. I said my prayers, and had milk for breakfast. The weather continued hot and dry. I danced my dance and wrote a letter till 11 o'clock and then went to the Virginia Coffeehouse and from thence to young Mr. Perry's to dinner, where I ate some Virginia pork. After dinner I settled some affairs and then drank tea with Mrs. Perry. Then I went to visit my daughters and saw the girls dance. My little daughter was better, thank God. About 6 o'clock I

1. Allen, created in 1711 Baron Bathurst, according to Cokayne 'a man of wit, taste, and learning, friend of Pope, Addison, etc.'

carried my daughter to visit Mrs. D-n-s, where we drank tea again till 8 o'clock, and then took a walk in the park till ten, and then I took leave and walked home, where I said my prayers.

16. I rose about 7 o'clock and read a chapter in Hebrew and no Greek. I said no prayers, but had milk for breakfast. The weather was cold and dry, the wind southeast. I settled some accounts and dusted my [c-ch] and put several things in order till 11 o'clock and then I went to Mr. U-t-n but he was out of town. Then I called at Mrs. S-n-l-t-n and stayed about quarter of an hour. Then I went to the market and bespoke a bed and other furniture for my chambers. Then I went to my chambers and stayed there till 2 o'clock and then walked home and had some broiled chicken for dinner. After dinner I slept a little and then read some English till six and then went to Will's Coffeehouse and wrote to Colonel Blakiston to take lodgings at Tunbridge. Then I went to St. James's Park where Colonel Smyth[2] gave a masque but the thunder and rain put an end to it about 10 o'clock and I went home and said my prayers.

17. I rose about 6 o'clock and read nothing because I packed up my things, which cost me some trouble. I neglected my prayers, but had milk for breakfast. The weather was very hot, the wind southeast. I removed several of my things about 2 o'clock and then went to Mr. Lindsay's to dinner and he looked very sour upon me. However, I bore it, and when I had Mrs. Lindsay by myself I told her what I heard about her and Colonel Murray and made her cry. I ate some roast mutton and stayed till 6 o'clock and then went and drank tea with my landlady. Then I went to Will's and from thence to the park, where I walked with Mrs. [Noel] and Mrs. P-p-y. Then I picked up a whore and committed uncleanness and ate some salmon for supper and about 12 o'clock walked home and said my prayers.

18. I rose about 6 o'clock but read nothing because I continued very busy in packing up my things in order to remove this day. I said a short prayer, and ate milk for breakfast. About 10 o'clock

2. Henry Smyth, alias Nevill of Holt, brother of Colonel Clement Nevill, was made a lieutenant colonel in 1717.

Captain G-th-s from Virginia came and stayed about half an hour and then proceeded to pack my things till 2 o'clock and then ate some boiled chicken for dinner. After dinner I put things in order and took a nap and about 4 o'clock carried away the rest of my things to my chamber where I went with them and about 6 o'clock went to my Lord Orrery's with Colonel Cecil and I stood godfather to Mrs. S-w-b-r-g daughter and gave two guineas to the midwife and one to the nurse. Then I went to the coffeehouse and from thence to my lodging, where I paid my landlord and my man and about 11 o'clock said my prayers.

19. I rose about 5 o'clock and got everything ready and about 6 o'clock with difficulty got the coach because it rained and thundered and went to my Lord Orrery's where I met my Lord Windsor and Colonel Cecil and drank a dish of chocolate and about 8 o'clock got into one of B-l-n-t coaches and crossed the ferry and went to Tunbridge. About two we got to Sevenoaks, where I found Mr. Lindsay and his wife. I ate some fowl and bacon for dinner. Colonel Fermor[3] and Mr. L-m-b-r-t came to us. About five we set out from hence and got to the Wells about seven and got lodgings at Mr. B-r-t at twenty-five shillings a room. Then we walked to the Wells and about nine returned to our lodgings, where I put my things in good order and then said my prayers.

20. I rose about 6 o'clock and read a chapter in Hebrew and two chapters in Greek. I said no prayers, but had milk for breakfast. The weather was clear and warm, the wind west. My Lord Percival and Colonel Blakiston came to see me and stayed about an hour. About 11 o'clock we went to church to prayers and after church to the Walk, where I played at several things and won about a guinea. About two we went home to dinner and I ate some roast goose. After dinner we gave a girl half a guinea each to set her up. About four I went to visit Mrs. Lindsay where I drank tea and about six went to the Walk where I played again and won about a guinea. Here we stayed till 10 o'clock and then went home and ate some milk and said my prayers.

3. John Fermor, lieutenant colonel of Rich's Dragoons. He had been governor of Minorca.

21. I rose about 6 o'clock and read a chapter in Hebrew and two chapters in Greek. I said no prayers, but had milk for breakfast. The weather was cloudy and warm, the wind west. About 9 o'clock my Lord Orrery and I went to visit my Lord Percival but he was from home. Then we walked to the wells, then to church, and then to the wells again, where I played at several things and won ten shillings. About two we went to dinner and I ate some venison. After dinner we drank a bottle till four and then went to visit Mrs. Lindsay and from thence to the wells, where I lost thirty shillings at hazard with the ladies. In the evening I went to the ball where the ladies took us out and particularly my Lady Isabel Scott[4] took me out to dance a French dance which I [obeyed]. About eleven I went home, washed my feet, and said my prayers.

22. I rose about 6 o'clock and read a chapter in Hebrew and two chapters in Greek. I said my prayers, and had milk for breakfast. The weather was cloudy and warm and it rained a little. Colonel Blakiston came to see me and about eleven we went to church. After church to the Walk, where I played and won a guinea and about 2 o'clock went home to dinner and ate some boiled chicken. After dinner we [tossed] a little till four and then went to the cold baths in our coach and six and about 6 o'clock came to the Walk and I played at hazard and lost two guineas. The Duchess of Montague[5] came last night. About 9 o'clock we left the Walk and went home and ate some milk for supper. I said my prayers.

23. I rose about 6 o'clock and read a chapter in Hebrew and two chapters in Greek. I said no prayers but had milk for breakfast. The weather continued dry and warm. I wrote a song upon poor Mr. Buckhurst. About 11 o'clock we went to church. After church I played at hazard and won two guineas and afterwards won a little at piquet of my Lady [Styles] and my Lord Orrery. About 2 o'clock I went to dine with Jack Sambrooke and ate some stewed crab. After

4. Lady Isabel Scott, daughter of Charles, 3rd Baron Cornwallis.

5. Mary Churchill, wife of John, 2nd Duke of Montague, daughter of the Duke of Marlborough, and until December 1717 lady of the bedchamber to the Princess of Wales.

dinner we drank some champagne and about six went to the Walk,
where I played at several things and won a little at all and got
acquainted with several ladies. Here we stayed till 9 o'clock and
then we walked home and ate some milk and said my prayers.

24. I rose about 6 o'clock and read a chapter in Hebrew and some
Greek. I neglected my prayers, but had milk for breakfast. The
weather continued dry and warm till noon. I wrote some English
till 10 o'clock and then went to Colonel Blakiston's and from thence
to church, after church to the Walk, where I played and lost about
ten shillings. I talked to several women till two when it rained and
we went to dinner and I ate some boiled mutton. Mr. L-m-b-r-t dined
with us. About 4 o'clock we returned to the Walk where I talked
abundance to my Lady [Styles]. I lost three guineas at [f-r-n], and
stayed till 10 o'clock on the Walk and then went home and had milk
for supper. I said my prayers.

25. I rose about 6 o'clock and read two chapters in Hebrew and
two chapters in Greek. I neglected my prayers, and had milk for
breakfast. The weather continued dry and clear, but a little windy.
About 9 o'clock we went to the wells because it was the last day
and about eleven went to prayers. After church I played and lost a
guinea. I talked to several ladies and walked about till 2 o'clock and
then I ate some crab for dinner. After dinner we returned to the
Walk again and then to church. After church we played at hazard
and I won four guineas. Then I went to the dance and talked abundantly to a lady and about 10 o'clock walked to my lodging and had
milk for supper. I packed up my things and said my prayers.

26. I rose about 5 o'clock and prepared to go to London. I said
my prayers and drank two dishes of chocolate at the coffeehouse.
Then I called upon my Lord Percival and found him up. I likewise
called on the widow but she was not stirring. About 8 o'clock we
set out and called on Colonel L-m-b-r-t at Sevenoaks and drank tea.
Then we proceeded to Farnborough and there had boiled chicken
for dinner, and about seven got to town almost choked with dust.
We lighted at Will's Coffeehouse and then went home to my

chambers and then called on my cousins Horsmanden but they were from home. Then I picked up a woman called Mrs. P-g-t and ate some boiled beef for supper and then carried her sister into the City and afterwards went to the bagnio and rogered her three times.

27. I rose about 9 o'clock and went to my chambers and put several things in order till 11 o'clock and then went into the City and dined with Dick Perry and ate some cold roast beef. After dinner we drank tea. Then I went home and put everything in order and then went to buy several things till nine and then went to Colonel Blakiston's and sat with him till almost ten and then Mrs. S-t-r called upon me in a coach but I would not go with her. I had milk for supper; about ten o'clock walked home and put several things in order and, having said my prayers, I lay for the first time in my chambers and slept very well, thank God, which I hope will make me prosper in them.

28. I rose about 6 o'clock and read a chapter in Hebrew and some Greek in Lucian. I neglected my prayers, but ate milk for breakfast. The weather continued dry and warm. I was exceedingly busy in unpacking my things and placing everything in order. About 11 o'clock my Lord Orrery did me the honor to call upon me and stayed about an hour. Then I worked very hard in the cellar till 3 o'clock and then only ate some milk for dinner. After dinner I put several things in order and about six went to Mr. M-n-l-y to fetch away the rest of my things and drank tea with Mrs. M-n-l-y. Then I went to Will's and sat with my Lord Orrery, my Lord Windsor, and Mr. C-m-p. Went to Crane Court to see the great snake 24 feet long and 20 inches round from the East Indies. Then we returned to the coffeehouse again and there I ate milk for supper and about ten walked home and said my prayers.

29. I rose about 6 o'clock and read a chapter in Hebrew and some Greek in Lucian. I neglected my prayers, but had milk for breakfast. The weather was still dry and cold. About 9 o'clock my neighbor M-d came to see me and stayed half an hour and then came Colonel Blakiston and stayed half an hour. Then came Mrs. S-t-r-d

and stayed half an hour. About 12 o'clock I went into the city and dined with Mrs. Lindsay and had some venison pasty. After dinner I went to Mr. [Tryon's] and drank tea where I saw the widow S-t-r-d, a pretty woman, and a great fortune. About six I took a place in the stagecoach for Tunbridge and then went home but found not my man. Then I went to Will's and from thence with my Lord Orrery to visit Mrs. Cook at the G-r-n B-l where we diverted ourselves for about an hour and then returned to Will's where I ate some milk for supper and about ten went home and said my prayers.

30. I rose about 6 o'clock and read nothing because I packed up my trunk for Tunbridge. I neglected my prayers, but had milk for breakfast. The weather continued dry and warm. Several persons came to me this morning and Mrs. S-t-r-d among the rest and brought me a pair of sheets. About 12 o'clock I went to my Lord Orrery's where I stayed to dinner and ate some boiled chicken. After dinner we went to the Temple where I was set down and I went home and from thence to see my daughters and learned that my little one was recovered of the smallpox which had been very favorably, thank God. Then I went to walk in the park and joined Mrs. D-n-s and Mrs. [Noel]. Then I walked to Will's and had milk and then walked home and said my prayers.

31. I rose about 6 o'clock and read a chapter in Hebrew but no Greek because I was busy about several matters. I neglected my prayers but had milk for breakfast. The weather was warm and dry. Several people came to me about business and among the rest Mrs. S-t-r-d. About 12 o'clock I went into the City to dine with Mr. Perry and ate some calf's head. Mrs. W-l-y dined there. After dinner I stayed and drank tea till four and then went to the bank to get bank bills for money. Then I went home and settled several matters and gave orders what I would have done in my absence. About 7 o'clock I went to Will's Coffeehouse and sat with my Lord Orrery till nine and then walked home and packed up my things and said my prayers.

August 1719

1. I rose about 4 o'clock and prepared everything for my journey to Tunbridge, and about six went to the stagecoach and with two gentlemen and one woman got out of town about 8 o'clock and about ten ate some bread and butter at Bromley and then I took a nap and about two got to Sevenoaks without anything remarkable. Here we had boiled chicken for dinner. About four we proceeded on our journey and got to the Wells about 7 o'clock and was set down at my lodging at T-th-y but I did not like my lodging but went to Mr. B-r-t and got a good lodging there. About eight I went upon the Walk and then went to the ball where was abundance of company and an entertainment. Here I stayed till twelve and sat and talked with Mrs. Lindsay till one and then said my prayers.

2. I rose about 7 o'clock and read a chapter in Hebrew and some Greek. I neglected my prayers but had milk for breakfast. It rained a little this morning but not enough to lay the dust. I danced my dance and about 10 o'clock went to church where we had a pretty good sermon. After church we walked more than an hour and then I returned home and dined with Mr. Lindsay and ate some broiled lamb. After dinner I went to my room and about 4 o'clock went again to church. After church we went upon the Walk and I treated Lady Percival and three of my Lord Abercorn's daughters[1] with tea and walked with several other ladies. About nine I went to sup with my cousin Horsmanden and ate some broiled mutton. Here I stayed till 11 o'clock and then went home and said my prayers.

3. I rose about 6 o'clock and read a chapter in Hebrew and some Greek. I said my prayers and had milk for breakfast. It continued dry

1. James Hamilton, 6th Earl of Abercorn, a member of the Privy Council, had four daughters: Elizabeth, who married William Brownlow; Mary, who married Henry Colley; Philippa, who married Benjamin Pratt; and Jane, who married Lord Archibald Hamilton.

and cold. I danced my dance, and about eleven went to church and from thence to the Walk where I played at several things and won two guineas and about 2 o'clock went to dine with my cousin Horsmanden and had roast goose for dinner. After dinner we sat and talked till 4 o'clock and then I went home and refreshed and then went to the Walk where I played again and lost a guinea. I talked to several women and about nine went to sup with Mr. Jack Sambrooke and ate some cold ham. We sat and were very merry till 11 o'clock and then we went home where I said my prayers.

4. I rose about 5 o'clock and read a chapter in Hebrew and some Greek. I said my prayers, and had milk for breakfast. It rained a little. I wrote some verses to ridicule Mr. Buckhurst's panegyrics. I danced my dance and about 11 o'clock went to chapel and from thence to the Walk where I found myself without spirits and did not play. I met with Colonel J-s-l-n and Mr. C-x. About 2 o'clock I went to Lord Percival's to dinner and ate some fish. In the afternoon we sat and talked till four and then I went home and took a nap and read some English till six and then went upon the Walk and played but neither won nor lost. About nine I went to the ball and was taken out and danced. About eleven I went home and supped with Mrs. Lindsay and ate some pigeon pie. I said my prayers.

5. I rose about 6 o'clock and read a chapter in Hebrew and some Greek. I said my prayers, and had milk for breakfast. The weather continued dry and cool; I danced my dance and then read some English till 11 o'clock and then went to church. After church I played at basset and lost three pounds but I won a pool at [t-r-k]. About 2 o'clock I dined, with Jack Sambrooke, with the Russian Ambassador and I ate some goose giblets. After dinner we drank coffee and then played at the fair chance and lost a crown. About 8 o'clock I went to a private ball where I danced with Lady Phil Pratt.[2] The Duchess of Montague was there. We had a fine supper and I ate some pigeon pie. We danced till 2 o'clock and then I went home but my partner went home about twelve. I said my prayers, &c.

2. Lady Philippa, daughter of Lord Abercorn, wife of Benjamin Pratt.

6. I rose about 7 o'clock and read a chapter in Hebrew and some Greek. I said my prayers, and had milk for breakfast. The weather continued dry and cold, the wind west. I danced my dance and about eleven went to church. After church I persuaded my Lady Percival to make a collection for a poor Greek slave and she got thirty pounds. I played a little for Lady Percival but lost. I dined with Lord Percival and ate partridge for dinner. Colonel J-s-l-n and his lady dined with us. About four I went home and took a nap and at six went to the Walk where I played a pool and lost it. Then we went to the medley, where was abundance of good company. At night I supped with Jack Sambrooke and ate some chicken. After supper we were merry till eleven and then went home and said my prayers.

7. I rose about 7 o'clock and read a chapter in Hebrew and some Greek. I said my prayers and had milk for breakfast. The weather continued dry and cold. I danced my dance and wrote a letter and about eleven went to church. After church I played a pool at [b-r-k-f] and lost five shillings. I lost thirty shillings at the fair chance. About 2 o'clock I went to Colonel J-s-l-n to dinner and ate some venison and Sir Thomas Colepeper[3] dined with us. About 4 o'clock I went home, took a nap, and read some English and about six returned to [...] where I played [f-r-n] and lost nothing. Then I played at hazard with the Duchess of Montague and my Lady Hinchinbrooke[4] and lost thirty shillings but won about two guineas at the fair chance. About ten I went to supper with Mrs. Lindsay and ate mutton cutlets and about twelve retired and said my prayers.

8. I rose about 6 o'clock and read a chapter in Hebrew and some Greek. I said my prayers, and had milk for breakfast. The weather continued dry and cold. About eight the two [married] daughters of Lord Abercorn went away. I danced my dance and about 11 o'clock went to church. After church I played and lost four pounds at the fair chance. About 2 o'clock I went to dine with my cousin Horsmanden and ate pigeon pie for dinner. After dinner I went

3. Sir Thomas Colepeper of Hollingbourne, Kent.

4. Elizabeth, daughter of Alexander Popham, wife of Edward Montague, Viscount Hinchinbrooke, and a lady of the bedchamber to the Princess of Wales.

home and took a nap and read some English and about six Will [Tryon] came and took a lodging in our house. Then I went and took a walk on the Walk and lost six pounds more. About nine I went to the ball and danced several French dances and then came and supped with Mrs. Lindsay and Will [Tryon] and ate some [w-t-r]. I neglected my prayers.

9. I rose about 7 o'clock and read a chapter in Hebrew and some Greek. I neglected my prayers, but had milk for breakfast. The weather continued dry and very hot. I danced my dance and about 10 o'clock went to church and heard an indifferent sermon. After church I went upon the Walk where I stayed till 2 o'clock and then dined at the tavern with Mr. Buckhurst and ate some boiled mutton. After dinner I went home and took a nap and read some English. About 6 o'clock I went upon the Walk and kept very much with Lady Buck and her sister. In the evening I went with Will [Tryon] and Molly F-s-t-r to the tavern and stayed half an hour and then I went to Jack Sambrooke's to supper and I ate apple pasties. We were very merry till eleven and then came home in chairs and said my prayers.

10. I rose about 6 o'clock and read a chapter in Hebrew and some Greek. I neglected my prayers, but had milk for breakfast. The weather continued dry and exceedingly hot. I danced my dance. I wrote some English till 11 o'clock and then went to church and from thence to the Walk where I lost ten shillings at commerce. I talked much to Sally Cornish. About 2 o'clock I dined at the tavern with several gentlemen and Mr. T-l-s-n among the rest, and ate some venison. After dinner I went home, took a nap, and read some English verse, and then went upon the Walk and spent most of my time with Sally Cornish and Lady Buck. However, I played a little at the fair chance and won about twenty shillings. I supped with Mr. Lindsay and Will [Tryon] was with us. It was exceedingly hot and I neglected my prayers.

11. I rose about 6 o'clock and read a chapter in Hebrew and some Greek. I said my prayers, and had milk for breakfast. The weather

was very hot and dry. I danced my dance and wrote some English till 11 o'clock and then I went to church. After church I played at basset and lost two guineas. I talked to several women till 2 o'clock and then went to dine at the tavern with several gentlemen and ate mutton. After dinner we talked till four and then I went home and took a nap and read some English till six and then went upon the Walk and lost three guineas at the fair chance which put me into the spleen very much. I treated Mrs. Sambrooke and her company with chocolate. It was exceedingly hot. However, I went to the ball at night and from thence went and supped with Mrs. Cornish and sat up till 4 o'clock till it was light when Will [Tyron] and Mr. G-l-d went away. Then I walked home and neglected my prayers.

12. I rose about 9 o'clock and read a chapter in Hebrew and some Greek. I said my prayers, and had milk for breakfast. The weather was very hot and dry. I danced my dance, and about 12 o'clock went to the Walk, where I talked to several ladies but did not play at all. About two I went to dinner with my cousin Horsmanden and ate roast chicken. After dinner I took a nap and then went home and read some English till 6 o'clock and then went again to the Walk and discoursed several ladies and drank coffee with Mrs. Sebright. About eight we went to the medley and after that I played a pool at [t-r-f-c] and about 11 o'clock went home to bed and said my prayers and slept extremely well.

13. I rose about 7 o'clock and read a chapter in Hebrew and some Greek. I said my prayers, and had milk for breakfast. The weather continued dry but clear. I danced my dance and read some English till eleven and then went to church. After church I went to the Walk where I played at piquet with Lady Buck and about 2 o'clock went to dine with Mr. Lethieullier, where I ate fish for dinner. Here was also Mr. F-k-n-r and Mr. D-r-k-y. We stayed till 5 o'clock and then returned to the Walk and I went home where I read some Latin and took a nap. About six I went to the Walk and won a raffle of thirteen guineas that cost me nothing because I won a guinea of Mr. B-c-n.

About 8 o'clock I went to the play and sat by Lady Jane Hamilton.[5] It rained extremely while we were here. About eleven I went home and said my prayers.

14. I rose about 6 o'clock and read a chapter in Hebrew and some Greek. I said my prayers, and had milk for breakfast. The weather was cold and cloudy, and it rained pretty much. Then I danced my dance and read some Latin till eleven and then went to church. After church I went upon the Walk where I played at lottery ticket and won a little. About 2 o'clock I went to dine with Jack Sambrooke and ate some chicken and bacon. After dinner I drank some coffee and about four we went to the Walk, from whence I went to my lodging and read some Latin till six and then returned to the Walk where I went one half with Mrs. C-m-t-n and we won twenty shillings apiece. About 8 o'clock we went to our private ball where I danced with Lady Jane Hamilton. There was a fine supper and I ate some tongue. We danced till 2 o'clock and then I went home in the chair and neglected my prayers, for which God forgive me.

15. I rose about 8 o'clock and read a chapter in Hebrew and some Greek. I said my prayers, and had milk for breakfast. The weather was cold and cloudy, the wind northwest. I danced my dance. About eleven I went to church. After church I went to the Walk and won a guinea at basset. About two I went to dine with my cousin Horsmanden and ate some roast turkey. After dinner Mrs. Lindsay came in and we drank tea. About five I went home and at six to the Walk, where I won two raffles and [gave] one to Mrs. [Shutz] and one to Mrs. C-m-t-n. About nine I went to the ball and danced four minuets. About eleven I went home and ate an apple pasty for supper. I said my prayers.

16. I rose about 7 o'clock and read a chapter in Hebrew and some Greek. I neglected my prayers, but had milk for breakfast. The weather was cold and clear, the wind north. I danced my dance and

5. Lady Jane Hamilton, wife of Lord Archibald Hamilton, daughter of Lord Abercorn and sister of Lord Paisley.

wrote some English. About ten-thirty I went to church where we had an indifferent sermon. After church we took a walk and diverted ourselves till 2 o'clock and then I dined with Mr. Lindsay, and Lady Buck and her sister dined there too. I ate some boiled chicken and after dinner Mrs. Cornish came in and sat with us till four and then we went to church and had a pretty good sermon. After church a party of us went to the cold baths, where we drank some Rhenish wine. Mr. Lindsay and his wife were out of humor. About seven we went to the Walk, where I gave coffee and stayed upon the Walk till ten and then I went home and said my prayers. I had some Germans that made a damn noise next to me.

17. I rose about 7 o'clock and read a chapter in Hebrew and some Greek. I neglected my prayers, but had milk for breakfast. The weather was cold and clear, the wind northwest. I danced my dance and wrote some English. About eleven I went to church. After church I went to the Walk, where I played at basset and lost twelve shillings. I dined with Mr. Lindsay and ate some goose roasted. After dinner I wrote some English till six and then went to the Walk and played at several things. They [f-l] a private ball without me and Major Smith and Mr. G-r-n-t-m. I played at several things and lost a little. I had a kind of a looseness. About eleven I came home, wrote some English, and read a little. The Germans continued to make a noise. Mr. Lindsay gave me twenty guineas.

18. I rose about 7 o'clock and read a chapter in Hebrew and some Greek. I said my prayers, and had milk for breakfast. The weather was cold and clear. I danced my dance and wrote some English till 11 o'clock, and then I went to church. After church I went to the Walk and won a guinea at the lottery but lost it again at basset. About 2 o'clock I went to dine with Mr. Lindsay and ate some boiled rabbit and onions. After dinner the Cornishes came in and I went with them to drink tea. I walked about and lost about two guineas at [f-r-n]. In the evening I came home with Mr. Lindsay, and so did Mr. W-r-s and his wife and I ate some partridge for supper and sat up till 1 o'clock and neglected my prayers.

19. I rose about 7 o'clock and read a chapter in Hebrew and some Greek. I said my prayers, and had milk for breakfast. The weather was cold and clear. I danced my dance and wrote some English till 11 o'clock and then went to church. After church I played and lost two guineas. My Lord C-s-t-m-n invited me to dinner and I ate some venison. After dinner I took my leave, being bound with the two Cornishes and Mrs. Lindsay to Penshurst, where we ate bread and butter and drank tea. Mr. N-t and three other gentlemen carried wine and fruit which we had in the bower in the park. About 9 o'clock we returned to the Walk, where I won a guinea at the ace of hearts. I invited the Duchess of Monmouth[6] and her lady to our ball with several other ladies. About ten I went home and said my prayers.

20. I rose about 7 o'clock and read a chapter in Hebrew and some Greek. I said my prayers, and had milk for breakfast. The weather was warm and dry. I danced my dance and read some French till 11 o'clock and then I went to the chapel and from thence to the Walk where I won a guinea at the lottery and lost about as much at lottery ticket. I dined at the tavern with several gentlemen and ate some roast mutton. After dinner I went home and read some English till six and then went to the Walk and lost six guineas at the fair chance. Then I walked about till eight and then we went to a private ball where Lady Buck was my partner. About twelve we went to supper and I ate some [fat eels]. About 3 o'clock I went home and neglected my prayers.

21. I rose about 8 o'clock and read a chapter in Hebrew and some Greek. I said my prayers, and had milk for breakfast. The weather was warm and clear, the wind southeast. I danced my dance and about 11 o'clock went to Mrs. Lindsay's room to breakfast where I found Lady Buck and her sister, but they ate nothing. About twelve we went upon the Walk, where I won a pool at commerce. At two I dined at the tavern with several gentlemen and Major O-n-b-y among the rest. I ate some roast mutton. After dinner I sat till 5

6. Anne Scott, widow of James, Duke of Monmouth, later married to Lord Cornwallis, but apparently still known as the Duchess of Monmouth.

o'clock and then I went home and read some English and took a nap. About six I went again to the Walk, where we played at lottery ticket and I lost fifteen shillings. I talked to several persons and about eleven went home and said my prayers.

22. I rose about 7 o'clock and read a chapter in Hebrew and some Greek. I neglected my prayers, and had milk for breakfast. I danced my dance and read some English till 11 o'clock and then I went to church and from thence to the Walk where I played and won twenty-four shillings at the ace of hearts and half a crown at basset. About 2 o'clock I went to dine with my cousin Horsmanden where I ate some roast mutton. After dinner we drank tea with Mrs. Lindsay and then went upon the Walk where I played again at the ace of hearts and won twenty-five shillings. Then I walked about till nine and then went to the ball and about eleven went to sup with Mrs. Lindsay, with Lady Buck, and ate some partridge. We were merry till 1 o'clock and then I put Lady Buck into her coach and then retired to bed and neglected my prayers, for which God forgive me. I wrote a letter to London.

23. I rose about 6 o'clock and read a chapter in Hebrew and some Greek. I said my prayers, and had milk for breakfast. I danced my dance, and about ten-thirty went to church where we had but an indifferent sermon. After church we went to the Walk, where I stayed till two and then went to dine with Mrs. Lindsay and ate some rabbit and onions. After dinner Mrs. Cornish came in. About three I retired to my chamber and took a nap. Then I read some English till six and then went upon the Walk and walked with Lady Percival and her sister and several others. About nine we went to Mrs. Lindsay's to supper with Mrs. Cornish, and I ate some chicken and bacon. Tom A-d-l-n and Mr. G-th-r supped with us. About eleven I retired and said my prayers.

24. I rose about 7 o'clock and read a chapter in Hebrew and some Greek. I neglected my prayers, and had milk for breakfast. I danced my dance and read some English and then wrote some verses upon

four ladies.[7] About eleven I went to church and after church went to the Walk and lost six pounds at the ace of hearts. About two I dined at the tavern and ate some fish. After dinner we drank a bottle till 4 o'clock and I went home and read till five and then returned to the Walk again and played at several things and lost my money. About 10 o'clock I took a walk and met with a woman and kissed her exceedingly. Then I went home and said my prayers.

25. I rose about 7 o'clock and read a chapter in Hebrew and some Greek. I said my prayers, and had milk for breakfast. The weather was cloudy and threatened rain but none came. I wrote verses all the morning till 1 o'clock and then went upon the Walk where I won a little at the ace of hearts and faro. Here I stayed till 2 o'clock and then dined at the tavern and ate mutton [cutlet] for dinner. After dinner Molly the fruit girl came and Mr. C-r-v-n and I kissed her. Then I went home and wrote some English till six and then returned to the Walk and won a little at the ace of hearts. About 10 o'clock I went to the public ball and talked abundantly to Mrs. U-x-l-y. About twelve I went home and neglected my prayers.

26. I rose about 7 o'clock and read a chapter in Hebrew and no Greek. I said my prayers and had milk for breakfast. The weather was cold and clear, the wind northwest. I wrote some English till eleven and then went to church and from thence to the Walk where I lost three pounds. Here I stayed till 3 o'clock and then dined at the tavern and ate roast veal. Captain G-r-m-w-d made me blush by telling me of Molly A-l-c. About five I went home and read some English till six and then went and drank tea with Sally Cornish and Mrs. Polhill, who is as handsome as an angel. I played a pool at commerce with Lady Buck and some others and about ten went home

7. Byrd's verses, thinly disguised under the pseudonym 'Mr. Burrard,' appeared in *Tunbrigalia: or, Tunbridge Miscellanies, For the Year 1719* (London, 1719). The ladies mentioned in these verses were the Duchess of Montague, Lady Hinchinbrooke, Lady Percival, Lady Ranelagh, Lady Isabella Scott, Lady Charlotte Scott, Lady Buck, and Mrs. Cornish (and in the same verse, Horsmanden, Hoar, Borrel, Lindsay, Searle), Mrs. Lethieullier, and Mrs. Polhill. See *Another Secret Diary of William Byrd*, 403–8.

and supped with Mrs. Lindsay and my cousin Horsmanden and neglected my prayers.

27. I rose about 8 o'clock and read some Greek and no Hebrew. I neglected my prayers, but had milk for breakfast. The weather was very cool and dry, the wind northwest. I wrote some English till eleven and then went to church. After church I went to the Walk where I played and won twenty shillings at the ace of hearts. I was invited to dine with Mr. Sambrooke but my cousin Horsmanden had engaged me before to dinner and I ate some mutton steaks. After dinner I went home and wrote some English and then took a nap till six and then returned to the Walk and won thirty shillings at the ace of hearts. About 9 o'clock we went to Mr. B-k-n-l ball which was very handsome. I danced with Sally Cornish, which Mr. A-d-l-n envied and would fain have quarreled at what I said but Sally Cornish kept it off. I ate some salmon [g-n-y]. I stayed till 2 o'clock when my partner went away and I went away likewise and found my man not come home. However, I sent for him and neglected my prayers.

28. I rose about 8 o'clock and read a chapter in Hebrew and some Greek. I neglected my prayers, but had milk for breakfast. The weather was cold and dry, the wind northwest. About nine I wrote some English and then went to visit Mrs. Lindsay in bed, where I found my cousin Horsmanden, which kept me from church. About twelve I went to the Walk, where I found Brigadier H-r-v-n and Colonel Cecil. I won thirty-five shillings at the ace of hearts. About two I dined with Mr. H-r-v-n, Colonel Cecil, and Major Smith and ate some boiled chicken for dinner. About five we went upon the Walk and I went home and adjusted myself and then returned to the Walk and drank tea with Mrs. Lindsay and the Cornishes. I won ten shillings at the ace of hearts and about seven we went to my Lord C-s-t-r-m-n ball, where I danced several French dances. My partner was Mrs. Sebright. I stayed till 2 o'clock and had two dishes of chocolate. Then came home and ate some bread and butter with Mrs. Lindsay and neglected my prayers.

29. I rose about 8 o'clock and read a chapter in Hebrew and a chapter in Greek. I said my prayers, and had milk for breakfast. The weather was cold and cloudy and threatened rain. I wrote a letter to London and about eleven went to church. After church I went to the Walk and lost ten guineas at the ace of hearts which was all the stake my Lady Buck and I had. Then I had time to talk with several ladies till dinner, when I ate some venison with Tom H-r-v-n and Colonel Cecil. After dinner I went home and read some English till six and then went to the Walk and won twenty shillings at hazard. Then I drank tea with Mrs. Cornish and stayed with her till she went away and then I went to visit Daniel Horsmanden, who had a swelled face, and ate roast beef for supper. Here I stayed till 11 o'clock and then went home and neglected my prayers, for which God forgive me.

30. I rose about 8 o'clock and read a chapter in Hebrew and some Greek in the Greek testament. I said my prayers, and had milk for breakfast. The weather was cold and clear. I danced my dance and about ten called on Mr. Lindsay, who came last night. Then I went to church and Dr. D-n-t gave us a dull sermon. After church I went to the Walk and talked to several ladies till 2 o'clock and then went to dine at the tavern with some of my friends. After dinner I went home and read some English and took a nap but was disturbed by Mr. B-k-n-l coming into the room. About six I went to the Walk and joined Mrs. Cornish and went with them and Mrs. Lindsay in their coach to take the air for about an hour. Then I treated them in one of the rooms with some tongue and some ham and Rhenish wine. However, about ten I went to sup with Mr. Lindsay, and Sir Charles Buck and my Lady went with us. I neglected my prayers.

31. I rose about 7 o'clock and read a chapter in Hebrew and some Greek in the Greek testament. I neglected my prayers, but had milk for breakfast. The weather was clear and warm. I danced my dance and wrote some English till 11 o'clock and then went to church and from thence to the Walk where I won about fifteen shillings at the ace of hearts. About 2 o'clock I went to dine with Mr. Lindsay and ate some duck. After dinner I retired to my room, read some English,

and took a nap till six and then returned to the Walk again where I talked abundance to Sally Cornish. I won twenty shillings at [f-r-n]. We drank tea with Tom H-r-v-n and then we went to Mr. Horsmanden's to supper and took Lady Buck and her sister with us, and I ate some cold venison pasty and we were very merry and did not part till two in the morning, when I went home and neglected my prayers.

September 1719

1. I rose about 7 o'clock and read a chapter in Hebrew and a chapter in Greek. I said my prayers, and had milk for breakfast. The weather was cold and cloudy, the wind west. I danced my dance and about eleven went to church and from thence to the Walk where I played at the ace of hearts and won ten shillings. I talked abundance to Sally Cornish and about two dined with her at Mrs. Lindsay's and ate some boiled rabbit and onions. After dinner I retired and took a nap and then read some English till 6 o'clock and then went to the Walk where I played at the ace of hearts and won two guineas. I gave tea to Mrs. D-r-x. At night I went to the ball and from thence to sup with my cousin Horsmanden, where I ate some fricassee of rabbit for supper. Mr. Lindsay and his lady supped with us, and Mr. B-n-s-n, and we went home about 2 o'clock and I neglected my prayers.

2. I rose about 8 o'clock and read a chapter in Hebrew and a chapter in Greek. I neglected my prayers, and had milk for breakfast. The weather was warm and clear. I danced my dance and read some English till 11 o'clock and then went to Mrs. Lindsay's room and from thence to the Walk where I played at several things and won fifty shillings. I talked to several persons and about 9 o'clock went to B-l-s ball which she gave for her wedding day and it was very handsome. I danced French dances and country dances with Lady Buck

till 11 o'clock and then went to Mrs. Cornish's to supper, where I ate some cold turkey and we sat up till 3 o'clock and then went home in chairs because it rained. I neglected my prayers.

3. I rose about 8 o'clock and read a chapter in Hebrew and a chapter in Greek. I said my prayers, and had milk for breakfast. The weather was cold and cloudy, the wind northwest. I danced my dance and about eleven went to church and from thence to the Walk where I wrote a song for Mrs. Cornish and won thirty shillings at the ace of hearts. I entertained Mrs. Lindsay and both the Cornishes at dinner and ate some fish. After dinner we drank tea and I wrote a letter to the man that Mrs. Lindsay gathered money for. Then I read some English till six and then went to the Walk and won a guinea at the ace of hearts. I talked abundance to Mrs. Sebright, then we heard Mr. B-r-r read a play and then went home to supper, and I entertained Sir Charles Buck and his family and ate cold chicken. We acted proverbs till twelve and then went to bed and I neglected my prayers.

4. I rose about 8 o'clock and read a chapter in Hebrew and a chapter in Greek. I neglected my prayers, but had milk for breakfast. I danced all my dances and wrote some English till eleven. Daniel Horsmanden came but did not stay. Then I went to the Walk and won thirty shillings at the ace of hearts. Then I talked to several ladies and read the news. About three I went home and dined with Mrs. Lindsay, and Major Smith dined there with us, and I ate some venison. Mrs. Lindsay said something that I took ill and looked very grave and would not go to the ball they had contrived. However, I drank two dishes of tea. About six I went to the Walk and won seventy shillings at the ace of hearts but thirty shillings of it was for Mrs. B-r-n. When everybody went to the ball I took the opportunity to go home to bed, which I did after washing my feet. My eye was a little sore. I said my prayers.

5. I rose about 7 o'clock and read a chapter in Hebrew and a chapter in Greek. I said my prayers, and had milk for breakfast. The weather was cold and overclouded, the wind east, and it rained a little. About 11 o'clock I went to church and from thence to the

Walk where I drank tea with Mr. Horsmanden and afterwards played at the ace of hearts and won ten, at [f-r-n] and won twenty shillings. Then I sat and talked to Mrs. Cornish till 3 o'clock and then went to dine with Lady Buck and ate some boiled chicken. Afterwards Mrs. Cornish walked with Mrs. Sebright and me in the fields. About five we went to the Walk and I went home and adjusted myself and then went to the Walk and won thirty shillings at the hearts. I gave B-l a half guinea for a [f-r-ing]. About nine I went to the ball and about eleven went home and said my prayers.

6. I rose about 7 o'clock and read a chapter in Hebrew and a chapter in Greek. I neglected my prayers, and had milk for breakfast. The weather was clear and warm, the wind west. I danced my dance and about ten went to visit my neighbor Lindsay and from thence to church, where we had a pretty good sermon. After church I went upon the Walk, a little out of humor about a lampoon that I was in with Mrs. Lindsay. Mrs. Lindsay and the two Cornishes dined with me and I ate some venison. After dinner went to walk in the grove and from thence went home and from thence to the Walk where I stayed till ten and then carried my cousin Horsmanden home to supper and ate some partridge. After supper we went to [little plays] till 12 o'clock and then I went to my chamber and packed up my things and said my prayers.

7. I rose about 5 o'clock and got everything ready to go to London and accordingly after drinking a dish of chocolate I went with Mrs. Lindsay and the two Cornishes and gave the horses some hay at Sevenoaks and proceeded from thence to Bromley where Colonel Harrison[1] and Colonel Cecil and Mr. Lindsay met us and I ate some roast goose for dinner. In the afternoon Colonel Harrison went with the ladies the rest of the journey and I went with Cecil and we got to London about 7 o'clock and I walked home and from thence went to see Mrs. S-t-r-d but she was from home; then to Mrs. Smith's, where I stayed till ten and then walked home, where I put several things in order and said my prayers.

1. Thomas Harrison, colonel of the Sixth Foot Regiment, 1708 to 1716, when he sold his colonelcy. A relative of Secretary of State Townshend.

8. I rose about 8 o'clock and read nothing because I put several things in order. I neglected my prayers, but had milk for breakfast. The weather continued hot and dry. About 11 o'clock I went to the Virginia Coffeehouse and from thence I went with Mr. Carter to Mr. Perry's and dined with Dick and ate some boiled mutton. After dinner I read some letters from Virginia and sat and talked till 4 o'clock and then went home and went from thence to visit Mrs. Smith with whom I drank tea and saw two women, a mother and daughter who stayed about two hours and then came Mrs. Johnson with whom I supped and ate some fricassee of rabbit and about ten went to bed with her and lay all night and rogered her twice.

9. I rose about 8 o'clock and went home where I read a little Hebrew but no Greek. I neglected my prayers, but had milk for breakfast. The weather continued hot and clear. Mr. Horsmanden came to my chamber and told me his sisters were with Lady Buck in Bow Street. There I went and found Mrs. Sebright with a black eye, having been overturned in the coach. About 2 o'clock I went to Pontack's where we had a fine haunch of venison and some other things. We stayed till 8 o'clock and then Mrs. Lindsay and the two Misses Cornish called on us to go to Southwark Fair. We were no sooner there but Sally Cornish was so ill she was forced to go away with her sister and Colonel Cecil and I gallanted them to G-v-n Garden and then took [my] leave and neglected my prayers.

10. I rose about 7 o'clock and read a chapter in Hebrew and some Greek in Lucian. I neglected my prayers, but had milk for breakfast. The weather was cold and cloudy. About eleven I went to visit my Lord Orrery, where I stayed to dinner and ate some boiled mutton. After dinner we sat and talked till five and then went to Will's Coffeehouse where I read the news and about six went to visit Sally Cornish and drank tea with her and stayed two hours and then went back to Will's where I sat and discoursed till nine and was angry with my man for not keeping his time better. About nine I went home and wrote in my journal till ten and then said my prayers.

11. I rose about seven and read a chapter in Hebrew and some Greek. I said my prayers, and had milk for breakfast. The weather

was cold and clear, the wind west. I put several things in order till 12 o'clock and then I went to visit Mrs. Southwell where I stayed to dinner and ate some boiled mutton. There was Lord Percival, Daniel Dering, and George Harrison, who were very merry till 5 o'clock and then I walked home and when I had given some orders took a walk in the garden for half an hour and then returned home where I wrote some English till nine and then came Mrs. S-t-r-d. I drank a glass of wine to our good rest and then went to bed before my man came home and rogered her three times. However I could not sleep and neglected my prayers.

12. I rose about 7 o'clock and let out my mistress but my man had like to have seen her. I read a chapter in Hebrew and some Greek in Lucian. I said my prayers, and sent for my wine from Mr. Southwell. I put several things in order till 2 o'clock and then ate some milk only for dinner. After dinner I put several things in order and wrote some English till 6 o'clock and then I called at the playhouse which was very full because it was the first time of acting.[2] However, I did not stay but went to the coffeehouse, where I sat with my Lord Orrery about 8 o'clock, and then I ate some milk and [t-k-t] bread for supper. After supper I was very sleepy and about nine went home in the chair. It rained hard. It continued to rain very much.

13. I rose about 8 o'clock and read a chapter in Hebrew and some Greek in Lucian. I said my prayers, and had milk for breakfast. The weather cleared up and was warmish. I danced my dance but did not go to church but sent my man. I wrote a letter and about 1 o'clock ate some milk and cream. After dinner I put several things in order and danced again, then I wrote more English. I resolved this day to go to Virginia to take care of my affairs. About 5 o'clock I walked to see my daughter but was displeased to find her without [gloves]. I learned that my little daughter continued still sick and was going into the country. Then I walked to Will's Coffeehouse where I spent the evening with my Lord Orrery and ate some milk for supper, and about nine walked home and said my prayers.

2. The first play of the season at Drury Lane was *Hamlet.*

14. I rose about 7 o'clock and read a chapter in Hebrew and some Greek in Lucian. I said my prayers, and had milk for breakfast. The weather was cold and cloudy, the wind northwest. About 9 o'clock I sent for my wine from Mr. U-t-n and about eleven went to visit Mr. U-t-n where I drank a dish of chocolate and then went to Mr. C-r-m-r about my ticket. Then I went into the City to Mr. H-t-l-y where I received a bill and ate some fish for dinner. After dinner we drank a bottle of champagne and then I went to Mr. Lindsay's where I settled accounts with Mrs. Lindsay and then went home, and from thence to Will's Coffeehouse, where I gave my Lord Orrery a book concerning Virginia. About eight I went to Mrs. Smith's where I met Molly and had some oysters for supper and about eleven we went to bed and I rogered her twice.

15. I rose about 9 o'clock and we drank [b-t-y] and about eleven I went home and read a chapter in Hebrew and no Greek. I neglected my prayers, and about 1 o'clock went to Mr. C-r-m-r but he was from home. Then I went to dine with Mr. U-t-n and ate some boiled mutton. After dinner we drank some Burgundy and about four went to visit Margaret Bellenden and stayed about an hour and then I walked home and put myself in order and then went to Mrs. Cornish's where I drank tea and was merry; Mrs. C-r being there, I did everything I could to make myself agreeable and stayed and supped and ate some oysters and then sat and talked till twelve and then went home and neglected my prayers.

16. I rose about 8 o'clock and read a chapter in Hebrew and some Greek in Lucian. I neglected my prayers, and had milk for breakfast. The weather was clear and warm, the wind northeast. About 11 o'clock I went and walked into the City to the Virginia Coffeehouse, where I talked with Captain Posford and several others and then walked to Mr. Perry's and dined with the old gentleman and ate some cold boiled beef. After dinner I went to visit Mrs. Perry and she showed us her daughter's fine presents from her lover who was very rich. Then came in the lover himself who seemed a good sort of a man. We drank tea and Mrs. B-r-k came and talked abundance. About five I walked home and walked from thence to the coffee-

house and from thence I went to Lady Guise's, where I sat till nine and then went home and said my prayers.

17. I rose about 7 o'clock and read a chapter in Hebrew and some Greek in Lucian. I neglected my prayers, but had milk for breakfast. The weather was cold and cloudy, the wind west. I danced my dance. I read several things relating to Virginia. About 12 o'clock Mr. G-n-ing came to me and stayed about half an hour. I read some English till 2 o'clock and then had milk and cream for dinner. After dinner I continued to read letters from Virginia till 6 o'clock and then I went to Lady Guise's and let her have three of my tickets for which she was to remain in my debt. About seven I went to Mrs. FitzHerbert's where I ate some boiled pork and drank some ale. About nine I walked away and picked up a girl whom I carried to the bagnio and rogered her twice very well. It rained abundance in the night.

18. I rose about 8 o'clock and went home about nine, where I read a chapter in Hebrew and some Greek. I said no prayers, but had milk for breakfast. The weather was cold and cloudy. About 11 o'clock Mr. M-d came to me and stayed about an hour. Then came my cousin Horsmanden and stayed quarter of an hour. About two I had milk and cream for dinner. After dinner I put several things in order and wrote a letter to Virginia till 6 o'clock and then came Mr. Horsmanden and we went into the City to Mr. Lindsay's but because they were not within we stopped to Mr. [Tryon's] till they came and then we played at [f-r-n] and I lost two guineas. About ten we went to supper and I ate some boiled beef. After supper we sat and talked till twelve and then we took leave and I went home but neglected my prayers and was out of humor.

19. I rose about 7 o'clock and read a chapter in Hebrew and some Greek in Lucian. I neglected my prayers, but had milk for breakfast. The weather was warm and clear. About 10 o'clock came Colonel Blakiston and I talked with him about making peace in Virginia. I put several things in order till 1 o'clock and then came Daniel Horsmanden and we went to dine at the Blue Post in Oldbourne and

ate some roast beef. After dinner we walked to my stonecutter and chose some marble for my chimney. Then we took a walk in Lincoln's Inn Garden till five and then I went home and wrote a letter till six and then walked to the playhouse at Drury Lane where I stayed the play and had the pleasure to see Mrs. D-r-x there. After the play I went to Will's and from thence home, where I said my prayers.

20. I rose about 7 o'clock and read a chapter in Hebrew but no Greek because I wrote a letter to Colonel Blakiston concerning reconcilement in Virginia. I neglected my prayers but had milk for breakfast. I danced my dance but went not to church myself but sent my man. About 12 o'clock came Mr. Horsmanden and we went together to dine with Mr. Will [Tryon] and ate some roast beef for dinner. In the afternoon we drank a bottle till 5 o'clock and then drank tea with the ladies. Then Daniel Horsmanden and I went to Will's Coffeehouse and from thence to visit Mrs. Cornish where we drank tea together. Here we found Mrs. D-r-x, very agreeable woman, and Mr. H-m-n the lover of Sally Cornish who seemed not to like our company, so about eight we took leave and I went home, read English, and said my prayers.

21. I rose about 6 o'clock and read a chapter in Hebrew and some Greek in Lucian. I said my prayers, and had milk for breakfast. The weather was cold and clear, the wind north. I danced my dance and wrote a letter to Virginia till 2 o'clock and then ate some milk and cream for dinner. In the afternoon I put several things in order and then wrote more letters to Virginia and then read some English till 5 o'clock when I went to visit Mrs. Southwell but she was from home. Then I walked in the park with the Muscovite Ambassador. Then I walked about the street to look for a whore but found none to my mind so I went to Will's Coffeehouse where I had milk for supper. About nine I walked home and said my prayers.

22. I rose about 6 o'clock and read a chapter in Hebrew and some Greek in Lucian. I said my prayers, and had milk for breakfast. The weather was cold and cloudy, the wind west. I danced my dance and then wrote a letter to Virginia till 11 o'clock and then I went into the City and dined with Dick Perry, and Mr. Isham dined with us, and I ate some chicken and bacon. After dinner we sat and talked, and drank tea. Mrs. C-r-d-k had dined with us. About 5 o'clock I took leave and walked to the Exchange and there took coach and went home where I found the joiner at work. Then I wrote a letter and then walked to see my daughter and found Mrs. T-r-v-r there. Here I stayed till 8 o'clock and then walked to Will's where I had milk and cream, and about ten walked home and said my prayers.

23. I rose about 7 o'clock and read a chapter in Hebrew and some Greek in Lucian. I neglected my prayers, and had milk for breakfast. The weather was cold and cloudy, the wind northeast. I danced my dance, and then wrote some English till 12 o'clock and then came Daniel Horsmanden and gave me a relation of his journey to Sir Charles Buck's. He stayed half an hour, and then I went to Mrs. Southwell's where I met my Lord T-m-n and my Lord Ashburnham. I dined with Betty alone and ate some fish. After dinner we talked very gravely till 5 o'clock and then I went home and wrote a letter till six and then Daniel Horsmanden came again and we went to visit a whore but she was from home. Then we went to Mrs. Smith's, where we had rack punch and a turkey for supper. There was a woman but we did nothing but stayed till 12 o'clock and then went home and I said my prayers. I dreamed I caused a coffin to be made for me to bury myself in but I changed my mind.

24. I rose about 7 o'clock and read a chapter in Hebrew and some Greek in Lucian. I said my prayers, and had milk for breakfast. The weather was cold and raining, the wind east. I danced my dance and about ten began to write letters till one and then went in my chariot into the City and dined at Pontack's and ate some boiled beef. After dinner Mr. H-l and I went to Lincoln's Inn where I wrote letters till five and then went to visit Mrs. Cornish and found dear Sally by herself and sat with her half an hour and then took leave because she went out. Then I went to Dame FitzHerbert's and ate some roast beef with her and stayed till 9 o'clock and then walked home in the dark, where I put several things in order and said my prayers.

25. I rose about 7 o'clock and read a chapter in Hebrew and some Greek in Lucian. I said my prayers, and had milk for breakfast. The weather was cloudy and cold, the wind northeast. I danced my dance and then wrote some English till eleven and then I called on Mr. Horsmanden and we went to Guildhall to see the tickets drawn. We sat in the Gallery about an hour but none of our tickets came up though I [beset] myself this morning. About two we returned and dined at Mr. Horsmanden's lodgings and I ate some boiled beef and I sent for a bottle of wine. After dinner I went home and wrote some English till seven and then we went to visit Mrs. Cook, another of my acquaintances, where I stayed about an hour and then went to Mrs. Smith's where I was to meet my mistress that lived in Firth Street. I ate some fricassee and was merry till 11 o'clock and then retired, and I rogered her twice.

26. I rose about 9 o'clock and we drank some milk coffee and about ten went home and read a chapter in Hebrew but no Greek. I neglected my prayers. However, I danced my dance. I put several things in order and wrote some letters till 2 o'clock and then walked to Mr. Horsmanden's to dinner and ate some pork and peas and we had a bottle of my wine. After dinner I walked home and wrote more letters till five and then went to visit Mrs. Cornish where I drank tea and Mrs. Lindsay and Mrs. C-r were there. We played at cards and I won a little. Then they gave us Barbados sweetmeats and about ten we ate some roast partridge for supper. They gave us some champagne and we were merry till twelve and then I went home and neglected my prayers.

27. I rose about 7 o'clock and read a chapter in Hebrew and some Greek in Lucian. I neglected my prayers, and had milk for breakfast. The weather was clear and cold, the wind northeast. About 10 o'clock came Mr. Page in his fine chariot and stayed till twelve when he carried me into the City to Mr. Lindsay's to dinner, where I ate some boiled beef. Both Mr. Lindsay and Mrs. Lindsay were indisposed. After dinner we all slept a little. About five drank tea and then Will [Tryon] came in and I took leave and went to Somerset House to visit Mrs. U-m-s, but they were from home. Then I walked to Mrs.

M-r-l-y where I found Mrs. U-m-s and sat with them about an hour
and then went home with Mrs. U-m-s and sat about an hour and
then walked home and said my prayers.

28. I rose about 7 o'clock and read nothing because I prepared to
go make my Lord Orkney the proposal of peace. I neglected my
prayers, but had milk for breakfast. The weather was clear and cold,
the wind east. About nine I danced my dance and at ten came old Mr.
Perry and carried me in my chariot to Colonel Blakiston's and from
thence we went all together to my Lord Orkney's. I found him on
the high rope but at last he agreed to write a letter by me, notwithstanding I had as he said treated him indifferently. About twelve we
took leave and Mr. Perry and I went to the Bishop of London where
we settled Mr. Blair's business and I ate some roast duck for dinner.
About four we took leave and I got home about five where I danced
my dance again. About six Mr. Horsmanden came and we went to
visit Mrs. Cook and I carried two bottles of wine with us. There we
supped and I ate some fricassee of chicken and were merry but did
nothing. However, we stayed till 12 o'clock, when I came home and
neglected my prayers.

29. I rose about 7 o'clock and I read a chapter in Hebrew and some
Greek in Lucian. I said my prayers, but had milk for breakfast. The
weather was clear and cold, the wind northeast. I put several things in
order and wrote some English till 2 o'clock and then walked to my
cousin Horsmanden's lodging to dinner and ate some goose. After
dinner we drank tea with our mistress till four and then I took a walk
in our garden and then went home and about five went in the chariot
to visit my daughter and stayed with her till seven. Then I went to
Mrs. [Andrews'] and drank tea and stayed with them till nine. Then
I went to Will's, where I drank a glass of cherry brandy, and about
ten walked to my chambers where I said my prayers.

30. I rose about 7 o'clock and read a chapter in Hebrew and some
Greek in Lucian. I said my prayers, and had boiled milk for breakfast. The weather was cold and cloudy, the wind east. I danced my
dance and wrote something for Colonel Blakiston till 11 o'clock and

then I went into the City and dined with Colonel Blakiston at old Mr. Perry's and ate some pheasant for dinner. After dinner we went to the other house where I learned that Sally Perry was to be married tomorrow. Here I drank tea and about 4 o'clock went home and adjusted myself and about six went to visit Mr. Southwell who came two days since from Ireland. About seven I went to Lady Guise's and sat with her about an hour and then walked to Will's and from thence home but picked up a girl by the way and committed uncleanness with her, for which God forgive me. I said my prayers.

October 1719

1. I rose about 7 o'clock and read a chapter in Hebrew and some Greek in Lucian. I said my prayers, and had milk for breakfast. The weather continued cold and clear, the wind east. I danced my dance and then wrote some English till 1 o'clock, when Mr. Horsmanden came and went with me into the City, where I entered my tickets and learned one was come up a blank. Then we returned to his lodgings where we had a hare for dinner. After dinner we discoursed till four and then took a walk in our garden till five and then went to visit Mrs. Lethieullier but she was from home. Then we went to Will's and from thence to the play, where was abundance of company and particularly Mrs. [Cambridge], as pretty as an angel. After the play I walked home and said my prayers. This day Miss Sarah Perry was married to Mr. S-n-s-m [*or* H-n-s-m].

2. I rose about 7 o'clock and read a chapter in Hebrew and some Greek in Lucian. I neglected my prayers, and had milk for breakfast. The weather was cold and cloudy, the wind east. I danced my dance and about 12 o'clock went to the Cockpit and consulted Tom Beake about my petition concerning my Council place. Then I called on

Mr. T-k-l at the Secretary's office and then went to dine with Mr. Southwell where I met Ned Blount and Mrs. FitzHerbert and ate some boiled pork. After dinner we sat and talked till 5 o'clock and then I took a walk in the park till six and then went to meet Molly H-r-t-n at Mrs. Smith's in Jermyn Street where I went to bed with her and lay till 9 o'clock but could do nothing. Then we had chicken for supper and I gave her two guineas and about twelve walked home and neglected my prayers.

3. I rose about 7 o'clock and read a chapter in Hebrew and some Greek in Lucian. I neglected my prayers, and had milk for breakfast. The weather was cold and clear, the wind east. I danced my dance and wrote some English till 2 o'clock and then ate only some boiled milk for dinner. In the afternoon I put several things in order till 4 o'clock and then went into the City and entered Mrs. Southwell's ticket at the office and then went to Mr. Perry's to pay my compliments to the bride and sat there two hours. Then I took leave and went to Will's and from thence to visit Mrs. B-r-t just come from France and sat there above an hour. Then I returned to Will's and ate some milk and then walked home and said my prayers. This day I had a blank come up in the lottery.

4. I rose about 7 o'clock and read a chapter in Hebrew and some Greek in Lucian. I said my prayers, and had milk for breakfast. The weather was cold and cloudy, the wind still at east. I danced my dance and about eleven went to Somerset Chapel and heard a pretty good sermon. After church I went home with Mrs. U-m-s after we had taken a walk in the garden and I ate some roast veal. After dinner we sat and talked of many things and about four Mrs. M-r-l-y and her sister came in and we drank tea till six and then I went to Misses Cornishes' but they were from home. Then I went to my Lord Islay's, just arrived from France, and drank a bottle of Hermitage and he told me of several things in France. About nine I went to Will's, had some milk, and walked home, washed my feet, and said my prayers.

5. I rose about 7 o'clock and read a chapter in Hebrew and some Greek in Lucian. I said my prayers, and had milk for breakfast. The

weather was cold and clear, the wind east. I danced my dance. Then I wrote some English till 1 o'clock and then went to Mr. Horsmanden's and dined with him and we had some veal roast. I returned home at three because the men were putting up the marble chimney, and wrote more English till 5 o'clock and then went to visit my daughter and sat with her till 7 o'clock and then went to Lady Guise's and sat with her till nine when I came away. I offered her any money she wanted which she told me she would accept. Then I walked to Will's where I ate some milk and then walked home and said my prayers.

6. I rose about 7 o'clock and read a chapter in Hebrew and some Greek in Lucian. I said my prayers and had milk for breakfast. The weather was clear and cold, the wind east. I danced my dance and then wrote some English till 2 o'clock and then ate only bread and cheese and drank milk. After dinner I wrote more English till 5 o'clock and then I went to visit my neighbor M-d who was not well and sat with him about an hour. Then I called in at the playhouse and went from thence to visit Misses Cornish but they were from home. Then I went to Misses [Sands'] and found them and sat with them about two hours and then went to Will's Coffeehouse and had milk for supper. Then I walked home and by the way endeavored to pick up a whore but could not. I neglected my prayers, for which God forgive me.

7. I rose about 7 o'clock and read a chapter in Hebrew and some Greek in Lucian. I said my prayers, and had milk for breakfast. The wind continued east and made the weather cold and clear. I danced my dance and put several things in order till 11 o'clock and then went into the City to the Virginia Coffeehouse and from thence I went and dined with old Mr. Perry and ate some roast mutton. George Turner dined with us and I took my passage with him for Virginia. After dinner I went to Dick Perry's and sat with them till five and then went home and found Mr. Horsmanden there and we called in at the play and from thence to Will's and then I went to Lady Guise's, lent her sixty pounds and then took leave and picked up a whore and carried her to the tavern where I gave her a supper and

we ate a broiled fowl. We did nothing but fool and parted about 11 o'clock and I walked home and neglected my prayers.

8. I rose about 7 o'clock and read a chapter in Hebrew and some Greek in Lucian. I said my prayers and had milk for breakfast. The weather was clear and cold, the wind east. I danced my dance and then began to make my will till 2 o'clock and then walked to Mr. Horsmanden's lodging where I ate some boiled chicken for dinner. After dinner we sat and talked till 4 o'clock and then I took a walk in our garden for half an hour and then went home where I found a maid that offered to go with me to Virginia and I agreed with her. About five I went to see my daughter who had a prize of twenty-five pounds in a lottery drawn this day. I carried her to Mrs. Cornish who was just going out. However we stayed about half an hour, and then went to Mrs. FitzHerbert's where we drank chocolate. About eight I sent home my daughter and went to Lady Guise's and lent her the rest of the sixty pounds. About nine I went to Will's and had milk for supper and read the news. I went home in the chair and said my prayers. It rained.

9. I rose about 7 o'clock and read a chapter in Hebrew and some Greek in Lucian. I said my prayers, and had milk for breakfast. The weather was warm and cloudy, the wind west. I danced my dance and then made an end of my will till 2 o'clock and then went to dine with my cousin Horsmanden and ate some boiled beef. After dinner I took a nap and about 4 o'clock walked in our garden and then went and was out of humor because my man stayed out. However, about five I went to my daughter's and took her to see the bride, Mrs. [H-s-m], and stayed there till 7 o'clock and then carried my daughter home and then went to visit Mrs. B-r-t and sat with her till nine and then went home and said my prayers. My man agreed to go with me to Virginia.

10. I rose about 7 o'clock and read a chapter in Hebrew and some Greek in Lucian. I said my prayers and had milk for breakfast. The weather was warm and cloudy, the wind west. I danced my dance and then wrote my will till 2 o'clock when I only ate some milk and

bread and cheese for dinner. In the afternoon I wrote more English till 4 o'clock and put several things in order till five and then went to Lady Guise's where I agreed to lend her forty pounds more. I drank some cherry brandy and saw the young girl that had a mind to go with me. Then I went to the play and had the pleasure to see Sally Cornish and her sister and many other ladies of my acquaintance. After the play I went to Will's and had some milk for supper and then walked home and said my prayers. I slept but indifferently. It rained a little.

11. I rose about 6 o'clock and read a chapter in Hebrew and some Greek in Lucian. I said my prayers, and had milk for breakfast. The weather was warm and cloudy, the wind west. I danced my dance and wrote some English till 11 o'clock and then I went to fetch my daughter to go to Mrs. Lindsay's to dinner and I ate some boiled turkey, and my cousin Horsmanden dined with us. After dinner Mrs. Lindsay and my daughter went to church and we men stayed and drank a bottle. After church we drank tea and Mr. Will G-r came in. About six I carried away my daughter home where I sat with her about an hour and then went and took a walk in our square and then went to visit my neighbor M-d and found him a little better and the doctor came in and I stayed till nine and then went home, washed my feet, and said my prayers.

12. I rose about 6 o'clock and read a chapter in Hebrew and some Greek in Lucian. I said my prayers, and had milk for breakfast. The weather was warm and cloudy, the wind west. I danced my dance and wrote some English till 11 o'clock and then went to my Lord Islay's but he was from home. Then I went to General Nicholson's but he was from home; then to Mr. Page's, and desired him to dine with Mr. Horsmanden with me, where I found Mr. H-n-r-s-n. We ate some roast beef for dinner and drank a little too much. About 4 o'clock I went to see Mr. Page's house and did not like it at all. Then I went to my lodging and from thence to Will's and from thence I went to meet my mistress at Mrs. Smith's and rogered her twice but it cost me ten guineas. Here I drank chocolate and gave my landlady

a guinea and went home about 11 o'clock and said my prayers. I slept very indifferently.

13. I rose about 7 o'clock and read a chapter in Hebrew, and some Greek in Lucian. I said my prayers and had milk for breakfast. The weather was warm and cloudy, the wind west. I danced my dance and wrote some English till 12 o'clock and then went to visit Mrs. Southwell, and she invited me to dinner. However, I went first to the Cockpit where I saw and spoke to the Duke of Argyll. I ate some boiled beef. After dinner we drank several healths together till 4 o'clock and I went to the Cornishes' and found them not; then I went to my Lady Guise's and lent her the rest of a hundred pounds. Here I stayed till 6 o'clock and then went to the play where I sat next to Mrs. [Cambridge] and talked abundance to her. After the play I went to Will's and had some milk and then went home in a chair. I said my prayers. I slept but indifferently.

14. I rose about 7 o'clock and read a chapter in Hebrew and some Greek in Lucian. I said my prayers, and had milk for breakfast. The weather was cold and cloudy, the wind west. I danced my dance and wrote some English till 11 o'clock and then went into the City and dispatched several matters. Then I went to the Virginia Coffeehouse and from thence to Dick Perry's to dinner where I ate some fish and Mr. Carter went with me. After dinner we sat and talked till 4 o'clock and then I went to Garraway's Coffeehouse and from thence to visit Sir Charles Cook, but he was from home. Then it rained and I went to Mr. Lindsay's where I found Mrs. Lindsay very ill. However, I played at faro and I lost three guineas and about 10 o'clock I ate some rice milk for supper and then went home and said my prayers.

15. I rose about 7 o'clock and read a chapter in Hebrew and some Greek in Lucian. I neglected my prayers, but had milk for breakfast. The weather was cold and cloudy and it rained sometimes. I danced my dance and wrote a letter to my Lady Mohun about my debt to which she returned an obliging answer. I put several things in order till 2 o'clock and then went to dine with my cousin Horsmanden and

ate some boiled chicken. After dinner we walked in Gray's Inn Garden till five and then I went to Will's Coffeehouse and from thence to meet my mistress at Mrs. Smith's where we ate walnuts and sack but she was indisposed, that I could not lay with her. The lot of twenty thousand pounds came up this day. About ten I came home and walked in the square and then went home and said my prayers.

16. I rose about 7 o'clock and read a chapter in Hebrew and some Greek in Lucian. I said my prayers, and had boiled milk for breakfast. The weather was warm and cloudy, the wind west. I danced my dance and about 11 o'clock went to my Lord Islay's and stayed there about an hour. Then I went to Colonel Blakiston's where I stayed to dine and ate some roast pigeon. Here I stayed till 4 o'clock and then went to Lady Guise, who told me she had begun to discourse Mrs. T-t-s about marriage. About 6 o'clock I went to visit Mrs. U-m-s where I drank tea and stayed till 8 o'clock; then I took a walk and picked up a woman and went with her to the tavern where we had a broiled fowl and afterwards I committed uncleanness for which God forgive me. About eleven I went home and neglected my prayers.

17. I rose about 7 o'clock and read a chapter in Hebrew and some Greek in Lucian. I neglected my prayers, and had boiled milk for breakfast. The weather was warm and clear, after having rained much in the morning. I danced my dance and about eleven went to Colonel Nicholson's but he was from home. Then to the Cockpit where I did some business and about one returned home. This morning I began to make a fire. About 2 o'clock Mr. Horsmanden and I dined near my lodging at the Blue Post and ate fish for dinner. About 4 o'clock we went to Islington to see my little daughter whom we found pretty well. About five we returned and I went first to Will's and then to the play where was but indifferent company. After the play I went to Will's and had some milk and then walked home and said my prayers.

18. I rose about 7 o'clock and read a chapter in Hebrew and some Greek in Lucian. I neglected my prayers, and had milk for breakfast.

The weather was clear and cold, the wind west. Then I danced my dance and put several things in order because I did not go to church. I read some English till 1 o'clock and then had some bread and cheese and milk for dinner. In the afternoon I read more English and danced again till 4 o'clock and then went to visit my neighbor M-d and sat with him about an hour and then took leave and went to visit Misses Cornish but missed them. Then I went to Mrs. [Andrews'] and drank tea with them and stayed till eight and then went to Mrs. U-m-s and ate some roast beef and drank a bottle of Burgundy and about 11 o'clock walked home and said my prayers.

19. I rose about 7 o'clock and read a chapter in Hebrew and some Greek in Lucian. I said my prayers, and had milk for breakfast. The weather was clear and cold, the wind west. I danced my dance. Annie Wilkinson came to make me a visit and stayed about an hour. Then came my old laundress, which I had before I left England. About 12 o'clock I went to Mr. Horsmanden's and with him into the City and called at several places and about 2 o'clock we returned to the Blue Post to dinner and I ate some roast mutton, and about four returned home and put myself in order and about five went to Will's and from thence to Lady Guise's where I stayed about an hour. Then I looked into the play and from thence went to Mrs. Lindsay's where I found Mrs. Cornish and Mrs. C-r. We were merry and ate some oysters for supper and about 10 o'clock I came with Mrs. Cornish to the Temple and from thence hacked it home where I said my prayers.

20. I rose about 7 o'clock and read a chapter in Hebrew and some Greek in Lucian. I said my prayers, and had milk for breakfast. The weather was clear and cold, the wind west. I danced my dance and about 10 o'clock went to Lord Islay's and because he was from home I went to the Cockpit and spoke to Mr. V-n-n about the committee and wrote to the Duke of Argyll about it. Then I went into the City and drank a dish of chocolate at Garraway's and from thence to Mr. Perry's to dine with the old gentleman and ate some boiled beef. I had several letters from Virginia. After dinner I went to visit Dick who had the gout and stayed till 5 o'clock and then went home and from thence to the play where I saw nobody I liked so went to Will's

and stayed about an hour, and then went to Mrs. Smith where I met a very tall woman and lay with her all night and rogered her three times.

21. I rose about 8 o'clock and gave my lass two guineas and drank some tea and milk and then went home, where I said my prayers and ate some milk. I read a chapter in Hebrew and about eleven came Suky Cole and told me her sister was gone away with Mr. G-n-ing. I put several things in order and received a letter from Lady Guise to invite me to dinner and about two I went there and Mrs. Ch-n-t-r-l dined there likewise. I ate some roast hare. After dinner I sat and talked till five and then went to Will's Coffeehouse where I sat with my Lord Orrery and Lord Islay till eight and read the news and had some milk for supper. Then I walked home and walked an hour in our square and about ten went home and said my prayers.

22. I rose about 7 o'clock and read some Greek in Lucian but no Hebrew. I said my prayers, and had milk for breakfast. The weather was cold and foggy, the wind northwest. I danced my dance and about 9 o'clock I went to my Lord Islay's where I made some of his broth and stayed till about 12 o'clock and then I went with him to the Cockpit to the Council but they were up before we came, so we went to my Lord Orrery's where I drank a dish of chocolate and stayed about an hour and then I went to Mr. Horsmanden's chamber and ate some boiled beef. After dinner I returned home where Captain Hastings[1] came to beg of me and I gave him a shilling. About five I went to visit Mrs. B-s where I drank tea and stayed an hour and then went to Mrs. FitzHerbert's and drank some ale and about nine went home and said my prayers.

23. I rose about 7 o'clock and read a chapter in Hebrew and some Greek in Lucian. I said my prayers, and had milk for breakfast. The weather was cold and clear, the wind east. I danced my dance and about 11 o'clock went to the Cockpit and talked with Mr. Sh-r-p about getting a committee for my business and he promised me he

1. Ferdinand Richard Hastings, captain and lieutenant colonel of the First Foot Guards.

would try. Here I stayed till 2 o'clock and then I had boiled milk and bread and cheese for dinner. In the afternoon I put several things in order till 4 o'clock, when I went to visit my daughter and sat with her an hour and then went into the City to Mr. Lindsay's where I played at cards till ten and then we went to supper and I ate some cold boiled beef. After supper we played at faro till twelve and then went home but neglected my prayers.

24. I rose about 7 o'clock and read a chapter in Hebrew and some Greek in Lucian. I said my prayers, and had boiled milk for breakfast. The weather was cold and clear, the wind east. I danced my dance and then went through the King's road to Putney and from thence to the Duke of Argyll's where I was favorably received by the Duke and he promised to write to the Governor of Virginia about me. Mr. C-r-y and Jenny Jeffreys dined there likewise and I ate some goose giblets. After dinner we sat till four and then I walked with Mr. C-r-y to his house where I ate abundance of grapes. We played at cards and I won five shillings. I ate some mutton cutlets for supper and about twelve we retired and I said my prayers.

25. I rose about 8 o'clock and read nothing. However, I said my prayers and danced my dance. The weather continued cold and clear, the wind east. About ten we drank our chocolate and then went to church, where Mr. B-r-d-y gave us a good sermon. After church I went to the coffeehouse and from thence to my Lord Percival's to dinner where I ate chicken fricassee. After dinner we sat and talked till four and then crossed the river to B-r-n-f-r with Daniel Dering and so proceeded to London and I went to Mrs. Cornish's where I found Mrs. Lindsay. We drank tea and were merry till ten and then went to supper and I ate some oysters, and then sat and talked till twelve and then I went home and said my prayers.

26. I rose about 7 o'clock and read a chapter in Hebrew and some Greek in Lucian. I neglected my prayers, and had boiled milk for breakfast. The weather continued cold and clear. About 11 o'clock I went to Lord Islay's to make broth where my Lord Orrery came and stayed with us an hour. About one I went to the Cockpit and

from thence to dine with Betty Southwell and Daniel Dering. I ate some boiled pork and we were very merry till 4 o'clock and then I went to Lady Guise's and sat with her till six and then went to Will's and sat with Lord Orrery till eight and then I went to visit Mrs. B-r-t but she was from home. Then to Mrs. U-m-s where I stayed to supper and ate some mutton cutlets and stayed till twelve and then walked home and neglected my prayers.

27. I rose about 7 o'clock and read a chapter in Hebrew and some Greek in Lucian. I neglected my prayers, and had boiled milk for breakfast. The weather was cold and clear, the wind northeast. I danced my dance. About 12 o'clock I went to the Cockpit, where I spoke with Tom Beake and drank a dish of chocolate and then returned home again and wrote two letters till 2 o'clock and then ate some boiled milk for dinner. After dinner I put several things in order and then wrote more letters till five and then went to Will's and read the news and about six went to the play with Lord Orrery. After the play I returned to Will's and had some milk for supper and about ten went home in a chair. This night I lay for the first time in my new chamber and said my prayers.

28. I rose about 7 o'clock and read a chapter in Hebrew and no Greek because I wrote some English. I said my prayers, and had milk for breakfast. The weather was warm and cloudy and it rained a little. About 10 o'clock came Mr. Albin and brought my paint box and several other things. About eleven I danced my dance and went into the City to the Virginia Coffeehouse and from thence to old Mr. Perry's to dinner where I ate some cold boiled beef. After dinner I wrote some English and then went to visit Mrs. Perry and sat with them half an hour. Then I went home and adjusted myself and about five went to the committee at the Cockpit where the lords agreed to recommend my case of Council to His Majesty. Then I went to Mrs. B-s and sat with her till 10 o'clock and then went home and said my prayers. The lords of the committee were exceedingly courteous to me.

29. I rose about 7 o'clock and read a chapter in Hebrew and some Greek in Lucian. I neglected my prayers but had boiled milk for

breakfast. The weather was warm and cloudy, the wind northwest. I danced my dance and settled some accounts till 11 o'clock and then came my Lord Percival and stayed about half an hour. Then I went to the Cockpit and by the way met Mr. B-r-n-t just come from Scotland with my Lord Islay. I saluted my friend Mr. B-r-n-t and then went to the Cockpit and thanked Mr. V-n-n for reading my paper to the committee last night. Then I went to bespeak a pair of boots in [Pall Mall] and then went home and ate some milk and bread and cheese for dinner. After dinner I wrote some English till three and then came Daniel Horsmanden and stayed about half an hour. About five I went to Mr. M-n-l-y and drank tea and then went to Will's and stayed till 8 o'clock and then walked about and carried a whore to the tavern and ate a roast chicken for supper. I committed uncleanness and about eleven went home and repented and said my prayers.

30. I rose about 7 o'clock and read a chapter in Hebrew and some Greek in Lucian. I neglected my prayers and had boiled milk for breakfast. The weather was cold and clear, the wind west. About 10 o'clock came Mr. B-r-n-t and we went together to the Duke of Argyll's and found him at my Lord Islay's but just going from thence. I went to my Lord Percival's and sat with him half an hour and then went to Lord Orrery's, but he was from home. Then to Colonel Blakiston's where I dined and ate some stewed duck. After dinner we sat and talked till five and then I went to Lady Guise's and stayed about an hour and then went to the play but did not stay but went to Will's where I sat the whole evening and learned many things concerning husbandry from my Lord B-n-l-y. I ate some milk for supper and about ten went home but found not my man there, but he stayed till 11 o'clock.

31. I rose about 7 o'clock and read a chapter in Hebrew and some Greek in Lucian. I said my prayers, and had milk for breakfast. The weather was cold and cloudy, and it rained, the wind northwest. I danced my dance. About 11 o'clock I called on Daniel Horsmanden and we went to Limehouse Hole on board of Captain Turner's ship. He received us with guns and I ate some pork and peas for dinner. After dinner we drank rack punch and I gave the captain ten guineas

for fresh provisions. We stayed here till almost 4 o'clock and then were sent away with more guns. We called on Mrs. Lindsay but she was from home; then we went to Will's and I went from thence with my Lord Orrery to the play. After the play I ate some milk and read the news and went home about 10 o'clock and said my prayers.

November 1719

1. I rose about 7 o'clock and read a chapter in Hebrew and some Greek in Lucian. I said my prayers, and had boiled milk for breakfast. The weather was clear and cold, the wind west. I danced my dance. About 11 o'clock came John Page and stayed about half an hour and then I went into the City to Mr. Lindsay's to dinner and ate some roast beef. After dinner we went to church and had a good sermon from Mr. H-s. After church we returned to Mr. Lindsay's and had tea and seed cakes. Here I stayed till 6 o'clock and then took leave and went to Will's where I stayed about an hour and then went to Mrs. B-r-t's where I sat and talked two hours till 9 o'clock and then I walked home, being very dry, where I settled several things in order and said my prayers.

2. I rose about 7 o'clock and read a chapter in Hebrew and some Greek in Lucian. I said my prayers, and had boiled milk for breakfast. The weather was clear and cold, the wind northwest. I danced my dance and then I wrote some English. About 11 o'clock I went to Lord Islay's where I made an end of the broth, and my Lord gave me some [p-r of l-m-n]. Then I went to Lord Orrery's where I dined and ate some venison. After dinner we drank a bottle till five and then went to Will's where I drank a dish of tea and then went home and from thence called at the new playhouse where the Prince was with very little company. Then I went to Lady Guise's and sat with her two hours and then walked home and by the way picked up Molly D-s-t and sat with her at her lodging an hour and then walked home and said my prayers.

3. I rose about 7 o'clock and read a chapter in Hebrew and some Greek in Lucian. I said my prayers, and had milk for breakfast. The weather was cold and cloudy and it snowed for half an hour. I danced my dance and wrote some English till 12 o'clock and then went to see my daughter and from thence into the City to Mr. Perry's and dined with Dick and ate some roast pigeon. After dinner we sat and talked and drank tea till 4 o'clock and then I went with Mr. Carter to Garraway's Coffeehouse and from thence I went to Mr. Lindsay's where I drank tea again and we played at cards and I won about thirty shillings. I stayed to supper and ate some fricassee of chicken. Mr. B-n-s-n and Mr. T-k-s-n played with us and I stayed till 12 o'clock and then went home and said my prayers.

4. I rose about 7 o'clock and read a chapter in Hebrew and some Greek. I said my prayers, and had boiled milk for breakfast. The weather was cold and cloudy, and it rained. I danced my dance and had several people come to me till 12 o'clock and then I went to the Cockpit and discoursed Mr. Beake and then went to Mr. Southwell's but there was nobody at home. Then I bought the chocolate pot and went home and had milk and bread and cheese for dinner. After dinner I wrote a letter to the Duke of Argyll[1] and put several things in order till 5 o'clock and then I went to Mr. Southwell's and sat with him half an hour; then to Misses Cornishes' but they were from home; then to Mrs. [Andrews'] and drank tea with them till eight and then to Will's where I ate some milk and about ten went home and said my prayers. It rained all night.

5. I rose about 7 o'clock and read a chapter in Hebrew and some Greek in Lucian. I said my prayers, and had boiled milk for breakfast. The weather was cold and it rained all day, the wind east. I

1. Byrd kept in his notebook a copy of the letter to the Duke of Argyll written on this date, concerning his relations with Spotswood. It is printed in *Another Secret Diary of William Byrd*, 368-71.

danced my dance. Several people came to me about business and I wrote a letter till 11 o'clock and then went to Lady Percival's to show her the way to make veal broth and we were busy about it till 2 o'clock when we dined and I ate some roast turkey. Sir Philip Parker[2] and his lady dined with us. After dinner we went about our cookery again till five and then I went to St. James's Coffeehouse and from thence to Mrs. B-s who was from home. Then to Lady Guise's and stayed about half an hour and then went to both plays but there was no company at either. Then I went to Will's, ate my milk and about ten went home and said my prayers.

6. I rose about 7 o'clock and read a chapter in Hebrew and some Greek in Lucian. I said my prayers, and had boiled milk for breakfast. The weather was cloudy and it rained abundance, the wind northeast. I danced my dance and wrote some English till 12 o'clock and then took up Mr. Horsmanden and went to the bank for some money and then went to the Virginia Coffeehouse and left a letter for Captain Turner. Then we went home and dined at the Blue Post and had boiled pork for dinner. After dinner I went home and put several things in order till five and then went to Lord Percival's and sat with my Lady till seven and then went to Mrs. B-s but she was from home. Then I went to Will's and found the Duke of Argyll and spoke to him about the letter he was to write to Virginia to the Governor. Then I went to the play with Lord Orrery but did not stay but went to Mrs. U-m-s where I found Margaret Bellenden. Here I ate an egg for supper and went home about twelve and said my prayers.

7. I rose about 7 o'clock and read a chapter in Hebrew and some Greek in Lucian. I said my prayers, and had boiled milk for breakfast. The weather was cold and cloudy, the wind east. I danced my dance and then wrote some English. Colonel Blakiston came and stayed about half an hour. About twelve I went into the City to Mr. Perry's and dined with the old gentleman and ate some roast beef. After dinner I went to visit Mrs. Perry and sat with her and her daughter till 4 o'clock and then went home and put myself in order

2. Sir Philip Parker was Lady Percival's father.

and then went to Will's where I saw the Duke of Argyll. From hence I went to the play and sat by myself. After the play I went to Leveridge's with Daniel Horsmanden, Mr. Carter, and Mr. Page and Mr. Clayton. We had broiled chicken for supper and drank rack punch till 2 o'clock and then went home and neglected my prayers. This day I laid up my chariot.

8. I rose about 7 o'clock and read a chapter in Hebrew and some Greek in Lucian. I neglected my prayers, but had milk for breakfast. The weather was cold and cloudy, and it rained a little. I went not to church because I was in haste to put up my things. I was very busy till 1 o'clock and then only ate some milk and bread and cheese for dinner. In the afternoon I put several things in order and about 5 o'clock went to Lady Guise's where I saw Sir Roger Braidshaigh, who told me his lady[3] was come with him. About six I went to Mrs. FitzHerbert's where I met Mr. Southwell, his son and sister and Peg Bellenden to supper. I ate some salmon and we were very merry till 10 o'clock and then I set them all home, called at Mrs. U-m-s and then went home and said my prayers. It rained all day.

9. I rose about 7 o'clock and read a chapter in Hebrew and some Greek in Lucian. I said my prayers and had boiled milk for breakfast. The weather was warm and cloudy, the wind west. I was very busy in packing up my things all day till 2 o'clock and then I only ate some boiled milk and bread and cheese for dinner. After dinner I continued to put up my things till 4 o'clock and then I went to visit my daughter and stayed with her about an hour and then went to Mrs. Lindsay's in the City but only he was at home so I stayed but a little and then went to Will [Tryon's] where I found abundance of people. Here I played at basset and won about twenty shillings. I stayed to supper and ate some roast duck. I stayed till eleven and then walked part of the way home and said my prayers.

10. I rose about 7 o'clock and read nothing because I wished to make an end of putting up my things. I said my prayers and had boiled milk for breakfast. The weather was clear and cold, the wind

3. Lady Braidshaigh was Rachel, sister of Sir John Guise.

northwest. About 10 o'clock came my Lord Percival and stayed about half an hour. Then came Colonel Blakiston and stayed half an hour. I sent for a cart to carry my things to Mr. Perry's and I went there myself about 12 o'clock and dined there with Colonel Blakiston and ate some roast beef. After dinner we went to the other house and I stayed till 4 o'clock and drank tea and then went to Garraway's and drank some cherry brandy, then called at my milliner's and went home and then to Will's where I saw the Duke of Argyll and he promised again to write a letter for me to Virginia. Then I went to visit my Lady Braidshaigh and saw the whole family and stayed there till 9 o'clock. Then I called in at the play and went to Will's where I ate milk and then walked home and said my prayers.

11. I rose about 7 o'clock and read nothing because I prepared to go out about business. However, I said my prayers, and had boiled milk for breakfast. The weather was cold and foggy, the wind east. About 10 o'clock came Mr. B-r-n-t but I could not stay with him, being obliged to go to Colonel Blakiston's with whom I went to Mr. Aislabie[4] about my account, who was very courteous to me. Then I went to my Lord Orkney, who promised to write to his lieutenant governor. Then I went to the Duke of Argyll's and stayed there about an hour and then to my Lord Orrery's who was from home; then to White's Chocolate House and then to Colonel Blakiston's to dinner and ate some wild duck. Here I stayed till 5 o'clock and then went to the park and walked and then to Will's where I stayed half an hour and then went with Lord Orrery to Mrs. B-r-t-n where we found two chambermaids that my Lord had ordered to be got for us and I rogered one of them and about 9 o'clock returned again to Will's where Betty S-t-r-d called on me in a coach and I went with her to the bagnio and rogered her twice, for which God forgive me.

12. I rose about 8 o'clock and went home and read nothing because I put several things in order. However, I said my prayers, and had boiled milk for breakfast. The weather was cold and cloudy, the wind east. I danced my dance and put several things in order till 1

4. John Aislabie, chancellor of the exchequer; a leader in the South Sea Company, a scheme for paying off the national debt, in 1719–20; after its collapse in 1720 he was committed to the Tower.

o'clock and then went to dine at Pontack's where I ate some fish. After dinner I walked to Mr. Perry's to inquire whether my things were sent aboard and found they were. Then I went and sat a little with Mrs. Perry and drank tea and stayed till 5 o'clock and then went home and from thence to Will's where I saw the Duke of Argyll. I stayed here the whole evening and had some milk for supper, and about 10 o'clock walked home and said my prayers and slept pretty well.

13. I rose about 7 o'clock and read a chapter in Hebrew and some Greek in Lucian. I said my prayers, and had boiled milk for breakfast. The weather was cold and clear, the wind east. I danced my dance. Mr. Horsmanden came and stayed half an hour and about eleven came another gentleman about Captain B-k-f-r ship. At eleven I went to my Lord Orrery's and sat with him about quarter of an hour because he was going out and then to Horace Walpole's and sat with him about an hour and then took my way towards Mrs. South-well's but she was from home. Then I walked in the park and went to Ozinda's and from thence to my Lord Orrery's to dinner and ate some fish. After dinner we walked in the garden and at five we went to Will's. I looked in at the play and then went with Mr. B-r-n-t to Mistress B-r-t and stayed about an hour. Then I returned to Will's again, ate some milk, and then walked home and said my prayers.

14. I rose about 7 o'clock and read a chapter in Hebrew and some Greek in Lucian. I neglected my prayers and had milk for breakfast. The weather was cold and clear, the wind southeast. I had several people come to me and Mr. Horsmanden among the rest. About 10 o'clock and something past, I went to the Duke of Argyll's and sat with him about an hour. Then I went to Lord Islay's but he was from home. Then to Mr. Southwell's and I found his sister and sat about an hour with her and then went to buy some things and then home, where I wrote some English and then went to dine with Lord Tyr-connel and ate some roast turkey. About five Mr. B-r-n-t and I went away to Will's where a woman called on me and I took Mr. B-r-n-t with me and we went to Red Lion Street to look for another woman and then went together to the tavern and ate a fricassee for supper

and were very merry and then went to the bagnio where I rogered my woman but once. Her name was Sally Cook. There was a terrible noise in the night like a woman crying.

15. I rose about 8 o'clock and Mr. B-r-n-t set me home where I read a chapter in Hebrew and some Greek in Lucian. I said my prayers, and had boiled milk for breakfast. About 11 o'clock came Mr. Page and carried me into the City to Mr. Lindsay's where I dined and ate some roast beef for dinner. In the afternoon we went to church and I slept a little there, for which God forgive me. After church we drank tea till 6 o'clock and then I walked to Paul's church and then took coach to Will's where I stayed till seven and then went to Mr. Southwell's where I met Lady Rich and her husband, my Lord [Southwell], Mrs. Bellenden and Robin Moore. We had a bowl of punch and I ate some roast venison for supper. We were very merry and stayed together till 12 o'clock and then I walked home and neglected my prayers.

16. I rose about 8 o'clock and read a chapter in Hebrew and some Greek in Lucian. I said my prayers, and had boiled milk for breakfast. The weather was cold and cloudy, the wind east. I danced my dance and paid my [tailor's] bill. About 11 o'clock I went to the Virginia Coffeehouse and spoke with Captain Turner and then went to Dick Perry's to dinner and ate some boiled beef. After dinner I sat and talked with them till 4 o'clock and then went home and carried the hamper with me that Mr. Lindsay gave me. From thence I went to Will's and from thence to Misses Cornishes' and found dear Sally at home and drank tea with her. About 8 o'clock Mrs. B-r-t-n came, who is a woman of good sense; we all ate some oysters together and Sally gave me a nutmeg grater to remember her by. Mrs. B-r-t-n and Betty went to Court but I stayed with Sally till 11 o'clock and then went home and said my prayers.

17. I rose about 8 o'clock and read a chapter in Hebrew and some Greek in Lucian. I said my prayers and had boiled milk for breakfast. The weather was clear and cold, the wind northwest. I danced my dance. About 10 o'clock came John Carter and stayed here till

1 o'clock. In the meanwhile came my Lord Orrery and stayed about an hour. Then came Colonel [Shutz] just come from the expedition. Then came Mr. F-l-y the prothonotary. I had nothing but milk and bread and cheese for dinner. After dinner I put several things in order till 4 o'clock and then came Mr. Horsmanden and stayed half an hour and I went to Lady Guise's to tell my maid to go to the ship on Thursday. About 6 o'clock I went to Lady Rich's where I met Mr. Southwell and his sister, my Lord [Southwell], Mrs. Bellenden and Robin Moore who were merry and I ate some boiled chicken for supper. We stayed till 12 o'clock and then I went home in a chair and said my prayers.

18. I rose about 8 o'clock and read a chapter in Hebrew and no Greek because I packed up my things. However, I said my prayers, and had milk for breakfast. The weather was warm and rained all day. About eleven I went to Sir Roger Braidshaigh and drank two dishes of chocolate and about twelve went to Lord Percival's and dined there and ate some roast pork. After dinner we drank tea till five and then I went to Will's Coffeehouse and spoke to the Duke of Argyll about his letter. About six I went to Mrs. Lindsay's and found Parson H-s there. We played at cards and I won fifteen shillings. About 10 o'clock we went to supper and I ate some stewed duck. About eleven I took leave and Mrs. Lindsay cried when I took my leave. I said my prayers.

19. I rose about 7 o'clock and read some Greek but no Hebrew because I packed up my things in order to go on board. However, I said my prayers, and had boiled milk for breakfast. The weather was warm and cloudy, the wind west. Several persons came to me about business and Colonel Blakiston came to visit me and stayed about half an hour. About 11 o'clock Mr. Carter and Mr. Horsmanden went with me to Billingsgate where we took water and went on board the *Spotswood* where we dined and I ate some pork and peas. I found my maid on board. I put my house in order and we had a bowl of rack punch. About four we went in the [r-] ashore with abundance of wind and walked to Ratcliffe Cross where we went into the tavern and had a bottle of wine and then took coach with which I set them

down and went to Mrs. Cornish's where I found little Lindsay who complained to me that her husband was jealous of me. I stayed till eleven and then went to Will's and had some milk and then went home in a chair and said my prayers.

20. I rose about seven and read nothing because I put several things in order. I said my prayers, and had boiled milk for breakfast. The weather was cold and clear, the wind northwest. I put several things in order till 11 o'clock and then I went to Lord Islay's where I stayed till 12 o'clock and then went to the Duke of Argyll's but he was from home; but I left the description of Virginia[5] for him and gave my Lord Islay another. Then I went to Lord Orrery's but he was from home. Then I went home and put several matters in order till two and then had boiled milk and bread and cheese for dinner. After dinner I settled several accounts till three and then came Daniel Horsmanden, when I put several papers into his hands relating to my business. About five I went to visit my daughter and about six carried her to my Lord Braidshaigh's where we stayed till eight and my daughter went with Lady Braidshaigh to my Lady Guise's and I went to Will's, where I met the Duke of Argyll and my other friends and drank two dishes of chocolate, and then went with Mr. B-r-n-t to Mrs. B-r-t and from thence to Court. About eleven I returned home and neglected my prayers.

21. I rose about 8 o'clock and read nothing because I had abundance of business to do. However, I said my prayers, and had boiled milk for breakfast. The weather was cold and clear, the wind north-

---

5. John Oldmixon, in the Preface to the 1741 edition of his *The British Empire in America* (first printed 1708) acknowledges his debt to a history of Virginia 'written with a great deal of spirit and judgment by a gentleman of the province, . . . Colonel Byrd, whom I knew when I was in the Temple' (1, x). A description of Virginia written by Byrd and translated into German by Samuel Jenner was published in Berne, Switzerland, in 1737 as *Neu-Gefundenes Eden*. See R. C. Beatty and W. J. Mulloy, *William Byrd's Natural History of Virginia* (Richmond, 1940). Byrd's MS 'History of the Dividing Line' is preceded by a brief history of Virginia. The description which he presented to the Duke of Argyll in 1719 may have been a version of the first, mentioned by Oldmixon, brought up to date; or the second, later revised and sent to Switzerland with proposals for a scheme of colonization; or the third, adapted as an introduction to the 'Dividing Line'; or still another description not otherwise known to us.

west. I put several things in order till 11 o'clock and then came Daniel Horsmanden and his brother Barrington and stayed half an hour. Then I went to Mr. U-t-n and drank a dish of chocolate with him. Then to my Lord Percival's and paid for my [apothecary shop]. Then to Colonel Blakiston's, but he was from home, but I saw his lady. Then I went to Mr. Southwell's to dinner, where I met Sir Roger Braidshaigh and his lady, my Lady Rich and her husband. I stayed with them till 5 o'clock and then went to Will's and from thence to Lady Guise's where I stayed an hour and then went to Mrs. U-m-s where I ate some veal steak for supper. Here I stayed till about 12 o'clock and then went home and neglected my prayers, for which God forgive me.

22. I rose about 8 o'clock and read a chapter in Hebrew and some Greek in Lucian. I said my prayers, and had boiled milk for breakfast. The weather was cold and clear, the wind northwest. I danced my dance and put several things in order till 2 o'clock and then I went to the Duke of Argyll's to dinner, where dined Sir Robert Rous and his lady and I ate some venison pasty. After dinner we sat and talked and the Duke was very kind to me and gave me a letter to the Lieutenant Governor. About 5 o'clock I took leave and went into the City to Mr. Perry's and supped with Dick Perry and ate some roast fowl. They seemed much concerned at my going away. About nine I took leave and walked home and by the way picked up a woman and committed uncleanness with her, for which God forgive me. About eleven I went home and wrote a letter. I neglected my prayers.

23. I rose about 8 o'clock and wrote some letters but read nothing. However, I said my prayers, and had boiled milk for breakfast. The weather was cold and cloudy, the wind west. I spent all the morning in packing up my things and gave Mr. Spencer[6] orders what to do in my chambers when I was gone. About 1 o'clock I went to Will's and

6. Mr. Spencer continued for some years to look after Byrd's chambers. In a letter to him of May 28, 1729, Byrd directed him to dispose of the chambers and gave careful directions for packing the books (MS in Colonial Williamsburg).

ate a jelly. Then to dine with Mr. U-t-n, and ate some boiled beef, and Mr. U-m-s dined with us. After dinner we sat and talked till 5 o'clock and then I went to my Lady Guise's and took leave of her and about seven to Colonel Blakiston's and took leave of him. Then I called in at the play and from thence went with Young in his chariot to Court but came from thence at ten and walked home and said a short prayer.

24. I rose about 5 o'clock and put everything in order to go away. I said my prayers and committed myself and my life to the Divine Providence. When Daniel Horsmanden and Mr. Carter came we drank chocolate and about 7 o'clock went out of town in a coach and six. At Dartford we ate some bread and butter, and dined at Rochester, and ate some fish for dinner. Nothing happened remarkable but it was dark before we got to Sittingbourne where we had roast mutton for supper. Here I learned that my uncle Rand[7] lay here last night. About 10 o'clock I retired and said my prayers.

25. I rose at 6 o'clock and read nothing nor did I eat anything for breakfast but got into the coach by seven. I said my prayers. The weather was clear and warm, the wind west. By the way I met a man that had been my servant whose name was Tom. He came from France and wanted to go with me to Virginia. About 11 o'clock we got to Canterbury and dined at the King's Head and invited Mr. G-s-l-n to dine with us. I ate some fish for dinner and about 2 o'clock we took leave of Mr. G-s-l-n and his son and went through a pleasant country to M-n-g-m where we found the family in great disorder. However, we had roast fowl for supper and a bowl of punch after supper. About eleven we retired and I neglected my prayers, for which God forgive me.

26. I rose about 8 o'clock and read some Greek. I said my prayers and had boiled milk for breakfast. The weather was cold and cloudy and it rained a little. I danced my dance. We played at piquet all the morning till dinner and then I ate some boiled beef. After dinner we took a walk, notwithstanding it was dirty and went to Upper Deal

7. Byrd's aunt Ursula Horsmanden married a Mr. Rand.

to visit my cousin Jenkins but he was from home. In returning we saw [Papey Hill] where my uncle [r-l d-n]. In the evening we sat with my cousin Betty who was in a deep consumption, and at night played again at piquet till supper. My cousin Jack paid me two guineas he had borrowed of me four years since. I ate some cold beef for supper. We sat and talked till 10 o'clock and then retired and I said my prayers. I wrote a letter to Mr. Perry.

27. I rose about 8 o'clock and read some Greek but no Hebrew. I said my prayers and had boiled milk for breakfast. The weather was cold and cloudy, the wind northwest. I danced my dance and about 9 o'clock the coach came for us and we took my cousin John Rand with us and we went to Dover but the weather did not favor us for it rained almost all the way. About 12 o'clock we got there and put up at the widow S-l-t-r, who was very handsome, and had tripe for dinner. We were very merry and stayed here till 2 o'clock and then went up to the castle that stands on the cliffs. About four we got home and had fish for supper. We sat and talked till ten and then retired and I kissed the maid and neglected my prayers.

28. I rose about 7 o'clock and read some Greek but no Hebrew. I said my prayers, and had boiled milk for breakfast. About 9 o'clock Daniel Horsmanden and Mr. Carter took leave and went away in my coach, notwithstanding the coachman was very drunk. I danced my dance and wrote some English till dinner and then ate roast veal. After dinner my uncle and cousin Jack took a walk to Northbourne and made a visit to the parson but he was from home. However, his wife entertained us with some strong beer. Then we walked home and read the news which Mr. D-d-s the parson brought us. I ate some boiled milk for supper and romped with Molly F-r-s-y and about 9 o'clock retired and kissed the maid so that I committed uncleanness, for which God forgive me.

29. I rose about 8 o'clock and read some Greek. I said my prayers, and had boiled milk for breakfast. The weather was cold and cloudy, and it rained a little. About 11 o'clock we went to church and Mr. D-d-s gave us a good sermon and then came home to dine with us and

I ate some roast mutton. After dinner it rained, that I could not walk so was content to romp with Molly F-r-s-y. In the evening we drank tea and then sat and talked till seven, when I ate some boiled milk for supper. After supper we sat and talked and romped a little. About ten I retired and kissed the maid and said my prayers.

30. I rose about 8 o'clock and I made the maid feel my roger. I said my prayers, and had boiled milk for breakfast. I read some Greek and settled several accounts. The weather was cold and cloudy, the wind west. I danced my dance and then read some English till dinner, when I ate some fish. After dinner we romped a little and the weather was so bad I could not walk out, so that I read more English till the evening, when Mr. B-l-d and Mr. D-d-s, two Northbourne ministers, came and stayed till 10 o'clock. I had milk for supper, and about 10 o'clock went to bed and neglected my prayers.

December 1719

1. I rose about 8 o'clock and read some Greek. I said my prayers, and had boiled milk for breakfast. The weather was cold and cloudy, the wind northwest. I danced my dance and wrote a letter to Mr. Perry. I read some English till dinner and then ate some boiled neat's tongue. After dinner several people came in to visit my uncle, among whom was the little parson of Northbourne and Mr. S-l-d-n. I went and sat with the women because they would not drink. I gave Sue the maid some nutmeg and onions for her ague. About 9 o'clock I ate some boiled milk for supper. Several people were out of humor. I bore it all right. We supped in my chambers and about ten went to bed and neglected my prayers.

2. I rose about 8 o'clock and read a chapter in Hebrew and some Greek. I said my prayers, and had boiled milk for breakfast. The weather was cold, the wind northeast. I danced my dance and wrote a letter to my cousin Ch-d-k by John Rand who was going there. I read some English till dinner and then ate some hashed beef. After dinner I took a walk of about three miles and almost tired myself. In the evening I read some English till supper and then ate some boiled turkey. After supper one of the maids was frightened into fits by a boy, which put all the family into a bustle. About nine I retired and took the maid by the cunt, which made me commit uncleanness, for which God forgive me.

3. I rose about 8 o'clock and read some Greek. I said my prayers, and had boiled milk for breakfast. The weather was clear and cold, the wind northeast and blowing fiercely. I danced my dance, and then read some English till dinner when I ate some stewed mutton. After dinner I received two letters from Daniel Horsmanden and then I walked to visit my cousin Jenkins and sat with them about half an hour, and then returned home and read some English till seven and then ate some boiled milk for supper. After supper I was so sleepy I could not hold open my eyes. About nine I retired and neglected my prayers, for which God forgive me.

4. I rose about 8 o'clock and read some Greek. I said my prayers and had boiled milk for breakfast. The wind was east, the weather cold and cloudy. Then I danced my dance. I wrote a letter to Daniel Horsmanden and about 10 o'clock my uncle and I walked to Deal and met Captain D-n in the street, but he did not invite us to dinner but Ned S-l-n-g-r did; but before dinner we went to see Mr. W-r-n who then invited us to dinner, but we excused ourselves. Then we called on John [Pye] [1] and went to dinner and I ate some boiled pork. We stayed with Ned S-l-n-g-r till 6 o'clock and then went home in my uncle's coach and I ate some broiled mutton for supper. We sat and talked till nine and then went to bed and I took the maid by the cunt and neglected my prayers.

1. Byrd mentions a cousin, John P – (probably Pye), a seaman, who visited him at Westover in 1709. See *The Secret Diary of William Byrd*, 120 *f*.

5. I rose about 8 o'clock and read some Greek. I said no prayers, but had boiled milk for breakfast. The weather continued cold and clear, the wind east. I danced my dance. About 10 o'clock I went with the girls to Mr. P-r-m-r and drank tea and then took a walk to Ripple and got home by twelve and found John [Pye] at home. I ate some roast rabbit. After dinner we sat and talked till four and then my cousin [Pye] went away and I ran to Deal and met Mr. [Pye] in his return. About five I returned home and read some English to the girls till seven and then ate some boiled milk. We sat and talked till nine and then retired and I said my prayers.

6. I rose about 8 o'clock and read a chapter in Hebrew and some Greek in Isocrates. I said my prayers and had boiled milk for breakfast. The weather was cold and clear, the wind southeast. I danced my dance. I wrote a letter to Sir Charles Wager. About 11 o'clock we went to church and Mr. D-d-s gave us a good sermon and came home with us to dinner, and I ate some boiled beef. My uncle was troubled with a toothache. After dinner I read some English to the girls because I could not walk because of the weather. In the evening I read more English till supper and then ate some boiled milk. I read again after supper till nine and then retired and said my prayers.

7. I rose about 8 o'clock and read some Greek and got some Hebrew words. I said my prayers and had boiled milk for breakfast. The weather was cold and cloudy. The wind continued at east, which kept the ship from coming down. However, about 11 o'clock I had a false alarm, for I had a messenger come from Mr. W-r-n that my ship was come, upon which I hastened down and when I came there it was a ship bound to the East Indies. I dined with Mr. W-r-n who is the King's storekeeper and a pretty man and his wife a good woman. I ate some salty fish. He showed me the King's stores. After dinner I drank tea and stayed till the evening, when I walked home, notwithstanding it rained a little. I found Mr. L-d there and ate some cold beef for supper. After supper we sat and talked till 9 o'clock and then I retired and said my prayers.

8. I rose about 8 o'clock and read a chapter in Hebrew and some Greek. I said my prayers, and had tea and bread and butter for breakfast, there being no milk. I danced my dance. I was a little out of humor for not having milk for breakfast. I read some English till dinner and then ate some roast beef. After dinner I read more English and then took a walk, notwithstanding it rained a little. The wind came to the north and at night it rained very much. I read some English to the ladies till seven and then we had boiled milk for supper. At night my uncle gave us a bowl of punch because it was Molly F-r-s-y birthday. About [...] I retired and took the maid by the cunt. I neglected my prayers.

9. I rose about 8 o'clock and read some Hebrew and some Greek. I said my prayers, and had boiled milk for breakfast. The weather was cold and cloudy, the wind west, so that I expected the ship every moment. I danced my dance and then read some English till dinner and then I ate some roast pork. After dinner I received a messenger that our ship was come into the Downs so I packed up my things and took leave of my friends and went in my uncle's coach to Deal and Mr. George W-r-n with me who was also come to tell me my ship was come. About four I got to Mr. W-r-n where I drank some wine and then went in his boat aboard, where I got safe and put my things in order but was a little sick. I ate no supper because of my indisposition, but sat up till ten and then retired but slept very little because of the noise. I said my prayers.

10. I rose about 8 o'clock and found myself very sick and vomited a little. I read a chapter in Hebrew and some Greek. I said my prayers and then put my things in order till dinner, when I ate some boiled beef; however I ate no breakfast, because of my indisposition, but a little veal broth. After dinner I took a walk for about an hour and then was driven in by the rain. Then I read some French and brought my maids into the cabin out of the cold and set them to work. I had some chocolate for supper which my maid Hannah made very good. The wind continued south. About 9 o'clock I went to bed and said my prayers. In the night a smuggler brought some brandy and I bought two half anchors at twenty shillings apiece.

11. I rose about 8 o'clock and read some Hebrew and some Greek. I said my prayers and had chocolate for breakfast. The weather was cold and clear, the wind still at south. I walked on the quarter deck about half an hour and then put my matters in order. The captain went ashore to buy several things and I continued aboard and ate some meat steaks for dinner. In the afternoon I put my matters in order till the evening and then took a walk of about a mile and then went and read some French till the captain came and then we talked and roasted chestnuts and had a bowl of punch and the captain told me his misfortunes in being cast away upon the Cape of Good Hope. About 9 o'clock I retired and said my prayers.

12. I rose about 8 o'clock and read a chapter in Hebrew and some Greek in Isocrates. I said my prayers, and had chocolate for breakfast, which my maid made very well. I wrote a letter to Mike Perry. Then I wrote some leaves in Coke's Littleton till dinner and then ate some boiled mutton not well dressed. After dinner I put several things in order and then I read some news till the evening and then took my evening walk for about half an hour. At night I read news aloud to the captain and we had some roast chestnuts and a bowl of punch but I drank very little of it. I read a little French but was hindered by my charity to the captain. About 9 o'clock I retired and said my prayers. I feared my gleet was returned again but, thank God, I was mistaken.

13. I rose about 8 o'clock and read a chapter in Hebrew and some Greek. I said my prayers, and had chocolate for breakfast. The weather was cold and cloudy, the wind southeast. Some of our neighbors loosed their topsails in order to weigh anchor but we thought the wind too scanty till 11 o'clock and then we agreed to weigh likewise. I took a walk and offered my service to the captain to read prayers but because they weighed anchor about 12 o'clock that was neglected. The wind was southeast and a moderate gale. We ran about four knots. I ate some boiled mutton for dinner. After dinner I read some English till the evening and then took my walk for about an hour and read more English and got a prayer by heart. I kept my

maid to read. About nine I retired and said my prayers but slept indifferently.

14. I rose about 8 o'clock and read a chapter in Hebrew and some Greek in Isocrates. I said my prayers and had chocolate for breakfast. The wind was east southeast, a fresh gale, and we went about eight knots all night and so continued. My man and my maid were both sick, but my girl kept very well. I read about nine leaves in Coke-Littleton till dinner and I ate some boiled mutton for dinner. After dinner I put several things in order and read more law till the evening, and then took a walk till 5 o'clock and then read some French and wrote some English. About 6 o'clock we reckoned ourselves even with the Straits and the wind continued very fair and fresh. I read some English and French till nine and then retired and said my prayers. I slept pretty well, thank God.

15. I rose about 8 o'clock and read a chapter in Hebrew and some Greek. I said my prayers, and had chocolate for breakfast. The weather was cold and cloudy, the wind east northeast and blowing fresh. I read some law and walked till dinner and then ate salt fish. After dinner I put several things in order and settled some accounts till evening and then took my walk but it blew so hard I could not walk with any pleasure. We saw a sail with French colors not very [low]. At night I read more law. Then I read some French, and then some English news till 9 o'clock when I retired and said my prayers but slept but indifferently because of the exceeding motion. My man continued very sick.

16. I rose about 8 o'clock and read a chapter in Hebrew and some Greek. I said my prayers, and had chocolate for breakfast. The weather was cold and cloudy, the wind still east northeast and very fresh, and we carried but little sail and the less because our consort could not keep up with us. About ten I took my walk and then read some law till dinner and then ate some boiled beef. After dinner I put several things in order and then settled my accounts till the evening and then took another walk. At night I read more law, though the captain had ordered a less candle than we used to have. Then I

read some French and then some news till 9 o'clock. We had some chestnuts roasted. I said my prayers and slept pretty well, thank God.

17. I rose about 8 o'clock and read a chapter in Hebrew and some Greek. I said my prayers, and had some cake and chocolate for breakfast. The weather was cold and cloudy, the wind still east northeast but not so fresh. We sailed, however, seven knots. I took my walk till eleven and then read some law till dinner and ate some plum pudding. After dinner I took a little walk, and then settled several accounts till the evening and then took a walk again. In the evening I read some news aloud to the captain and then read some French till 9 o'clock and then retired and said my prayers. I slept but indifferently because the ship rolled exceedingly so that I had a bottle of cherry brandy broken that was given me by Lady Guise.

18. I rose about 8 o'clock and read a chapter in Hebrew and some Greek. I said my prayers, and had cake and chocolate for breakfast. The weather was moderate and cloudy, the wind east northeast but not fresh. We discovered a sail to the south but she made from us. I walked a little because the mainsail was upon the deck and then read some law till dinner and then ate some roast beef. After dinner I took a walk till 2 o'clock and then settled several accounts till the evening, and then took another walk. My man was a little sick again and so was my girl Annie. At night I read more law and then read some news aloud to the captain. Afterwards I read some French till 9 o'clock and then retired and said my prayers.

19. I rose about 8 o'clock and read a chapter in Hebrew and some Greek. I said my prayers, and had cake and chocolate for breakfast. The weather was warm and cloudy, the wind northeast but moderate. I took a walk till 10 o'clock and then read some law. My man was pretty well again and so was my girl. I ate some cold roast beef for dinner. After dinner I took a walk till two and then settled several accounts till 4 o'clock. Then I gave the officers and the men to each a bottle of brandy and some sugar to drink to their wives, and the captain and I had a bowl of punch and some roast chestnuts and I read some news aloud till 8 o'clock and then my maid Hannah

washed my feet. About nine I retired and said my prayers. I slept well because we had but little motion, having the wind more on our quarter.

20. I rose about 8 o'clock and read a chapter in Hebrew and some Greek. I said my prayers and had cake and chocolate for breakfast. The weather was warm and clear, the wind southeast, and moderate. About ten I read prayers to the ship's company on the quarter deck, and then took a walk and then wrote a prayer till dinner and then ate some pork and peas. After dinner I put several things in order about my person, and then wrote some English till three when I read prayers to the ship's company again and then wrote more prayers till four and then took a walk. In the evening I read a sermon to my people and the captain. Then I read some French and wrote more prayers till 9 o'clock and then retired and said my prayers. The doctor came not to prayers because I had given him nothing.

21. I rose about 7 o'clock and read a chapter in Hebrew and some Greek. I said my prayers devoutly, and had cake and chocolate for breakfast. The weather was clear and warm, the wind south and little of it. I took a walk till ten and then read some law till dinner and then ate some hashed fowl. After dinner I walked for half an hour, and then settled some accounts and read some English till the evening, and then took a walk for about an hour, and then read some news to the captain, and then some French to myself till 9 o'clock, and then retired and said my prayers, but slept indifferently, being disturbed in my dreams about Westover.

22. I rose about 7 o'clock and read a chapter in Hebrew and some Greek. I said my prayers, and had cake and chocolate for breakfast. The weather was warm and clear, the wind about south and moderate. I took a walk and then read some law till dinner and then ate some boiled beef. After dinner I took a little walk. The people took down the mizzen topmast. Then I wrote some English till the evening and then took a walk for about an hour and then read some news and afterwards some French till 9 o'clock, when I retired and said my prayers. I slept pretty well but when I woke could not stir my left hand till some time.

23. I rose about 7 o'clock and read a chapter in Hebrew and some Greek. I said my prayers devoutly, and had cake and chocolate for breakfast. The weather was cloudy and cold, the wind southeast, a good gale. About 9 o'clock I took my walk till ten and then read some law till dinner, and then ate some cold boiled beef. After dinner I took a walk for half an hour and then wrote some English till the evening and then I took a walk. At night I read some news to the captain and then read some French till 9 o'clock and then retired and said my prayers and slept pretty well, thank God. My people were sick again.

24. I rose about 7 o'clock and read a chapter in Hebrew and some Greek. I said my prayers and had cake and chocolate for breakfast. The weather was warm and cloudy, the wind about south and moderate. About 7 o'clock we supposed we were abreast with the island of St. Mary's, to the south of it about eight leagues. I took a walk till ten and then read some law till dinner and then ate some boiled beef. After dinner I took a walk till 2 o'clock and then wrote some English till four. Then I took another walk till six. Then I read some French and afterwards some news aloud to the captain till nine, when I retired and said my prayers. I slept but indifferently being disturbed by a passenger that got drunk.

25. I rose about 7 o'clock and read a chapter in Hebrew and some Greek. I said my prayers, and had cake and [chocolate for] breakfast. The weather was warm and cloudy, the wind south and moderate. I took a walk till ten and then I read prayers to the ship's company and then wrote a prayer in English till dinner, when we had plum pudding and boiled mutton. After dinner I took a walk till three and then read prayers again and afterwards read some English till four and then took a walk. At night I read some French and the captain and I ate some roast chestnuts and drank a bowl of punch and we talked abundantly together. About nine I retired and said my prayers.

26. I rose about 7 o'clock and read a chapter in Hebrew and some Greek. I said my prayers, and had cake and chocolate for breakfast. The weather was warm and clear, the wind southeast and pretty fresh. I took a walk till ten and then read some law till dinner, when I ate some hashed mutton of my maid's dressing. After dinner I took a little walk till 2 o'clock and then wrote some English till four. I gave the officers and the men some brandy and sugar to make punch to drink to their wives and mistresses and then took another walk till six and then read some French till seven; then I read some news to the captain till eight; then my maid Hannah washed my feet and about nine I retired and said my prayers. I slept but indifferently because I dreamed I was clapped.

27. I rose about 7 o'clock and read a chapter in Hebrew and some Greek. I said my prayers, and had cake and chocolate for breakfast. The weather was warm and clear, the wind about southeast and almost calm. This day we got our awning up to keep us from the sun, and about ten I read prayers to the ship's company. Then I got a prayer by heart and read some French till dinner and then ate broiled mutton. It grew calm in the afternoon and I took a walk till 2 o'clock and then read prayers in public again. Then I wrote some English till the evening and then took a walk. At night I read some French and then read a sermon to the captain and my maids till 9 o'clock, and then I retired and said my prayers but slept indifferently.

28. I rose about 6 o'clock and read a chapter in Hebrew and some Greek. I said my prayers, and had cake and chocolate for breakfast. The weather was cloudy and cold, the wind north and about 7 o'clock began to blow fresh, after it had been calm all night. I took a walk till ten and then read some law. My man was sick again with the great motion of the ship. I ate broiled mutton for dinner. After dinner I took a walk and then wrote some English till the evening and then I walked again but it blew pretty cold at north. I read some French and then some news to the captain. Then I ate some cake. About nine I retired and said my prayers, but slept very indifferently because of the motion of the ship.

29. I rose about 6 o'clock and read a chapter in Hebrew and some Greek. I said my prayers and had cake and chocolate for breakfast. The weather was clear and warm, the wind about east. My man was better. I took a walk till ten and then read law. Mr. Turner began to write some things for me. We had a sea-pie for dinner which the captain took the trouble to make himself. After dinner I took a walk till two and then wrote some English and picked over my sound apples from the rotten. At night I read some news to the captain. We had a bowl of punch and ate some roast chestnuts and I drank too much. About nine I retired and said my prayers. I was wakened with something like the apparition of my daughter Evelyn and soon after dreamed she died that moment of the smallpox, which God forbid. I dreamed she died about three o'clock in the morning at London. It rained much.

30. I rose about 6 o'clock and read a chapter in Hebrew and some Greek. I said my prayers, and had cake and chocolate for breakfast. I was melancholy from my dream about my daughter Evelyn. However, I walked and afterwards read some law till dinner, and then ate some roast fowl. After dinner I put several things in order and then took a walk, notwithstanding the ship had great motion. Then I wrote some English till the evening and examined Mr. Turner's writing. Then I took a walk again and at night read some French and then some news to the captain till 9 o'clock. It lightened and looked dirty astern. I slept pretty well till 4 o'clock and then the captain saw a light at the head of the topmast like a star, which often happens at sea.

31. I rose about 6 o'clock and read a chapter in Hebrew and some Greek. I said my prayers, and had cake and chocolate for breakfast. The weather was cloudy and cold, the wind east, and it blew very fresh. It rained so that I could not walk. Therefore I read more law till dinner, when I ate some mutton steak. After dinner I took a walk till two and then wrote some English till four and then took another walk till night, and then read some French and read some news to the captain. About nine I went to bed and neglected my prayers and could not sleep almost all night for the great motion of the ship, which rolled about intolerably the whole night long.

January 1720

1. I rose about 6 o'clock and read a chapter in Hebrew and some Greek. I said my prayers, and had cake and chocolate for breakfast. The weather was clear and warm, the wind east and moderate. About nine I took a walk and then read some law. I ordered my maid Annie to write a little every day. I ate some roast beef. After dinner I took a walk till 2 o'clock and then wrote some English till 4 o'clock and then took a walk again till six. Then the captain gave me a bowl of punch for the sake of the day and we had some roast chestnuts. I read some French and then read news to the captain. About 9 o'clock I found myself sleepy and retired and said my prayers and slept pretty well, thank God.

2. I rose about 6 o'clock and read a chapter in Hebrew and some Greek. I said my prayers, and had cake and chocolate for breakfast. The weather was warm and cloudy, the wind west for the first time this voyage. I took a walk till 9 o'clock and then read some law. I gave Mr. Turner some cake for writing for me. I ate some boiled beef for my dinner. After dinner I took a walk till two and then wrote some English till four when I ate three apples and then took a walk again till six and then read some French and some news to the captain. I gave some brandy and sugar to the officers and men to drink to their inclination. Mr. O-m-s got drunk and cursed me without provocation. I said little to him because he was drunk. About nine I retired and said my prayers.

3. I rose about 6 o'clock and found I had got cold, I believe by washing my cabin. I read, however, a chapter in Hebrew and some Greek. I said my prayers and had cake and chocolate for breakfast. Mr. O-m-s came of himself and asked my pardon for cursing me last night. About ten I read prayers to the ship's company and read some

English. The wind was west, which put our captain out of humor but the weather was clear and wind very moderate. I ate some pork and peas for dinner. In the afternoon I put some things in order and then read prayers again, and wrote some English. My cold fell into my eye and made it sore. I took a walk and in the evening read some English as long as my eye would let me. About eight I retired and said my prayers.

4. I rose about 6 o'clock and read a chapter in Hebrew and some Greek. I said my prayers, and had cake and chocolate for breakfast. I found my eye better because my indisposition went away in a small looseness. I had two loose stools. I took a walk and then read some law till dinner and then I ate some hashed fowl. After dinner I put several things in order and took a walk till two and then I wrote some English till four and then took another walk till night, when the wind grew calm. I read some English to the captain and we had some chestnuts and a bowl of punch. About 9 o'clock I retired and said my prayers and slept pretty well, thank God.

5. I rose about 6 o'clock and read a chapter in Hebrew and some Greek. I said my prayers, and had cake and chocolate for breakfast. The weather was warm and clear and little or no wind. My eye was pretty well again. About nine I took a walk and read some law till dinner and then ate some sea-pie. After dinner I put several things in order instead of walking and then I wrote some English till the evening and then took a walk till night and then read some French and some English to the captain aloud. I set some copy for my people who all took to writing. About nine I retired and said my prayers and slept pretty well, thank God.

6. I rose about 6 o'clock and read a chapter in Hebrew and some Greek. I said my prayers, and had cake and chocolate for breakfast. The weather was clear and warm, the wind west but very little, almost calm. I took a walk and then read some law till dinner and then ate some boiled beef. After dinner I took a walk till two and then wrote some English till the evening and then walked again. The weather was very pleasant and temperate. At night I wrote more

English till 8 o'clock and then I read some French till nine, when I retired and said my prayers. I slept but indifferently.

7. I rose about 6 o'clock and read a chapter in Hebrew and some Greek. I said my prayers, and had cake and chocolate for breakfast. The weather was temperate and clear but quite calm. There was a great disturbance about a man that lay with the servant woman and she got a suit of clothes from the boy but nobody was punished, by which it appears the captain had no authority. I read some law till dinner and then ate some roast fowl. After dinner I put several things in order because it was too hot to walk. Then I wrote some English till the evening and then walked for about an hour, and then I read some French and some English till 9 o'clock and then retired and said my prayers and dreamed that my daughter appeared to me with one hand only, from whence I [judged] that one of my daughters is dead, and because it was the left hand that was left, I concluded that the youngest daughter is alive and the other dead, as I dreamed before.

8. I rose about 6 o'clock and read a chapter in Hebrew and some Greek. I said my prayers, and had cake and veal broth for breakfast. The weather was warm and clear, the wind northwest. There was a great commotion among the people in the ship, and the captain beat one of the servants because he would not pick oakum. I read some law till dinner and then ate some salt fish and eggs. After dinner I put several things in order but it was too hot to walk. I read some English till the evening and then walked about an hour. At night I read a little French and some English till eight and then I made Annie wash my legs. About nine I retired and said my prayers and slept pretty well, thank God.

9. I rose about 6 o'clock and read a chapter in Hebrew and some Greek. I said my prayers and had cake and veal broth for breakfast. The weather was clear and cool, the wind northeast and fresh. I took a walk till nine and then read some law till dinner and then I ate some boiled beef. After dinner I put several things in order because it was too hot to walk; then I read some English till the evening, and then I took a walk till night, when the captain gave me a bowl of punch

and we had some chestnuts roasted. I gave brandy and sugar to the people as usual, only instead of the first mess of the officers I gave to the second. I read some French and some English to the captain till 9 o'clock and then I retired and slept very bad, being too hot.

10. I rose about 6 o'clock and read a chapter in Hebrew and some Greek. I said my prayers and had cake and veal broth for breakfast. The weather was clear and warm, the wind southeast and fresh. At ten we went to prayers. Then I read some English and got a prayer by heart. I ate some hogs' haslet for dinner. After dinner I took a nap because I slept but little last night. About three I read prayers again and afterwards read some English till four and then took a walk and in my life I never saw so fine an evening. I read some English only, because I was very sleepy. About eight I retired and said my prayers. I slept pretty well till 2 o'clock and very little afterwards.

11. I rose about 6 o'clock and read a chapter in Hebrew and some Greek. I said my prayers, and had cake and veal broth for breakfast. The weather was clear and warm, the wind south and pretty fresh. I took a walk till nine and then read some law till dinner and then ate some roast pork. After dinner I put several things in order and then took a walk till two and then wrote some English till the evening, when it began to blow hard. At night I wrote some English and read some French till 9 o'clock and then retired and said my prayers and slept till 2 o'clock pretty well but afterwards ill.

12. I rose about 6 o'clock and read a chapter in Hebrew and some Greek. I said my prayers and ate cake and veal broth for breakfast. The weather was cold and cloudy, the wind northwest and fresh. My girl Annie was sick. I read some law till dinner and then ate some plum pudding. After dinner I put several things in order till two and then wrote some English till the evening and then took a walk till night and then wrote more English till eight and then read some English till nine and then retired and said my prayers. I slept but indifferently because the ship rolled intolerably.

13. I rose about 6 o'clock and read a chapter in Hebrew and some Greek. I said my prayers, and had cake and veal broth for breakfast. The wind was northeast and the weather cool and cloudy. I took a walk and then read law till dinner and then ate some boiled pork. My maid Annie was better and began to write and walk again. I took a walk and then wrote some English till the evening. Took a walk again till night and then wrote more English till eight and then read some English till 9 o'clock and then retired and said my prayers and slept pretty well, thank God.

14. I rose about 6 o'clock and read a chapter in Hebrew and some Greek. I said my prayers, and had cake and veal broth for breakfast. The weather was cold and cloudy, the wind northeast and fresh. I took a walk till nine and then read law till dinner. I ate some roast fowl. After dinner I put several things in order and did not take my walk but wrote some English till four and then was hindered from walking by the rain. It blew very fresh and we went at a great rate. At night I wrote more English till 8 o'clock and then read some English till nine and then retired and said my prayers but slept indifferently.

15. I rose about six and read a chapter in Hebrew and some Greek. I said my prayers, and had cake and broth for breakfast. The weather was cold and cloudy, the wind northeast, and blowing fresh. I took my walk till nine and then read law till dinner and then I ate some roast fowl. After dinner I put several things in order and then took a walk and then wrote some English till the evening, and then took a walk till night, and then wrote more English till 8 o'clock when I read some English and then retired and said my prayers and slept very well, thank God.

16. I rose about 6 o'clock and read a chapter in Hebrew and some Greek. I said my prayers, and had cake and veal broth for breakfast. The wind was northeast and blew little, the weather cold and cloudy. I took a walk and then read some law till dinner, when I ate some duck very well dressed. After dinner I put several things in order and then wrote some English till the evening and then took a walk

at night, and then read some of my writings to the captain and we
had a bowl of punch and I ate some cake and cheese and some chestnuts. Then I read some English till nine and retired and said my
prayers.

17. I rose about 6 o'clock and read a chapter in Hebrew and some
Greek. I said my prayers, and had cake and broth for breakfast. I
gave abundance of cake away to the men because it was mouldy. The
weather was clear and warm, the wind north but almost calm. About
ten I read prayers to the ship's company and then took a walk. I got
a prayer by heart and read some English till the evening and then
took a walk till night when I read some English till 9 o'clock and then
I retired and found I had a sore throat. I slept but indifferently. We
had very fine weather. We expect to see Bermudas.

18. I rose about 6 o'clock and read a chapter in Hebrew and some
Greek. I said my prayers and had cake and broth for breakfast. The
weather was warm and clear, the wind south but very little. I took a
walk till nine and then read some law till dinner, and then ate some
hashed fowl. After dinner I put several things in order and did not
walk because it was hot. I read several letters and other papers relating to Virginia, and ate two apples. In the evening I took a walk
till night, when I read more papers till 8 o'clock and then read some
English till nine and then retired but slept indifferently. We expected to see Bermudas but failed.

19. I rose about 6 o'clock and read a chapter in Hebrew and some
Greek. I said my prayers and had cake and broth for breakfast. The
weather was clear and hot, the wind southwest. I took a walk. We
hoped still to see Bermudas but could not so we believe we were to
the west of it. I read some law till dinner and then ate some roast
fowl. After dinner I put several things in order and then wrote some
English till the evening but I was hindered from walking by the rain.
At night I wrote more English till eight and then read some English
till nine and then retired, said my prayers, and slept pretty well, thank
God.

20. I rose about 6 o'clock and read a chapter in Hebrew and some Greek, and then said my prayers, and had cake and broth for breakfast. The wind was northeast and pretty fresh and cold. We saw a [gannet]. I took my walk and then read some law till dinner and then I ate some sea-pie. After dinner I put several things in order and then wrote some English till the evening and then took a walk but was forced to put on my coat for it was grown very cold. At night I wrote more English till 9 o'clock and then I retired and said my prayers and slept but indifferently.

21. I rose about 6 o'clock and read a chapter in Hebrew and some Greek. I said my prayers, and had cake and broth for breakfast. The weather was cold and clear, the wind northwest and blowing fresh and cold. However, I took my walk till nine and then read some law till dinner and then ate some haslet. After dinner I put several things in order and then wrote some English till the evening and then walked a little but was driven in by the rain. At night I wrote more English till 8 o'clock and then read English till nine and then retired and said my prayers but slept extremely ill because of the ship's motion. A bird blew aboard called a murre.

22. I rose about 6 o'clock and read a chapter in Hebrew and some Greek. I said my prayers, and had cake and broth for breakfast. The weather was cold and clear, the wind northwest. I took a walk. The bird that blew aboard we cast into the water and it dove and we saw it no more. I read some law till dinner and then ate some roast pork. After dinner I put several things in order and then wrote some English till the evening and then took a walk. At night I wrote more English till 9 o'clock and then retired and said my prayers but could not sleep at all for there blew a terrible storm all night that threw everything about the cabin and overset my great chest. The storm continued all night with thunder and lightning which seemed very near us.

23. I rose about 7 o'clock and read a chapter in Hebrew and a little Greek, but the motion of the ship made me sick with my want of sleep. I said my prayers, and ate some cake for breakfast. The storm

continued. I took a nap till 12 o'clock and then ate some broiled pork for dinner. After dinner I put several things in order and wrote nothing but read several papers till the evening. I could not walk because it rained and blew very hard. At night the captain and I had a bowl of punch and I ate some bread and cheese. Then I read some English and said my prayers but slept very indifferently because it blew violently.

24. I rose about 6 o'clock and read a chapter in Hebrew and some Greek. I said my prayers, and had cake and broth for breakfast. The weather was cloudy, cold, and stormy, the wind northwest. I read some English till 10 o'clock and then read prayers to the ship's company. Then I got a prayer by heart till dinner and ate some more broiled pork. The steward fell down and hurt himself. After dinner I put several things in order and then read some English till the evening and then walked about the cabin, for it was so wet and cold I could not look out. At night I read more English till 8 o'clock and then retired and said my prayers and slept better than I ever did aboard ship, for the water grew smooth and quiet.

25. I rose about 7 o'clock and read a chapter in Hebrew and some Greek. I said my prayers, and had cake and broth for breakfast. The weather was clear and cold, the wind southwest and almost calm. I walked till ten and then read some law till dinner and then I ate some plum pudding. After dinner I put several things in order and then wrote more English till the evening, and then took a walk till six and then wrote more English. The wind shifted often upon us that we weathered the ship several times. About nine I retired and said my prayers but slept indifferently. Some part of the night it blew very hard.

26. I rose about 6 o'clock and read a chapter in Hebrew and some Greek. I said my prayers, and had cake and broth for breakfast. The weather was cold and cloudy and the wind blew violently at north. However I took a walk and then read law till dinner and then ate roast pork and began to drink beer. After dinner I put several things in order and then wrote some English till the evening and then be-

cause it was bad weather I could not walk. At night I wrote more English till 9 o'clock and then retired but slept but indifferently because I had Cape Hatteras in my head. However, I said my prayers.

27. I rose about 6 o'clock and read a chapter in Hebrew and some Greek. I said my prayers and had nothing for breakfast because the fire was made so late. The weather was cold and cloudy, the wind northeast. About 9 o'clock we saw the color of the water was changed so we sounded the lead and found about twenty fathoms water which made us act to get clear of Cape Hatteras. I walked a little and then read some law till dinner and then ate some roast duck. After dinner I put several things in order and then read some English till 5 o'clock and then took my walk, notwithstanding it blew very hard at night. I read some English till nine and then retired, said my prayers, and slept pretty well, thank God.

28. I rose about 6 o'clock and read a chapter in Hebrew and some Greek. I said my prayers and had cake and broth for breakfast. The weather was clear and warm, the wind southeast and pretty moderate. I took a walk till nine and then read some law till dinner and then ate some roast fowl. After dinner I put several things in order and drew off my keg of brandy, but upon inquiry I found I had lost four bottles that were in the steward's custody. He swore he had not meddled with them, but I believed him not. Then I wrote some English till the evening and then took my walk. About six we found ground again. The captain paid me a bowl of punch that I won. I read some English to him till 9 o'clock and then I retired, but slept indifferently. However, I said my prayers.

29. I rose about 6 o'clock and read a chapter in Hebrew and some Greek. I said my prayers, and had cake and broth for breakfast. The weather was clear and cold, the wind northeast. About 9 o'clock we saw the land about five leagues from us. I took a walk till ten and then wrote some English and put several things in order till dinner when I ate some pork and peas. After dinner I put several things in order again till four and then took a walk. It was very cold. At night I

wrote more English till 8 o'clock and then read some English till nine and then retired and slept pretty well and said my prayers.

30. I rose about 6 o'clock and read a chapter in Hebrew and some Greek. I said my prayers and had cake and broth for breakfast. The weather was cold and cloudy, the wind southeast and it rained. We saw land all the morning, notwithstanding it was very dark. I put several things in order and wrote some English till dinner, when I ate some roast fowl. After dinner there came up a terrible northeaster just as we were entering the Cape that almost carried away all our mast. It was a grief to us to take our departure thus from the Cape. However, it is the fortune of the sea. It was very cold and the ship rolled intolerably. I wrote some English till the evening and went to bed at six to keep myself warm but could not sleep the whole night for the motion of the ship. However, I said my prayers.

31. I rose about 8 o'clock and found the storm continued and it was so cold that I only read a chapter in Hebrew and a little Greek. I said my prayers, and ate some cake for breakfast. The motion of the ship remained very bad and carried the captain's quarters and him to leeward and broke his head and one of the seamen broke a hole through the gallery door. We had nothing for dinner but bread and cheese because the cook could make no fire. I could do very little all day because of the cold and the motion of the ship and we drove about three miles out of our way without any sail. But in the evening we set the mainsail, notwithstanding the storm, and did not tumble so much. In the evening the storm abated. I read some English and went to bed about 7 o'clock but it was so cold I could hardly keep myself warm. However, I said my prayers and slept pretty well, thank God.

February 1720

1. I rose about 7 o'clock and read a chapter in Hebrew and some Greek. I said my prayers, and had cake and broth for breakfast. The weather was exceedingly cold, the wind still northwest but moderate. My maid Hannah had an ague. I took a walk and then wrote some English till dinner when I ate some salt beef and a pease pudding. After dinner I wrote some English till the evening and then took a walk till night and then read some English till 9 o'clock ·when I retired and said my prayers. I slept pretty well, and had a nocturnal pollution not altogether asleep. We found ground at about twenty fathoms.

2. I rose about 7 o'clock and read a chapter in Hebrew and some Greek. I said my prayers, and had cake and broth for breakfast. The weather was cold and cloudy, the wind south, and it rained a little. We had ground at seven fathoms. I wrote some English till dinner and then ate some roast flesh. After dinner I wrote more English till the evening. We saw land again but it was calm that we could not approach till the evening and then we sailed into the Cape with a moderate gale and sailed in about seven leagues and then came to anchor, for which God be praised. I wrote several things and finished my business till nine and then retired and said my prayers and slept very well, thank God.

3. I rose about 7 o'clock and read a chapter in Hebrew but no Greek because I prepared to go ashore. However, I said my prayers, and had cake and broth for breakfast. About ten we weighed anchor but the wind was not favorable so we got but a little way and came again to anchor and had roast pork for dinner. It grew cold, the wind west, and pretty fresh. I wrote a bill of exchange for twenty-eight pounds and gave it the captain and because he told me it was too little

I tore it and said I would give him more. We drank a bottle of wine and talked of several matters till 9 o'clock and then I retired and said my prayers.

4. I rose about 7 o'clock and read nothing because I prepared to go ashore. I said my prayers, and had broth for breakfast, all my cake being gone. The weather was clear in the morning but grew cloudy about 11 o'clock and the wind blew fresh against us that we could make but a poor hand of it. I ate some plum pudding for dinner full of plums because it was to be the last. About 2 o'clock Mr. A-n-s came aboard for letters and told me all the news of the country. I was resolved to go ashore and therefore desired the captain to set me ashore at Captain Smith's which he granted and gave me nine guns at parting. It was two hours before I could get to the shore and then I gave the seamen ten shillings. Captain Smith received me very courteously and I had boiled milk for supper. I perceived I had the piles a little and in the night they grew very bad, hindering my sleep very much. I said a short prayer. It was very cold.

5. I rose about 8 o'clock but found my piles very bad and they gave me abundance of pain. However, I said a short prayer, and had boiled milk for breakfast. The weather was clear and cold, the wind northwest. About 12 o'clock I was in such pain I was forced to go to bed again where I had a little nap and could eat nothing for dinner but in the morning I had sent for Dr. Blair,[1] who did not come till the evening, when I was let blood and anointed with oil of [marsh-mallow]. I was a little easier and ate some chicken broth. The doctor stayed all night but I was the whole night in pain and could not sleep. In the morning I had more chicken broth and the doctor went away. My man Joe anointed me night and morning. It was very cold.

6. I slept a little after waking the whole night. I said a short prayer and had chicken broth for breakfast. Doctor Blair went away. I was a little easier, thank God, and began to get up but could not sit without great uneasiness. I ate some minced chicken. After dinner Colo-

1. Archibald Blair, a physician, brother of Commissary James Blair, was a member of the House of Burgesses from James City County.

nel Smith[2] came to see me, as Mr. A-n-s had done in the morning. The Colonel told me all the news. He was so kind as to stay all night. I ate some chicken broth for supper and was pretty well, thank God, but could not sit but the only place where I was easy was abed. I slept pretty well, thank God.

7. I found myself better and had milk and potato for breakfast. I said a short prayer. After breakfast Colonel Smith went away and Phil Lightfoot[3] came to see me and offered me his chariot to go to Williamsburg tomorrow. I thanked him kindly and accepted his offer. He stayed about two hours and then left me and went with my landlord to church. I sat up a little while but could not sit very easy, though I was better, thank God. My landlord sat with me a good while and at night I ate some potato and milk and said my prayers. I slept pretty well, thank God. My maid went last night to Major Custis.[4]

8. I rose about 9 o'clock. I said a short prayer and had milk and potato for breakfast. I was pretty easy, thank God. It was 11 o'clock before Mr. Lightfoot and his chariot came. Then I gave the servants ten shillings and took leave of my good landlord and went to Williamsburg and by the way overtook Major Custis and went to his house where several gentlemen came to see me, and particularly Colonel Ludwell,[5] Mr. Blair,[6] Mr. Roscow,[7] Frank Lightfoot,[8] Ben

2. Colonel John Smith, member of the Council of Virginia and a governor of the College of William and Mary. The Captain Smith with whom Byrd was staying was probably of the same Gloucester County family.

3. Colonel Philip Lightfoot, of Sandy Point, Charles City County, member of the Council, one of the richest men in Virginia.

4. John Custis, of Queen's Creek, had been married to Frances Parke, sister of Lucy Parke Byrd.

5. Colonel Philip Ludwell, II, Green Springs, James City County, member of the Council, trustee of the College, and vestryman of Bruton Parish.

6. James Blair, Commissary to Virginia from the Bishop of London; founder and president of the College of William and Mary, and member of the Council.

7. James Roscow, to whom Byrd had sold the office of receiver general.

8. Francis Lightfoot, presumably the brother of Colonel Philip Lightfoot.

Harrison,[9] and John Randolph.[10] By the last I sent a letter to the Governor with several others that I brought to him from England. Dr. Blair came likewise and he and Mr. Roscow dined with us and I ate some goose. My goods came to town in the Major's cart and were put into his store. I ate some milk and potato for supper and about 9 o'clock retired and was pretty easy, thank God.

9. I rose about 8 o'clock and ate milk and potato. I found myself pretty easy, thank God, and said my prayers. The weather was warm and cloudy. About 10 o'clock John Randolph brought me the answer from the Governor that put an end to all my thoughts of peace. Major Holloway[11] happened to be by and Major Custis. I took the Governor's answer in writing and then read it to John Randolph that we might be sure it was right. Then came the Commissary and he and Major Holloway dined with us and I ate some roast turkey. After dinner we sat and talked of the public affairs. I wondered Mr. Clayton[12] came not among my visitors but it was for fear of the Governor which kept several other gentlemen from coming. At night I had potato and milk and about 9 o'clock retired and said my prayers. I found myself better, thank God.

10. I rose about 8 o'clock and said my prayers and had potato and milk for breakfast. Then I sent my man to Mr. Clayton's to let him know if I was not sick I should have waited on him, which courteous reproach brought him about 10 o'clock. I sat with him half an hour and then took leave of him and the Major and went in Colonel Ludwell's coach to his house[13] where I got about 12 o'clock and found

9. Benjamin Harrison, the young son of Byrd's old friend and neighbor, Benjamin Harrison of Berkeley, who died in 1710.

10. John Randolph, son of Colonel William Randolph I.

11. Major John Holloway, a member of the House of Burgesses for York County, later elected speaker.

12. John Clayton, attorney general for Virginia, and a burgess for James City County.

13. Colonel Ludwell's home at Green Springs, about five miles from Williamsburg, was an estate settled by Sir William Berkeley, governor of Virginia. It came into the Ludwell family when Berkeley's widow married Philip Ludwell, Sr.

the family well. Stith Bolling and Will Drummond dined with us, and I ate some bacon. After dinner the Colonel and I discoursed of several matters and I read some of my work to him with which he seemed well satisfied. In the evening we drank tea and my cousin Hannah[14] sang and played on the b-s-l. We sat and talked till ten and then retired and I slept pretty well, thank God.

11. I rose about 8 o'clock and found myself much better, thank God. I said a short prayer, and had milk for breakfast. About 11 o'clock Mr. Blair came and then Mr. Holloway and I read several of my papers and we discoursed of several things relating to the Governor till dinner and then I ate some bacon. After dinner we read more of my papers till the evening and then we drank tea and heard Miss Hannah sing, who has a pretty voice. We sat and talked till 10 o'clock and then retired and I neglected my prayers but slept pretty well, thank God.

12. I rose about 8 o'clock and was better, thank God. I said my prayers and had milk and potato for breakfast. I wrote several letters to England and got the Colonel's man to copy them. Mr. Blair and Mr. Holloway went away and the Colonel and I took a walk in the orchard, notwithstanding the wind blew cold. I let them taste of my broth, which they liked very well. I ate some boiled beef for dinner. After dinner I made an end of writing my letters and desired Colonel Ludwell to give them to Captain Randolph. I said my prayers and slept pretty well, thank God. It was exceedingly cold, the wind northwest.

13. I rose about 8 o'clock and found myself pretty easy. I said my prayers and ate some roast duck for breakfast because I was to travel. The weather was cold again. About 10 o'clock I took leave and was carried to the ferry in Colonel Ludwell's coach where we warmed ourselves and then were carried over the river where I found Colonel Hill's[15] coach ready to receive us on the other side. Then I proceeded

14. Daughter of Philip Ludwell. In 1722 she married Thomas Lee.

15. They crossed the Chickahominy River, probably at Barrett's Ferry. Colonel Edward Hill lived at Shirley on the James River, near Westover.

home but very slow because the roads were fresh and I did not get home till the evening, when I found. thank God, all things got lately in pretty good order. I kept Colonel Hill's coach all night. I ate some boiled beef for supper and then retired and slept pretty well.

14. I rose about 7 o'clock and read nothing because I went to look upon everything and to rummage. I had boiled milk for breakfast, but neglected my prayers. The weather was cold and clear. I found several things extremely amiss and many matters in which my cousin Brayne had been to blame. However, I gave him gentle words but told him of his faults. Among the rest I found he had spoiled my guns and drunk up abundance of my wine. However, I carried it kindly to him. I could not go to church but invited my cousin Harrison[16] and her son to dinner with me and I ate some boiled beef. After dinner we sat and talked till the evening and then she went away and I took a walk and read a little and ate milk and potato for supper. I said my prayers and slept pretty well. I began to kiss my girl Annie.

15. I rose about 7 o'clock and read a chapter in Hebrew and some Greek. I said my prayers, and had boiled milk for breakfast. I put several things in order till about 12 o'clock and then came Drury Stith[17] and his son John Stith and Colonel Eppes to dine with me, but I told them I was to dine with Mrs. Harrison and invited them to go with me which they all did except John Stith and I ate some boiled beef. After dinner my cousin Grymes came to visit me but not finding me came to Mrs. Harrison's and in the evening walked home with me and we talked about state affairs till 10 o'clock and then retired. I neglected my prayers, for which God forgive me.

16. I rose about 6 o'clock and read a little Hebrew and a little Greek. I said my prayers, and had chocolate for breakfast. The weather was warm and cloudy, the wind northeast. We took a walk and then walked to Mrs. Harrison's but returned back to dine with me and I would have brought Mrs. Harrison with me but she would

16. Elizabeth Burwell, widow of Benjamin Harrison, of Berkeley, adjacent to Westover on the James River.

17. Drury Stith of Charles City County.

not come; however, my cousin Ben came and dined with us and I ate some boiled pork. After dinner we sat and talked till the evening and then Major Mumford[18] came. We walked with Mr. Grymes almost as far as Mrs. Harrison's where he lay, and Major Mumford returned home with me and we talked of all my affairs till 9 o'clock and then retired and said my prayers.

17. I rose about 7 o'clock and read nothing because I had business to do with Major Mumford. However, I said my prayers and had milk for breakfast, but the Major had chocolate. We talked of several matters till about 11 o'clock when Dick Cocke came and stayed to dinner and I ate some roast beef. While we were at dinner young Parson Robinson[19] came and dined with us. After dinner we sat and talked till about 4 o'clock, when the Major and the rest of the company took their leave, when I took a walk about the plantation till the evening, and then read some Hebrew and some Greek and about 9 o'clock went to bed and kissed Annie till I spent, for which God forgive me.

18. I rose about 7 o'clock and read a chapter in Hebrew and some Greek. I said my prayers, and had milk and potato for breakfast. The weather was clear and warm, the wind west. I put several things in order till 12 o'clock and then Frank Hardyman and Llewellin Eppes came to dine with me and I gave them some boiled pork. They stayed after dinner till 4 o'clock and then went away. Henry Anderson came and brought me word that all was well above at my quarters at the Falls. In the evening he and I took a walk about the plantation. He stayed all night and I wrote a letter for him to carry to the overseer. We talked of several things but he told me he had found a coal mine near the Falls of very good coal. We talked till 9 o'clock and then retired and I said my prayers.

18. Major Robert Mumford, a burgess from Prince George County, Byrd's lawyer and general business agent.

19. James Robertson, minister of Westover Church. (Byrd wrote 'Robinson' and 'Robertson' interchangeably.)

19. I rose about 7 o'clock and read a chapter in Hebrew and some Greek. I said my prayers, and had potato and milk for breakfast. The weather was clear and warm, the wind northwest. I put several things in order till 12 o'clock and then Captain Harwood[20] and his kinsman came to visit me and stayed to dinner and I ate some boiled beef. After dinner we sat and talked of the public affairs and I found them against the court. I seemed to favor their party and gained their hearts. About 4 o'clock they took leave and I walked about the plantation till the evening and then wrote in my journal till nine and then retired and said my prayers.

20. I rose about 7 o'clock and read a chapter in Hebrew and some Greek. I said my prayers, and had milk and potato for breakfast. The weather was cold and it rained for about an hour. I continued to put several things in order till dinner and then I ate some tripe and [cow-heel] with only my cousin Brayne. After dinner I put more things in order till the evening and then took a walk about the plantation. My overseer asked leave to go to Mr. Bland's[21] and Captain Turner's man brought me several things from Major Mumford. I had a quarrel with my man Joe and beat him for being very saucy, after which he was very sullen and very good. In the evening I wrote in my journal till nine and then retired and said my prayers.

21. I rose about 7 o'clock and read a chapter in Hebrew and some Greek and had milk and potato for breakfast. The weather was clear and cold, the wind northwest. I put several things in order, notwithstanding it was Sunday. I sent my people to prayers, though I could not go to them myself. Mrs. Harrison sent me some fish and I invited her and her son to come to dine with me and about one they brought Master Frank Lightfoot with them. I ate some fish. After dinner Frank went away but Mrs. Harrison stayed till the evening and then I took a walk till the evening [sic] and wrote in my journal and then retired.

22. I rose about 7 o'clock and read a chapter in Hebrew and some Greek. I said my prayers, and had milk and potato for breakfast. The

20. Captain Samuel Harwood, burgess from Charles City County.
21. Richard Bland of Jordan's Point, across the James River from Westover.

weather was cold and clear, the wind northwest. I put several matters in order till 11 o'clock and then came Ned Goodrich[22] to whom I showed my public papers. About 1 o'clock came Colonel Randolph[23] and his brother Dick,[24] Parson Robinson, and Parson Finney[25] and they all dined with me and I ate some boiled beef. After dinner we walked in the garden till four and then the company went away and I took a walk about the plantation. After dinner John Grills and John Banister[26] came and stayed a little while but went away again with Mr. Goodrich across the river. I wrote in my journal till nine and then retired and said my prayers.

23. I rose about 7 o'clock and read a chapter in Hebrew and some Greek. I said my prayers, and had boiled milk for breakfast. The weather was clear and cold, the wind northwest. I was very busy in putting things in order till dinner and then I ate some broiled pork with my cousin Brayne only. After dinner I put more things in order till about 4 o'clock when Captain Posford came and stayed about an hour and told me he was going to Williamsburg. When he was gone I took a little walk but it looked as if it would rain. In the evening I wrote in my journal till nine and then retired and said my prayers.

24. I rose about 6 o'clock and read a chapter in Hebrew and some Greek. I said my prayers, and had milk and potato for breakfast. The weather was cold and cloudy, the wind northeast. Till 2 o'clock I put things in order and then ate some roast duck. After dinner Captain Harrison[27] came and I caused some victuals to be got for him and I

22. Colonel Edward Goodrich, burgess from Prince George County until his death in November, 1720.

23. Colonel William Randolph II, eldest son of William Randolph I of Turkey Island, burgess from Henrico County.

24. Richard Randolph of Curles, fifth son of Colonel William Randolph I.

25. William Finney, minister of Henrico Parish.

26. John Banister, son of the botanist John Banister, who had been a friend of Byrd's father. Banister acted as a business manager for Byrd. In 1724 he became collector of the upper James River District.

27. Captain Henry Harrison, a burgess from Surry County.

ate some roast pigeon with him again. I read to him several of my books of what I had done in England and talked everything over with him, because he was a man of factor in the House of Burgesses. At night we drank a bottle of wine till 9 o'clock and then retired and I said my prayers but committed uncleanness with Annie.

25. I rose about 6 o'clock and read a chapter in Hebrew and some Greek. I said my prayers, and drank chocolate with Captain Harrison. The weather was cold and clear, the wind north. The captain and I took a walk in the garden and talked of many things relating to the public till 12 o'clock and then came Captain L-s and a stranger with him and then came Mr. Clayton and then Colonel Harrison[28] and I ate some roast turkey. After dinner we sat and talked till 4 o'clock and then Captain Harrison and Captain L-s went away and then Mr. Clayton, but the Colonel stayed with me all night and we talked of many things till 10 o'clock and then retired and I committed uncleanness again with Annie, for which God forgive me.

26. I rose about 6 o'clock and read nothing because I wrote a letter to the Falls. I neglected my prayers, but drank chocolate with Captain [i.e. Colonel] Harrison. The weather was clear and warm. About 8 o'clock the Colonel and I walked to Mrs. Harrison's where we drank tea. Mr. Clayton went away to Williamsburg about 10 o'clock but the Colonel and I dined with my neighbor and I ate some bacon. After dinner we sat and talked till 3 o'clock and then I waited on the Colonel to the ferry where I took my leave. This day there came a beef and fourteen hogs from the Falls which were killed. I walked about the plantation till the evening and then read some Greek. I wrote in my journal till 9 o'clock and then retired and said my prayers.

27. I rose about 6 o'clock and read a chapter in Hebrew and a little Greek. I said my prayers, and had milk and potato for breakfast. The weather was clear and warm, the wind west. I put several things in order and examined matters till 11 o'clock, when Captains Posford

28. Colonel Nathaniel Harrison, of Wakefield, Surry County, a member of the Council (brother of Henry).

and Turner came and dined with me and I ate some hogs haslet. After dinner came my old gardener Tom Cross. About 4 o'clock the captains went away and I walked about with the gardener and talked abundantly with him about the garden. In the evening I talked with my man Frank who came from above. I read some Greek and washed my feet. About 9 o'clock I retired and said my prayers.

28. I rose about 6 o'clock and read a chapter in Hebrew and some Greek. I said my prayers, and had milk and potato for breakfast. The weather was clear and warm, the wind east. I put several things in order till 11 o'clock when Major Mumford came and I went with him to church where I saw many of my old friends who were glad to see me. Mr. Robinson gave us a sermon pretty good. After church I invited Colonel Hill and his daughter[29] and Drury Stith and his family but the last would not come, so took Captain Posford and Captain Turner and ate some roast beef. After dinner we sat and talked till 4 o'clock and then all went away but Major Mumford and he and I took a walk about the plantation and talked of many matters. In the evening I ordered something for Tom Cross that was sick and about nine retired and said my prayers.

29. I rose about 6 o'clock and read nothing because Major Mumford and I talked of several matters and I gave several orders before we went to Mr. Bland's. I said my prayers and had chocolate for breakfast with the Major. About 9 o'clock Captain Posford came and called us to go in his boat. We took up Mrs. Harrison and Mrs. Duke[30] by the way and got about 11 o'clock to Mr. Bland's and found him very much indisposed but very glad to see me. Here we found Mrs. Stith. We did not dine till 3 o'clock and then I ate some fish. After dinner we drank tea and about 5 o'clock took leave. I counselled Mr. Bland to drink milk from the cow every day which he promised me to take. We set Mrs. Harrison home and Captain Posford and I walked to my house and drank a glass of wine and then he went aboard. I inquired into the affairs of my family and about nine retired and said my prayers.

29. Elizabeth, daughter of Colonel Hill, later married John Carter.

30. Elizabeth Taylor Duke, widow of Henry Duke.

March 1720

1. I rose about 6 o'clock and read a chapter in Hebrew and some Greek in Isocrates. I said my prayers, and had milk and potato for breakfast. The weather was warm and cloudy, the wind southeast. I put several things in order till 11 o'clock and then Major Bolling came and I gave him my papers to read relating to Virginia. I set my boy to filling up the jugs of wine that my Cousin Brayne had emptied. Just before dinner came Robin Hix,[1] and the Major and he both dined with me and I ate some pie. After dinner we sat and talked till 4 o'clock and then my company went away. I had several of my people take sick and went to visit them. In the evening I walked to Mrs. Harrison's where I stayed till 8 o'clock and then walked home and was taken in the rain and very wet before I got home but I shifted myself and drank a glass of malmsey. I said my prayers. It rained almost all night.

2. I rose about 6 o'clock and read a chapter in Hebrew and some Greek. I said my prayers and had boiled milk for breakfast. The weather was warm and it rained a little. I had four people sick and I gave them physic and walked to the quarters to see them. I wrote a letter to England and then put several things in order till dinner and then several gentlemen came from the courthouse and dined with me, among whom was my old shipmate Mr. [Adam]. I ate some boiled beef. After dinner most of the company went away and I wrote a letter to Mr. Poythress and then took a walk and saw my sick people again and found them pretty well, thank God. At night I wrote to Mr. Bland in order to send it tomorrow morning. I said my prayers. It rained and thundered very much this night.

1. Robert Hix, an Indian trader and neighbor of Byrd.

3. I rose about 6 o'clock and read a chapter in Hebrew and some Greek. I said my prayers, and had milk for breakfast. The weather was cold and cloudy, the wind north. My people were better, thank God. My cousin Brayne and I had many quarrels about my affairs. I put several things in order and wrote a letter till dinner and then ate some stewed duck by myself for cousin Brayne was from home to get something that he had lent. After dinner I put several things in order and then wrote more letters and then took a walk till the evening and then wrote more letters till 9 o'clock and then retired and said my prayers.

4. I rose about 6 o'clock and read a chapter in Hebrew and some Greek. I said my prayers, and had milk and potato for breakfast. The weather was cold and clear, the wind north. My people were all well but Jenny, thank God. My cousin Brayne and I had many scolds. I wrote a letter to England and put several things in order till dinner and then I ate some tripe. After dinner Mr. Salle[2] and Mr. Dennis came and I talked a good deal to them and was very kind to them. My bricklayer came from Mr. Bland's. I took a walk with him about the plantation till the evening and then I wrote a letter to my brother Beverley[3] from whom I had received one. I said my prayers.

5. I rose about 6 o'clock and read a chapter in Hebrew and some Greek. I said my prayers and had milk for breakfast. The weather was warm and cloudy, the wind southwest. My people were pretty well, thank God. I put several things in order till about 11 o'clock and then came Major Kennon[4] to visit me. He stayed to dinner and I ate some roast beef. After dinner we sat about half an hour and then he went away and I put several things in order in the library and in the house till the evening when it rained so much that I could not walk.

2. Probably Abraham Salle, of Manakin Town, a Huguenot settlement on the upper James River.

3. Colonel Robert Beverley, who had married Byrd's sister Ursula, was author of *The History and Present State of Virginia* (1705). He lived at Beverley Park, King and Queen County.

4. Major William Kennon, sheriff of Henrico County.

At night I wrote some English till 9 o'clock and then retired and said my prayers.

6. I rose about 6 o'clock and read a chapter in Hebrew and some Greek. I said my prayers, and had milk and potato for breakfast. The weather was cold and clear, the wind northwest. I put several things in order in the library and danced my dance. I intended to go to prayers but my people did not tell me when the clerk came. I ate some roast beef for dinner. In the afternoon I walked in the garden and then danced again and put several things in order till the evening and then I walked about the plantation, and made a visit to the sick people at the quarters. At night I wrote a letter to England till 9 o'clock and then retired and said my prayers. I committed uncleanness.

7. I rose about 6 o'clock and read a chapter in Hebrew and some Greek. I said my prayers, and had milk for breakfast. The weather was clear and cold, the wind west. I put several things in order and then wrote a letter to England and then walked in the garden till dinner and then I ate some snipe. After dinner I put several things in order again about the house and worked hard till the evening and then I took a walk about the plantation and visited my bricklayer and found him working well. At night I wrote some English and ate some toast and milk. About 9 o'clock I said my prayers and retired.

8. I rose about 6 o'clock and read a chapter in Hebrew and some Greek. I said my prayers, and had boiled milk for breakfast. The weather was cold and clear, the wind east. I set several things in order and sent my cousin Brayne to Prince George Court to get in a debt. About 12 o'clock came Captain Posford and Mr. G-r-y but could not stay. I dined by myself and ate some fish. After dinner I walked in the garden and put everything in order in the library and the house and in the evening walked about the plantation. At night I wrote a letter to England till nine and then retired and said my prayers. It rained abundantly.

9. I rose about six and read a chapter in Hebrew and some Greek. I said my prayers, and had milk and potato for breakfast. The weather was cloudy and it rained in the morning till 10 o'clock and then held up. About twelve Captain Posford sent his boat for me to go on board his ship and when I came there I found Colonel Randolph and his brother Dick and Captain Drury Stith and John Stith. We were received very courteously with guns and I ate some bacon for dinner. After dinner we drank the King's health and were pretty merry and every time Captain Posford fired Captain Turner did the like. Here I stayed till 9 o'clock and then went home in the Captain's boat and I gave the people a crown. I said my prayers.

10. I rose about six and read nothing because I wrote letters all the morning to England. However, I said my prayers, and had milk and potato for breakfast. The weather was clear and warm, the wind southeast. I walked in the garden and put several things in order till dinner, and then ate some fish. After dinner I put several things in order till three and then Mrs. Duke came [with] a daughter of Captain Mallory.[5] They stayed till five and then I walked with them to Mrs. Harrison's where I found Mrs. Anderson[6] and her daughter. Here I stayed with them till 9 o'clock and then walked home and said my prayers. I felt Annie's belly this morning.

11. I rose about six and read a chapter in Hebrew and some Greek. I said my prayers and had boiled milk for breakfast. The weather was cold and clear, the wind west. I put several things in order and sealed up my letters that were to go by Captain Turner. About 1 o'clock came Mrs. Harrison, Mrs. Anderson and her daughter, Mrs. Duke and Mrs. Mallory and Ben Harrison to dine with me and I ate some pie for dinner. After dinner the ladies stayed till the evening and then went away and I took a walk about the plantation. At night I wrote some English and said my prayers.

5. Probably one of the daughters of Francis Mallory, sheriff of Prince George County, who died in 1719.

6. Mrs. Frances Anderson, widow of Reverend Charles Anderson, rector of Westover Parish from 1694 to 1718.

12. I rose about 6 o'clock and read a chapter in Hebrew and some Greek. I said my prayers, and had milk and potato for breakfast. The weather was cold and clear, the wind northwest. I put several things in order till 11 o'clock and then Major Mumford came with his son that he is sending to England. He went away but returned soon with Colonel Eppes and Captain Turner. They all dined with me and I ate some [cowheel]. After dinner I settled accounts with Captain Turner and took leave of him and the rest of the company and then took a walk about the plantation. I gave a peacock and hen to Mrs. Harrison. In the evening I settled several matters till 9 o'clock. I ate some milk and said my prayers.

13. I rose about 6 o'clock and read a chapter in Hebrew and some Greek. I said my prayers, and had milk for breakfast. The weather was cold and clear and a little frost, the wind east. I danced my dance and adjusted myself to go to church which I did about 11 o'clock and had a good sermon from Captain Robinson. After church I invited Drury Stith and his family and Colonel Eppes and his son to dinner and I ate some roast beef. We sat and talked till 5 o'clock and then the company departed except Major Mumford who stayed all night and we took a walk till the evening and then sat and talked till 10 o'clock and then I retired and said my prayers.

14. I rose about six and made Annie a visit. Then I read some Hebrew but no Greek because I did business with Major Mumford. I said my prayers and had chocolate for breakfast. The weather was cold and cloudy and it rained in the morning. So we settled several accounts till 11 o'clock and then took a walk about the plantation till dinner and then I ate some boiled beef. After dinner the Major went away and my people set him over the river and then I sent them aboard ship to get my letters and I received two only by Captain Llewellyn, who was sick. I liked not the contents of them. The sloop came down and brought shingles, &c. We lit a kiln of lime, notwithstanding it rained. I wrote a letter, ate some milk, and then retired and said my prayers. I slept but ill, because the cats kept me awake.

15. I rose about 6 o'clock and read a chapter in Hebrew and some Greek. I said my prayers and had milk and potato for breakfast. The weather was cold and cloudy, the wind southeast, and it rained much. I wrote a letter to send to New Kent by my cousin Brayne but he was thrown from his horse and bruised very much so could not go, but was bled and put to bed, where he vomited exceedingly. I ate some cold beef for dinner because the pork that was dressed was not good. After dinner I read some news and then danced my dance and then walked about the plantation. At night I ate some milk and wrote a letter to Major Mumford till 9 o'clock and then retired and said my prayers.

16. I rose about 6 o'clock and read a chapter in Hebrew and some Greek. I said my prayers, and had boiled milk for breakfast. The weather was cold and cloudy, the wind north and a small frost. I danced my dance and then settled several accounts and looked over several papers till dinner and then I ate some fish and sent my cousin Brayne some pudding, who was better, notwithstanding he lay abed all day. After dinner I put several things in order in the library till 6 o'clock and then took a walk about the plantation and at night read some news and gave audience to my people till 9 o'clock and then retired and said my prayers.

17. I rose about 6 o'clock and read a chapter in Hebrew and some Greek. I said my prayers, and had milk for breakfast. The weather was cold and clear, the wind west. I danced my dance and then settled several accounts and then walked to see my people at work. Mr. Brayne was better and wanted some brandy but I let him know to expect no such physic. I ate some boiled beef for dinner. After dinner I put several things in order in the library till 3 o'clock and then my things came from Captain Llewellyn and I unpacked several of them. I had a pain in my toe like the gout but moderate. In the evening I was in pain with my foot. Then I read some news till 9 o'clock, ate some milk, retired, and said my prayers. My sleep was very sweet.

18. I rose about 6 o'clock and read a chapter in Hebrew and some Greek. I said my prayers and had milk for breakfast. The weather was cold and clear, the wind east. I put several things in order till 10 o'clock and then I received a letter from Colonel Harrison which told me that the Duke of Argyll was made Governor of Virginia and that I was made his lieutenant governor. I wrote an answer to the Colonel and thanked him for his news, but did not believe it. My foot was better, thank God, and so was my cousin Brayne. I ate some stewed duck for dinner. After dinner I put several things in order and unpacked some things at the store. I walked about the garden very much. At night I read some news and discoursed my people and ate some toast and milk and about nine retired and said my prayers.

19. I rose about 6 o'clock and read a chapter in Hebrew and some Greek. I said my prayers, and had milk for breakfast. The weather was cold and clear, the wind northwest. I sent my boat to Appomattox and made a present of my wife's saddle to Mr. Mumford's daughter. I put several things in order and wrote a letter to the Falls. John Hardyman came to dine with me and I ate some pork and pease pudding for dinner. After dinner I settled accounts with Mr. Hardyman and he went away. Then came Captain L-s. I assisted my gardener to lay out some of the garden. In the evening I ate some toast and milk and wrote a letter. Then I had my feet washed till 9 o'clock and then retired and said my prayers. It snowed in the night pretty much.

20. I rose about 6 o'clock and read a chapter in Hebrew and some Greek. I said my prayers and had milk for breakfast. The weather began to clear up, the wind north and cold. I danced my dance and about 11 o'clock I went with my family to church where Dick W-l-t-n read prayers. Then I returned to dinner and ate some boiled beef. After dinner I put several things in order and then walked to Mrs. Harrison's where I found Mrs. Frank Hardyman. I stayed with them till the evening and then walked home and found Captain L-s-l-n people. I sent some [cheese] to Mrs. Harrison for a woman [that was] ready to lie in. I wrote a letter to Mr. Mumford and gave my orders to my people and about nine retired and said my prayers.

2 1. I rose about 6 o'clock and read a chapter in Hebrew and some Greek. I said my prayers, and had milk for breakfast. The weather was clear and cold, the wind west. My sloop went to Appomattox for tobacco and John Brayne set out for New Kent. I put several things in order till 11 o'clock and then Ben Harrison went with me on board Captain L-s-l-n to dinner where came Captain Stith. Poor L-s-l-n was lame but cheerful and entertained us very well. I ate some pork and peas. After dinner we had a bowl of punch and were merry. John Stith just called but did not stay but Captain L-s dined with us. We had several guns and stayed till 9 o'clock and ate some cold bacon and then returned and I was almost drunk but behaved very well and sent Billy home with Ben Harrison and retired but neglected my prayers.

2 2. I rose about six and read a chapter in Hebrew and some Greek. I said my prayers, and had milk and potato for breakfast. I found myself out of order after drinking. The weather was cold and clear, the wind west. I danced my dance and walked much in the garden. I settled some accounts and put things in order till dinner and then I ate some ox cheek. After dinner I put several things in order till 4 o'clock and then I read some English till the evening and then I took a walk about the plantation, and at night read some news till 9 o'clock and then retired and said my prayers. The bricklayer was taken sick and bled.

2 3. I rose about 6 o'clock and read a chapter in Hebrew and some Greek. I said my prayers, and had milk for breakfast. The weather was cold and clear, the wind northwest. The bricklayer took physic but it worked indifferently. I was out of humor at several things about my [house] and furniture. About 11 o'clock I got upon my horse to go to Colonel Hill's and Ben Harrison went with me. We got there about twelve and found Drury Stith there. We had a good dinner but I ate only bacon. After dinner we stayed till 5 o'clock and then I came home and I talked with my people and read some English till 9 o'clock and then retired and said my prayers.

2 4. I rose about 6 o'clock and read a chapter in Hebrew and some Greek in Isocrates. I said my prayers and had milk and potato for

breakfast. The weather was cold and a little frost, the wind northwest. My bricklayer was well again. I walked to Mrs. Harrison's in
hopes to procession my land[7] but the parson did not come, so that I
came back again about 1 o'clock and ate some roast beef for dinner.
Just after I had done Parson Fontaine[8] came and took the rest of my
dinner and then we walked about the garden and plantation. He is a
pretty kind of man and did not sign the address. At night we had
some buttered potatoes and drank a bottle of cider and sat and talked
till about 9 o'clock and then retired and I neglected my prayers.

25. I rose about 6 o'clock and read a chapter in Hebrew and some
Greek. I said my prayers, and had chocolate for breakfast. The
weather was warm and clear, the wind southwest. I walked about
with the parson till 10 o'clock and then he took leave and I could not
persuade him to stay and dine. I danced my dance and wrote in my
journal. I set a boy about cleaning the [w-t] till dinner and then ate
some fish. After dinner I put several things in order and read some
English till the evening when I walked about the plantation. At night
I read some English and ate milk for supper. At nine I said my
prayers.

26. I rose about 6 o'clock and read a chapter in Hebrew and some
Greek. I said my prayers and had boiled milk for breakfast. The
weather was warm and cloudy, but it rained a little. I danced my
dance and settled several accounts till 11 o'clock and then took a
walk in the garden till twelve when George Walker came and I
showed him everything with which he was well pleased. I ate some
[cowheel] for dinner. After dinner I walked with George Walker
to Mrs. Harrison's and then he went to Colonel Hill's and I walked

7. Every four years, under the supervision of the vestry, each man was obliged
to 'procession' or to walk along the boundaries of his land and renew the marks on
trees which indicated these boundaries. See *William and Mary Quarterly*, 3rd
Ser., VI (1949), 416-36.

8. Peter Fontaine, a Huguenot, came to Virginia in 1716, and was minister of
Westover Parish, 1720–57. He was chaplain on the boundary commission with Byrd
in 1728. His brother, Francis Fontaine, came to Virginia in 1720 and was minister
of St. Margaret's Parish in Caroline County, 1721–2.

home and Mrs. Harrison walked part of the way with me. Then I looked over my people and walked in the garden till the evening when I read some English. I ate some milk and said my prayers.

27. I rose about 6 o'clock and read a chapter in Hebrew and some Greek. I said my prayers, and had boiled milk for breakfast. The weather was warm and cloudy and it rained a little, the wind southwest. I put several things in order and danced my dance. About eleven I went to church where old Parson Robinson[9] gave us a sermon. After church I invited Colonel Eppes, Frank Hardyman and his wife and Mrs. Duke and Captain L-s to dine with us and I ate some roast beef. After dinner we sat and talked and walked in the garden till 5 o'clock and then the company went away and my cousin Brayne came from New Kent and I was displeased with his proceedings. I took a walk and at night wrote three letters and then retired and said my prayers. I committed uncleanness by kissing Annie.

28. I rose about 6 o'clock and read a chapter in Hebrew and some Greek. I said my prayers, and had boiled milk for breakfast. The weather was cold and clear, the wind northeast. I danced my dance and settled several accounts and then walked about the plantation and saw my people at work. My man Jack was sick and I caused him to be bled. I read some English till dinner and then ate some roast beef. After dinner I put several things in order till 4 o'clock and then George Walker came to let me taste of his wine. He stayed about an hour and then I walked about the plantation till night and then ate some milk and said my prayers.

29. I rose about 6 o'clock and read a chapter in Hebrew and some Greek. I said my prayers, and had boiled milk for breakfast. The weather was dark and cloudy, the wind southeast. I danced my dance and put several things in order. About 10 o'clock came George Walker and Mr. Cargill[10] and about eleven came Frank Hardyman and his wife and we went aboard Captain L-s about 1 o'clock in the rain,

9. George Robertson, minister of Bristol Parish, 1693–1739.

10. Reverend John Cargill, minister of Southwark Parish, in Surry County, 1708–23.

where we dined very indifferently and I ate some salt beef and pea soup. We were pretty merry; however, it rained all day and all the evening so that at last I agreed to go with Mrs. Duke home provided they would all dine with me tomorrow, so I wrote a letter home and then we went to Mrs. Duke's where we sat and talked till 10 o'clock and then Mr. Cargill and I lay together. I neglected my prayers.

30. I rose about 6 o'clock and read nothing but talked with Mr. Cargill abundantly of the Commissary. The weather was cloudy and warm and threatened more rain. About 9 o'clock I ate some rice milk for breakfast. Then I took a walk and Mr. Cargill went away. About 12 o'clock Captain L-s sent the boat to carry us to my house and we got there about 1 o'clock and Mr. Hardyman and his wife and her two sisters[11] with us. I ate some boiled beef. After dinner we walked in the garden and talked till 4 o'clock and then the company all went away but Mrs. Duke and she went over the river about 6 o'clock and Captain C-k came very drunk to my house and I walked with him to Mrs. Harrison's to keep him from falling down the bank. There I found his wife and stayed about half an hour and then returned home where I had a petition against my man Joe who would not allow the people small beer. I did them right and about nine retired and said my prayers. It rained all night.

31. I rose about 6 o'clock and read a chapter in Hebrew and some Greek. I said my prayers, and had boiled milk for breakfast. The weather was cold and cloudy, the wind northwest, and it rained a little. I danced my dance and then wrote several letters to send to Williamsburg by my cousin Brayne. Then I wrote a letter to England and then walked in the garden till dinner and then ate some roast beef. After dinner I walked to see my workmen and my people in the garden and then wrote another letter to England and in the evening walked about the plantation. At night I read some English and ate some milk till 9 o'clock and then retired and said my prayers.

11. Mrs. Frank Hardyman, Mrs. John Hardyman, Mrs. Greenhill, and Mrs. Duke were sisters, daughters of Mr. Taylor.

April 1720

1. I rose about 6 o'clock and read a chapter in Hebrew and some Greek. I said my prayers, and had milk and potato for breakfast. The wind was northwest, the weather cold and clear. I danced my dance and walked about to see my people, who began this day to pull down the [wash-house]. I wrote a letter to England and then walked in the garden till dinner and then I ate some [cowheel.] After dinner I put several things in order and then read some English and walked much among my people. I sent 200 bushels of salt to Appomattox in the evening. I took a walk about the plantation till the evening and at night ate some milk and wrote a letter to Appomattox, and read some English till 9 o'clock and then retired.

2. I rose about 6 o'clock and read a chapter in Hebrew and some Greek. I said my prayers and had milk for breakfast. The weather was clear and cold, the wind northwest. I danced my dance and then walked about to see my people work, and then settled several accounts and put several things in order till one o'clock and then came George Walker and Captain L-s to dine with me and I ate some pork and pease pudding. After dinner I settled accounts with Captain L-s and then they both went away and I walked to see my people, who made a good day's work and I gave them a dram in the evening. The [n-t-king] and two other Indians came and I gave them victuals and put them over the river. At night I read some English till nine, ate some milk, and then retired and said my prayers.

3. I rose about 6 o'clock and read a chapter in Hebrew and some Greek. I said my prayers, and had milk for breakfast. The weather was warm and clear, the wind southwest. I danced my dance and walked in the garden till 11 o'clock and then I went to church where

the clerk read prayers. After church I came home and read some Latin till dinner and then ate some boiled beef. After dinner I walked a little and then took a nap. Then my cousin Brayne returned from Williamsburg but could get me no freight but brought me several excuses from the masters of the ships. In the evening I walked about the plantation till the evening [*sic*] and then I wrote a letter to Major Merriweather[1] about my tobacco in New Kent. I had my feet washed and about 9 o'clock retired and said my prayers.

4. I rose about 6 o'clock and read a chapter in Hebrew and some Greek. I said my prayers, and had milk for breakfast. The weather was warm and clear, the wind west. My maid Rose had endeavored to steal a sheep from Jack, for which reason I caused her to be whipped. About 10 o'clock I went over the river and went to visit good Mr. Bland whom I found extremely ill, so that he just knew me. I could not forbear crying to see my friend so bad. I ate some cider and toast and about 2 o'clock took leave and went with John Grills to Major Mumford's but called at John's house and stayed a little while and drank some good beer, then proceeded to the Major's and found him and his family in good health. I ate some turkey and then John Grills returned to Mr. Bland's again. The Major and I sat and talked of many things and about 9 o'clock I retired and said my prayers.

5. I rose about 6 o'clock and read a chapter in Hebrew and a little Greek. I said my prayers, and had chocolate for breakfast. The weather was warm and clear, the wind northwest. I gave the Major's five daughters each twenty pounds for a piece of plate. I walked about and we talked till about 11 o'clock and then the company began to come that were designed for the christening. There came abundance of company and I and Dick Kennon with Jenny Bolling[2] were gossips. We danced a little before dinner and then I ate some bacon and fowl. After dinner we danced and were merry and at night some danced and some drank and we were all pleased till 10

1. Major Nicholas Merriweather, a burgess from New Kent County.

2. Probably Jane Bolling, daughter of Major John Bolling, and her cousin Richard Kennon. 'Gossips' were godparents.

o'clock and then the company went home and we went to bed and I said my prayers.

6. I rose about 7 o'clock and read a little Greek. I said a short prayer, and had chocolate for breakfast. The weather was cloudy and warm, the wind west. We settled several matters and the girls and I danced till 11 o'clock and then we took leave of the ladies and the Major and I went to dine with Will Kennon, and there Parson Robinson met us and Major Bolling.[3] I ate some ox cheek. After dinner we sat and talked till 4 o'clock and then went to Major Bolling's where we drank punch and several good things, but ate nothing having dined pretty late. Mrs. Bolling is a clean, good woman and everybody was very courteous to me. We kept Parson Robinson with us and were very merry and good humored till 11 o'clock and then retired and I said my prayers. It rained and thundered in the night. I slept but indifferently.

7. I rose about 7 o'clock and read nothing. However, I said my prayers, and had chocolate for breakfast. The weather was cloudy and cold, the wind northwest. About 10 o'clock we took leave and rode twelve miles to Hal Anderson's where we dined and I ate some bacon. After dinner we went to Falling Creek, which I found in great disorder and the mill could but just go. From thence to the Falls and from thence over the river to all the plantations, which were in good order and the people all well, thank God. Parson Robinson and . . . for supper. I said my prayers and slept very well, thank God. Two of my people pretended to be sick but only pretended.

8. I rose about 6 o'clock and read nothing but gave several orders about everything. I said my prayers, and had milk for breakfast. The weather was cold and clear, the wind northwest. About 9 o'clock we rode to Kensington, which plantation I found in good order and all the people well, thank God. From thence we returned direct to Falling Creek, where I stayed about half an hour and then went away to return home and Major Mumford and Parson Robinson went with

3. Major John Bolling, of Cobbs, on the Appomattox River. His wife was Mary Kennon.

me as far as Abraham Womack's and there I took leave of them and went to Colonel Hill's, whom I found indisposed with the gout. Here I drank some tea and then took leave and returned home where I found all well, thank God. I received a letter from Hal Harrison by which I learned his family was very sick. I ate some milk and about nine retired and said my prayers.

9. I rose about six and read a chapter in Hebrew and no Greek, because I prepared to go to Mr. Bland's funeral. I said my prayers and had milk and potato for breakfast. I had three stools. About 10 o'clock Captain L-s-l-n sent his boat to carry me to Mr. Bland's. I took nobody with me but my overseer. I got there about 12 o'clock and soon after there came abundance of company, of both sexes. We had a sermon and everything that was necessary for the occasion. Everybody was very courteous to me and I was the same to everybody. I ate some cake and drank some mulled wine. About 6 o'clock I returned home and Mrs. Duke came with me in the boat and set me home and then went on. I had letters from New Kent that told me all was well, thank God. I ate some milk and about 9 o'clock retired and said my prayers.

10. I rose about 6 o'clock and read a chapter in Hebrew and some Greek. I said my prayers, and had milk and potato for breakfast. The weather was warm and clear, the wind southwest. I danced my dance and walked in the garden. Then I prepared for church and about 11 o'clock walked there and we had an indifferent sermon from Mr. Robinson. After church I invited Drury Stith and his family and the parson to dinner but the latter would not go. We ate some roast mutton for dinner. After dinner we walked in the garden and I showed them several rarities. About 5 o'clock they went home and I walked about the plantation and saw several things till the evening and then I wrote two letters to New Kent. I ate some milk and retired about 9 o'clock and said my prayers.

11. I rose about 6 o'clock and read a chapter in Hebrew and some Greek. I said my prayers, and had boiled milk for breakfast. The weather was warm and clear, the wind east. I danced my dance and

walked about to see my people. Then I settled several accounts and put several things in order till dinner when I ate some boiled mutton. After dinner I walked to my workmen and then put several things in order in the library till the evening and then I took a walk about the plantation. At night I gave the bricklayer a bottle of rum for laying the bricks. I washed my feet and about 9 o'clock retired and said my prayers.

12. I rose about 6 o'clock and read a chapter in Hebrew and some Greek. I said my prayers, and had boiled milk for breakfast. The weather was clear and warm, the wind southeast. I danced my dance and walked among my workmen. I sent John Brayne over the river to get in debts at Prince George Court, but he had no success. I settled several accounts till dinner and then ate some roast mutton. After dinner I walked about and put several things in order, and then read some English till the evening and then walked about the plantation. At night I wrote some English. I had two women sick but I took them in time. At night came Mr. Mumford and John Banister that I intend to set over my affairs in New Kent. We drank cider and talked till 10 o'clock and then retired, and I said my prayers.

13. I rose about 6 o'clock and read a chapter in Hebrew and some Greek. I said my prayers and had milk for breakfast, though the Major and John Banister had chocolate. The weather was clear and warm, the wind southeast. About 10 o'clock George Walker sent his boat and we went on board the ship that brought servants and from thence went with the Major and Dick Randolph on board George Walker's ship to dinner and I ate some pork and peas. After dinner we had a bowl of punch and then went on board Captain L-s-l-n where I saw Colonel Allen and Ned Goodrich. Here we drank punch till 9 o'clock and then we ate bread and cheese and about 10 o'clock we went home and I carried the Major, Dick Randolph, and Major Kennon home with me and retired and said my prayers. It rained in the night.

14. I rose about 6 o'clock but read nothing because I was forced to attend the company. However, I said my prayers and drank choc-

olate for breakfast. The weather was cloudy and it rained a little. However I ventured to go about 11 o'clock to Captain Drury Stith's and parted with my company at Herring Creek. The Captain and his lady were very courteous to me and I ate some roast turkey. After dinner one of his daughters sang and the other danced with me and we were merry till 6 o'clock and then I took leave and returned home and found some of my New Kent people had brought me two steers and told me that my people were all well, thank God. I wrote a letter to one of my overseers and about 9 o'clock retired and said my prayers.

15. I rose about 6 o'clock and read a chapter in Hebrew and some Greek. I said my prayers, and had boiled milk for breakfast. The weather was clear and warm, the wind west. I danced my dance and read some English till 11 o'clock and then went to church where we had the Sacrament, which I took with devotion. After church I went home by myself, being a fast day[4] and ate some asparagus and eggs. After dinner I took a nap and then read some English till the evening, and then took a walk about the plantation and saw my people, who had a holiday. At night I ate some milk, read some English and said my prayers.

16. I rose about 6 o'clock and read a chapter in Hebrew and some Greek. I said my prayers, and had boiled milk for breakfast. The weather was clear and very cold, the wind north. I danced my dance and then walked about among my people to see everybody at their business. Then I settled several accounts till dinner and then ate some ox cheek. After dinner I put several things in order and then settled some accounts and then went to my people and was with them till 5 o'clock when Captain L-s came and gave me bills of lading. He stayed with me till six and then I took a walk about the plantation. At night I talked with my people and read some English till 9 o'clock when I retired and said my prayers.

17. I rose about 6 o'clock and read a chapter in Hebrew and some Greek. I said my prayers and had milk for breakfast. The weather

4. This was Good Friday.

was clear and cold, the wind northeast. I danced my dance and then read some English and walked some time in the garden. We had no prayers because the clerk did not come till it was too late. I ate some roast beef by myself because Mr. Brayne went to Frank Hardyman's. After dinner I took a nap and then read more English till the evening and then took a walk about the plantation. My man S-y told me of some of Tom's tricks and particularly that he went to the fishing place for three hours together. I scolded at Tom about it. At night I ate some milk and washed my feet; at 9 o'clock retired.

18. I rose about 6 o'clock and read a chapter in Hebrew and some Greek. I said my prayers, and had milk for breakfast. The weather was clear and warm, the wind southwest. I danced my dance and settled several accounts and walked in the garden and then read some Latin till dinner when I ate some boiled mutton. After dinner I put several things in order and then read some English. About 9 o'clock I heard nine guns and sent my boat to inquire if any ship was come in and to get my letters. My people returned home that I gave leave to go abroad. At night I ate some milk and prepared for my journey tomorrow. My man Bob brought word that all was well at the Falls, thank God. My people brought word that Captain Ned Randolph was come in.

19. I rose about 6 o'clock and read a chapter in Hebrew and some Greek. I said my prayers, and had milk for breakfast. The weather was cold and clear, the wind southwest. About 9 o'clock came Major Mumford and John Banister to go with me to New Kent. Accordingly I gave orders in my family and then went to Mrs. Stith's to breakfast where I ate some bacon. About 2 o'clock we took leave and I went to Mr. Adams' where we were courteously entertained but I ate nothing but milk for supper. Here we [saw] old Mrs. F-l-t who was very hearty. About nine we retired and I said my prayers.

20. I rose about 6 o'clock and read a chapter in Hebrew and no Greek. I said my prayers, and had milk for breakfast. The weather was cold and clear, the wind southwest. About 8 o'clock we took leave and Mr. Adams went with us to Major Merriweather's where

we got about 11 o'clock. He received me very courteously and we ate some milk and drank some wine to stay our stomachs and then the Major went good part of the way with us and we got to the quarters about 2 o'clock. I saw all the people at my quarters and found several faults but they had done abundance of work. Cornelius Dabney came over the river to me and told me all was well, thank God. At night we went to Mrs. Anderson's where we were kindly entertained and I ate milk for supper. About nine we retired and I said my prayers. Here was abundance of chinches.

21. I rose about 6 o'clock and read nothing because we intended to go away early. However, we had chocolate for breakfast and about eight took our leave and returned again to the quarters and went over the river where I found everything in very good order and the people all particularly well, men, women, and children, thank God. About 2 o'clock we dined at the quarters where Cornelius lived and I ate some bacon. About 4 o'clock we returned over the river and went to Major Merriweather's where we got about 6 o'clock and he was courteous to us and talked freely of the government. About seven I ate some salt beef for supper and about ten we retired. The weather was very hot so that I slept very indifferently but better than the night before. I said my prayers. It rained in the night.

22. I rose about 6 o'clock and read nothing because I prepared for my journey. However, I said my prayers, and had chocolate for breakfast. The rain hindered us from taking our leave so soon as we intended; however about ten we set out and it rained good part of the way. When we came to the bridge we ate some biscuits and drank some punch; while we were thus employed Mr. Adams came by and went with us as far as Drury Stith's where we found Mr. [Griffin].[5] Here we stayed about half an hour and then proceeded home where I found all well, thank God. We had some fish and cold roast beef but I ate of the last only. About five the Major and John Banister took leave and went over the river and I walked about the plantation, not-

5. Probably the Reverend Charles Griffin, head of the Indian school at the College of William and Mary, formerly master of an Indian school at Christanna.

withstanding I was exceedingly tired. I neglected my prayers and committed uncleanness with Annie, for which God forgive me.

23. I rose about 6 o'clock and read a chapter in Hebrew and some Greek. I said my prayers, and had milk for breakfast. The weather was warm and clear, the wind west. I danced my dance and then put several accounts in order. I took a walk to see my people at work till dinner and then I ate some [cowheel]. After dinner I put several things in order and received several letters from England by Major Bolling's man. I read some English and then walked about the plantation. At night I gave audience to my people and read some English. I ate some milk and about nine retired and said my prayers.

24. I rose about 6 o'clock and read a chapter in Hebrew and some Greek. I said my prayers, and had boiled milk for breakfast. The weather was warm and clear, the wind northeast. I resolved to go to town because I understood that my order was come for my being restored to the Council.[6] I gave the necessary orders and having eaten some roast beef I committed my family to the protection of God and rode to Green Springs but by the way met Colonel Hill and Colonel Randolph, who could tell me no news. About six I got to Colonel Ludwell's where I found Mr. Commissary and Mr. Holloway. The Colonel gave me a letter from Mr. Southwell and in it my order of Council. We talked of several things and I ate some milk and about 10 o'clock retired and said my prayers. It rained in the night.

25. I rose about six and read nothing because Mr. Commissary came into my chamber and talked with me half an hour about his affairs. I drank some chocolate for breakfast and about 10 o'clock the Colonel and I went in his chariot to town where I found another letter with the King's order of Council. I went with some of my friends to the capitol where I presented my orders of Council to the Governor and told him I should have waited upon him to his house but that the message I had received from him at my first coming had discouraged me. He told me he would obey the King's order but

6. See the King's order in council to restore Byrd to the Council of Virginia, dated January 8, 1719/20, in *Calendar of Virginia State Papers*, I, 194-5

if I had come without it he would not have admitted me. Then he railed at me most violently before all the people but I answered him without any fear or any manner and came off with credit. However, he did not swear me so I loitered about till the court was up and then dined with the Council and ate some boiled beef. In the evening we went to Colonel Ludwell's house and then I walked to Major Custis' where I lay and about 10 o'clock retired and said my prayers. Colonel Carter[7] came to town.

26. I rose about 6 o'clock and read nothing because I wanted to get the Council together in order to my being sworn. About 8 o'clock I called at Dr. Blair's, where I drank a dish of chocolate and then we went to the capitol where I was sworn and then went down to court where I sat till 1 o'clock and then to talk with some of my friends till the court rose and then we went to dinner and I ate some boiled mutton. After dinner we walked to the bowling green where I gave the woman a pistole to encourage the green. Then we called at Colonel Ludwell's and then I walked home and by the way beat my man for being drunk and saucy. I sat with the Major about half an hour and then retired and said my prayers. The Governor was not at court.

27. I rose about 6 o'clock and read some English. I ate milk and potatoes for breakfast and then reprimanded my man before Major Custis for being drunk last night. Then I walked to my chamber and read some English and got my room in order. About 10 o'clock came Colonel Ludwell and then we walked to court where we sat till four and then came to dinner and I ate some roast mutton. After dinner I went to Colonel Ludwell's to see my cousin Hannah and I drank some tea and found several ladies there. About 8 o'clock we walked to Colonel Carter's lodging where we discoursed about some 'treasonable' matters and sat there till 10 o'clock and then walked home to bed and said my prayers.

7. Robert ('King') Carter, of Corotoman, member of the Council; agent for the Fairfax family, proprietors of the Northern Neck; member of the board of William and Mary College.

28. I rose about 6 o'clock and read some English only and said my prayers. I had milk and potato for breakfast. About eight I walked to my lodgings and wrote some English till 10 o'clock and then came Colonel Harrison and the Commissary. Then we went to court and I sat there till two and then came off to talk with Captain O-r-d and discoursed him much about my quarrel with the Governor. About four I ate some boiled beef for dinner. After dinner we sat and talked till 6 o'clock and then took a walk and then returned to Colonel Ludwell's where we drank tea and then six of the Council [met] about the complaint to be made against the Governor, but we did not finish. However we stayed together till almost 11 o'clock and then I walked home and neglected my prayers.

29. I rose about 6 o'clock and read a chapter in Hebrew and some Greek. I said my prayers, and had milk for breakfast. The weather continued dry and clear, the wind west. About ten Mr. Commissary came to my lodgings and we walked to the court and then went into Council where there passed abundance of hard words between the Governor and Council about Colonel Ludwell and Mr. Commissary for about two hours till of a sudden the clouds cleared away and we began to be perfectly good friends and we agreed upon terms of lasting reconciliation, to the great surprise of ourselves and everybody else.[8] The Governor invited us to dinner and entertained us very hospitably and the guns were fired and there was illumination all the town over and everybody expressed great joy. The Governor kissed us all round and gave me a kiss more than other people. We had also a concert of music at the Governor's and drank the necessary healths till 11 o'clock and then we took leave and walked home and said my prayers.

8. This reconciliation between the Governor and his adversaries is described in a private letter from Virginia preserved among the papers of the Board of Trade in the Public Record Office: '. . . then he [the Governor] began to play his old game of dissimulation and when they least thought of it he melted them with a most humble desire of peace and friendship and would agree with them in all things and saluted them with a Judas's kiss, and came from the council chamber to the bar and saluted Mr. Holloway who had also been his adversary. This humble disposition was agreeable to all and there were great rejoicings throughout the town for this sudden and unexpected reconciliation.' (October 5, 1721).

30. I rose about 6 o'clock and read some English and then said my prayers and had milk for breakfast. I was prepared to go and make the Governor a visit but he prevented me by coming to me first and was exceedingly courteous. He stayed about half an hour, and then I went to wait on the Secretary[9] but he was from home. However, his lady came out and his pretty daughter and I drank some tea and about ten went to the capitol and sat there till two and then went to my dinner and ate some boiled mutton. After dinner I went to my lodging and read some Greek and settled some accounts till six and then the Governor's coach came to carry me to the landing to partake of Captain Wharwood's[10] treat. Here we were treated handsomely and were very merry till 10 o'clock and then we took leave of the Captain, and the Governor set me home and I said my prayers. The weather continued very warm and dry.

May 1720

1. I rose about 6 o'clock and read a chapter in Hebrew and some Greek. I said my prayers, and had milk for breakfast. The weather was hot and dry, the wind west. About 10 o'clock I went to church and sat in councillors' seat and Mr. Commissary gave us a sermon about peace. After dinner I went to dine with the Governor and ate some boiled mutton. After dinner we sat till 2 o'clock and then went to church again and Mr. Seagood[1] preached. After church I walked to the Commissary's where I saw Betty Cocke who is very pretty,

9. William Cocke, secretary of state for Virginia, 1712-20. His wife was Elizabeth Catesby.

10. Captain Wharwood (or Whorwood), of His Majesty's Ship *Rye*. *Journals of the House of Burgesses*, I, 303-4.

1. George Seagood, rector of Sittenbourne Parish, Richmond and King George counties.

and drank some tea and stayed till 9 o'clock and then walked home and wrote. I said my prayers and then washed my feet. It was very hot, which made me sleep very indifferently.

2. I rose about six and read a chapter in Hebrew and some Greek. I said my prayers, and had milk for breakfast. The weather continued hot and dry, the wind west. I danced my dance. About 8 o'clock I went to wait on the Governor, who received me very courteously and gave me some chocolate, and I gave Mrs. Russell[2] some chicken broth, which both the Governor and Mrs. Russell approved. Then I took leave and went to Dr. Blair's and from thence to Mr. Randolph's where we drank tea. Then we called on Colonel Ludwell and from thence I went to my rooms, where I settled several accounts and then went to the capitol where we stayed till four and then I dined with the Governor and ate some boiled beef. After dinner we sat and talked till 9 o'clock and then I walked home and said my prayers.

3. I rose about 6 o'clock and read nothing because I wrote a letter to the Duke of Argyll. I neglected my prayers, and had milk for breakfast. The weather continued dry and warm, the wind west. I went to visit my Aunt Ludwell[3] and stayed there about an hour and then came to my lodgings and wrote a letter. Then I went to court and then to the Council and about 4 o'clock we went to dinner and I ate some boiled beef. After dinner we went all to visit Mrs. Bray[4] but she was from home. Then we went to Mrs. Archer's who gave us some tea. Then we forced ourselves on Colonel Jones[5] and drank a bottle of wine till 9 o'clock and then walked home and said my prayers.

4. I rose about 6 o'clock and read nothing because I went out early. However, I said my prayers, and had milk for breakfast. The

2. Mrs. Katharine Russell, Spotswood's mistress. See *The Secret Diary of William Byrd,* 206 *et passim.*

3. Lucy Parke's mother was Jane Ludwell; 'Aunt Ludwell' is probably Colonel Ludwell's wife, Hannah Harrison.

4. Widow of Colonel David Bray, who died in 1717.

5. Thomas Jones, a burgess, represented the College.

weather was warm and dry, the wind west. About 8 o'clock I went to my rooms where I wrote a letter to England. Then I went to the General Court where I sat till twelve and then went away when Colonel Ludwell's case came on. Then I returned again to my rooms and settled some accounts till 4 o'clock and then we went to dinner and I ate some boiled beef. In the evening I went to the College in Mr. President's coach and Mr. Commissary gave us an entertainment where the Governor and Council were present and most of the ladies and gentlemen in town. I danced with Mrs. Russell. At 10 o'clock we went to supper and I ate some cheese cake. About 2 o'clock I went home and neglected my prayers.

5. I rose about 6 o'clock and read nothing because I got ready to wait upon the Governor. However, I said my prayers, and had milk for breakfast. The weather continued warm and dry, the wind west. About 9 o'clock I waited on the Governor and he received me very courteously but because he was busy I stayed about quarter of an hour; then I went to my rooms and wrote some English and then went to Council where we made sheriffs and did several other things and about 4 o'clock went to dine at the club where we were treated and I ate some boiled beef. After dinner I took a walk with Jimmy Roscow and talked with him about several matters relating to us. Then I walked home and sat about half an hour with the Major and then retired and said my prayers.

6. I rose about 6 o'clock and read nothing because I went out to settle accounts with several people, particularly with Mr. Roscow, who seemed to grudge paying me my part of the salary. However, he paid me and I drank tea with him and then went to put my things in order to go out of town. However, I went to wait on Mrs. Cocke after I had taken leave of the Governor and she asked me to dine there which I agreed to do with Major Custis and ate some roast veal. After dinner I drank some tea and about 4 o'clock took leave and went to Green Springs in Colonel Ludwell's coach where I was courteously treated and ate some milk and strawberries. My cousin Hannah gave us a song and about ten I retired and said my prayers. It rained abundance this night, thank God.

7. I rose about 6 o'clock and read nothing because I prepared to go home. However, I said my prayers and had some chocolate first and then pigeon pie for breakfast. The weather was cold and cloudy, the wind west. About 9 o'clock I took leave and proceeded to the ferry where I discharged my debt and then went to Mrs. Stith's where I found a very sensible man called Mr. G-r-y. Here I ate some fried pigeon and about 4 o'clock went home where I found all well, thank God, but understood my cousin Brayne had been disordered, for which I gave him a good scolding. Then I walked about and found everything in pretty good order and much the better for the rain that fell last night. I ate some milk and at night committed uncleanness with Annie and neglected my prayers.

8. I rose about 6 o'clock and read a chapter in Hebrew and some Greek. I said my prayers, and had boiled milk for breakfast. The weather was clear and warm, the wind southwest. About 10 o'clock came Captain Ned Randolph and stayed with me till church time and then we walked to church where I was glad to meet all my neighbors in good health. Mr. Robinson gave us a sleepy sermon. Then I took Mrs. Harrison and her son, Mrs. Hamlin, Mrs. Duke, and Colonel Eppes to dinner and I ate some roast ham and chicken. After dinner we sat and talked till 6 o'clock and then I walked home with Mrs. Harrison and stayed there to supper and ate some strawberries and cream and then walked home and said my prayers. In the morning I committed uncleanness with Annie, for which God forgive me.

9. I rose about 6 o'clock and read a chapter in Hebrew and some Greek. I said my prayers, and had milk and potato for breakfast. The weather was warm and clear, the wind southwest. About 10 o'clock came two of Major Bolling's daughters, one of Major Mumford's, and Drury Bolling and young Jack Bolling. About eleven Captain Randolph sent his boat and we all went aboard his ship where was all the people that had attended the [birthday]. I ate some roast lamb. After dinner we danced and toasted all the healths consequent to the good agreement of the Governor and Council and I began the Governor's health. We were very merry till 9 o'clock and then I ate some

ham and about eleven I took leave and had fifteen guns from three ships.

10. I rose about 6 o'clock and read a chapter in Hebrew and some Greek. I said my prayers, and had boiled milk for breakfast. The weather was hot and clear, the wind west. About 9 o'clock came Colonel Allen and Dick Cocke and stayed till eleven and then went over the river to Prince George Court. About 1 o'clock came Major Bolling's son and two daughters, Major Mumford's two daughters, Dick Randolph, Drury Bolling, and Captain Tom Bolling and Mrs. Duke, who all dined with me and I ate some boiled beef. After dinner we sat and talked till 5 o'clock and then the company took leave and I walked about the plantation, talked with my people, said my prayers, and retired.

11. I rose about 6 o'clock and read a chapter in Hebrew and some Greek. I said my prayers, and had boiled milk for breakfast. The weather was warm and cloudy, the wind north. I danced my dance. Then I settled several accounts till 1 o'clock. It rained all the morning pretty hard. I ate some boiled mutton for dinner. In the afternoon I settled more accounts till 5 o'clock and then read some French till night and then I took a walk in the garden. I was out of humor and spoke cross to everybody. Annie washed my feet. I said my prayers but committed uncleanness, for which God forgive me.

12. I rose about 6 o'clock and read a chapter in Hebrew and some Greek. I said my prayers, and had boiled milk for breakfast. The weather was cold and cloudy, the wind northeast. I danced my dance and then wrote several things and settled several accounts till 1 o'clock and then Captain [Webster] and Mr. [Thornton] came and dined with me and I ate some roast mutton. After dinner I paid the Captain thirteen pounds for the pipe of wine that George Walker sold me and then both of them went away and I wrote several letters to my overseers till the evening and then took a walk about the plantation. At night I discoursed with my people and gave John F-l orders to go to my plantation in New Kent tomorrow. I said my prayers and slept very indifferently.

13. I rose about 5 o'clock and read a chapter in Hebrew and some Greek. I said my prayers, and had boiled milk for breakfast. The weather was cold and cloudy, the wind southwest. I danced my dance and put several things in order and read news till dinner and then ate some boiled mutton. After dinner I took a small nap till 3 o'clock and then wrote some letters to England till the evening and then went into the garden to eat cherries. Then I walked to Mrs. Harrison's and ate more cherries and sat and talked about Ben's going to England till 9 o'clock and then I walked home in the dark and found all the family well, thank God. I talked with my people and then committed uncleanness, for which God forgive me. I neglected my prayers and slept with abundance of disturbance.

14. I rose about 5 o'clock and read a chapter in Hebrew and some Greek. I said my prayers, and had boiled milk for breakfast. The weather was warm and cloudy, the wind south. I danced my dance and then settled several accounts and wrote a long letter to England and saw my people work till dinner when I ate some fish. After dinner I read some news then wrote more letters to England and settled several matters. It thundered and rained violently for about two hours. In the evening I walked about home because it threatened to rain. At night I talked with my people and said my prayers.

15. I rose about 5 o'clock and read a chapter in Hebrew and some Greek. I said my prayers and had boiled milk for breakfast. The weather was warm and clear, the wind northwest. I danced my dance. I scolded at Mr. Brayne and my servants for stealing the cherries and bade Mr. Brayne go about his business. I wrote some English till it was time to go to church and then walked there and found Mrs. Harrison. Dick read prayers to us and after church I walked home with Mrs. Harrison and dined with her and ate some chicken pie. After dinner we sat and talked of many things till the evening and then I walked home and looked over several matters. John F-l came from my quarters at the Falls and New Kent and told me everybody was well, thank God. I talked with my people and said my prayers, but was out of humor at several matters relating to my overseer.

16. I rose about 5 o'clock and read a chapter in Hebrew and some
Greek. I said my prayers and had boiled milk for breakfast. The
weather was clear and cold, the wind southwest. I danced my dance
and wrote a letter to England and then went into the garden and ate
some cherries and then wrote more letters till about 1 o'clock and
then came Mr. Poythress and dined with me and I ate some boiled
beef. After dinner I settled some accounts with Mr. Poythress till 4
o'clock and then he went away and I wrote more letters to England
till six and then Ben Harrison came and walked about with me till
night and then we drank a pint of wine between us till 10 o'clock and
then he took leave and I talked with some of my people and then
retired and slept but indifferently.

17. I rose about 5 o'clock and read a chapter in Hebrew and some
Greek. I said my prayers and had boiled milk for breakfast. The
weather was clear and cold, the wind northeast. I danced my dance.
I resolved to go to Mrs. Anderson's. However, before I went I wrote
a letter to England and about 11 o'clock rode to Mrs. Anderson's
where I found Jack Stith and his wife[6] and soon after came David
Bray[7] and Mr. S-w-n-y, a sensible man. About 3 o'clock we dined
and I ate some bacon. After dinner Drury Stith who was also there
carried David Bray and Mr. S-w-n-y to his plantation at Sapony and
then we that were left behind drank coffee. About 5 o'clock I returned home and walked about the plantation and found Will and
S-y lame. I ate some milk and about 9 o'clock retired. It rained
violently.

18. I rose about 5 o'clock and read a chapter in Hebrew and some
Greek. I said my prayers, and had boiled milk for breakfast. The
weather was cold and cloudy, the wind south. I danced my dance
and then wrote a letter to England. Then I went into the garden to
eat cherries and then settled some accounts till dinner and then Colonel Eppes came in and I ate some [brown peas]. After dinner the
Colonel and I settled accounts and then he went away and then

6. John Stith's wife was Elizabeth, daughter of Mrs. Anderson.

7. Son of Colonel David Bray and Mrs. Judith Bray.

came Mrs. Hamlin and Mrs. Duke and stayed about an hour and ate some cherries and then went over the river, and I took a walk about the plantation. At night I talked with my people, said my prayers, and then retired and committed uncleanness with Annie, for which God forgive me. It blew pretty hard.

19. I rose about 5 o'clock and read a chapter in Hebrew and some Greek. I said my prayers and had boiled milk for breakfast. The weather was cold and clear, the wind northwest. I danced my dance and then wrote a letter to England and settled several accounts till 12 o'clock and then ate some cherries and then wrote more English till dinner when I ate some boiled pork. After dinner I took a nap and then wrote more letters till the evening. We began to raze our kitchen. In the evening I took a walk about the plantation. At night I talked with my people and gave them a dram and some cherries to the people at the quarters who were very thankful. The wind blew hard at northwest and made it very cold. I slept but indifferently.

20. I rose about 5 o'clock and read a chapter in Hebrew and some Greek. I said my prayers and had boiled milk for breakfast. The weather was cold and clear, the wind north. I danced my dance. Then I wrote some English till 10 o'clock and then went into the garden and gathered cherries. Then I wrote more letters till 12 o'clock and then read in the library till dinner when I ate some [cowheel]. After dinner I took a little nap and then wrote more letters to England till the evening when I took a walk to Mrs. Harrison's but she was from home. Then I walked about my own plantation. At night I caused cherries to be given to all my people about the house. I talked with my people, ate some milk, and about 9 o'clock retired and said my prayers.

21. I rose about 5 o'clock and read a chapter in Hebrew and some Greek. I said my prayers and had boiled milk for breakfast. The weather was cold and cloudy, the wind southwest. I danced my dance. I wrote a letter to Falling Creek and sent the tailor up with it. I went into the garden and ate cherries and then wrote a letter to England. About 12 o'clock came John Randolph, his brother Ned,

Captain Tom Bolling and Mr. P-k and dined with me and we had mutton pie for dinner. In the afternoon we played at billiards till 5 o'clock and then took leave. In the evening I took a walk and met Mrs. Harrison who had been at Mrs. Hamlin's who was very sick. We consulted what to do and resolved to let her blood. She went and in returning told me our patient was better. My bricklayer's brother and sister came to see him and brought three [g-r-n] along with them. I talked with my people and said my prayers.

22. I rose about 5 o'clock and read a chapter in Hebrew and some Greek. I said my prayers, and had boiled milk for breakfast. The weather was warm and cloudy, the wind southwest. I danced my dance and then wrote a letter to England till 11 o'clock and then came Major Mumford and John Banister and I walked to church with them. The Major had been sick of an ague. Mr. Robinson gave us a good sermon. After church I invited the Major, John Grills and his wife, with Colonel Eppes to dinner but Banister would not come for fear of losing his passage. I ate some roast duck. After dinner we sat and talked till 5 o'clock when I went over the river to visit Mrs. Hamlin who was sick. There I found Mr. Cargill and his wife but Mrs. Harrison went with me. About 7 o'clock I returned and took a walk with the Major till eight. Then we sat and talked till ten and then retired, when I said my prayers and made Annie feel about my person.

23. I rose about 5 o'clock and read a chapter in Hebrew and some Greek. I said my prayers, and had chocolate for breakfast with the Major. The weather was exceedingly hot and cloudy and about 10 o'clock it thundered, and rained about eleven, but before that the Major went aboard ship. I wrote a letter to England till 11 o'clock, and then reprimanded my maid Hannah for being particular to go above all the rest. About 12 o'clock came Colonel Eppes and we went aboard Captain P-r-s-n brigantine where we dined and I ate some roast pig. After dinner we were very merry and stayed there till 9 o'clock and then called at Mrs. Hamlin's to inquire how she did and found her a little better. Then I carried Colonel Eppes and Major

Mumford home with me. I neglected my prayers, for which God forgive me.

24. I rose about 5 o'clock and read nothing either in Hebrew or in Greek. I neglected my prayers because of my company. The weather was cold and clear, the wind north. The Colonel went away after he had his chocolate but Major Mumford stayed and we played at billiards. Then I wrote some English till 12 o'clock and then came Parson Cargill and Captain P-r-s-n and dined with us and I ate some roast bacon. After dinner there came six Sapony Indians[8] and I entertained them with rum and victuals. About 4 o'clock my company went away and then I took a nap and then wrote a letter to England. In the evening I took a walk to Mrs. Harrison's and stayed about an hour and then returned, talked with my people, and retired and said a short prayer.

25. I rose about 5 o'clock and read a chapter in Hebrew and some Greek. I said a short prayer, and had boiled milk for breakfast. The weather was cold and cloudy and it rained. However, Captain L-s-l-n sent his boat for me and about 12 o'clock I went aboard and he gave me the compliment of five guns. Soon after came Captain Ned Randolph, Major Robin Bolling, his brother Tom, and Dick Randolph and Jack Stith who all dined with us and I ate some fowl and bacon. After dinner we played at dice and I lost a pistole and in the evening took leave and went to visit Mrs. Hamlin and found her very bad and I gave her the best advice I could and then came home, talked with my people, and learned that Jenny was sick. I committed uncleanness with Annie and then prayed to God to forgive me.

26. I rose about 5 o'clock and read a chapter in Hebrew and some Greek. I neglected my prayers, and had boiled milk for breakfast. The weather was cloudy and cold, the wind east. About 7 o'clock came Billy Hamlin to get some barley cinnamon water for his mother and I sent half a pint. Then came Captain Ned Randolph and drank chocolate with me and then came Ben Harrison and I gave them some strong water. About ten he went away and I walked about and

8. The Sapony was an eastern Siouan tribe, now extinct.

visited my people and walked in the garden till dinner and then ate some roast [g-r]. After dinner I put several things in order and then wrote more letters and saw my people work till the evening and then I took a walk to Mrs. Harrison's and sat with her about an hour and then returned home, talked with my people, and said my prayers.

27. I rose about 5 o'clock and read a chapter in Hebrew and some Greek. I said my prayers, and had boiled milk for breakfast. The weather was clear and cold, the wind north. I danced my dance and then prepared to go to Colonel Harrison's and therefore put every-thing in order for that journey. About 12 o'clock came Ben Harrison and Mr. [Jefferson] and I ate some bacon and cold sallet. Mr. [Jefferson] gave me a [calumet of peace of two nations]. About one we went over the river and found Mrs. Hamlin very ill and Mrs. Harri-son with her and I advised that she might take a vomit. About 3 o'clock we proceeded on our journey and got to Colonel Harrison's by six, but not finding him at home we followed him on board Cap-tain Randolph where we sat about an hour and then returned and I ate a fricassee of lamb for supper. Then we sat and talked till ten and then retired and I neglected my prayers, for which God forgive me. I slept well.

28. I rose about 7 o'clock and read a chapter in Hebrew and some Greek. I said my prayers, and drank some chocolate for breakfast with the rest of the company. The weather was clear and cold, the wind northwest. The Colonel and I played at piquet and I won five shillings. Then we walked in the garden till dinner and I ate some boiled beef. After dinner came Mr. Richardson and his wife and we played at piquet again till the evening and I won about ten shillings. We ran a race in the garden. Mr. Lightfoot and his lady and Mr. Cargill dined with us but the two first went away. Then we played at lottery ticket and I won nothing, and then played a pool at piquet and I won ten shillings. About twelve we went to bed and I neglected my prayers. I slept very well. My horse got away.

29. I rose about 7 o'clock and read a chapter in Hebrew and no Greek. I said my prayers, and had chocolate for breakfast. The

weather was cold and clear but [...]. We did not go to church but they sat and talked till 12 o'clock and then went over the river to Mr. Lightfoot's to dinner and carried Mrs. Richardson with us but her husband went home. Here Mr. [Jefferson] came and I ate some bacon but ate too much. After dinner we took a walk to see Mrs. Jones, but she was from home. Then Mr. Lightfoot and I shot in the bow till the evening and then we took leave and returned to Colonel Harrison's where we sat and talked till 10 o'clock and then retired and I said my prayers and slept pretty well. Mr. Cargill went to church and carried Ben Harrison with him and stayed away all night.

30. I rose about 7 o'clock and read some Greek. I said my prayers, and had chocolate for breakfast. The weather was cold and cloudy. About 10 o'clock we took leave of Mrs. Harrison and the Colonel went with us to his brother the Captain's where we got about 12 o'clock and were very courteously received and here Ben Harrison and Mr. Cargill joined us again. About 2 o'clock we went to dinner and I ate some fish. While we were at dinner came Mr. Richardson and a parson that came from South Carolina. After dinner there came a violent storm of hail and broke all the windows, which it might easy do because the hailstones were as big as hens' eggs. The wind also blew so hard that it threw down a new house. When the storm was over we played at several games and I won about three pounds. We drank good rack punch and were merry till 12 o'clock and then retired and Colonel Harrison and I lay together. I neglected my prayers.

31. I rose about 8 o'clock and read some Greek. I said a short prayer, and had tea and bread and butter for breakfast. The weather was cold and cloudy. However, we took leave about 10 o'clock of all our kind friends and Ben Harrison and Mr. Cargill and I rode to Mrs. Hamlin's who we found sick still but asleep and therefore I could not see her. I found some of my people sick but we had escaped the hail, thank God. About 1 o'clock I walked to Mrs. Harrison's to dinner where I found my two cousins Bassett. I ate some chicken pie. After dinner we played at [...], romped, and sat and talked till the evening, and then I walked home. It had rained great part of the

afternoon. I found my bricklayer sick of an ague and several others ill and lame; among the rest S-y was very lame and so was old John. I committed uncleanness with Annie, for which God forgive me.

June 1720

1. I rose about 5 o'clock and read a chapter in Hebrew and some Greek. I said my prayers, and had boiled milk for breakfast. The weather was cold and cloudy, the wind northeast. I danced my dance and wrote a letter to Major Mumford and sent John F-l with it. I settled several accounts till dinner and then ate some fish. After dinner came Frank Lightfoot and Mr. W-l-k and saw my garden and library, and Mr. W-l-k was much pleased with the seats. Then I read some English till the evening and then took a walk to my neighbor Harrison's where we were merry with my cousins Bassett, and Colonel Allen came and increased our company. We played at [little plays] till 9 o'clock and then I took leave and walked home and found my family pretty well, thank God. I talked with several of them and then retired and said my prayers.

2. I rose about 5 o'clock and read a chapter in Hebrew and some Greek. I said my prayers, and had milk for breakfast. The weather was cloudy but it did not rain. I put several things in order and wrote to Captain Bolling and sent John F-l with it. I read some English. My bricklayer had an ague and I ordered him a vomit. About 12 o'clock came my cousin Harrison, her son, my two cousins Bassett and Colonel Allen to dinner and I ate some roast capon. After dinner we went into the library and talked and then went and ate fruit till 6 o'clock and then the company took leave and I walked with them most of the way and then returned and washed my feet. I talked with several of my people and then retired and said my prayers.

3. I rose about 5 o'clock and read a chapter in Hebrew and some Greek. I said my prayers, and had milk and potato for breakfast. The weather was cold and cloudy, the wind northeast. I danced my dance. I began to give my bricklayer the bark, by which he missed his fit. I wrote a letter to England till dinner and then I ate some minced fowl. After dinner I put several things in order and looked to my workmen till the evening and then I took a walk about the plantation and went to Mrs. Harrison's to visit her and my cousins Bassett and found Colonel Allen with his mistress. I sat with them till 9 o'clock and then walked home and found my family well. I talked with my people and said my prayers.

4. I rose about 5 o'clock and read a chapter in Hebrew and some Greek. I said my prayers and had boiled milk for breakfast. The weather was warm and clear, the wind southwest. Tom Cross, my old gardener, came from Williamsburg and brought me a letter from Major Custis. I gave the overseer and people and G-r-f-r leave to go abroad. I wrote a letter to England till dinner and then ate some fish. After dinner I put several things in order and then wrote more letters till the evening and then took a walk about the plantation and into the orchard. At night I said my prayers, talked with my people, and then retired.

5. I rose about 5 o'clock and read a chapter in Hebrew and some Greek. I said my prayers, and had milk and potato for breakfast. The weather was cold and clear. I danced my dance and cleaned my teeth. About 10 o'clock came Captain Tom Bolling and Mrs. Duke. The captain came to borrow a horse, which I lent him. About eleven I walked to church, where I received the Sacrament and invited Colonel Hill, Mrs. Anderson, John Stith and his wife, Mrs. Greenhill,[1] and Parson Robinson's daughter to dinner and ate some beans and bacon. After dinner the company went away soon because I went with Colonel Hill to Mrs. Harrison's, it being the last day that my cousins Bassett stayed. I continued with them all the afternoon and at night walked home, talked with my people, and said my prayers.

1. Mrs. Joseph Greenhill, sister of Mrs. Duke.

6. I rose about 5 o'clock and read nothing because I wrote letters to Williamsburg and to my overseers in New Kent. I said no prayers, but had boiled milk for breakfast. About 8 o'clock I rode to Mrs. Harrison's where I breakfasted again with the ladies. About 9 o'clock I went with them about three miles in their coach and then took leave and rode back again to Mrs. Harrison's and then waited on her to Frank Hardyman's to the christening of his son, where was abundance of company. I ate some chicken pie. After dinner we danced till the evening and were very merry and I danced a jig with Mrs. Harrison. In the evening we took leave and I went home with Mrs. Harrison and then walked to my own house where I found there had been a quarrel between Sam and Hannah in which Sam had been in the wrong, for which I reprimanded him. My people came home from the Falls and told me there was a great want of corn, which made me much out of humor.

7. I rose about 5 o'clock and read a chapter in Hebrew and some Greek. I said my prayers, and had boiled milk for breakfast. The weather was cold and clear, the wind south. I danced my dance. About 10 o'clock came Henry Anderson from the Falls and told me all was well above. He paid me some money and told me of all my business. About 11 came Mrs. Richardson and a minister and another gentleman that came lately from Carolina. I received them very courteously and showed them the garden and library, with which they were pleased. They stayed to dinner with me and ate some boiled mutton. After dinner we sat and talked till 4 o'clock and then the rain held and the company went away and I read some . . .

8. I rose about 5 o'clock and read a chapter in Hebrew and some Greek. I said my prayers, and had boiled milk for breakfast. The weather was cold and clear, the wind southwest. Mrs. Hamlin died yesterday morning. I danced my dance. I walked to the quarters to see my man S-y whose leg was swollen very much, and ordered him a stupe three times a day. Then I went into the garden and ate some cherries, and then wrote a letter to England. Then I read some Latin in Horace till dinner and then ate some fish. After dinner two men came from New Kent about business and I ordered them some

victuals. Then came Colonel Eppes, Captain Bolling, and Mrs. Duke and stayed till the evening and then I took a walk and ate some black cherries. At night I talked with my people and committed uncleanness with Annie.

9. I rose about 5 o'clock and wrote two letters to send by John F-l to New Kent Court. Then I read a chapter in Hebrew and some Greek. I said my prayers, and had boiled milk for breakfast. The weather was exceedingly hot and cloudy, the wind southwest. I danced my dance and then ordered my people to [draw] the pipe of wine I had of George Walker. Then I wrote some English and read some Latin till dinner and then ate some boiled mutton. After dinner I read more Latin and walked among my people. About 5 o'clock came Mr. Clayton, Mr. Harrison, and young Mr. Edwards and soon after they came we had a violent gust and abundance of rain and thunder. However, we drank three bottles of George Walker's till 10 o'clock and then the company took leave and I retired and neglected my prayers, for which God forgive me.

10. I rose about 5 o'clock and read a chapter in Hebrew and some Greek. I said my prayers, and had boiled milk for breakfast. The weather continued hot, notwithstanding the rain, the wind southwest and very cloudy. I was very busy in the cellar till 10 o'clock and then read some Latin till twelve and then came Mrs. Harrison and Mr. Clayton. Soon after them came Colonel Hill and Mrs. Greenhill and last of all came our parson Robinson to dine with me and I ate some beans and bacon. After dinner we walked to the church to see poor Mrs. Hamlin buried and hear her funeral sermon. I asked Mr. Cargill and his wife to walk down but they excused themselves. Then I returned home and read more Latin till the evening, when I was hindered in my walk by the rain. I talked with my people and said my prayers.

11. I rose about 5 o'clock and read a chapter in Hebrew and some Greek. I said my prayers, and had boiled milk for breakfast. The weather was hot and cloudy, the wind west. I danced my dance and about 10 o'clock walked into the churchyard to see Mr. Harrison do

justice upon two of his people for selling his corn. Then I returned
and read some Latin till 12 o'clock and then took a little nap till dinner and then ate some cold beef and sallet. After dinner I slept again
a little and then read more Latin till about 3 o'clock when there came
a terrible clap of thunder and damaged the pigeonhouse and killed
sixteen sheep that lay under it for shelter. I caused the throats of the
sheep to be cut and gave them to the people. In the evening I took a
walk and ate some cherries and at night washed my feet. Then talked
with my people and retired and said my prayers. I slept but indifferently because of the mosquitoes.

_12._ I rose about 5 o'clock and read a chapter in Hebrew and some
Greek. I said my prayers and had boiled milk for breakfast. The
weather was very hot and clear, the wind west. I danced my dance
and cleaned my teeth. It was very hot so that I could not go to
church, but I sent my people there to prayers. I read some Latin till
dinner and then ate some roast veal. After dinner I took a nap and Mr.
R-s-t-n, one of my overseers, came to justify himself against some
accusations. Then I read more Latin till the evening and then took a
walk about the plantation till night and then washed my feet. I gave
directions to my people and then retired and said my prayers.

_13._ I rose about 3 o'clock and said my prayers and got ready to
meet Colonel Hill in order to go to Williamsburg, and accordingly
about 5 o'clock I met him at Herring Creek and went with him in his
coach about ten miles and then we took horses and at the ferry I ate
some hoecake and onions and then we proceeded to Green Springs,
where I ate more milk. Then we played at piquet and took a nap till
the afternoon and then came Colonel Ludwell and Frank Lightfoot
from Williamsburg. I ate some fried chicken for dinner. After dinner Mr. Lightfoot went away and we sat and talked till ten when I
found myself very sleepy and retired but did not say my prayers, for
which God forgive me. I had a little looseness.

_14._ I rose about 6 o'clock and read some English. I said my
prayers, and ate some milk for breakfast. The weather was pretty
cold, the wind east. About 8 o'clock Colonel Ludwell, Colonel Hill,

and I went in Colonel Ludwell's coach to Williamsburg and when we had adjusted ourselves Colonel Ludwell and I went to visit Mrs. Russell and there I drank two dishes of chocolate and about 12 o'clock went to the capitol where we found Colonel Bassett, Colonel Harrison, Mr. President, Mr. Secretary, and Colonel Page.[2] We went and were sworn in court and then tried a man for burning Colonel Hill's house. Then I discoursed Mr. Pratt about Mr. Brook who I agreed to make my general overseer and to give him 10 per cent. Then we took leave of our friends and returned to Green Springs where I ate some milk and about 9 o'clock retired but neglected my prayers, for which God forgive me.

15. I rose about 4 o'clock and drank two dishes of chocolate but because it threatened rain we stayed till seven and then I ate some milk and about eight took leave and met Colonel Hill's coach ten miles from my house and then got into it and we came together to the creek and then I mounted my horse and took leave of the Colonel and rode home, where I found all well, thank God. I put several things in order till dinner and then ate some fish. After dinner I took a nap for about half an hour and then read some Latin till 5 o'clock and then came Mr. Harrison and his mother and brought me some apricots. They stayed till seven and then I walked almost home with them and then returned and examined my people and then retired and said my prayers.

16. I rose about 5 o'clock and read a chapter in Hebrew and some Greek. I said my prayers, and had boiled milk for breakfast. The weather was cold and cloudy, the wind east. I danced my dance. My looseness continued. Then I overlooked my people and then wrote a letter to England and then read some Latin till dinner and then I ate some beans and bacon. After dinner I took a nap and then wrote more letters and read more Latin till the evening and then I took a walk about the plantation and mended the spring at the quarters and then walked to see the wheat. Then I came home and talked with my people and then retired and said my prayers but slept indifferently.

2. William Bassett, Nathaniel Harrison, Edmund Jenings (president), William Cocke (secretary), and Mann Page, all members of the Council.

17. I rose about 5 o'clock and read a chapter in Hebrew and some Greek. I said my prayers, and had boiled milk for breakfast. The weather was cold and clear, the wind southwest. My sloop came down this morning and I found my man Johnny drunk, for which when I threatened to beat him he said I should not so I had him whipped and gave him thirty lashes. I danced my dance. I read some Latin till dinner and then ate some cold ham and sallet. After dinner I took a nap and then cut some sugar in pieces. Then I took a walk about the plantation and ate some cherries. At night I talked with the people, retired and said my prayers. I received an account that one of my quarters was burnt in New Kent. My looseness was better.

18. I rose about 5 o'clock and read a chapter in Hebrew and some Greek. I wrote two letters to New Kent. I said my prayers, and had boiled milk for breakfast. The weather was very hot, the wind southwest. I danced my dance and read some Latin. Mr. Brayne talked of carrying away his things and going over the river to Mr. Braxton's.[3] I offered him his passage if he chose to go to England but that he refused. I wrote more letters to the Falls till dinner and then ate some battered eggs. After dinner I went to beat the white sugar and then read some Latin till the evening and then walked about the plantation but found it exceedingly hot. At night I gave a bottle of rum to the people, talked with some of them, then retired and said my prayers.

19. I rose about 5 o'clock and read a chapter in Hebrew and some Greek. I said my prayers, and had boiled milk for breakfast. The weather was exceedingly hot, the wind southwest. I danced my dance. I did not go to church because of the great heat, but read some Latin. After church I sent to invite some of the company to dinner and there came Colonel Eppes, Captain Bolling, Captain Eppes, and Mr. Frank Hardyman. I ate some fricassee of hare. After dinner we sat and talked till 5 o'clock and then I sent to Mrs. Harrison's for Colonel Hill's coach and went there and found several ladies, Mrs. Richardson, Hannah Ludwell, and Hannah Harrison, Mr. Lightfoot

3. George Braxton, a burgess from King and Queen County.

and his lady. Here I stayed till 9 o'clock and then walked home and was exceedingly hot. I talked with my people and then retired and said my prayers.

20. I rose about 5 o'clock and read a chapter in Hebrew and some Greek. I said my prayers, and had boiled milk for breakfast. The weather continued very hot. However, about 8 o'clock I went to Mrs. Harrison's in a boat and ate some milk there. We played at piquet and shot with bows and I won five bits. Sometimes we romped and sometimes talked and complained of the heat till dinner and then I ate some hashed lamb. After dinner we romped again and drank abundance of water. We played at piquet again and I stayed till 8 o'clock and then took leave and walked home and found everything well, thank God. I talked with my people and said my prayers and then retired and slept but indifferently because of the exceedingly great heat.

21. I rose about 5 o'clock and read a chapter in Hebrew and some Greek. I neglected to say my prayers, but had milk for breakfast. The weather continued very hot and we began to cut down our wheat. About 9 o'clock came Frank Lightfoot and we played at billiards and then at piquet and I won two bits. Then we sat and talked till dinner when I ate some beans and bacon. After dinner we agreed to take a nap and slept about an hour and then I received a letter from New Kent that told me William R-s-t-n was run away. Then Mr. Lightfoot and I played again at piquet till the evening and then walked about the garden till night and then he went away and I gave my people a bowl of punch and they had a fiddle and danced and I walked in the garden till ten and then committed uncleanness with Annie. I said my prayers.

22. I rose about 5 o'clock and wrote a letter to New Kent. Then I read a chapter in Hebrew and some Greek. I said my prayers and had milk for breakfast. The weather continued hot. I wrote a comic letter to Mr. Lightfoot to invite him and the ladies to dinner, but he wrote me word the ladies could not come for want of a horse. My people made an end of reaping about 12 o'clock, and I sent away the sloop

to fetch [sh-l] [4] and sent Will with them. I ate some mutton pie. After dinner I took a nap and then read some Latin and lolled about till the evening and then I took a walk in the orchard and ate cherries and then took a walk about the plantation. At night I had my feet washed and walked about in the garden till late. I said my prayers.

23. I rose about 5 o'clock and read a chapter in Hebrew and some Greek. I said my prayers, and had milk for breakfast. The weather was very hot but the wind was fresh at southwest. I read some Latin and took a nap till 12 o'clock and then came Mr. Richardson and his wife, Miss Ludwell and Miss Harrison, Mrs. Harrison and her son, and the two Miss Blands to dine with me. Mr. Lightfoot and his lady came not because she was sick. I entertained them handsomely and ate some bacon and French beans. After dinner we had a bowl of punch and then some tea. It rained very much this afternoon. The good company stayed with me till 7 o'clock and then all went away and I took a walk, said a short prayer, talked with my people, and retired.

24. I rose about 5 o'clock and read a chapter in Hebrew and some Greek. I said my prayers, and had boiled milk for breakfast. The weather was cold and cloudy, the wind west. My man Ned was sick. About 9 o'clock I walked to Mrs. Harrison's and there played at piquet and shot in the bow. About 11 o'clock came Mrs. Randolph and dined with us and I ate some roast shoat. After dinner I took a nap and then we played again at piquet and I lost three bits. In the evening we drank some punch and young Jack Bolling came. About 8 o'clock I took leave of Hannah Ludwell and Hannah Harrison and Frank Lightfoot and then walked home and talked with my people and neglected my prayers. I slept pretty well, thank God.

25. I rose about 5 o'clock and read a chapter in Hebrew and some Greek. I said my prayers, and had milk for breakfast. The weather was very hot and clear, the wind west. I read some Latin till about 11 o'clock and then came young Stanhope about my land at Taskanask

4. Perhaps 'shingles' from the sawmill at the Falls. 'Shells' or 'shale' are other possibilities.

but we came to no determination. About 12 o'clock came Mrs. Harrison, Mrs. Randolph, two Misses Bland, and Mrs. Lightfoot and Miss F-t-s-y to dine with me and I ate some hashed chicken. After dinner we had a bowl of punch and were merry. The company stayed till 5 o'clock and then went away just as it began to rain. Then it rained about an hour and then I took a walk in the garden. At night I talked with my people, had my feet washed, and then retired and neglected my prayers. John F-l had an ague.

26. I rose about 5 o'clock and read a chapter in Hebrew and some Greek. I said my prayers and had milk for breakfast. The weather was cold, the wind northwest and clear. I danced my dance and then read some Latin till 11 o'clock when Major Mumford came, who stayed with me till dinner and I ate some boiled mutton. After dinner we sat and talked about all our affairs and took a nap and in the evening walked about the plantation and overlooked everything. At night Captain Bolling's boat came for Major Mumford and an invitation for me to come aboard tomorrow. I talked with all my people and said my prayers and then retired but was exceedingly troubled with mosquitoes.

27. I rose about 5 o'clock and read a chapter in Hebrew and some Greek. I said my prayers and had milk for breakfast. The weather was hot, the wind south. My overseer removed this day from hence to New Kent. I began to tar the house and then came Major John Bolling and sat with me till 12 o'clock and then Captain Bolling's boat came to carry me aboard his ship, where I found Major Mumford and Robin Bolling and Drury Bolling. The captain received me kindly and I ate some boiled lamb. After dinner we had a bowl of punch and were merry and continued so till 8 o'clock and then we ate some cold lamb for supper. About ten I came home with Majors Bolling and Mumford and went immediately to bed without saying my prayers and slept very ill.

28. I rose about 5 o'clock and read nothing because I had company. Major Bolling went away about 6 o'clock but Major Mumford stayed and drank some chocolate but I ate milk. I said my prayers. About

eight Major Mumford went across the river. Then I wrote a letter to England till 11 o'clock and then came Colonel Eppes to give me a small bill of exchange but did not stay. About one came Captain Bray to dine with me and I ate some boiled mutton. After dinner we both took a nap. It rained and thundered pretty much; however, he went away about 4 o'clock and I read some Latin till the evening and then took a walk into the orchard and about the plantation. At night I washed my feet, discoursed my people, and retired and said my prayers and slept pretty well, thank God.

29. I rose about 5 o'clock and read a chapter in Hebrew and some Greek. I said my prayers, and had milk for breakfast. The weather was hot and clear, the wind southwest. I danced my dance and then settled some accounts. About 11 o'clock came Captain Bray and brought me a letter and bill of exchange from Colonel Hill. He stayed about half an hour and then I read some Latin till dinner and then ate some bacon and sallet. After dinner I put some things in order in the library and then read more Latin till the evening and then took a walk to see my people at work. G-f-r, one of my carpenters, broke his shin. In the evening I sent Mrs. Harrison some pears and plums. Then came young John Bolling and would have nothing but milk for supper. I talked with my people, retired, and said my prayers.

30. I rose about 5 o'clock and read a chapter in Hebrew and some Greek. I said my prayers, and had milk for breakfast. John Bolling went away to the races in Surry, notwithstanding it was like to be very hot. I danced my dance and then settled several accounts. Then I read some Latin till dinner and then ate some fish. After dinner I took a nap and then beat some sugar, which made me very weary. Then I read more Latin till the evening and then took a walk to my people who were reaping the oats. At night I gave them a bowl of punch. I said my prayers and retired. I sent Mrs. Harrison a great fish. It was exceedingly hot without one breath of wind, so that the people at the races must have been melted.

July 1720

1. I rose about 5 o'clock and read a chapter in Hebrew and some Greek. I said my prayers, and had milk for breakfast. The weather was clear and very hot, the wind southwest. I danced my dance and then settled several accounts till 11 o'clock and then I read some Latin till dinner when I ate some cold bacon but could eat very little. After dinner I took a nap which disordered me very much. Then I read more Latin till the evening but was so hot that I drank abundance of wine and water and some punch. About sunset I took a walk to Mrs. Harrison's and ordered my servants to carry her some fruit. She gave me a syllabub and I stayed till ten and then walked home and committed uncleanness with Annie. I slept but indifferently because I was bit by mosquitoes.

2. I rose about 5 o'clock and read a chapter in Hebrew and some Greek in Lucian. I said my prayers, and had milk for breakfast. The weather was clear, the wind northwest. I put several things in order and then settled several accounts and then read some Latin till dinner and then I had no stomach. However I ate some hashed mutton. After dinner I took a nap and then read more Latin and drank a sneaker of punch to keep me from being dry. The weather was so cool that I was forced to put on my coat. Then I took a walk about the plantation and shot an old dog with an arrow for flying at me but did not kill him. At night I talked with my people and gave them all a dram. I slept better this night than I had done a long time because it was cool.

3. I rose about 5 o'clock and read a chapter in Hebrew and some Greek. I said my prayers, and had milk for breakfast. The weather continued cold and clear, the wind northwest. I danced my dance and then wrote a letter till 11 o'clock and then walked to church where Mr. Robinson gave us a good sermon. After church I took

home Colonel Hill, Mrs. Anderson, Mrs. Duke, Mrs. Frank Hardy-man and the parson and ate some roast chicken for dinner. After dinner we drank tea and were merry till 5 o'clock and then the company took leave and I walked with Mrs. Anderson to Mrs. Harrison's and stayed there about an hour and then returned home and found all well, thank God. I talked with my people and retired and said my prayers and slept very well, because it was cool.

4. I rose about 5 o'clock and read a chapter in Hebrew and some Greek. I said my prayers, and had milk for breakfast. The weather continued cold and clear, the wind west. I danced my dance and then settled several accounts and then read some Latin. I wrote a letter to Williamsburg till dinner and then ate some hashed chicken. After dinner I took a nap and then read more Latin till the evening and then took a walk about the plantation and met with Mrs. Duke waiting for the ferry and gave her some pears. At night I talked with my people and gave them a bowl of punch because the house was covered in. I walked in the garden and said my prayers and slept very well, thank God.

5. I rose about 5 o'clock and read nothing because I prepared to go to Colonel Randolph's. However, I said my prayers, and had milk for breakfast. The weather was cold and clear. About 6 o'clock I took horse and got to Colonel Randolph's[1] about eight and found Colonel Harrison there. He went up in his sloop and called there. I drank some tea and then we sat and talked and were merry till dinner and then I ate some roast chicken. After dinner we had a bowl of rack punch over which we were very merry till the evening and then Colonel Harrison went to Dick Cocke's[2] and I rode home and got there about 10 o'clock. I said my prayers and thanked God for finding all my people and affairs well. I slept very well because it was cool.

6. I rose about 5 o'clock and read a chapter in Hebrew and some Greek in Lucian. I said my prayers, and had milk for breakfast. The

1. Colonel Randolph lived at Turkey Island, Henrico County, up the river from Westover.

2. At Bremo, Henrico County, west of Turkey Island.

weather continued very cool and dry. I danced my dance and then settled several accounts. Then I read some Latin till one o'clock when Mr. Randolph of Weyanoke, Major John Eppes, Mr. Harwood and Billy Hamlin came to dine with me and I ate roast mutton. After dinner they stayed about an hour but had very little to say. When they took leave I walked to see my people and then to Mrs. Harrison's where I found Colonel Hill and abundance of company. Here I stayed till night and then walked home and found Annie sick of an ague. I talked with my people and then retired and said my prayers.

7. I rose about 5 o'clock and read a chapter in Hebrew and some Greek in Lucian. I said my prayers, and had milk for breakfast. The weather began to be hot again, the wind southwest. I danced my dance. I gave Annie a vomit that worked indifferently. Then I wrote a letter to Major Mumford and afterwards read some Latin till 1 o'clock when Colonel Hill and Mrs. Anderson came and when we were at dinner came Mrs. Duke and Mrs. Hardyman. I ate some fish for dinner. After dinner the company went away to court and I read some Latin till evening and then took a walk. It rained abundantly this afternoon and this evening, thank God, according to my prayers. This morning old G-n-t-r came to show my people to dig a well. Bob was taken with a fever and ague. About 9 o'clock I retired and said my prayers.

8. I rose about 5 o'clock and read a chapter in Hebrew and some Greek in Lucian. I said my prayers, and had milk for breakfast. The weather was cold after the rain, and cloudy, the wind northwest. I danced my dance and then settled several accounts and put several things in order till 12 o'clock. Then I read some Latin till dinner and ate some broiled fish. After dinner I put several things in order and read some Latin in Horace till the evening. My man Bob had a vomit for an ague. In the evening I took a walk to Mrs. Harrison's where I found the whole family indisposed. I drank some syllabub and stayed till 9 o'clock and then walked home and talked with my people. John had the piles for which I gave him some burnt [sh-y] and hogs' lard. I said my prayers and slept very well, thank God.

9. I rose about 5 o'clock and read a chapter in Hebrew and some Greek. I said my prayers, and had milk for breakfast. The weather continued cold and clear, the wind northwest. I danced my dance. I settled some accounts and walked to see my people work. Then I read some Latin till dinner and then ate some boiled mutton. After dinner I took a nap till 3 o'clock and then put several things in order till five and then read more Latin. About six came Frank Lightfoot and stayed till eight. We played at billiards and I beat him and then walked to the end of my pasture with him and then returned and talked with my people and gave them a dram. About nine I said my prayers and retired and slept very well, thank God.

10. I rose about 5 o'clock and read a chapter in Hebrew and some Greek. I said my prayers, and had milk for breakfast. The weather continued cold and clear, the wind northwest. I danced my dance and cleaned my teeth according to custom. About 11 o'clock I went to church where the clerk read prayers, after which I went to Mrs. Harrison's to dinner, where I ate some dried beef. After dinner we sat and talked all the afternoon. About 4 o'clock Mr. Fontaine came and we were very merry till 7 o'clock and then I walked home where I found all well, thank God. Then I talked with my people and then retired and said my prayers.

11. I rose about 5 o'clock and read a chapter in Hebrew and some Greek. I said my prayers, and had milk for breakfast. The weather was clear and warm, the wind southwest. I danced my dance and put several things in order till 11 o'clock and then came Mr. Fontaine and we played at billiards till 12 o'clock and then we looked upon prints till dinner and I ate some roast chicken. After dinner we remembered all our friends in England and he went away about three and I read nothing because I looked after my people. In the evening I walked in the orchard and about the plantation. At night I talked with my people. I said my prayers and retired about 9 o'clock and committed uncleanness with Annie. I slept very well, thank God.

12. I rose about 5 o'clock and read a chapter in Hebrew and some Greek. I said my prayers and had milk for breakfast. The weather

was clear and warm, the wind southwest. I danced my dance. My man Sam was almost drunk. Billy Wilkins fell from the roof of the library by the slipping of the ladder. I caused him to be bled and to take [a-r-s salt], which made all safe. I settled several accounts till dinner and then ate some [c-t] broth and apple dumpling. After dinner I nodded a little and then read some Latin till the evening and then I carried to Mrs. Harrison some fruit and wished them a good journey to Colonel Bassett's, where they go tomorrow. I received several letters from England. I talked with my people and said my prayers and slept but indifferently because I ate too much fruit.

13. I rose about 5 o'clock and read a chapter in Hebrew and some Greek in Lucian. I said my prayers and had milk for breakfast. The weather was warm and clear, the wind southwest. I danced my dance and put several things in order. Then I read some news till dinner and then ate some hashed chicken. After dinner I put several things in order and then took a little nap. Afterwards I read some Latin till the evening and then I walked into the orchard and ate so many plums that I could not sleep. I talked much with my people and gave them all a dram and then went to bed but could not sleep. I said my prayers.

14. I rose about 5 o'clock and read a chapter in Hebrew and some Greek in Lucian. I said my prayers, and had milk for breakfast. The weather was cold and cloudy, the wind southwest. I read some news till ten and then walked to see my people at work and then read more English till dinner and then I ate some fish. After dinner I put several things in order and then wrote more news. It rained a little but not enough to wet the ground. Then I read some Latin till the evening and then took a walk and drank some warm milk. Then I talked with my people and gave them a dram. About 9 o'clock came Major Mumford and Dick Kennon who had been at York to buy Negroes. I gave them some cold bacon and cucumbers and we drank a bottle of wine and then retired and I said my prayers and slept pretty well, thank God. The Major brought me an English letter.

15. I rose about 5 o'clock and read nothing because of my company, but we played at billiards and I won half a crown. I said my

prayers and had milk for breakfast. The weather was warm and clear. About 8 o'clock the gentlemen went away. I wrote some English and read some Latin till dinner and then I ate some hog's tongue and [cymlings]. After dinner I oiled the closet doors and then read some Latin till the evening and then took a walk, though I could not walk far because it rained a little. At night came Ben Harrison and brought me some letters from Colonel Bassett that came from England. He stayed about an hour. Then I talked with my people and said my prayers and retired and slept pretty well, thank God.

16. I rose about 5 o'clock and read a chapter in Hebrew and some Greek. I said my prayers, and had milk for breakfast. The weather was cold and cloudy, the wind southwest. I danced my dance and read some news till 12 o'clock and then read some Latin till dinner when I ate some bacon and eggs. After dinner I put several things in order till the evening and then took a walk, notwithstanding it had rained abundantly, thank God. At night I gave my people some punch and talked with several of them, and about 9 o'clock said my prayers and retired.

17. I rose about 5 o'clock and read a chapter in Hebrew and some Greek. I said my prayers, and had milk for breakfast. The weather was cold and cloudy, the wind southwest. I danced my dance and put several things in order till 11 o'clock and then I went to church, where we had an indifferent sermon. After church Colonel Harrison came ashore from his sloop and he and ten more of the congregation went home with me to dinner and I ate roast lamb. After dinner we sat and talked till 5 o'clock and then the company went away and Colonel Harrison went aboard his sloop again and I took a walk and prepared everything to go from home tomorrow. I talked with my people and then said my prayers and retired and slept pretty well, thank God.

18. I rose about 4 o'clock and said my prayers and drank some warm milk. About six I was over the river and intended to go to Colonel Harrison's boat, mistook my way and went to Mr. Richardson's and found him sick, but his lady was well. I drank tea and ate

bread and butter and about twelve we went over the creek and rode all to Colonel Harrison's³ where we found Frank Lightfoot. I ate watermelon and about three we dined and I ate some boiled beef. After dinner we played a pool at piquet and I lost about a crown. We drank a bowl of punch and were merry till 10 o'clock and then retired and I said my prayers.

19. I rose about 4 o'clock and said a short prayer. Then we drank some chocolate and about 6 o'clock Colonel Harrison and I took leave and went to Williamsburg, going by the way of S-w-n-y, where we arrived about 11 o'clock and as soon as we dressed we went to the Governor's and talked abundantly of things till two, when we went to dinner and I ate some boiled beef. After dinner we sat and drank punch and were merry till 11 o'clock, when I went to Major Custis' in the Governor's coach because it had rained abundance. I said my prayers and slept pretty well, thank God.

20. I rose about 6 o'clock and ate some milk. I said a short prayer and then walked with the Major in his garden, into which he had put gravel. About nine the Major and I walked to the Secretary's where we saw the ladies and drank tea. Here I stayed till ten and then went with the Secretary to the capitol where every councillor was present. Part of our business was to judge of the complaints against Parson Robinson.⁴ We agreed to have an Assembly the second of November next. About 2 o'clock we went and dined with the Governor and I ate some roast veal. After dinner we sat till 5 o'clock and then took leave and I went to Major Custis' and from thence to the College to the Commissary's and found Mrs. Russell and Mrs. Ludwell there. I stayed till 7 o'clock and then Colonel Ludwell and I rode by ourselves to Green Springs, where I ate some milk and some fruit and about 10 o'clock retired and neglected my prayers, for which God forgive me.

21. I rose about 4 o'clock and drank some chocolate and about five took leave of the Colonel and passed the ferry about six and got home

3. Colonel Nathaniel Harrison lived at Wakefield, Surry County.

4. James Robertson, the minister of Westover Church, was accused of uttering false speeches against the Crown.

about 10 o'clock and found all pretty well, thank God. I put several things in order and wrote in my journal. Then I read some Greek till dinner and then ate some fish. After dinner I took a nap and then put several things in order till the evening and then I took a walk about the plantation but before I could see everything there came up a black cloud and it began to rain and rained abundantly. I talked with my people and said my prayers. I committed uncleanness with Annie, for which God forgive me.

22. I rose about 5 o'clock and read a chapter in Hebrew and some Greek in Lucian. I said my prayers, and had milk for breakfast. The weather was cold and cloudy, the wind southwest. I danced my dance. Then I looked over my people and wrote some English till 12 o'clock and then read some Latin till dinner when I ate some bacon fraise. After dinner I put several things in order and then read some news and some Latin till the evening when it rained and hindered me from walking about the plantation. However, when it held up I walked in the garden and then talked with my people and about 9 o'clock said my prayers and retired.

23. I rose about 5 o'clock and read a chapter in Hebrew and some Greek in Lucian. I said my prayers, and had milk for breakfast. The weather was warm and clear, the wind southwest. I danced my dance. I settled several accounts and put things in order and then read some Latin till dinner, when I ate some tongue. After dinner I put several things in order and read some old letters from Lady Sherard[5] till the evening and then I took a walk about the plantation and called on Ben Harrison but he was gone to Major Mumford's. In the evening I talked with my people and Jack told me of some horses that had destroyed a hogshead of tobacco and I gave him orders to shoot them as not being fit to live. I said my prayers and retired.

5. Mary Calverley, wife of Bennet Sherard, 3rd Baron Sherard, later Viscount Sherard and Earl of Harborough, was known to Byrd before and after her marriage in 1696; she died in 1702. Among Byrd's letters is a character of Mary Calverley as 'Melantha.' Baron Sherard may have been connected with the family of Sherards of Lobthorpe, kin of Byrd through the Parke family. See *Another Secret Diary of William Byrd*, 228.

24. I rose about 5 o'clock and read a chapter in Hebrew and some Greek in Lucian. I said my prayers, and had milk for breakfast. The weather was clear and hot, the wind west. I danced my dance and wrote three letters to my overseers above. Then I read some Latin till dinner because it was so hot I could not dress me to go to prayers. I ate some broiled fish. After dinner I took a nap and then read some English and then some Latin till the evening and then I took a walk about the plantation and ate some fruit. At night I talked with my people and gave them some cider. Then I said my prayers and retired and committed uncleanness.

25. I rose about 5 o'clock and sent John F-l to my upper plantation to inquire how everything goes. I read a chapter in Hebrew and some Greek in Lucian. I said my prayers, and had milk for breakfast. The weather was warm and clear, the wind southwest. I danced my dance and then settled several people's accounts till dinner when I ate some bacon and eggs. After dinner I put several things in order and then wrote letters to several gentlemen that owe me money. Then I read some Latin in Horace till the evening and then took a walk about the plantation. At night I talked with my people and gave them all some cider. Then I took a walk in the garden, said my prayers and retired and dreamed that Mr. Bland came to me and told me that good people were happy but must first pass through the fire to prove them and I persuaded him to sing to me as they [sort] above, which he did, but Mrs. Harrison sang with him and hindered me from hearing him.

26. I rose about 5 o'clock and read a chapter in Hebrew and some Greek. I said my prayers, and had milk for breakfast. The weather was exceedingly hot without wind. However, I danced my dance, and then wrote an account of my vision to Mrs. Harrison. Then read some Latin till dinner and then ate some fish. After dinner I put several things in order and then settled several accounts. It rained about 5 o'clock for about half an hour. Mr. Harrison came and we ate some watermelon. When he went away I took a walk in the garden till it was dark. Then I talked with my people and gave them some cider. I said my prayers and retired.

27. I rose about 5 o'clock and read a chapter in Hebrew and some Greek. I said my prayers, and had milk for breakfast. The weather was cold and cloudy, the wind southwest . . . dined with me and I ate some boiled chicken. After dinner we sat and talked till 4 o'clock and then Mr. Harrison went away. I read some Latin till the evening when we took Sam G-r-d-n mares eating tobacco. I sent to Sam and threatened hard that I would make him pay the damage. John F-l came from above and let me know how everything did, that they were well, thank God, but wanting rain, which God grant them. I walked about the plantation, talked with my people, said my prayers, and committed uncleanness, for which God forgive me. I was out of humor and slept very ill.

28. I rose about 5 o'clock and read a chapter in Hebrew and some Greek in Lucian. I said my prayers, and had milk for breakfast. The weather was very hot and cloudy, the wind southwest. I danced my dance. I wrote some English till 11 o'clock and then came Drury Stith's son and paid me the money he owed. I asked him to stay to dinner and I ate some boiled mutton. After dinner we ate some fruit and then played at billiards till the evening and then he took leave and I gave him a little cat to carry to his sister and some fruit. At night I took a walk, after having written a letter to Mr. Anderson. Then I talked with my people and said my prayers, and retired.

29. I rose about 4 o'clock and got ready to go to visit Mr. [Cocke] the [b-r-m-r] and call upon Mr. Harrison. I said a short prayer and drank warm milk. It rained by the way and made me a little wet. However, I got there about 9 o'clock though we stayed by the way under a tree. Mr. [Cocke] received us very courteously and about ten we ate some fried chicken. Then we took a walk about his grounds about two miles. Then we returned and talked and I read some things to them. About 4 o'clock we ate again and I ate some boiled mutton and about six took leave and rode home, but were wet because the rain overtook us again. When I came home I shifted myself and drank some malmsey. My family was all well, thank God. I talked with my people and said my prayers.

30. I rose about 5 o'clock and read a chapter in Hebrew and some Greek. I said my prayers, and had milk for breakfast. The weather was warm and cloudy. I danced my dance. I agreed to lend Mrs. O-l-t that came last night fifty upon the security of four Negroes, and wrote a letter to Mr. Anderson about it. Then wrote some English and walked about to see my people till dinner and then ate some bacon and eggs. After dinner I put several things in order and then wrote some Latin till the evening. Sam asked leave to go to Mr. Bland's. It rained a little so that I could walk only in the garden. At night I talked with the people and said my prayers and slept pretty well. I committed uncleanness with Annie, for which God forgive me.

31. I rose about 5 o'clock and read a chapter in Hebrew and some Greek. I said my prayers, and had milk for breakfast. The weather was cold and cloudy, the wind west. Billy Wilkins' father came to excuse his son's going home. About eleven I went to church and Mr. Robinson gave us a good sermon. After church I asked Colonel Eppes and his daughter, Frank Hardyman and his wife, Mrs. Duke and Mrs. [Underhill] to dine with me and I ate some roast chicken. After dinner we sat and talked till 6 o'clock and then the company went away and I took a walk in the garden till night and then talked with my people, said my prayers, and retired and dreamed I went to England and left my business in disorder. I slept pretty well, thank God.

August 1720

1. I rose about 5 o'clock and read a chapter in Hebrew and some Greek in Lucian. I said my prayers, and had milk for breakfast. The weather was cold and cloudy, the wind west. I danced my dance. I

wrote some English and then read some Latin till dinner, when I ate some fish. After dinner I took a little nap and then wrote more English and read more Latin till the evening and then took a walk about the plantation and ate some fruit. At night I discoursed my people about their business and then said my prayers and slept very ill but dreamed that the Governor was here.

2. I rose about 5 o'clock and read a chapter in Hebrew and some Greek in Lucian. I said my prayers, and had milk for breakfast. The weather was cold and cloudy, the wind west. I danced my dance. Sam G-r-d-n mare broke into my pasture, of which I sent him word and let him know I would shoot her if she came there again. I wrote some English till dinner and then ate some fish again. After dinner I put several things in order and then wrote two letters to Williamsburg till the evening and then took a walk about the plantation. At night I talked with my people and particularly with Tom who had taken a vomit because he had an ague. His vomit had worked very well and he was better, thank God. I said my prayers and retired, but committed uncleanness, for which God forgive me.

3. I rose about 5 o'clock and read a chapter in Hebrew and some Greek in Lucian. I said my prayers, and had milk for breakfast. The weather was warm and clear, the wind northwest. I danced my dance. Then I settled several accounts and wrote some letters till 12 o'clock and then came Ben Harrison, Mrs. Frank Hardyman, Mrs. Anderson, her daughter and Mrs. Duke. After them came Major Bolling, but he would not stay. Then came Colonel Hill and I ate some [l-m-d]. After dinner several went away and came again but about six they all went away and it began to rain very hard. I ordered all my people to go hang tobacco because it came on so fast. Then I talked with the boys and said my prayers and about nine retired and slept indifferently.

4. I rose about 5 o'clock and read a chapter in Hebrew and some Greek in Lucian. I said my prayers, and had milk for breakfast. The weather was warm and clear, the wind southeast. I danced my dance. Jenny B-s-n was whipped for several faults. I looked over the work

of my people and then wrote some English till 12 o'clock and then read some Latin till dinner. After dinner I put some things in order and then read some English and then wrote again till the evening, when I walked about the plantation. At night I talked with my people and ordered everybody to go hang tobacco. Then I said my prayers and retired and slept indifferently.

5. I rose about 5 o'clock and read a chapter in Hebrew and some Greek in Lucian. I said my prayers, and had milk for breakfast. The weather was warm and clear, the wind southwest. I danced my dance and then wrote some English till 12 o'clock and then read some Latin till dinner, when I ate some cold roast lamb. After dinner I put several things in order in the library and then wrote more English till 6 o'clock and then read more Latin. At night I talked with my people and refused to let P-p-l go to see his wife. Then I walked in the garden, said my prayers, and retired. It rained abundance after I was abed.

6. I rose about 5 o'clock and read a chapter in Hebrew and some Greek in Lucian. I said my prayers, and had milk for breakfast. The weather was clear and cold, the wind north. I danced my dance and then prepared to go to the race at Captain Drury Stith's and got there about 11 o'clock and stayed till one before the races began. Abundance of people were there. It was 4 o'clock before we went to dinner and then I ate some hog's head. After dinner we walked to the field again and saw more races and about 6 o'clock I took leave of the company and returned home, where I talked with my people, said my prayers, and retired. Colonel Ludwell sent me word the Governor would come Tuesday.

7. I rose about 5 o'clock and read a chapter in Hebrew and some Greek in Lucian. I said my prayers, and had milk for breakfast. The weather was cool and cloudy and it rained a little in the morning. I danced my dance and then read a sermon till 11 o'clock and then went to church and heard the clerk read prayers. After church Major Mumford came and dined with me and I ate some roast chicken. After dinner we sat and talked and took a walk about the plantation

and got soaked which made me change my clothes. My people almost all got drunk with cider I had given them, for which I was very angry with them and threatened to punish them that I should ever see drunk again. I committed uncleanness with Annie, for which God forgive me. However, I said my prayers.

8. I rose about 5 o'clock and read a chapter in Hebrew and no Greek because I talked with Major Mumford. I said my prayers, and had chocolate for breakfast. The weather was very cool and cloudy. The Major and I played at billiards and I won a crown. Then we walked to Ben Harrison's and brought him back with us to dinner and I ate some hashed chicken. After dinner we played at billiards and then had a bowl of punch. Then we took a walk about the plantation. At night I talked with my people and prepared everything for the Governor's coming tomorrow. Colonel Ludwell told me in his letter that Mr. Dick Perry was dead. I said a short prayer and retired.

9. I rose about 5 o'clock and read nothing because I talked with the Major and prepared for the Governor's coming to dine with me this day. I ate some chocolate for breakfast. About nine the Major went away and I got everything in great order long before the Governor came, who came not till 5 o'clock and there came with him Colonel Ludwell, the Secretary and his son, and John Randolph. I received them at the outer gate and about six we went to dinner and had four dishes of courses. Just before we sat down the Secretary's son fainted away and at dinner the Governor fainted away likewise. At night we drank some claret and old Madeira but the Governor was going to faint again. So we put him to bed and the rest of the company sat up till 11 o'clock and then retired. I persuaded Annie to come to bed but she did not consent. I neglected to say my prayers. I received letters from England that told me of Dick Perry's death the 16th of April last.

10. I rose about 5 o'clock and got everything put in the best order I could. I read some Greek before the company was up and said my prayers. The weather was cool and cloudy, the wind northeast. About 9 o'clock we had tea and chocolate for breakfast and I made

John Randolph governor of the tea table. About 11 o'clock I waited on the Governor to Colonel Hill's to dinner where several gentlemen met me. About 3 o'clock we went to dinner and I ate some boiled mutton. After dinner we went to Colonel Randolph's in his boat, only the Secretary took leave and went to Mrs. Harrison's. About 7 o'clock we got to Colonel Randolph's where we found the table finely covered. We sat and drank some punch till 8 o'clock and then I ate some chicken for supper. About ten we went to bed and I slept very well, only I neglected my prayers, for which God forgive me.

11. I rose about 6 o'clock and Colonel Ludwell and I walked to visit old Mrs. Randolph[1] and the Governor came to us afterwards. I neglected my prayers and about 9 o'clock we walked back to the Colonel's and I ate some chicken pie for breakfast. About 11 o'clock we returned in the Colonel's boat to Colonel Hill's and proceeded from thence to Mr. Hardyman's where we drank strong water but found Mrs. Hardyman very dirty. From thence we rode to Mrs. Harrison's to dinner where there was abundance of company and I ate some fried veal. After dinner we were very merry, only Colonel Hill had a headache. I lent Mrs. Harrison on this occasion my knives and gilt, and her servant broke one of my knives. In the evening the Governor, Mr. Randolph, and young Mr. Cocke walked to my house where we drank a bottle and went to bed about 11 o'clock and I kissed Annie and committed uncleanness, for which God forgive me.

12. I rose about 5 o'clock and read nothing because I put everything in order to wait on the Governor. About 8 o'clock we had tea and chocolate and several gentlemen came to breakfast with us. It rained a little in the morning, which gave me hopes the Governor would stay, but I could not persuade him, so about 10 o'clock he took leave and our gentlemen waited on him about eight miles but I waited on him to Frank Lightfoot's,[2] but by the way had some rain. About 2 o'clock we ate some bread and butter with Frank and then went

1. Probably Mary Isham, widow of William Randolph I of Turkey Island.

2. At Sandy Point, west of the Chickahominy River.

over the river to Colonel Harrison's where we dined and I ate some veal. After dinner we were very merry till 11 o'clock and then retired and I neglected my prayers, for which God forgive me. I slept very well.

13. I rose about 6 o'clock and read some English. I said my prayers, and ate some roast chicken for breakfast. The weather was cold and clear, the wind northwest. The Colonel was much indisposed. Captain Harrison and Ned Goodrich came here to wait on the Governor. About 11 o'clock we went in Frank Lightfoot's boat to Colonel Ludwell's landing where his coach carried the Governor and me to the house. I ate some calf's head for dinner. I played at piquet with John Randolph and lost ten shillings. About 5 o'clock the Governor took leave and went to Williamsburg, but I stayed and Frank Lightfoot. Mr. Grymes and his wife[3] were here. The men took a walk in the evening and at night I ate some peaches and milk for supper and about 11 o'clock we retired but I neglected my prayers.

14. I rose about 6 o'clock and read some Greek. I said my prayers, and ate some chicken pie for breakfast. The weather was warm and clear, the wind west. About 10 o'clock the ladies went in the coach and the gentlemen rode to church where Mr. Jones[4] gave us a good sermon. After church we returned to Colonel Ludwell's to dinner and I ate some boiled veal and bacon. After dinner we sat and talked till 6 o'clock and I wrote a letter to Major Custis. Then Frank Lightfoot and I took leave and went in the Colonel's coach to the ferry and there met our horses that carried us to Mr. Lightfoot's where Parson Fontaine received us and we drank a bowl of punch and were merry. We sent to know how Colonel Harrison did and learned he was very well again. About ten we retired and I said my prayers.

3. Mrs. John Grymes, Lucy Ludwell, sister of Philip Ludwell.

4. Reverend Hugh Jones, professor of mathematics at William and Mary College, 1717–21, chaplain of the House of Burgesses, and author of *The Present State of Virginia* (1724). See the editor's introduction to Jones' *The Present State of Virginia*, ed. Richard L. Morton (Chapel Hill, N.C., 1956).

15. I rose about 5 o'clock and had chocolate for breakfast and then Frank and the parson paid me the compliment to ride with me to the road where I took leave of them and had a pleasant journey home, where I found all well, thank God. I put everything in order and then wrote a letter to Mrs. Harrison and read some Greek till dinner and then ate some fish. After dinner I put several things in order and then committed uncleanness with Annie in the library. Then I read some English till the evening and walked about the plantation. P-p-l and G-r-f-r came from above and told me everybody was well, thank God. I gave all the people a dram, said my prayers, and then retired and slept very well, thank God.

16. I rose about 5 o'clock and read a chapter in Hebrew and some Greek in Lucian. I said my prayers, and had milk for breakfast. The weather was clear and warm, the wind southwest. I danced my dance. I sent Mrs. Harrison some fish and told her I would come and dine with her and about 12 o'clock I went there and by the way ran after some horses that were getting into the pasture. I ate some bacon for dinner. After dinner we sat and talked of several things till the evening and then I walked home and talked with my people. I was out of humor. When my people hung tobacco some of the pieces fell down and hurt one of the women. I said my prayers, or else I believe it would have killed her. I slept very well, thank God.

17. I rose about 5 o'clock and read a chapter in Hebrew and some Greek in Lucian. I said my prayers, and had milk for breakfast. The weather was hot and clear, the wind southwest. I danced my dance. My sloop returned this morning with [sh-l]. I wrote some English till dinner and then ate some boiled mutton. After dinner I put several things in order and then read some Latin till the evening and then took a walk and with my arrow shot Sam G-r-d-n mare in the back. At night Mr. Lightfoot's smith came to be cured of his indisposition. I was angry with G-f-r for putting up the [rungs] so that they fell down and with Ned for leaving the oxen by themselves to break the cart. I talked with my people and said my prayers, but committed uncleanness with Annie, for which God forgive me.

18. I rose about 5 o'clock and read a chapter in Hebrew and some Greek in Lucian. I said my prayers, and had milk for breakfast. The weather was clear and warm, the wind southwest. However, I got ready to go to Captain Drury Stith's to the marriage of his daughter Mary[5] and accordingly called on Mrs. Harrison about 10 o'clock and waited on her there and found abundance of company and old Mrs. Bolling[6] among them. About 2 o'clock we went to dinner and I ate some roast veal. After dinner we danced and were merry till 6 o'clock and then I waited on Mrs. Harrison home and from thence proceeded to my own house, where I found all well, thank God, only John was bad with his hand, into which he had run the [fang of a cat].

19. I rose about 5 o'clock and read a chapter in Hebrew and some Greek. I said my prayers, and had milk for breakfast. The weather was warm and cloudy, the wind southwest. I danced my dance and walked to see my people work. Then I wrote some English till dinner and then ate some bacon and eggs. After dinner I put several things in order and then wrote more English and then read some Latin till the evening, when it rained. Captain Friend came ashore and desired some bread for his people, which I gave him. In the evening I took a walk about the plantation and at night talked with my people and said my prayers. It rained in the night.

20. I rose about 5 o'clock and read a chapter in Hebrew and some Greek in Lucian. I said my prayers, and had milk for breakfast. It rained this morning, the wind north. I danced my dance. I wrote some English and looked after my people till dinner and then ate some bacon and French beans. After dinner I put several things in order and wrote more English till the evening and then Frank Lightfoot came and we played at billiards. In about an hour he took leave and returned to Mrs. Harrison's but the rain hindered . . .

5. Mary, daughter of Drury Stith, married Buller Herbert, a grandson of Lord Herbert.

6. Probably Anne Stith, widow of Robert Bolling of Kippax.

21. I rose about 5 o'clock and read a chapter in Hebrew but no Greek because I prepared to go over the river to Major Mumford's and notwithstanding it rained a little I went about 7 o'clock and got to the Major's about eleven and found them all well. I said my prayers by the way and about 12 o'clock we went to church, where the clerk read prayers because Parson Robinson was gone to Williamsburg. Major Kennon, John and Drury Bolling were at church and went home with the Major to dinner, and so did Dick Kennon, and I ate some roast shoat. After dinner we drank a bowl of punch till the evening and then the company went away and the Major and I took a walk. We sat and talked till 9 o'clock and then I retired and said my prayers but slept very indifferently.

22. I rose about 7 o'clock and read some Greek and then dressed myself and said my prayers devoutly. About 9 o'clock we went to breakfast and I ate some apple pie and milk. Then we walked to see the [still] at work and I learned the way of making the [sawed fence]. About 1 o'clock we went over the river[7] to dine with Dick Kennon where Major Kennon met me and Mrs. Bolling and her son, and I ate some boiled lamb for dinner. After dinner we played at cards and I won six bits. Here we stayed till dark and then returned to Major Mumford's where we sat up till [*sic*] and talked till 9 o'clock and I was so hot that I walked naked in the chamber till ten. Felt an inclination for a woman. I said a short prayer and slept pretty well.

23. I rose about 7 o'clock and read some Greek and then dressed myself and said my prayers and about 9 o'clock I had apple pie and milk for breakfast. The weather was extremely hot. We sat and talked till 12 o'clock and then went over the river and called on Dick Kennon, where we found the Major and Drury Bolling and they went with us to Major Bolling's to dinner. By the way we called on Hal Randolph[8] for half an hour and drank a glass of claret and then proceeded on our way but were overtaken by a great shower of

7. The Kennons and Bollings lived on the north side of the Appomattox River.

8. Henry Randolph of Chatsworth, sixth son of Colonel William Randolph 1.

rain and were very wet and got to Major Bolling's about 3 o'clock. The Major was not yet returned but we had a good dinner and I ate some boiled beef. After dinner the Major came from Williamsburg but brought no news. We played at cards and drank punch all the evening till 11 o'clock and then retired. I said my prayers and slept pretty well, thank God.

24. I rose about 7 o'clock and read some Greek and then dressed myself and about 8 o'clock drank some chocolate for breakfast. I said a short prayer. About ten I took leave and John Bolling went with me to Colonel Hill's where I found old Parson Robinson. Here we stayed and drank tea and ate bread and butter till 2 o'clock and I went home and John Bolling went to see Ben Harrison. I got home about 3 o'clock and found all well, thank God. Mr. Stanhope and I agreed at last about the land at Taskanask. My man John was better in his hand. In the evening I took a walk to Mrs. Harrison's where I ate some roast beef. She was not very well. About nine I walked home and committed uncleanness with Annie, for which God forgive me.

25. I rose about 5 o'clock and read a chapter in Hebrew and some Greek. I said my prayers, and had milk for breakfast. The weather was clear and hot, the wind west. I danced my dance and wrote a letter to Hal Anderson and then came Sam Harwood and his uncle and stayed quarter of an hour. About 1 o'clock I walked to the courthouse to see the people choose burgesses and they chose John Stith and Sam Harwood. I brought six ladies home to dinner and ate some fish. After dinner we returned to the courthouse again to see the [behavior] of the people, which was extravagant, but Sam Harwood was courteous even to his adversary. About 7 o'clock I walked home and carried Mrs. Duke with me and Sam Harwood's daughters till Sam Harwood called for them. I talked with my people, said my prayers, and slept pretty well, thank God, because it was cool.

26. I rose about 5 o'clock and read a chapter in Hebrew and some Greek. I said my prayers, and had milk for breakfast. The weather was cool and clear, the wind northwest. I danced my dance and then walked to see my people work. Then I wrote some English till twelve

and then read Latin till dinner when I ate bacon and French beans. After dinner I took a little nap and then put several things in order. Afterwards I wrote more English and then read more Latin till the evening and then walked to Mrs. Harrison's whom I found indisposed but I persuaded her to take the bark. About eight I returned home and talked with my people and said my prayers.

27. I rose about 5 o'clock and read a chapter in Hebrew and some Greek. I said my prayers, and had milk for breakfast. The weather was cool and clear, the wind west. I danced my dance and then walked to see my people. Then I wrote some English and after that some Latin till dinner, when I ate some boiled crab. After dinner I put several things in order. Then I read some news, and then some English in the library till the evening, when I took a walk about the plantation. At night I talked with my people about their several businesses, said my prayers, and retired. I slept exceedingly well, thank God, and dreamed the King's daughter was in love with me.

28. I rose about 5 o'clock and read a chapter in Hebrew and some Greek. I said my prayers, and had milk and potato for breakfast. The weather was clear and cold, the wind north. I danced my dance and then read some English till 11 o'clock and then walked to church where I slept in the sermon, for which God forgive me. After church I asked Frank Hardyman and his wife, the parson, and Mrs. Duke to dine with me and I ate some roast shoat. After dinner we sat and talked till about 6 o'clock and then all the company went away and I took a walk about the plantation. At night I talked with my people and said my prayers and slept pretty well. I dreamed I made love to a young sister and made her in love with me while I intended to get the older.

29. I rose about 5 o'clock and read a chapter in Hebrew and some Greek. I said my prayers, and had milk for breakfast. The weather was cold and clear, the wind north. I danced my dance. I looked after my people and then wrote some English till twelve and then read some Latin till dinner and ate some crabs for dinner. In the afternoon I put several things in order and then wrote more English till 4

o'clock, when Mrs. Duke and Mrs. [Underhill] came to inquire what Mr. [Underhill] stole from me and I let her know what it was and then told her that for her sake I would not prosecute him. In the evening they went away and I took a walk about the plantation. At night I talked with my servants and said my prayers.

30. I rose about 5 o'clock and as soon as I was dressed I said my prayers and recommended my family to the Divine Protection and then rode to Frank Hardyman's where I drank tea with them and then Frank and I went with Colonel Eppes to Varina to the election of burgesses in the upper county,[9] where we went to visit Mr. Finney who gave us nothing but small beer. Then I went to John Bolling's from whose house we walked to the courthouse where I found Mrs. Randolph, the two Blands and Mrs. Eppes. Colonel Randolph and his brother Tom had the great number of votes by their great industry. When all was over I walked back to John Bolling's where I dined and ate some bacon. After dinner I took leave and Major Mumford and I went over the river and rode to his house where we got about 9 o'clock and John Banister went with us. I said my prayers.

31. I rose about 7 o'clock and read some English. I said my prayers and had apple pie and milk for breakfast. The weather was very warm and clear, the wind south. I agreed with John Banister to live at Westover and I would give him thirty pounds a year current money. Then we walked to Mr. Herbert's[10] who brought his wife home yesterday. Then we went over the river and went to Major Bolling's and dined with him and I ate some roast lamb. After dinner we took leave and went home by way of the Hundred[11] and found everybody well, thank God, except Billy Wilkins and Ned. I talked with my people and said my prayers. I slept but indifferently because it was very hot.

9. Henrico County.

10. Buller Herbert, bridegroom of Mary Stith.

11. Bermuda Hundred.

September 1720

1. I rose about 5 o'clock and read a chapter in Hebrew and some Greek. I said my prayers, and had milk and potato for breakfast. The weather was warm and cloudy. I danced my dance and then wrote some English till dinner, when I ate some roast pork. After dinner I put several things in order and then wrote more English till the evening, when I took a walk to Mrs. Harrison's where I ate some milk and apples and some fruit. Here I stayed and talked till 8 o'clock and then walked home and talked with several of my people till nine and then retired and said a short prayer.

2. I rose about 6 o'clock and read a chapter in Hebrew and some Greek. I said my prayers, and had milk for breakfast. The weather was cold and cloudy, the wind southeast and threatening rain. I danced my dance and then walked to see my people beat cider. Then I wrote some English till dinner when I ate some bacon and French beans. After dinner I put several things in order and then wrote more English till the evening, when I took a walk but went not far because it threatened rain. I talked with my people and said my prayers, but at night had the misfortune to commit uncleanness with Annie. It rained in the night pretty much.

3. I rose about 6 o'clock and read a chapter in Hebrew and some Greek in Lucian. I said my prayers, and had milk and potato for breakfast. The weather was cool and clear, the wind northwest. I danced my dance. I walked to see my people work. Then I wrote some English till about 11 o'clock, when Mr. O-l-g-v came to settle Mr. P-l-t account with me. Then I read some Latin till dinner, when I ate some crab for dinner. After dinner I put several things in order and caused F-r-b-y to be whipped because she stole peaches and then

told a lie. I read more Latin till the evening, and then I took a walk
about the plantation. At night I gave the people some cider, had my
feet washed, talked with my people, said my prayers, and then retired
and slept pretty well, thank God.

4. I rose about 6 o'clock and read a chapter in Hebrew and some
Greek in Lucian. I said my prayers devoutly, and had milk and potato
for breakfast. The weather was clear and cool, the wind northwest.
I read some English till 11 o'clock and then walked to church, where
Dick read prayers to us and after church I walked to Mrs. Harrison's
to dinner, where I ate some fowl and bacon. Mrs. Sarah Hardyman
dined with us. Mrs. Harrison herself was indisposed. After dinner we
sat and talked and drank coffee till the evening and then I took leave
and walked home, where I found all well, thank God. I talked with
my people and said my prayers and then I tempted Annie to let me
feel her, but she would not let me, for which she is to be commended
and for which God be praised.

5. I rose about 6 o'clock and read a chapter in Hebrew and some
Greek in Lucian. I said my prayers, and had milk and potato for
breakfast. The weather was cold and cloudy, the wind north. I
danced my dance. I wrote two letters and received the news that Mrs.
Lightfoot was brought to bed of a girl last night. I sent my boat to
Mr. Lightfoot's for coal. I wrote some English till dinner and then
ate some bacon and eggs. After dinner I put several things in order
and then read some Latin till the evening, and then took a walk
about the plantation and looked after all my people. At night I said
my prayers and slept but indifferently.

6. I rose about 6 o'clock and read a chapter in Hebrew and some
Greek in Lucian. I said my prayers, and had milk and potato for
breakfast. The weather was cold and clear, the wind southeast. I
danced my dance. Then I went to see my people work and then
wrote some English till dinner and in the afternoon put several things
in order and then wrote more English and read some Latin. My
bricklayer had an ague but I learned nothing of it till night. In the
evening I took a walk about the plantation and at night talked with

my people, said my prayers, and committed uncleanness with Annie, for which God forgive me.

7. I rose about 6 o'clock and read a chapter in Hebrew and some Greek in Lucian. I said my prayers and had milk for breakfast. The weather was cold and cloudy and it threatened rain. I read some law to look for cases to serve Mrs. Harrison's business[1] and about 2 o'clock I went to court, where I met her and soon after came Mr. Roscow and Mr. Cole[2] to visit me. These two gentlemen and Colonel Harrison and Colonel Hill dined with me and I ate some boiled beef. After dinner it rained abundance. However, Colonel Hill would go home, but the other gentlemen stayed and we drank a bottle of wine and were merry but about nine Colonel Harrison went to Mrs. Harrison's and I retired and said a short prayer.

8. I rose about 6 o'clock and read some Greek before the gentlemen rose and when they were up we played at billiards till breakfast, and then I drank some chocolate and about ten we walked to Mrs. Harrison's where we ate another breakfast and for my part I ate some fried chicken. Then we went over the river to Prince George courthouse to the great race between Captain Harrison and Robin Bolling, and I lost thirty shillings. About [sic] we had a dinner there and I ate some boiled beef. Mrs. Duke and Mrs. O-n-t were there and dined with us. About 6 o'clock we returned over the river and Major Kennon and Major Mumford followed us and we ate some bacon and chicken for supper and laughed and were merry till 10 o'clock and then retired and committed uncleanness with Annie, for which God forgive me. Colonel Harrison's lady was at Mrs. Harrison's.

9. I rose about 6 o'clock and read nothing but played at billiards till breakfast and then I drank two dishes of chocolate. About 9 o'clock we walked again to Mrs. Harrison's in order to go again over the river to the same place to see another race, where I won about

1. Mrs. Harrison was trying to prove her title to lands held by Benjamin Harrison before his death.

2. William Cole was burgess from Warwick County.

three pounds, but we were disappointed of our dinner because the woman was sick. I was much tired and played at piquet with Frank Lightfoot and lost a little. Here we stayed till sunset again and then Colonel Harrison and Frank Lightfoot, Frank Taylor and Mrs. P-r-s went home with me to supper and we all ate abundantly because we had no dinner and I ate some lamb pie. After supper we were exceedingly merry till 11 o'clock and then all the gentlemen except Mr. Cole and Mr. Roscow walked by moonshine to Mrs. Harrison's. I neglected my prayers, for which God forgive me.

10. I rose about 6 o'clock and read a chapter in Hebrew and some Greek. I said my prayers, and had veal broth for breakfast, but the gentlemen had meat. I showed them the granary and the kitchen garden and about 10 o'clock they took leave and went away and then I walked about to see my business and people work and then read some Latin. I had whipped Moll for lying if Hannah had not asked for her. I ate some roast lamb for dinner. After dinner I took a nap and then read more Latin till the evening and then I took a walk about the plantation. At night I talked with my people and then read Latin till 9 o'clock. Then I said my prayers and retired and slept very well, thank God.

11. I rose about 6 o'clock and read a chapter in Hebrew and some Greek. I said my prayers, and had milk and potato for breakfast. The weather was cold and clear, the wind northeast. I danced my dance, cleaned my teeth, and got ready to go to church, where Mr. Robinson gave us an indifferent sermon. After church I invited Colonel Eppes and his daughter, Frank Hardyman and his wife, and Mrs. Duke to dinner and ate some veal and bacon. After dinner we sat and talked till the evening and then the company went away and I walked about the plantation. At night I talked with my people. I ordered all my people some cider. I read some English till 9 o'clock and then said my prayers and committed uncleanness with Annie, for which God forgive me. I slept very well.

12. I rose about 6 o'clock and read a chapter in Hebrew and some Greek. I said my prayers, and had boiled milk for breakfast. The

weather was cool and foggy, the wind southwest. I danced my dance. I walked to see my people work and then wrote three letters till dinner and then ate some roast veal. After dinner I put several things in order and then read some Latin. About 3 o'clock Major Kennon sent his boat for twenty-five bushels of salt and Major Mumford sent his cooper. About four I walked to Mrs. Harrison's where I sat and talked till sunset and then returned home and talked with my people. Then I read some Latin. My maid Annie had an ague. About nine I said my prayers and retired. I slept very well, thank God. We beat cider.

13. I rose about 6 o'clock and read a chapter in Hebrew and some Greek in Lucian. I said my prayers, and had milk and potato for breakfast. The weather was cool and clear, the wind southwest. I danced my dance. We beat cider again and then I settled some accounts and wrote a letter. About eleven I ate some bread and butter and then came Mrs. Duke and I went with her to Frank Hardyman's and from thence to Colonel Eppes's with Frank and his wife. Here we found Lewellin Eppes [and] his wife. The Colonel received us kindly but things were in no great order. However, I ate some [fraise of fowls]. After dinner we rode all to visit Colonel Hill, who fell from his horse and received some hurt. Here I stayed about quarter of an hour and then rode home where I found all well except Annie who had an ague. I talked with my people and gave them some cider. Then I read a sermon and about nine said my prayers and retired, but slept indifferently.

14. I rose about 6 o'clock and read a chapter in Hebrew and some Greek in Lucian. I said my prayers, and had milk for breakfast. The weather was hot and cloudy, the wind . . . My sloop went up about noon to the Falls and I wrote three letters till dinner and then ate some veal cutlets. After dinner I put several things in order and then wrote another letter. One of my people came from the Falls and brought word that one of my boys had broken his leg. I walked about the plantation till the evening and then talked with my people. Then I read some English, said my prayers, and slept but indifferently. Annie continued sick, notwithstanding she took the bark.

15. I rose about 6 o'clock and read a chapter in Hebrew and some Greek. I said my prayers, and had milk for breakfast. The weather was very hot and clear, the wind southwest. I danced my dance and then took a walk to see my people work. Then I wrote some English and read some Latin till dinner, when I ate some boiled beef. After dinner I put some things in order and then read more Latin and wrote a letter till the evening, when I walked about the plantation. At night I gave most of the people a dram and made them beat cider till 10 o'clock. I read a sermon in Tillotson, said my prayers, and about nine retired and said my prayers.

16. I rose about 6 o'clock and read a chapter in Hebrew and some Greek in Lucian. I said my prayers and had milk for breakfast. The weather was grown very cold and cloudy, the wind northeast. I danced my dance. I prepared to go out but was hindered a little by Mr. G-r-y who came to advise me about his health and I gave him the best advice I could. About eleven I rode to Frank Hardyman's and from thence walked with him and his wife to Lewellin Eppes's, where Colonel Eppes, Mrs. Anderson, Miss Hill, and John Stith's wife came and dined with us and I ate some fowl and bacon. After dinner Drury Stith came and about five I took leave and rode home, where I found everybody well except Annie, who had a fever this day. I read a sermon in Dr. Tillotson, talked with my people, said my prayers, and retired about 9 o'clock and slept pretty well.

17. I rose about 6 o'clock and read a chapter in Hebrew and some Greek in Lucian. I said my prayers, and had milk for breakfast. The weather was cold and cloudy, the wind southeast and threatening rain. I danced my dance. Then I walked to see my people work. Then we put things in order in the cellar. I ran after the hogs that got into the corn and read English till dinner when I ate some roast beef. After dinner I put several things in order and then worked again in the cellar till the evening, when I took a walk about the plantation and when I returned I found my brother Duke[3] and his wife. I re-

3. James Duke, sheriff of James City County; since Byrd refers to his wife as 'sister' and as an aunt of Susan Brayne (daughter of Byrd's sister Susan), it seems likely that Mrs. Duke was Byrd's sister Mary.

ceived them kindly. I gave them souse, fish, and roast beef for supper. We talked till about 9 o'clock and then retired. I said my prayers and slept pretty well, thank God.

18. I rose about 6 o'clock and read a chapter in Hebrew and some Greek. I said my prayers, and had milk for breakfast. The weather was cold and cloudy, the wind east. I danced my dance and about 11 o'clock we walked to church, where the clerk read prayers. After church we went home and Mrs. Harrison went with us to dinner and I ate some boiled beef. After dinner we sat and talked till the evening and then walked with Mrs. Harrison almost home and then returned and sat and talked all the evening till 9 o'clock and then we retired and I said a short prayer and wrote two letters. I slept pretty well, thank God.

19. I rose about 6 o'clock and read a chapter in Hebrew and some Greek in Lucian. I said my prayers, and had chocolate for breakfast. My brother went this morning to visit Colonel Eppes and I desired him to bring him to dinner. I sent home Mr. Mumford's cooper with a letter of thanks. The weather was cloudy and warm. I danced my dance. I scolded at John F-l for stealing the people's potatoes. About 12 o'clock came Mrs. Duke and her lawyer, Mr. Poythress, and dined with my brother and sister Duke and I ate some pork collops. After dinner we sat and talked and then I went and put up my things. In the evening we sat to drink several healths till 9 o'clock and then retired and I said my prayers and packed up my things, and slept very well, thank God.

20. I rose about 5 o'clock and said my prayers and then got everything ready for my journey. Then I drank two dishes of chocolate and took leave and left all the company there. I rode with pleasure because it was a cool morning and said several prayers by the way. I got to New Kent courthouse about 11 o'clock and there had some milk. Here I saw Dr. Burbage[4] and treated him with a bottle of English beer. He rode a little way with me and I got well to Colonel

4. Robert Burbage, physician, of New Kent County.

Bassett's [5] about 2 o'clock where I was received courteously and about three we went to dinner and I ate some roast beef. After dinner we sat and talked about an hour and then the Colonel and I took a walk and in the evening I sat with my cousin A-l-n who had a fever and took the bark. About 7 o'clock I drank two dishes of chocolate. About nine I retired and said my prayers and slept pretty well, thank God.

21. I rose about 6 o'clock and read a little Hebrew and a little Greek. I said my prayers, and ate some milk for breakfast. The weather was cloudy and it rained a little all day, the wind northeast. I showed several things to Colonel Bassett of my writing and then went and talked with the ladies till 2 o'clock, when we went to dinner and I ate some roast turkey. After dinner we sat and talked till 5 o'clock and then we drank coffee. Then I read some English to the ladies and then talked till eight and then we drank chocolate and talked till ten and then retired and I said my prayers. It continued to rain, the wind northeast. I slept well, thank God.

22. I rose about 6 o'clock and read some Hebrew but no Greek. I said my prayers, and had rice milk for breakfast. It continued to rain a little, the wind northeast. I packed up my things and about 10 o'clock took leave and went in Colonel Bassett's coach with Mrs. Corbin to the brick house and from thence we went in Colonel Bassett's boat to Colonel Corbin's where we got about 1 o'clock and the tide was so high we could not get over it without difficulty. Colonel Bassett went with us. Colonel Corbin [6] received us very courteously and about three we went to dinner and I ate some beans and bacon. After dinner we walked to see the new house that was building. About 5 o'clock Colonel Bassett returned home and we walked a little and then drank a bowl of punch made of arrack. We sat and talked till ten and then retired and I said my prayers. It rained exceedingly all night.

5. Colonel Bassett lived at Eltham, New Kent County, on the York River.

6. Colonel Gawin Corbin, a burgess from Middlesex County, lived on the north side of the York River.

23. I rose about 6 o'clock and read a chapter in Hebrew, but no Greek. I said my prayers, and drank chocolate. The weather was cloudy, the wind southwest. About 9 o'clock I ate some milk. Then I read all my papers to Colonel Corbin and his lady, concerning what I did in England. Then we talked and walked till 2 o'clock, when I ate some boiled tongue and chicken. After dinner we went to see the workmen build the new house. Then we took a walk and at night we drank a little bowl of arrack punch and then had some chocolate. We talked and were merry till 10 o'clock and then I retired and read some Greek till almost eleven and then said my prayers.

24. I rose about 6 o'clock and read a chapter in Hebrew but no Greek. I said my prayers, and had first chocolate and then milk for breakfast. The weather was warm and cloudy, the wind west. About 10 o'clock we took leave and Colonel Corbin and I went in his coach and six to John Grymes's[7] which is about sixteen miles, where we found him in an ague but his wife was well, thank God. We talked about several matters till 3 o'clock and then I ate some boiled beef for dinner. After dinner we walked about the garden, which was pretty, till the evening and then we sat and talked till about nine when I retired and read some Greek and put several things in order and then said my prayers and retired.

25. I rose about 6 o'clock and read a chapter in Hebrew and then said my prayers. The weather continued cloudy, and it rained a little, the wind northeast. I ate some milk for breakfast. About 9 o'clock Tom R-d came over the river and about eleven came John Wormeley and Matt Kemp to visit me and just before dinner came Charles Grymes.[8] I ate some boiled beef. After dinner we sat and talked and could not walk because the weather was misty. Mr. Corbin went to church after breakfast to talk with people about his election. John Grymes continued sick. The company stayed all night except Tom

7. John Grymes lived at Brandon, Middlesex County, on the Rappahannock River.

8. John Wormeley of Rosegill, on the Rappahannock, Matthew Kemp, and Charles Grymes, brother of John Grymes, all of Middlesex County.

R-d and we sat and talked till 9 o'clock and then we retired and I said my prayers and read some Greek.

26. I rose about 6 o'clock and read a chapter in Hebrew. I said my prayers and had milk for breakfast. The weather was warm and cloudy, the wind northeast. We persuaded John Grymes to take the bark and about 12 o'clock took leave and I went with John Wormeley in his chariot to his house where we got about one and about two dined and I ate some boiled beef. After dinner we walked about the plantation which is very pretty and then played at billiards and I lost about ten shillings. At night we drank about a pint of rack punch apiece and about 11 o'clock retired and I was forced to lie with Dr. Blair because there was abundance of company in the house. Mrs. Wormeley was indisposed so that we neither saw her nor any other woman. I said my prayers. Joe R-ng was very sick.

27. I rose about 7 o'clock and read some English only. I said a short prayer, and had milk tea for breakfast. The weather was warm and clear, the wind southwest. About 10 o'clock Jack Wormeley and Charles Grymes went to the election and left Dr. Blair and me at home. We walked and then played at piquet and then played at billiards, and I won about a crown. Then we ate bread and butter to stay our stomachs, and diverted ourselves till about 4 o'clock, and then came Mr. Corbin, Harry Armistead,[9] Dr. [Downing]. These gentlemen told me that Corbin and John Grymes were the burgesses. About five we went to dinner and I ate some roast beef. After dinner we had a bowl of rack punch and Mr. C-ch, a very [horrid] fellow, came very drunk. About eleven we retired and I said my prayers.

28. I rose about 7 o'clock and read nothing because of the company. I neglected my prayers, but had milk and tea for breakfast. The weather continued warm, the wind southeast. About 11 o'clock I took leave of the gentlemen, and John Wormeley went with us to M-t-m ferry in Mr. Grymes's coach and from thence were set over

9. Colonel Henry Armistead, of Hesse, Gloucester County.

the river at Colonel Carter's.[10] The Colonel met us with abundant courtesy and about 4 o'clock went to dinner and there I saw Miss Anne Carter,[11] a very agreeable girl. I ate some chicken fricassee. After dinner the ladies took leave and retired and we drank some rack punch till 11 o'clock and then retired and I lay in the fine room and slept very well, thank God. It rained pretty much.

29. I rose about 7 o'clock and read nothing but English. I neglected to say my prayers, but had milk tea for breakfast. The weather was clear and cool, the wind northwest. We played at cards and I lost two bits. Then we took a walk about the plantation and then sat and talked till dinner when I ate some roast duck. After dinner Jack Wormeley took leave, and Charles Grymes came in the evening. We took a walk till the evening and then played at cards and took on the ladies and played with them till 10 o'clock when I retired and said my prayers. Charles Grymes told us his brother was sick again.

30. I rose about 7 o'clock and read a chapter in Hebrew and some Greek. I said my prayers, and had milk tea for breakfast. The weather was cool and clear, the wind northwest. About 10 o'clock we played at cards and I lost a little. About 12 o'clock Captain P-n-g-t and his daughter came and Mr. Stagg, the dance master, and I danced a minuet with Mrs. Anne Carter and Miss P-n-g-t. About 2 o'clock we dined and I ate some boiled beef. After dinner we danced again, French dances and country dances, and drank some rack punch and played at cards till 11 o'clock and then we retired.

10. Corotoman, on the Rappahannock River in Lancaster County.

11. Anne, daughter of Colonel Carter, married Ben Harrison about 1722.

October 1720

1. I rose about 7 o'clock and read a chapter in Hebrew and some Greek. I said my prayers, and had milk tea for breakfast. The weather was cold and clear, the wind northeast. I packed up my things with intention to go after breakfast, but the Colonel persuaded me to stay till after dinner, so we played at cards till 12 o'clock and then came Colonel Page and his lady and Major Burwell.[1] I ate some boiled chicken. In the afternoon we took leave of the Colonel and his fine daughters and the rest of the company and went over the river to M-t-s-m where we met Major Burwell's lady going to her husband at Colonel Carter's and I handed her to the boat. Then we went to Mr. Grymes to his house in his coach, where we found them pretty well. I said my prayers.

2. I rose about 7 o'clock and read a chapter in Hebrew and some Greek. The weather was cold and cloudy, the wind northeast. About 10 o'clock we went in the coach to church with Mrs. Grymes, where we found Mr. Wormeley and all the citizens of Urbanna. Mr. Yates[2] gave us a good sermon. After church I talked to all the citizens of Urbanna and then returned in the coach to Mr. Grymes's to dinner and ate some boiled beef. After dinner we took leave and Mr. Wormeley went with the doctor and me to Mr. Armistead's in his wherry and got there about 7 o'clock and were kindly received by Mr. Armistead and his lady. We drank a bowl of rack punch and about 10 o'clock retired and I neglected my prayers, for which God forgive me.

1. Lewis Burwell, son of Nathaniel; his wife was Mary Willis.

2. Bartholomew Yates, minister of Christ Church Parish, Middlesex County, 1703–34.

3. I rose about 7 o'clock and read a chapter in Hebrew and some Greek. I said my prayers, and had bread and butter and tea for breakfast. The weather was cold and cloudy, the wind northeast. Then we walked to see his horses run. Then we returned to the house and saw Mr. Stagg teach his scholars to dance. Then we played at cards and I lost a little till dinner and then I ate some hashed chicken. After dinner we took a walk about the plantation and at night played at cards again. Parson Jones[3] dined here and Parson Wye[4] lives in the house. We had some rack punch and sat up till 10 o'clock and then retired without saying my prayers.

4. I rose about 7 o'clock and read some Greek. I said my prayers, and had toast and butter and tea for breakfast. The weather was cold and clear, the wind northwest. About ten the doctor and I took leave and rode away in a journey of twenty miles to Colonel Lewis'[5] where we got about 2 o'clock and found the Colonel at home and he received us kindly and I ate some broiled beef. After dinner we took a walk about the plantation and at night Mr. Brook came and I talked with him about my business at the Falls. At night we drank a bottle of claret and sat and talked till 10 o'clock and then retired and I said my prayers. I committed uncleanness.

5. I rose about 7 o'clock and read nothing. However, I said a short prayer, and had [c-l-r] beef for breakfast. The weather was cold and clear, the wind northwest. About 10 o'clock I drank two glasses of sack and then we took leave of Colonel Lewis and rode to H-l Bay where we saw my cousin Martin. Her husband was gone abroad; however, we stayed about an hour with her and then went over the

3. Reverend Emanuel Jones, minister of Petworth Parish, Gloucester County.

4. William Wye, appointed missionary to Goose Creek, South Carolina, in 1717; his credentials were said to have been forged and his appointment was canceled. Edwin L. Goodwin, *The Colonial Church in Virginia* (London, 1927), 318.

5. John Lewis, of Warner Hall, Gloucester County, on the Severn River near the Bay.

river and rode to Colonel Digges's,[6] who received us kindly and we dined there and I ate some roast beef. After dinner we drank a bottle of claret and then took leave and rode to Williamsburg, where I went to wait on the Governor, where I found Captain Wharwood, Captain Martin,[7] and several others. I stayed about an hour and then went to the Commissary's where I drank two dishes of chocolate, and Mrs. Stith[8] and Mrs. Keith were with us. Here I stayed till 10 o'clock and then walked home and read some Greek and said my prayers. I slept pretty well, thank God.

6. I rose about 7 o'clock and read a chapter in Hebrew and some Greek. I said my prayers, and had boiled milk for breakfast. The weather was clear and warm, the wind west. About 8 o'clock the Commissary, Mrs. Stith, and Mrs. Keith came to see us and stayed till ten and then I walked to the Governor's where I saw Mrs. Russell. Here I stayed till 12 o'clock and then walked to Dr. Blair's and from thence to the College to the Commissary's lodging where I took my leave and rode to Green Springs, where I found Mr. Corbin and his lady, Colonel Allen and his lady. I ate some boiled beef for dinner. After dinner I took a walk and at night sat and talked till about 9 o'clock and then took leave and retired and slept pretty well, thank God.

7. . . . . the wind west. About 10 o'clock Colonel Corbin and his lady, Colonel Allen and his lady, and Colonel Ludwell and I went to

6. Cole Digges was elected a burgess by Warwick County but did not serve as he was sworn a member of the Council on September 15, 1720. He lived at Bellfield, on the York River.

7. Captain John Martin was sent by the Governor and Council in command of a brig to St. Augustine with a flag of truce to stop privateering. Captain Wharwood supplied armament from his ship, the *Rye*. Martin lost his vessel. See *The Journals of the House of Burgesses*, I, 303–4.

8. Mrs. Mary (Randolph) Stith, widow of Captain John Stith, who boarded and lodged the masters and scholars of the College 'in the neatest and most regular and plentiful manner.' Hugh Jones, *Present State of Virginia*, ed. Richard Morton (Chapel Hill, N.C., 1956), 68, 186. Her son William later became president of the College.

Williamsburg, where we made first a visit to Major Custis, who was a little better, thank God. Then we went to the Governor's, who was from home. Then we went to the President's, where we found the Governor. The President gave us some strong water. Then we went to sit in Council in the capitol where we agreed to fit out a sloop to go with a flag of truce to St. Augustine. We appointed Captain Martin to command her. About 4 o'clock we went to dine with the Governor with the company that came from Colonel Ludwell's this morning and I took some roast pig. After dinner we sat about an hour and then Colonel Ludwell and I went to Green Springs, where we talked till nine and then we retired and I said my prayers.

8. I rose about 7 o'clock and read a chapter in Hebrew and some Greek. I said my prayers, and had boiled milk for breakfast. The weather was clear and cold, the wind northwest. About 9 o'clock I took leave and rode home in five hours and nothing remarkable happened by the way. I got home about 2 o'clock and found all well, thank God, and all my business in good order. About 3 o'clock I ate some blue-wing for dinner and then put several things in order till the evening, when I took a walk about the plantation. At night I talked with my people and gave them some cider, and then wrote some English till 8 o'clock and then retired and said my prayers.

9. I rose about 7 o'clock and read a chapter in Hebrew and some Greek in Lucian. I said my prayers, and had milk and potato for breakfast. The weather was cold and clear, the wind north. I danced my dance and then put several things in order till church and then about eleven I went and found all my neighbors well and glad to see me. After church I invited Mrs. Harrison, her son and daughter, Colonel Eppes and his son and daughter, and Mrs. Duke and her daughter to dinner with me and I ate some pork. After dinner we sat and talked and about 4 o'clock they all took leave and I walked about the plantation. At night I talked with my people and gave orders and then read some Greek till 8 o'clock. Then I said my prayers and retired.

10. I rose about 7 o'clock and read a chapter in Hebrew and some Greek in Lucian. I said my prayers, and had boiled milk for breakfast. The weather was cold and clear, the wind southwest. I danced my dance. Then I took a walk to see my people work and then wrote a letter to the Falls. Then came Captain Lewellin Eppes and stayed about an hour; then came Major Mumford and John Banister and dined with me and I ate some boiled pork. After dinner we took a walk about the plantation and in the evening drank some cider and talked several matters till 9 o'clock and then retired. I said a short prayer and slept but indifferently. It rained all night.

11. I rose about 7 o'clock and read a little Greek. I said my prayers, and had boiled milk for breakfast and my friends had chocolate. The weather continued rainy, the wind northeast. Then we played at billiards and the Major beat me two games. Then I wrote some English while he and Banister played. John Banister came to begin his year. The Major, notwithstanding it rained, would not stay but went to Prince George Court. I ate some fish for dinner. After dinner I began to pack up my things for the General Court. In the evening I could not go out to walk because it continued to rain. At night John Banister and I discoursed about several matters till 8 o'clock and then we retired. I said my prayers and slept pretty well, thank God.

12. I rose about 7 o'clock and read nothing because I prepared for my going to town. I said my prayers, and had boiled milk for breakfast. It continued to rain and I continued to pack up my things all the morning till dinner and then I ate some fish. After dinner I put several things in order and let all my people know what they were to do in my absence. In the evening came several of my overseers from New Kent and I learned that all my people were well, thank God. They told me of several of their wants and made several complaints, of which little notice is to be taken. In the evening I took a walk and at night wrote what orders I had to leave in writing. About ten I said my prayers and retired.

13. I rose about 7 o'clock and put all my business in order for my journey. I said my prayers, and had boiled milk for breakfast. The weather was warm and clear, the wind southwest. About nine young John Bolling came but I left John Banister to entertain him and gave him chocolate. About ten I committed my family to the Divine protection and rode with my two overseers to New Kent. I called at the courthouse where I executed conveyances to Mr. M-r-s and Mr. Stanhope. Colonel Bassett was there and took Major Merriweather and myself home with him, where I was courteously entertained and ate beef for supper. We sat and talked till 10 o'clock and then retired and I said my prayers.

14. I rose about 7 o'clock and read a little Greek. I said my prayers, and had rice milk for breakfast. The weather was exceedingly hot and clear. However, about 10 o'clock I took leave and rode to Williamsburg, but my horse was almost tired and so was I likewise. However I got about 2 o'clock to Major Custis' where I ate some bacon and eggs for dinner. About 4 o'clock I sent for Harry Cary[9] and took lodgings at his house. Then came Dr. Blair and I went with him to the Governor's, who received me gravely. I told him I had heard he had been told that I had been busy at elections and justified myself from that calumny. I went from hence to the Commissary's where I drank some ale and ate some cake and about nine walked to Major Custis' where I lay. I neglected my prayers, for which God forgive me.

15. I rose about 7 o'clock and read nothing because I wished to put my lodging in order. However, I said my prayers, and had boiled milk for breakfast. The weather continued warm and clear, the wind southwest. I talked half an hour with Major Custis and then walked to my house and put things in order there. About ten I waited on the President and went with him to the Governor's. About eleven we went to court and sat till one and then sat in Council about some letters from the Governor of Pennsylvania. Then we went to the Governor's to dinner and I ate some tongue and udder. About five I took leave and walked with the Commissary to my lodging and from

9. Henry Cary, a builder of Williamsburg; he built the president's house at the College.

thence to the College where I saw Mrs. Keith and Mrs. Stith. I sat there and talked till nine and then went to my new lodging, where I put everything in order. It continued hot. I neglected my prayers, for which God forgive me.

16. I rose about 7 o'clock and read a chapter in Hebrew and some Greek. I said my prayers, and had boiled milk for breakfast. The weather changed and grew cold and it rained, the wind northwest. I read some English. The Secretary called on me about eleven but did not stay because he was going to his [p-s-r-t]. I could not go to church because it rained, but I put several things in order till 1 o'clock and then the doctor sent his coach for me and I went to dine with him and ate some roast beef and there dined with us a Frenchman from Martinique. Then we went to church and Mr. Fontaine preached. After church we went back again with the Secretary and carried the Commissary and his brother with us and there we spent the evening and drank a bottle of good claret till nine and then walked home, read the Commissary's Latin verses, and said my prayers.

17. I rose about 7 o'clock, and read a chapter in Hebrew and some Greek. I said my prayers, and had boiled milk for breakfast. The weather was cold and clear, the wind northwest. I read some Latin till 10 o'clock and then came the Commissary and stayed about half an hour. Then I walked to the capitol and sat in court till 12 o'clock and then because I had nobody to dine with at the ordinary I went to dine with the Commissary and ate some chicken and bacon. After dinner we sat and talked till the evening and then drank coffee. At night we sent for Mrs. Stith and played at cards till 9 o'clock and I lost two bits. About nine I walked home and read some English and said my prayers.

18. I rose about 7 o'clock and read a chapter in Hebrew and some Greek in Lucian. I said my prayers, and had milk for breakfast. The weather continued cold and clear, the wind northwest. I read some French and then about 10 o'clock walked to the capitol and by the way called at the President's. About 11 o'clock we sat, and finished the business about one, and then I walked to Colonel Ludwell's and from thence with him to the College, where we dined with the Commissary and I ate some beefsteak. After dinner we called on Mrs. Stith and then Colonel Ludwell and I took leave and walked to his house where I stayed all the evening and about 6 o'clock came John Grymes, his wife, and his sister. I sat with them about an hour and then walked home and read some French. I said my prayers.

19. I rose about 7 o'clock and read a chapter in Hebrew and some Greek in Lucian. I said my prayers, and had milk for breakfast. The weather was warm and clear, the wind east. About 8 o'clock came Dr. [Lomax] and Major Custis, and after them Colonel Bassett and he went away and came again in half an hour and then I walked with him and we called at Colonel Digges's lodging but he was from home. Then to Colonel Lewis' but he was from home; then to the President's, and we sat with him till 11 o'clock when the Governor came and we went to court and sat there all day till 7 o'clock and then we went to dinner and I ate some roast goose. After supper I went with Colonel Bassett to see his lady and sat with them till ten and then went home and learned that my man was drunk. He kept out of my way. I said my prayers.

[20.] ... reproved my man for having been drunk and threatened to have him to be publicly corrected in case he ever served me so again. About 10 o'clock I walked to Colonel Bassett's where I saw abundance of ladies. About eleven we walked to court where we sat till four and then went to dinner and I ate some boiled beef, and we entertained four gentlemen between Colonel Ludwell and me. Then we walked to Colonel Bassett's and from thence to the capitol where Mr. Stagg gave a ball and Mrs. Anne Carter was at it. I talked to her and several other ladies and about ten we came home, where I said my prayers and retired. I committed uncleanness.

21. I rose about 7 o'clock and read a chapter in Hebrew and a little Greek. I said my prayers, and had boiled milk for breakfast. The weather was clear and cold, the wind northwest. About 9 o'clock I walked to Colonel Carter's lodgings where I drank tea with the ladies. About 11 o'clock we went to court and sat there all day till the eve-

ning upon a grave case. At night we ate some boiled pork for supper and about 8 o'clock went to the Governor's assembly, where I talked abundantly to the ladies and danced with my cousin Grymes. I asked Mrs. Anne Carter to dance a minuet but she pretended she was tired and yet danced soon after with Mr. Armistead, without any meaning but only for want of knowing the world. About 11 o'clock I waited on the ladies to their coach and went home with Mrs. Bassett. I said my prayers.

22. I rose about 7 o'clock and read a chapter in Hebrew and some Greek. I said my prayers, and had boiled milk for supper. The weather was cold and cloudy, the wind northwest. About 9 o'clock I went to Colonel Bassett's and took leave of the ladies. Then I walked to the Governor's and showed him my [arrears]. Then I went to Dr. Blair's to see Mrs. Armistead[10] and then to Colonel Ludwell's to breakfast, where was Miss Anne Carter and her sister Burwell,[11] and I ate some boiled beef. About 12 o'clock I went to the capitol and in court the Secretary was struck with a fit of an apoplexy and died immediately and fell upon me. This made a great consternation. About two I dined at [B-c-c] and ate some wild duck. Then Colonel Carter and I went in Colonel Corbin's coach and six to the mouth of Queen's Creek and so over the river to Colonel Page's[12] where we ate some beefsteak and about 11 o'clock retired. I lay with Colonel Carter, and neglected my prayers, for which God forgive me.

23. I rose about 7 o'clock and read nothing but talked with Colonel Carter. I neglected my prayers, for which God forgive me. The weather was cold and clear, the wind northwest. I drank some tea for breakfast and about 11 o'clock we went in the coach to church, where Mr. Hughes[13] gave us a good sermon. After church we went

10. Martha Burwell, wife of Henry Armistead.

11. Mrs. Nathaniel Burwell was Elizabeth, daughter of Robert Carter.

12. Rosewell, on the York River, Gloucester County.

13. Reverend Thomas Hughes, who came to Virginia in 1716, was minister of Abingdon Parish, Gloucester County, 1719 to 1744.

to dine with Mr. Burwell,[14] where there was abundance of company and I ate some boiled beef. After dinner we took a little walk and then I talked about an hour with the ladies. Then we drank a bottle of punch and were merry till 10 o'clock and then I retired with Colonel Carter. I said a short prayer and slept but little because the Colonel snored and rose in the night to smoke his pipe. Mrs. Bray died this day of the flux.

24. I rose about 7 o'clock and read nothing but wrote a letter to Mr. Brook. I said my prayers, and had tea and bread and butter for breakfast. The weather was cold and clear, the wind west. About 11 o'clock we took leave of Mr. Burwell and the ladies and went to Colonel Page's in the coach and called on Mr. Pratt by the way, who was not yet recovered. We stayed at Colonel Page's about an hour and then came over the river in his boat and got to the college landing about 2 o'clock. I walked to Williamsburg and went to my lodgings to change my clothes because I was to go to the Secretary's funeral. Then I went to court and sat till 5 o'clock and then went to dine and then I ate some boiled pork. About 8 o'clock we went to the funeral, which was well managed by the Governor.[15] About ten I returned home and said my prayers.

25. I rose about 7 o'clock and read a chapter in Hebrew and some Greek in Lucian. I said my prayers, and had boiled milk for breakfast. The weather was cold and it rained very much all day. About 11 o'clock Major Holloway sent his chariot for me to carry me to the capitol. Otherwise I could not have gone. About twelve the court sat and rose again about three and then we went to dinner and I ate some roast mutton. After dinner we played at cards all the evening and I lost five bits. About ten I went home by the light of a candle and lantern where I said my prayers and slept very well, thank God.

14. Nathaniel Burwell, of Carter's Creek, Gloucester County, a burgess.

15. Dr. Cocke's tablet in Bruton Church read: ' . . . Alexander Spotswood . . . with the principal gentlemen of the country, attended his funeral, and, weeping, saw the corpse interred at the west side of the altar, in Bruton Church.' *William and Mary College Quarterly*, 1st ser., XVI (1907–8), 16.

26. I rose about 7 o'clock and read a chapter in Hebrew and some Greek in Lucian. I said my prayers, and had boiled milk for breakfast. The weather was warm and clear, the wind west. About 9 o'clock Major Custis came and stayed about half an hour and then I walked to Colonel Carter's lodging where I gave Stagg a guinea for his ball. Then Colonel Carter and I took a walk till eleven and then sat in court till 3 o'clock when we went to dinner and I ate some boiled beef. After dinner about 4 o'clock we went to Mrs. Bray's[16] funeral and I held up the pall. Then I walked to Colonel Bassett's lodging and sat and drank a bottle of wine with him and about nine walked to my own lodging and talked with my landlady till almost ten and then retired and said my prayers.

27. I rose about 7 o'clock and read a chapter in Hebrew and some Greek. I said my prayers, and had milk and potato for breakfast. The weather was clear and cool, the wind northwest. I wrote a letter to the Duke of Argyll till 10 o'clock and then came Colonel Bassett and I walked with him to court and sat there till 2 o'clock and then went to dine with Colonel Jenings where I ate some roast chicken, and John Grymes dined with us and after dinner he and I took a walk to the landing and then went to visit Jack Custis and sat with him about half an hour and then went to the College to visit the Commissary and sat half an hour with him and then went to Colonel Ludwell's and sat half an hour with him and then went to Colonel Bassett's and sat there about an hour and then I walked home and said my prayers.

28. I rose about 7 o'clock and wrote a chapter in Hebrew and some Greek. I said my prayers, and had milk for breakfast. The weather was cool and clear, the wind northwest. About 10 o'clock I went to wait on the Governor to let him know I should go out of town and desired him to dispense with my absence [sic]. Then I went to Colonel Carter's and gave him my letter to the Duke of Argyll and to his

16. Mrs. Bray, widow of Colonel David Bray, was buried in Bruton churchyard. See William Meade, *Old Churches, Ministers and Families of Virginia* (Philadelphia, 1857), I, 199.

son for getting the Secretary's place.[17] About eleven we went to court and I sat till one and then went into Colonel Ludwell's coach and drove to Green Springs, where I got by three o'clock and then ate some wild fowl for dinner. After dinner my cousin Grymes went in the coach to Williamsburg and I took a walk with the other ladies. At night we played at cards and ate nuts till 10 o'clock and then I took leave and neglected my prayers.

29. I rose about 7 o'clock and read some French. I said my prayers, and ate some roast shoat for breakfast. The weather was cold and clear, the wind northwest. About 10 o'clock I took leave and rode on Mrs. Ludwell's horse and got home without any accident about 3 o'clock and found everybody well, thank God, and all my affairs in good order. I ate some bacon and eggs. After dinner I took a walk with John Banister and at night talked with my people about their several businesses and with Banister till 8 o'clock and then I committed uncleanness with Annie, for which God forgive me. I neglected my prayers, in which I did very wrong.

30. I rose about 7 o'clock and read a chapter in Hebrew and some Greek in Lucian. I said my prayers, and had boiled milk for breakfast. The weather was clear and warm, the wind north. I danced my dance. About 11 o'clock I walked to church where the clerk read prayers. Then I walked with John Banister to see his mother and there I found Mrs. Eppes and Mrs. Hardyman and Mrs. Taylor. I ate some roast goose. We had very good cider. Here I stayed till the evening and then walked home and found my family pretty well, only the tailor had a looseness. Mr. Thornton also sent to me for wine and I sent it him for his wife. At night I talked with all my people and read some Greek. I said my prayers.

17. Spotswood had written on the day of Cocke's death recommending Jenings for the place of secretary (*Official Letters of Alexander Spotswood*, II, 343). Byrd's recommendation of John Carter (still in England) carried weight; Carter was made secretary of state on his return to Virginia in 1722.

31. I rose about 7 o'clock and read nothing because I had many things to settle before I went to Williamsburg. However, I said my prayers, and had boiled milk for breakfast. The weather was clear and warm, the wind east. I wrote a letter and settled several accounts till dinner and then I ate some roast beef. After dinner I put several things in order and then wrote more English till the evening, when Major Mumford came and Banister with him. After them came Mr. Brook with an overseer for the Falls. I gave them some ducks for supper and some roast beef. We sat and talked till about 9 o'clock and then retired. I neglected my prayers, for which God forgive me. After I was abed Major John Bolling came and I ordered him everything he wanted but did not get up.

November 1720

1. I rose about 5 o'clock and wrote a letter and put my affairs in order. I said my prayers, and ate some cold roast beef for breakfast. The weather was clear and warm, the wind west. About 9 o'clock Mr. Brook and Banister went to the Falls and about ten I committed my family to Providence and went with Major Bolling, Major Mumford, and Ben Harrison and Billy Hamlin to Green Springs and there everybody left me and I went to visit my Aunt by myself and ate some boiled beef for dinner. After dinner we had the pleasure to hear my cousin Hannah sing and young Mr. Lee[1] was there. At night the girls put a drawn sword and common prayer book open at the matrimony on my head and made me dream of my mistress Annie Carter. I neglected my prayers, for which God forgive me.

1. Thomas Lee later married Hannah Ludwell.

2. I rose about 7 o'clock and read only a little French. I said my prayers, and had potato and milk for breakfast. The weather was cloudy and warm, the wind west. About ten I took leave of my Aunt and went in the chair with the girls to Williamsburg. I changed my clothes and then walked to the capitol and found the court sitting. About one we rose and walked to Colonel Ludwell's where he gave me abundance of English letters, and among the rest one from my Lord Orrery. About three we dined and I ate some boiled beef. Then we took a little walk and in the evening the House of Burgesses met and chose Mr. Holloway speaker by a majority of eleven. Then we walked to Colonel Ludwell's again and played at cards and I won seven shillings. About ten I walked home and put several things in order. I said my prayers.

3. I rose about 7 o'clock and read a chapter in Hebrew and some Greek. I said my prayers, and had boiled milk for breakfast. The weather was cold and clear, the wind northwest. I wrote a letter to England and about 11 o'clock walked to court, where we finished the business and about 2 o'clock the Governor made his speech to both houses of Assembly and the Speaker made his speech. About 3 o'clock we rose and went to dinner. I ate some roast turkey. After dinner we took a walk to visit the Commissary where we found several ladies. Here we stayed till 7 o'clock and then walked to the Governor's to the assembly where was abundance of company and I danced with Mrs. Russell. I drank three dishes of chocolate and about 10 o'clock walked to Colonel Ludwell's where we learned what the House of Burgesses had done and about eleven I went home and said my prayers.

4. I rose about 7 o'clock and read a chapter in Hebrew and some Greek. I said my prayers, and had boiled milk for breakfast. The weather was cold and clear, the wind southwest. I danced my dance, and then wrote a letter to England till 12 o'clock and then walked to the capitol and sat in the upper house of Assembly. I moved an address to the Governor, and I was ordered to draw it, with Mr. Commissary and Colonel Beverley, and accordingly I did draw one till 3 o'clock and then I ate some fish. After dinner we went to the committee

where we agreed upon the address and showed it to the rest of the Council and then went to Mr. [Graffenried's]² ball, where I danced four dances and ate some plumcake. We stayed till 10 o'clock and then I walked home and said my prayers.

5. I rose about 7 o'clock and read a chapter in Hebrew and some Greek. I said my prayers, and had boiled milk for breakfast. The weather was cold and cloudy, the wind northeast. About ten I walked to Colonel Carter's lodgings, where I sat about half an hour and then we went to the capitol where after some dispute we passed the address without an amendment and then the Commissary, Colonel Digges, and I were sent to know when the Governor would receive it and he returned for answer that he would come to the Council chamber which he did about 1 o'clock and returned a kind answer. The Burgesses also presented their address and were answered very kindly. Then we went to dinner and I ate some boiled mutton. After dinner I took leave of Colonel Carter because he went out of town and I took a walk till the evening and then went to see the Commissary and stayed there till 9 o'clock and then went home and found Colonel Carter and several gentlemen at my lodgings. I stayed with them about half an hour and then retired and said my prayers.

6. I rose about 7 o'clock and wrote a chapter in Hebrew and some Greek. I said my prayers, and had boiled milk for breakfast. The weather was cold and it snowed all day so that few people went to church and there was only prayers but I could not go so that I had time to read my letters from England till 1 o'clock and then my landlord Mr. Cary invited me to dinner with Major Merriweather and I ate some roast beef. After dinner we sat and talked till the evening and then, notwithstanding the snow, Mr. Cary and I walked to visit Major Custis and sat with him about two hours and then returned and I washed my feet but neglected my prayers, for which God forgive me. Major Mumford came this day to visit me but would not dine with us.

2. Probably Christopher Graffenried, son of Christopher de Graffenried, founder of New Bern, N.C. He and his wife may have had an inn in Williamsburg at this time. See note in *Another Secret Diary of William Byrd*, 86.

7. I rose about 7 o'clock and found it continued to snow. I read a chapter in Hebrew and some Greek in Lucian. I said my prayers, and had boiled milk for breakfast. I wrote some English for the House of Burgesses and a letter to Colonel Randolph. About 12 o'clock I went to the President's and sat with him about an hour and then went to the Governor's with him in his coach to dine with the Governor with the rest of the gentlemen of the Council, and I ate some boiled venison. After dinner we sat and talked about several matters relating to the Assembly till about 6 o'clock and then I went home with Colonel Ludwell and several of the Burgesses came to us and we talked of the public business till nine and then I went home in Colonel Ludwell's coach and wrote some English till 11 o'clock and then retired and said my prayers.

8. I rose about 7 o'clock and read a chapter in Hebrew and some Greek in Lucian. I said my prayers, and had boiled milk for breakfast. The weather was warm and cloudy and foggy. I read some English till 11 o'clock and then walked to visit Major Mumford and found him and walked with him to the capitol; from thence I went with him to Colonel Jenings' and stayed about half an hour. Then because none of the Council were like to dine with me, I went to the College and dined with the Commissary and ate roast mutton. After dinner we sat and talked till 5 o'clock and then I made a visit to Mrs. Cocke and found her very well considering her condition. Here I found Mrs. Pratt and sat with them till seven and then Mrs. Robinson set me home in her coach and I sat with Mrs. Cary[3] till nine and then read some news. I said my prayers and retired.

9. I rose about 7 o'clock and read a chapter in Hebrew and some Greek in Lucian. I said my prayers, and had boiled milk for breakfast. The weather was warm and cloudy, the wind southeast. About 9 o'clock came Colonel Harrison and sat with me about an hour. Then I dressed me and walked to Dr. Blair's where I drank a dish of tea and then walked to Mrs. Sullivan's and played a pool of piquet with Colonel Harrison and Harry Willis. About two we walked to the capitol and talked with the Governor about the address to the

3. Mrs. Cary was Anne Edwards, second wife of Henry Cary.

King and then returned to Sullivan's and ate some fish for dinner. After dinner Charles Grymes and I took a walk and then went to Colonel Ludwell's and there played at piquet and lost fifteen shillings. About eight I walked home in the rain and wrote some English and said my prayers.

10. I rose about 7 o'clock and read a chapter in Hebrew and some Greek in Lucian. I said my prayers, and had boiled milk for breakfast. The weather was very cool, the wind northwest. I read some news till 11 o'clock and then walked to the capitol where we had nothing to do but talk with our friends till two and then we dined and I ate some roast beef. After dinner Colonel Harrison and I walked to Colonel Bassett's where we found all his ladies. We sat and talked till seven and then went to the Governor's assembly, where was abundance of company. We danced till ten and then I played at piquet till eleven and I won about twenty shillings. Then we ate some cold beef and drank a bottle till one and then took leave and I walked home, where I neglected my prayers.

11. I rose about 7 o'clock and read a chapter in Hebrew and some Greek in Lucian. I said my prayers, and had boiled milk for breakfast. The weather was cold and clear, the wind west. About 9 o'clock Colonel Harrison and I went to the Governor's to talk freely with him about the affairs of the Assembly and particularly about the Governor's house and we brought him to a good temper about it. Then I went home and settled some matters and the Commissary came to visit me. Then I walked to the capitol where we sat in Council till 3 o'clock and then went to dinner and I ate some wild ducks. After dinner Colonel Harrison and I played at piquet and I lost a crown. Then we walked to Colonel Ludwell's and there found Mrs. Harrison and Mrs. Bassett and talked with them till 8 o'clock and then went to Colonel Bassett's and stayed an hour and then I went home and said my prayers.

12. I rose about 7 o'clock and read a chapter in Hebrew and some Greek in Lucian. I said my prayers, and had boiled milk for breakfast. The weather was cold and clear, the wind north. About 9

o'clock came Major [Braxton] and sat with me about an hour. Then I dressed and went to Colonel Bassett's and from thence to the capitol where we had a Council about a peace among the Indians. Here we sat till 2 o'clock and then I walked to Colonel Bassett's to dine with the ladies because the Colonel was gone home. After dinner I walked to the Commissary's where I stayed about an hour and then returned to Colonel Bassett's again and found abundance of company. We acted proverbs and were merry till 8 o'clock and then I ate some cold venison pasty. About nine I came home and said my prayers.

13. I rose about 7 o'clock and read a chapter in Hebrew and some Greek in Lucian. I said my prayers, and had boiled milk for breakfast. The weather was cold and clear, the wind northwest. I put myself in order and about 11 o'clock walked with Colonel Allen to church and carried the ladies into the council pew. Mr. Wye gave us a long sermon in which he flattered the Governor very much. After dinner I went home with the Governor to dinner and ate some venison pasty. After dinner we sat till 3 o'clock and then went again to church and I slept in sermon time, for which God forgive me. After church I went to visit Mrs. Cocke with my cousin Harrison and my cousin Bassett and stayed there about two hours and then I went home with these two ladies and said my prayers.

14. I rose about 7 o'clock and read a chapter in Hebrew and some Greek in Lucian. I said my prayers, and had boiled milk for breakfast. The weather was clear and cold, the wind southwest. About 9 o'clock came Major Custis and sat with me about an hour and then I walked to Mr. Robinson's[4] where my cousins Bassett were. Here I stayed about an hour and then met with my brother Duke who told me my sister and her fireside were well. About 2 o'clock I walked home with the Commissary and ate some roast goose. After dinner we sat a little and then I took leave and went to Mrs. Bassett's and by the way met Captain Hunt who desired me to be his security, but I refused him, thank God. About 7 o'clock I got home and said my prayers. I slept very well, thank God.

4. John Robinson, of Essex County, member of the Council, a nephew of the Bishop of London.

15. I rose about 7 o'clock and read a chapter in Hebrew and some Greek in Lucian. I said my prayers, and had boiled milk for breakfast. The weather was cold and clear, the wind southwest. About 10 o'clock the Commissary came and sat about half an hour with me and then we walked away together to visit Colonel Ludwell, but he was from home. Then we walked up the town and met Colonel Harrison just come to town. About 2 o'clock I walked to the College with the Commissary where I dined and all the family of the Bassetts and Harrisons, about twenty in number, and I ate some venison pasty. After dinner we sat and talked till 6 o'clock and then walked to Colonel Bassett's and found Mrs. Burwell there just come to town. Here I spent my evening till 9 o'clock and then went home and said my prayers.

16. I rose about 7 o'clock and read a chapter in Hebrew and some Greek. I said my prayers, and had boiled milk for breakfast. The weather was clear and warm, the wind southwest. Major Burwell called on me and stayed about half an hour. I sent to know how the Governor did and at his desire went to wait on him and he showed us the [draft] of the upper part of the country.[5] About 12 o'clock we walked to the capitol and sat there till one and met the Burgesses in a conference. We sat till about 3 o'clock and then went to dinner and ate some boiled beef. After dinner Colonel Carter, Colonel Lewis, and I took a walk till six and then went to the President's house to meet the rest of the Council. Here we stayed till eight and then walked to Colonel Ludwell's where we saw abundance of ladies. About nine I took leave and walked home and said my prayers.

17. I rose about 7 o'clock and read a chapter in Hebrew and no Greek. I said my prayers, and had boiled milk for breakfast. The weather was clear and warm. About ten I walked to Colonel Ludwell's and then walked with him to the capitol where we received some letters from England. About twelve we went into the Council and then went to the conference, where we agreed in everything. The Governor and both houses were present. About three we went

5. Spotswood was planning the establishment of two new counties (Brunswick and Spotsylvania) to protect the mountain frontier.

to dinner and I ate some boiled beef and then walked home to put myself in order to go to the Governor's assembly but first I called on Colonel Ludwell and went from thence with Colonel Bassett in the President's coach. At the assembly I danced with Mrs. Russell. About ten I went to supper and ate some bacon and chicken and then we danced again. After that I stayed till two and then walked home and neglected my prayers. When I went to bed I found some hair cut and put into my bed by Mrs. Allen and Hannah Ludwell, against whom I swore revenge.

18. I rose about 7 o'clock and read a chapter in Hebrew and a little Greek in Lucian. I said my prayers, and had boiled milk for breakfast. The weather was warm and clear, the wind west. About ten I went to drink tea with Mr. Roscow and his lady and then walked with Colonel Carter, Colonel Ludwell, and Colonel Bassett to the landing on the Queen's Creek and called on Tom Jones. At our return thence we went to dinner and I ate some boiled pork. After dinner we played at cards and then Colonel Carter and I walked again till the evening. We parted and endeavored to pick up a whore but could not find one. Then I went to Colonel Ludwell's and from thence to Colonel Bassett's, where I spent the evening till 10 o'clock and then went home and wrote two letters and neglected my prayers, for which God forgive me.

19. I rose about 7 o'clock and read a chapter in Hebrew and some Greek. I said my prayers, and had boiled milk for breakfast. The weather was warm and cloudy and it began to rain. About 8 o'clock Major Merriweather came and sat with me about half an hour. Then came John F-l and let me know that all was pretty well at home only somebody had broke my store and stole three gallons of rum. I sent home my foul linen by him and then read some news till 11 o'clock and then went with Colonel Bassett in his coach to the capitol where we sat till 2 o'clock and then went to the Colonel's house to dinner and I ate some roast ducks. After dinner I went to visit Mrs. Ludwell where we played at [little plays] and were merry till eleven and then I came home in Colonel Ludwell's coach and said my prayers.

20. I rose about 7 o'clock and read a chapter in Hebrew and some Greek. I said my prayers, and had boiled milk for breakfast. The weather was warm and clear, the wind west. I read some English till 11 o'clock and then went to church and Mr. Commissary gave us a sermon. After church the Governor asked me to dine with him and a Mrs. B— dined there, and the Speaker. I ate some venison pasty. After dinner we went again to church where I slept a little, God forgive me. After church Mr. Roscow and I took a walk to the landing and at our return went to visit Colonel Jenings, where we drank tea and ate some cheesecake. Here we stayed till 9 o'clock and Colonel Presley[6] was with us. Then I walked home and read some English till ten and then retired and said my prayers. I committed uncleanness, for which God forgive me.

21. I rose about 7 o'clock and read a chapter in Hebrew and some Greek. I said my prayers, and had boiled milk for breakfast. The weather was clear and warm, the wind southwest. I settled several accounts till 11 o'clock and then walked to Major Custis' where I stayed about half an hour. Then I went to Colonel Bassett's and sat with the girls about an hour and then went to Colonel Ludwell's and stayed there about an hour. I likewise went to see the [musician]. About 2 o'clock I walked with the Commissary to the College to dinner and ate some cold turkey. After dinner I walked into the town, took a walk with Colonel Carter and then went to Colonel Ludwell's where we found the Governor. We sat and talked politics till nine and then the Governor left us and half an hour after him I walked home and said my prayers. I was out of humor with Colonel Randolph to a great degree.

22. I rose about 7 o'clock and read a chapter in Hebrew and some Greek. I said my prayers, and had milk for breakfast. The weather was clear and warm, the wind west. I wrote some English till 11 o'clock and then walked to Colonel Ludwell's and from thence to the capitol where we had a conference with the Burgesses, and then read several bills till 3 o'clock and then ate some mutton pie. After dinner Mr. Grymes and I took a walk till night and then I went to

6. Colonel Peter Presley, burgess from Northumberland County.

Colonel Bassett's where was abundance of company and we acted proverbs and were very merry till 11 o'clock and then I walked home and said my prayers.

23. I rose about 7 o'clock and read a chapter in Hebrew and some Greek in Lucian. I said my prayers, and had boiled milk for breakfast. The weather was clear and cold, the wind northeast. My boat came down with my clothes and brought me an account that all my family were well, thank God, and that Tom had stole my rum out of the store, for which I ordered him to be severely whipped. About twelve I went to the Governor's where the Governor saw me and told me that my claim should be granted and that he would speak to his people about it. We sat till 3 o'clock and then went to dinner and I ate some roast turkey. After dinner we took a walk till the evening and then walked to Colonel Ludwell's where we played at cards and I won a little and about 10 o'clock walked home and said my prayers.

24. I rose about 7 o'clock and read a chapter in Hebrew and some Greek in Lucian. I said my prayers, and had boiled milk for breakfast. The weather was cold and clear, the wind west. I went to the Governor's about 9 o'clock and talked several matters with him. Then I walked to Colonel Bassett's to see Mrs. Corbin who had been sick and about eleven walked with the Colonel to the capitol where we sat to business till 3 o'clock and then I went to dine with Colonel Jenings with Colonel Bassett's family and ate some boiled tongue. About . . . o'clock we went to the assembly at the Commissary's where I danced with Mrs. Russell and then played at piquet with Colonel Harrison and won five shillings, and about . . .

25. I rose about 7 o'clock and read a chapter in Hebrew and some Greek in Lucian. I said my prayers, and had boiled milk for breakfast. The weather was cold and clear, the wind west. I wrote an address to the King and about 11 o'clock the Commissary called on me and we walked to Colonel Bassett's and took him to the capitol, where we passed several bills till 2 o'clock and then Colonel Harrison and I played at piquet till dinner, when I ate some stewed [swan]. After dinner Colonel Carter and I took a walk and I went to visit Mr. Presi-

dent, where we found the Governor and abundance of company that agreed to visit him this evening. Here I played at cards and lost twenty shillings and stayed till 12 o'clock and then walked home and said my prayers.

26. I rose about 7 o'clock and read a chapter in Hebrew and some Greek in Lucian. I said my prayers, and had boiled milk for breakfast. The weather was cold and clear, the wind west. About nine I walked to Colonel Bassett's but found nobody at home. Then I walked to Colonel Ludwell's to make Mr. Grymes a visit and found him better. Then I walked to the capitol and from thence to dinner about 2 o'clock and ate some roast duck. After dinner I took a walk by myself to the landing and in the evening went again to Colonel Ludwell's to make another visit to Mr. Grymes. Then I went down to the ladies and played at cards till 10 o'clock. Colonel Bassett's family went out of town this morning. I said my prayers.

27. I rose about 7 o'clock and read a chapter in Hebrew and some Greek in Lucian. I said my prayers and had boiled milk for breakfast. The weather was cold and clear, the wind northwest. I cleaned my teeth and put several things in order till 11 o'clock and then went to church where Mr. Jones gave us a sermon about the mountains. After church the Governor took me home to dinner and I ate some giblet pie. Mrs. Russell looked as if she had ... About 3 o'clock we went to church and Mr. Jones gave us another sermon on the same subject. After church I took a walk to the landing and then went to visit Mrs. Cocke, where I stayed about an hour and then went to Colonel Ludwell's and found everybody going to bed about 7 o'clock. However, I stayed about half an hour and then walked home and said my prayers.

28. I rose about 7 o'clock and read some Greek in Lucian, and a chapter in Hebrew. I said my prayers, and had boiled milk for breakfast. The weather was warm and cloudy, the wind southwest. I wrote some English. I took the white woman by the cunt. She told she was out of order else she should not [matter it.] I went not out till 2 o'clock and then went to Colonel Ludwell's house and there Colonel Carter came and we stayed to dinner and I ate some wild duck. After

dinner we sat and talked till the evening and then we played at cards and I won a little. We played till 10 o'clock. Mr. Grymes was indisposed. However, we stayed till eleven and then went home in the coach and I set Colonel Carter home at his lodgings and then went home myself and said my prayers.

29. I rose about 7 o'clock and read a chapter in Hebrew and some Greek in Lucian. I said my prayers, and had boiled milk for breakfast. The weather was warm and cloudy, the wind west. I wrote some English till 11 o'clock and then walked to visit Mr. Grymes who had a fever and purge. About twelve we walked to the capitol and sat there till two and then went to dinner and I ate some roast goose. After dinner Colonel Carter and I took a walk till 6 o'clock and then went to Colonel Ludwell's where we agreed to play at cards and I won six bits. We were very merry till 10 o'clock and then I walked home and said my prayers.

30. I rose about 7 o'clock and read a chapter in Hebrew and some Greek in Lucian. I said my prayers, and had boiled milk for breakfast. The weather was warm and cloudy, the wind west. About ten I walked with Colonel Harrison to the Governor's where we talked freely with him. Then we walked to the capitol where we sat very close till 3 o'clock and then went to dinner. Captain Wharwood dined with us and I ate some chicken and bacon. After dinner we sat about an hour and then Colonel Carter, Colonel Ludwell, and I went to Colonel Jenings to sit upon the [administration] between the Colonel and Parson Jones about a Negro of the college that came by his death by Mr. Jones's means. About eight we played at cards and I lost four bits and went not home till 12 o'clock and I said my prayers.

December 1720

1. I rose about 7 o'clock and read a chapter in Hebrew and some Greek in Lucian. I said my prayers, and had boiled milk for breakfast. It rained very much all day, the wind southwest. Mr. Fontaine came to talk with me about our parish and I promised him my interest. I read some English till 11 o'clock and then Colonel Ludwell came and took me in the coach to the capitol where I went to prayers and afterwards to the committee to hear Tom Lee's trial which lasted all day.[1] However, about 3 o'clock I went away to dinner and we had roast mutton. After dinner Colonel Harrison and I played at piquet and then four of us went to whisk and I lost six bits and about 10 o'clock went home in Colonel Ludwell's coach and said my prayers. It snowed and grew very cold.

2. I rose about 7 o'clock and read a chapter in Hebrew and some Greek in Lucian. I said my prayers and had boiled milk for breakfast. The weather was cold and clear, the wind north. I wrote some English till ten and then came Major Custis and sat with me about half an hour. About eleven I walked to Colonel Ludwell's and found Mr. Grymes better, thank God. Then we walked to the capitol where we sat till near 3 o'clock and then went to dinner and I ate some boiled mutton. After dinner Colonel Carter and I took a walk and then went to Colonel Jenings' to deliver to him our [awards]. Then Colonel Harrison came to us and we played at cards and I lost ten shillings and about 11 o'clock went home and said my prayers. I dreamed that I had notice given me that I should die suddenly in six or seven days.

1. It was claimed that Thomas Lee was illegally returned a burgess from Westmoreland County. The committee of elections and privileges, after reviewing the qualifications of voters, decided that Daniel McCarty had more votes than Lee and accordingly the former took his seat. See *Journals of the House of Burgesses of Virginia*, ed. H.R. McIlwaine (Richmond, Va., 1905–15), I, 260, 294.

3. I rose about 7 o'clock and read a chapter in Hebrew and some Greek in Lucian. I said my prayers, and had boiled milk for breakfast. The weather was cold and clear, the wind west. About 10 o'clock I went to Colonel Ludwell's and stayed there about an hour and then walked to the capitol to prayers. Afterwards I met Captain Wharwood and about 2 o'clock went to dinner and ate some fish. Colonel Page and Major Burwell dined with us and after dinner they all went away together in order to go to York River and I took a walk of about two hours and then walked after two women but in vain so about 6 o'clock I went home and sat with my landlord and his wife till seven and then read some English. Colonel Harrison told me he dreamed there was a funeral at Westover, which agreed with my dream last night and made me begin to think there was something in it.

4. I rose about 7 o'clock and read a chapter in Hebrew and some Greek in Lucian. I said my prayers, and had boiled milk for breakfast. The weather was cold and cloudy, the wind southwest, and about 9 o'clock it began to rain and rained a little all day. However, I walked to church where the Commissary preached a good sermon. After church the Governor asked me to dine with him but the Commissary had invited me before so I walked to the College to dinner and ate some pork boiled. After dinner we sat and talked and went into church in the afternoon because it continued to rain. For that reason, too, I stayed all the evening till 8 o'clock and then I sent to beg the favor of Major Holloway to lend me his chariot which he was so kind as to do and I took leave and went home and read some English and said my prayers. After I was in bed the maid of the house came into my chamber and I felt her and committed uncleanness but did not roger her.

5. I rose about 7 o'clock and read a chapter in Hebrew and some Greek in Lucian. I said my prayers, and had boiled milk for breakfast. The weather was cold and cloudy, the wind northeast. I wrote some English till 11 o'clock and then went to visit Major Mumford but he was from home. Then I went to Colonel Jenings' but he was from home but Miss H-r-n-t-n asked me to go in which I did and sat with her half an hour, and then I went to the Attorney's and stayed about

half an hour and then to Sullivan's where I found Major Mumford and persuaded him to take a vomit. Then I walked with Colonel Ludwell and Colonel Carter to the College and we dined with Mr. Commissary and I ate some boiled beef. After dinner I went to Major Mumford's lodgings and gave him a vomit and then went to Colonel Ludwell's and played at cards and lost twenty shillings. About ten I walked home and said my prayers. It snowed a little. I had a sty upon my eye.

6. I rose about 7 o'clock and read a chapter in Hebrew and some Greek in Lucian. I said my prayers and had boiled milk for breakfast. The weather was cold and clear, the wind west. I wrote some English and then went to visit the President and asked him to favor our bill but he refused me. Then I walked to the capitol where we sat till 3 o'clock . . . at cards and I lost eight shillings. About ten I went home and said my prayers.

7. I rose about 7 o'clock and read a chapter in Hebrew and some Greek. I said my prayers, and had boiled milk for breakfast. The weather was cold and clear, the wind northwest. About ten I walked to Major Mumford's lodgings and found him disordered with a little fever for which I gave him the bark. Then I went to visit Mr. Grymes and then walked to the capitol where we sat till 3 o'clock and then went to dinner and I ate some boiled mutton. Then Colonel Carter and I took a walk and afterwards I walked to Colonel Ludwell's where we played at cards and I won twelve shillings. About ten I walked home and found it very cold. One of Mr. Cary's chimneys was on fire but they soon put it out. I said my prayers and slept very well, thank God almighty.

8. I rose about 7 o'clock and read a chapter in Hebrew and some Greek in Lucian. I said my prayers, and had boiled milk for breakfast. The weather was cold and clear, the wind southwest. I read some news till 10 o'clock and then I wrote a letter to Westover and then Colonel Bassett came and sat with me quarter of an hour. About twelve I walked to the capitol where we sat and heard several bills read till 3 o'clock and then we went to dinner and I ate some boiled

pork. After dinner Colonel Carter and I took a walk till 5 o'clock and then I went to Colonel Ludwell's where we agreed upon the address to the King about the two new counties.[2] About 8 o'clock we walked to the Governor's where I played at cards and lost four pounds, and went home about 11 o'clock and said my prayers.

9. I rose about 7 o'clock and read a chapter in Hebrew and some Greek in Lucian. I said my prayers, and had boiled milk for breakfast. The weather was cold and clear, the wind west. I felt the breasts of the Negro girl which she resisted a little. I put several things in order and then walked to the Governor who received me very kindly. Then I called on Mr. Digges but he was from home. Then I walked to the capitol where with much difficulty we passed the bill about Charles City County.[3] We did several other things and then went to dinner and I ate some roast mutton. After dinner I walked a little to pick up a woman and found none, and then went to the place where we dine and played at cards till 10 o'clock and I won a little and then walked home and said my prayers.

10. I rose about 7 o'clock and read a chapter in Hebrew and some Greek in Lucian. I said my prayers, and had boiled milk for breakfast. The weather was cold and clear, the wind west. About 10 o'clock came Mr. Grymes and stayed about an hour and then I walked with him to the capitol where we sat about two hours and then Colonel Carter and I went to dine with the Governor and I ate some stewed turkey. After dinner we sat and drank a bottle till 7 o'clock and then Colonel Carter and I took a walk to the President's where we played at cards and I won seven shillings. Then we ate

2. 'An Act for Erecting the Counties of Spotsylvania and Brunswick, etc.' was passed December 8. The address to the King is printed in the *Journals of the House of Burgesses*, I, 298-9. In November the assembly had passed bills for dividing two other counties. See 'An Act for Dividing Richmond County' (into Richmond and King George counties) and 'An Act for Dividing New Kent County' (into New Kent and Hanover counties), in M. P. Robinson, *Virginia Counties* (Richmond, Va., 1916), 199-201.

3. This was a bill for enlarging the county and consolidating the parts of the parishes of Westover and Weyanoke on the north side of the James River and the part of Wallingford Parish on the west side of the Chickahominy River. See *Journals of the House of Burgesses*, I, 296.

some oysters and sat and talked till ten and then I walked home and I found John F-l there who told me all was well at home. I said my prayers.

11. I rose about 7 o'clock and read a chapter in Hebrew and some Greek in Lucian. I said my prayers, and had boiled milk for breakfast. The weather was cold and clear, the wind northwest. About 11 o'clock Colonel Carter and Colonel Jenings called upon me and I walked to church with them where Mr. Cargill preached a good sermon. I was invited to three several places but dined with the Governor and ate some boiled venison. The Governor told us people were in abundance of confusion about their stocks.[4] After dinner Captain Martin came and told us his misfortune of losing his vessel. Then Colonel Carter and I took a walk and in the evening went to the College to visit the Commissary and ate some mince pie with him and about ten I took leave and walked home and said my prayers.

12. I rose about 7 o'clock and read a chapter in Hebrew and some Greek in Lucian. I said my prayers and had boiled milk for breakfast. The weather was warm and clear, the wind west. I dressed myself about 10 o'clock and went to Colonel Jenings' and there drank tea and about eleven went with Colonel Carter and him to the Governor's to compliment him upon his birthday but found him in his gown. Then we went to see Mr. Robinson who was sick of a fever and from thence to the capitol where we sat about three hours till 4 o'clock and then went to dinner and I ate some boiled pork. About 6 o'clock we went to the Governor's in Colonel Jenings' coach, who received us kindly. We played at stock jobbing for the Indian cabinet and I gave Betty Bland the chance of one card and Hannah Ludwell the chance of the other but neither won. I danced country dances and stayed till 11 o'clock and then waited on Hannah Ludwell home and then went home myself and said my prayers.

13. I rose about 7 o'clock and read a chapter in Hebrew and some Greek in Lucian. I said my prayers, and had boiled milk for breakfast. The weather was clear and warm, the wind southwest. About

4. Probably stock in the South Sea Company, which collapsed in 1720.

9 o'clock came Colonel Corbin and John Grymes and stayed with me about half an hour and then I dressed and went out to Colonel Ludwell's and sat there with the ladies about half an hour and then walked to the capitol where we sat about two hours and then went to Sullivan's where Colonel Harrison and I played at piquet till dinner and then I ate some boiled beef. After dinner Colonel Carter and I took a walk and then I went to Colonel Ludwell's again and from thence to the College where Tom Lee and David Bray gave a ball. Here I danced with Mrs. Russell and about ten walked home and said my prayers.

14. I rose about 7 o'clock and read a chapter in Hebrew and some Greek in Lucian. I said my prayers, and had boiled milk for breakfast. The weather was warm and clear, the wind southwest. Billy Beverley[5] came to see me and stayed about an hour and about ten I walked to Colonel Ludwell's and took leave of the ladies, who were going to Green Springs. Then I walked to the capitol where we sat about Captain Martin till 3 o'clock and then went to dinner and I ate some roast beef. Nat Burwell came and told me the House had agreed to give me four hundred pounds for my services and expenses in general.[6] Then Colonel Carter and I took a walk and at night I went to Colonel Ludwell's where we played at cards and about ten I went home and said my prayers.

15. I rose about 7 o'clock and read a chapter in Hebrew and some Greek in Lucian. I said my prayers, and had boiled milk for breakfast. The weather was cold and cloudy, the wind northeast. Mr. Custis came to see me and so did Major Merriweather and stayed about half an hour. Then I walked to the capitol and we sat about several bills and the House of Burgesses brought up my resolution about the four hundred pounds which put the Governor out of humor and he said not one word about it. At 4 o'clock we rose and

5. Billy Beverley was Byrd's nephew William, son of Robert Beverley and Ursula Byrd.

6. On December 14, 1720, the House of Burgesses appointed William Byrd 'to solicit in Great Britain the subject matter of the address of the Council and Burgesses to His Majesty,' and other matters. *Journal of the House of Burgesses*, I, 300.

went to dinner and I ate some boiled beef. After dinner I walked to Colonel Ludwell's, where we played at cards and I lost a crown, and stayed till 10 o'clock and then walked home and said my prayers. I slept but indifferently.

16. I rose about 7 o'clock and read a chapter in Hebrew and some Greek in Lucian. I said my prayers, and had boiled milk for breakfast. The weather was cold and clear, the wind northwest. About 10 o'clock I went to Colonel Ludwell's to take leave of Mrs. Grymes and then walked to the capitol where we sat till 4 o'clock and then went to dinner and I ate some fish. After dinner Colonel Carter, Colonel Lewis and I took a walk till the evening and then I walked to Colonel Ludwell's where I found Major Merriweather, Dr. Blair, Mr. Burwell, and Mr. Grymes. We talked politics till 9 o'clock and then I took leave and walked home. The wind got to the northeast and blew exceedingly cold. I said my prayers.

17. I rose about 7 o'clock and read a chapter in Hebrew and some Greek. I said my prayers, and had boiled milk for breakfast. The weather was cold and clear, the wind northwest. I put up my things and about 10 o'clock Mr. Commissary came to visit me and about eleven we went together to Colonel Bassett's and from thence to the capitol to prayers. Then we sat upon business till 3 o'clock. The Governor continued out of humor all the time. Then we went to dinner and I ate some beefsteak till the evening. John F-l came from home and let me know all was well, thank God. My boat also came down and I ordered my things on board, notwithstanding it was very cold, for fear the cargo should be frozen. In the evening Colonel Lewis and I took a walk and at night I went to Colonel Jenings' and lost ten shillings and came home about eleven and said my prayers. My man complained Mr. Cary had beat him.

18. . . . About 10 o'clock Colonel Corbin came. However, I got ready to go to church by 11 o'clock, notwithstanding it was very cold, and the Commissary gave us a good sermon. After church Colonel Carter, Colonel Lewis, and I went to the Commissary's to dinner and I ate some roast turkey and chine. After dinner we sat and

talked for two hours and then drank coffee; about 5 o'clock we went to visit Major Custis, where we walked in his garden and then I ate some potato and milk and about 9 o'clock I took leave and walked home, where I read some English and said my prayers.

19. I rose about 7 o'clock and read a chapter in Hebrew and some Greek in Lucian. I said my prayers, and had boiled milk for breakfast. The weather was much warmer, the wind southwest. I wrote some English till 11 o'clock and then walked to the capitol where I was told the Governor would not pass my four hundred pounds except I would give bond to take nothing in his prerogative.[7] About twelve we sat and my resolution was passed in the Council, notwithstanding a paper of the Governor was left with Colonel Jenings to dissuade the Council from it. About four we went to dinner and I ate some boiled beef. After dinner I went to Colonel Ludwell's to frame the address with the rest of the committee. Afterwards they played at cards. Mr. Grymes was indisposed again. About 10 o'clock I went home and read some news.

20. I rose about 7 o'clock and read a chapter in Hebrew and some Greek in Lucian. I said my prayers, and had boiled milk for breakfast. The weather was warm and clear, the wind southwest. About 10 o'clock I walked to visit Mr. Grymes, who was indisposed. Then I walked to prayers and afterwards had some talk with the Governor about giving bond not to meddle with anything relating to the government beside what was mentioned in my instructions, but I refused to give such bond absolutely if he would sign a warrant for all the money in the Treasurer's hands, and so we parted. Then we had a court of admiralty and condemned a man for piracy.[8] Then we went to dinner and I ate some boiled mutton. After dinner Colonel

7. The Governor wished to amend the bill to include a provision 'that the instructions to be given . . . be signed by the Governor and that the Solicitor enter into bond to the Governor not to meddle in Great Britain with any other affair of this government than what shall be contained in his said instructions.' Ibid. 308.

8. The seacoast was menaced by buccaneers, against whom Spotswood waged a vigorous campaign. In 1718 the notorious Teach ('Blackbeard') was killed by an expedition which Spotswood sent out. In 1720 Virginia hanged four pirates in chains as a warning to others.

Harrison and I walked to visit Mrs. Cocke and stayed there till seven
and then went to Dr. Blair's where I stayed till eight and then went
home where I found Harry Cary very sick. I just called to see him
and then retired and said my prayers.

21. I rose about 7 o'clock and read a chapter in Hebrew and some
Greek in Lucian. I said my prayers, and had boiled milk for breakfast. The weather was warm and cloudy, the wind southwest. It
rained pretty much. I wrote some English and about 11 o'clock went
to the capitol to prayers and then into the Council room where the
Governor endeavored to show how reasonable it was that I should give
bond not to meddle with anything but what was in my instructions,
but he was answered very fully. The House gave very good reasons
why they could not go into the Governor's amendment.[9] About 4
o'clock we went to dinner and I ate some stewed pork. After dinner
I walked to visit John Grymes and found him better. Here I played
at cards and lost a little till 9 o'clock and then walked home, read
some news, and said my prayers.

22. I rose about 7 o'clock and read a chapter in Hebrew and some
Greek in Lucian. I said my prayers, and had boiled milk for breakfast. The weather was warm and clear, the wind southwest. Several
gentlemen came to visit to take leave and about 10 o'clock I went to
Colonel Ludwell's to take leave of John Grymes, who went away
not very well. Then I went to Mrs. Sullivan's and settled accounts
with her and then walked to the capitol wherein we sat and disposed
several matters, being in hopes to go home but we reckoned without
our host. But we went to dinner about three and I ate roast goose.
After dinner Colonel Carter went away, and Colonel Page, and then
Colonel Lewis and I took a walk and at night went to the President's
where I lost twenty shillings to Colonel Harrison and about ten I
walked home and said my prayers.

9. The message to the Governor was that 'we are entirely ignorant of any other
affairs relating to this government intended to be by him meddled in' and that they
hoped 'you will not now deprive the country of a person so capable and in all respects
most proper for this employment by insisting on the proposed addition to our resolve.'
Journals of the House of Burgesses, I, 309–10.

23. I rose about 7 o'clock and read nothing because I prepared to go with Colonel Harrison and Colonel Ludwell to take leave of the Governor because I would not be wanting in civility, notwithstanding I had been indifferently treated by him. Accordingly we went and we argued the business but he came off but poorly with his bond. I desired him not to keep the Assembly any longer on my account and begged he would put an end to it.[10] I went to Mr. Clayton's and paid him a little money. Then went to take leave of my landlady and gave the servants ten shillings. Then went to the capitol where I told the Governor I had rather my tongue to be cut out than it should be tied up from doing my country service. About four Colonel Ludwell and I went out of town to Green Springs, where I ate some fried pork. Then we played at cards till ten and then I retired and said my prayers.

24. I rose about 7 o'clock and read a little English. I said my prayers, and had chocolate for breakfast. The weather was warm and clear, the wind west. About 10 o'clock I took leave and got to the ferry about eleven. I got into the boat with my man servant and would not let Colonel Randolph's man go with us who was just coming after me with John Stith. About 3 o'clock I got home and found all well, thank God, but I scarcely knew the place again because of the alteration. I ate some beef head for dinner. In the evening I took a walk with Banister till night and then I wrote two letters, one to Major Mumford, the other to Mr. Anderson. I had a letter from the Falls that told me all was well. I said my prayers but committed uncleanness with Annie, for which God forgive me. It rained exceedingly in the night.

25. I rose about 7 o'clock and read a chapter in Hebrew and some Greek. I said my prayers, and had boiled milk for breakfast. It continued to rain very much. However, Bob went to the Falls before I

10. The Governor explained that his motive was 'to take away temptation from unquiet spirits who might be disposed to sow again the seeds of contention.' Ibid. 313–14. In the end the Governor had to give way and the bill was passed. Byrd was back in England by the middle of 1722.

was up. I danced my dance. It rained so much we had no church, so I read some English at home till dinner and then I ate some haslet. After dinner Banister and I sat and talked because the rain would not let us go out. However, in the evening I walked a little in the garden. At night I talked with my people and read a sermon of Tillotson till 9 o'clock and then went to bed and committed uncleanness with Annie, for which God forgive me, and I was very sorry for it. I slept pretty well, thank God.

26. I rose about 7 o'clock and read a chapter in Hebrew and some Greek in Lucian. I said my prayers, and had boiled milk for breakfast. The weather was clear and cold, the wind north. Banister went over the river to see his mother and I put many things in order. I danced my dance and wrote some English till noon and then walked to Mrs. Harrison's to dinner and ate some roast chicken. After dinner I sat and talked with her about many things and told her the treatment I had from the Governor with relation to the four hundred pounds. Ben was from home. I stayed here till 4 o'clock and then walked home and found all my family well, thank God. I read some English and was resolved to avoid playing the fool with Annie. I said my prayers and slept pretty well, thank God.

27. I rose about 7 o'clock and read a chapter in Hebrew and some Greek in Lucian. I said my prayers, and had boiled milk for breakfast. The weather was clear and cold, the wind northwest. I danced my dance and then settled several accounts and read some Latin till dinner and then I ate some [cowheel]. After dinner I put several things in order and then danced my dance again till the evening and then took a walk about the plantation and found everything in pretty good condition. At night I talked with my people and with Sam among the rest who came home according to his promise but Bob did not come till I was abed. I read some English till 9 o'clock and then said my prayers and resolved to forbear Annie by God's grace.

28. I rose about 7 o'clock and read a chapter in Hebrew and some Greek. I said my prayers, and had boiled milk for breakfast. The weather was cold and clear, the wind northwest. I talked with Tom

Cross, who came last night, about my garden and got him to lay out that part that was new. I set all my people to work except Sam who said it was not fortunate to work on this day.[11] About 12 o'clock came Captain Drury Stith and a little after came Colonel Hill, Mrs. Harrison and Mr. [Griffin] and dined with me and I ate some roast duck. After dinner we sat and talked till the evening and then the company went away and I walked home with Mrs. Harrison. At night I talked with my people and found Sam was not come home. I read some English till nine and then said my prayers. Sam was not come when I went to bed.

29. I rose about 7 o'clock and read a chapter in Hebrew and some Greek. I said my prayers, and had milk and potato for breakfast. The weather was warm and clear, the wind west. About 11 o'clock Parson Robinson came to talk with me about the parish but I told him Mr. Fontaine had spoken with me first. I reprimanded Sam for staying so late out last night. I wrote some English till 11 o'clock and then [nephew] Beverley came from Colonel Randolph's and dined with me and I ate some . . . again, for which God of his excessive goodness forgive me. I said a short prayer. Sixteen hogs came from the Falls.

30. I rose about 7 o'clock and read a chapter in Hebrew but no Greek. I said my prayers, and had boiled milk for breakfast. The weather was cold and clear, the wind northwest. Mr. Beverley and I walked about and saw my people at work, and then I wrote a letter to the Falls by Frank that came down with the hogs, which we killed this day. About 2 o'clock came Captain Harwood, the Burgess, and dined with me and I ate some roast goose. After dinner we sat and talked about an hour and then Mr. Beverley went away and Captain Harwood likewise and then Ben Harrison came and stayed about half an hour and I walked with him some part of his way. At night I wrote two letters to send by the gardener and gave him twenty-six shillings for two days' work and he was so affronted that he sent me back a pistole and went away in the night. I talked with my people and about nine returned and said a short prayer and slept but indifferently.

11. This was Childermas Day.

31. I rose about 7 o'clock and read a chapter in Hebrew and no Greek. I said my prayers, and had boiled milk for breakfast. The weather was warm and clear, the wind west. I danced my dance and then helped Tom plant the trees. Then I read some Latin till dinner when I ate some broiled goose. After dinner I put several things in order and then read more Latin. Then I looked after my people . . . and in the evening walked about the plantation. At night I received letters from my overseers in New Kent by which I learned that all was well, thank God. I talked with several of my people and then read some English in the *Whole Duty of Man*[12] which edified me very much. About 9 o'clock I said my prayers and retired and slept but indifferently. My sloop went away to the Falls.

January 1721

1. I rose about 7 o'clock and read a chapter in Hebrew and some Greek in Lucian. I said my prayers, and had boiled milk for breakfast. The weather was warm and clear, the wind west. I danced my dance and put myself in order till eleven and then I walked to church where Mr. Jones preached. I invited Mrs. Harrison, the widow Stith, Mr. Jones, Colonel Hill, and his daughter to dinner and I ate some boiled pork. After dinner I showed Mr. Jones the library and we talked till the evening and then all the company went away and I took a walk about the plantation. At night I wrote letters to my overseers in New Kent. Then I read some English till 9 o'clock, then washed my feet, said my prayers, and retired, and slept very ill and thought I should have vomited.

12. [Richard Allestree], *The Whole Duty of Man, Necessary for All Families, With Private Devotions for Several Occasions* (1658).

2. I rose about 7 o'clock and read a chapter in Hebrew and some Greek in Lucian. I said my prayers, and had boiled milk for breakfast. The weather was cold and cloudy, the wind northeast. I danced my dance and then settled several accounts and wrote some English till 1 o'clock when Banister came home. I ate some roast pork for dinner. After dinner I sat and talked with Banister about an hour and then went into the library and read some Latin and danced my dance again and walked about in the library because it rained and I could not walk abroad. At night I gave quarters to a traveller and entertained him with victuals and cider. I talked with my people and read some English till 9 o'clock and then said my prayers devoutly and slept very well, thank God, and dreamed I was very dear to the King and he made me Secretary of State and I advised with my Lord Oxford how to manage that great office.

3. I rose about 7 o'clock and read a chapter in Hebrew and some Greek in Lucian. I said my prayers, and had boiled milk for breakfast. The weather was cold and clear, the wind northwest. I danced my dance. Then I put my business in order and about 11 o'clock went over the river to Captain Harrison's where I got about 3 o'clock and was courteously received. About four we went to dinner and I ate some fish. In the afternoon came Mr. Simons[1] and stayed with us all night. We sat and talked politics till 9 o'clock and then I retired and said my prayers. Mrs. Hannah Ludwell and Hannah Harrison came.

4. I rose about 7 o'clock and read nothing in Hebrew or Greek. However, I said my prayers, and had tea and bread and butter for breakfast. The weather was cold and clear, the wind northwest. About 11 o'clock we took leave and I rode with Hannah Ludwell and Hannah Harrison to Colonel Harrison's where we got about twelve. We found all this family well. The Colonel came not home till about 3 o'clock and then we went to dinner and I ate some boiled beef. In the evening came Colonel Ludwell, who came from his plantation at night. We played at cards and I lost a little. About 8 o'clock came Mr. Graffenried to teach the Colonel's children to dance. About 11

1. Henry Harrison and John Simons were burgesses from Surry County.

o'clock we retired and I said my prayers. Colonel Ludwell and I lay together.

5. I rose about 7 o'clock and read a little English. I said my prayers, and had sausage for breakfast. The weather continued cold and clear, the wind northwest. About 12 o'clock we all went over the river in the Colonel's boat to Mr. Lightfoot's where we found Phil Lightfoot and Mr. Armistead, his wife's brother. We had a handsome dinner and I ate some boiled tongue. After dinner we sat and talked till 4 o'clock and Colonel Ludwell went home but we played at piquet and I lost twenty shillings. About 8 o'clock we returned over the river and found one of the Colonel's chimneys on fire, but it was soon put out. We played at cards at night till 11 o'clock and then retired. I said a short prayer.

6. I rose about 7 o'clock and read some English till nine. I said my prayers, and ate some boiled milk for breakfast. The weather was cold and clear, the wind northwest. Several persons came, Captain Harrison and his lady, Mr. Edwards and his son,[2] Mr. Richardson and his wife, Mr. Cargill and his wife and daughter, who all came before dinner. I ate some roast mutton. After dinner we played at piquet and I lost twenty shillings. Then we acted proverbs and were merry till one o'clock . . . retired and Parson Cargill and I lay together. We danced country dances about two hours before we acted proverbs and Mr. Graffenried played to . . . be a good sort of man.

[Several pages of the manuscript are missing. The diary continues on February 13, 1721.]

2. Perhaps Benjamin Edwards, who had married Elizabeth Harrison, a sister of Colonel Harrison. They had a son Benjamin. Captain Henry Harrison's wife was Elizabeth (Smith) Harrison. Hannah (Mrs. Philip) Ludwell was another sister and Elizabeth (Burwell) Harrison a sister-in-law.

February 1721

[13.] . . . I talked with my people and then read some English and wrote till 9 o'clock and then said my prayers and retired. I had not a stool in two days.

14. I rose about 6 o'clock and read a chapter in Hebrew and some Greek in Lucian. I said my prayers, and had boiled milk for breakfast. The weather was cold and clear, the wind northwest. I danced my dance and was griped in my gut and had a loose stool or two and was indisposed. However, I wrote some English till dinner, when I ate some fish. After dinner I walked to Mrs. Harrison's but she had no [cheese]. I sat with her till the evening and then walked home and received a letter from Major Mumford and a letter from England that the plague was there. At night I wrote some English till 9 o'clock and talked with my people, said my prayers, and then retired.

15. I rose about 6 o'clock and read a chapter in Hebrew and some Greek in Lucian. I said my prayers, and had boiled milk for breakfast. The weather was clear and warm, the wind southwest. About 10 o'clock I went over the river and rode to John Grills' but he was from home. However, I sat with his wife and she gave me some sausage and eggs and stayed till 3 o'clock and then went on to Major Mumford's but he was gone to Colonel Randolph's to settle my account, but about an hour after me he came and Major Kennon with him, who kindly invited me to his house but I excused myself. I ate some boiled beef for supper and then Major Kennon went away and we sat and talked till 9 o'clock and then retired and I said my prayers.

16. I rose about 7 o'clock and read a little English. I said my prayers, and had milk for breakfast. The weather was fair in the morning

but about 11 o'clock it began to rain and continued to rain the whole day. However, John Grills came and settled accounts with me and paid me his debt and then stayed and dined with us and I ate some fowl and bacon. After dinner it continued to rain and so to help out bad air we drank a bowl of punch and sat and talked till the evening and then Grills went away and we sat all the evening and discoursed of several things till 9 o'clock and then I retired and neglected my prayers, for which God forgive me.

17. I rose about 7 o'clock and read some English and said my prayers. It continued to rain a little and was very cold, the wind northeast. I ate some hoecakes and milk for breakfast and then resolved not to go for fear of being wet. We walked to see Mr. Herbert and stayed there about an hour and then returned to Major Mumford's to dinner and I ate some boiled beef. After dinner we sat and talked and I read a little in *Hudibras* till the evening, when we had a bowl of punch again. We sat and talked of several subjects till 9 o'clock and then I retired and neglected my prayers again, for which God forgive me.

18. I rose about 7 o'clock and read some English. I said my prayers, and had some chocolate for breakfast. The weather was cold and clear, the wind northwest. About 10 o'clock I took leave of the ladies and the Major and I went to Major John Bolling's where we had another breakfast of sausage and eggs. I stayed till 2 o'clock and then took leave of the ladies and Major Mumford and Major Bolling went with me to the Hundred where I took leave of him and proceeded home where I found all pretty well, thank God. I walked about the plantation till night and then wrote three letters and talked with my people till 9 o'clock and then said my prayers and kissed Annie.

19. I rose about 7 o'clock and read a chapter in Hebrew and some Greek in Lucian. I said my prayers, and had boiled milk for breakfast. The weather was clear and warm, the wind west. I put several things in order. About 10 o'clock John Banister went over the river to go home and about eleven I walked to church where we had prayers but there was only my family. After church I walked to Mrs. Harrison's where we dined and I ate some roast beef. Colonel Eppes

dined there likewise. After dinner we sat and talked till the evening and then the Colonel took horse and I walked home, where I found all well, thank God. My people had their cider and I talked with several of them. At night I wrote in my journal and then read some English till 9 o'clock and then retired. I said my prayers and committed uncleanness with Annie, God forgive me.

20. I rose about 7 o'clock and read a chapter in Hebrew and some Greek in Lucian. I said my prayers, and had veal broth for breakfast, because I had taken three Anderson's [pills]. My physic worked three times. However, I wrote some English concerning the plague[1] till dinner and then ate some boiled mutton. After dinner I put several things in order and then wrote more English till the evening and then danced my dance again and afterwards walked about the plantation. I was displeased with John F-l for being so careless as to run [scissors] into his thigh. At night I talked with my people, read some English and said my prayers and slept pretty well, thank God.

21. I rose about 6 o'clock and read a chapter in Hebrew and some Greek in Lucian. I said my prayers, and had boiled milk for breakfast. The weather was cold and clear, the wind northwest. John F-l had a fever and I ordered him a vomit, which worked pretty well. I danced my dance and then wrote some English till dinner when I ate some roast mutton. After dinner I put several things in order till 3 o'clock and then came Jimmy Roscow who brought me some English letters. I gave him some dinner as soon as it could be prepared and we sat and talked of many things and drank a bottle of wine till the evening, and then I said my prayers and retired. I kissed Annie and slept indifferently. My sloop came down from above.

22. I rose about 6 o'clock and read a chapter in Hebrew and no Greek. I neglected my prayers, for which God forgive me, but had boiled milk for breakfast. The weather was clear and cold, the wind northeast. I danced my dance and then talked with Mr. Roscow till

1. The *Discourse Concerning the Plague,* published anonymously in London in 1721, is believed to be the work Byrd was writing; it is reprinted in *Another Secret Diary of William Byrd,* 411–43.

ten when we took a walk to Mrs. Harrison's where we sat and talked till dinner and I ate very heartily. After dinner we sat by a good fire and were merry till 3 o'clock and then Mr. Roscow went away to Colonel Randolph's and I walked home and sent away my sloop with tobacco to Captain L-p at Sapony. Then I took a walk about the plantation till the evening and then came my people from the Falls with a steer and told me all was well. I wrote some English, said my prayers, and retired.

23. I rose about 6 o'clock and read a chapter in Hebrew and some Greek in Lucian. I said my prayers, and had boiled milk for breakfast. The weather was cold and cloudy, the wind northwest. I danced my dance. I wrote a letter to the Falls. I walked about among my people to see they minded their business till dinner and then ate some hashed mutton. After dinner I put several things in order and then walked out and with Tom marked out where I would have the ditch. John F-l was indisposed with his lameness so that he could not walk. In the evening I walked about the plantation. At night I talked with my people and then read some English till 9 o'clock when I said my prayers but committed uncleanness with Annie, for which God forgive me.

24. I rose about 6 o'clock and read a chapter in Hebrew and some Greek. I said my prayers, and had boiled milk for breakfast. The weather was cold and clear, the wind northwest. I danced my dance and then wrote some English about the plague. Then I walked to see my people work till dinner when I ate some boiled beef. After dinner I put several things in order and then read some news. Old Bess was sick and I ordered her a vomit. In the evening I walked to see Mrs. Harrison where I sat and talked till 8 o'clock and then returned home and found all well, thank God. I read some news till 10 o'clock and then said my prayers and retired.

25. I rose about 6 o'clock and read a chapter in Hebrew and some Greek in Lucian. I said my prayers, and had milk and potato for breakfast. The weather was cold and clear, the wind northwest. I danced my dance and then wrote some English. About ten my sloop

returned from carrying my tobacco on board. Then I walked to see my people work till dinner when I ate some roast duck. After dinner I put several things in order and then wrote more English till 4 o'clock when Mr. Fontaine and his brother-in-law came and I gave them some victuals and we sat and talked French all the evening till 9 o'clock and then we retired and I said my prayers and slept but indifferently.

26. I rose about 6 o'clock and read a chapter in Hebrew and some Greek. I said my prayers, and had chocolate for breakfast with my company. The weather was cold and clear, the wind northwest. I danced my dance and put several things in order till 11 o'clock and then I walked to church where was a great congregation. After church I asked Frank ... and his wife to walk home with me and Mrs. Duke. When I came there I found Captain Wharwood, John Blair,[2] and John Bolling, and while we were at dinner ... came and I ate some boiled beef. After dinner we sat and talked till the evening and then came Mr. Roscow and we had a bowl of [d-p-n-s] but Colonel Ludwell and Mr. .... and went to Mrs. Harrison's but the Captain, John Blair, and I sat up till eleven and then I committed uncleanness with Annie, for which God forgive me.

27. I rose about 6 o'clock and read a chapter in Hebrew but no Greek. I said my prayers, and had no breakfast at home but about nine we walked to Mrs. Harrison's, where I had some chocolate for breakfast. Here we stayed till 12 o'clock and then persuaded Mrs. Harrison and Colonel Ludwell to go dine with me but Mr. Roscow would not stay. So we walked home, where I entertained my company as well as I could and ate some boiled chicken for dinner. After dinner we drank a bowl of punch till the evening and then Mrs. Harrison and Colonel Ludwell went to Mrs. Harrison's house and the Captain, John Blair, and I stayed and drank punch till the Captain and I had almost quarreled about the women that I brought with me. About 12 o'clock I retired in bad humor and slept but indifferently.

2. John, son of Dr. Archibald Blair, and nephew of the Commissary.

28. I rose about 6 o'clock and read nothing because I got every-thing in order. However, I said my prayers shortly. The weather was warm and clear, the wind southwest. About 8 o'clock came Colonel Ludwell to breakfast with us and I ate some mutton pie. Then I put my family in order and about 10 o'clock we went aboard the Cap-tain's little yawl and sailed down the river to Frank Lightfoot's where we dined and I ate some boiled beef. Colonel Harrison came to us but we could not persuade him to go with us to Colonel Ludwell's. About 5 o'clock we took leave and sailed down to Colonel Ludwell's landing and from thence in his coach to the house, where we were courteously entertained, and found Ben Harrison there. I was very sleepy and about eleven retired and said my prayers.

March 1721

1. I rose about 7 o'clock and read nothing but got ready as soon as I could. However, I said my prayers and went to the company. I ate some hogs' feet for breakfast. The weather was warm and clear, the wind southwest. About 10 o'clock Captain Wharwood went in Colonel Ludwell's coach and he and Colonel Harrison rode their horses to Williamsburg where we went to wait on the Governor, who received us courteously. Then I went to see my landlady, Mrs. Cary, and then walked to the capitol, where we sat in Council about Cap-tain Martin's account and the disposition of the money given to the sailors that went with him but we could get no commission of the peace for our county, for which reason I can't guess. About 5 o'clock we went to dine with the Governor, where I ate some roast pigeon. We stayed till seven and then returned to Green Springs again where we found Major Burwell with the rest of the company, and Captain Martin. We played at proverbs and were merry till 12 o'clock when I said my prayers and slept very well, thank God.

2. I rose about 7 o'clock and read nothing, but got myself ready to join the good company. However, I said my prayers and found the weather warm and clear. I ate some neats' tongue for breakfast. Captain Martin and I played at piquet and I won six bits and then he and all the company went away but the Commissary came in his stead and we talked about several matters relating to myself. About three we went to dinner and I ate some boiled beef. After dinner we sat and talked till five and then the Commissary went away and the Colonel and I took a walk to see his improvements. At night we sat and talked about several matters till ten and then retired and I said my prayers and slept pretty well, thank God Almighty.

3. I rose about 7 o'clock and read nothing but got myself ready. However, I said my prayers and had milk and potato for breakfast. The weather was cold and . . . the wind northwest. About 10 o'clock I took leave and gave the servants eight bits. I discharged all my debts to both ferries and then proceeded home, where I found all well, thank God. I walked about the garden and found my people had minded their business during my absence. I ate some hashed duck and then put several things in order till the evening and then took a walk about the plantation. At night I discoursed all my people and Billy desired leave to fight with Joe to try the mastery and I gave him leave. I washed my feet and then committed uncleanness with Annie, for which God forgive me.

4. I rose about 7 o'clock and read a chapter in Hebrew and some Greek. I said my prayers, and had milk and potato for breakfast. The weather was cold and clear, the wind northwest. I danced my dance. Last night Jenny P-r-s came to ask leave for Sam G-r-d-n to fish. I kissed her and was kind to her and gave her some physic and some wine. Billy Wilkins beat Joe because he would not fight. I settled some accounts and read some English till dinner when I ate some boiled mutton. After dinner I put several things in order till 5 o'clock and then walked to Mrs. Harrison's and sat with her the whole evening till 9 o'clock and then by the light of the moon walked home and talked with my people and about ten said my prayers and retired and slept pretty well. This night I got a cold.

5. I rose about 7 o'clock and read a chapter in Hebrew and some Greek in Lucian. I said my prayers, and had boiled milk for breakfast. The weather was cold and clear, the wind north. I danced my dance and put myself in order and then looked over some books in the library and then walked in the garden till 12 o'clock when I thought I saw Mrs. Duke come over the river in the ferry and so I walked to the landing and there found her and her daughter and I invited them down. About the same time came Mrs. Harrison and [Libby] Goodrich, and I ate some fish for dinner. After dinner came Ben Harrison and Mr. Graffenried but would not stay. In the evening the ladies went to Mrs. Harrison's and I took a walk about the plantation. In the evening I talked with my people and then wrote some letters till nine and then said my prayers and retired. My cold was worse.

6. I rose about 7 o'clock and read nothing because I prepared to go to the Falls, and gave the necessary orders. I said my prayers, and had milk and potato for breakfast. The weather was warm and cloudy, the wind west. My man Abraham broke his shin and was very lame. About 11 o'clock I ate some cold roast beef and then I got on my horse and rode to Frank Hardyman's, notwithstanding it rained a little, where I found abundance of company met to learn to dance. I was persuaded by the . . . and the company to stay to dinner and ate some fish for dinner. Colonel Randolph's lady[1] and Drury Stith and his two daughters dined with us and Colonel Hill and his [daughter]. . . . I resolved to stay all night and we danced country dances and Mrs. [Hunt] was my partner. We sat up till 10 o'clock and then Mr. Graffenried and I lay together. My cold continued bad. However, I slept pretty well, thank God. Some of the Nottoway Indians[2] came and danced.

7. I rose about 7 o'clock and read nothing but got myself ready as soon as I could. I neglected my prayers, but had chocolate for breakfast. Abundance of the Sapony Indians came to get a passport to the

1. Mrs. William Randolph was Elizabeth Beverley.

2. Like the Sapony, the Nottoway were an eastern Siouan tribe, now believed extinct.

Pamunkey town[3] and sang one of their songs. About 9 o'clock I took leave and rode to Colonel Hill's where I drank more chocolate. About ten I went over the river and found it extremely cold. However, I rode to Henry Anderson's and with him to Falling Creek where Major Mumford overtook us. The sawmill made a shift to go. Here I found Dick, the miller, sick. Then we proceeded to the Falls where we found a Negro woman very sick, and old Tony. Major Mumford let them blood. About 4 o'clock we ate some pork and then rode to the people at work on the island. At night we had two bowls of brandy punch and sat up till ten and then I retired and found a clean little bed for myself and another for Major Mumford.

8. I rose about 7 o'clock and read nothing but got ready and said a short prayer. I talked with Will Bass, Mr. F-r-m-r and Page P-n-s about several matters and then ate some hoecakes and milk. It rained a little. However, about 10 o'clock I visited the sick and found them better, though the woman had miscarried. Then we returned to Falling Creek where I visited the sick miller again and then we proceeded to Mr. Anderson's where I ate some boiled beef and received some money. His wife was in a deep consumption. About 3 o'clock we took leave and rode to Major John Bolling's where we were courteously received by the little woman and she sent for her husband who was from home, and he came through the rain to us. In the evening I ate some fowl and bacon and then had a bowl of punch and drank of it till 10 o'clock and then retired.

9. I rose about 7 o'clock and read some English. I said my prayers, and had chocolate for breakfast. I found it had rained abundance in the night, the wind northeast. We offered to go away but they persuaded us to stay till dinner, which we had about 1 o'clock and I ate roast chicken. After dinner I took leave of the ladies but the Major went with me to the Hundred, but Major Mumford went right home. About 4 o'clock I crossed the river and got home about seven and

3. The Pamunkey Indians still retain their tribal organization and live on the reservation set aside for them in the seventeenth century in King William County. Near by live the Mattaponi Indians, the only other 'reservation' Indians in Virginia today. Hugh Jones, *Present State of Virginia*, ed. Richard L. Morton (Chapel Hill, N.C., 1956). 172-3.

found all well, thank God, and all my business in good order. I walked about the plantation in the evening and found the people had obeyed my orders. At night I talked with my people and gave them some cider and then wrote in my journal till 9 o'clock and said my prayers. I asked Annie to come to bed to me but she would not be prevailed with. My cold continued but not very violent.

10. I rose about 6 o'clock and read a chapter in Hebrew and some Greek in Lucian. I said my prayers, and had boiled milk for breakfast. The weather was clear and cold, the wind west. I danced my dance and then wrote some English till dinner when I ate some roast mutton. After dinner I put several things in order and then wrote more English till the evening, when I walked about the plantation and saw all my people at work. At night I talked with my people about their several businesses and then wrote some English again till 9 o'clock and then I committed uncleanness with Annie, for which God forgive me.

11. I rose about 6 o'clock and read a chapter in Hebrew and some Greek in Lucian. I said my prayers, and had boiled milk for breakfast. The weather was warm and cloudy, the wind northwest. I danced my dance and then wrote some English and walked in the garden till dinner and just as I sat down came Mrs. Duke and her daughter and son and I ate some [cowheel]. After dinner I walked with Mrs. Duke to the landing and when I returned I found Jenny P-r-s come to bring back my bottle in which I gave her something for her indisposition. I kissed her and felt her breasts for about two hours and then she walked off and I wrote some English till the evening and then walked about the plantation. At night I talked with my people and then wrote more English till 9 o'clock and then said my prayers and retired.

12. I rose about 6 o'clock and read a chapter in Hebrew and some Greek in Lucian. I said my prayers, and had boiled milk for breakfast. The weather was cold and clear, the wind northwest. I danced my dance and sent Mrs. Harrison some fish and then put several things in order till 11 o'clock and then walked to church where we had

prayers. After church I returned home to dinner and ate some boiled beef. After dinner I put some things in order and then took a walk to Mrs. Harrison's who told me Colonel Page's house was burnt to the ground,[4] which I was much concerned to hear. I sat with my neighbor till the evening and ate apples and then took a walk home and talked with my people and then wrote some English till nine when I washed my feet and said my prayers. Annie lay down with me but I only kissed her.

13. I rose about 6 o'clock and read a chapter in Hebrew and some Greek in Lucian. I said my prayers, and had boiled milk for breakfast. The weather was warm and clear, the wind east. I danced my dance and sent away my boat to Colonel Ludwell's for some fig trees. Then I wrote some English till dinner when I ate some roast beef. After dinner I put several things in order and then wrote more English till the evening when I walked to the old plantation to meet Jenny P-r-s but the whore did not come. I stayed there about two hours and then returned home. I received some wild turkey and several other things by Major Mumford's boat with a letter from the Major. I wrote several letters to Williamsburg by Sam who is designed [for] there tomorrow. Then I wrote some English till nine and then said my prayers and kissed Annie.

14. I rose about 6 o'clock and read a chapter in Hebrew and some Greek in Lucian. I said my prayers, and had boiled milk for breakfast. The weather was cold and cloudy, the wind northeast. Mr. Will Harrison brought me some money from Captain Harrison. I dispatched Major Mumford's boat and wrote a letter to him. I danced my dance and then I wrote some English till 1 o'clock when the Frenchman came again about buying some land and there was another man with him. They dined with me and I ate some boiled beef. After dinner it began to rain and continued till night when it snowed a little. I wrote some more English till the evening when I could not walk for the rain.

4. Robert Carter, writing on March 8, reported that Colonel 'Cage's' house and barn had burned to the ground. See *Letters of Robert Carter*, 1720–1727, ed. Louis B. Wright (San Marino, Calif., 1940), 90.

At night I talked with my people about their business and then wrote more English till 10 o'clock and then I said my prayers and retired.

15. I rose about 6 o'clock and read a chapter in Hebrew and some Greek in Lucian. I said my prayers, and had boiled milk for breakfast. The weather was cloudy, the wind northeast. I danced my dance and then wrote some English till dinner when I ate some hashed mutton. I scolded at Joe for taking the wine but I was sorry for it because it proved a mistake. After dinner I put several things in order and then wrote more English till the evening when I took a walk about the plantation and overlooked my business. About 6 o'clock I received a letter from the Falls that told me my sick people were better, thank God, and all things well. At night I examined John F-l about settling his administration and told him I would not keep him any longer. I talked with my people and said my prayers.

16. I rose about 6 o'clock and read a chapter in Hebrew and some Greek in Lucian. I said my prayers and had boiled milk for breakfast. The weather was clear and warm, the wind west. I danced my dance, and then wrote my book fair about the plague and made a good beginning till dinner when I ate some hashed duck. After dinner I put some things in order and then wrote more English till the evening, when I took a walk about the plantation. This day we began to turf the bowling green. At night I talked with my people and gave orders for sending away the sloop and then wrote more English till 9 o'clock and then said my prayers.

17. I rose about 6 o'clock and read a chapter in Hebrew and some Greek in Lucian. I said my prayers, and had boiled milk for breakfast. The weather was warm and foggy, the wind east. I danced my dance. Sam came late last night from Williamsburg and brought me a letter from Major Custis. I wrote some English till dinner and then ate some hashed beef. After dinner I put several things in order and walked to see my people work but about 3 o'clock it began to rain and continued raining till 10 o'clock at night. I wrote some English till the evening. Sam went into the [sink] to see whether there was anything to stop the water. I took a walk in the gallery. At night I talked with my

people and wrote more English till 9 o'clock and then said my prayers. I committed uncleanness with Annie, God forgive me.

18. I rose about 6 o'clock and read a chapter in Hebrew and some Greek in Lucian. I said my prayers, and had boiled milk for breakfast. The weather was clear and warm, the wind west. I danced my dance and then wrote some English and walked among my people to see them work. I dined not till 2 o'clock in expectation of the parson but he came not, so I ate some fish by myself, but soon after dinner came my cousin Suky Brayne[5] being put away by Mr. Beverley. I gave her and the man that came with her some fish. About four o'clock the man went away and the parson and Mr. Harrison came and stayed about an hour and then returned to Mrs. Harrison's. I sat and talked with my people and afterwards with my cousin till 9 o'clock and I said my prayers.

19. I rose about 6 o'clock and read a chapter in Hebrew and some Greek in Lucian. I said my prayers, and had boiled milk for breakfast. The weather was clear and cold, the wind west. I [dreamed] the ships were come in and so I talked with Captain Turner about my tobacco. I danced my dance and about 11 o'clock went to church where Mr. Fontaine gave us a good sermon. After church I invited Colonel Hill, his daughter, and Mrs. Greenhill, Mrs. Duke, and Colonel Eppes to dine. My cousin Brayne went to dine with Mrs. Harrison. I ate some wild turkey. After dinner we sat and talked till the evening and then Mrs. Duke went over the river in my boat and the rest of the company went away and I took a walk. At night I talked first with my people and then with my cousin till nine when I said my prayers and then retired and slept very well, thank God.

20. I rose about 6 o'clock and read a chapter in Hebrew and some Greek in Lucian. I said my prayers, and had boiled milk for breakfast. The weather was clear and cold, the wind northwest. I danced my dance and then walked to see my people work. Then I wrote some English till dinner when I ate some hashed beef. After dinner I put several things in order and about 3 o'clock came John Banister and I

5. Byrd's niece, the daughter of his sister Susan and John Brayne of England.

walked about with him for about an hour and then wrote more English till the evening and then took a walk to the old plantation but saw nobody. At night I was out of humor and sat and talked with my cousin and Banister till 9 o'clock and then had my feet washed. I said a short prayer.

21. I rose about 6 o'clock and read a chapter in Hebrew and some Greek in Lucian. I said my prayers and had boiled milk for breakfast. The weather was clear and cloudy, the wind west. I danced my dance and then wrote some English till dinner when I ate some fish. After dinner I put several things in order and then walked about to see my people at their business. About 4 o'clock came young John Bolling and brought me a letter from Colonel Harrison in which he gave me hints about a new governor. I gave John Bolling some fish and mince pie. In the evening he went away home and I took a walk about the plantation. At night I talked with my people till nine and then said my prayers.

22. I rose about 6 o'clock and read a chapter in Hebrew and some Greek. I said my prayers, and had boiled milk for breakfast. The weather was clear and cold, the wind northwest. I danced my dance and then took a walk in the garden to see my people work. Then I read over my book about the plague and corrected it till dinner and then I ate some boiled beef. After dinner I put some things in order and then walked to Mrs. Harrison's where I read over my book and she liked it very much. Here I stayed till the evening and then returned home and talked with my people and afterwards with Banister and my cousin till 9 o'clock when I said my prayers and retired but after I was in bed I committed uncleanness with my maid Annie, for which God forgive me.

23. I rose about 6 o'clock and read a chapter in Hebrew and some Greek in Lucian. I said my prayers, and had boiled milk for breakfast. The weather was cold and clear, the wind south. I danced my dance and then walked in the garden to see my people proceed in their business. I wrote a letter to England till 12 o'clock and then came Mrs. Harrison to dine with me and I ate some boiled fowl.

After dinner came Colonel Eppes but the victuals was brought again for him. Then we sat and talked till 4 o'clock when seventeen of the Nottoway Indians came and I gave them some rum and victuals. Then I took a walk about the plantation. At night I read and my cousin read some English till 9 o'clock and then I said my prayers and retired.

24. I rose about 6 o'clock and read a chapter in Hebrew and some Greek in Lucian. I said my prayers, and had boiled milk for breakfast. The weather was cold and cloudy, the wind northeast. I danced my dance. Then I walked about the garden to see my people lay the turf. Then I wrote two letters to England till dinner and ate some hashed wild turkey. After dinner I showed some Indians my house and garden and then I wrote another letter to England. It rained a little. In the evening I took a walk about the plantation, notwithstanding I was indisposed in my stomach with wind. At night I talked with my people till nine and then said my prayers.

25. I rose about 6 o'clock and read a chapter in Hebrew and some Greek in Lucian. I said my prayers and had boiled milk for breakfast. The weather was warm and cloudy and it rained a little in the morning but held up again so that about 11 o'clock I recommended my family to God and about seven miles off the rain overtook me and I put into James [Jones]. In half an hour I proceeded to [Wilcox's] and there the rain made me take up again. Here I ate some bacon and eggs and in about an hour went to Mr. Lightfoot's where I was courteously received and ate some milk and hoecakes and at night Captain C-p came and we drank punch till eleven and were merry and then retired and I neglected my prayers but slept pretty well, thank God.

26. I rose about 7 o'clock and read some English. I said my prayers, and had milk and hoecakes for breakfast. The weather was cold and clear, the wind west. Colonel Harrison just came and breakfasted with us and then returned and I read some of my plague book to him. About 10 o'clock we rode to church where Mr. Fontaine gave us a sermon that I had heard before. After church we returned to Mr. Lightfoot's and the parson and Mr. Harwood with us and I ate some

boiled beef. After dinner I sat about an hour and then took leave and Mr. Lightfoot and Captain C-p went with me into the [main] road and from thence I proceeded by myself to Green Springs. My stomach was disordered by wind exceedingly. I was courteously received by everybody and at night I took an Anderson's pill and retired about eleven and slept pretty well, thank God.

27. I rose about 7 o'clock and read some English. I said a short prayer, and had some broiled mutton for breakfast. My pill worked three times. The weather was clear and cold and about 10 o'clock we rode to Williamsburg where I went to visit Major Custis and walked in his garden, which was much improved. Then I rode to the College where Colonel Ludwell met me and talked with the Commissary about his business and I dined with him and I ate some boiled goose. After dinner we walked to [B-c-c] where we found several of the governors of the College who were at dinner. When they made an end we all walked to the College where we resolved to state the case of the Commissary fairly and agreed to have the business of his salary there determined. About 9 o'clock Colonel Ludwell and I returned to Green Springs, where we found Mrs. Bassett and Mrs. Allen and Lucy Bassett and Will Edwards. We sat and talked till twelve and then retired and I slept pretty well, thank God.

28. I rose about 7 o'clock and read nothing. I said a short prayer, and ate some bacon for breakfast. The weather continued cold and clear, the wind west. About 10 o'clock Colonel Ludwell and I went again to Williamsburg to meet the governors of the College. We judged several things and heard a very false memorial of Parson Jones in which we did nothing. We did several other matters till 3 o'clock and then I took Major Burwell and carried him to Green Springs in the coach where we dined and I ate some roast pigeon. After dinner we sat and talked till night and then we acted proverbs and were very merry till 12 o'clock and then we retired and I slept pretty well, thank God.

29. I rose about 7 o'clock and read nothing. I said a short prayer, and ate [stuffed] beef for breakfast. The weather was warm and

cloudy, the wind southwest. However about 10 o'clock I took leave of the good company and rode home in five hours without being wet. I found all well, thank God, and learned that all was well at my plantation. I walked about the garden and discoursed Banister about my business. Annie was indisposed with an ague. About 5 o'clock I danced my dance and then ate some milk and hoecakes for supper. In the evening I took a walk about the plantation and at night talked with my people till 9 o'clock and then said a short prayer and slept but indifferently. It rained a little all night.

30. I rose about 6 o'clock and read a chapter in Hebrew and some Greek in Lucian. I said my prayers, and had boiled milk for breakfast. The weather was warm and cloudy, the wind north. I wrote a letter to the Falls and sent away the sloop. I danced my dance. I gave Annie a vomit for her ague, which worked but indifferently. Then I walked in the garden and wrote some English till dinner when I ate some hashed beef. After dinner I put several things in order and then took a walk and then read some Latin till the evening, when I danced again. It rained pretty much so that I could not walk. At night I talked with my people till nine and then said my prayers and retired and slept but indifferently. It rained abundantly in the night.

31. I rose about 6 o'clock and read a chapter in Hebrew and some Greek in Lucian. I said my prayers, and had boiled milk for breakfast. The weather was cold and cloudy, the wind northeast. I danced my dance. Annie had her ague again. I read some English till dinner and then ate boiled beef. After dinner I put several things in order and then walked to Mrs. Harrison's and sat with her till five and then walked to the old plantation in hopes to see Jenny P-r-s but did not succeed, so I returned and talked with my people till 9 o'clock and then said my prayers and slept but indifferently. There came four Indians.

April 1721

1. I rose about 6 o'clock and read a chapter in Hebrew and some Greek in Lucian. I said my prayers, and had boiled milk for breakfast. The weather was warm and clear, the wind west. I walked about and saw my people working about several things. About 12 o'clock came Mr. Stanhope and another man about land. They stayed to dinner with me and I ate some [cowheel]. After dinner I showed them all my contrivances, with which they were well pleased, and about 4 o'clock they went away. I sent John and P-p-l to Falling Creek to help trim the sloop. About 5 o'clock came Rice Jones from the upper county to talk about the repair of my mill and dam at Falling Creek. In the evening I took a walk about the plantation and at night talked with my people and said my prayers. I wrote two letters to the Falls.

2. I rose about 6 o'clock and read a chapter in Hebrew and some Greek in Lucian. I said my prayers, and had boiled milk for breakfast. The weather was warm and clear, the wind southwest. I danced my dance and walked about the garden till 11 o'clock and then I went to church to prayers and then returned and read some English till dinner when I ate some boiled beef. After dinner I sat and talked with Banister and then walked about the garden. Mrs. Brayne took a vomit that worked very well. I read more English and took a walk in the orchard and kitchen garden and ordered Captain C-p man some cider, who came to see the garden. In the evening I took a walk about the plantation and at night talked with my people till nine and then said my prayers and retired and slept pretty well, thank God.

3. I rose about 6 o'clock and read a chapter in Hebrew and some Greek in Lucian. I said my prayers and had milk and Indian hoe-

cakes for breakfast. The weather was cold and clear, the wind west. I danced my dance. I sent to invite Mr. Clayton and Mr. Lightfoot who were at next house to dinner but they excused themselves. However, about 10 o'clock Mr. Clayton came and stayed about an hour and then proceeded to Williamsburg. I wrote some English till dinner and then ate some roast beef. After dinner I put several things in order and then read some English till the evening when Mr. Lightfoot came and walked about the garden and then played at piquet till 9 o'clock when he went away and I retired and committed uncleanness with Annie, for which God forgive me.

4. I rose about 6 o'clock and read a chapter in Hebrew and some Greek in Lucian. I said my prayers, and had milk and hoecakes for breakfast. The weather was warm and cloudy, the wind southwest. I danced my dance and then came Mr. Lightfoot and Captain C-p and the Captain and I settled our business and he gave me bills of lading and I gave him my letters and my book about the plague to deliver to Mr. Perry. Then we played at billiards till 11 o'clock and then having drunk some [r-t-t] they went away. I ate some boiled mutton for dinner. In the afternoon came Dr. Blair, who had been with Colonel Eppes. We walked in the garden and in the evening I walked with him almost to Mrs. Harrison's. At night I talked with my people till nine and then said my prayers and retired.

5. I rose about 6 o'clock and read a chapter in Hebrew and some Greek in Lucian. I said my prayers and had milk and hoecakes for breakfast. The weather was cold and cloudy, the wind north. I danced my dance and walked about in the garden. Then I wrote some English till 12 o'clock and then came Drury Stith about some business and stayed about half an hour and then I walked to the court where I joined with some gentlemen to save a poor girl from whipping that had a bastard. I invited Mr. W-m-s, Bowler Cocke, and Major Bolling to dinner and I ate some boiled beef. After dinner we walked about the garden and then went to court again where I stayed about an hour and then walked home and then about the plantation. At night I talked with my people till 9 o'clock and then

said my prayers and afterwards committed uncleanness with Annie, for which God forgive me.

6. I rose about 6 o'clock and read a chapter in Hebrew and some Greek in Lucian. I said my prayers, and had milk and hoecakes for breakfast. The weather was cold and clear, the wind east. I sent my cousin Brayne to visit her aunt Duke and wrote a letter to my sister. I danced my dance and then wrote some English till dinner when I ate some hashed mutton. After dinner I took a nap and then walked to Mrs. Harrison's where I sat and talked till 6 o'clock and then returned home and found Sam had set the [kiln] on fire and the wind blew direct upon the woodpile. I set a watch all night upon it and wrote a letter to my brother Duke to excuse myself from lending him one hundred pounds. I talked with my people and said a short prayer and retired and slept very ill.

7. I rose about 6 o'clock and read a chapter in Hebrew and some Greek in Lucian. I said my prayers, and had milk and hoecakes for breakfast. The weather was cold and cloudy, the wind southwest. I danced my dance. I furnished Banister with six pounds in money and then gave him leave to go home and wrote a letter by him to Major Mumford. I walked to see my people work and then wrote some English till dinner when I ate some broiled beef and asparagus. After dinner I put several things in order and then wrote more English till the evening and then I took a walk about the plantation. When I returned I found Ralph [Hunt] from my quarters at New Kent who told me all my people were well, thank God. I talked with my people and had my feet washed and then said my prayers and retired. It rained in the night.

8. I rose about 6 o'clock and read a chapter in Hebrew and some Greek in Plutarch. I said my prayers, and had [b-l] and hoecakes for breakfast. The weather was cold and cloudy, the wind northeast. I danced my dance and then walked about to see my people work. Then I wrote some English till dinner and ate some hashed mutton. Soon after dinner came Mr. Fontaine and I gave him some fish. Then we took a walk about the main garden till the evening.

The parson told me that four ships were come into York River. At night I talked with my people and then read my book to him about the plague. I said my prayers and retired about 10 o'clock.

9. I rose about 6 o'clock and read a chapter in Hebrew and some Greek in the common prayer book. I said my prayers, and had some chocolate for breakfast with Mr. Fontaine. The weather was cold and cloudy, the wind southwest. I danced my dance and seemed well disposed to receive the Sacrament by resolving to mend my life. After church I invited Mrs. Duke and Mrs. [Hunt], Colonel Eppes and one Mr. G-ing who came to court Mrs. [Hunt]. I ate some roast turkey. After dinner we sat and talked till 5 o'clock and then it began to rain and they resolved to stay all night. We drank several things and were merry till 10 o'clock and I kissed Mrs. [Hunt] several times and she was not very unwilling. I neglected my prayers for which God forgive me.

10. I rose about 6 o'clock and read a chapter in Hebrew and no Greek, because I entertained my company. I gave them a dram and Mrs. [Hunt] took one likewise. I ate battered eggs for breakfast. Then we took a walk and I showed Mr. G-ing all my contrivances. About 10 o'clock I sent for Mrs. Harrison and she came and dined with us and I ate some boiled chicken. After dinner it rained again very violently for about an hour and then my company went away and I walked in the garden. At night I talked to my people till nine and then said my prayers, but committed uncleanness with Annie, for which God forgive me.

11. I rose about 6 o'clock and read a chapter in Hebrew and some Greek in Plutarch. I said my prayers, and had milk and hoecakes for breakfast. It rained a little this morning. I danced my dance and then walked about the garden to see my people work. Then I wrote some English till dinner and then ate some hashed turkey. After dinner I put several things in order and then read some Latin till the evening. It rained abundantly so that I could not walk about the plantation. At night came Major Mumford and Banister from Prince George Court and I gave them some hashed beef and fish for supper. Then

we sat and talked about several things till 10 o'clock and then I said my prayers and retired.

12. I rose about 6 o'clock and read a chapter in Homer and a little Greek. I said my prayers, and had milk and potato for breakfast. I found myself very much troubled with wind. The Major and I played at billiards and I lost. Then we took a walk to Mrs. Harrison's where we found Hannah Harrison. We talked till twelve and then we offered to return but we were invited to stay to dinner and I ate some boiled beef. After dinner we sat and talked of several things till the evening and then took leave. The Major and I walked about the kitchen garden and then about the orchard. At night I talked with my people and about ten took two of Anderson's pills, said my prayers, and retired, and slept pretty well. Bob and John came from above.

13. I rose about six o'clock and I read a chapter in Hebrew and some Greek in Plutarch. I said my prayers, and had veal broth for breakfast. The weather was cold and cloudy, the wind northeast. I danced my dance. About 9 o'clock Major Mumford went away and I walked about the garden to see my people work till about 12 o'clock and then came Will Hamlin and Mrs. [Hunt] and soon after them Mrs. Harrison and Hannah Harrison and then Colonel Hill, who all dined with me and I ate some roast turkey. After dinner came Mrs. Stith and brought me a letter from John Carter. The company all went away about 5 o'clock and I walked home with Mrs. Harrison and then returned. It rained a little. I talked with my people till 9 o'clock and then said my prayers and took a pill.

14. I rose about 6 o'clock and read a chapter in Hebrew and some Greek in Plutarch. I said my prayers, and had boiled milk for breakfast. The weather was cold and cloudy, the wind north. I danced my dance and had five stools. Then I walked about to see my people work and then settled several accounts till dinner when I ate some cold roast beef. After dinner I put several matters in order and then read some Latin till the evening when Mrs. Duke and Mrs. [Hunt] called and I walked with them in the garden. Dick Cocke brought

me some letters from England and one from my daughters, who were well, thank God. Then I walked about the plantation and at night talked with my people till 9 o'clock and then said my prayers and I took one Anderson's pill and slept pretty well.

15. I rose about 6 o'clock and read a chapter in Hebrew and some Greek in Plutarch. I said my prayers, and had boiled milk for breakfast. The weather was cold and clear, the wind northwest. I danced my dance. Several Nottoway Indians came here to get over the river. I walked about to see my people work and then wrote some English till dinner. After dinner I put several things in order and then prepared my business to go to Williamsburg. In the evening came Mr. Harrison and told me all the news he had at New Kent Court and I walked with him almost home and then returned and found it extremely cold so that my people covered their plants again. At night I talked with my people till 9 o'clock and then said my prayers but committed uncleanness with Annie, for which God forgive me. I rose in the night to shit.

16. I rose about 6 o'clock and read nothing. I found myself indisposed with a bloody flux. I sent away my trunk to Williamsburg in my boat. I said my prayers and had milk and [milo] for breakfast. I put everything in order and recommended my family to the protection of the Almighty and then rode to Green Springs, but by the way had two stools. I stayed at the ferry about an hour because the man was gone out. However, I got over the river well at last, notwithstanding the wind blew violently, and about 3 o'clock got to Green Springs where I found all well; however I was indisposed and could eat nothing. However, in the evening I drank a gallon of thin broth in which [milo] and [camphor] had been boiled which washed me very well and about 10 o'clock took a [composing] drink and slept very well after I said a short prayer for my recovery. Captain Bradby dined here.

17. I rose about 6 o'clock and read nothing, but found myself much better, thank God. I said my prayers and had mutton broth for breakfast. The weather was cold and clear, the wind west. About

10 o'clock we took leave and rode to town and I went to my lodging and put everything in order and then went and gave orders for my boat to return home. Then I went to the capitol where we sat till 3 o'clock and then went to dinner where I ate some boiled mutton and broth. After dinner we took a little walk with Colonel Ludwell and Colonel Harrison and in the evening I went home and read my letters and put my things in order and at night said a short prayer and took my [composing] drink.

18. I rose about 6 o'clock and read a chapter in Hebrew and some Greek in Lucian. I said my prayers, and had boiled milk for break-fast. The weather was warm and cloudy, the wind south. I found myself better, thank God. This morning I received the sad news of Billy Brayne's[1] death, from Mr. B-r-n-t, for which I was sincerely concerned. About 10 o'clock I went to wait on Governor Keith[2] and sat with him about an hour and then went to court where I sat till 4 o'clock and then we went to dinner and ate some boiled mutton and broth. After dinner Captain W-r-r came and sat with us about an hour and then came Mr. [Griffin] and brought the new master of the grammar school with him. Colonel Harrison and I were courteous to him for about an hour more. Then I walked home and read some English and said my prayers. I slept pretty well, thank God.

19. I rose about 6 o'clock and read a chapter in Hebrew and some Greek in Lucian. I said my prayers, and had boiled milk for break-fast. The weather was warm and cloudy and it rained a little. I wrote a letter and about 9 o'clock went to Colonel Ludwell's where I found only the ladies. I stayed about half an hour and then went to Mr. Roscow's who was not stirring, but I found Mrs. Molly Hardyman and I talked to her about her coming here as a witness.[3]

1. Byrd's nephew, orphaned son of Susan Byrd and John Brayne, had lived at Westover after 1710 and in 1712 was sent to the College.

2. Sir William Keith, governor of Pennsylvania, 1717–26.

3. Probably to appear at the trial of James Robertson. John Hardyman was a witness of the event and as he did not report the incident he was suspended as sheriff of the county.

Then I went to . . . till 2 o'clock and then went to dinner and Governor Keith dined with us with his two friends and I ate some boiled beef. After dinner the Governor came and sat with us a little and then carried our gentlemen away and we went to court and sat about an hour and then took a walk. Then I walked to Colonel Ludwell's and from thence to the Governor's where we drank rack punch till ten and then I walked home and said my prayers.

20. I rose about 6 o'clock and read a chapter in Hebrew and some Greek in Lucian. I said my prayers, and had boiled milk for breakfast. The weather was cold and cloudy, the wind northwest. I wrote several letters to my quarters in New Kent. About 10 o'clock I walked to the President's where I saw Mrs. H-r-n-t-n and her daughter. Here I stayed about an hour and then walked to the capitol where we tried several criminals. About one I went out and ate some broth and then returned again and sat till five and then went to dinner and I ate some roast mutton. After dinner Colonel Harrison and I walked to visit Mrs. Cocke where we stayed about two hours and then I walked to Colonel Ludwell's where Mrs. Russell came and talked abundantly. About ten I walked home and said a short prayer.

21. I rose about 6 o'clock and read a chapter in Hebrew and some Greek in Lucian. I said my prayers, and had boiled milk for breakfast. The weather was warm and cloudy. About nine I went to Colonel Bassett's where I ate another breakfast of tea and bread and butter. Then I went to court where Parson Robinson was tried and found guilty though some pains was taken by the church to soften matters. About a [o-r] lady came to justify him but to no purpose. At five we went to dinner and I ate some boiled mutton. At night I went and discoursed Mr. Roscow and forgave him his bargain and then went to the Governor's where was an assembly and I danced with Mrs. Russell and stayed till 12 o'clock and then went home and neglected my prayers, for which God forgive me.

22. I rose about 6 o'clock and read a chapter in Hebrew and some Greek in Lucian. I said my prayers, and had boiled milk for break-

fast. The weather was warm and cloudy, the wind southwest. Colonel Corbin and Will Edwards came and stayed half an hour and then Colonel Harrison and stayed half an hour and then I walked to the capitol to endeavor to find Captain [Hunt] and I found him and he paid me the debt he owed. Then I walked to the capitol and there we sat till 4 o'clock and then I went to dine with the Commissary and ate some boiled mutton. After dinner came in Mrs. Randolph and Mrs. Ludwell. Mr. Brook called on me and told me all was well above, thank God. In the evening I took a walk and then went to Mrs. Bassett's and spent the evening till ten and then went home and neglected my prayers, for which God forgive me.

23. I rose about 6 o'clock and read a chapter in Hebrew and some Greek in Lucian. I said my prayers, and had boiled milk for breakfast. The weather was cold and clear, the wind west. I put several things in order and about 10 o'clock went to Mrs. Bassett's and from thence to church where Mr. Scott[4] gave us an indifferent sermon. After church the Governor asked me to dine with him but I was engaged to Mrs. Bassett, where I ate some roast chicken. After dinner we sat and talked and Mrs. Russell and Mrs. H-r-n-t-n came and several gentlemen. In the evening we went to walk in Major Custis' garden and the Major was very gallant. About 8 o'clock I went home and read some English and washed my feet and said my prayers.

24. I rose about 6 o'clock and read a chapter in Hebrew and some Greek in Lucian. I said my prayers, and had boiled milk for breakfast. The weather was cold and clear, the wind west. I read some English and then wrote a letter to England till ten. Then I went to Mrs. Bassett's and just inquired after their health and then walked to Dr. Blair's and from thence to Colonel Ludwell's where Ben Harrison gave me a letter from home where all were well, thank God. Then I walked to Mrs. Sullivan's and ate some broth and then went to the capitol where we sat till four and then went to dinner and Colonel Carter and Colonel Lewis dined with us and Jack Wormeley

4. Alexander Scott, minister of Overwharton Parish, Stafford County, from 1711 to 1738.

dined with us also. Then Colonel Carter and I took a walk and in the evening I called on James Roscow and then walked to Mrs. Bassett's and sat about an hour and then went home and said my prayers and slept pretty well, thank God.

25. I rose about 6 o'clock and read a chapter in Hebrew and some Greek in Lucian. I said my prayers, and had boiled milk for breakfast. The weather was warm and cloudy, the wind . . . to England and settled some accounts till 10 o'clock and then came Colonel Ludwell and I walked with him to Colonel Bassett's and walked from . . . capitol but before I sat in court I drank a dish of chocolate. Then we passed judgment upon Parson Robinson and sat a little in Council and about four rose and went to dinner and I ate some boiled mutton. After dinner we walked to see Mrs. Grymes just come to town and from thence we went to the play, which they acted tolerably well. When this was done I went home and said my prayers.

26. I rose about 6 o'clock and read a chapter in Hebrew and some Greek in Lucian. I said my prayers, and had boiled milk for breakfast. The weather was warm and cloudy, the wind southwest. I wrote a letter to England about the Receiver General's place. Then I walked to Colonel Ludwell's and from thence to Colonel Bassett's and from thence to the capitol and by the way drank some chocolate and then sat in court till 5 o'clock. The Governor invited me to dinner and I ate some pigeon and bacon. After dinner we drank a bottle of claret and then went to the play but I stayed not above two acts. Then I walked home and read a letter I had received from Mr. Perry about my debt. I neglected my prayers, for which God forgive me, and slept but indifferently.

27. I rose about 6 o'clock and read a chapter in Hebrew and some Greek in Lucian. I said my prayers, and had boiled milk for breakfast. The weather was cold and cloudy, the wind northwest. I wrote a letter to England, and then walked to Colonel Bassett's where I drank two dishes of chocolate and then walked with the Colonel to the capitol where we sat till five and then adjourned to the Council chamber where the Governor could make no impression upon us,

notwithstanding he endeavored it very much. About six we went to dinner and I ate some roast beef. After dinner we took a walk and then I went to Jimmy Roscow's who was from home and then to Colonel Bassett's where I sat till 10 o'clock and then walked home and neglected my prayers, for which God forgive me.

28. I rose about 6 o'clock and read a chapter in Hebrew and some Greek in Lucian. I said my prayers, and had boiled milk for breakfast. The weather was cold and clear, the wind northwest. I wrote a letter home and sent it by Dick W-l-t-n. About 9 o'clock came Isham Randolph and then came Sir William Keith and then Billy Beverley and stayed till about 10 o'clock. Then I went to take leave of my cousin Bassett who went out of town, and there drank a dish of chocolate. Then Colonel Bassett and I went to the Governor's to take leave of Sir William Keith and went with him a little way out of town as did abundance of gentlemen at the Governor's request. Then we went to court and sat till five and then went to dinner and I ate some boiled beef. After dinner Colonel Carter and I took a walk and then I went home and wrote a letter. I neglected to say my prayers, for which God forgive me. Mr. Brook called on me in his way to the Falls.

29. I rose about 6 o'clock and read a chapter in Hebrew and some Greek in Lucian. I said my prayers, and had boiled milk for breakfast. The weather was clear and cold, the wind northwest. Colonel Harrison came and we agreed about the Receiver General's place and the bond that he should give. About 10 o'clock I went to Colonel Bassett's, where I ate another breakfast and then took leave of Mrs. Bassett, who went out of town. Then we walked to court and sat till two and then I went to my lodgings and prepared to go to Green Springs and about three went with Mr. Grymes to the College where I ate some goose giblets. Then I called to see Mrs. Stith and then we proceeded to Green Springs in Colonel Ludwell's coach and got there about seven. We talked and were merry till eight and then took a walk. Then I ate some potato and milk and about ten went to bed. I neglected my prayers, for which God forgive me.

30. I rose about 7 o'clock and read some English. I said my prayers and had milk and potato for breakfast. The weather was warm and clear, the wind southwest. Isham Randolph came time enough to breakfast with us. About ten some of the company went to Colonel Harrison's and the rest went to church, but I stayed at home and wrote two . . . After dinner we drank and were merry and Ben Harrison desired me to speak to Colonel Carter about his pretension to his daughter. . . . sat and talked till 9 o'clock and then retired and I neglected my prayers, for which God forgive me.

May 1721

1. I rose about 6 o'clock and read some English. I said my prayers, and had some cold bacon for breakfast. The weather was warm and cloudy, the wind southwest. About 9 o'clock we took leave and went in the coach to Williamsburg and there put myself in order and about 12 o'clock went to the capitol where we sat till four and then adjourned and went to dinner and I ate some boiled beef. After dinner several persons came in and we drank a bottle of claret. In the evening Major Mumford came to me and told me all was well at home but he told me he could not let me have any land. About 9 o'clock I walked [home] and said my prayers. It rained a little in the night.

2. I rose about 6 o'clock and read nothing because I wrote several letters to England. I said my prayers, and had boiled milk for breakfast. The weather was cold and cloudy. About 10 o'clock I went to the capitol where we sat very close till 4 o'clock and then we went

to dinner and I ate some boiled mutton. After dinner we sat and talked till 7 o'clock and then I looked into the play but did not like the company. Then I took a walk to meet some women but met none so I went home and wrote a letter and neglected my prayers, for which God forgive me.

3. I rose about 6 o'clock and read a chapter in Hebrew and some Greek. I said my prayers, and had milk for breakfast. The weather was cold and cloudy and it rained a little. I wrote a letter to England and then went to the Council where we learned that Captain Turner had been plundered by the pirates. About twelve we went into court where I sat about two hours and then went with Captain Posford to Dr. Blair's to dinner and I ate some roast pork. After dinner we went to the bowling green and I won a bit. Then I went with Colonel Carter to Colonel Jones's and we played at cards and I lost a little and about 10 o'clock walked home and neglected my prayers. It rained and thundered in the night.

4. I rose about 6 o'clock and read a chapter in Hebrew and some Greek. I said my prayers, and had boiled milk for breakfast. The weather was cold and cloudy and it rained a little. Mr. Fontaine came and stayed about an hour. Then I went to the Governor to beg that he would spare me some bulbs for my garden and he was pleased to give me some orange trees. Then I went to Colonel Carter and interceded with him for Ben Harrison and at last obtained leave for him to wait on the Colonel at Rappahannock. Then I went to the capitol where we sat till four and then went to dinner and I ate some chicken and bacon. Then we walked to the bowling green and from thence to Colonel Bassett's where we were kindly entertained till ten and then I walked home and said my prayers.

5. I rose about 6 o'clock and read a chapter in Hebrew and some Greek. I said my prayers and had boiled milk for breakfast. The weather was cold and cloudy, the wind northeast. I packed up my things and wrote a letter to Mr. Nelson to spare me some land. Then came John F-l from Westover and told me all was well, thank God. Then I went to the Governor's and drank with Mrs. Russell, the

Governor being rode to York. My business was to get the bulbs and orange trees that the Governor promised me; accordingly I got them and sent them to the landing. Then I went to the capitol where we sat in court till 2 o'clock and then I went with Colonel Harrison to Dr. Blair's to see Mrs. Richardson before she went away and there I dined and ate some pigeon pie. After dinner we walked to the bowling green where I lost five shillings. Then we returned to court and finished the business. Then I walked to the College to see the Commissary where I sat about an hour and then walked home and said my prayers.

6. I rose about 6 o'clock and read a chapter in Hebrew and some Greek. I said my prayers, and had boiled milk for breakfast. The weather was cold and cloudy, the wind northwest. About 8 o'clock I went to settle accounts with Dr. Blair and several others and then ate another breakfast with Colonel Ludwell. Then I paid Harry Cary for the tobacco he [sold] me. Then I went to wait on the Governor to know what I was to give him for his bulbs but he said they cost him nothing and therefore that I should . . . I thanked him and then walked to the capitol where we sat in Council till 5 o'clock and then took leave and we took horse and then rode . . . bacon and sallet and bacon, and sat and talked till ten and then retired and I said my prayers.

[7]. [I rose about 6 o'clock] and read nothing. However, I said my prayers and had boiled milk for breakfast. The weather was clear and cold, the wind northwest. About . . . some boiled beef for breakfast and about ten the family went to church and Ben Harrison and I took leave and rode home where we got about three . . . where I found Banister, who told me all was well. Here I ate some bacon and eggs and sallet and stayed till 5 o'clock and walked home and saw everything in good order, thank God. I talked with my people and about 9 o'clock retired and Annie came to bed to me and I committed uncleanness with her, for which God forgive me.

8. I rose about 6 o'clock and read a chapter in Hebrew and some Greek in Plutarch. I said my prayers, and had boiled milk for break-

fast. The weather was cold and clear, the wind southwest. I danced my dance and then settled some accounts and talked with Will Bass and Mr. P-n-s and wrote a letter to Mr. Brook till dinner when I ate some roast haslet. After dinner I put several things in order and unpacked several goods till the evening and then I took a walk about the plantation. At night I talked with my people and said my prayers and about 9 o'clock retired and slept pretty well, thank God.

9. I rose about 6 o'clock and read a chapter in Hebrew and some Greek in Plutarch. I said my prayers, and had potato milk for breakfast. The weather was clear and warm, the wind west. Captain L-s came about 7 o'clock and ate some milk with me and then came Captain L-s [sic] and Captain Bolling and stayed about an hour. I walked to see my people work till 12 o'clock and then came Parson Fontaine and soon after came Mrs. Harrison to dine with me and I ate some boiled beef. After dinner we sat and talked and were merry till 6 o'clock and then came Ben Harrison and stayed a little while and then we all walked home with Mrs. Harrison and drank some cider and then the parson and I returned and about 10 o'clock retired and I kissed Annie. It rained a little.

10. I rose about 6 o'clock and read a chapter in Hebrew and some Greek in Plutarch. I said my prayers, and had chocolate for breakfast. The weather was cold and clear, the wind northeast. I danced my dance and played at bowls with Mr. Fontaine till 8 o'clock and then he went away and I settled several accounts till dinner and then I ate some broiled pork. After dinner I put several things in order and then read some English till the evening and then took a walk about the plantation and then took a turn in the garden. At night I talked with my people, washed my feet, and committed uncleanness with Annie, for which God forgive me.

11. I rose about 6 o'clock and read nothing because Mr. Harrison came to take me into Surry to the horse race and Mr. Tullitt's [1] brother came with him. I said my prayers and had some milk and hoecakes for breakfast. About half after seven we went over the

1. John Tullitt, a builder in Williamsburg.

river and we overtook Captain Isham Randolph, Captain Tom Bolling and Mr. Adams and rode with them to Captain Harrison's,
where we drank some chocolate and then rode about two miles to
the race, where was abundance of people and Mr. Simons' white
horse beat the Captain's Spaniard and I won ten shillings. Here we
settled the freight at seven pounds a ton. It rained, so that about
4 o'clock Isham Randolph and I rode back to the Captain's where
we had a good supper and I ate some chicken pie. Then we drank
some rack punch till 11 o'clock and then I retired and Isham Randolph and I lay together. I neglected my prayers, for which God
forgive me.

12. I rose about 7 o'clock and read nothing because I got ready
to go to the company. I said my prayers and had chocolate for
breakfast. Then we sat and talked till 9 o'clock and then Captain
Posford and I took leave and I rode home where I got about eleven
and found some of my people sick, likewise a [d-r-b-y] who told
me all were well in New Kent, thank God. I walked about till dinner
and then I ate some broiled pork and after dinner I took a small nap
and then read a chapter in Hebrew and some Greek and put several
things in order till the evening, and then walked about the plantation.
About 3 o'clock it rained very hard for about half an hour. At night
I talked with my people and about 9 o'clock said my prayers and
retired.

[13]. . . .

[14]. . . . in Hebrew and some Greek in Plutarch. I said my
prayers, and had milk and hoecakes for breakfast. The weather was
cold and cloudy, the wind west. I danced my dance and cleaned my
teeth and put several things in order till 11 o'clock and then I went
to prayers where there was nobody [. . .] except my family. After
church I walked to Mrs. Harrison's to dinner and ate some . . . After
dinner we sat and talked till the evening and Tom Bolling, Colonel
Cole, and Mr. [Lightfoot] were there. In the evening I took leave
and walked home and talked with my people and at night committed uncleanness with Annie, for which God forgive me.

15. I rose about 5 o'clock and read a chapter in Hebrew and some Greek in Plutarch. I said my prayers, and had hoecakes and milk for breakfast. The weather was clear and warm, the wind southwest. I danced my dance. I settled several accounts and read a little Latin till 12 o'clock when Frank Lightfoot and Ben Harrison came, notwithstanding it was very hot. Frank and I played at piquet till dinner and then I ate some roast pork. Then we played at billiards for about two hours and then at bowls and I won seven bits. At night I walked home and I talked with my people and ordered some cider to some seamen that came to meet Captain Randolph but he did not come. I said my prayers and retired and slept very ill because of the heat.

16. I rose about 5 o'clock and read a chapter in Hebrew and some Greek in Plutarch. I said my prayers, and had hoecakes and milk for breakfast. The weather was warm and cloudy, the wind southeast, and it rained about 10 o'clock. I settled some accounts and then read some English till dinner when I ate some broiled pork. After dinner I put several things in order and then took a nap. Afterwards I read some Latin till the evening and then walked about the garden. At night I talked with my people. Several guns were fired at Swinyards about 5 o'clock. I said my prayers and retired and slept very well, thank God.

17. I rose about 5 o'clock and read a chapter in Hebrew and some Greek in Plutarch. I said my prayers and had boiled milk for breakfast. The weather was cool and cloudy, the wind east. I danced my dance and then walked in the kitchen garden and ate cherries. Then I wrote some English and walked to see my people work. Just before dinner it rained again abundantly. I ate some green peas. After dinner I took a nap and then read some news and put several things in order. Then I read some Latin till the evening but could not walk because of the rain. I talked with my people and about nine retired and slept very well, thank God.

18. I rose about 5 o'clock and read a chapter in Hebrew and some Greek in Plutarch. I said my prayers, and had boiled milk for breakfast. The weather continued cloudy, the wind southwest. I danced my dance. Then I walked to see my people work and afterwards wrote some English till dinner, when I ate some dried beef. After dinner I took a nap and then put several things in order and read some news. Then walked to see my people work. Then read some Latin till the evening. Then took a walk about the plantation. At night came Banister. I talked with all my people and then said my prayers and retired and slept indifferently.

19. I rose about 5 o'clock and read a chapter in Hebrew and some Greek in Plutarch. I said my prayers and had boiled milk for breakfast. The weather was warm and clear. I danced my dance and then walked to see my people work. Then I wrote some English and settled several accounts. About 11 o'clock came . . . that Mr. Cole intended to tell the Governor that I intended to keep a letter of his that came enclosed from Mr. Perry. He . . . broiled pork and had a little nap after dinner. Then I put several things in order and read some Latin . . . At night I talked with my people and said my prayers . . .

HISTORY OF THE DIVIDING LINE

BEFORE I enter upon the journal of the line between Virginia and North Carolina, it will be necessary to clear the way to it, by showing how the other British colonies on the Main have, one after another, been carved out of Virginia, by grants from His Majesty's royal predecessors. All that part of the northern American continent now under the dominion of the King of Great Britain, and stretching quite as far as the cape of Florida, went at first under the general name of Virginia.

. . .

[An account of the settlement of the colonies is omitted.]

. . .

Both the French and the Spaniards had, in the name of their respective monarchs, long ago taken possession of that part of the northern continent that now goes by the name of Carolina; but finding it produced neither gold nor silver, as they greedily expected, and meeting such returns from the Indians as their own cruelty and treachery deserved, they totally abandoned it. In this deserted condition that country lay for the space of ninety years, till King Charles the second, finding it a derelict, granted it away to the Earl of Clarendon and others by his royal charter dated March the 24th, 1663. The boundary of that grant towards Virginia was a due west line from Luck Island (the same as Colleton Island), lying in 36 degrees of north latitude, quite to the South Sea.

But afterwards Sir William Berkeley, who was one of the grantees and at that time governor of Virginia, finding a territory of thirty-one miles in breadth between the inhabited part of Virginia and the above-mentioned boundary of Carolina, advised the Lord Clarendon of it. And his lordship had interest enough with the King to obtain a second patent to include it, dated June the 30th, 1665.

This last grant describes the bounds between Virginia and Carolina in these words: 'To run from the north end of Currituck Inlet, due west to Weyanoke Creek, lying within or about the degree of thirty-six and thirty minutes of northern latitude, and from thence west, in a direct line, as far as the South Sea.' Without question, this boundary was well known at the time the charter was granted, but in a long course of years Weyanoke Creek lost its name, so that it became a controversy where it lay. Some ancient persons in Virginia affirmed it was the same with Wicocon, and others again in Carolina were as positive it was Nottoway River.

In the meantime, the people on the frontiers entered for land and took out patents by guess, either from the King or the lords proprietors. But the Crown was like to be the loser by this incertainty, because the terms both of taking up and seating land were easier much in Carolina. The yearly taxes to the public were likewise there less burdensome, which laid Virginia under a plain disadvantage.

This consideration put that government upon entering into measures with North Carolina to terminate the dispute and settle a certain boundary between the two colonies. All the difficulty was, to find out which was truly Weyanoke Creek. The difference was too considerable to be given up by either side, there being a territory of fifteen miles betwixt the two streams in controversy.

However, till that matter could be adjusted it was agreed on both sides that no lands at all should be granted within the disputed bounds. Virginia observed this agreement punctually, but I am sorry I can't say the same of North Carolina. The great officers of that province were loath to lose the fees accruing from the grants of land,

and so private interest got the better of public spirit; and I wish that were the only place in the world where such politics are fashionable.

All the steps that were taken afterwards in that affair will best appear by the report of the Virginia commissioners, recited in the order of council given at St. James's, March the 1st, 1710 . . .

It must be owned, the report of those gentlemen was severe upon the then commissioners of North Carolina, and particularly upon Mr. Moseley. I won't take upon me to say with how much justice they said so many hard things, though it had been fairer play to have given the parties accused a copy of such representations, that they might have answered what they could for themselves.

But since that was not done, I must beg leave to say thus much in behalf of Mr. Moseley, that he was not much in the wrong to find fault with the quadrant produced by the surveyors of Virginia, because that instrument placed the mouth of Nottoway River in the latitude of 37 degrees; whereas, by an accurate observation made since, it appears to lie in 36° 30½′, so that there was an error of near 30 minutes, either in the instrument or in those who made use of it.

Besides, it is evident the mouth of Nottoway River agrees much better with the latitude, wherein the Carolina charter supposed Weyanoke Creek (namely, in or about 36° 30′), than it does with Wicocon Creek, which is about fifteen miles more southerly.

This being manifest, the intention of the King's grant will be pretty exactly answered, by a due west line drawn from Currituck Inlet to the mouth of Nottoway River, for which reason 'tis probable that was formerly called Weyanoke Creek, and might change its name when the Nottoway Indians came to live upon it, which was since the date of the last Carolina charter.

The lieutenant governor of Virginia, at that time Colonel Spotswood, searching into the bottom of this affair, made very equitable proposals to Mr. Eden, at that time governor of North Carolina, in order to put an end to this controversy. These, being formed into preliminaries, were signed by both governors and transmitted to England, where they had the honor to be ratified by His late Majesty and assented to by the lords proprietors of Carolina.

Accordingly an order was sent by the late King to Mr. Gooch, afterwards lieutenant governor of Virginia, to pursue those preliminaries exactly. In obedience thereunto he was pleased to appoint three of the council of that colony to be commissioners on the part of Virginia, who, in conjunction with others to be named by the governor of North Carolina, were to settle the boundary between the two governments upon the plan of the above-mentioned articles.

Two experienced surveyors were at the same time directed to wait upon the commissioners, Mr. Mayo, who made the accurate map of Barbadoes, and Mr. Irvine, the mathematic professor of William and Mary College. And because a good number of men were to go upon this expedition, a chaplain was appointed to attend them, and the rather because the people of the frontiers of North Carolina, who have no minister near them, might have an opportunity to get themselves and their children baptized.

Of these proceedings on our part, immediate notice was sent to Sir Richard Everard, governor of North Carolina, who was desired to name commissioners for that province, to meet those of Virginia at Currituck Inlet the spring following. Accordingly he appointed four members of the council of that province to take care of the interests of the lords proprietors. Of these, Mr. Moseley was to serve in a double capacity, both as commissioner and surveyor. For that reason there was but one other surveyor from thence, Mr. Swan. All the persons being thus agreed upon, they settled the time of meeting to be at Currituck, March the 5th, 1728.

In the meantime, the requisite preparations were made for so long and tiresome a journey; and because there was much work to be done and some danger from the Indians, in the uninhabited part of the country, it was necessary to provide a competent number of men. Accordingly, seventeen able hands were listed on the part of Virginia, who were most of them Indian traders and expert woodsmen.

[Feb.] 27.　These good men were ordered to come armed with a musket and a tomahawk or large hatchet, and provided with a sufficient quantity of ammunition.

They likewise brought provisions of their own for ten days, after which time they were to be furnished by the government. Their march was appointed to be on the 27th of February, on which day one of the commissioners met them at their rendezvous, and proceeded with them as far as Colonel Allen's. This gentleman is a great economist and skilled in all the arts of living well at an easy expense.

28.   They proceeded in good order through Surry County, as far as the widow Allen's, who had copied Solomon's complete housewife exactly. At this gentlewoman's house, the other two commissioners had appointed to join them, but were detained by some accident at Williamsburg longer than their appointment.

29.   They pursued their march through the Isle of Wight, and observed a most dreadful havoc made by a late hurricane, which happened in August, 1726. The violence of it had not reached above a quarter of a mile in breadth but within that compass had leveled all before it. Both trees and houses were laid flat on the ground and several things hurled to an incredible distance. 'Tis happy such violent gusts are confined to so narrow a channel, because they carry desolation wherever they go. In the evening they reached Mr. Godwin's, on the south branch of Nansemond River, where they were treated with abundance of primitive hospitality.

March 1.   This gentleman was so kind as to shorten their journey by setting them over the river. They coasted the northeast side of the Dismal for several miles together, and found all the grounds bordering upon it very full of sloughs. The trees that grew near it looked very reverend, with the long moss that hung dangling from their branches. Both cattle and horses eat this moss greedily in winter when other provender is scarce, though it is apt to scour them at first. In that moist soil, too, grew abundance of that kind of myrtle which bears the candle-berries. There was likewise here and there a gall bush, which is a beautiful evergreen and may be cut into any shape. It derives its name from its berries turning water black, like the galls of an oak.

When this shrub is transplanted into gardens, it will not thrive without frequent watering.

The two other commissioners came up with them just at their journey's end, and that evening they arrived all together at Mr. Crawford's, who lives on the south branch of Elizabeth River, over against Norfolk. Here the commissioners left the men with all the horses and heavy baggage, and crossed the river with their servants only, for fear of making a famine in the town.

Norfolk has most the air of a town of any in Virginia. There were then near 20 brigantines and sloops riding at the wharves, and often-times they have more. It has all the advantages of situation requisite for trade and navigation. There is a secure harbor for a good number of ships of any burthen. Their river divides itself into three several branches, which are all navigable. The town is so near the sea that its vessels may sail in and out in a few hours. Their trade is chiefly to the West Indies, whither they export abundance of beef, pork, flour and lumber. The worst of it is, they contribute much towards debauch-ing the country by importing abundance of rum, which, like gin in Great Britain, breaks the constitution, vitiates the morals, and ruins the industry of most of the poor people of this country. This place is the mart for most of the commodities produced in the adjacent parts of North Carolina. They have a pretty deal of lumber from the bor-derers on the Dismal, who make bold with the King's land there-abouts without the least ceremony. They not only maintain their stocks upon it, but get boards, shingles and other lumber out of it in great abundance.

The town is built on a level spot of ground upon Elizabeth River, the banks whereof are neither so high as to make the landing of goods troublesome, or so low as to be in danger of overflowing. The streets are straight and adorned with several good houses, which increase every day. It is not a town of ordinaries and public houses, like most others in this country, but the inhabitants consist of merchants, ship-carpenters and other useful artisans, with sailors enough to manage their navigation. With all these conveniences, it lies under the two great disadvantages that most of the towns in Holland do by having neither good air nor good water. The two cardinal virtues that make a place thrive, industry and frugality, are seen here in perfection; and so long as they can banish luxury and idleness, the town will remain in a happy and flourishing condition.

The method of building wharves here is after the following man-ner. They lay down long pine logs that reach from the shore to the edge of the channel. These are bound fast together by cross pieces notched into them, according to the architecture of the log houses in North Carolina. A wharf built thus will stand several years, in spite of the worm, which bites here very much, but may be soon repaired in a place where so many pines grow in the neighborhood.

The commissioners endeavored, in this town, to list three more men to serve as guides in that dirty part of the country, but found that these people knew just enough of that frightful place to avoid it.

They had been told that those netherlands were full of bogs, of marshes and swamps, not fit for human creatures to engage in, and this was reason enough for them not to hazard their persons. So they told us, flat and plain, that we might e'en daggle through the mire by ourselves for them.

The worst of it was, we could not learn from anybody in this town what route to take to Currituck Inlet; till at last we had the fortune to meet with a borderer upon North Carolina, who made a rough sketch of that part of the country. Thus, upon seeing how the land lay, we determined to march directly to Prescot Landing upon Northwest River and proceed thence by water to the place where our line was to begin.

4. In pursuance of this resolution we crossed the river this morning to Powder Point, where we all took horse; and the grandees of the town with great courtesy conducted us ten miles on our way, as far as the long bridge built over the south branch of the river. The parson of the parish, Mr. Marsden, a painful apostle from the Society, made one in this ceremonious cavalcade.

At the bridge these gentlemen, wishing us a good deliverance, returned, and then a troop of light horse escorted us as far as Prescot Landing upon Northwest River. Care had been taken beforehand to provide two periaugas to lie ready at that place to transport us to Currituck Inlet. Our zeal was so great to get thither at the time appointed, that we hardly allowed ourselves leisure to eat, which in truth we had the less stomach to, by reason the dinner was served up by the landlord, whose nose stood on such ticklish terms that it was in danger of falling into the dish. We therefore made our repast very short, and then embarked with only the surveyors and nine chosen men, leaving the rest at Mr. W———n's to take care of the horses and baggage. There we also left our chaplain, with the charitable intent that the gentiles round about might have time and opportunity, if they pleased, of getting themselves and their children baptized.

We rowed down Northwest River about eighteen miles, as far as the mouth of it, where it empties itself into Albemarle Sound. It was really a delightful sight, all the way, to see the banks of the river adorned with myrtle, laurel and bay trees, which preserve their verdure the year round, though it must be owned that these beautiful plants, sacred to Venus and Apollo, grow commonly in very dirty soil. The river is in most places fifty or sixty yards wide, without spreading much wider at the mouth. 'Tis remarkable it was never known to ebb and flow till the year 1713, when a violent storm opened a new inlet about five miles south of the old one; since which convulsion, the old inlet is almost choked up by the shifting of the sand and grows both narrower and shoaler every day.

It was dark before we could reach the mouth of the river, where our wayward stars directed us to a miserable cottage. The landlord was lately removed bag and baggage from Maryland, through a strong antipathy he had to work and paying his debts. For want of our tent we were obliged to shelter ourselves in this wretched hovel, where we were almost devoured by vermin of various kinds. However, we were above complaining, being all philosophers enough to improve such slender distresses into mirth and good humor.

5.   The day being now come, on which we had agreed to meet the commissioners of North Carolina, we embarked very early, which we could the easier do, having no temptation to stay where we were. We shaped our course along the south end of Knot's Island, there being no passage open on the north.

Farther still to the southward of us we discovered two smaller islands that go by the names of Bell's and Church's isles. We also saw a small New England sloop riding in the sound, a little to the south of our course. She had come in at the new inlet, as all other vessels have done since the opening of it. This navigation is a little difficult and fit only for vessels that draw no more than ten feet water.

The trade hither is engrossed by the saints of New England, who carry off a great deal of tobacco without troubling themselves with paying that impertinent duty of a penny a pound.

It was just noon before we arrived at Currituck Inlet, which is now so shallow that the breakers fly over it with a horrible sound and at the same time afford a very wild prospect. On the north side of the inlet the high land terminated in a bluff point from which a spit of land extended itself towards the southeast full half a mile. The inlet lies between that spit and another on the south of it, leaving an opening of not quite a mile, which at this day is not practicable for any vessel whatsoever. And as shallow as it now is, it continues to fill up more and more, both the wind and waves rolling in the sands from the eastern shoals.

About two o'clock in the afternoon we were joined by two of the Carolina commissioners, attended by Mr. S[wa]n, their surveyor. The other two were not quite so punctual, which was the more unlucky for us because there could be no sport till they came. These gentlemen, it seems, had the Carolina commission in their keeping, notwithstanding which they could not forbear paying too much regard to a proverb—fashionable in their country—not to make more haste than good speed.

However, that we who were punctual might not spend our precious time unprofitably, we took the several bearings of the coast. We also surveyed part of the adjacent high land, which had scarcely any trees growing upon it but cedars. Among the shrubs we were showed here and there a bush of Carolina tea called Japon, which is one species of the Phylarea. This is an evergreen, the leaves whereof have some resemblance to tea, but differ very widely both in taste and flavor. We also found some few plants of the spired-leaf silkgrass, which is likewise an evergreen, bearing on a lofty stem a large cluster of flowers of a pale yellow. Of the leaves of this plant the people thereabouts twist very strong cordage.

A virtuoso might divert himself here very well in picking up shells of various hue and figure, and amongst the rest that species of conch shell which the Indian peak is made of. The extremities of these shells are blue and the rest white, so that peak of both these colors are drilled out of one and the same shell, serving the natives both for ornament and money, and are esteemed by them far beyond gold and silver.

The cedars were of singular use to us in the absence of our tent, which we had left with the rest of the baggage for fear of overloading the periaugas. We made a circular hedge of the branches of this tree, wrought so close together as to fence us against the cold winds. We then kindled a rousing fire in the center of it, and lay round it like so many knights templars. But as comfortable as this lodging was, the surveyors turned out about two in the morning to try the varia-

tion by a meridian taken from the north star, and found it to be somewhat less than three degrees west.

The commissioners of the neighboring colony came better provided for the belly than the business. They brought not above two
men along with them that would put their hands to anything but the
kettle and the frying-pan. These spent so much of their industry that
way that they had as little spirit as inclination for work.

6.   At noon, having a perfect observation, we found the latitude of
Currituck Inlet to be 36° 31'.

Whilst we were busied about these necessary matters, our skipper
rowed to an oyster bank just by and loaded his periauga with oysters
as savory and well-tasted as those from Colchester or Walfleet, and
had the advantage of them, too, by being much larger and fatter.

About three in the afternoon the two lag commissioners arrived
and after a few decent excuses for making us wait told us they were
ready to enter upon business as soon as we pleased. The first step was
to produce our respective powers, and the commission from each governor was distinctly read, and copies of them interchangeably delivered.

It was observed by our Carolina friends that the latter part of the
Virginia commission had something in it a little too lordly and positive. In answer to which we told them 'twas necessary to make it
thus peremptory, lest the present commissioners might go upon as
fruitless an errand as their predecessors. The former commissioners
were tied down to act in exact conjunction with those of Carolina
and so could not advance one step farther or one jot faster than they
were pleased to permit them. The memory of that disappointment,
therefore, induced the government of Virginia to give fuller powers
to the present commissioners by authorizing them to go on with the
work by themselves in case those of Carolina should prove unreasonable and refuse to join with them in carrying the business to execution. And all this was done lest His Majesty's gracious intention
should be frustrated a second time.

After both commissions were considered, the first question was,
where the dividing line was to begin. This begat a warm debate; the
Virginia commissioners contending, with a great deal of reason, to begin at the end of the spit of sand which was undoubtedly the north

shore of Currituck Inlet. But those of Carolina insisted strenuously that the point of high land ought rather to be the place of beginning, because that was fixed and certain, whereas the spit of sand was ever shifting and did actually run out farther now than formerly. The contest lasted some hours with great vehemence, neither party receding from their opinion that night. But next morning, Mr. M[oseley], to convince us he was not that obstinate person he had been represented, yielded to our reasons and found means to bring over his colleagues.

Here we began already to reap the benefit of those peremptory words in our commission, which in truth added some weight to our reasons. Nevertheless, because positive proof was made by the oaths of two credible witnesses, that the spit of sand had advanced 200 yards towards the inlet since the controversy first began, we were willing for peace's sake to make them that allowance. Accordingly we fixed our beginning about that distance north of the inlet and there ordered a cedar post to be driven deep into the sand for our beginning. While we continued here we were told that on the south shore not far from the inlet dwelt a marooner that modestly called himself a hermit, though he forfeited that name by suffering a wanton female to cohabit with him.

His habitation was a bower covered with bark after the Indian fashion, which in that mild situation protected him pretty well from the weather. Like the ravens, he neither plowed nor sowed but subsisted chiefly upon oysters which his handmaid made a shift to gather from the adjacent rocks. Sometimes, too, for change of diet, he sent her to drive up the neighbor's cows, to moisten their mouths with a little milk. But as for raiment, he depended mostly upon his length of beard, and she upon her length of hair, part of which she brought decently forward, and the rest dangled behind quite down to her rump, like one of Herodotus' East Indian pigmies. Thus did these wretches live in a dirty state of nature, and were mere Adamites, innocence only excepted.

7. This morning the surveyors began to run the dividing line from the cedar post we had driven into the sand, allowing near three degrees for the variation. Without making this just allowance, we should not have obeyed His Majesty's order in running a due west

WILLIAM BYRD OF VIRGINIA

line. It seems the former commissioners had not been so exact, which gave our friends of Carolina but too just an exception to their proceedings. The line cut Dosier's Island, consisting only of a flat sand, with here and there an humble shrub growing upon it. From thence it crossed over a narrow arm of the Sound into Knot's Island, and there split a plantation belonging to William Harding.

The day being far spent, we encamped in this man's pasture, though it lay very low and the season now inclined people to aguish distempers. He suffered us to cut cedar branches for our enclosure and other wood for firing, to correct the moist air and drive away the damps. Our landlady in the days of her youth, it seems, had been a laundress in the Temple, and talked over her adventures in that station with as much pleasure as an old soldier talks over his battles and distempers, and I believe with as many additions to the truth. The soil is good in many places of this island, and the extent of it pretty large. It lies in the form of a wedge: the south end of it is several miles over, but towards the norrh it sharpens into a point. It is a plentiful place for stock, by reason of the wide marshes adjacent to it and because of its warm situation. But the inhabitants pay a little dear for this convenience by losing as much blood in the summer season by the infinite number of mosquitoes as all their beef and pork can recruit in the winter.

The sheep are as large as in Lincolnshire because they are never pinched by cold or hunger. The whole island was hitherto reckoned to lie in Virginia, but now our line has given the greater part of it to Carolina. The principal freeholder here is Mr. White, who keeps open house for all travelers that either debt or shipwreck happens to cast in his way.

8. By break of day we sent away our largest periauga with the baggage, round the south end of Knot's Island, with orders to the men to wait for us in the mouth of North River. Soon after we embarked ourselves on board the smaller vessel, with intent, if possible, to find a passage round the north end of the island.

We found this navigation very difficult, by reason of the continued shoals, and often stuck fast aground; for though the sound spreads many miles, yet it is in most places extremely shallow and requires a skillful pilot to steer even a canoe safe over it. It was almost as hard to keep our temper as to keep the channel in this provoking situation. But the most impatient amongst us stroked down their choler and swallowed their curses, lest, if they suffered them to break out, they might sound like complaining, which was expressly forbid as the first step to sedition.

At a distance we descried several islands to the northward of us, the largest of which goes by the name of Cedar Island. Our periauga stuck so often that we had a fair chance to be benighted in this wide water, which must certainly have been our fate had we not luckily spied a canoe that was giving a fortune-teller a cast from Princess Anne County over to North Carolina. But, as conjurers are sometimes mistaken, the man mistrusted we were officers of justice in pursuit of a young wench he had carried off along with him. We gave the canoe chase for more than an hour, and when we came up with her threatened to make them all prisoners unless they would direct us into the right channel. By the pilotage of these people we rowed up an arm of the Sound called the Back Bay till we came to the head of it. There we were stopped by a miry pocoson full half a mile in breadth, through which we were obliged to daggle on foot, plunging now and then, though we picked our way, up to the knees in mud. At the end of this charming walk we gained the terra firma of Princess Anne County. In that dirty condition we were afterwards obliged to foot it two miles, as far as John Heath's plantation, where we expected to meet the surveyors and the men who waited upon them.

While we were performing this tedious voyage, they had carried the line through the firm land of Knot's Island where it was no more than half a mile wide. After that they traversed a large marsh that was exceedingly miry and extended to an arm of the Back Bay. They crossed that water in a canoe which we had ordered round for that purpose, and then waded over another marsh that reached quite to the highland of Princess Anne. Both these marshes together make a breadth of five miles, in which the men frequently sunk up to the middle, without muttering the least complaint. On the contrary, they turned all these disasters into merriment.

It was discovered by this day's work that Knot's Island was improperly so called, being in truth no more than a peninsula. The northwest side of it is only divided from the main by the great marsh above-mentioned, which is seldom totally overflowed. Instead of that, it might by the labor of a few trenches be drained into firm meadow, capable of grazing as many cattle as Job, in his best estate, was master of. In the miry condition it now lies, it feeds great numbers in the winter, though when the weather grows warm they are driven thence by the mighty armies of mosquitoes, which are the plague of the lower part of Carolina as much as the flies were formerly of Egypt (and some rabbis think those flies were no other than mosquitoes).

All the people in the neighborhood flocked to John Heath's to behold such rarities as they fancied us to be. The men left their beloved chimney corners, the good women their spinning wheels, and some, of more curiosity than ordinary, rose out of their sick beds to come and stare at us. They looked upon us as a troop of knight errants who were running this great risk of our lives, as they imagined, for the public weal; and some of the gravest of them questioned much whether we were not all criminals condemned to this dirty work for offenses against the state. What puzzled them most was what could make our men so very light-hearted under such intolerable drudgery. 'Ye have little reason to be merry, my masters,' said one of them, with a very solemn face, 'I fancy the pocoson you must struggle with tomorrow will make you change your note and try what metal you are made of. Ye are, to be sure, the first of human race that ever had the boldness to attempt it, and I dare say will be the last. If, therefore, you have any worldly goods to dispose of, my advice is that you make your wills this very night, for fear you die intestate tomorrow.' But, alas! these frightful tales were so far from disheartening the men, that they served only to whet their resolution.

9.   The surveyors entered early upon their business this morning, and ran the line through Mr. Eyland's plantation, as far as the banks of North River. They passed over it in the periauga and landed in Gibbs's marsh, which was a mile in breadth and tolerably firm. They trudged through this marsh without much difficulty as far as the high land, which promised more fertility than any they had seen in these lower parts. But this firm land lasted not long before they came upon the dreadful pocoson they had been threatened with. Nor did they

find it one jot better than it had been painted to them. The beavers and otters had rendered it quite impassable for any creature but themselves.

Our poor fellows had much ado to drag their legs after them in this quagmire but, disdaining to be balked, they could hardly be persuaded from pressing forward by the surveyors, who found it absolutely necessary to make a traverse in the deepest place to prevent their sticking fast in the mire and becoming a certain prey to the turkey buzzards.

This horrible day's work ended two miles to the northward of Mr. Merchant's plantation, divided from Northwest River by a narrow swamp, which is causewayed over. We took up our quarters in the open field not far from the house, correcting, by a fire as large as a Roman funeral pile, the aguish exhalations arising from the sunken grounds that surrounded us.

The neck of land included betwixt North River and Northwest River, with the adjacent marsh, belonged formerly to Governor Gibbs but since his decease to Colonel Bladen, in right of his first lady, who was Mr. Gibbs's daughter. It would be a valuable tract of land in any country but North Carolina, where, for want of navigation and commerce, the best estate affords little more than a coarse subsistence.

10. The Sabbath happened very opportunely to give some ease to our jaded people, who rested religiously from every work but that of cooking the kettle. We observed very few cornfields in our walks, and those very small, which seemed the stranger to us because we could see no other tokens of husbandry or improvement. But upon further inquiry, we were given to understand people only made corn for themselves and not for their stocks, which know very well how to get their own living. Both cattle and hogs ramble in the neighboring marshes and swamps, where they maintain themselves the whole winter long and are not fetched home till the spring. Thus these indolent wretches, during one half of the year, lose the advantage of the milk of their cattle, as well as their dung, and many of the poor creatures perish in the mire, into the bargain, by this ill management. Some who pique themselves more upon industry than their neighbors will now and then, in compliment to their cattle, cut down a tree

whose limbs are loaden with the moss aforementioned. The trouble would be too great to climb the tree in order to gather this provender, but the shortest way (which in this country is always counted the best) is to fell it, just like the lazy Indians, who do the same by such trees as bear fruit, and so make one harvest for all. By this bad husbandry milk is so scarce in the winter season that were a big-bellied woman to long for it, she would lose her longing. And in truth I believe this is often the case, and at the same time a very good reason why so many people in this province are marked with a custard complexion.

The only business here is raising of hogs, which is managed with the least trouble and affords the diet they are most fond of. The truth of it is, the inhabitants of North Carolina devour so much swine's flesh that it fills them full of gross humors. For want, too, of a constant supply of salt, they are commonly obliged to eat it fresh, and that begets the highest taint of scurvy. Thus, whenever a severe cold happens to constitutions thus vitiated, 'tis apt to improve into the yaws, called there very justly the country distemper. This has all the symptoms of the pox, with this aggravation, that no preparation of mercury will touch it. First it seizes the throat, next the palate, and lastly shows its spite to the poor nose, of which 'tis apt in a small time treacherously to undermine the foundation. This calamity is so common and familiar here that it ceases to be a scandal, and in the disputes that happen about beauty the noses have in some companies much ado to carry it. Nay, 'tis said that once, after three good pork years, a motion had like to have been made in the house of burgesses, that a man with a nose should be incapable of holding any place of profit in the province; which extraordinary motion could never have been intended without some hopes of a majority.

Thus, considering the foul and pernicious effects of eating swine's flesh in a hot country, it was wisely forbidden and made an abomination to the Jews, who lived much in the same latitude with Carolina.

11. We ordered the surveyors early to their business, who were blessed with pretty dry grounds for three miles together. But they paid dear for it in the next two, consisting of one continued frightful pocoson, which no creatures but those of the amphibious kind ever had ventured into before. This filthy quagmire did in earnest put the men's courage to a trial, and though I can't say it made them lose

their patience, yet they lost their humor for joking. They kept their gravity like so many Spaniards, so that a man might then have taken his opportunity to plunge up to the chin without danger of being laughed at. However, this unusual composure of countenance could not fairly be called complaining. Their day's work ended at the mouth of Northern's Creek, which empties itself into Northwest River; though we chose to quarter a little higher up the river, near Mossy Point. This we did for the convenience of an old house to shelter our persons and baggage from the rain which threatened us hard. We judged the thing right, for there fell an heavy shower in the night that drove the most hardy of us into the house. Though indeed our case was not much mended by retreating thither, because that tenement having not long before been used as a pork store, the moisture of the air dissolved the salt that lay scattered on the floor, and made it as wet within doors as without. However, the swamps and marshes we were lately accustomed to had made such beavers and otters of us that nobody caught the least cold.

We had encamped so early that we found time in the evening to walk near half a mile into the woods. There we came upon a family of mulattoes that called themselves free, though by the shyness of the master of the house, who took care to keep least in sight, their freedom seemed a little doubtful. It is certain many slaves shelter themselves in this obscure part of the world, nor will any of their righteous neighbors discover them. On the contrary, they find their account in settling such fugitives on some out-of-the-way corner of their land to raise stocks for a mean and inconsiderable share, well knowing their condition makes it necessary for them to submit to any terms. Nor were these worthy borderers content to shelter runaway slaves, but debtors and criminals have often met with the like indulgence. But if the government of North Carolina has encouraged this unneighborly policy in order to increase their people, it is no more than what ancient Rome did before them, which was made a city of refuge for all debtors and fugitives, and from that wretched beginning grew up in time to be mistress of a great part of the world. And considering how fortune delights in bringing great things out of small, who knows but Carolina may, one time or other, come to be the seat of some other great empire?

12. Everything had been so soaked with the rain that we were obliged to lie by a good part of the morning and dry them. However, that time was not lost, because it gave the surveyors an opportunity of platting off their work and taking the course of the river. It likewise helped to recruit the spirits of the men, who had been a little harassed with yesterday's march. Notwithstanding all this, we crossed the river before noon and advanced our line three miles. It was not possible to make more of it, by reason good part of the way was either marsh or pocoson. The line cut two or three plantations, leaving part of them in Virginia and part of them in Carolina. This was a case that happened frequently, to the great inconvenience of the owners, who were therefore obliged to take out two patents and pay for a new survey in each government.

In the evening we took up our quarters in Mr. Ballance's pasture, a little above the bridge built over Northwest River. There we discharged the two periaugas, which in truth had been very serviceable in transporting us over the many waters in that dirty and difficult part of our business. Our landlord had a tolerable good house and clean furniture, and yet we could not be tempted to lodge in it. We chose rather to lie in the open field, for fear of growing too tender. A clear sky, spangled with stars, was our canopy, which being the last thing we saw before we fell asleep gave us magnificent dreams. The truth of it is, we took so much pleasure in that natural kind of lodging that I think at the foot of the account, mankind are great losers by the luxury of feather beds and warm apartments.

The curiosity of beholding so new and withal so sweet a method of encamping brought one of the Senators of North Carolina to make us a midnight visit. But he was so very clamorous in his commendations of it, that the sentinel, not seeing his quality either through his habit or behavior, had like to have treated him roughly. After excusing the unseasonableness of his visit and letting us know he was a parliament man, he swore he was so taken with our lodging that he would set fire to his house as soon as he got home and teach his wife and children to lie, like us, in the open field.

13. Early this morning our chaplain repaired to us with the men we had left at Mr. Wilson's. We had sent for them the evening before to relieve those who had the labor-oar from Currituck Inlet. But

to our great surprise they petitioned not to be relieved, hoping to gain immortal reputation by being the first of mankind that ventured through the great Dismal. But the rest being equally ambitious of the same honor, it was but fair to decide their pretensions by lot. After fortune had declared herself, those which she had excluded offered money to the happy persons to go in their stead. But Hercules would have as soon sold the glory of cleansing the Augean stables, which was pretty near the same sort of work. No sooner was the controversy at an end but we sent those unfortunate fellows back to their quarters whom chance had condemned to remain upon firm land and sleep in a whole skin. In the meanwhile the surveyors carried the line three miles, which was no contemptible day's work, considering how cruelly they were entangled with briers and gall bushes. The leaf of this last shrub bespeaks it to be of the alaternus family.

Our work ended within a quarter of a mile of the Dismal abovementioned, where the ground began to be already full of sunken holes and slashes, which had, here and there, some few reeds growing in them. 'Tis hardly credible how little the bordering inhabitants were acquainted with this mighty swamp, notwithstanding they had lived their whole lives within smell of it. Yet as great strangers as they were to it they pretended to be very exact in their account of its dimensions and were positive it could not be above seven or eight miles wide, but knew no more of the matter than star-gazers know of the distance of the fixed stars. At the same time, they were simple enough to amuse our men with idle stories of the lions, panthers and alligators they were like to encounter in that dreadful place. In short, we saw plainly there was no intelligence of this terra incognita to be got but from our own experience. For that reason it was resolved to make the requisite dispositions to enter it next morning. We allotted every one of the surveyors for this painful enterprise, with twelve men to attend them. Fewer than that could not be employed in clearing the way, carrying the chain, marking the trees, and bearing the necessary bedding and provisions. Nor would the commissioners themselves have spared their persons on this occasion, but for fear of adding to the poor men's burthen while they were certain they could add nothing to their resolution.

We quartered with our friend and fellow traveler, William Wilkins, who had been our faithful pilot to Currituck and lived about a mile from the place where the line ended. Everything looked so very clean and the furniture so neat that we were tempted to lodge within doors. But the novelty of being shut up so close quite spoiled our rest, nor did we breathe so free by abundance as when we lay in the open air.

14.   Before nine of the clock this morning the provisions, bedding and other necessaries were made up into packs for the men to carry on their shoulders into the Dismal. They were victualed for eight days at full allowance, nobody doubting but that would be abundantly sufficient to carry them through that inhospitable place; nor indeed was it possible for the poor fellows to stagger under more. As it was, their loads weighed from sixty to seventy pounds, in just proportion to the strength of those who were to bear them.

'Twould have been unconscionable to have saddled them with burthens heavier than that, when they were to lug them through a filthy bog, which was hardly practicable with no burthen at all. Besides this luggage at their backs, they were obliged to measure the distance, mark the trees, and clear the way for the surveyors every step they went. It was really a pleasure to see with how much cheerfulness they undertook, and with how much spirit they went through all this drudgery. For their greater safety, the commissioners took care to furnish them with Peruvian bark, rhubarb and hipocoacanah, in case they might happen in that wet journey to be taken with fevers or fluxes.

Although there was no need of example to inflame persons already so cheerful, yet to enter the people with the better grace, the author and two more of the commissioners accompanied them half a mile into the Dismal. The skirts of it were thinly planted with dwarf reeds and gall bushes, but when we got into the Dismal itself, we found the reeds grew there much taller and closer, and, to mend the matter, were so interlaced with bamboo briers that there was no scuffling through them without the help of pioneers. At the same time we found the ground moist and trembling under our feet like a quagmire, insomuch that it was an easy matter to run a ten-foot pole up to the head in it without exerting any uncommon strength to do it. Two of the men, whose burthens were the least cumbersome, had orders to march before with their tomahawks and clear the way in order to make an opening for the surveyors. By their assistance we made a shift to push the line half a mile in three hours, and then reached a small piece of firm land, about a hundred yards wide, standing up above the rest like an island. Here the people were glad to lay down their loads and take a little refreshment, while the happy man whose lot it was to carry the jug of rum began already, like Æsop's bread-carriers, to find it grow a good deal lighter.

After reposing about an hour, the commissioners recommended vigor and constancy to their fellow-travelers, by whom they were answered with three cheerful huzzas, in token of obedience. This ceremony was no sooner over but they took up their burthens and attended the motion of the surveyors, who, though they worked with all their might, could reach but one mile farther, the same obstacles still attending them which they had met with in the morning. However small this distance may seem to such as are used to travel at their ease, yet our poor men, who were obliged to work with an unwieldy load at their backs, had reason to think it a long way; especially in a bog where they had no firm footing, but every step made a deep impression which was instantly filled with water. At the same time they were laboring with their hands to cut down the reeds, which were ten feet high, their legs were hampered with the briers. Besides, the weather happened to be very warm, and the tallness of the reeds kept off every friendly breeze from coming to refresh them. And indeed it was a little provoking to hear the wind whistling among the branches of the white cedars, which grew here and there amongst the reeds, and at the same time not have the comfort to feel the least breath of it.

In the meantime the three commissioners returned out of the Dismal the same way they went in and having joined their brethren proceeded that night as far as Mr. Wilson's. This worthy person lives within sight of the Dismal, in the skirts whereof his stocks range and maintain themselves all the winter, and yet he knew as little of it as he did of Terra Australis Incognita. He told us a Canterbury tale of a North Briton whose curiosity spurred him a long way into this great desert, as he called it, near twenty years ago, but he having no compass nor seeing the sun for several days together wandered about till he was almost famished; but at last he bethought himself of a secret his countrymen make use of to pilot themselves in a dark day. He took a fat louse out of his collar and exposed it to the open day on a piece of white paper which he brought along with him for his journal. The poor insect, having no eyelids turned himself about till he found the darkest part of the heavens, and so made the best of his way towards the north. By this direction he steered himself safe out, and gave such a frightful account of the monsters he saw and the distresses he underwent that no mortal since has been hardy enough to go upon the like dangerous discovery.

15. The surveyors pursued their work with all diligence, but still found the soil of the Dismal so spongy that the water oozed up into every footstep they took. To their sorrow, too, they found the reeds and briers more firmly interwoven than they did the day before. But the greatest grievance was from large cypresses which the wind had blown down and heaped upon one another. On the limbs of most of them grew sharp snags, pointing every way like so many pikes, that required much pains and caution to avoid. These trees being evergreens, and shooting their large tops very high, are easily overset by every gust of wind, because there is no firm earth to steady their roots. Thus many of them were laid prostrate, to the great encumbrance of the way. Such variety of difficulties made the business go on heavily, insomuch that from morning till night the line could advance no farther than one mile and thirty-one poles. Never was rum, that cordial of life, found more necessary than it was in this dirty place. It did not only recruit the people's spirits, now almost jaded with fatigue, but served to correct the badness of the water, and at the same time to resist the malignity of the air. Whenever the men wanted to drink, which was very often, they had nothing more to do but to make a hole and the water bubbled up in a moment. But it was far from being either clear or well tasted, and had besides a physical effect, from the tincture it received from the roots of the shrubs and trees that grew in the neighborhood.

While the surveyors were thus painfully employed, the commissioners discharged the long score they had with Mr. Wilson for the men and horses which had been quartered upon him during our expedition to Currituck. From thence we marched in good order along the east side of the Dismal, and passed the long bridge that lies over the south branch of Elizabeth River. At the end of eighteen miles we reached Timothy Ivy's plantation, where we pitched our tent for the first time, and were furnished with everything the place afforded. We perceived the happy effects of industry in this family, in which every one looked tidy and clean and carried in their countenances the cheerful marks of plenty. We saw no drones there, which are but too common, alas, in that part of the world. Though in truth the distemper of laziness seizes the men oftener much than the women. These last spin, weave and knit, all with their own hands, while their husbands, depending on the bounty of the climate, are slothful in everything but getting of children, and in that only instance make themselves useful members of an infant colony.

There is but little wool in that province, though cotton grows very kindly, and, so far south, is seldom nipped by the frost. The good women mix this with their wool for their outer garments; though, for want of fulling, that kind of manufacture is open and sleazy. Flax likewise thrives there extremely, being perhaps as fine as any in the world, and I question not might, with a little care and pains, be brought to rival that of Egypt; and yet the men are here so intolerable lazy they seldom take the trouble to propagate it.

16. The line was this day carried one mile and a half and sixteen poles. The soil continued soft and miry, but fuller of trees, especially white cedars. Many of these, too, were thrown down and piled in heaps, high enough for a good Muscovite fortification. The worst of it was, the poor fellows began now to be troubled with fluxes, occasioned by bad water and moist lodging; but chewing of rhubarb kept that malady within bounds.

In the meantime the commissioners decamped early in the morning and made a march of twenty-five miles, as far as Mr. Andrew Mead's, who lives upon Nansemond River. They were no sooner got under the shelter of that hospitable roof but it began to rain hard and continued so to do great part of the night. This gave them much pain for their friends in the Dismal, whose sufferings spoiled their taste for the good cheer wherewith they were entertained themselves. However, late that evening, these poor men had the fortune to come upon another terra firma, which was the luckier for them, because the lower ground, by the rain that fell, was made a fitter lodging for tadpoles than men. In our journey we remarked that the north side of this great swamp lies higher than either the east or the west, nor were the approaches to it so full of sunken grounds. We passed by no less than two Quaker meeting houses, one of which had an awkward ornament on the west end of it, that seemed to ape a steeple. I must own I expected no such piece of foppery from a sect of so much outside simplicity. That persuasion prevails much in the lower end of Nansemond County, for want of ministers to pilot the people a decenter way to heaven. The ill reputation of tobacco planted in those lower parishes makes the clergy unwilling to accept of them, unless it be such whose abilities are as mean as their pay. Thus, whether the churches be quite void or but indifferently filled, the Quakers will have an opportunity of gaining proselytes. 'Tis a wonder no popish missionaries are sent from Maryland to labor in this neglected vineyard, who we know have zeal enough to traverse sea and land on the meritorious errand of making converts. Nor is it less strange that some wolf in sheep's clothing arrives not from New England to lead astray a flock that has no shepherd. People uninstructed in any religion are ready to embrace the first that offers. It is natural for helpless man to adore his Maker in some form or other, and were there any exception to this rule, I should suspect it to be among the Hottentots of the Cape of Good Hope and of North Carolina.

There fell a great deal of rain in the night, accompanied with a strong wind. The fellow-feeling we had for the poor Dismalites on account of this unkind weather rendered the down we laid upon uneasy. We fancied them half-drowned in their wet lodging, with the trees blowing down about their ears. These were the gloomy images our fears suggested; though it was so much uneasiness clear gain. They happened to come off much better, by being luckily encamped on the dry piece of ground afore-mentioned.

17. They were, however, forced to keep the Sabbath in spite of their teeth, contrary to the dispensation our good chaplain had given them. Indeed, their short allowance of provision would have justified their making the best of their way, without distinction of days. 'Twas certainly a work both of necessity and self-preservation to save themselves from starving. Nevertheless, the hard rain had made every-

thing so thoroughly wet that it was quite impossible to do any business. They therefore made a virtue of what they could not help, and contentedly rested in their dry situation.

Since the surveyors had entered the Dismal, they had laid eyes on no living creature: neither bird nor beast, insect nor reptile came in view. Doubtless the eternal shade that broods over this mighty bog and hinders the sunbeams from blessing the ground makes it an uncomfortable habitation for anything that has life. Not so much as a Zealand frog could endure so aguish a situation. It had one beauty, however, that delighted the eye, though at the expense of all the other senses: the moisture of the soil preserves a continual verdure, and makes every plant an evergreen, but at the same time the foul damps ascend without ceasing, corrupt the air, and render it unfit for respiration. Not even a turkey buzzard will venture to fly over it, no more than the Italian vultures will over the filthy Lake Avernus, or the birds in the Holy Land over the Salt Sea where Sodom and Gomorrah formerly stood.

In these sad circumstances, the kindest thing we could do for our suffering friends was to give them a place in the Litany. Our chaplain, for his part, did his office and rubbed us up with a seasonable sermon. This was quite a new thing to our brethren of North Carolina, who live in a climate where no clergyman can breathe any more than spiders in Ireland.

For want of men in holy orders, both the members of the council and justices of the peace are empowered by the laws of that country to marry all those who will not take one another's word; but for the ceremony of christening their children, they trust that to chance. If a parson come in their way, they will crave a cast of his office, as they call it, else they are content their offspring should remain as arrant pagans as themselves. They account it among their greatest advantages that they are not priest-ridden, not remembering that the clergy is rarely guilty of bestriding such as have the misfortune to be poor. One thing may be said for the inhabitants of that province, that they are not troubled with any religious fumes and have the least superstition of any people living. They do not know Sunday from any other day, any more than Robinson Crusoe did, which would give them a great advantage were they given to be industrious. But they keep so many Sabbaths every week, that their disregard of the seventh day has no manner of cruelty in it, either to servants or cattle.

It was with some difficulty we could make our people quit the good cheer they met with at this house, so it was late before we took our departure; but to make us amends, our landlord was so good as to conduct us ten miles on our way, as far as the Cypress Swamp, which drains itself into the Dismal. Eight miles beyond that we forded the waters of the Coropeak, which tend the same way as do many others on that side. In six miles more we reached the plantation of Mr. Thomas Spight, a grandee of North Carolina. We found the good man upon his crutches, being crippled with the gout in both his knees. Here we flattered ourselves we should by this time meet with good tiding of the surveyors, but had reckoned, alas! without our host: on the contrary, we were told the Dismal was at least thirty miles wide in that place. However, as nobody could say this on his own knowledge, we ordered guns to be fired and a drum to be beaten, but received no answer, unless it was from that prating nymph Echo, who, like a loquacious wife, will always have the last word, and sometimes return three for one.

18. It was indeed no wonder our signal was not heard at that time by the people in the Dismal, because in truth, they had not then penetrated one third of their way. They had that morning fallen to work with great vigor; and finding the ground better than ordinary, drove on the line two miles and thirty-eight poles. This was reckoned an Herculean day's work, and yet they would not have stopped there, had not an impenetrable cedar thicket checked their industry. Our landlord had seated himself on the borders of this Dismal, for the advantage of the green food his cattle find there all winter, and for the rooting that supports his hogs. This, I own, is some convenience to his purse for which his whole family pay dear in their persons, for they are devoured by mosquitoes all the summer and have agues every spring and fall which corrupt all the juices of their bodies, give them a cadaverous complexion, and besides a lazy, creeping habit, which they never get rid of.

19. We ordered several men to patrol on the edge of the Dismal, both towards the north and towards the south, and to fire guns at proper distances. This they performed very punctually, but could

hear nothing in return, nor gain any sort of intelligence. In the mean-time whole flocks of women and children flew hither to stare at us with as much curiosity as if we had lately landed from Bantam or Morocco. Some borderers, too, had a great mind to know where the line would come out, being for the most part apprehensive lest their lands should be taken into Virginia. In that case they must have sub-mitted to some sort of order and government; whereas in North Carolina every one does what seems best in his own eyes. There were some good women that brought their children to be baptized, but brought no capons along with them to make the solemnity cheerful. In the meantime it was strange that none came to be married in such a multitude, if it had only been for the novelty of having their hands joined by one in holy orders. Yet so it was, that though our chaplain christened above an hundred, he did not marry so much as one couple during the whole expedition. But marriage is reckoned a lay contract in Carolina, as I said before, and a country justice can tie the fatal knot there as fast as an archbishop. None of our visitors could, how-ever, tell us any news of the surveyors, nor indeed was it possible any of them should at that time, they being still laboring in the midst of the Dismal. It seems they were able to carry the line this day no further than one mile and sixty-one poles, and that whole distance was through a miry cedar bog, where the ground trembled under their feet most frightfully. In many places, too, their passage was retarded by a great number of fallen trees that lay horsing upon one another. Though many circumstances concurred to make this an un-wholesome situation, yet the poor men had no time to be sick, nor can one conceive a more calamitous case than it would have been to be laid up in that uncomfortable quagmire. Never were patients more tractable or willing to take physic than these honest fellows; but it was from a dread of laying their bones in a bog that would soon spew them up again. That consideration also put them upon more caution about their lodging. They first covered the ground with square pieces of cypress bark, which now, in the spring, they could easily slip off the tree for that purpose. On this they spread their bedding; but unhappily the weight and warmth of their bodies made the water rise up betwixt the joints of the bark, to their great inconvenience. Thus they lay not only moist, but also exceedingly cold, because their fires were continually going out. For no sooner was the trash upon the surface burnt away, but immediately the fire was extinguished by the moisture of the soil, insomuch that it was great part of the sentinel's business to rekindle it again in a fresh place every quarter of an hour. Nor could they indeed do their duty better because cold was the only enemy they had to guard against in a miserable morass where nothing can inhabit.

20. We could get no tidings yet of our brave adventurers, notwithstanding we despatched men to the likeliest stations to inquire after them. They were still scuffling in the mire, and could not possibly forward the line this whole day more than one mile and sixty-four chains. Every step of this day's work was through a cedar bog, where the trees were somewhat smaller and grew more into a thicket. It was now a great misfortune to the men to find their provisions grow less as their labor grew greater; they were all forced to come to short allowance, and consequently to work hard without filling their bellies. Though this was very severe upon English stomachs, yet the people were so far from being discomfited at it, that they still kept up their good humour, and merrily told a young fellow in the company, who looked very plump and wholesome, that he must expect to go first to pot, if matters should come to extremity. This was only said by way of jest, yet it made him thoughtful in earnest. However, for the present he returned them a very civil answer, letting them know that, dead or alive, he should be glad to be useful to such worthy good friends. But, after all, this humorous saying had one very good effect, for that younker, who before was a little inclined by his constitution to be lazy, grew on a sudden extremely industrious, that so there might be less occasion to carbonade him for the good of his fellow travelers. While our friends were thus embarrassed in the Dismal, the commissioners began to lie under great uneasiness for them. They knew very well their provisions must by this time begin to fall short, nor could they conceive any likely means of a supply. At this time of the year both the cattle and hogs had forsaken the skirts of the Dismal, invited by the springing grass on the firm land. All our hopes were that Providence would cause some wild game to fall in their way, or else direct them to a wholesome vegetable for subsistence. In short they were haunted with so many frights on this

occasion that they were in truth more uneasy than the persons whose case they lamented.

We had several visitors from Edenton, in the afternoon, that came with Mr. Gale, who had prudently left us at Currituck, to scuffle through that dirty country by ourselves. These gentlemen, having good noses, had smelled out, at thirty miles' distance, the precious liquor with which the liberality of our good friend Mr. Mead had just before supplied us. That generous person had judged very right, that we were now got out of the latitude of drink proper for men in affliction, and therefore was so good as to send his cart loaden with all sorts of refreshments, for which the commissioners returned him their thanks, and the chaplain his blessing.

21. The surveyors and their attendants began now in good earnest to be alarmed with apprehensions of famine, nor could they forbear looking with some sort of appetite upon a dog which had been the faithful companion of their travels. Their provisions were now near exhausted. They had this morning made the last distribution, that so each might husband his small pittance as he pleased. Now it was that the fresh colored young man began to tremble, every joint of him, having dreamed the night before that the Indians were about to barbecue him over live coals. The prospect of famine determined the people at last, with one consent, to abandon the line for the present, which advanced but slowly, and make the best of their way to firm land. Accordingly they set off very early, and by the help of the compass which they carried along with them steered a direct westwardly course. They marched from morning till night, and computed their journey to amount to about four miles, which was a great way, considering the difficulties of the ground. It was all along a cedar swamp, so dirty and perplexed that if they had not traveled for their lives they could not have reached so far. On their way they espied a turkey buzzard that flew prodigiously high to get above the noisome exhalations that ascend from that filthy place. This they were willing to understand as a good omen, according to the superstitions of the ancients, who had great faith in the flight of vultures. However, after all this tedious journey, they could yet discover no end of their toil, which made them very pensive, especially after they had eat the last morsel of their provisions. But to their unspeak-

able comfort, when all was hushed in the evening, they heard the cattle low and the dogs bark very distinctly, which to men in that distress was more delightful music than Faustina or Farinelli could have made. In the meantime the commissioners could get no news of them from any of their visitors, who assembled from every point of the compass. But the good landlord had visitors of another kind while we were there, that is to say, some industrious masters of ships that lay in Nansemond River. These worthy commanders came to bespeak tobacco from these parts to make up their loadings, in contempt of the Virginia law which positively forbade their taking in any made in North Carolina. Nor was this restraint at all unreasonable; because they have no law in Carolina, either to mend the quality or lessen the quantity of tobacco, or so much as to prevent the turning out of seconds, all which cases have been provided against by the laws of Virginia. Wherefore, there can be no reason why the inhabitants of that province should have the same advantage of shipping their tobacco in our parts, when they will by no means submit to the same restrictions that we do.

22. Our patrol happened not to go far enough to the northward this morning; if they had, the people in the Dismal might have heard the report of their guns. For this reason they returned without any tidings, which threw us into a great though unnecessary perplexity. This was now the ninth day since they entered into that inhospitable swamp, and consequently we had reason to believe their provisions were quite spent. We knew they worked hard and therefore would eat heartily so long as they had wherewithal to recruit their spirits, not imagining the swamp so wide as they found it. Had we been able to guess where the line would come out, we would have sent men to meet them with a fresh supply; but as we could know nothing of that, and as we had neither compass nor surveyor to guide a messenger on such an errand, we were unwilling to expose him to no purpose; therefore, all we were able to do for them, in so great an extremity, was to recommend them to a merciful Providence. However long we might think the time, yet we were cautious of showing our uneasiness, for fear of mortifying our landlord. He had done his best for us, and therefore we were unwilling he should think us dissatisfied with our entertainment. In the midst of our concern, we were most agree-

ably surprised, just after dinner, with the news that the Dismalites were all safe.

· · ·

[A short passage describing delays of the surveyors in the Dismal Swamp is omitted.]

· · ·

24.   This being Sunday, we had a numerous congregation, which flocked to our quarters from all the adjacent country. The news that our surveyors were come out of the Dismal increased the number very much, because it would give them an opportunity of guessing, at least, whereabouts the line would cut, whereby they might form some judgment whether they belonged to Virginia or Carolina. Those who had taken up land within the disputed bounds were in great pain lest it should be found to lie in Virginia; because this being done contrary to an express order of that government, the patentees had great reason to fear they should in that case have lost their land. But their apprehensions were now at an end, when they understood that all the territory which had been controverted was like to be left in Carolina. In the afternoon, those who were to reenter the Dismal were furnished with the necessary provisions, and ordered to repair the overnight to their landlord, Peter Brinkley's, that they might be ready to begin their business early on Monday morning. Mr. Irvine was excused from the fatigue, in compliment to his lungs; but Mr. Mayo and Mr. Swan were robust enough to return upon that painful service, and, to do them justice, they went with great alacrity. The truth was, they now knew the worst of it; and could guess pretty near at the time when they might hope to return to land again.

25.   The air was chilled this morning with a smart northwest wind, which favored the Dismalites in their dirty march. They returned by the path they had made in coming out, and with great industry arrived in the evening at the spot where the line had been discontinued. After so long and laborious a journey, they were glad to repose themselves on their couches of cypress-bark, where their sleep was as sweet as it would have been on a bed of Finland down. In the meantime we who stayed behind had nothing to do but to make the

best observations we could upon that part of the country. The soil
of our landlord's plantation, though none of the best, seemed more
fertile than any thereabouts, where the ground is near as sandy as the
deserts of Africa and consequently barren. The road leading from
thence to Edenton, being in distance about twenty-seven miles, lies
upon a ridge called Sandy Ridge, which is so wretchedly poor that it
will not bring potatoes. The pines in this part of the country are of a
different species from those that grow in Virginia: their bearded
leaves are much longer and their cones much larger. Each cell contains a seed of the size and figure of a black-eyed pea, which, shedding in November, is very good mast for hogs, and fattens them in a
short time. The smallest of these pines are full of cones which are
eight or nine inches long, and each affords commonly sixty or seventy
seeds. This kind of mast has the advantage of all other by being more
constant and less liable to be nipped by the frost or eaten by the cater-
pillars. The trees also abound more with turpentine and consequently
yield more tar than either the yellow or the white pine; and for the
same reason make more durable timber for building. The inhabitants
hereabouts pick up knots of lightwood in abundance, which they
burn into tar and then carry it to Norfolk or Nansemond for a market. The tar made in this method is the less valuable, because it is said
to burn the cordage, though it is full as good for all other uses as that
made in Sweden and Muscovy.

Surely there is no place in the world where the inhabitants live with
less labor than in North Carolina. It approaches nearer to the description of Lubberland than any other, by the great felicity of the
climate, the easiness of raising provisions, and the slothfulness of the
people. Indian corn is of so great increase that a little pains will sub-
sist a very large family with bread, and then they may have meat
without any pains at all, by the help of the low grounds and the great
variety of mast that grows on the high land. The men, for their parts,
just like the Indians, impose all the work upon the poor women. They
make their wives rise out of their beds early in the morning, at the
same time that they lie and snore till the sun has risen one-third of his
course and dispersed all the unwholesome damps. Then, after stretching and yawning for half an hour, they light their pipes, and under
the protection of a cloud of smoke venture out into the open air;

though, if it happens to be never so little cold, they quickly return shivering into the chimney corner. When the weather is mild, they stand leaning with both their arms upon the cornfield fence, and gravely consider whether they had best go and take a small heat at the hoe: but generally find reasons to put it off till another time. Thus they loiter away their lives, like Solomon's sluggard, with their arms across, and at the winding up of the year scarcely have bread to eat. To speak the truth, 'tis a thorough aversion to labor that makes people file off to North Carolina, where plenty and a warm sun confirm them in their disposition to laziness for their whole lives.

26.   Since we were like to be confined to this place till the people returned out of the Dismal, 'twas agreed that our chaplain might safely take a turn to Edenton, to preach the Gospel to the infidels there and christen their children. He was accompanied thither by Mr. Little, one of the Carolina commissioners, who, to show his regard for the church, offered to treat him on the road with a fricassee of rum. They fried half a dozen rashers of very fat bacon in a pint of rum, both which being dished up together, served the company at once both for meat and drink. Most of the rum they get in this country comes from New England and is so bad and unwholesome that it is not improperly called 'kill-devil.' It is distilled there from foreign molasses, which, if skillfully managed, yields near gallon for gallon. Their molasses comes from the same country and has the name of 'long sugar' in Carolina, I suppose from the ropiness of it, and serves all the purposes of sugar, both in their eating and drinking. When they entertain their friends bountifully, they fail not to set before them a capacious bowl of Bombo, so called from the admiral of that name. This is a compound of rum and water in equal parts, made palatable with the said long sugar. As good humor begins to flow, and the bowl to ebb, they take care to replenish it with sheer rum, of which there always is a reserve under the table.

But such generous doings happen only when that balsam of life is plenty; for they have often such melancholy times, that neither land-graves nor cassiques can procure one drop for their wives when they lie in or are troubled with the colic or vapors. Very few in this country have the industry to plant orchards, which in a dearth of rum might supply them with much better liquor. The truth is, there is one inconvenience that easily discourages lazy people from making this improvement: very often, in autumn, when the apples begin to ripen, they are visited with numerous flights of parakeets that bite all the fruit to pieces in a moment for the sake of the kernels. The havoc they make is sometimes so great that whole orchards are laid waste in spite of all the noises that can be made or mawkins that can be dressed up to fright them away. These ravenous birds visit North Carolina only during the warm season, and so soon as the cold begins to come on retire back towards the sun. They rarely venture so far north as Virginia, except in a very hot summer, when they visit the most southern parts of it. They are very beautiful; but like some other pretty creatures, are apt to be loud and mischievous.

27. Betwixt this and Edenton there are many thuckleberry slashes, which afford a convenient harbor for wolves and foxes. The first of these wild beasts is not so large and fierce as they are in other countries more northerly. He will not attack a man in the keenest of his hunger, but run away from him as from an animal more mischievous than himself. The foxes are much bolder, and will sometimes not only make a stand but likewise assault any one that would balk them of their prey. The inhabitants hereabouts take the trouble to dig abundance of wolfpits, so deep and perpendicular that when a wolf is once tempted into them he can no more scramble out again than a husband who has taken the leap can scramble out of matrimony.

Most of the houses in this part of the country are loghouses, covered with pine or cypress shingles three feet long and one broad. They are hung upon laths with pegs, and their doors, too, turn upon wooden hinges and have wooden locks to secure them, so that the building is finished without nails or other ironwork. They also set up their pales without any nails at all, and indeed more securely than those that are nailed. There are three rails mortised into the posts, the lowest of which serves as a sill with a groove in the middle big enough to receive the end of the pales: the middle part of the pale rests against the inside of the next rail, and the top of it is brought forward to the outside of the uppermost. Such wreathing of the pales in and out makes them stand firm, and much harder to unfix than when nailed in the ordinary way.

Within three or four miles of Edenton the soil appears to be a little more fertile, though it is much cut with slashes which seem all to have a tendency towards the Dismal. This town is situated on the north side of Albemarle Sound, which is there about five miles over. A dirty slash runs all along the back of it, which in the summer is a foul annoyance and furnishes abundance of that Carolina plague, mosquitoes. There may be forty or fifty houses, most of them small and built without expense. A citizen here is counted extravagant if he has ambition enough to aspire to a brick chimney. Justice herself is but indifferently lodged, the courthouse having much the air of a common tobacco-house. I believe this is the only metropolis in the Christian or Mohammedan world where there is neither church, chapel, mosque, synagogue, or any other place of public worship of any sect or religion whatsoever. What little devotion there may happen to be is much more private than their vices. The people seem easy without a minister as long as they are exempted from paying him. Sometimes the Society for Propagating the Gospel has had the charity to send over missionaries to this country; but unfortunately the priest has been too lewd for the people, or, which oftener happens, they too lewd for the priest. For these reasons these reverend gentlemen have always left their flocks as arrant heathen as they found them. Thus much, however, may be said for the inhabitants of Edenton, that not a soul has the least taint of hypocrisy or superstition, acting very frankly and above-board in all their excesses.

Provisions here are extremely cheap and extremely good, so that people may live plentifully at a trifling expense. Nothing is dear but law, physic, and strong drink, which are all bad in their kind, and the last they get with so much difficulty that they are never guilty of the sin of suffering it to sour upon their hands. Their vanity generally lies not so much in having a handsome dining room, as a handsome house of office: in this kind of structure they are really extravagant. They are rarely guilty of flattering or making any court to their governors, but treat them with all the excesses of freedom and familiarity. They are of opinion their rulers would be apt to grow insolent if they grew rich, and for that reason take care to keep them poorer and more dependent, if possible, than the saints in New England used to do their governors. They have very little coin, so they are forced to carry on their home traffic with paper money. This is the only cash that will tarry in the country, and for that reason the discount goes on increasing between that and real money, and will do so to the end of the chapter.

. . .

[A short passage describing routine difficulties is omitted.]

. . .

April 1. The surveyors, getting now upon better ground quite disengaged from underwoods, pushed on the line almost twelve miles. They left Somerton Chapel near two miles to the northwards, so that there was now no place of public worship left in the whole province of North Carolina.

The high land of North Carolina was barren and covered with a deep sand; and the low grounds were wet and boggy, insomuch that several of our horses were mired and gave us frequent opportunities to show our horsemanship.

The line cut William Spight's plantation in two, leaving little more than his dwelling house and orchard in Virginia. Sundry other plantations were split in the same unlucky manner, which made the owners accountable to both governments. Wherever we passed we constantly found the borderers laid it to heart if their land was taken into Virginia: they chose much rather to belong to Carolina, where they pay no tribute, either to God or to Cæsar. Another reason was that the government there is so loose and the laws are so feebly executed that, like those in the neighborhood of Sidon formerly, every one does just what seems good in his own eyes. If the governor's hands have been weak in that province, under the authority of the lord proprietors, much weaker then were the hands of the magistrate, who, though he might have had virtue enough to endeavor to punish offenders, which very rarely happened, yet that virtue had been quite impotent, for want of ability to put it in execution. Besides, there might have been some danger, perhaps, in venturing to be so rigorous, for fear of undergoing the fate of an honest justice in Currituck precinct. This bold magistrate, it seems, taking upon him to order a fellow to the stocks for being disorderly in his drink, was for his intemperate zeal carried thither himself, and narrowly escaped being whipped by the rabble into the bargain.

This easy day's work carried the line to the banks of Somerton Creek, that runs out of Chowan River a little below the mouth of Nottoway.

2. In less than a mile from Somerton Creek the line was carried to Blackwater, which is the name of the upper part of Chowan, running some miles above the mouth of Nottoway. It must be observed that Chowan, after taking a compass round the most beautiful part of North Carolina, empties itself into Albemarle Sound a few miles above Edenton. The tide flows seven or eight miles higher than where the river changes its name and is navigable thus high for any small vessel. Our line intersected it exactly half a mile to the northward of Nottoway. However, in obedience to His Majesty's command, we directed the surveyors to come down the river as far as the mouth of Nottoway in order to continue our true west line from thence. Thus we found the mouth of Nottoway to lie no more than half a minute farther to the northward than Mr. Lawson had formerly done. That gentleman's observation, it seems, placed it in 36° 30′, and our working made it out to be 36° 30½′—a very inconsiderable variance.

The surveyors crossed the river over against the middle of the mouth of Nottoway, where it was about eighty yards wide. From thence they ran the line about half a mile through a dirty pocoson, as far as an Indian field. Here we took up our lodging in a moist situation, having the pocoson above mentioned on one side of us, and a swamp on the other.

In this camp three of the Meherrin Indians made us a visit. They told us that the small remains of their nation had deserted their ancient town, situated near the mouth of Meherrin River, for fear of the Catawbas, who had killed fourteen of their people the year before; and the few that survived that calamity had taken refuge amongst the English on the east side of Chowan. Though, if the complaint of these Indians were true, they are hardly used by our Carolina friends. But they are the less to be pitied, because they have ever been reputed the most false and treacherous to the English of all the Indians in the neighborhood.

Not far from the place where we lay, I observed a large oak which had been blown up by the roots, the body of which was shivered into perfect strings, and was, in truth, the most violent effects of lightning I ever saw.

But the most curious instance of that dreadful meteor happened at York, where a man was killed near a pine tree in which the lightning made a hole before it struck the man, and left an exact figure of the tree upon his breast, with all its branches, to the wonder of all that beheld it, in which I shall be more particular hereafter.

. . .

[With the advance of spring, rattlesnakes began to crawl out of their winter quarters; in view of this hazard, the surveyors agreed to abandon the undertaking until the autumn. A short passage of routine description is omitted.]

. . .

7. The next day being Sunday, we ordered notice to be sent to all the neighborhood that there would be a sermon at this place, and an opportunity of christening their children. But the likelihood of rain got the better of their devotion, and what perhaps might still be a stronger motive, of their curiosity. In the morning we despatched a runner to the Nottoway town to let the Indians know we intended them a visit that evening, and our honest landlord was so kind as to be our pilot thither, being about four miles from his house. Accordingly in the afternoon we marched in good order to the town, where the female scouts, stationed on an eminence for that purpose, had no sooner spied us but they gave notice of our approach to their fellow citizens by continual whoops and cries, which could not possibly have been more dismal at the sight of their most implacable enemies. This signal assembled all their great men, who received us in a body and conducted us into the fort.

This fort was a square piece of ground inclosed with substantial puncheons, or strong palisades, about ten feet high, and leaning a little outwards to make a scalade more difficult. Each side of the square might be about a hundred yards long, with loopholes at proper distances, through which they may fire upon the enemy. Within this inclosure we found bark cabins sufficient to lodge all their people in case they should be obliged to retire thither. These cabins are no other but close arbors made of saplings, arched at the top, and covered so well with bark as to be proof against all weather. The fire is made in the middle, according to the Hibernian fashion, the smoke whereof finds no other vent but at the door, and so keeps the whole family warm at the expense both of their eyes and complexion. The Indians have no standing furniture in their cabins but hurdles to repose their persons upon which they cover with mats or deerskins. We were conducted to the best apartments in the fort, which just before had been made ready for our reception, and adorned with new mats that were sweet and clean. The young men had painted themselves in a hideous manner, not so much for ornament as terror. In that frightful equipage they entertained us with sundry war dances wherein they endeavored to look as formidable as possible. The instrument they danced to was an Indian drum, that is, a large gourd with a skin braced taut over the mouth of it. The dancers all sang to this music, keeping exact time with their feet, while their heads and arms were screwed into a thousand menacing postures. Upon this occasion the ladies had arrayed themselves in all their finery. They were wrapped in their red and blue match coats, thrown so negligently about them that their mahogany skins appeared in several parts, like the Lacedæmonian damsels of old. Their hair was braided with white and blue peak, and hung gracefully in a large roll upon their shoulders.

This peak consists of small cylinders cut out of a conch shell, drilled through and strung like beads. It serves them both for money and jewels, the blue being of much greater value than the white, for the same reason that Ethiopian mistresses in France are dearer than French, because they are more scarce. The women wear necklaces and bracelets of these precious materials when they have a mind to appear lovely. Though their complexions be a little sad-colored, yet their shapes are very straight and well proportioned. Their faces are seldom handsome, yet they have an air of innocence and bashfulness, that with a little less dirt would not fail to make them desirable.

Such charms might have had their full effect upon men who had been so long deprived of female conversation, but that the whole winter's soil was so crusted on the skins of those dark angels that it required a very strong appetite to approach them. The bear's oil, with which they anoint their persons all over, makes their skins soft, and at the same time protects them from every species of vermin that use to be troublesome to other uncleanly people. We were unluckily so many that they could not well make us the compliment of bed-fellows, according to the Indian rules of hospitality, though a grave matron whispered one of the commissioners very civilly in the ear, that if her daughter had been but one year older, she should have been at his devotion.

It is by no means a loss of reputation among the Indians for damsels that are single to have intrigues with the men; on the contrary, they count it an argument of superior merit to be liked by a great number of gallants. However, like the ladies that game they are a little mer-cenary in their amours and seldom bestow their favors out of stark love and kindness. But after these women have once appropriated their charms by marriage, they are from thenceforth faithful to their vows, and will hardly ever be tempted by an agreeable gallant, or be provoked by a brutal or even by a fumbling husband to go astray. The little work that is done among the Indians is done by the poor women, while the men are quite idle, or at most employed only in the gentle-manly diversions of hunting and fishing.

In this, as well as in their wars, they use nothing but firearms, which they purchase of the English for skins. Bows and arrows are grown into disuse, except only amongst their boys. Nor is it ill policy, but on the contrary very prudent, thus to furnish the Indians with firearms, because it makes them depend entirely upon the English, not only for their trade, but even for their subsistence. Besides, they were really able to do more mischief while they made use of arrows, of which they would let silently fly several in a minute with wonderful dex-terity, whereas now they hardly ever discharge their firelocks more than once, which they insidiously do from behind a tree, and then re-tire as nimbly as the Dutch horse used to do now and then formerly in Flanders.

We put the Indians to no expense but only of a little corn for our horses, for which in gratitude we cheered their hearts with what rum we had left, which they love better than they do their wives and chil-dren. Though these Indians dwell among the English and see in what plenty a little industry enables them to live, yet they choose to continue in their stupid idleness, and to suffer all the inconveniences of dirt, cold and want, rather than to disturb their heads with care, or defile their hands with labor.

The whole number of people belonging to the Nottoway town, if you include women and children, amount to about two hundred. These are the only Indians of any consequence now remaining within the limits of Virginia. The rest are either removed or dwindled to a very inconsiderable number, either by destroying one another or else by the smallpox and other diseases—though nothing has been so fatal to them as their ungovernable passion for rum, with which, I am sorry to say it, they have been but too liberally supplied by the English that live near them.

And here I must lament the bad success Mr. Boyle's charity has hitherto had towards converting any of these poor heathens to Christianity. Many children of our neighboring Indians have been brought up in the college of William and Mary. They have been taught to read and write, and have been carefully instructed in the principles of the Christian religion, till they came to be men. Yet after they returned home, instead of civilizing and converting the rest, they have immediately relapsed into infidelity and barbarism themselves.

And some of them, too, have made the worst use of the knowledge they acquired among the English by employing it against their benefactors. Besides, as they unhappily forget all the good they learn, and remember the ill, they are apt to be more vicious and disorderly than the rest of their countrymen.

I ought not to quit this subject without doing justice to the great prudence of Colonel Spotswood in this affair. That gentleman was lieutenant governor of Virginia when Carolina was engaged in a bloody war with the Indians. At that critical time it was thought expedient to keep a watchful eye upon our tributary savages, who we knew had nothing to keep them to their duty but their fears. Then it was that he demanded of each nation a competent number of their great men's children to be sent to the college, where they served as so many hostages for the good behavior of the rest, and at the same time were themselves principled in the Christian religion. He also placed a schoolmaster among the Sapony Indians, at the salary of fifty

pounds per annum, to instruct their children. The person that undertook that charitable work was Mr. Charles Griffin, a man of good
family, who by the innocence of his life and the sweetness of his
temper was perfectly well qualified for that pious undertaking. Besides, he had so much the secret of mixing pleasure with instruction
that he had not a scholar who did not love him affectionately. Such
talents must needs have been blest with a proportionable success, had
he not been unluckily removed to the college, by which he left the
good work he had begun unfinished. In short, all the pains he had
taken among the infidels had no other effect but to make them something cleanlier than other Indians are. The care Colonel Spotswood
took to tincture the Indian children with Christianity produced the
following epigram, which was not published during his administration, for fear it might then have looked like flattery.

> Long has the furious priest essayed in vain,
> With sword and faggot, infidels to gain,
> But now the milder soldier wisely tries
> By gentler methods to unveil their eyes.
> Wonders apart, he knew 'twere vain t'engage
> The fix'd preventions of misguided age.
> With fairer hopes he forms the Indian youth
> To early manners, probity and truth.
> The lion's whelp thus, on the Libian shore, ⎫
> Is tamed and gentled by the artful Moor, ⎬
> Not the grim sire, inured to blood before. ⎭

I'm sorry I can't give a better account of the state of the poor Indians with respect to Christianity, although a great deal of pains has
been and still continues to be taken with them. For my part, I must be
of opinion, as I hinted before, that there is but one way of converting
these poor infidels and reclaiming them from barbarity, and that is,
charitably to intermarry with them, according to the modern policy
of the most Christian King in Canada and Louisiana. Had the English
done this at the first settlement of the colony, the infidelity of the Indians had been worn out at this day, with their dark complexions, and
the country had swarmed with people more than it does with insects.
It was certainly an unreasonable nicety that prevented their entering

into so good-natured an alliance. All nations of men have the same natural dignity, and we all know that very bright talents may be lodged under a very dark skin. The principal difference between one people and another proceeds only from the different opportunities of improvement. The Indians by no means want understanding, and are in their figure tall and well-proportioned. Even their copper-colored complexion would admit of blanching, if not in the first, at the farthest in the second generation. I may safely venture to say, the Indian women would have made altogether as honest wives for the first planters as the damsels they used to purchase from aboard the ships. It is strange, therefore, that any good Christian should have refused a wholesome, straight bed-fellow, when he might have had so fair a portion with her as the merit of saving her soul.

8. We rested on our clean mats very comfortably, though alone, and the next morning went to the toilet of some of the Indian ladies, where, what with the charms of their persons and the smoke of their apartments, we were almost blinded. They offered to give us silkgrass baskets of their own making, which were modestly refused, knowing that an Indian present, like that of a nun, is a liberality put out to interest, and a bribe placed to the greatest advantage. Our chaplain observed with concern that the ruffles of some of our fellow travelers were a little discolored with puccoon, wherewith the good man had been told those ladies used to improve their invisible charms.

About 10 o'clock we marched out of town in good order, and the war captains saluted us with a volley of small arms. From thence we proceeded over Black-water bridge to Colonel Henry Harrison's, where we congratulated each other upon our return into Christendom.

Thus ended our progress for this season, which we may justly say was attended with all the success that could be expected. Besides the punctual performance of what was committed to us, we had the pleasure to bring back every one of our company in perfect health. And this we must acknowledge to be a singular blessing, considering the difficulties and dangers to which they had been exposed. We had reason to fear the many waters and sunken grounds through which we were obliged to wade might have thrown the men into sundry acute distempers; especially the Dismal, where the soil was so full of water, and the air so full of damps, that nothing but a Dutchman could live in them. Indeed, the foundation of all our success was the exceeding dry season. It rained during the whole journey but rarely, and then, as when Herod built his temple, only in the night or upon the Sabbath, when it was no hindrance at all to our progress.

The tenth of September being thought a little too soon for the commissioners to meet, in order to proceed on the line, on account of snakes, it was agreed to put it off to the twentieth of the same month, of which due notice was sent to the Carolina commissioners.

[Sept.] 19. We, on the part of Virginia, that we might be sure to be punctual, arrived at Mr. Kinchin's, the place appointed, on the nineteenth, after a journey of three days, in which nothing remarkable happened. We found three of the Carolina commissioners had taken possession of the house, having come thither by water from Edenton. By the great quantity of provisions these gentlemen brought, and the few men they had to eat them, we were afraid they intended to carry the line to the South Sea. They had five hundred pounds of bacon and dried beef, and five hundred pounds of biscuit, and not above three or four men. The misfortune was, they forgot to provide horses to carry their good things, or else trusted to the incertainty of hiring them here, which, considering the place, was leaving too much to that jilt, hazard. On our part we had taken better care, being completely furnished with everything necessary for transporting our baggage and provisions. Indeed we brought no other provisions out with us but a thousand pounds of bread, and had faith enough to depend on Providence for our meat, being desirous to husband the public money as much as possible. We had no less than twenty men, besides the chaplain, the surveyors and all the servants, to be subsisted upon this bread. However, that it might hold out the better, our men had been ordered to provide themselves at home with provision for ten days, in which time we judged we should get beyond the inhabitants, where forest game of all sorts was like to be plenty at that time of the year.

20. This being the day appointed for our rendezvous, great part of it was spent in the careful fixing our baggage and assembling our men, who were ordered to meet us here. We took care to examine their arms, and made proof of the powder provided for the expedi-

tion. Our provision-horses had been hindered by the rain from coming up exactly at the day; but this delay was the less disappointment, by reason of the ten days' subsistence the men had been directed to provide for themselves. Mr. Moseley did not join us till the afternoon, nor Mr. Swan till several days later.

Mr. Kinchin had unadvisedly sold the men a little brandy of his own making, which produced much disorder, causing some to be too choleric, and others too loving; insomuch that a damsel who assisted in the kitchen had certainly suffered what the nuns call martyrdom, had she not capitulated a little too soon. This outrage would have called for some severe discipline, had she not bashfully withdrawn herself early in the morning, and so carried off the evidence.

. . .

[A passage of about 8700 words is omitted. It describes the daily routine of the surveyors, the efforts of the hunters to keep the camp supplied with game, and some of the customs of the Indians.]

. . .

[Oct.] 12. We were so cruelly entangled with bushes and grape-vines all day that we could advance the line no farther than five miles and twenty-eight poles. The vines grow very thick in these woods, twining lovingly round the trees almost everywhere, especially to the saplings. This makes it evident how natural both the soil and climate of this country are to vines, though I believe most to our own vines. The grapes we commonly met with were black, though there be two or three kinds of white grapes that grow wild. The black are very sweet, but small, because the strength of the vine spends itself in wood; though without question a proper culture would make the same grapes both larger and sweeter. But, with all these disadvantages, I have drunk tolerably good wine pressed from them, though made without skill. There is then good reason to believe it might admit of great improvement, if rightly managed.

Our Indian killed a bear, of two years old, that was feasting on these grapes. He was very fat, as they generally are in that season of the year. In the fall, the flesh of this animal has a high relish, different from that of other creatures, though inclining nearest to that of pork, or rather of wild boar. A true woodsman prefers this sort of meat to that of the fattest venison, not only for the *haut gout*, but also because the fat of it is well tasted, and never rises in the stomach. Another proof of the goodness of this meat is that it is less apt to corrupt than any other with which we are acquainted. As agreeable as such rich diet was to the men, yet we who were not accustomed to it tasted it at first with some sort of squeamishness, that animal being of the dog kind; though a little use soon reconciled us to this American venison. And that its being of the dog kind might give us the less disgust, we had the example of that ancient and polite people, the Chinese, who reckon dog's flesh too good for any under the quality of a mandarin. This beast is in truth a very clean feeder, living, while the season lasts, upon acorns, chestnuts and chinquapins, wild honey and wild grapes. They are naturally not carnivorous, unless hunger constrain them to it after the mast is all gone, and the product of the woods quite exhausted. They are not provident enough to lay up any hoard, like the squirrels, nor can they, after all, live very long upon licking their paws, as Sir John Mandeville and some other travelers tell us, but are forced in the winter months to quit the mountains and visit the inhabitants. Their errand is then to surprise a poor hog at a pinch to keep from starving. And to show that they are not flesh-eaters by trade, they devour their prey very awkwardly. They don't kill it right out and feast upon its blood and entrails, like other ravenous beasts, but having, after a fair pursuit, seized it with their paws, they begin first upon the rump, and so devour one collop after another, till they come to the vitals, the poor animal crying all the while for several minutes together. However, in so doing, Bruin acts a little imprudently, because the dismal outcry of the hog alarms the neighborhood, and 'tis odds but he pays the forfeit with his life before he can secure his retreat.

But bears soon grow weary of this unnatural diet, and about January, when there is nothing to be gotten in the woods, they retire into some cave or hollow tree, where they sleep away two or three months very comfortably. But then they quit their holes in March, when the fish begin to run up the rivers, on which they are forced to keep Lent till some fruit or berry comes in season. But bears are fondest of chestnuts, which grow plentifully towards the mountains, upon very large trees, where the soil happens to be rich. We were curious to know how it happened that many of the outward branches of those trees came to be broke off in that solitary place, and were informed that the bears are so discreet as not to trust their unwieldy bodies on the smaller limbs of the tree, that would not bear their weight; but after venturing as far as is safe, which they can judge to an inch, they bite off the end of the branch, which falling down, they are content to finish their repast upon the ground. In the same cautious manner they secure the acorns that grow on the weaker limbs of the oak. And it must be allowed that in these instances a bear carries instinct a great way and acts more reasonably than many of his betters who indiscreetly venture upon frail projects that will not bear them.

. . .

[A long passage of about 14,000 words covering the period from October 13 to October 30 is omitted. This passage describes the activities of the Indian hunters and the fauna and flora of the countryside, and relates the daily activities of the surveyors.]

. . .

[30.] In the evening one of the men knocked down an opossum, which is a harmless little beast that will seldom go out of your way, and if you take hold of it, it will only grin and hardly ever bite. The flesh was well tasted and tender, approaching nearest to pig, which it also resembles in bigness. The color of its fur was a goose gray, with a swine's snout, and a tail like a rat, but at least a foot long. By twisting this tail about the arm of a tree, it will hang with all its weight and swing to anything it wants to take hold of. It has five claws on the forefeet of equal length, but the hinder feet have only four claws, and a sort of thumb standing off at a proper distance. Their feet being thus formed qualify them for climbing up trees to catch little birds, which they are very fond of. But the greatest particularity of this creature, and which distinguishes it from most others that we are acquainted with, is the false belly of the female, into which her young retreat in time of danger. She can draw the slit, which is the inlet into this pouch, so close, that you must look narrowly to find it, especially if she happen to be a virgin. Within the false belly may be seen seven or eight teats, on which the young ones grow from their first formation till they are big enough to fall off, like ripe fruit from a tree.

This is so odd a method of generation, that I should not have believed it without the testimony of mine own eyes. Besides a knowing and credible person has assured me he has more than once observed the embryo opossums growing to the teat before they were completely shaped, and afterwards watched their daily growth till they were big enough for birth. And all this he could the more easily pry into, because the dam was so perfectly gentle and harmless, that he could handle her just as he pleased. I could hardly persuade myself to publish a thing so contrary to the course that nature takes in the production of other animals, unless it were a matter commonly believed in all countries where that creature is produced, and has been often observed by persons of undoubted credit and understanding. They say that the leather-winged bats produce their young in the same uncommon manner. And that young sharks at sea, and the young vipers ashore, run down the throats of their dams when they are closely pursued.

The frequent crossing of Crooked Creek, and mounting the steep banks of it, gave the finishing stroke to the foundering of our horses; and no less than two of them made a full stop here, and would not advance a foot farther, either by fair means or foul. We had a dreamer of dreams amongst us, who warned me in the morning to take care of myself, or I should infallibly fall into the creek; I thanked him kindly and used what caution I could, but was not able, it seems, to avoid my destiny, for my horse made a false step and laid me down at my full length in the water. This was enough to bring dreaming into credit, and I think it much for the honor of our expedition, that it was graced not only with a priest but also with a prophet. We were so perplexed with this serpentine creek, as well as in passing the branches of the Irvine (which were swelled since we saw them before) that we could reach but five miles this whole day. In the evening we pitched our tent near Miry Creek (though an uncomfortable place to lodge in) purely for the advantage of the canes.

Our hunters killed a large doe and two bears, which made all other misfortunes easy. Certainly no Tartar ever loved horseflesh, or Hottentot guts and garbage, better than woodsmen do bear. The truth of it is, it may be proper food perhaps for such as work or ride it off, but, with our chaplain's leave, who loved it much, I think it not a very proper diet for saints, because 'tis apt to make them a little too rampant.

And now, for the good of mankind and for the better peopling an infant colony which has no want but that of inhabitants, I will venture to publish a secret of importance which our Indian disclosed to me. I asked him the reason why few or none of his countrywomen were barren. To which curious question he answered, with a broad grin upon his face, they had an infallible secret for that. Upon my being importunate to know what the secret might be, he informed me that, if any Indian woman did not prove with child at a decent time after marriage, the husband, to save his reputation with the women, forthwith entered into a bear-diet for six weeks, which in that time makes him so vigorous that he grows exceedingly impertinent to his poor wife, and 'tis great odds but he makes her a mother in nine months. And thus much I am able to say, besides, for the reputation of the bear diet, that all the married men of our company were joyful fathers within forty weeks after they got home, and most of the single men had children sworn to them within the same time, our chaplain always excepted, who, with much ado, made a shift to cast out that importunate kind of devil, by dint of fasting and prayer.

Nov. 1. By the negligence of one of the men in not hobbling his horse, he straggled so far that he could not be found. This stopped us all the morning long; yet, because our time should not be entirely lost, we endeavored to observe the latitude at twelve o'clock. Though our observation was not perfect, by reason the wind blew a little too fresh, however, by such a one as we could make, we found ourselves in 36° 20′ only. Notwithstanding our being thus delayed, and the unevenness of the ground over which we were obliged to walk (for most of us served now in the infantry) we traveled no less than six miles; though, as merciful as we were to our poor beasts, another of 'em tired by the way and was left behind for the wolves and panthers to feast upon.

As we marched along, we had the fortune to kill a brace of bucks, as many bears, and one wild turkey. But this was carrying sport to wantonness because we butchered more than we were able to transport. We ordered the deer to be quartered and divided amongst the horses for the lighter carriage, and recommended the bears to our daily attendants, the turkey-buzzards. We always chose to carry venison along with us rather than bear, not only because it was less cumbersome, but likewise because the people could eat it without bread, which was now almost spent. Whereas the other, being richer food, lay too heavy upon the stomach, unless it were lightened by something farinaceous. This is what I thought proper to remark, for the service of all those whose business or diversion shall oblige them to live any time in the woods. And because I am persuaded that very useful matters may be found out by searching this great wilderness, especially the upper parts of it about the mountains, I conceive it will help to engage able men in that good work, if I recommend a wholesome kind of food, of very small weight and very great nourishment, that will secure them from starving in case they should be so unlucky as to meet with no game. The chief discouragement at present from penetrating far into the woods is the trouble of carrying a load of provisions. I must own famine is a frightful monster, and for that reason to be guarded against as well as we can. But the common precautions against it are so burthensome that people cannot tarry long out and go far enough from home to make any effectual discovery. The portable provisions I would furnish our foresters withal are gluebroth and rockahominy: one contains the essence of bread, the other of meat. The best way of making glue-broth is after the following method: Take a leg of beef, veal, venison, or any other young meat, because old meat will not so easily jelly. Pare off all the fat, in which there is no nutriment, and of the lean make a very strong broth, after the usual manner, by boiling the meat to rags till all the goodness be out. After skimming off what fat remains, pour the broth into a wide stew-pan, well tinned, and let it simmer over a gentle, even fire, till it comes to a thick jelly. Then take it off and set it over boiling water, which is an evener heat, and not so apt to burn the broth to the vessel. Over that let it evaporate, stirring it very often till it be reduced, when cold, into a solid substance like glue. Then cut it into small pieces, laying them single in the cold, that they may dry the sooner. When the pieces are perfectly dry, put them into a canister, and they will be good, if kept dry, a whole East Indian voyage. This glue is so strong, that two or three drams, dissolved in boiling water with a little salt, will make half a pint of good broth, and if you should be faint with fasting or fatigue, let a small piece of this glue melt in your mouth, and you will find yourself surprisingly refreshed. One pound of this cookery would keep a man in good heart above a month, and is not only nourishing but likewise very wholesome. Particularly it is good against fluxes, which woodsmen are very liable to by lying too near the moist ground and guzzling too much cold water. But as it will be only used now and then, in times of scarcity, when game is wanting, two pounds of it will be enough for a journey of six months. But this broth will be still more heartening, if you thicken every mess with half a spoonful of rockahominy, which is nothing but Indian corn parched without burning, and reduced to powder. The fire drives out all the watery parts of the corn, leaving the strength of it behind, and this being very dry, becomes much lighter for carriage and less liable to be spoiled by the moist air. Thus half a dozen pounds of this sprightful bread will sustain a man for as many months, pro- vided he husband it well, and always spare it when he meets with venison, which, as I said before, may be very safely eaten without any bread at all. By what I have said, a man need not encumber him- self with more than eight or ten pounds of provisions, though he continue half a year in the woods. These and his gun will support him very well during that time, without the least danger of keeping one single fast. And though some of his days may be what the French call *jours maigres*, yet there will happen no more of those than will be necessary for his health, and to carry off the excesses of the days of plenty, when our travelers will be apt to indulge their lawless appetites too much.

. . .

[A short passage relating the activities from November 2 to No- vember 7 is omitted.]

7. After crossing the Dan, we made a march of eight miles over hills and dales as far as the next ford of that river. And now we were by practice become such very able footmen that we easily out-walked our horses and could have marched much farther, had it not been in pity to their weakness. Besides, here was plenty of canes, which was reason enough to make us shorten our journey. Our gun-ners did great execution as they went along, killing no less than two braces of deer, and as many wild turkeys.

Though practice will soon make a man of tolerable vigor an able footman, yet, as a help to bear fatigue I used to chew a root of gin-seng as I walked along. This kept up my spirits, and made me trip away as nimbly in my half jack-boots as younger men could do in their shoes. This plant is in high esteem in China, where it sells for its weight in silver. Indeed it does not grow there, but in the mountains of Tartary, to which place the emperor of China sends ten thousand men every year on purpose to gather it. But it grows so scattering there, that even so many hands can bring home no great quantity. In-deed it is a vegetable of so many virtues that Providence has planted it very thin in every country that has the happiness to produce it. Nor indeed is mankind worthy of so great a blessing, since health and long life are commonly abused to ill purposes. This noble plant grows likewise at the cape of Good Hope, where it is called kanna and is in wonderful esteem among the Hottentots. It grows also on the north-ern continent of America, near the mountains, but as sparingly as truth and public spirit. It answers exactly both to the figure and vir-tue of that which grows in Tartary, so that there can be no doubt of its being the same. Its virtues are, that it gives an uncommon warmth and vigor to the blood, and frisks the spirits, beyond any other cor-dial. It cheers the heart even of a man that has a bad wife, and makes him look down with great composure on the crosses of the world. It promotes insensible perspiration, dissolves all phlegmatic and viscous humors that are apt to obstruct the narrow channels of the nerves. It helps the memory, and would quicken even Helvetian dullness. 'Tis friendly to the lungs, much more than scolding itself. It comforts the stomach and strengthens the bowels, preventing all colics and fluxes. In one word, it will make a man live a great while, and very well while he does live. And what is more, it will even make old age

amiable, by rendering it lively, cheerful, and good-humored. However, 'tis of little use in the feats of love, as a great prince once found,
who, hearing of its invigorating quality, sent as far as China for some
of it, though his ladies could not boast of any advantage thereby.

.   .   .

[A passage relating events from November 7 to November 15 is
omitted. In this passage Byrd discusses the Indians who formerly inhabited the region, the annoyance suffered from horseflies and ticks,
the danger from spider bites, and the killing of a buffalo.]

.   .   .

15. About three miles from our camp we passed Great Creek, and
then, after traversing very barren grounds for five miles together, we
crossed the Trading Path, and soon after had the pleasure of reaching
the uppermost inhabitant. This was a plantation belonging to Colonel
Mumford, where our men almost burst themselves with potatoes and
milk. Yet, as great a curiosity as a house was to us foresters, still we
chose to lie in the tent, as being much the cleaner and sweeter lodging.

The Trading Path above mentioned receives its name from being
the route the traders take with their caravans, when they go to traffic
with the Catawbas and other southern Indians. The Catawbas live
about two hundred and fifty miles beyond Roanoke River, and yet
our traders find their account in transporting goods from Virginia to
trade with them at their own town. The common method of carrying
on this Indian commerce is as follows: Gentlemen send for goods
proper for such a trade from England, and then either venture them
out at their own risk to the Indian towns, or else credit some traders
with them of substance and reputation, to be paid in skins at a certain
price agreed betwixt them. The goods for the Indian trade consist
chiefly in guns, powder, shot, hatchets (which the Indians call tomahawks,) kettles, red and blue planes, Duffields, Stroudwater blankets,
and some cutlery wares, brass rings and other trinkets. These wares
are made up into packs and carried upon horses, each load being from
one hundred and fifty to two hundred pounds, with which they are
able to travel about twenty miles a day, if forage happen to be plentiful. Formerly a hundred horses have been employed in one of these

Indian caravans, under the conduct of fifteen or sixteen persons only, but now the trade is much impaired, insomuch that they seldom go with half that number.

The course from Roanoke to the Catawbas is laid down nearest southwest, and lies through a fine country that is watered by several beautiful rivers. Those of the greatest note are, first, Tar river, which is the upper part of Pamptico, Flat River, Little River and Eno River, all three branches of Neuse. Between Eno and Saxapahaw rivers are the Haw old fields, which have the reputation of containing the most fertile high land in this part of the world, lying in a body of about fifty thousand acres. This Saxapahaw is the upper part of Cape Fair River, the falls of which lie many miles below the Trading Path. Some mountains overlook this rich spot of land, from whence all the soil washes down into the plain, and is the cause of its exceeding fertility. Not far from thence the path crosses Aramanchy River, a branch of Saxapahaw, and about forty miles beyond that, Deep River, which is the north branch of Peedee. Then forty miles beyond that, the path intersects the Yadkin, which is there half a mile over, and is supposed to be the south branch of the same Peedee. The soil is exceedingly rich on both sides the Yadkin, abounding in rank grass and prodigiously large trees; and for plenty of fish, fowl and venison, is inferior to no part of the northern continent. There the traders commonly lie still for some days, to recruit their horses' flesh as well as to recover their own spirits.

Six miles further is Crane Creek, so named from its being the rendezvous of great armies of cranes, which wage a more cruel war at this day with the frogs and the fish than they used to do with the pigmies in the days of Homer. About three-score miles more bring you to the first town of the Catawbas, called Nauvasa, situated on the banks of Santee River. Besides this town there are five others belonging to the same nation, lying all on the same stream, within the distance of twenty miles. These Indians were all called formerly by the general name of the Usherees, and were a very numerous and powerful people. But the frequent slaughters made upon them by the northern Indians, and, what has been still more destructive by far, the intemperance and foul distempers introduced amongst them by the Carolina traders, have now reduced their numbers to a little more than four hundred fighting men, besides women and children. It is a charming place where they live, the air very wholesome, the soil fertile, and the winters ever mild and serene.

In Santee River, as in several others of Carolina, a small kind of alligator is frequently seen, which perfumes the water with a musky smell. They seldom exceed eight feet in length in these parts, whereas, near the equinoctial, they come up to twelve or fourteen. And the heat of the climate don't only make them bigger, but more fierce and voracious. They watch the cattle there when they come to drink and cool themselves in the river; and because they are not able to drag them into the deep water, they make up by stratagem what they want in force. They swallow great stones, the weight of which, being added to their strength, enables them to tug a moderate cow under water, and as soon as they have drowned her, they discharge the stones out of their maw and then feast upon the carcass.

However, as fierce and as strong as these monsters are, the Indians will surprise them napping as they float upon the surface, get astride upon their necks, then whip a short piece of wood like a truncheon into their jaws, and holding the ends with their two hands, hinder them from diving by keeping their mouths open, and when they are almost spent, they will make to the shore, where their riders knock them on the head and eat them. This amphibious animal is a smaller kind of crocodile, having the same shape exactly, only the crocodile of the Nile is twice as long, being when full grown from twenty to thirty feet. This enormous length is the more to be wondered at, because the crocodile is hatched from an egg very little larger than that of a goose. It has a long head, which it can open very wide, with very sharp and strong teeth. Their eyes are small, their legs short, with claws upon their feet. Their tail makes half the length of their body, and the whole is guarded with hard, impenetrable scales, except the belly, which is much softer and smoother. They keep much upon the land in the day time, but towards the evening retire into the water to avoid the cold dews of the night. They run pretty fast right forward, but are very awkward and slow in turning, by reason of their unwieldy length. It is an error that they have no tongue, without which they could hardly swallow their food; but in eating they move the upper jaw only, contrary to all other animals. The way of catching them in Egypt is with a strong hook fixed to the end of a chain and baited with a joint of pork, which they are very fond of. But a live hog is generally tied near, the cry of which allures them to the hook. This account of the crocodile will agree in most particulars with the alligator, only the bigness of the last cannot entitle it to the name of 'leviathan,' which Job gave formerly to the crocodile, and not to the whale, as some interpreters would make us believe.

So soon as the Catawba Indians are informed of the approach of the Virginia caravans, they send a detachment of their warriors to bid them welcome, and escort them safe to their town, where they are received with great marks of distinction. And their courtesies to the Virginia traders, I dare say, are very sincere, because they sell them better goods and better pennyworths than the traders of Carolina. They commonly reside among the Indians till they have bartered their goods away for skins, with which they load their horses and come back by the same path they went. There are generally some Carolina traders that constantly live among the Catawbas, and pretend to exercise a dictatorial authority over them. These petty rulers don't only teach the honester savages all sorts of debauchery, but are unfair in their dealings, and use them with all kinds of oppression. Nor has their behavior been at all better to the rest of the Indian nations among whom they reside, by abusing their women and evil-entreating their men; and by the way, this was the true reason of the fatal war which the nations roundabout made upon Carolina in the year 1713. Then it was that all the neighboring Indians, grown weary of the tyranny and injustice with which they had been abused for many years, resolved to endure their bondage no longer, but entered into general confederacy against their oppressors of Carolina. The Indians opened the war by knocking most of those little tyrants on the head that dwelt amongst them under pretense of regulating their commerce, and from thence carried their resentment so far as to endanger both North and South Carolina.

16. We gave orders that the horses should pass Roanoke River at Monisep Ford, while most of the baggage was transported in a canoe. We landed at the plantation of Cornelius Keith, where I beheld the wretchedest scene of poverty I had ever met with in this happy part of the world. The man, his wife and six small children, lived in a pen,

like so many cattle, without any roof over their heads but that of heaven. And this was their airy residence in the day time, but then there was a fodder stack not far from this inclosure, in which the whole family sheltered themselves anights and in bad weather. However, 'twas almost worth while to be as poor as this man was, to be as perfectly contented. All his wants proceeded from indolence, and not from misfortune. He had good land, as well as good health and good limbs to work it, and, besides, had a trade very useful to all the inhabitants round about. He could make and set up quern stones very well, and had proper materials for that purpose just at hand, if he could have taken the pains to fetch them. There is no other kind of mills in those remote parts, and therefore if the man would have worked at his trade he might have lived very comfortably. The poor woman had a little more industry, and spun cotton enough to make a thin covering for her own and her children's nakedness.

I am sorry to say it, but idleness is the general character of the men in the southern part of this colony as well as in North Carolina. The air is so mild, and the soil so fruitful, that very little labor is required to fill their bellies, especially where the woods afford such plenty of game. These advantages discharge the men from the necessity of killing themselves with work, and then for the other article of raiment, a very little of that will suffice in so temperate a climate. But so much as is absolutely necessary falls to the good women's share to provide. They all spin, weave and knit, whereby they make a good shift to clothe the whole family; and to their credit be it recorded, many of them do it very completely, and thereby reproach their husbands' laziness in the most inoffensive way, that is to say, by discovering a better spirit of industry in themselves.

From hence we moved forward to Colonel Mumford's other plantation, under the care of Miles Riley, where, by that gentleman's directions, we were again supplied with many good things. Here it was we discharged our worthy friend and fellow traveler, Mr. Bearskin, who had so plentifully supplied us with provisions during our long expedition. We rewarded him to his heart's content, so that he returned to his town loaden with riches and the reputation of having been a great discoverer.

17. This being Sunday, we were seasonably put in mind how much

we were obliged to be thankful for our happy return to the inhabitants. Indeed, we had great reason to reflect with gratitude on the signal mercies we had received. First, that we had, day by day, been fed by the bountiful hand of Providence in the desolate wilderness, insomuch that if any of our people wanted one single meal during the whole expedition, it was entirely owing to their own imprudent management. Secondly, that not one man of our whole company had any violent distemper or bad accident befall him, from one end of the line to the other. The very worst that happened was, that one of them gave himself a smart cut on the pan of his knee with a tomahawk, which we had the good fortune to cure in a short time, without the help of a surgeon. As for the misadventures of sticking in the mire and falling into rivers and creeks, they were rather subjects of mirth than complaint, and served only to diversify our travels with a little farcical variety. And, lastly, that many uncommon incidents have concurred to prosper our undertaking.

We had not only a dry spring before we went out, but the preceding winter, and even a year or two before, had been much drier than ordinary. This made not only the Dismal, but likewise most of the sunken grounds near the seaside, just hard enough to bear us, which otherwise had been quite impassable. And the whole time we were upon the business, which was in all about sixteen weeks, we were never catched in the rain except once, nor was our progress interrupted by bad weather above three or four days at most. Besides all this, we were surprised by no Indian enemy, but all of us brought our scalps back safe upon our heads. This cruel method of scalping of enemies is practiced by all the savages in America, and perhaps is not the least proof of their original from the northern inhabitants of Asia. Among the ancient Scythians it was constantly used, who carried about these hairy scalps as trophies of victory. They served them, too, as towels at home and trappings for their horses abroad. But these were not content with the skin of their enemies' heads, but also made use of their skulls for cups to drink out of upon high festival days, and made greater ostentation of them than if they had been made of gold or the purest crystal.

Besides the duties of the day, we christened one of our men who had been bred a Quaker. The man desired this of his own mere motion, without being tampered with by the parson, who was willing every one should go to Heaven his own way. But whether he did it by the conviction of his own reason, or to get rid of some troublesome forms and restraints, to which the saints of that persuasion are subject, I can't positively say.

18. We proceeded over a level road twelve miles, as far as George Hix's plantation, on the south side Meherrin River, our course being for the most part northeast. By the way we hired a cart to transport our baggage, that we might the better befriend our jaded horses. Within two miles of our journey's end this day, we met the express we had sent the Saturday before to give notice of our arrival. He had been almost as expeditious as a carrier pigeon, riding in two days no less than two hundred miles.

All the grandees of the Sapony nation did us the honor to repair hither to meet us, and our worthy friend and fellow traveler, Bearskin, appeared among the gravest of them in his robes of ceremony. Four young ladies of the first quality came with them, who had more the air of cleanliness than any copper-colored beauties I had ever seen; yet we resisted all their charms, notwithstanding the long fast we had kept from the sex, and the bear diet we had been so long engaged in. Nor can I say the price they set upon their charms was at all exorbitant. A princess for a pair of red stockings can't, surely, be thought buying repentance much too dear.

The men had something great and venerable in their countenances, beyond the common mien of savages; and indeed they ever had the reputation of being the honestest, as well as the bravest Indians we have ever been acquainted with. This people is now made up of the remnants of several other nations, of which the most considerable are the Sapony, the Occaneches, and Steukenhocks, who not finding themselves separately numerous enough for their defense, have agreed to unite into one body, and all of them now go under the name of the Sapony. Each of these was formerly a distinct nation, or rather a several clan or canton of the same nation, speaking the same language, and using the same customs. But their perpetual wars against all other Indians in time reduced them so low as to make it necessary to join forces together.

They dwelt formerly not far below the mountains, upon Yadkin

River, about two hundred miles west and by south from the falls of Roanoke. But about twenty-five years ago they took refuge in Virginia, being no longer in condition to make head not only against the northern Indians, who are their implacable enemies, but also against most of those to the south. All the nations round about, bearing in mind the havoc these Indians used formerly to make among their ancestors in the insolence of their power, did at length avenge it home upon them, and made them glad to apply to this government for protection. Colonel Spotswood, our then lieutenant governor, having a good opinion of their fidelity and courage, settled them at Christanna, ten miles north of Roanoke, upon the belief that they would be a good barrier on that side of the country against the incursion of all foreign Indians. And in earnest they would have served well enough for that purpose, if the white people in the neighborhood had not debauched their morals and ruined their health with rum, which was the cause of many disorders and ended at last in a barbarous murder committed by one of these Indians when he was drunk, for which the poor wretch was executed when he was sober. It was matter of great concern to them, however, that one of their grandees should be put to so ignominious a death. All Indians have as great an aversion to hanging as the Muscovites, though perhaps not for the same cleanly reason: these last believing that the soul of one that dies in this manner, being forced to sally out of the body at the postern, must needs be defiled. The Sapony took this execution so much to heart, that they soon after quitted their settlement and removed in a body to the Catawbas. The daughter of the Tetero king went away with the Sapony, but being the last of her nation, and fearing she should not be treated according to her rank, poisoned herself, like an old Roman, with the root of the trumpet plant. Her father died two years before, who was the most intrepid Indian we have been acquainted with. He had made himself terrible to all other Indians by his exploits, and had escaped so many dangers that he was esteemed invulnerable. But at last he died of a pleurisy, the last man of his race and nation, leaving only that unhappy daughter behind him, who would not long survive him.

The most uncommon circumstance in this Indian visit was that they all came on horseback, which was certainly intended for a piece of state, because the distance was but three miles, and 'tis likely they had walked afoot twice as far to catch their horses. The men rode more awkwardly than any Dutch sailor, and the ladies bestrode their palfreys a la mode de France, but were so bashful about it that there was no persuading them to mount till they were quite out of our sight. The French women used to ride a-straddle, not so much to make them sit firmer in the saddle, as from the hopes the same thing might peradventure befall them that once happened to the nun of Orleans, who, escaping out of a nunnery, took post en cavalier, and in ten miles' hard riding had the good fortune to have all the tokens of a man break out upon her. This piece of history ought to be the more credible, because it leans upon much the same degree of proof as the tale of Bishop Burnet's two Italian nuns, who, according to his lordship's account, underwent the same happy metamorphosis, probably by some other violent exercise.

19. From hence we despatched the cart with our baggage under a guard, and crossed Meherrin River, which was not thirty yards wide in that place. By the help of fresh horses that had been sent us, we now began to mend our pace, which was also quickened by the strong inclinations we had to get home. In the distance of five miles we forded Meherrin Creek, which was very near as broad as the river. About eight miles farther we came to Sturgeon Creek, so called from the dexterity an Occaneche Indian showed there in catching one of those royal fish, which was performed after the following manner. In the summer time 'tis no unusual thing for sturgeons to sleep on the surface of the water, and one of them having wandered up into this creek in the spring, was floating in that drowsy condition. The Indian above mentioned ran up to the neck into the creek a little below the place where he discovered the fish, expecting the stream would soon bring his game down to him. He judged the matter right, and as soon as it came within his reach, he whipped a running noose over his jowl. This waked the sturgeon, which being strong in its own element darted immediately under water and dragged the Indian after him. The man made it a point of honor to keep his hold, which he did to the apparent danger of being drowned. Sometimes both the Indian and the fish disappeared for a quarter of a minute, and then rose at some distance from where they dived. At this rate they continued flouncing about, sometimes above and sometimes under water, for a

considerable time, till at last the hero suffocated his adversary and haled his body ashore in triumph.

About six miles beyond that, we passed over Wicco-quoi Creek, named so from the multitude of rocks over which the water tumbles in a fresh, with a bellowing noise. Not far from where we went over is a rock much higher than the rest, that strikes the eye with agreeable horror, and near it a very talkative echo, that, like a fluent helpmeet, will return her good man seven words for one, and after all be sure to have the last. It speaks not only the language of men, but also of birds and beasts, and often a single wild goose is cheated into the belief that some of his company are not far off, by hearing his own cry multiplied; and 'tis pleasant to see in what a flutter the poor bird is, when he finds himself disappointed. On the banks of this creek are very broad low grounds in many places, and abundance of good high land, though a little subject to floods.

We had but two miles more to Captain Embry's, where we found the housekeeping much better than the house. Our bountiful land-lady had set her oven and all her spits, pots, gridirons and saucepans to work, to diversify our entertainment, though after all it proved but a Mohammedan feast, there being nothing to drink but water. The worst of it was, we had unluckily outrid the baggage, and for that reason were obliged to lodge very sociably in the same apartment with the family, where, reckoning women and children, we mustered in all no less than nine persons, who all pigged lovingly together.

20. In the morning Colonel Bolling, who had been surveying in the neighborhood, and Mr. Walker, who dwelt not far off, came to visit us; and the last of these worthy gentlemen, fearing that our drinking so much water might incline us to pleurisies, brought us a kind supply both of wine and cider. It was noon before we could disengage ourselves from the courtesies of this place, and then the two gentlemen above mentioned were so good as to accompany us that day's journey, though they could by no means approve of our Lithuanian fashion of dismounting now and then in order to walk part of the way on foot.

We crossed Nottoway River not far from our landlord's house, where it seemed to be about twenty-five yards over. This river divides the county of Prince George from that of Brunswick. We had not gone eight miles farther before our eyes were blessed with the sight of Sapony chapel, which was the first house of prayer we had seen for more than two calendar months. About three miles beyond that, we passed over Stony Creek, where one of those that guarded the baggage killed a polecat, upon which he made a comfortable repast. Those of his company were so squeamish they could not be persuaded at first to taste, as they said, of so unsavory an animal; but seeing the man smack his lips with more pleasure than usual, they ventured at last to be of his mess, and instead of finding the flesh rank and high-tasted, they owned it to be the sweetest morsel they had ever eat in their lives. The ill savor of this little beast lies altogether in its urine, which nature has made so detestably ill-scented on purpose to furnish a helpless creature with something to defend itself. For as some brutes have horns and hoofs, and others are armed with claws, teeth and tusks for their defense; and as some spit a sort of poison at their adversaries, like the paco; and others dart quills at their pursuers, like the porcupine; and as some have no weapons to help themselves but their tongue, and others none but their tails; so the poor polecat's safety lies altogether in the irresistible stench of its water; insomuch that when it finds itself in danger from an enemy, it moistens its bushy tail plentifully with this liquid ammunition, and then, with great fury, sprinkles it like a shower of rain full into the eyes of its assailant, by which it gains time to make its escape. Nor is the polecat the only animal that defends itself by a stink. At the cape of Good Hope is a little beast called a stinker, as big as a fox and shaped like a ferret, which being pursued has no way to save himself but by farting and squittering, and then such a stench ensues that none of its pursuers can possibly stand it.

At the end of thirty good miles, we arrived in the evening at Colonel Bolling's, where first, from a primitive course of life, we began to relapse into luxury. This gentleman lives within hearing of the falls of Appomattox River, which are very noisy whenever a flood happens to roll a greater stream than ordinary over the rocks. The river is navigable for small craft as high as the falls, and at some distance from thence fetches a compass, and runs nearly parallel with James River almost as high as the mountains. While the commissioners fared sumptuously here, the poor chaplain and two surveyors, stopped ten miles short at a poor planter's house, in pity to their horses, made a St. Anthony's meal, that is, they supped upon the pickings of what stuck in their teeth ever since breakfast. But to make them amends, the good man laid them in his own bed, where they all three nestled together in one cotton sheet and one of brown ozna-burgs, made still something browner by two months' copious perspiration.

21. But those worthy gentlemen were so alert in the morning after their light supper, that they came up with us before breakfast, and honestly paid their stomachs all they owed them.

We made no more than a Sabbath day's journey from this to the next hospitable house, namely, that of our great benefactor, Colonel Mumford. We had already been much befriended by this gentleman, who, besides sending orders to his overseers at Roanoke to let us want for nothing, had, in the beginning of our business, been so kind as to recommend most of the men to us who were the faithful partners of our fatigue. Although in most other achievements those who com-mand are apt to take all the honor to themselves of what perhaps was more owing to the vigor of those who were under them, yet I must be more just, and allow these brave fellows their full share of credit for the service we performed, and must declare, that it was in a great measure owing to their spirit and indefatigable industry that we over-came many obstacles in the course of our line, which till then had been esteemed insurmountable. Nor must I at the same time omit to do justice to the surveyors, and particularly to Mr. Mayo, who, be-sides an eminent degree of skill, encountered the same hardships and underwent the same fatigue that the forwardest of the men did, and that with as much cheerfulness as if pain had been his pleasure, and difficulty his real diversion. Here we discharged the few men we had left, who were all as ragged as the Gibeonite ambassadors, though, at the same time, their rags were very honorable by the service they had so vigorously performed in making them so.

22. A little before noon we all took leave and dispersed to our several habitations, where we were so happy as to find all our families well. This crowned all our other blessings, and made our journey as prosperous as it had been painful. Thus ended our second expedition, in which we extended the line within the shadow of the Cherokee

HISTORY OF THE DIVIDING LINE

Mountains, where we were obliged to set up our pillars, like Hercules, and return home. We had now, upon the whole, been out sixteen weeks, including going and returning, and had traveled at least six hundred miles, and no small part of that distance on foot. Below, towards the seaside, our course lay through marshes, swamps, and great waters; and above, over steep hills, craggy rocks, and thickets, hardly penetrable. Notwithstanding this variety of hardships, we may say, without vanity, that we faithfully obeyed the King's orders, and performed the business effectually in which we had the honor to be employed.

Nor can we by any means reproach ourselves of having put the Crown to any exorbitant expense in this difficult affair, the whole charge, from beginning to end, amounting to no more than one thousand pounds. But let no one concerned in this painful expedition complain of the scantiness of his pay, so long as His Majesty has been graciously pleased to add to our reward the honor of his royal approbation, and to declare, notwithstanding the desertion of the Carolina commissioners, that the line by us run shall hereafter stand as the true boundary betwixt the governments of Virginia and North Carolina.

.   .   .

[The names of the members of the expedition and the statement of expenses are omitted.]

A JOURNEY TO THE LAND OF EDEN

In the Year 1733

[BYRD set out from Westover on September 15, 1733, with two servants and four horses to visit his lands on the borders of North Carolina. He was joined by Major William Mayo, one of the surveyors on the expedition to survey the dividing line, Peter Jones, another member of the former expedition, John Banister, Major Mumford, and several others who made up the party. He traveled by easy stages, observing conditions at other plantations that he had acquired. On September 19 he went over lands that he owned near the falls of the James River, described the terrain, and wrote that he had laid out the cities of Richmond and Petersburg:

The land seems good enough for corn along the river, but a quarter of a mile back it is broken and full of stones. After satisfying my curiosity, I returned the way I came and shot the same strait back again and paddled down the river to the company. When we got home, we laid the foundation of two large cities: one at Shacco's to be called Richmond, and the other at the point of Appomattox River to be called Petersburg. These Major Mayo offered to lay into lots without fee or reward. The truth of it is, these two places being the uppermost landing of James and Appomattox rivers are naturally intended for marts where the traffic of the outer inhabitants must center. Thus we did not build castles only but also cities in the air.

By September 25 the party reached the Dan River and crossed. Byrd had injured his knee but not seriously enough to hinder his traveling.]

25. The weather now befriending us, we despatched our little affairs in good time, and marched in a body to the line. It was already grown very dim, by reason many of the marked trees were burnt or blown down. However, we made shift, after riding little more than half a mile, to find it, and having once found it, stuck as close to it as we could. After a march of two miles, we got upon Cane Creek, where we saw the same havoc amongst the old canes that we had observed in other places, and a whole forest of young ones springing up in their stead. We pursued our journey over hills and dales till we arrived at the second ford of the Dan, which we passed with no other damage than sopping a little of our bread, and shipping some water at the tops of our boots. The late rains having been a little immoderate, had raised the water and made a current in the river.

We drove on four miles farther to a plentiful run of very clear water, and quartered on a rising ground a bow-shot from it. We had no sooner pitched the tents, but one of our woodsmen alarmed us with the news that he had followed the track of a great body of Indians to the place where they had lately encamped. That there he had found no less than ten huts, the poles whereof had green leaves still fresh upon them. That each of these huts had sheltered at least ten Indians, who, by some infallible marks, must have been northern Indians. That they must need have taken their departure from thence no longer ago than the day before, having erected those huts to protect themselves from the late heavy rains. These tidings I could perceive were a little shocking to some of the company, and particularly the little Major, whose tongue had never lain still, was taken speechless for sixteen hours. I put as good a countenance upon the matter as I could, assuring my fellow travelers, that the northern Indians were at peace with us, and although one or two of them may now and then commit a robbery or a murder (as other rogues do), yet nationally and avowedly they would not venture to hurt us. And in case they were Catawbas, the danger would be as little from them, because they are too fond of our trade to lose it for the pleasure of shedding a little English blood. But supposing the worst, that they might break through all the rules of self-interest and attack us, yet we ought to stand bravely on our defense, and sell our lives as dear as we could. That we should have no more fear on this occasion than just to make us more watchful and better provided to receive the enemy, if they had the spirit to venture upon us. This reasoning of mine, though it could not remove the panic, yet it abated something of the palpitation, and made us double our guard. However, I found it took off the edge of most of our appetites for everything but the rum bottle, which was more in favor than ever, because of its cordial quality. I hurt my other knee this afternoon, but not enough to spoil either my dancing or my stomach.

26. We liked the place so little that we were glad to leave it this morning as soon as we could. For that reason we were all on horseback before nine, and after riding four miles arrived at the mouth of Sable Creek. On the eastern bank of that creek, six paces from the mouth, and just at the brink of the river Dan, stands a sugar tree, which is the beginning of my fine tract of land in Carolina, called the Land of Eden. I caused the initial letters of my name to be cut on a large poplar and beech near my corner, for the more easy finding it another time. We then made a beginning of my survey, directing our course due south from the sugar tree above-mentioned. In a little way we perceived the creek forked, and the western branch was wide enough to merit the name of a river. That to the east was much less, which we intersected with this course. We ran southerly a mile, and found the land good all the way, only towards the end of it we saw the trees destroyed in such a manner that there were hardly any left to mark my bounds. Having finished this course, we encamped in a charming peninsula, formed by the western branch of the creek. It contained about forty acres of very rich land, gradually descending to the creek, and is a delightful situation for the manor house. My servant had fed so intemperately upon bear, that it gave him a scouring, and that was followed by the piles, which made riding worse to him than purgatory. But anointing with the fat of the same bear, he soon grew easy again.

27. We were stirring early from this enchanting place, and ran eight miles of my back line, which tended south eighty-four and a half westerly. We found the land uneven, but tolerably good, though

very thin of trees, and those that were standing fit for little but fuel and fence-rails. Some conflagration had effectually opened the country, and made room for the air to circulate. We crossed both the branches of Lowland Creek, and sundry other rills of fine water. From every eminence we discovered the mountains to the northwest of us, though they seemed to be a long way off. Here the air felt very refreshing and agreeable to the lungs, having no swamps or marshes to taint it. Nor was this the only good effect it had, but it likewise made us very hungry, so that we were forced to halt and pacify our appetites with a frugal repast out of our pockets, which we washed down with water from a purling stream just by. My knees pained me very much, though I broke not the laws of traveling by uttering the least complaint. Measuring and marking spent so much of our time that we could advance no further than eight miles, and the chain carriers thought that a great way.

In the evening we took up our quarters in the low-grounds of the river, which our scouts informed us was but two hundred yards ahead of us. This was no small surprise, because we had flattered ourselves that this back line would not have intersected the Dan at all; but we found ourselves mistaken, and plainly perceived that it ran more southerly than we imagined, and in all likelihood pierces the mountains where they form an amphitheater. The venison here was lean; and the misfortune was we met no bear in so open a country, to grease the way and make it slip down. In the night our sentinel alarmed us with an idle suspicion that he heard the Indian whistle (which amongst them is a signal for attacking their enemies). This made every one stand manfully to his arms in a moment, and I found nobody more undismayed in this surprise, than Mr. Bannister; but after we had put ourselves in battle array, we discovered this whistle to be nothing but the nocturnal note of a little harmless bird that inhabits those woods. We were glad to find the mistake, and commending the sentinel for his great vigilance, composed our noble spirits again to rest till the morning. However, some of the company dreamed of nothing but scalping all the rest of the night.

28. We snapped up our breakfast as fast as we could, that we might have the more leisure to pick our way over a very bad ford across the river. Though, bad as it was, we all got safe on the other side. We

were no sooner landed, but we found ourselves like to encounter a
very rough and almost impassable thicket. However, we scuffled
through it without any dismay or complaint. This was a copse of
young saplings, consisting of oak, hickory and sassafras, which are
the growth of a fertile soil. We gained no more than two miles in
three hours in this perplexed place, and after that had the pleasure to
issue out into opener woods. The land was generally good, though
pretty bare of timber, and particularly we traversed a rich level of
at least two miles. Our whole day's journey amounted not quite to
five miles, by reason we had been so hampered at our first setting out.
We were glad to take up our quarters early in a piece of fine low-
grounds, lying about a mile north of the river. Thus we perceived the
river edged away gently towards the south, and never likely to come
in the way of our course again. Nevertheless, the last time we saw it,
it kept much the same breadth and depth that it had where it divided
its waters from the Staunton, and in all likelihood holds its own quite
as high as the mountains.

29. In measuring a mile and a half farther we reached the lower
ford of the Irvin, which branches from the Dan about two miles to
the south southeast of this place. This river was very near threescore
yards over, and in many places pretty deep. From thence, in little
more than a mile, we came to the end of this course, being in length
fifteen miles and eighty-eight poles. And so far the land held reasonably good; but when we came to run our northern course of three
miles, to the place where the country line intersects the same Irvin
higher up, we passed over nothing but stony hills, and barren
grounds, clothed with little timber, and refreshed with less water.
All my hopes were in the riches that might lie underground, there
being many goodly tokens of mines. The stones which paved the
river, both by their weight and color, promised abundance of metal;
but whether it be silver, lead or copper, is beyond our skill to discern.
We also discovered many shows of marble, of a white ground, with
streaks of red and purple. So that 'tis possible the treasure in the
bowels of the earth may make ample amends for the poverty of its
surface.

We encamped on the bank of this river, a little below the dividing
line, and near the lower end of an island half a mile long, which, for

the metallic appearances, we dignified with the name of Potosi. In our way to this place we treed a bear, of so mighty a bulk that when we fetched her down she almost made an earthquake. But neither the shot nor the fall disabled her so much, but she had like to have hugged one of our dogs to death in the violence of her embrace. We exercised the discipline of the woods by tossing a very careless servant in a blanket, for losing one of our axes.

30. This being Sunday, we were glad to rest from our labors; and to help restore our vigor, several of us plunged into the river, notwithstanding it was a frosty morning. One of our Indians went in along with us, and taught us their way of swimming. They strike not out both hands together, but alternately one after another, whereby they are able to swim both farther and faster than we do. Near the camp grew several large chestnut trees very full of chestnuts. Our men were too lazy to climb the trees for the sake of the fruit, but, like the Indians, chose rather to cut them down, regardless of those that were to come after. Nor did they esteem such kind of work any breach of the sabbath, so long as it helped to fill their bellies. One of the Indians shot a bear, which he lugged about half a mile for the good of the company. These gentiles have no distinction of days, but make every day a sabbath, except when they go out to war or a hunting, and then they will undergo incredible fatigues. Of other work the men do none, thinking it below the dignity of their sex, but make the poor women do all the drudgery. They have a blind tradition amongst them, that work was first laid upon mankind by the fault of a female, and therefore 'tis but just that sex should do the greatest part of it. This they plead in their excuse; but the true reason is that the weakest must always go to the wall, and superiority has from the beginning ungenerously imposed slavery on those who are not able to resist it.

October 1. I plunged once more into the river Irvin this morning, for a small cold I had caught, and was entirely cured by it. We ran the three-mile course from a white oak standing on my corner upon the western bank of the river, and intersected the place, where we ended the back line exactly, and fixed that corner at a hickory. We steered south from thence about a mile, and then came upon the Dan, which thereabouts makes but narrow lowgrounds. We forded it

about a mile and a half to the westward of the place where the Irvin
runs into it. When we were over, we determined to ride down the
river on that side, and for three miles found the high-land come close
down to it, pretty barren and uneven. But then on a sudden the scene
changed and we were surprised with an opening of large extent,
where the Sauro Indians once lived, who had been a considerable
nation. But the frequent inroads of the Senecas annoyed them incessantly, and obliged them to remove from this fine situation about
thirty years ago. They then retired more southerly, as far as Pee Dee
River, and incorporated with the Kewawees, where a remnant of
them is still surviving. It must have been a great misfortune to them
to be obliged to abandon so beautiful a dwelling, where the air is
wholesome, and the soil equal in fertility to any in the world. The
river is about eighty yards wide, always confined within its lofty
banks, and rolling down its waters, as sweet as milk, and as clear as
crystal. There runs a charming level, of more than a mile square, that
will bring forth like the lands of Egypt, without being overflowed
once a year. There is scarce a shrub in view to intercept your
prospect, but grass as high as a man on horseback. Towards the
woods there is a gentle ascent, till your sight is intercepted by an
eminence that overlooks the whole landscape. This sweet place is
bounded to the east by a fine stream, called Sauro Creek, which running out of the Dan and tending westerly makes the whole a peninsula. I could not quit this pleasant situation without regret, but often
faced about to take a parting look at it as far as I could see, and so indeed did all the rest of the company. But at last we left it quite out of
sight, and continued our course down the river, till where it intersects my back line, which was about five miles below Sauro Town.
We took up our quarters at the same camp where we had a little
before been alarmed with the supposed Indian whistle, which we
could hardly get out of our heads. However, it did not spoil our rest;
but we dreamed all night of the delights of Tempe and the Elysian
Fields.

2. We awaked early from these innocent dreams, and took our
way along my back line till we came to the corner of it. From thence
we slanted to the country line, and kept down as far as the next ford-
ing place to the river, making in the whole eighteen miles. We breathed

all the way in pure air, which seemed friendly of the lungs and circulated the blood and spirits very briskly. Happy will be the people destined for so wholesome a situation, where they may live to fullness of days, and which is much better still, with much content and gaiety of heart. On every rising ground we faced about to take our leave of the mountains, which still showed their towering heads. The ground was uneven, rising into hills, and sinking into valleys great part of the way, but the soil was good, abounding in most places with a greasy black mold.

We took up our quarters on the western bank of the river, where we had forded it at our coming up. One of our men, Joseph Colson by name, a timorous, lazy fellow, had squandered away his bread, and grew very uneasy when his own ravening had reduced him to short allowance. He was one of those drones who love to do little and eat much, and are never in humor unless their bellies are full. According to this wrong turn of constitution, when he found he could no longer revel in plenty, he began to break the rules by complaining and threatening to desert. This had like to have brought him to the blanket, but his submission reprieved him. Though bread grew a little scanty with us, we had venison in abundance, which a true woodsman can eat contentedly without any bread at all. But bear's flesh needs something of the farinaceous to make it pass easily off the stomach.

In the night we heard a dog bark at some distance, as we thought, when we saw all our own dogs lying about the fire. This was another alarm; but we soon discovered it to be a wolf, which will sometimes bark very like a dog, but something shriller.

3. The fine season continuing, we made the most of it by leaving our quarters as soon as possible. We began to measure and mark the bounds of Major Mayo's land on the south of the country line. In order to do this we marched round the bent of the river, but he being obliged to make a traverse, we could reach no farther than four miles. In the distance of about a mile from where we lay, we crossed Cliff Creek, which confined its stream within such high banks that it was difficult to find a passage over. We kept close to the river, and two miles farther came to Hix's Creek, where abundance of canes lay dry and prostrate on the ground, having suffered in the late septennial

slaughter of that vegetable. A mile after that we forded another stream, which we call Hatcher's Creek, from two Indian traders of that name, who used formerly to carry goods to the Sauro Indians. Near the banks of this creek I found a large beech tree, with the following inscription cut upon the bark of it, 'J. H., H. H., B. B., lay here the 24th of May, 1673.' It was not difficult to fill up these initials with the following names, Joseph Hatcher, Henry Hatcher and Benjamin Bullington, three Indian traders, [who] had lodged near that place sixty years before, in their way to the Sauro town. But the strangest part of the story was this, that these letters cut in the bark should remain perfectly legible so long. Nay, if no accident befalls the tree, which appears to be still in a flourishing condition, I doubt not but this piece of antiquity may be read many years hence. We may also learn from it that the beech is a very long-lived tree, of which there are many exceedingly large in these woods. The Major took in a pretty deal of rich low-ground into his survey, but unhappily left a greater quantity out, which proves the weakness of making entries by guess. We found the Dan fordable hereabouts in most places. One of the Indians shot a wild goose, that was very lousy, which nevertheless was good meat, and proved those contemptible tasters to be no bad tasters. However, for those stomachs that were so unhappy as to be squeamish, there was plenty of fat bear, we having killed two in this day's march.

4. I caused the men to use double diligence to assist Major Mayo in fixing the bounds of his land, because he had taken a great deal of pains about mine. We therefore mounted our horses as soon as we had swallowed our breakfast. Till that is duly performed a woodsman makes a conscience of exposing himself to any fatigue. We proceeded then in his survey, and made an end before night, though most of the company were of opinion the land was hardly worth the trouble. It seemed most of it before below the character the discoverers had given him of it. We fixed his eastern corner on Cocquade Creek, and then continued our march, over the hills and far away along the country line two miles farther. Nor had we stopped there, unless a likelihood of rain had obliged us to encamp on an eminence where we were in no danger of being overflowed. Peter Jones had a smart fit of an ague, which shook him severely, though he bore it like

a man; but the small Major had a small fever and bore it like a child. He groaned as if he had been in labor, and thought verily it would be his fate to die like a mutinous Israelite in the wilderness, and be buried under a heap of stones. The rain was so kind as to give us leisure to secure ourselves against it, but came however time enough to interrupt our cookery, so that we supped as temperately as so many philosophers, and kept ourselves snug within our tents. The worst part of the story was that the sentinels could hardly keep our fires from being extinguished by the heaviness of the shower.

5. Our invalids found themselves in traveling condition this morning, and began to conceive hopes of returning home and dying in their own beds. We pursued our journey through uneven and perplexed woods, and in the thickest of them had the fortune to knock down a young buffalo, two years old. Providence threw this vast animal in our way very seasonably, just as our provisions began to fail us. And it was the more welcome too because it was change of diet, which of all varieties, next to that of bedfellows, is the most agreeable. We had lived upon venison and bear 'til our stomachs loathed them almost as much as the Hebrews of old did their quails. Our butchers were so unhandy at their business that we grew very lank before we could get our dinner. But when it came, we found it equal in goodness to the best beef. They made it the longer because they kept sucking the water out of the guts, in imitation of the Catawba Indians, upon the belief that it is a great cordial, and will even make them drunk, or at least very gay.

We encamped upon Hico River, pretty high up, and had much ado to get our house in order before a heavy shower descended upon us. I was in pain lest our sick men might suffer by the rain, but might have spared myself the concern, because it had the effect of a cold bath upon them and drove away their distemper, or rather changed it into a canine appetite that devoured all before it. It rained smartly all night long, which made our situation on the low-ground more fit for otters than men.

6. We had abundance of drying work this morning after the clouds broke away and showed the sun to the happy earth. It was impossible for us to strike the tents till the afternoon, and then we took our departure and made an easy march of four miles to another

branch of Hico River, which we called Jesuit's Creek, because it misled us. We lugged as many of the dainty pieces of the buffalo along with us as our poor horses could carry, envying the wolves the pleasure of such luxurious diet. Our quarters were taken upon a delightful eminence that scornfully overlooked the creek and afforded us a dry habitation. We made our supper on the tongue and udder of the buffalo, which were so good that a Cardinal Legate might have made a comfortable meal upon them during the carnival. Nor was this all, but we had still a rarer morsel, the bunch rising up between the shoulders of this animal, which is very tender and very fat. The primings of a young doe, which one of the men brought to the camp, were slighted amidst these dainties, nor would even our servants be fobbed off with cates so common.

The low-grounds of this creek are wide in many places, and rich, but seem to lie within reach of every inundation; and this is commonly the case with most low-grounds that lie either on the rivers or on the creeks that run into them. So great an inconvenience lessens their value very much, and makes high-land that is just tolerable of greater advantage to the owner. There he will be more likely to reap the fruits of his industry every year, and not run the risk, after all his toil, to see the sweat of his brow carried down the stream, and perhaps many of his cattle drowned into the bargain. Perhaps in times to come people may bank their low-grounds as they do in Europe, to confine the water within its natural bounds to prevent these inconveniences.

7. The scarcity of bread, joined to the impatience of some of our company, laid us under a kind of necessity to hasten our return home. For that reason we thought we might be excused for making a sabbath day's journey of about five miles, as far as our old camp upon Sugar Tree Creek. On our way we forded Buffalo Creek, which also empties its waters into Hico River. The woods we rode through were open, and the soil very promising, great part thereof being low-grounds, full of tall and large trees. A she bear had the ill luck to cross our way, which was large enough to afford us several luxurious meals.

I paid for violating the sabbath by losing a pair of gold buttons. I pitched my tent on the very spot I had done when we ran the dividing line between Virginia and Carolina. The beech whose bark recorded the names of the Carolina Commissioners was still standing, and we did them the justice to add to their names a sketch of their characters.

We got our house in order time enough to walk about and make some slight observations. There were sugar trees innumerable growing in the low-grounds of this creek, from which it received its name. They were many of them as tall as large hickories, with trunks from fifteen to twenty inches through. The woodpeckers, for the pleasure of the sweet juice which these trees yield, pierce the bark in many places and do great damage, though the trees live a great while under all these wounds. There grows an infinite quantity of maidenhair, which seems to delight most in rich grounds. The sorrel tree is frequent there, whose leaves, brewed in beer, are good in dropsies, green-sickness, and cachexies. We also saw in this place abundance of papaw trees, the wood whereof the Indians make very dry on purpose to rub fire out of it. Their method of doing it is this: they hold one of these dry sticks in each hand, and by rubbing them hard and quick together, rarify the air in such a manner as to fetch fire in ten minutes. Whenever they offer any sacrifice to their God, they look upon it as a profanation to make use of fire already kindled, but produce fresh virgin fire for that purpose by rubbing two of these sticks together that never had been used before on any occasion.

8. After fortifying ourself with a bear breakfast, Major Mayo took what help he thought necessary, and began to survey the land with which the Commissioners of Carolina had presented him upon this creek. After running the bounds, the Major was a little disappointed in the goodness of the land, but as it had cost him nothing it could be no bad pennyworth, as his upper tract really was.

While that business was carrying on, I took my old friend and fellow traveler, Tom Wilson, and went to view the land I had entered for upon this creek, on the north of the country line. We rode down the stream about six miles, crossing it sundry times, and found very wide low grounds on both sides of it, only we observed, wherever the low-grounds were broad on one side the creek, they were narrow on the other. The highlands we were obliged to pass over were very good, and in some places descended so gradually to the edge of the low-grounds that they formed very agreeable prospects and pleasant situations for building.

About four miles from the line, Sugar Tree Creek emptied itself into the Hico, which with that addition swelled into a fine river. In this space we saw the most, and most promising good land we had met with in all our travels. In our way we shot a doe, but she not falling immediately, we had lost our game had not the ravens, by their croaking, conducted us to the thicket where she fell. We plunged the carcass of the deer into the water, to secure it from these ominous birds till we returned, but an hour afterwards were surprised with the sight of a wolf which had been fishing for it and devoured one side. We knocked down an ancient she bear that had no flesh upon her bones, so we left it to the freebooters of the forest. In coming back to the camp we discovered a solitary bull buffalo, which boldly stood his ground, contrary to the custom of that shy animal; we spared his life, from a principle of never slaughtering an innocent creature to no purpose. However, we made ourselves some diversion by trying if he would face our dogs. He was so far from retreating at their approach that he ran at them with great fierceness, cocking up his ridiculous little tail and grunting like a hog. The dogs in the meantime only played about him, not venturing within reach of his horns, and by their nimbleness came off with a whole skin.

All these adventures we related at our return to the camp, and what was more to the purpose, we carried to them the side of venison which the wolf had vouchsafed to leave us. After we had composed ourselves to rest, our horses ran up to our camp as fast as their hobbles would let them. This was to some of us a certain argument that Indians were near, whose scent the horses can no more endure than they can their figures; though it was more likely they had been scared by a panther or some other wild beast, the glaring of whose eyes are very terrifying to them in a dark night.

9. Major Mayo's survey being no more than half done, we were obliged to amuse ourselves another day in this place. And that the time might not be quite lost, we put our garments and baggage into good repair. I for my part never spent a day so well during the whole voyage. I had an impertinent tooth in my upper jaw that had been loose for some time, and made me chew with great caution. Particularly I could not grind a biscuit but with much deliberation and presence of mind. Tooth-drawers we had none amongst us, nor any

of the instruments they make use of. However, invention supplied this want very happily, and I contrived to get rid of this troublesome companion by cutting a caper. I caused a twine to be fastened round the root of my tooth, about a fathom in length, and then tied the other end to the snag of a log that lay upon the ground, in such a manner that I could just stand upright. Having adjusted my string in this manner, I bent my knees enough to enable me to spring vigorously off the ground, as perpendicularly as I could. The force of the leap drew out the tooth with so much ease that I felt nothing of it, nor should have believed it was come away, unless I had seen it dangling at the end of the string. An under tooth may be fetched out by standing off the ground and fastening your string at due distance above you. And having so fixed your gear, jump off your standing, and the weight of your body, added to the force of the spring, will prize out your tooth with less pain than any operator upon earth could draw it. This new way of tooth-drawing, being so silently and deliberately performed, both surprised and delighted all that were present, who could not guess what I was going about. I immediately found the benefit of getting rid of this troublesome companion by eating my supper with more comfort than I had done during the whole expedition.

10. In the morning we made an end of our bread and all the rest of our provision, so that now we began to travel pretty light. All the company were witnesses how good the land was upon Sugar Tree Creek, because we rode down it four miles till it fell into Hico River. Then we directed our course over the highland, thinking to shorten our way to Tom Wilson's quarter. Nevertheless, it was our fortune to fall upon the Hico again, and then kept within sight of it several miles together, till we came near the mouth. Its banks were high and full of precipices on the east side, but it afforded some low-grounds on the west. Within two miles of the mouth are good shows of copper mines, as Harry Morris told me, but we saw nothing of them. It runs into the Dan just below a large fall, but the chain of rocks don't reach quite cross the river, to intercept the navigation.

About a mile below lives Aaron Pinston, at a quarter belonging to Thomas Wilson, upon Tewahominy Creek. This man is the highest inhabitant on the south side of the Dan, and yet reckons himself perfectly safe from danger. And if the bears, wolves, and panthers were

as harmless as the Indians, his stock might be so too. Tom Wilson offered to knock down a steer for us, but I would by no means accept
of his generosity. However, we were glad of a few of his peas and
potatoes and some rashers of his bacon, upon which we made good
cheer. This plantation lies about a mile from the mouth of Tewahominy, and about the same distance from the mouth of Hico River, and
contains a good piece of land. The edifice was only a log house,
affording a very free passage for the air through every part of it, nor
was the cleanliness of it any temptation to lie out of our tents, so we
encamped once more, for the last time, in the open field.

11. I tipped our landlady with what I imagined a full reward for
the trouble we had given her, and then mounted our horses, which
pricked up their ears after the two meals they had eaten of corn. In
the distance of about a mile we reached the Dan, which we forded
with some difficulty into the fork. The water was pretty high in the
river, and the current something rapid, nevertheless all the company
got over safe with only a little water in their boots. After traversing
the fork, which was there at least two good miles across, we forded
the Staunton into a little island, and then the narrow branch of the
same to the mainland.

We took Major Mumford's tenant in our way, where we moistened our throats with a little milk, and then proceeded in good order to Blue Stone Castle. My landlady received us with a grim sort of
a welcome, which I did not expect, since I brought her husband back
in good health, though perhaps that might be the reason. 'Tis sure
something or other did tease her, and she was a female of too strong
passions to know how to dissemble. However, she was so civil as to
get us a good dinner, which I was the better pleased with because Col.
Cock and Mr. Mumford came time enough to partake of it. The Colonel had been surveying land in these parts, and particularly that on
which Mr. Stith's copper mine lies, as likewise a tract on which Cornelius Cargill has fine appearances. He had but a poor opinion of Mr.
Stith's mine, foretelling it would be all labor in vain, but thought
something better of Mr. Cargill's. After dinner these gentlemen took
their leaves, and at the same time I discharged two of my fellow
travelers, Thomas Wilson and Joseph Colson, after having made
their hearts merry, and giving each of them a piece of gold to rub

their eyes with. We now returned to that evil custom of lying in a house, and an evil one it is when ten or a dozen people are forced to pig together in a room, as we did, and were troubled with the squalling of peevish, dirty children into the bargain.

12. We ate our fill of potatoes and milk, which seems delicious fare to those who have made a campaign in the woods. I then took my first minister, Harry Morris, up the hill, and marked out the place where Blue Stone Castle was to stand and overlook the adjacent country. After that I put my friend in mind of many things he had done amiss, which he promised faithfully to reform. I was so much an infidel to his fair speeches (having been many times deceived by them), that I was forced to threaten him with my highest displeasure unless he mended his conduct very much. I also let him know that he was not only to correct his own errors, but likewise those of his wife, since the power certainly belonged to him in virtue of his conjugal authority. He scratched his head at this last admonition, from whence I inferred that the gray mare was the better horse.

We gave our heavy baggage two hours' start and about noon followed them, and in twelve miles reached John Butcher's, calling by the way for Master Mumford in order to take him along with us. Mr. Butcher received us kindly and we had a true Roanoke entertainment of pork upon pork, and pork again upon that. He told us he had been one of the first seated in that remote part of the country, and in the beginning had been forced, like the great Nebuchadnezzar, to live a considerable time upon grass. This honest man set a mighty value on the mine he fancied he had in his pasture, and showed us some of the ore, which he was made to believe was a gray copper and would certainly make his fortune. But there is a bad distemper rages in those parts, that grows very epidemical. The people are all mine mad, and neglecting to make corn, starve their families in hopes to live in great plenty hereafter. Mr. Stith was the first that was seized with the frenzy, and has spread the contagion far and near. As you ride along the woods, you see all the large stones knocked to pieces, nor can a poor marcasite rest quietly in its bed for these curious inquirers. Our conversation ran altogether upon this darling subject 'til the hour came for our lying in bulk together.

13. After breaking our fast with a sea of milk and potatoes, we

took our leave, and I crossed my landlady's hand with a piece of money. She refused the offer at first, but, like a true woman, accepted of it when it was put home to her. She told me the utmost she was able to do for me was a trifle in comparison of some favor I had formerly done her; but what that favor was, neither I could recollect, nor did she think proper to explain. Though it threatened rain, we proceeded on our journey and jogged on in the new road for twenty miles, that is as far as it was cleared at that time, and found it would soon come to be a very good one after it was well grubbed.

. . .

[The narrative concludes with a brief account of the journey home; a list of the eleven white men, three Indians, three Negroes, twenty horses, and four dogs that made up the party; a plat of Byrd's 'twenty thousand acres in North Carolina'; and a table of mileages between the points travelled.]

. . .

A PROGRESS TO THE MINES

In the Year 1732

SEPTEMBER 18. For the pleasure of the good company of Mrs. Byrd, and her little governor, my son, I went about half way to the falls in the chariot. There we halted, not far from a purling stream, and upon the stump of a propagate oak picked the bones of a piece of roast beef. By the spirit which that gave me, I was the better able to part with the dear companions of my travels and to perform the rest of my journey on horseback by myself.

I reached Shacco's before two o'clock and crossed the river to the mills. I had the grief to find them both stand as still for the want of water as a dead woman's tongue for want of breath. It had rained so little for many weeks above the falls, that the Naiads had hardly water enough left to wash their faces. However, as we ought to turn all our misfortunes to the best advantage, I directed Mr. Booker, my first minister there, to make use of the lowness of the water for blowing up the rocks at the mouth of the canal. For that purpose I ordered iron drills to be made about two foot long, pointed with steel, chisel fashion, in order to make holes, into which we put our cartridges of powder, containing each about three ounces. There wanted skill among my engineers to choose the best parts of the stone for boring that we might blow to the most advantage. They made all their holes quite perpendicular, whereas they should have humored the grain of the stone for the more effectual execution. I ordered the points of the drills to be made chisel way, rather than the diamond, that they might need to be seldomer repaired, though in stone the diamond points would make the most despatch. The water now flowed out of the river so slowly that the miller was obliged to pond it up in the canal by setting open the flood-gates at the mouth and shutting those close at the mill. By this contrivance, he was able at any time to grind two or three bushels, either for his choice customers, or for the use of my plantations.

Then I walked to the place where they broke the flax, which is wrought with much greater ease than the hemp, and is much better for spinning. From thence I paid a visit to the weaver, who needed a little of Minerva's inspiration to make the most of a piece of cloth. Then I looked in upon my Caledonian spinster, who was mended more in her looks than in her humor. However, she promised much, though at the same time intended to perform little. She is too high-spirited for Mr. Booker, who hates to have his sweet temper ruffled, and will rather suffer matters to go a little wrong sometimes than give his righteous spirit any uneasiness. He is very honest and would make an admirable overseer where servants will do as they are bid. But eye-servants, who want abundance of overlooking, are not so proper to be committed to his care. I found myself out of order, and for that reason retired early; yet with all this precaution had a gentle fever in the night, but towards morning nature set open all her gates and drove it out in a plentiful perspiration.

19. The worst of this fever was that it put me to the necessity of taking another ounce of bark. I moistened every dose with a little brandy and filled the glass up with water, which is the least nauseous way of taking this popish medicine, and besides hinders it from purging. After I had swallowed a few poached eggs, we rode down to the mouth of the canal, and from thence crossed over to the broad Rock Island in a canoe. Our errand was to view some iron ore, which we dug up in two places. That on the surface seemed very spongy and poor, which gave us no great encouragement to search deeper, nor did the quantity appear to be very great. However, for my greater satisfaction, I ordered a hand to dig there for some time this winter. We walked from one end of the island to the other, being about half

a mile in length, and found the soil very good, and too high for any flood, less than that of Deucalion, to do the least damage. There is a very wild prospect both upward and downward, the river being full of rocks, over which the stream tumbled with a murmur loud enough to drown the notes of a scolding wife. This island would make an agreeable hermitage for any good Christian who had a mind to retire from the world.

Mr. Booker told me how Dr. Ireton had cured him once of a looseness which had been upon him two whole years. He ordered him a dose of rhubarb, with directions to take twenty-five drops of laudanum so soon as he had had two physical stools. Then he rested one day, and the next he ordered him another dose of the same quantity of laudanum to be taken, also after the second stool. When this was done, he finished the cure by giving him twenty drops of laudanum every night for five nights running. The doctor insisted upon the necessity of stopping the operation of the rhubarb before it worked quite off, that what remained behind might strengthen the bowels. I was punctual in swallowing my bark, and that I might use exercise upon it, rode to Prince's Folly, and my Lord's islands, where I saw very fine corn.

In the meantime Vulcan came in order to make the drills for boring the rocks, and gave me his parole he would, by the grace of God, attend the works till they were finished, which he performed as lamely as if he had been to labor for a dead horse and not for ready money. I made a North Carolina dinner upon fresh pork, though we had a plate of green peas after it, by way of desert, for the safety of our noses. Then my first minister and I had some serious conversation about my affairs, and I find nothing disturbed his peaceable spirit so much as the misbehavior of the spinster above-mentioned. I told him I could not pity a man who had it always in his power to do himself and her justice, and would not. If she were a drunkard, a scold, a thief, or a slanderer, we had wholesome laws that would make her back smart for the diversion of her other members, and 'twas his fault he had not put those wholesome severities in execution. I retired in decent time to my own apartment, and slept very comfortably upon my bark, forgetting all the little crosses arising from overseers and Negroes.

20. I continued the bark, and then tossed down my poached eggs with as much ease as some good breeders slip children into the world. About nine I left the prudentest orders I could think of with my vizier and then crossed the river to Shacco's. I made a running visit to three of my quarters, where, besides finding all the people well, I had the pleasure to see better crops than usual both of corn and tobacco. I parted there with my intendant, and pursued my journey to Mr. Randolph's, at Tuckahoe, without meeting with any adventure by the way. Here I found Mrs. Fleming, who was packing up her baggage with design to follow her husband the next day, who was gone to a new settlement in Goochland. Both he and she have been about seven years persuading themselves to remove to that retired part of the country, though they had the two strong arguments of health and interest for so doing. The widow smiled graciously upon me and entertained me very handsomely. Here I learned all the tragical story of her daughter's humble marriage with her uncle's overseer. Besides the meanness of this mortal's aspect, the man has not one visible qualification, except impudence, to recommend him to a female's inclinations. But there is sometimes such a charm in that Hibernian endowment, that frail woman can't withstand it, though it stand alone without any other recommendation. Had she run away with a gentleman or a pretty fellow, there might have been some excuse for her, though he were of inferior fortune: but to stoop to a dirty plebeian, without any kind of merit, is the lowest prostitution. I found the family justly enraged at it; and though I had more good nature than to join in her condemnation, yet I could devise no excuse for so senseless a prank as this young gentlewoman had played. Here good drink was more scarce than good victuals, the family being reduced to the last bottle of wine, which was therefore husbanded very carefully. But the water was excellent. The heir of the family did not come home till late in the evening. He is a pretty young man, but had the misfortune to become his own master too soon. This puts young fellows upon wrong pursuits, before they have sense to judge rightly for themselves. Though at the same time they have a strange conceit of their own sufficiency when they grow near twenty years old, especially if they happen to have a small smattering of learning. 'Tis then they fancy themselves wiser than all their tutors and governors,

which makes them headstrong to all advice, and above all reproof
and admonition.

21. I was sorry in the morning to find myself stopped in my career
by bad weather brought upon us by a northeast wind. This drives a
world of raw unkindly vapors upon us from Newfoundland, laden
with blight, coughs, and pleurisies. However, I complained not, lest I
might be suspected to be tired of the good company. Though Mrs.
Fleming was not so much upon her guard, but mutinied strongly at
the rain that hindered her from pursuing her dear husband. I said
what I could to comfort a gentlewoman under so sad a disappointment. I told her a husband that stayed so much at home as hers did,
could be no such violent rarity, as for a woman to venture her precious health to go daggling through the rain after him, or to be miserable if she happened to be prevented. That it was prudent for married people to fast sometimes from one another, that they might come
together again with the better stomach. That the best things in this
world, if constantly used, are apt to be cloying, which a little absence
and abstinence would prevent. This was strange doctrine to a fond
female, who fancies people should love with as little reason after
marriage as before.

In the afternoon Monsieur Marij, the minister of the parish, came
to make me a visit. He had been a Romish priest, but found reasons,
either spiritual or temporal, to quit that gay religion. The fault of this
new convert is that he looks for as much respect from his Protestant
flock as is paid to the popish clergy, which our ill-bred Huguenots do
not understand. Madam Marij had so much curiosity as to want to
come too; but another horse was wanting, and she believed it would
have too vulgar an air to ride behind her husband. This woman was
of the true exchange breed, full of discourse but void of discretion,
and married a parson, with the idle hopes he might some time or other
come to be His Grace of Canterbury. The gray mare is the better
horse in that family, and the poor man submits to her wild vagaries
for peace' sake. She has just enough of the fine lady to run in debt and
be of no signification in her household. And the only thing that can
prevent her from undoing her loving husband will be that nobody
will trust them beyond the sixteen thousand, which is soon run out
in a Goochland store. The way of dealing there is for some small mer-

chant or peddler to buy a Scots pennyworth of goods, and clap 150 per cent upon that. At this rate the parson can't be paid much more for his preaching than 'tis worth. No sooner was our visitor retired, but the facetious widow was so kind as to let me into all this secret history, but was at the same time exceedingly sorry that the woman should be so indiscreet and the man so tame as to be governed by an unprofitable and fantastical wife.

22. We had another wet day to try both Mrs. Fleming's patience and my good breeding. The northeast wind commonly sticks by us three or four days, filling the atmosphere with damps, injurious both to man and beast. The worst of it was, we had no good liquor to warm our blood and fortify our spirits against so strong a malignity. However, I was cheerful under all these misfortunes, and expressed no concern but a decent fear lest my long visit might be troublesome. Since I was like to have thus much leisure, I endeavored to find out what subject a dull married man could introduce that might best bring the widow to the use of her tongue. At length I discovered she was a notable quack, and therefore paid that regard to her knowledge as to put some questions to her about the bad distemper that raged then in the country. I mean the bloody flux, that was brought us in the Negro-ship consigned to Col. Braxton. She told me she made use of very simple remedies in that case, with very good success. She did the business either with hartshorn drink that had plantain leaves boiled in it, or else with a strong decoction of St. Andrew's Cross, in new milk instead of water. I agreed with her that those remedies might be very good, but would be more effectual after a dose or two of Indian physic.

But for fear this conversation might be too grave for a widow, I turned the discourse and began to talk of plays, and finding her taste lay most towards comedy, I offered my service to read one to her, which she kindly accepted. She produced the second part of *The Beggar's Opera*, which had diverted the town for forty nights successively and gained four thousand pounds to the author. This was not owing altogether to the wit or humor that sparkled in it, but to some political reflections that seemed to hit the ministry. But the great advantage of the author was that his interest was solicited by the Duchess of Queensbury, which no man could refuse who had but half an eye in his head, or half a guinea in his pocket. Her Grace, like death, spared nobody, but even took my Lord Selkirk in for two guineas, to repair which extravagance he lived upon Scots herrings two months afterwards. But the best story was, she made a very smart officer in His Majesty's guards give her a guinea, who swearing at the same time 'twas all he had in the world, she sent him fifty for it the next day, to reward his obedience. After having acquainted my company with the history of the play, I read three acts of it and left Mrs. Fleming and Mr. Randolph to finish it, who read as well as most actors do at a rehearsal. Thus we killed the time and triumphed over the bad weather.

23. The clouds continued to drive from the northeast and to menace us with more rain. But as the lady resolved to venture through it, I thought it a shame for me to venture to flinch. Therefore, after fortifying myself with two capacious dishes of coffee, and making my compliments to the ladies, I mounted, and Mr. Randolph was so kind as to be my guide.

At the distance of about three miles, in a path as narrow as that which leads to heaven, but much more dirty, we reached the homely dwelling of the Reverend Mr. Marij. His land is much more barren than his wife, and needs all Mr. Bradley's skill in agriculture to make it bring corn.

Thence we proceeded five miles farther, to a mill of Mr. Randolph's that is apt to stand still when there falls but little rain, and to be carried away when there falls a great deal.

. . .

[Byrd continues his journey toward Germanna where he is to visit Alexander Spotswood, who has been a pioneer in developing iron mines and furnaces in Virginia. On the way he visits some old friends, Mr. and Mrs. Chiswell, and is disappointed to discover that Mrs. Chiswell, whom he has not seen in twenty-four years, has aged sadly. After discussing with Mr. Chiswell the techniques of iron-mining and smelting he proceeds on his journey.]

. . .

Then I came into the main county road, that leads from Fredericksburg to Germanna, which last place I reached in ten miles more. This famous town consists of Col. Spotswood's enchanted castle on one side of the street, and a baker's dozen of ruinous tenements on the other, where so many German families had dwelt some years ago, but are now removed ten miles higher, in the fork of Rappahannock, to land of their own. There had also been a chapel about a bow-shot from the Colonel's house at the end of an avenue of cherry trees, but some pious people had lately burnt it down, with intent to get another built nearer to their own homes. Here I arrived about three o'clock and found only Mrs. Spotswood at home, who received her old acquaintance with many a gracious smile. I was carried into a room elegantly set off with pier glasses, the largest of which came soon after to an odd misfortune. Amongst other favorite animals that cheered this lady's solitude, a brace of tame deer ran familiarly about the house, and one of them came to stare at me as a stranger. But unluckily spying his own figure in the glass, he made a spring over the tea table that stood under it and shattered the glass to pieces, and falling back upon the tea table, made a terrible fracas among the china. This exploit was so sudden, and accompanied with such a noise, that it surprised me and perfectly frightened Mrs. Spotswood. But it was worth all the damage to show the moderation and good humor with which she bore this disaster.

In the evening the noble Colonel came home from his mines, who saluted me very civilly, and Mrs. Spotswood's sister, Miss Theky, who had been to meet him *en cavalier*, was so kind too as to bid me welcome. We talked over a legend of old stories, supped about nine, and then prattled with the ladies till it was time for a traveler to retire.

In the meantime I observed my old friend to be very uxorious, and exceedingly fond of his children. This was so opposite to the maxims he used to preach up before he was married, that I could not forbear rubbing up the memory of them. But he gave a very good-natured turn to his change of sentiments, by alleging that whoever brings a poor gentlewoman into so solitary a place, from all her friends and acquaintance, would be ungrateful not to use her and all that belongs to her with all possible tenderness.

28. We all kept snug in our several apartments till nine, except Miss Theky, who was the housewife of the family. At that hour we met over a pot of coffee, which was not quite strong enough to give us the palsy. After breakfast the Colonel and I left the ladies to their domestic affairs and took a turn in the garden, which has nothing beautiful but three terrace walks that fall in slopes one below another. I let him understand that besides the pleasure of paying him a visit, I came to be instructed by so great a master in the mystery of making of iron, wherein he had led the way, and was the Tubal Cain of Virginia. He corrected me a little there, by assuring me he was not only the first in this country, but the first in North America, who had erected a regular furnace. That they ran altogether upon bloomeries in New England and Pennsylvania, till his example had made them attempt greater works. But in this last colony, they have so few ships to carry their iron to Great Britain, that they must be content to make it only for their own use, and must be obliged to manufacture it when they have done. That he hoped he had done the country very great service by setting so good an example. That the four furnaces now at work in Virginia circulated a great sum of money for provisions and all other necessaries in the adjacent counties. That they took off a great number of hands from planting tobacco, and employed them in works that produced a large sum of money in England to the persons concerned, whereby the country is so much the richer. That they are besides a considerable advantage to Great Britain, because it lessens the quantity of bar iron imported from Spain, Holland, Sweden, Denmark and Muscovy, which used to be no less than twenty thousand tons yearly, though at the same time no sow iron is imported thither from any country but only from the plantations. For most of this bar iron they do not only pay silver, but our friends in the Baltic are so nice, they even expect to be paid all in crown pieces. On the contrary, all the iron they receive from the plantations, they pay for it in their own manufactures, and send for it in their own shipping.

Then I inquired after his own mines, and hoped, as he was the first that engaged in this great undertaking, that he had brought them to the most perfection. He told me he had iron in several parts of his great tract of land, consisting of forty-five thousand acres. But that the mine he was at work upon was thirteen miles below Germanna. That his ore (which was very rich) he raised a mile from his furnace, and was obliged to cart the iron when it was made, fifteen miles to Massaponux, a plantation he had upon Rappahannock River; but that the road was exceeding good, gently declining all the way, and had no more than one hill to go up in the whole journey. For this reason his loaded carts went it in a day without difficulty. He said it was true his works were of the oldest standing: but that his long absence in England, and the wretched management of Mr. Greame, whom he had entrusted with his affairs, had put him back very much. That what with neglect and severity, above eighty of his slaves were lost while he was in England, and most of his cattle starved. That his furnace stood still great part of the time, and all his plantations ran to ruin. That indeed he was rightly served for committing his affairs to the care of a mathematician, whose thoughts were always among the stars. That nevertheless, since his return, he had applied himself to rectify his steward's mistakes and bring his business again into order. That now he had contrived to do everything with his own people, except raising the mine and running the iron, by which he had contracted his expense very much. Nay, he believed that by his directions he could bring sensible Negroes to perform those parts of the work tolerably well. But at the same time he gave me to understand that his furnace had done no great feats lately, because he had been taken up in building an air furnace at Massaponux, which he had now brought to perfection, and should be thereby able to furnish the whole country with all sorts of cast iron, as cheap and as good as ever came from England. I told him he must do one thing more to have a full vent for those commodities, he must keep a shallop running into all the rivers, to carry his wares home to people's own doors. And if he would do that I would set a good example and take off a whole ton of them.

Our conversation on this subject continued till dinner, which was both elegant and plentiful. The afternoon was devoted to the ladies, who showed me one of their most beautiful walks. They conducted me through a shady lane to the landing, and by the way made me drink some very fine water that issued from a marble fountain and ran incessantly. Just behind it was a covered bench, where Miss Theky often sat and bewailed her virginity. Then we proceeded to the river, which is the south branch of Rappahannock, about fifty yards wide, and so rapid that the ferry boat is drawn over by a chain, and therefore called the Rapidan. At night we drank prosperity to all the Colonel's projects in a bowl of rack punch, and then retired to our devotions.

· · ·

[Byrd recounts in detail his conversations with Spotswood about mining and politics. He visits Spotswood's mines and furnaces and then proceeds to Fredericksburg where he stays with Colonel Harry Willis, who shows him around. 'Besides Col. Willis, who is the top man of the place, there are only one merchant, a tailor, a smith, and an ordinary keeper,' Byrd comments, 'though I must not forget Mrs. Levingstone, who acts here in the double capacity of a doctress and a coffee woman. And were this a populous city, she is qualified to exercise two other callings.' Completing his visit with Colonel Willis on October 4, Byrd departs for his plantations on the upper James River and at last reaches Westover on October 9.]

· · ·

INDEX

RESEARCH LIBRARY
OF
COLONIAL AMERICANA

An Arno Press Collection

Histories

Acrelius, Israel. **A History of New Sweden;** Or, The Settlements
on the River Delaware . . . Translated with an Introduction
and Notes by William M. Reynolds. Historical Society of
Pennsylvania, MEMOIRS, XI, Philadelphia, 1874.

Belknap, Jeremy. **The History of New Hampshire.** 3 vols., Vol. 1—
Philadelphia, 1784 (Reprinted Boston, 1792), Vol. 2—Boston,
1791, Vol. 3—Boston, 1792.

Browne, Patrick. **The Civil and Natural History of Jamaica.** In
Three Parts . . . London, 1756. Includes 1789 edition
Linnaean index.

[Burke, Edmund]. **An Account of the European Settlements in
America.** In Six Parts . . . London, 1777. Two volumes in one.

Chalmers, George. **An Introduction to the History of the Revolt
of the American Colonies:** Being a Comprehensive View of
Its Origin, Derived From the State Papers Contained in
the Public Offices of Great Britain. London, 1845. Two
volumes in one.

Douglass, William. **A Summary, Historical and Political, of the
First Planting, Progressive Improvements, and Present State
of the British Settlements in North-America.** Boston, 1749–
1752. Two volumes in one.

Edwards, Bryan. **The History, Civil and Commercial, of the
British Colonies in the West Indies.** Dublin, 1793–1794. Two
volumes in one.

Hughes, Griffith. **The Natural History of Barbados.** In Ten Books.
London, 1750.

[Franklin, Benjamin]. **An Historical Review of the Constitution and Government of Pennsylvania, From Its Origin . . .** London, 1759.

Hubbard, William. **A General History of New England, From the Discovery to MDCLXXX.** (*In* Massachusetts Historical Society, COLLECTIONS, Series 2, vol. 5, 6, 1815. Reprinted 1848.)

Hutchinson, Thomas. **The History of the Colony of Massachusetts Bay** . . . 3 vols., Boston, 1764–1828.

Keith, Sir William. **The History of the British Plantations in America** . . . London, 1738.

Long, Edward. **The History of Jamaica:** Or, General Survey of the Antient and Modern State of that Island . . . 3 vols., London, 1774.

Mather, Cotton. **Magnalia Christi Americana; Or, The Ecclesiastical History of New-England From . . . the Year 1620, Unto the Year . . . 1698. In Seven Books.** London, 1702.

Mather, Increase. **A Relation of the Troubles Which Have Hapned in New-England, By Reason of the Indians There From the Year 1614 to the Year 1675** . . . Boston, 1677.

Smith, Samuel. **The History of the Colony of Nova-Caesaria, Or New-Jersey** . . . **to the Year 1721** . . . Burlington, N.J., 1765.

Thomas, Sir Dalby. **An Historical Account of the Rise and Growth of the West-India Collonies,** and of the Great Advantages They are to England, in Respect to Trade. London, 1690.

Trumbull, Benjamin. **A Complete History of Connecticut,** Civil and Ecclesiastical, From the Emigration of Its First Planters, From England, in the Year 1630, to the Year 1764; and to the Close of the Indian Wars . . . New Haven, 1818. Two volumes in one.

Personal Narratives and Promotional Literature

Byrd, William. **The Secret Diary of William Byrd of Westover, 1709–1712,** edited by Louis B. Wright and Marion Tinling. Richmond, Va., 1941.

Byrd, William. **The London Diary (1717–1721) and Other Writings,** edited by Louis B. Wright and Marion Tinling. New York, 1958.

A Genuine Narrative of the Intended Conspiracy of the Negroes
at Antigua. Extracted From an Authentic Copy of a Report,
Made to the Chief Governor of the Carabee Islands, by the
Commissioners, or Judges Appointed to Try the Conspirators.
Dublin, 1737.

Gookin, Daniel. **An Historical Account of the Doings and
Sufferings of the Christian Indians in New England in the
Years 1675, 1676, 1677** . . . (*In* American Antiquarian
Society, Worcester, Mass. ARCHAEOLOGIA
AMERICANA. TRANSACTIONS AND COLLECTIONS.
Cambridge, 1836. vol. 2.)

Gookin, Daniel. **Historical Collections of the Indians in New
England.** Of Their Several Nations, Numbers, Customs,
Manners, Religion and Government, Before the English
Planted There . . . Boston, 1792.

Morton, Thomas. **New English Canaan or New Canaan.**
Containing an Abstract of New England, Composed in
Three Books . . . Amsterdam, 1637.

Sewall, Samuel. **Diary of Samuel Sewall, 1674–1729.** (*In*
Massachusetts Historical Society. COLLECTIONS, 5th
Series, V–VII, 1878–1882.) Three volumes.

Virginia: Four Personal Narratives. (Hamor, Ralph. *A True
Discourse on the Present Estate of Virginia . . . Till the
18 of June 1614 . . .* London, 1615/Hariot, Thomas. *A Briefe
and True Report of the New Found Land of Virginia . . .*
London, 1588/Percy, George. *A Trewe Relacyon of the
Proceedings and Ocurrentes of Momente Which Have
Happened in Virginia From . . . 1609, Until . . . 1612.*
(In *Tyler's Quarterly Historical and Genealogical Magazine,*
Vol. III, 1922.) /Rolf, John. *Virginia in 1616.* (In *Virginia
Historical Register and Literary Advertiser,* Vol. I,
No. III, July, 1848.) New York, 1972.

Winthrop, John. **The History of New England From 1630–1649.**
Edited by James Savage. Boston, 1825–1826. Two volumes
in one.

New England Puritan Tracts of the Seventeenth Century

Cobbett, Thomas. **The Civil Magistrate's Power in Matters of
Religion Modestly Debated** . . . London, 1653.

Cotton, John. **The Bloudy Tenent, Washed, and Made White in
the Bloud of the Lambe** . . . London, 1647.

Cotton, John. **A Brief Exposition with Practical Observations Upon the Whole Book of Canticles.** London, 1655.

Cotton, John. **Christ the Fountaine of Life:** Or, Sundry Choyce Sermons on Part of the Fift Chapter of the First Epistle of St. John. London, 1651.

Cotton, John. **Two Sermons.** (*Gods Mercie Mixed with His Justice* . . . London, 1641/*The True Constitution of a Particular Visible Church, Proved by Scripture* . . . London, 1642.) New York, 1972.

Eliot, John. **The Christian Commonwealth:** Or, The Civil Policy of the Rising Kingdom of Jesus Christ. London, 1659.

Hooker, Thomas. **The Application of Redemption,** By the Effectual Work of the Word, and Spirit of Christ, for the Bringing Home of Lost Sinners to God. London, 1657.

H[ooker], T[homas]. **The Christian's Two Chiefe Lessons,** Viz. Selfe Deniall, and Selfe Tryall . . . London, 1640.

Hooker, Thomas. **A Survey of the Summe of Church-Discipline** Wherein the Way of the Churches of New England is Warranted Out of the Word, and All Exceptions of Weight, Which Are Made Against It, Answered . . . London, 1648.

Increase Mather Vs. Solomon Stoddard: Two Puritan Tracts. (Mather, Increase. *The Order of the Gospel, Professed and Practised by the Churches of Christ in New-England* . . . Boston, 1700/Stoddard, Solomon. *The Doctrine of Instituted Churches Explained, and Proved From the Word of God.* London, 1700.) New York, 1972.

Mather, Cotton. **Ratio Disciplinae Fratrum Nov-Anglorum.** A Faithful Account of the Discipline Professed and Practised, in the Churches of New England. Boston, 1726.

Mather, Richard. **Church Covenant:** Two Tracts. (*Church-Government and Church-Covenant Discussed, in an Answer to the Elders of the Severall Churches in New-England* . . . London, 1643/*An Apologie of the Churches in New-England for Church-Covenant, Or, A Discourse Touching the Covenant Between God and Men, and Especially Concerning Church-Covenant* . . . London, 1643.) New York, 1972.

The Imperial System

[Blenman, Jonathan]. **Remarks on Several Acts of Parliament Relating More Especially to the Colonies Abroad** . . . London, 1742.

British Imperialism: Three Documents. (Berkeley, George. *A Proposal for the Better Supplying of Churches in our Foreign Plantations, and for Converting the Savage Americans to Christianity by a College to be Erected in the Summer Islands, Otherwise Called the Isles of Bermuda* . . . London, 1724/[Fothergill, John]. *Considerations Relative to the North American Colonies.* London, 1765/*A Letter to a Member of Parliament Concerning the Naval-Store Bill* . . . London, 1720.) New York, 1972.

Coke, Roger. **A Discourse of Trade** . . . London, 1670.

[D'Avenant, Charles]. **An Essay Upon the Government of the English Plantations on the Continent of America** (1701). An Anonymous Virginian's Proposals for Liberty Under the British Crown, With Two Memoranda by William Byrd. Edited by Louis B. Wright. San Marino, Calif., 1945.

Dummer, Jeremiah. **A Defence of the New-England Charters** . . . London, 1721.

Gee, Joshua. **The Trade and Navigation of Great Britain Considered:** Shewing that Surest Way for a Nation to Increase in Riches, is to Prevent the Importation of Such Foreign Commodities as May Be Rais'd at Home. London, 1729.

[Little, Otis]. **The State of Trade in the Northern Colonies Considered;** With an Account of Their Produce, and a Particular Description of Nova Scotia . . . London, 1748.

Tucker, Jos[iah]. **The True Interest of Britain, Set Forth in Regard to the Colonies:** And the Only Means of Living in Peace and Harmony With Them, Including Five Different Plans for Effecting this Desirable Event . . . Philadelphia, 1776.

073639

Byrd, William

The London diary
(1717-1721) and
other writings

78

DATE DUE
